CRAFTS SUPPLY SOURCE BOOK

FIFTH EDITION

The comprehensive shop-by-mail guide
for thousands of craft materials

MARGARET A. BOYD

BETTERWAY BOOKS
CINCINNATI, OHIO

ACKNOWLEDGMENTS

My appreciation to all the companies that responded for this fifth edition of the book. A special thanks to Patti Boyd, my dear daughter-in-law and dear friend, who marshalled the hundreds of new listings, rounded up the former companies, and virtually made this edition possible. She is a light for all.

And again to my family and friends for their support..

Library of Congress Cataloging-in-Publication Data

Boyd, Margaret Ann.
    Crafts supply sourcebook / Margaret A. Boyd.—5th ed.
        p.   cm.
    Includes bibliographical references and index.
    ISBN 1-55870-506-6 (pbk. : alk. paper)
    1. Handicraft—United States—Equipment and supplies—Directories. 2. Handicraft—Canada—Equipment and supplies—Directories. I. Title.
TT12.B683   1999
745.5'029'473—dc21   98-43318
                                                  CIP

Editor: Roseann Biederman
Production coordinator: Kristen Heller
Production editor: Jeff Crump
Cover design: Brian Roeth
Cover photography: Brian Steege/Guildhaus Photographics

In memory of my creative grandmothers,
Johanna Pribyl and Elizabeth Jane Munnerlyn.

GUIDE TO THE LISTINGS IN THIS BOOK

The listings in this book are divided into three sections: general arts and crafts; needlecrafts, sewing and fiber arts; and resources. Within these sections are more than fifty categories to help you easily locate the supplies you need.

Most suppliers listed here are retailers serving the hobbyist or professional craftsperson. Many also offer wholesale prices to legitimate businesses; when this is the case, there will be a note following the "Discounts" heading. A few of the suppliers listed are manufacturers and sell wholesale only. They are listed here so you will be able to contact them to find a retailer that carries their supplies.

The listings include all available contact information: name of business or catalog, mailing addresses, phone and fax numbers and E-mail addresses when provided by the company. This contact information is followed by a list of supplies available following the "Offers" heading. When available, the listing will also include how you can get more information. Often a company requests a SASE (self-addressed stamped envelope). SASEs should be #10 business-sized envelopes. When the business asks for a large SASE, include a large, manila envelope with double the postage. Be sure you also include a specific request for the information you need.

If a store location is available in addition to the mail-order services provided, the listing will include the address of that location and, when provided, the hours during which the location is open to the public. Finally, any discounts offered, as well as any credit cards accepted, are included if the company provided them.

Listings in the *Crafts Supply Sourcebook* are free. They are not advertisements, and the author and publisher are not endorsing the businesses listed here. Our aim is to provide you with a number of possibilities so you can make choices that are right for your own business or hobby.

The listings were compiled and verified by mail by the author. Most listings were also checked over the phone by the publisher prior to publication. We have tried to be as accurate as possible; still, the crafts supply market is constantly changing, so companies listed may go out of business or make changes in the merchandise they offer. The publisher cannot be responsible for any losses resulting from using this book, such as the cost of postage for mail that is returned to sender. Postal rates fluctuate. Always verify current rates with your post office.

Comments and contributions are welcome for future editions. May your days be full of the light of creative expression!

Margaret A. Boyd
P.O. Box 6232-FW
Augusta, GA 30906

Contents

INTRODUCTION

The fifth edition of this sourcebook includes hundreds of new and exciting supply sources, as well as updated information on the sources included in previous editions. These wonderful companies provide materials that inspire us to even more creatively innovative craft design and work.

Behind every catalog are dedicated business professionals who share their wares and often their experience as well. The literature offered on inquiry may include technical hints that help us avoid pitfalls and produce more satisfying results with greater ease. Often the value of what we can learn far outweighs the cost of the literature.

With that in mind, I urge you to explore your areas of interest and other areas, too—they can lead to new pathways of creation. Whatever you create, enjoy!

Margaret A. Boyd

General Arts & Crafts

Airbrushing

Also see Artist's Supplies, Graphics & Printing; General Craft Supplies; Paints, Finishes & Adhesives.

BADGER AIR-BRUSH CO.
9128 W. Belmont Ave.
Franklin Park IL 60131
Contact: Jan Myers or Ken Schlotfeldt
Phone: (847)678-3104
Fax: (847)671-4352
Offers: Manufacturers of airbrushes and airbrush-related accessories—paints, stencils and compressors.
Catalog: 32 pages, 4-color. Free.
Phone Orders: M-F, 8:30-4:30 CST.
Discounts: Sell to distributors and select retailers.

BEAR AIR
(formerly Jurak)
15 Tech Circle
Natick MA 01760
Contact: Sue Winslow
Phone: (800)232-7247
Fax: (508)655-3390
Offers: All brands of airbrushes, supplies and videos. Compressors and paints. Full line of airbrush supplies.
Catalog: 92 pages.
Phone Orders: 8-6 EST.
Mail Orders: Will ship to Canada, US and foreign.
Discounts: Up to 20%.
Accepts: American Express, MasterCard, Visa, C.O.D.

DICK BLICK
Dept. CB
P.O. Box 1267
Galesburg IL 61402-1267
Phone: (309)343-6181
Offers: Full line of art/sculpture and other materials and equipment: soapstone, alabaster, stone sculpture tool sets. Modeling: instant papier-mâchés, Sculptamold, plastercraft gauze, plaster of Paris (and molds), Sculpey, FIMO, modeling clays. Clays: Mexican pottery, Marblex, Westwood ovencraft, others. Also offers Egyptian paste, earthenware and other kitchen-fired clays, plus glazes, ceramic and modeling tools/sets and aids.
Accepts: American Express, Discover, MasterCard, Visa

LOU DAVIS WHOLESALE
Dept. CS8
N3211 County Rd. H. N.
Lake Geneva WI 53147
Phone: (414)248-2000 or (800)748-7991
Offers: Brand-name craft and ceramic supplies, including music movements in more than 200 tunes, chalks, paints, spray finishes, airbrushes and compressors, clock movements, doll-making supplies, lamp parts and accessories, brushes, magnets, glitter, abrasives, adhesives and cleaning tools.
Catalog: $2 (refundable with order).
Accepts: Discover, MasterCard, Visa

8 STAR SALES
P.O. Box 351928
10 S. Holland-Sylvania Rd. #208
Toledo OH 43635-1928
Contact: Matt Baker
Phone: (419)868-8127
Fax: (419)868-7603
E-mail: airbrush8@aol.com
Website: http://members.aol.com/airbrush8
Offers: 17 videotapes on how to airbrush. Artists Rob Prior and Pamela Shanteau. Best quality video and audio and most professional training.
Catalog: 2-3 folds, $2.50 (refundable).
Phone Orders: 24 hours (800)687-5005.
Mail Orders: Will ship anywhere, prepayment required.
Discounts: Sells wholesale to legitimate businesses.
Accepts: American Express, Discover, MasterCard, Visa

JERRY'S ARTARAMA
P.O. Box 58638
Raleigh NC 27658
Contact: Ira Allen
Phone: (919)878-6782
Fax: (919)873-9565
E-mail: jartist@aol.com
Website: www.jerryscatalog.com
Store Location: Locations in Deerfield Beach FL, Bellerose NY, West Hartford CT, Rochester NY and Ft. Collins CO.
Offers: Paints, brushes, inks, mediums, drawing equipment, markers, pastels and crayons, tapes and adhesives, sprays, canvas, airbrush portfolios, fabric art, printmaking supplies, sculpture supplies, picture frames and mats, furniture and equipment for art studios.
Catalog: $2. 150 pages, color/b&w.
Phone Orders: M-F, 8:30-8; Sat, 11-5 EST.

Mail Orders: US, Canada, foreign. Prepay or credit card.
Accepts: American Express, Discover, MasterCard, Visa

KEMPER ENTERPRISES, INC.

13595 12th St.
Chino CA 91710
Contact: Katie Munday
Phone: (800)388-5367 or (909)627-6191
Fax: (909)627-4008
E-mail: thetoolady@aol.com
Offers: Manufacturer and designer of tools for painting that include the Fluid Writer, Wipe-Out tool that erases mistakes, faux finishing tools and a spray gun cleaner set.
Catalog: Free. 70+ pages color. Please send $1.50 for p&h.
Phone Orders: Customer service hours are M-F, 8-4:30 PST.
Mail Orders: Can expect order to ship within 2 days of receipt. Ship domestic and international through UPS.
Discounts: Sell wholesale to businesses. For account qualifications and status please contact.
Accepts: Discover, MasterCard, Visa, International Money Order, bank wire transfer in American dollars only

JOE KUBERT ART & GRAPHIC SUPPLY

37A Myrtle Ave.
Dover NJ 07801
Phone: (973)328-3266
Fax: (973)328-7283
Store Location: At above address. M-F, 10-6; Sat, 9-4.
Offers: Artist's, cartoonist's, and graphic art materials, including boards, papers (art, parchments, drafting, etching, rag, others), paints, finger paints, brushes, palettes, pens, crayons, chalk, pencils, pastels, airbrushes, airbrush sets, calligraphy pens/inks, drafting materials/equipment and Pantographs. Also carries mat/paper cutters, projectors, easels, canvas, stretcher strips, graphic and printing supplies, frisket, grids, films, Letraset letters, tapes, film, waxers, light boxes, projectors, furniture, plus etching, block printing and silkscreen supplies and equipment, tools, knives and books.
Catalog: $4.

LIQUID NEON

5130 E. Charleston Blvd., Suite 5-52
Las Vegas NV 89122
Contact: Karen LaPratt
Phone: (702)641-7142
Fax: (702)641-7001
Offers: Rubber stamps, foil, glue, E-Z Airbrushing.
Catalog: Color, 24 pages and insert. $3.
Phone Orders: M-F, 8-5 PST.
Mail Orders: Retail orders accompanied by payment. Wholesale orders: minimum first order $150, subsequent order $75.
Accepts: check, money order

NORTH LIGHT BOOKS

1507 Dana Ave.
Cincinnati OH 45207
Phone: (513)531-2222

Offers: Art instruction books covering painting portraits, florals. Offers instruction in landscapes, nature, textures, flowers, weather, animals, people, urban settings and wildlife. Covers techniques for basics, such as color, light and values, acrylics, watercolors, oils, airbrush, screen printing and silk fabrics. Drawing and pastel titles are also available. Write.

OTT'S DISCOUNT ART SUPPLY

102 Hungate Dr.
Greenville NC 27858
Phone: (800)356-3289
Fax: (919)756-2397
Website: www.otts.com
Offers: A full range of pencils, charcoal, artist's papers and other materials. Airbrushes, canvas, brushes and books.
Catalog: Free.

PAASCHE AIRBRUSH CO.

7440 W. Lawrence Ave.
Harwood Heights IL 60656
Phone: (708)867-9191
E-mail: paascheair@aol.com
Website: www.paascheairbrush.com
Offers: Airbrushes, including gravity feed and siphon single and double action models; airbrush sets for paints, varnish, lacquers and others. Accessories, air compressors, sprayers, equipment and supplies for air etching/spraying are also available. Also offers an air etching video. Manufacturer. Free literature.
Discounts: Call for current discounts.

PEARL

Dept. CSS
308 Canal St.
New York NY 10013
Phone: (212)431-7932 or (800)221-6845
Fax: (212)431-6798
Website: www.pearlpaint.com
Store Location: 20 stores, coast-to-coast.
Offers: Extensive artist's supplies (including known brands). Carries paints—oils, acrylics, watercolors, gouache, egg temperas, encaustics, vinyl matte, lettering enamel, gold leaf, specialty paints and various mediums. Also carries paint accessories and tools, including sculpture, wood carving, framers, others. Also offers airbrushes and printmaking supplies, studio accessories, easels, mannequins, silk paint and dyes, equipment, furniture and others. Provides international mail order. We special order anything.
Catalog: Write for list. Fine art catalog, $1.50.
Discounts: Quantity; teachers, institutions and professionals; large order discounts negotiable.
Accepts: American Express, Discover, MasterCard, Visa, check, money order

SAX ARTS & CRAFTS

P.O. Box 510710
New Berlin WI 53151
Phone: (414)784-6880

Offers: Artist's supplies (known brands), including paints, brushes, palette knives, boxes, organizers, trays, markers, pens. Also carries sumi supplies, airbrush kits/accessories and compressors, paints, inks, canvas, stretchers, tools, easels, boards, plus a full line of papers, boards, mats and cutters. Also offers frames, framing tools and supplies, knives, scissors, adhesives, paper cutters, waxers, glue guns, tapes, punches and pencils. Carries artists' aids, such as mannequins and models. Drafting items, calligraphy and lettering tools, light boxes, mounting presses, film, projectors, photography supplies, magnifier lamps and furniture are also available. Stocks block printing supplies and presses, etching, screen printing items/kits, T-shirt printing machines, photo and speed screen supplies, videos (art, craft), filmstrips and books.

Catalog: $5 (refundable).

Discounts: Quantity, wholesale to legitimate resellers.

Accepts: American Express, Discover, MasterCard, Visa

V.E.A.S. PRODUCTIONS

P.O. Box 278

Troy MI 48099

Contact: Valynn Davenport

Phone: (248)584-2020 or (810)293-6931

E-mail: gemartschl@aol.com

Website: http://members.aol.com/gemartschl/

Store Location: Troy MI location.

Offers: Instructional learning video programs on how to airbrush paint, graphic and mural painting, gold leafing, glass etching, pinstriping, automotive painting and sign-lettering techniques. "Street Art" manual.

Catalog: Free. Send #10 SASE envelope.

Phone Orders: Yes.

Mail Orders: At above address.

Discounts: Wholesalers 50%.

Art Instruction

Also see Artist's Supplies, Graphics & Printing; Books & Booksellers; Publications; Associations.

CARTOON OPPORTUNITIES
(formerly Cartoonerama)
P.O. Box 248
Chalfont PA 18914
Contact: Bill Keough
Phone: (215)822-9158
Fax: (215)822-9158
E-mail: billkeo@erols.com
Offers: Newsletter lists cartoon markets for professional cartoonists.

TONY COUCH
5840 Musket Lane
Stone Mountain GA 30087
Phone: (800)491-7870
Offers: 10 art instruction workshop videos on painting and drawing, given by Tony Couch.

FLORA & CO. MULTIMEDIA
P.O. Box 8263
Albuquerque NM 87198
Contact: Jan Flora
Phone: (505)255-9988
Fax: (505)255-9988
E-mail: crafts@floraco.com
Website: floraco.com
Offers: Silkscreen instruction video, adapted to the home workshop, demonstrating techniques for reproducing patterns on fabric, wood, paper, plastics and other flat surfaces; a workbook is included. Also puppet making. Send SASE.
Phone Orders: Yes. Fax 24 hours a day.
Mail Orders: Immediate shipment.
Accepts: American Express, Discover, MasterCard, Visa

BEEBE HOPPER
731 Beech Ave.
Chula Vista CA 91910
Phone: (619)420-8766
Offers: Instruction books in decorative arts (featherstroke technique), painting wildfowl and landscapes. Send SASE.

DAVID LARSON PRODUCTIONS
(formerly Perfect Palette)
5910 N. Lilly Rd.
Menomonee Falls WI 53051
Contact: Kate Larson

Phone: (414)252-4122
Fax: (414)252-3833
E-mail: katel@craftnet.org
Website: http://www.craftnet.org/ppal
Offers: Perfect Palette decorative painting in all skill levels and mediums: oil, acrylic, watercolor, pen and ink, faux finishes and fabric.
Catalog: Full-line color. $2 (refundable). Newest releases flyer is free.
Phone Orders: (800)839-0306. M-F, 8:30-5 CST.
Mail Orders: Perfect Palette, P.O. Box 25286, Milwaukee WI 53225. Will ship to US, Canada and overseas. Prepayment required.
Discounts: To legitimate businesses with minimum requirements.
Accepts: Discover, MasterCard, Visa

LILIEDAHL PUBLICATIONS
11814 Coursey Blvd. #498
Baton Rouge LA 70816
Contact: Johnnie Liliedahl
Phone: (504)769-8586
Fax: (504)769-8586
E-mail: lilipubs@ix.netcom.com
Offers: Art instruction videos on realist and old master methods; oil painting and drawing. Painting accessories.
Catalog: Free 30-page catalog.
Phone Orders: 24 hours.
Mail Orders: Free shipping in US.
Discounts: Wholesale to distributors.
Accepts: MasterCard, Visa

MAJIC OF MAINE
1065 Riverside Dr.
Auburn ME 04210
Phone: (207)782-5650
Fax: (207)795-6490
E-mail: cspencer@cybertours.com
Store Location: At above address.
Offers: Instructional videos of painting wildlife into landscapes (bear, fish, birds, moose and deer). Offers sales and rentals. Video production service.
Catalog: Free brochure.
Discounts: Sells wholesale.

NORTH LIGHT ART SCHOOL
1507 Dana Ave.
Cincinnati OH 45207
Offers: Home-study art course from professionals including a series of basic studies, perspective, techniques for pencil, color, painting and others. Write.

NORTH LIGHT BOOKS

1507 Dana Ave.
Cincinnati OH 45207
Phone: (513)531-2222
Offers: Art instruction books covering painting portraits, florals. Offers instruction in landscapes, nature, textures, flowers, weather, animals, people, urban settings and wildlife. Covers techniques for basics, such as color, light and values, acrylics, watercolors, oils, airbrush, screen printing and silk fabrics. Drawing and pastel titles are also available. Write.

NOVA COLOR ARTISTS' ACRYLIC PAINT

5894 Blackwelder St.
Culver City CA 90232
Phone: (213)870-6000
Store Location: At above address.
Offers: Artists' acrylic paint factory direct. Over 80 colors in 4-ounce tubes, pints, quarts and gallons. All mediums. Gesso, pearls and metallics.
Catalog: Free price list and color chart.
Phone Orders: M-F, 8:30-5 PST.
Mail Orders: Ship UPS, all US and Canada. Credit card or prepayment.
Discounts: Factory direct prices for all customers.
Accepts: MasterCard, Visa

SIGNILAR ART VIDEOS

P.O. Box 278-CS
Sanbornton NH 03269
Contact: Joanne Boyce
Phone: (800)205-4904
Fax: (603)934-6525
Website: signilar.com
Offers: Master artists demonstrations on videos. Broadcast quality. Sculpting demonstrations with Bruno Lucchesi and Jan D'Esopo. Painting demonstrations with David A. Leffel, Burton Silverman, Ken Davies and Lajos Markos.
Catalog: Free.
Accepts: Discover, MasterCard, Visa, check

V.E.A.S. PRODUCTIONS

P.O. Box 278
Troy MI 48099
Contact: Valynn Davenport
Phone: (248)584-2020 or (810)293-6931
E-mail: gemartschl@aol.com
Website: http://members.aol.com/gemartschl/
Store Location: Troy MI location.
Offers: Instructional learning video programs on how to airbrush paint, graphic and mural painting, gold leafing, glass etching, pinstriping, automotive painting and sign-lettering techniques. "Street Art" manual.
Catalog: Free. Send #10 SASE envelope.
Phone Orders: Yes.
Mail Orders: At above address.
Discounts: Wholesalers 50%.

VIDEO LEARNING LIBRARY

(formerly Art Video Library)
5777 Azalea Dr.
Grants Pass OR 97526
Phone: (541)479-7140
Offers: Over 1,200 art instruction videos for sale or rent. Members may rent videos at low cost and elect to apply rent to purchase. Videos cover acrylics, oils, watercolors, pastels, drawing, color, anatomy, perspective, still life, landscapes, airbrushing and portraits. Instructors include Carter, Demeres, Sargent, Burton, Kelly, Jenkins, Palluth, Blackman, Graham, Flannery, Pike, Marchenko, Boyle, Vilppu, Lee, Pitard and Harris.
Catalog: Free.

Artist's Supplies, Graphics & Printing

Also see Paints, Finishes & Adhesives; Tole & Decorative Crafts; Books & Booksellers; Publications; Associations; other specific categories.

ACCENT
100 North St.
Bloomsbury NJ 08804
Contact: Elizabeth Weaver
Phone: (908)479-4124
Fax: (908)479-6885
Website: www.accentproducts.com
Store Location: Contact your local dealer or Accent for a dealer near you.
Offers: Full line of decorative and craft products. Acrylic paint, brushes, faux finishing and memory books are our specialty.

ALCHEMIST PAINT & VARNISHES
P.O. Box 272
Hills Ville VA 24343
Contact: Donald C. Fels, owner
Phone: (540)728-5326
E-mail: donald@amberalchemy.com
Offers: Painting mediums. Specializing in antique and old masters painting mediums: amber varnishes, Baroque oil and Oil of Florence.
Catalog: Call for catalog info.
Phone Orders: Wholesale, retail.

ART SUPPLY WAREHOUSE
5325 Departure Dr.
Raleigh NC 27616
Phone: (800)995-6778 or (919)878-5077
Fax: (919)878-5075
Website: www.aswexpress.com
Offers: A full range of artist's supplies including paints, canvas, brushes, frames, easels, paper, airbrushing supplies and much, much more.
Catalog: Free catalog.
Phone Orders: Yes.
Mail Orders: At above address.
Accepts: Discover, MasterCard, Visa

ARTISAN/SANTA FE, INC.
717 Canyon Rd.
Santa Fe NM 87501
Phone: (800)331-6375
Offers: Artist's supplies including Holbein products and hard-to-find items. Full line of oils and watercolors for professionals also available.

THE ARTIST'S CLUB
P.O. Box 8930
Vancouver WA 98668
Phone: (800)845-6507
Offers: Tole painting/country home. Unpainted wood decorations, including Christmas ornaments and decorations, spring bunnies, watering cans and others. Also offers painting projects, paints, brushes, tools and instruction books.
Catalog: Free.
Accepts: American Express, Discover, JCB, MasterCard, Visa

BLACK HORSE FINE ART SUPPLY
70 S. Winooski Ave., Suite 204
Burlington VT 05401
Contact: John E. Bates
Phone: (802)658-1695
Fax: (802)660-1977
E-mail: jebvt@together.net
Store Location: (802)860-4972
Offers: Fine art supplies featuring Holbein art materials.
Catalog: $2.50 ($5 off order over $30).
Phone Orders: 7 days a week, 24 hours a day.
Mail Orders: US and Canada, including AK, HI and PR.
Discounts: 30-50% off every day.
Accepts: American Express, MasterCard, Visa

DICK BLICK
Dept. CB
P.O. Box 1267
Galesburg IL 61402-1267
Phone: (309)343-6181
Offers: Full line of art/sculpture and other materials and equipment: soapstone, alabaster, stone sculpture tool sets. Modeling: instant papier-mâchés, Sculptamold, plastercraft gauze, plaster of Paris (and molds), Sculpey, FIMO, modeling clays. Clays: Mexican pottery, Marblex, Westwood ovencraft, others. Also offers Egyptian paste, earthenware and other kitchen-fired clays, plus glazes, ceramic and modeling tools/sets and aids.
Accepts: American Express, Discover, MasterCard, Visa

CHATHAM ART DISTRIBUTORS, INC.
P.O. Box 3851
Frederick MD 21705
Phone: (800)822-4747
Fax: (301)631-0108
Offers: Decorative art supplies, including painting surfaces,

tools, paints and brushes. Also carries books.
Catalog: Write for catalog.

CHEAP JOE'S ART STUFF
374 Industrial Park Dr.
Boone NC 28607
Phone: (800)227-2788
Offers: Artist's supplies, such as papers (known brands) and a line of art supplies at reduced cost including professional colors (oils, watercolors, acrylics and others).
Catalog: Free.

CHROMA, INC.
205 Bucky Dr.
Lititz PA 17543
Phone: (800)257-8278
Fax: (717)626-9292
E-mail: info@chroma-inc.com
Website: www.chroma-inc.com
Offers: Jo Sonja's acrylics, Atelier studio acrylics, archival oils, Chromacryl Student acrylics, Chromacryl Junior, liquid temperas, private label manufacturer, gesso, drawing inks and finger paints.
Catalog: Available for each product line.
Phone Orders: Yes.
Mail Orders: Will ship to US and Canada.
Discounts: Sells to distributors, retail accounts and individuals who do not have a local source.
Accepts: MasterCard, Visa

CONRAD MACHINE CO.
1525 S. Warner
Whitehall MI 49461
Phone: (616)893-7455
Offers: Etching and lithography presses (2 sizes), Convertible Press (hand-driven model) and optional accessories. Carries table and floor model presses, plus re-manufactured presses in 12″ to 36″ sizes.
Catalog: Free. Request trade-ins list.
Discounts: Quantity; sells wholesale.

DALER-ROWNEY, INC.
(formerly Robert Simmons)
2 Corporate Dr.
Cranbury NJ 08512
Phone: (609)655-5252
Offers: Robert Simmons brushes for watercolors, oils and acrylics, plus brushes for crafts, artwork, ceramics, hobbies and lettering. Styles available include tole decorative brushes and ceramic brushes. Also offers Fabric Master brushes, base coaters (flat, round) and scrubbers (nylon). Bamboo brushes, brushes for plaster crafts and china painting, brush sets in most sizes and styles. Books are also available. Also manufactures oil, watercolor, acrylic paint, liquid acrylic. Contact your dealer or write.

LOU DAVIS WHOLESALE
Dept. CS8
N3211 County Rd. H. N.
Lake Geneva WI 53147
Phone: (414)248-2000 or (800)748-7991
Offers: Brand-name craft and ceramic supplies, including music movements in more than 200 tunes. Chalks, paints, spray finishes, airbrushes and compressors. Clock movements, doll-making supplies, lamp parts and accessories. Brushes, magnets, glitter, abrasives, adhesives and cleaning tools.
Catalog: $2 (refundable with order).
Accepts: Discover, MasterCard, Visa

GRAFIX
19499 Miles Rd.
Cleveland OH 44128
Contact: Hayley Prendergast
Phone: (216)581-9050
Fax: (216)581-9041
E-mail: info@grafixarts.com
Website: www.grafixarts.com
Offers: Plastic films and creative products for design, art, drafting, graphics and crafts; Dura-Lar, Clear-Lay, acetate, masking and drafting film; Frisket film, Incredible Art Products, Funky films, Funky fur and convenience packs.
Catalog: 6-page brochure with pricing.
Phone Orders: M-F, 8:30-5 EST.
Mail Orders: Global; f.o.b. Cleveland OH.
Discounts: Wholesale to legitimate businesses.
Accepts: MasterCard, Visa, C.O.D.

GRAPHIC CHEM & INK CO.
P.O. Box 27
728 N. Yale Ave.
Villa Park IL 60181
Phone: (800)465-7382
Fax: (630)832-6064
E-mail: graphchem@aol.com
Offers: Printmaking supplies. Block printing line includes linoleum and wood blocks, brayers and cutting tools. Lithographic line includes gums, asphaltum, tusche and rollers (rubber, KU Leather, NuClear). Carries litho stones in many sizes, KU Leather and composition, inks, a variety of papers and other supplies, etching and silkscreen materials. Write.
Catalog: Free.
Phone Orders: Yes.
Mail Orders: Call above number.
Accepts: American Express, MasterCard, Visa

GRAPHIC MEDIA CO.
1518 N. Highland Ave.
Los Angeles CA 90028
Phone: (800)408-6242
Offers: Art supplies in a wide range of name brands, including Grumbacher, Winsor & Newton, Liquitex, Mountblanc, Waterman, Parker, Pelikan, 3M, Letraset and others.

Catalog: $5 (refundable).
Discounts: 20-60%.

GRUMBACHER

P.O. Box 68
100 North St.
Bloomsbury NJ 08804
Phone: (908)479-4124
Website: www.grumbacher.com
Offers: Full lines of artist's supplies, including paints and brushes for artists and sign painters, Golden Edge synthetic brushes, mediums and other tools and equipment.
Catalog: Contact your dealer or send SASE.

THE HEALTHY LIGHTING CATALOG

(formerly Verilux)
P.O. Box 2455
Stamford CT 06906
Contact: Judy Maxson
Phone: (888)544-4865
Fax: (888)544-4861
E-mail: verilux@aol.com
Website: www.ergolight.com
Offers: "Instant Sun" full spectrum studio lighting for accurate evaluation of color intensity, value and hues across the entire visible spectrum. Call or write.
Accepts: American Express, MasterCard, Visa

HK HOLBEIN, INC.

P.O. Box 555
20 Commerce St.
Williston VT 05495-0555
Contact: Timothy S. Hopper
Phone: (802)862-4573
Fax: (802)658-5889
Website: www.holbeinhk.com
Offers: Holbein artist quality oil color, watercolor, acrylics, Acryla Gouache, Duo Aqua watersoluble oil color, liquid acrylics, airbrush colors, airbrushes and a full line of tole and decorative brushes.
Catalog: 100 pages, color. Consumers $7, retailers no charge.
Phone Orders: Yes.
Discounts: Sells wholesale to legitimate retail businesses.
Accepts: MasterCard, Visa

THE ITALIAN ART STORE

84 Maple Ave.
Morristown NJ 07960
Contact: Claude Bernard
Phone: (800)643-6440 or (973)644-2717
Fax: (973)644-5074
Store Location: At above address; M-F, 9-5.
Offers: Finest artist materials from all over the world at 40-70% discount. Wholesale prices. Free shipping on $100 orders.
Catalog: Free. 60 pages.
Phone Orders: M-F, 9-5 EST.

Mail Orders: Yes. Will ship to Canada.
Discounts: 40-70%. Wholesale pricing.
Accepts: Discover, MasterCard, Visa

JERRY'S ARTARAMA

P.O. Box 58638
Raleigh NC 27658
Contact: Ira Allen
Phone: (919)878-6782
Fax: (919)873-9565
E-mail: jartist@aol.com
Website: www.jerryscatalog.com
Store Location: Locations in Deerfield Beach FL, Bellerose NY, West Hartford CT, Rochester NY and Ft. Collins CO.
Offers: Paints, brushes, inks, mediums, drawing equipment, markers, pastels and crayons, tapes and adhesives, sprays, canvas, airbrush, portfolios, fabric art, printmaking supplies, sculpture supplies, picture frames and mats, furniture and equipment for art studios.
Catalog: $2. 150 pages, color/b&w.
Phone Orders: M-F, 8:30-8; Sat, 11-5 EST.
Mail Orders: US, Canada, foreign. Prepay or credit card.
Accepts: American Express, Discover, MasterCard, Visa

KEMPER ENTERPRISES, INC.

13595 12th St.
Chino CA 91710
Contact: Katie Munday
Phone: (800)388-5367 or (909)627-6191
Fax: (909)627-4008
E-mail: thetoolady@aol.com
Offers: Manufacturer and designer of tools for painting that include the Fluid Writer, Wipe-Out tool that erases mistakes, faux finishing tools and a spray gun cleaner set.
Catalog: Free. 70+ pages color. Please send $1.50 for p&h.
Phone Orders: Customer service hours are M-F, 8-4:30 PST.
Mail Orders: Can expect order to ship within 2 days of receipt. Ship domestic and international through UPS.
Discounts: Sell wholesale to businesses. For account qualifications and status please contact.
Accepts: Discover, MasterCard, Visa, International Money Order, bank wire transfer in American dollars only

JOE KUBERT ART & GRAPHIC SUPPLY

37A Myrtle Ave.
Dover NJ 07801
Phone: (973)328-3266
Fax: (973)328-7283
Store Location: At above address. M-F, 10-6; Sat, 9-4.
Offers: Artist's, cartoonist's, and graphic art materials, including boards, papers (art, parchments, drafting, etching, rag, others), paints, finger paints, brushes, palettes, pens, crayons, chalk, pencils, pastels, airbrushes, airbrush sets, calligraphy pens/inks, drafting materials/equipment and Pantographs. Also carries mat/paper cutters, projectors, easels, canvas, stretcher strips, graphic and printing supplies, frisket, grids, films, Letraset letters, tapes, film, waxers, light boxes, projectors, furniture, plus etching, block printing and

silkscreen supplies and equipment, tools, knives and books.
Catalog: $4.

OTT'S DISCOUNT ART SUPPLY
102 Hungate Dr.
Greenville NC 27858
Phone: (800)356-3289
Fax: (919)756-2397
Website: www.otts.com
Offers: A full range of pencils, charcoal, artist's papers and other materials. Airbrushes, canvas, brushes and books.
Catalog: Free.

PAASCHE AIRBRUSH CO.
7440 W. Lawrence Ave.
Harwood Heights IL 60656
Phone: (708)867-9191
E-mail: paascheair@aol.com
Website: www.paascheairbrush.com
Offers: Airbrushes, including gravity feed and siphon single and double action models; airbrush sets for paints, varnish, lacquers and others. Accessories, air compressors, sprayers, equipment and supplies for air etching/spraying are also available. Also offers an air etching video. Manufacturer. Free literature.
Discounts: Call for current discounts.

PEARL
Dept. CSS
308 Canal St.
New York NY 10013
Phone: (212)431-7932 or (800)221-6845
Fax: (212)431-6798
Website: www.pearlpaint.com
Store Location: 20 stores, coast-to-coast.
Offers: Extensive artist's supplies (including known brands). Carries paints—oils, acrylics, watercolors, gouache, egg temperas, encaustics, vinyl matte, lettering enamel, gold leaf, specialty paints and various mediums. Also carries paint accessories and tools, including sculpture, wood carving, framers, others. Also offers airbrushes and printmaking supplies, studio accessories, easels, mannequins, silk paint and dyes, equipment, furniture and others. Provides international mail order. We special order anything.
Catalog: Write for list. Fine art catalog, $1.50.
Discounts: Quantity; teachers, institutions and professionals; large order discounts negotiable.
Accepts: American Express, Discover, MasterCard, Visa, check, money order

PENTEL OF AMERICA, LTD.
2805 Columbia St.
Torrance CA 90509
Contact: Janet Quan, public relations coordinator
Phone: (310)320-3831, ext. 253
Fax: (310)320-4036
E-mail: pr@pentel.com
Website: http://www.pentel.com

Offers: An extensive line of pens, including porous, markers, projection, white, ceramic tip, correction and permanent pens. Also offers drafting pencils, erasers and Roll'N Glue adhesive. Contact your dealer or send SASE.

PERMA COLOR
226 E. Tremont
Charlotte NC 28203
Phone: (704)333-9201
Website: http://members.aol.com/hmmcn/
Offers: Dry pigments standard, pearlescents, bronze powders, iridescents, Rabbitskin glue, gesso-primed panels, Kolinsky sable brushes. Specialty items, including talc, kaolin, gums, binders, gesso and graphite. Send SASE.
Discounts: Quantity; teachers and institutions. Sells wholesale to legitimate businesses and professionals.

PRINTMAKERS MACHINE CO., INC.
P.O. Box 71
724 N. Yale
Villa Park IL 60181-0071
Contact: Dean Clark
Phone: (800)992-5970
Fax: (630)832-6064
Offers: Presses, for all printmaking. Etching, lithographic, combination presses and monotype presses.
Catalog: Free upon request.
Phone Orders: Yes.
Mail Orders: At above address.

REX GRAPHIC SUPPLY
P.O. Box 6626
Raritan Center
Edison NJ 08816-6626
Contact: Ron Thomas
Phone: (732)613-8777 or (800)367-3952
Fax: (732)390-8065
E-mail: ront@home.com
Offers: Complete line of drafting, engineering, graphic art and school/office supplies. Featuring The Creator graphic arts table, the Original True Angle, Hyglo 6-in-1 Rotary Craft Punch, the Ring Pen and Craft Cutts decorative edged scissors.
Catalog: Free.
Phone Orders: M-F, 9-5 EST.
Mail Orders: Prepayment required. Allow 2-4 weeks for delivery. Other address: P.O. Box 24238, Tempe AZ 85285. (602)921-9266 or (800)821-7125.
Discounts: Sells wholesale to trade.
Accepts: MasterCard, Visa

SAX ARTS & CRAFTS
P.O. Box 510710
New Berlin WI 53151
Phone: (414)784-6880
Offers: Artist's supplies (known brands), including paints, brushes, palette knives, boxes, organizers, trays, markers, pens. Also carries sumi supplies, airbrush kits/accessories

and compressors, paints, inks, canvas, stretchers, tools, easels, boards, plus a full line of papers, boards, mats and cutters. Also offers frames, framing tools and supplies, knives, scissors, adhesives, paper cutters, waxers, glue guns, tapes, punches and pencils. Carries artists' aids, such as mannequins and models. Drafting items, calligraphy and lettering tools, light boxes, mounting presses, film, projectors, photography supplies, magnifier lamps and furniture are also available. Stocks block printing supplies and presses, etching and screen printing items/kits, T-shirt printing machines, photo and speed screen supplies, videos (art, craft), filmstrips and books.

Catalog: $5 (refundable).
Discounts: Quantity, wholesale to legitimate resellers.
Accepts: American Express, Discover, MasterCard, Visa

DANIEL SMITH ARTISTS' MATERIALS
P.O. Box 84268
4150 First Ave. S.
Seattle WA 98124-5568
Contact: Kathleen Connally, sales manager
Phone: (800)426-6740 (US and Canada) or (206)223-9599
Fax: (800)238-4065
E-mail: dsartmtrl@aol.com
Store Location: At above address, Bellevue WA.
Offers: Watercolors, acrylics, oil paints and printmaking inks, pastels and drawing materials. Over 700 types, sizes and colors of artists' papers. Glass paints, dry pigments, gilding and bookbinding materials. Canvas, panels, stretcher bars and studio furniture. Reasonably priced custom-cut frames are a specialty.
Catalog: 180 pages, color. $5 (refundable). Free supplements.
Phone Orders: M-F, 6-5; Sat, 9-5 PST.
Mail Orders: Ship worldwide. Most orders ship the same day they are placed.
Accepts: American Express, Discover, MasterCard, Visa

USARTQUEST, INC.
P.O. Box 88
Chelsea MI 48118
Contact: Susan Pickering Rothamel
Phone: (800)200-7848
Fax: (734)475-7622
E-mail: aqsue@aol.com
Website: www.usartquest.com

Offers: Unique high-quality fine art materials. Sole distributor for decorative mica for fine art. Videos, Perfect Paper adhesive, tapes, papers and accessories for arts and crafts.
Catalog: Retail-online only (wholesale) catalog available.
Phone Orders: M-F, 9-6 EST.
Mail Orders: International.
Discounts: Wholesale/distributors.
Accepts: American Express, MasterCard, Visa

UTRECHT MANUFACTURING CORP.
33 35th St.
Brooklyn NY 11232
Phone: (718)768-2525 or (800)223-9132
Website: www.utrechtart.com
Store Location: 12 stores, coast-to-coast.
Offers: Professional artists' oil paints, watercolors, acrylic paints, brushes, stretchers, paper converters and other major brand art supplies, such as papers, colors, canvases and more.
Catalog: Free.

V.E.A.S. PRODUCTIONS
P.O. Box 278
Troy MI 48099
Contact: Valynn Davenport
Phone: (248)584-2020 or (810)293-6931
E-mail: gemartschl@aol.com
Website: http://members.aol.com/gemartschl/
Store Location: Troy MI location.
Offers: Instructional learning video programs on how to airbrush paint, graphic and mural painting, gold leafing, glass etching, pinstriping, automotive painting and sign lettering techniques. "Street Art" manual.
Catalog: Free. Send #10 SASE envelope.
Phone Orders: Yes.
Mail Orders: At above address.
Discounts: Wholesalers 50%.

WINSOR & NEWTON
P.O. Box 1396
Piscataway NJ 08855-1396
Phone: (732)562-0770
Fax: (732)562-0941
Website: www.winsornewton.com
Offers: Artist's colors and brushes, including watercolors, oil colors, acrylic colors, Artisan water mixable oil colors and mediums, Kolinsky sable brushes, Regency Gold, craft brushes and many others. Manufacturer only. Does not sell to individuals.

Basketry & Seat Weaving

Also see Batik & Dyeing; Native American & Frontier Crafts; Nature Crafts; Knitting & Crochet.

ALLEN'S BASKETWORKS
P.O. Box 82638
Portland OR 97282
Phone: (503)238-6384
Offers: Basketry supplies (domestic and imported) and basic basket kits. Also carries reeds (round, flat, flat oval), rattan, cane, raffia, pine needles, seagrass, fiber rush (paper), "Richard's bean twine," basket feet, hoops, many handles, wooden bases and dyes. Tools available include awls, pliers and scissors. We carry basketry books and also a complete line of supplies for pine needle baskets.
Catalog: SASE.
Discounts: Sells wholesale.

BASKET BEGINNINGS
25 W. Tioga St.
Tunkhannock PA 18657-1422
Phone: (717)836-6080
Fax: (717)836-6224
Offers: Basket and fiber art products, including natural, hand-gathered, hand-dyed materials, Irish waxed linen and a line of unusual beads.
Catalog: Free.
Phone Orders: Yes.
Mail Orders: At above address.
Accepts: American Express, MasterCard, Visa

CANE & BASKET SUPPLY CO.
1283 S. Cochran Ave.
Los Angeles CA 90019
Contact: Bill Fimpler
Phone: (213)939-9644
Fax: (213)939-7237
E-mail: cabasu@2cowherd.net
Store Location: At above address.
Offers: Caning and basket weaving supplies, instruction books and basket kits, raffia, wax linen thread, pine needles, flat reeds, round reeds, hoops, handles, fiber rush, genuine rush, seagrass, gourds, rattan poles and bamboo poles.
Catalog: 24 pages. $2, refundable.
Phone Orders: M-F, 8:30-5:30 PST.
Mail Orders: Worldwide.
Discounts: To the trade and professional crafters.
Accepts: American Express, Diners Club, Discover, Master-Card, Visa

THE CANING SHOP
Dept. CSS
926 Gilman St.
Berkeley CA 94710
Phone: (800)544-3373
Fax: (510)527-7718
Website: http://www.caning.com
Offers: Basketry and chair caning supplies including cane and webbing, spline, Danish seat cord, rawhide and rubber webbing, Shaker tapes, reed splint, fiber rush, Hong Kong grass, ash splint, braided raffia, willowsticks and reed. Also carries rattan poles, Kooboo and whole rattans, pine needles, hickory and palm bark, paper rush, jute roving, date palm stalks, pressed fiber seats, basket kits and hoops. Tools available include awls, chisels, clamps, knives, clippers, shears, sliver grippers and cutters. Gourds and a gourd crafting book, videos, books, Ukranian egg decorating supplies, books and videos are also available.
Catalog: $2 (refundable).
Discounts: Quantity; teachers and institutions.
Accepts: Discover, MasterCard, Visa

CONNECTICUT CANE & REED
P.O. Box 762
331 Broad St.
Manchester CT 06045
Phone: (860)646-6586
Fax: (860)649-2221
E-mail: ctcanereed@msn.com
Store Location: At above address. M-F, 9-6; Sat, 10-5.
Offers: "Finestkind" basketry and chair seating materials. New England-made solid oak hoops, handles and market basket rims, as well as slotted pine bases and a variety of stool kits. Specializing in Shaker Tape for chair seating and basketry made 100% in the US. Publishes and distributes the highly acclaimed book *Chair Seat Weaving for Antique Chairs* by Marion Burr Sober. Can accommodate special requests and needs on orders large and small.
Phone Orders: (800)227-8498. M-F, 9-5; Sat, 10-4 EST.
Mail Orders: We ship everywhere, prepayment required, allow 1-2 weeks for delivery.
Discounts: Quantity discounts.
Accepts: American Express, Discover, MasterCard, Visa

COUNTRY BASKETS
90 Polikoff Rd.
Ashley Falls MA 01222
Phone: (413)229-2655
Offers: Shaker style and other original black ash basket-making kits and molds.
Catalog: Send SASE.

THE COUNTRY SEAT, INC.
Dept. CSS
1013 Old Philly Pike
Kempton PA 19529-9321
Phone: (610)756-6124
Fax: (610)756-0088
E-mail: ctryseat@fast.net
Website: http://www.countryseat.com
Store Location: At above address. M, 12-7; T-F, 9-5;
Sat, 9-1.
Offers: A complete line of basketry and chair seating supplies including natural and pre-dyed reeds, hoops, handles, basket kits for all skill levels, Nantucket supplies, basket accents and over 800 books and patterns.
Catalog: Send large SASE (3 stamps).
Phone Orders: Worldwide shipment. Discover, MasterCard or Visa required.
Mail Orders: Worldwide shipment.
Discounts: Quantity.
Accepts: Discover, MasterCard, Visa, check, money order

FRANK'S CANE & RUSH SUPPLY
7252 Heil Ave.
Huntington Beach CA 92647
Phone: (714)847-0707
Offers: Basket and seat weaving supplies, including bamboo and rattan poles, cane and binder cane, cane webbing, reed spline, fiber and wire rush, Danish cord, sugar palm, raw coconut fiber, fiber wicker and braids, round reeds, oriental sea grass, rice straw, raffia and sisal. Also has woodware, cutting tools, accessories, basket and furniture kits, upholstery supplies include cords, strips, tools, edgings, polyfilament and brass hardware. Tools include awls, wire twisters, cutters, templates and calipers.
Catalog: Free.
Discounts: Quantity; sells wholesale to legitimate businesses.
Accepts: American Express, Discover, MasterCard, Visa

GH PRODUCTIONS, INC.
Dept. CS
P.O. Box 621
Scottsville KY 42164
Contact: Scott Gilbert
Phone: (502)237-4821
Fax: (502)237-5137
E-mail: ghprod@nctc.com
Website: basketmakerscatalog.com
Store Location: Scottsville KY location.
Offers: Basket making and chair bottoming supplies, including flat and round reed and cane; basket kits; waxed linen thread, Shaker tape, basket handles, tools and othes. Also offers books.
Catalog: 32 pages. Free.
Phone Orders: (800)447-7008. M-F, 8-4:30 CST.
Mail Orders: Ship US and Canada. Prepaid.

Discounts: Sells wholesale to legitimate businesses.
Accepts: Discover, MasterCard, Visa

GRATIOT LAKE BASKETRY
HC1, Box 16
Mohawk MI 49950
Phone: (906)337-5116
Fax: (906)337-4260
E-mail: glbasketry@worldnet.att.net
Offers: Basketry supplies, including white pulute, maple, black walnut, cherry, 6 types of reeds, ash splint, poplar, seagrass, cane bindings, slab and chair rattan and cane webbing, birch, cedar, elm bark, honeysuckle, black ash. Also carries spline tools, kits, dyes, handles, hoops and embellishments. Florida materials include grapevines and philodendron sheaths. Also has patterns and books.
Catalog: Free catalog and newsletter.
Discounts: Quantity; teachers and institutions.

JAM CREATIONS
P.O. Box 764
1900 W. Wardlow Rd.
Highland MI 48357
Contact: Joan Moore
Phone: (248)887-5045
E-mail: jambasket@aol.com
Offers: Patterns for basket making. Books, including *Tribute*—23 patterns for all levels, and *Tole Sampler*, beginning to intermediate basket weaving and painting patterns.
Catalog: Catalog list with text and prices with retail.

JOHN MCGUIRE
398 S. Main
Geneva NY 14456
Phone: (315)781-1251
Store Location: Geneva NY.
Offers: Basketry supplies including Nantucket and Shaker style kits, wooden and resin molds, Nantucket, cane, reed, cherry, hickory, white oak rims, cherry bases, oak staves, bone decorations. Also offers black ash, cedar, bear grass, round and flat reed, splint cutting machines, tabletop shavehorses, drawknives, cutters, nippers, handles, dyes and instructional books. Also holds classes.
Catalog: Send large SASE for 32-page catalog.
Discounts: Quantity.

THE NORESTA CANE & REED
320 Western Ave.
Allegan MI 49010
Phone: (616)673-3249
Offers: Basketry supplies including press cane, hank cane, rush, splint, wicker, flat and round reeds, hoops, handles, dyes, basketry tools and books. Holds classes.
Catalog: $2.
Discounts: Sells wholesale.

NORTH CAROLINA BASKET WORKS

P.O. Box 744
Vass NC 28394
Phone: (800)338-4972
Offers: A distinctive selection of basketry kits, plus a complete line of supplies, including reeds, other naturals, and a large selection of handmade white oak handles. Also carries Nantucket and Shaker hardwood molds—accurate reproductions; rental is available on selected molds.
Discounts: Quantity.

OZARK BASKETRY SUPPLIES

P.O. Box 599
Fayetteville AR 72702
Phone: (501)442-9292
Offers: Supplies including basketry kits, tools, chair canes, handles, hoops, materials, chair seating supplies and dyes. Low priced. Carries over 100 books.
Catalog: $1.
Discounts: Sells wholesale.
Accepts: MasterCard, Visa

PACIFIC WEAVE/THE BASKETRY SCHOOL CONFERENCES

P.O. Box 15457
Seattle WA 98115-0457
Contact: Leslye Coe/Michelle Berg
Phone: (206)523-8955 or (800)879-3283
Fax: (206) 523-8981
Offers: Basketry materials including NW natural materials, books and tools. Basketry conferences.
Catalog: (800)879-3283.
Phone Orders: (800)879-3283.
Mail Orders: (800)879-3283.

PLYMOUTH REED & CANE SUPPLY

1200 W. Ann Arbor Rd.
Plymouth MI 48170
Phone: (734)455-2150
Fax: (734)455-9984
Store Location: At above address.
Offers: Basket-making supplies including natural weaving products, handles, hoops, tools, Old Village Collection basketry kits, chair seating materials, dyes, stencils and books. Write.
Discounts: Wholesale prices available.
Accepts: Discover, MasterCard, Visa

ROYALWOOD, LTD.

517-CSS Woodville Rd.
Mansfield OH 44907
Phone: (419)526-1630 or (800)526-1630
Store Location: At above address.
Offers: Basketry supplies including Irish waxed linen, a line of reed and other naturals, hoops, handles, dyes, accessories, basketry kits, brown ash, tools and molds.
Catalog: $2.
Discounts: Quantity.

SAX ARTS & CRAFTS

P.O. Box 510710
2405 S. Calhoun Rd.
New Berlin WI 53151
Phone: (414)784-6880
Offers: Artist's supplies (known brands), including a full line of weaving looms and aids, yarns, weaving kits, rug/craft yarns, embroidery/crewel threads, rug hook frames and aids, canvas, hoops, burlap and felt. Indian beading, beads, feathers, macrame, basketry and batik supplies, fabric paints, airbrush kits and inks, stencil films, trims, foam, stained glass kits, etching and beveled glass supplies and supplies for decoupage, jewelry making, leather, casting, plastics, wood and metal working are also available.
Catalog: $5 (refundable).
Discounts: Quantity, sells wholesale to legitimate businesses.

SIMPLY DE-VINE

654 Kendall Rd.
Cave Junction OR 97523
Contact: Meri Gerber
Phone: (541)592-3752
Fax: (541)592-4424
Store Location: At above address (Foris Winery).
Offers: Grapevine wreaths: teardrops, heart, oval, matted back and others. Carries baskets, bundles and cane wreaths. Manufacturer. Special orders service.
Phone Orders: M-F, 8-5 PST.
Mail Orders: In the US. Allow 1-3 weeks for delivery.
Discounts: Wholesale.
Accepts: MasterCard, Visa

V.I. REED & CANE

8522 Lakeview Bay Rd.
Rogers AR 72756
Contact: Linda Hebert
Phone: (501)789-2639
Fax: (501)789-2639
E-mail: linhebert@aol.com
Website: www.basketweaving.com
Offers: Full range of basket weaving and seat weaving supplies: kits, patterns (by Basketry Studio A), reed, cane, hoops, handles, Linda Hebert instructional videos, cane webbing, seagrass, fiber rush and more. Absolutely guaranteed superior quality. Custom T-shirts and aprons for your guild.
Catalog: Free.
Phone Orders: (800)852-0025.
Mail Orders: Ships anywhere. Most orders shipped within 24 hours.
Discounts: Low minimums for wholesale kits.
Accepts: American Express, Discover, MasterCard, Visa

VICTORIAN VIDEO

930 Massachusetts
Lawrence KS 66044
Contact: Jim and Susan Bateman
Phone: (785)842-4333 or (800)848-0284 (orders)

Fax: (785)842-0794
E-mail: yarnbarn@idir.net
Website: www.victorianvid.com
Store Location: At above address. M-Sat, 9:30-5:30 (Th until 8); Sun, 1-4.
Offers: How-to-craft videos cover beading, weaving, spinning, dyeing, knitting, crochet, basketry, sewing, quilting, needlework, lace making and more. Over 180 videos to choose from.
Catalog: Free. 34 pages.
Phone Orders: (800)848-0284. M-Sat, 9:30-5:30 CST.
Mail Orders: Yes. Prompt service.
Discounts: Retail; wholesale to legitimate businesses.
Accepts: Discover, MasterCard, Visa, check, money order

WEST VIRGINIA BASKETRY SUPPLY

(formerly Virginia Basket Supply)
Rt. 71, Box 26A
Glenville WV 26351
Contact: Carol Ross
Phone: (304)462-7638
E-mail: carolross@neumedia.net
Website: www.neumedia.net/~carolross
Offers: Basketry materials, including honeysuckle, cattails and yucca.
Catalog: Yes.
Phone Orders: Yes.
Mail Orders: Yes.
Accepts: check, money order

WALTERS BASKET WILLOW CROFT

RR 1, Box 127D
Washington Island WI 54246
Phone: (920)847-2276

Offers: Basketry materials include English basket willow (imported from Bristol, England) and propagated root, which comes with instructions for growing your own materials. Send SASE.
Discounts: Coupons and quantity discounts available.

WOODCREEK FARMS, INC.

12419 Jerry City Rd.
Cygnet OH 43413
Contact: Sales staff
Phone (800)664-1630
Fax: (419)655-2224
E-mail: woodcreek@wcnet.org
Website: www.woodcreekfarms.com
Store Location: At above address. M-F, 9-5 EST.
Offers: Dried flowers, herbs, wreaths, swags, assorted supplies, baskets and wall mounts. Everlasting dried flowers and herbs in plug trays. Live plants for spring planting.
Catalog: Free.
Phone Orders: M-F, 9-5 EST.
Mail Orders: UPS or mail. US or Canada. Prepayment to Canada. Short delivery time.
Discounts: We only sell wholesale; tax number needed.
Accepts: Discover, MasterCard, Visa

WOVEN SPIRIT BASKETRY

820 Albee Road W., Casey Key Plaza
Nokomis FL 34275
Phone: (941)485-6730
Store Location: At above address.
Offers: Full line of basket-making supplies, equipment and books.
Catalog: $2 (refundable).

Bead Crafts

Also see General Craft Supplies; Native American & Frontier Crafts; Jewelry Making & Lapidary; Miniature Making, Miniatures & Dollhouses; related categories.

ALICE'S STAINED GLASS (ASG)
Dept. CS
P.O. Box 552
Glendale AZ 85311-0552
Contact: Alice or Tammy
Phone: (602)939-7260
Fax: (602)939-8044
Store Location: Call ahead for appointment.
Offers: Glass bead-making supplies, videos and books; glass mosaic supplies and books; glass art-related supplies; handmade glass beads for the discriminating jeweler; and private bead-making classes.
Catalog: SASE for specific areas. 9,000-item "Big Book," $8 including postage.
Phone Orders: Yes.
Mail Orders: Worldwide shipping.
Discounts: Wholesale bead-making supplies to legitimate businesses.
Accepts: MasterCard, Visa (No C.O.D.)

BALLY BEAD CO.
2304 Ridge Rd.
Rockwall TX 75087
Phone: (972)771-4515 or (800)543-0280
Fax: (972)722-1979
E-mail: ballybead@worldnet.att.net
Website: http://www.ballybead.com
Store Location: At above address.
Offers: Jewelry making supplies, including gemstones, fetishes, Heishi, old coins and other ethnic items. Beads include Austrian and Czech crystal types, antique silver, seed, 14K gold-filled, sterling and plated types. Designer jewelry parts, angel parts, jewelry chains, ethnic and Santa Fe looks, and others. Beading supplies and classes also available.
Catalog: $4.95 (refundable).
Phone Orders: Yes.
Mail Orders: At above address.
Discounts: Discounts built into quantity purchases.
Accepts: Discover, MasterCard, Visa

BATON ROUGE BEAD CO.
15959 Hewwood, Suite F
Baton Rouge LA 70816
Contact: Carolyn Haley

Phone: (504)755-1332
Fax: (504)755-1334
Store Location: Baton Rouge LA location; M-F, 10-6; Sat, 10-4.
Offers: Seed beads—all kinds—14/0-6/10. Bugle beads, Japanese Delicas, Czech glass beads, handmade lampworked beads, natural stone beads, trade beads, Indian beads, bone and horn beads, crystal beads, fetishes and charms, memory wire, dichroic glass pendants, finished beads and jewelry, beading classes and freshwater pearls and silk.
Catalog: Price list $1.
Phone Orders: Yes.
Mail Orders: Same-day shipping.
Discounts: Quantity.
Accepts: MasterCard, Visa, check (order held until check clears), money order

THE BEAD DIRECTORY
P.O. Box 10103
Oakland CA 94610
Contact: Linda Benmour or Jody McDonnell
Phone: (707)569-0338
Fax: (415)664-4252
Offers: The most comprehensive collection of bead sources available. Wholesale, retail and mail-order sources. Over 600 of the best sources for beads and bead supplies. Also bead bazaars, bead makers, bead-making supplies, books, classes and museums.
Catalog: 270 pages. New section: Internet sites.
Phone Orders: Yes.
Mail Orders: Shipping costs are $3.50 US, $5 Canada and $9 foreign.
Accepts: MasterCard, Visa

BEAD IT! BEADS FROM AROUND THE WORLD
152 S. Montezuma
Prescott AZ 86303
Contact: Alessandra Scamaroo
Phone: (520)778-0220
Fax: (520)445-6270
E-mail: mail.beadit.com
Website: www.beadit.com
Store Location: Locations in Prescott AZ, Minneapolis MN, St. Louis MO and El Paso TX.
Offers: Beads, including Czech glass seeds; druks, rondelles, vintage German, antique trade beads, new Indian glass and gemstones. GF and SS beads and closures. How-to books, tools and supplies.
Catalog: New color catalog. Call for info.
Phone Orders: (800)657-0304.

Mail Orders: At above address.
Discounts: Quantity discounts.
Accepts: Discover, MasterCard, Visa

THE BEAD TREE
67 Blacksmith Shop Rd., Box 682
West Falmouth MA 02574
Contact: JoAnn Allard
Phone: (508)548-4665
Fax: (508)540-0507
E-mail: beadtree@aol.com
Store Location: At above address. M, W, F and Sun, 1-5.
Offers: Strands of beads from all over the world, seed beads 11/0, 8/0, 6/0 and Delicas, over 200 charms, findings in gold, silver, GF and sterling.
Catalog: $2.
Phone Orders: Yes.
Mail Orders: Yes.
Discounts: Over $50—10%.
Accepts: MasterCard, Visa

BEADCATS
Dept. CS
P.O. Box 2840
Wilsonville OR 97070-2840
Contact: Virginia or Carol
Phone: (503)625-2323
Fax: (503)625-4329
E-mail: carol@beadcats.com
Website: beadcats.com
Store Location: No walk-ins. Call 1 week in advance for appointment.
Offers: Expert service by Virginia Blakelock and Carol Perrenoud. Hundreds of colors of modern and antique Czech, Italian, French and Japanese seed beads, sizes 3/0-24/0, including Delicas, 3-cuts and charlottes. Their own pressed bead factory in Bohemia uses proprietary molds and rare glasses to produce beads you'll find nowhere else. Also a huge selection of colored threads and beading supplies.
Catalog: On-line. Also 50-page paper for $2.
Phone Orders: M-F, 10-4 PST.
Mail Orders: Will ship anywhere in the world, usually within 1 working day, prepaid or C.O.D.
Discounts: Wholesale, $100 minimum, special catalog available.
Accepts: Discover, MasterCard, Visa, business and personal check

BEADY EYED WOMEN, ENTERPRISES
P.O. Box 60691
San Diego CA 92166
Contact: Jeannette Cook or Vicki Star
Phone: (619)469-0254 or (760)633-1247
Fax: (760)633-1225
E-mail: vstar3@aol.com
Website: beadyeyedwomen.com
Offers: Beading books, amulet pouch patterns and kits, classes, bead party necklace kit and beading retreats.

Catalog: Quarterly newsletter. $12 per year.
Phone Orders: M-Th, 10-4 PST.
Mail Orders: Yes.
Discounts: Wholesale to bead stores.
Accepts: Discover, MasterCard and Visa

BEADZIP
2316-C Sarah Lane
Falls Church VA 22043
Phone: (703)849-8463
Offers: Beads, including glass, from areas worldwide—India, Czech, Peking and others. Also offers American Studio and African trade beads, seed beads, crystals, Bali silver, brass, copper, precious metal and plate, heishi, amber, enamel, cloisonne, porcelain, gemstones, bone, shell, wood, cinnabar and others. Jewelry findings, stringing materials, tools, supplies and books also available.
Catalog: Has design ideas. $5 (refundable).

BEYOND BEADERY
P.O. Box 460
Rollinsville CO 80474
Contact: Betcey Ventrella
Phone: (303)258-9389 or (800)840-5548
Fax: (303)258-9394
E-mail: beyondbd@earthnet.net
Website: http://members.aol.com/beyondbead
Store Location: By appointment only.
Offers: Thousands and thousands of Czech and Japanese glass seed beads, Japanese Delicas and antiques, Swarovski Austrian crystals and cut and pressed glass. Over a hundred how-to-bead books. Beading needles, threads, cords—all the things you need to bead.
Catalog: $2. 40 pages with color inserts.
Phone Orders: (800)840-5548. M-F, 9-5 MST.
Mail Orders: All orders shipped within 24 hours. No minimums.
Accepts: American Express, Discover, MasterCard, Visa

BOONE TRADING COMPANY
P.O. Box BB
562 Coyote Rd.
Brinnon WA 98320
Phone: (360)796-4330
Offers: Ivory carving and scrimshaw materials including legal pre-embargo elephant ivory, walrus, fossil walrus, mammoth, hippo and warthog. Available in a variety of forms including tusks, chunks, slabs, scrap, polished ivory jewelry and buckle blanks and beads. Also offers ivory carvings and scrimshaw, related books and tools, animal skulls, shark teeth, old trade beads, pearl shell and more.
Catalog: $1. 40 pages, illustrated.
Discounts: Sells wholesale to businesses.
Accepts: MasterCard, Visa

BOVIS BEAD CO.
P.O. Box 13345
Tucson AZ 85732
Contact: Pierre G. Bovis

Phone: (520)318-9512
Fax: (520)318-0023
Store Location: 4500 E. Speedway Blvd., Tucson AZ 85732.
Offers: Rare antique beads from remote areas of the world—Africa, Asia, Europe and Americas; French glass beads: "white hearts," old-time American Indian colors; French brass and copper beads; French spinning wheel to string beads; beads of all material, sizes and shapes; and bone and horn hairpipe beads. Beading supplies: needles, cords and sinew. American Indian craft supplies and more.
Catalog: $5 prepaid.
Phone Orders: Yes.
Mail Orders: Yes.
Discounts: All at wholesale prices.
Accepts: cash, check, money order—no credit cards

CAL-ART BEADS & THINGS

(formerly L.C. Smith's Beads)
P.O. Box 189
Jacksonville OR 97530
Contact: Cal or Alice Smith
Phone: (541)899-1557
Fax: (541)899-1557
Store Location: 155 N. Third St., Jacksonville OR 97530
Offers: Glassblowing and lampworkers supplies: books, kilns, Pyrex and soft glass, tools, torches, scales, diamond files, drills, plastic zip bags, trays and displays, videos, jeweler tools and supplies. Glass bottles and beads.
Catalog: Glass, $2; Jeweler's supplies, color $5.
Phone Orders: 7 days, 10-5.
Mail Orders: Yes.
Discounts: Resale and schools.
Accepts: American Express, Discover, MasterCard, Visa

CARAVAN BEADS, INC.

449 Forest Ave.
Portland ME 04101
Contact: Barry Kahn, president
Phone: (207)761-2503
Fax: (207)874-2664
E-mail: info@caravanbeads.com
Website: www.caravanbeads.com
Store Location: Retail store at above address. Also Chicago IL, Dover NH, and Wilmington NC.
Offers: Direct importer of Miyuki Japanese beads including 550 colors of Delicas 11/O and 6/O seed beads, 4mm cubes, triangles and bugles. Also import and distribute Japanese Miracle beads and Chinese freshwater pearls.
Catalog: Free price lists. Check website for regular updates on new stuff.
Phone Orders: (800)230-8941.
Discounts: Wholesale to stores, designers and other resellers.
Accepts: all major credit cards

CENTER FOR THE STUDY OF BEADWORK

P.O. Box 13719-CSC
Portland OR 97213
Contact: Alice Scherer

Phone: (503)657-0583
Fax: (503)657-0583
Website: www.europa.com/~alice
Offers: Beadwork books, resources and a newsletter. Books include authentic techniques and data, specific tribal and regional beading, patterns and data.
Catalog: $2.50, including sample newsletter.
Phone Orders: Yes; leave on machine.
Mail Orders: Yes.

COCHRAN'S CRAFTS

845 Willow Rd.
Lancaster PA 17601
Phone: (717)392-1687
Offers: Brass, silver and nickel-plated beads, including plain, fluted, swirl, bone hairpipe, F Czech and Japanese seed beads and antique trade beads. Sinew, findings, nymo thread and over 100 books of bead research and instructions.
Catalog: $1.

COLUMBINE BEADS

2723 Loch Haven Dr.
Ijamsville MD 21754
Contact: Linda Agar-Hendrix
Phone: (800)638-6947 or (301)865-5047
Fax: (301)865-1016
Offers: Imported Japanese square, twisted hex, magmata, triangle and foil.
Catalog: $3.50 (refundable with $20 order).
Discounts: Sells wholesale by ½ kilos.
Accepts: MasterCard, Visa

DABL'S PERETTE'S AFRICAN BEAD GALLERY

P.O. Box 711
1257 Washington Blvd.
Detroit MI 48226
Contact: Olayame Dabl's
Phone: (313)964-4247
Fax: (313)964-4281
Store Location: At above address. M-Sat, 12-9.
Offers: Perhaps Michigan's largest selection of African beads, textile and carvings. Thousands of rare, old and new items. Traditional mask, figures and metal. Beads from 1600s-1900s.
Catalog: 48 pages, 8½×11 b&w. $5 p&h.
Phone Orders: (800)530-6830. M-F, 12-5.
Mail Orders: Will ship anywhere, C.O.D. or prepayment.
Discounts: Sells wholesale and retail.
Accepts: check, money order

DJENNE BEADS & ART

Trapper's Alley
508 Monroe #202
Detroit MI 48226
Contact: Mahamadou Sumareh
Phone: (313)965-6620
Fax: (313)965-2060
E-mail: aa6887@wayne.edu

Website: In the process.
Store Location: Greektown in downtown Detroit.
Offers: Kuba cloth, Kente cloth, Mud cloth, antique baskets, beadwork, kaigle beads, clothing, yoruba beadwork, drums, body oils.
Catalog: Call for info.
Mail Orders: Yes.

DOUBLE JOY BEADS

7121 E. Shauraro Dr.
Scottsdale AZ 85254
Phone: (602)998-4495
Fax: (602)443-9540
Offers: Line of solid copper beads and jewelry findings.
Catalog: For copper beads and finding vintage beads and Swarovski crystals. (800)497-3702.

DRUMBEAT INDIAN ARTS

(formerly Canyon Records & Indian Arts)
4143 N. 16th St.
Phoenix AZ 85016
Phone: (602)266-4823
Offers: Beads in a variety of types and sizes—seeds, recailles, bugles, crow, hexagon, metal and bone. Also carries threads, quills, furs, shells, feathers, findings and shawl fringes. Write for craft list.

EAGLECRAFTS, INC.

168 W. 12th St.
Ogden UT 84404
Contact: Sue Smith
Phone: (801)393-3991
Fax: (801)745-0903
E-mail: eglcrafts@aol.com
Store Location: Eagle Feather Trading Post at above address. M-Sat, 9-6.
Offers: Beads of all kinds from all over the world. Beading supplies, Indian and mountain man craft supplies, kits, books, frontier clothing patterns, finished beadwork, leather, feathers, findings, gifts, looms, mandellas, Pendleton, conchos, pottery, belt buckles.
Catalog: 148 pages, 18 color charts. $4 ($5 off first order).
Phone Orders: (801)393-3991. M-Sat, 9-6 MST.
Mail Orders: Will ship worldwide; prepayment, C.O.D. or account required.
Discounts: 10% to qualified craftsmen; wholesale to legitimate businesses.
Accepts: Discover, MasterCard, Visa

ELVEE/ROSENBERG, INC.

11 W. 37th St.
New York NY 10018-6235
Contact: Melanie Holzberg
Phone: (212)575-0767
Fax: (212)575-0931
Store Location: Showroom located at above address. M-F, 9-4.
Offers: Simulated pearls and fashion beads, glass, plastic,

naturals, sterling silver, electroplated beads, cabochons and findings. Custom orders accepted including dyeing, pearlizing and electroplating. Vintage and unusual beads in stock. New fashion beads available every season. Spanish-speaking personnel available.
Catalog: Available for basic items.
Phone Orders: M-F, 9-5 EST.
Mail Orders: Will ship within US and Canada. Exporting available. Usually ship within a few days.
Discounts: Sells wholesale to legitimate businesses only.
Accepts: American Express, MasterCard, Visa

EVENING STAR DESIGNS

200 Merrimack St., Suite 401
Haverhill MA 01830
Contact: Carolyn S. Cibik or Valerie Kelley
Phone: (978)372-3473 or (800)666-3562
Fax: (978)372-6535
E-mail: evening.star.designs@worldnet.att.net
Website: http://home.att.net/~evening.star.design
Offers: Crazy quilting supplies: fancy fabrics, lace, trim, ribbon, embroidery threads, silk ribbon, metallic braid and ribbon, beads, (glass, mother-of-pearl, semiprecious stone, porcelain, crystal and more), buttons, books, patterns and kits.
Catalog: $3.
Phone Orders: Yes.
Mail Orders: At above address.
Accepts: MasterCard, Visa, check, money order

FIREFLY EMBROIDERIES

P.O. Box 304
Davisburg MI 48350
Phone: (800)447-6218
E-mail: ffbead@mich.com
Offers: Beaded embroidery kits with glass beads, sequins, pattern, needles and fabric in a variety of designs for clothing, jewelry and accessories. Also offers Pinzazz beaded stickpin kits and Razzmatazz beaded barrette kits. Luminette beaded lampshade kits.
Catalog: $2.

GAMEPLAN VIDEOS

(formerly Gameplan/Abstract)
2233 McKinley Ave.
Berkeley CA 94703
Phone: (510)843-9969
Offers: 14 instructional videos on polymer clay crafting by Tony Hughes, including *Beginning Workshop*, *Bead Shapes* and *Mixing Media*. Also offers videos on recreating turquoise, lapis, bone, jade, amber and coral.
Catalog: Free.

GAMPEL SUPPLY

11 W. 37th St.
New York NY 10018-6235
Contact: Ira Zagoren
Phone: (212)398-9222
Fax: (212)575-0931

Store Location: At above address. M-F, 9-5.

Offers: Bead stringing and jewelry making supplies, tools, adhesives, findings, wire, needles, threads, cording, beads, bead boards, books and much more. Spanish-speaking personnel available.

Catalog: Free. Available upon request.

Phone Orders: M-F, 9-5 EST.

Mail Orders: Will ship C.O.D., cash, prepaid or credit card. Will ship within a few days.

Discounts: Sells wholesale to legitimate businesses.

Accepts: American Express, MasterCard, Visa

GARDEN OF BEADIN'

P.O. Box 1535

Redway CA 95542-3105

Contact: Charlotte Silverstein

Phone: (707)923-9120

Fax: (707)923-9160

E-mail: beads@asis.com

Website: www.a1server.com/beadluv

Store Location: 752 Redwood Dr., Gaberville CA 95542-3105

Offers: Beads, including bugles, glass seed in full range of colors and sizes; crow, pony, hex, crystal and other gemstone colors; Czech drops, crystal faceted, glass and crystal. Carries wood, venetian, satin glass and pseudo trade types.

Catalog: Free. 64 pages, color.

Phone Orders: (800)BEAD-LUV.

Mail Orders: Global shipping.

Discounts: On quantity and orders over $150 (20%).

Accepts: American Express, Discover, MasterCard, Visa

GOLDEN HANDS PRESS

(formerly Art to Wear)

5 Crescent Pl. S. #2

St. Petersburg FL 33711

Contact: Bob Poris

Phone: (813)867-3711

Fax: (813)867-4211

Offers: 2 bead-stringing books: *Step-by-Step Bead Stringing* by Ruth F. Poris, $7.99 + shipping and *Advanced Beadwork* by Ruth F. Poris, $14.99 + shipping. Bead stringing (jeweler's) tools such as pliers, tweezers, scissors, pin vises and awls. Also carries bead boards, needles, tips, crimps, tiger-tails, cable chains, foxtails, boullion wire, needle cards, silk cones, spool cord kits and jewelry findings. Beads include sterling, 14K, gold-filled types, semiprecious gemstone beads and freshwater pearls. Carries designer bead kits and books.

Phone Orders: M-F, 10-5 EST.

Mail Orders: Yes; prepayment.

Discounts: Depends on quantity for wholesalers, distributors, etc.

Accepts: MasterCard, Visa

HIRSCH DESIGNS

7000 N. 16th St., Suite 120-181

Phoenix AZ 85020

Contact: Fran Hirsch

Phone: (602)861-2961

Fax: (602)331-8306

E-mail: franhir@juno.com

Offers: Delica beads from Miyuki, antique beads from Toho, colored thread, beading needles, square tubes. Next day shipping.

Catalog: $3. Color.

Phone Orders: M-F, 10-5. Some Saturdays.

Mail Orders: To most anywhere.

Discounts: Wholesale to businesses.

Accepts: Discover, MasterCard, Visa

HOUSE OF ONYX

The Aaron Bldg.

120 N. Main St.

Greenville KY 42345-1504

Contact: Fred Rowe III, president

Phone: (800)844-3100

Fax: (502)338-9605

E-mail: onyx@muhlon.com

Website: www.houseofonyx.com

Store Location: At above address.

Offers: Genuine gemstone beads (loose), gold and silver chains and bead-stringing cords. Gemologists: appraisals and lab services.

Catalog: Monthly. Free.

Phone Orders: Yes.

Mail Orders: US only. Immediate shipments.

Discounts: 75% maximum.

Accepts: MasterCard, Visa, check, cash

J P IMPORTED

3350 D Fulton Rd., Box 258

Fulton CA 95439

Contact: Jeff Pines

Phone: (707)541-0301

Fax: (707)541-0301

E-mail: jpimport@sonic.net

Store Location: Wholesale; only by appointment.

Offers: We carry a large selection of venetian glass and hand-painted ceramic beads specializing in animals.

Catalog: Available upon request.

Phone Orders: M-F, 10-2 PST or fax anytime.

Mail Orders: US and Canada. Retail prepayment required.

Discounts: Wholesale to legitimate businesses.

Accepts: MasterCard, Visa

MANGUM'S BEADER'S PARADISE, INC.

(formerly Mangum's Western Wear)
P.O. Box 362
Blackfoot ID 83221
Phone: (208)785-9967 or (208)785-1838
Offers: Seed beads (down to size 24); will match color swatches.
Catalog: $1.

MARGOLA CORP.

48 W. 37th St.
New York NY 10018
Contact: Neil J. Chalfin
Phone: (212)695-1115
Fax: (212)594-0071
E-mail: margola@erols.com
Website: www.margola.com
Store Location: At above address. M-F, 8-6.
Offers: Czech beads: seed, 2-cut, 3-cut, bugle, druk, firepolish, crystal beads, glass and crystal quality rhinestones, jewelry findings, nailheads, settings, glass pearls and Japanese and Chinese urea pearls. Metallized beads, puff fabric trim, iron-on rhinestones bulk and iron-on rhinestone motifs.
Catalog: Various per products category.
Phone Orders: M-F, 8-5 EST.
Mail Orders: Will ship to US and Canada. Terms net 10 EOM to accounts who can produce acceptable credit references.
Discounts: Sells wholesale.
Accepts: MasterCard, Visa, prepay check, C.O.D.

MORNING LIGHT EMPORIUM

P.O. Box 1155
Paonia CO 81428
Phone: (970)527-4493
Offers: Glass beads, including crow, pony, 11/O and 14/O seed beads, bugles, chevrons, metal and bone. Also offers beading thread, needles and books.
Catalog: Free.

THE NAME GAME

505 S. Beverly Dr. #123
Beverly Hills CA 90212
Phone: (310)284-3434
Offers: Line of letter and symbol beads of wood in English, Greek, Hebrew and American Sign Language. Send SASE.
Discounts: Sells wholesale.

NATURAL TOUCH

P.O. Box 855
San Anselmo CA 94979
Contact: Judy Tomsky
Phone: (415)257-4104
Fax: (415)451-0124
E-mail: ntbeads@aol.com
Store Location: Showroom. Call for details.

Offers: Recycled glass beads from Indonesia. Unique folded silver beads, brass metal spacers, antique trade beads, stones and adornments. Wide variety of components, findings and stones for the jewelry oriented, hobbyist and designers. Also good for decorators.
Catalog: 4-color. $3.
Phone Orders: Accepted 24 hours.
Mail Orders: Will ship.
Discounts: Sells wholesale to business licensed companies.
Accepts: MasterCard, Visa

ORNAMENTAL RESOURCES, INC.

P.O. Box 3010
Idaho Springs CO 80452
Phone: (800)876-ORNA
Website: www.ornabead.com
Offers: Complete lines of glass beads, including faceted, cut, foiled, decorated, fancy, metal, ceramic, plastic, bone, stone, shell, bugles, pony and seed beads in all sizes. Collectors' beads, metal stampings, chains, appliqué materials, rhinestones, studs, sequins, glass jewels, tassels, buckles and buttons. Also offers beading tools and supplies and design assistance. $25 minimum order. Call or write.
Catalog: $15 (with one year's supplements).

PERSONALITY PLUS

38 US Rt. 4 E.
Mendon VT 05701
Contact: Jean Pearson
Phone: (802)773-9377
E-mail: pearson@vermontel.com
Website: www.beadz.com
Store Location: At above address.
Offers: Bead emporium with over 1,900 varieties of beads and findings. Worktables, free instruction. Open T-Sat, 10-5; Sun, 1-5. Other hours by appointment.
Catalog: Free.
Phone Orders: (802)773-1516. M-F, 9-5 EST.
Mail Orders: Requests to above address. Prepayment required.
Accepts: Discover, MasterCard, Novus, Visa

PROMENADE'S LE BEAD SHOP

1970 13th St.
Boulder CO 80302
Phone: (303)440-4807
Offers: Full line of beadwork supplies (for beaded jewelry, trim on clothing and other). Also carries beading kits, threads, needles and bead instruction booklets for earrings, clothing and other articles.
Catalog: $2.50 (refundable).

RISHASHAY

300 Evans Ave.
Missoula MT 59801
Contact: John P. Anderson

Phone: (800)517-3311
Fax: (406)549-3467
Offers: Handmade silver beads from Indonesia.
Catalog: 34 pages, color. $5 (refunded with first order).
Phone Orders: 9-5 MST.
Mail Orders: At above address. Same-day shipping on orders received before 12 noon MST.
Discounts: Wholesale and retail.
Accepts: American Express, Discover, MasterCard, Visa

SCOTTSDALE BEAD SUPPLY
3625 N. Marshall Way
Scottsdale AZ 85251
Contact: Kelly or Mike Charveaux
Phone: (602)945-5988
Fax: (602)945-4248
Website: www.scottsdalebeadsupply.com
Store Location: At above address.
Offers: Direct importers of Balinese silver beads, Czech beads, Indian, Japanese Delicas. Very large assortment of custom lamp beads. Manufacturers of dichroic glass donuts and pendants, cabochons and our own custom sterling charms and pendants.
Catalog: $5 (refundable on first order).
Phone Orders: $50 minimum.
Mail Orders: $50 minimum.
Discounts: Wholesale and retail.
Accepts: MasterCard, Visa

SHIPWRECK BEADS
2727 Westmoor Court SW
Olympia WA 98502
Phone: (360)754-2323
E-mail: sales@shipwreck-beads.com
Website: www.shipwreck-beads.com
Store Location: At above address.
Offers: Beads: Czech glass, gemstone, metallics, crystal, seed, wood, bone, buffalo horn, plastic, antique, trade and others, plus beading supplies and tools, jewelry findings and books.
Catalog: 108 pages, full color. $4.
Phone Orders: 7 days a week, 9-6 PST.

Discounts: Quantity; sells wholesale to legitimate businesses and professionals.
Accepts: Discover, MasterCard, Visa, net terms on approved credit

UNIVERSAL SYNERGETICS BEADCATS
P.O. Box 2840
Wilsonville OR 97070-2840
Contact: Carol or Virginia
Phone: (503)625-2323
Fax: (503)625-4329
E-mail: orders@beadcats.com
Website: www.beadcats.com
Offers: Seed beads (11/O-22/O); bugle beads; and Czech pressed glass beads in the shape of drops, pendants, leaves and flowers. Bead sample cards available. Colored nylon beading thread, findings, books, needles and many beading supplies.
Catalog: $2.
Phone Orders: M-F, 10-4 PST.
Mail Orders: Orders shipped within 24 hours. Ship overseas air parcel post insured.
Discounts: Wholesale. $100 minimum orders; ¼ kilo minimum per bead.
Accepts: Discover, MasterCard, Visa, check, money order

VEON CREATIONS
3565 State Rd. V
DeSoto MO 63020
Contact: Char or Veon
Phone: (314)586-5377
Fax: (314)586-5377
E-mail: veonbds@jcn1.com
Website: www.jcn1.com/veonbds
Store Location: At above address. M-F, 11-7 CST.
Offers: Beads, beadworking supplies, jewelry findings, bead and crafts how-to books, American Indian heritage books and Indian craft supplies. *Creative Beaded Earrings*, Volumes 1-4 (retail and wholesale).
Catalog: Bead & Supplies, $4. Book $4.
Phone Orders: M-F, 11-7 CST.
Mail Orders: Will ship to US and Canada. Prepaid required.
Discounts: Bulk discounts on beads. Wholesale *Creative Beaded Earrings*, Volumes 1-4.
Accepts: MasterCard, Visa, check, money order

Ceramics

Also see Artist's Supplies, Graphics & Printing; General Craft Supplies; Sculpture & Modeling; Doll & Toy Making—Rigid. Note the many custom services available in this chapter.

AEGEAN SPONGE CO., INC.
4722 Memphis Ave.
Cleveland OH 44144
Contact: Althea Psarras
Phone: (216)749-1927
Fax: (216)749-2110
E-mail: jplimnos@worldnet.att.net
Website: www.craftroom.com/aegeansponge
Offers: Natural and synthetic sponges and a variety of tools. Ceramic supplies available include Christmas tree lights and sets, lightbulbs, clock movements, music boxes, turntables, lusters, chalks, abrasives, brushes, liquid gold and spray finishes.
Catalog: Wholesale catalog available.
Phone Orders: Yes.
Mail Orders: Yes.
Discounts: Available.
Accepts: MasterCard, Visa, check, money order

AFTOSA
1034 Ohio Ave.
Richmond CA 94804
Phone: (510)233-0334 or (800)231-0397
Website: www.aftosa.com
Offers: Supportive items including votive chimneys, lamp kits, candles, mini-lamp kits and shades, stoppers, dispenser pumps and wire whips. Also carries jewelry findings for pins and earrings, plus wax resist.
Catalog: Free.
Accepts: American Express, Discover, MasterCard, Visa

AIM KILNS
350 SW Wake Robin
Corvallis OR 97333
Phone: (800)647-1624
Fax: (541)758-8051
Offers: Doll kiln (designed by doll makers for doll makers), 15 amps, cone 10, 8″ square, with shut off infinite switch. Write or call.
Discounts: Sells wholesale to established distributors.

ALBERTA'S MOLDS, INC.
P.O. Box 2018
Atascadero CA 93423
Contact: Alberta Gaskell (California office)

Phone: (805)466-9255
Fax: (805)466-5961
E-mail: info@albertas.com
Website: webmaster@albertas.com
Store Location: Other location: 1209 ESI Dr., Springdale AR 72764.
Offers: Full line of ceramic molds including classic, Early American, novelty/holiday figures, animals, music box carousels and dinnerware.
Catalog: $10 ($7 + $3 for postage).
Phone Orders: (805)466-9255.
Mail Orders: At P.O. Box.
Discounts: To bona fide ceramic businesses.

AMERICAN ART CLAY CO., INC.
4717 W. 16th St.
Indianapolis IN 46222
Contact: Nancy Elliott
Phone: (317)244-6871 or (800)374-1600
Fax: (317)248-9300
E-mail: amacobrent@aol.com
Website: www.amaco.com
Offers: AMACO ceramic supplies and glazes. Clays include firing, nonfiring, modeling and other types. Over 475 colors of glazes and underglazes available from low fire to high fire. Electric kilns include economical round models and high-fire square models, all available with Select Fire computer control. Other products include potter's wheels, slab rollers, brushes, tools and supplies.
Catalog: Free.
Phone Orders: M-F, 8-5 EST.
Mail Orders: Prepayment required. Will ship to US and Canada.
Discounts: Manufacturer—sells through distributors.
Accepts: Discover, MasterCard, Visa

ARNEL'S, INC.
2330 SE Harney St.
Portland OR 97202
Contact: Marc W. Dransfeldt
Phone: (503)236-8540
Fax: (503)236-6494
Store Location: At above address. M-F, 8:30-5.
Offers: Ceramic pottery molds designed for slip-casting with earthenware slip, stoneware or porcelain. Over 500 designs. Dinnerware, seasonal, figurines, Victorian, animal figures, ethnic and lots more.
Catalog: Full color. $7 (refundable).
Phone Orders: (800)2AR-NELS. M-F, 8:30-5 PST.

Mail Orders: At above address. Canadian customers add $3 additional for p&h.

Discounts: Available upon request for customers with legitimate businesses.

Accepts: American Express, Discover, MasterCard, Visa, check, money order

ATLANTIC MOLD CORP.

55 Main St.

Trenton NJ 08620

Phone: (609)581-0880

Fax: (609)581-0467

Offers: Ceramic molds for figurines (children, historical, doll parts, birds, animals and others), Christmas items (nativity, angels, candles, dishes and Santas) and Easter and other holiday designs. Also offers spaceman/craft molds, decoratives, plaques, vases, clocks, containers, beer steins, emblems, chess sets, planters, platters, casseroles, cookie jars, bathroom items and bases. Accessories available include lamp parts, sets, Lanshire clock movements and Lucite lights. Manufacturer. Contact your dealer.

Catalog: $8.50, color.

Accepts: MasterCard, Visa

DICK BLICK

Dept. CB

P.O. Box 1267

Galesburg IL 61402-1267

Phone: (309)343-6181

Offers: Full line of art/sculpture and other materials and equipment: soapstone, alabaster, stone sculpture tool sets. Modeling: instant papier-mâchés, Sculptamold, plastercraft gauze, plaster of Paris (and molds), Sculpey, FIMO, modeling clays. Clays: Mexican pottery, Marblex, Westwood ovencraft, others. Also offers Egyptian paste, earthenware and other kitchen-fired clays, plus glazes, ceramic and modeling tools/sets and aids.

Accepts: American Express, Discover, MasterCard, Visa

B&W TILE CO., INC.

14600 S. Western Ave.

Gardena CA 90249

Contact: Debbie

Phone: (310)538-9579

Fax: (310)538-2190

Store Location: At above address. Also 3325 Russell St., Riverside CA 92501. Phone: (909)715-4620. Fax: (909)515-4630. M-F, 8-5; Sat, 8-4.

Offers: Ceramic and bisque tile, trims and tile supplies. Manufacturer of ceramic and bisque products; showroom at both stores.

Catalog: $1. Shows shapes and sizes.

Phone Orders: M-F, 8-5 PST.

Mail Orders: Will ship to US and Canada.

Discounts: Dealers welcome.

Accepts: MasterCard, Visa

BRICKYARD CERAMICS & CRAFTS

4721 W. 16th St.

Speedway IN 46222

Contact: Order desk

Phone: (800)677-3289

Fax: (800)248-9300

Store Location: At above address. M-F, 9-4:30; W, 9-8; Sat, 9-3.

Offers: Ceramics supplies: kilns, glazes, tools, clay, wheels and more. Crafts: Friendly Clay, Friendly Plastics, cotton press, stamps, candle supplies and more.

Catalog: Free AMACO catalog.

Phone Orders: M-F, 9-4:30.

Mail Orders: Worldwide. Fast delivery.

Discounts: Sells wholesale to legitimate businesses.

Accepts: Discover, MasterCard, Visa, C.O.D.

CHARLES A. CASPER

Rt. 1, Box 379

May TX 76857

Contact: Charles A. Casper

Phone: (915)643-2388

Offers: Native American peace pipe kits, pipe bowl molds and wooden stems. Authentic native pot and ostrich egg molds.

Catalog: Send five 32¢ stamps for prices.

Mail Orders: Will ship to US.

CERAMIC BUG SUPPLIES

17220 Garden Valley Rd.

Woodstock IL 60098

Contact: Daniel E. Schneider

Phone: (815)568-7663

Fax: (815)568-7659

Store Location: At above address.

Offers: Robert Simmons brushes, Mayco Colors, ceramic bug slip marbleizer and ceramic bug slip. Lots of used and never used molds. Kilns, new and used, repairs and parts.

Phone Orders: Yes.

Mail Orders: Yes.

Discounts: As apply.

Accepts: check, money order

CERAMIC CREATIONS

144 Hollyvale Dr.

Houston TX 77060

Phone: (713)448-2515

Fax: (713)448-1675

Offers: Ceramic bisque and greenware, including Native American, holidays, country items, angels, cherubs, cookie jars, teapots, canisters and lots of African figurines and plaques for children and adults.

Catalog: $5.95.

Discounts: Quantity. Dealers only.

CERAMIC RESTORATION
2015 N. Dobson Rd.
Suite 4, Box 59
Chandler AZ 85224
Offers: Instruction for restoration of damaged porcelains, ceramics and collectibles. Restoration videos with detailed examples also available. Also offers 8 explanatory lessons and a selection of professional supplies. Send large SASE.

CERAMICORNER DECALS
626 N. San Gabriel Ave.
Azusa CA 91792
Contact: Mike Boehm
Phone: (626)969-1456
Fax: (626)334-6639
Offers: Decals for ceramics. Large variety of open stock designs plus custom printing service.
Catalog: 79-page decal catalog and custom printing information. $8, postpaid.
Phone Orders: (800)423-8543.
Mail Orders: Yes.

CREATIVE CERAMICS
9815 Reeck
Allen Park MI 48101
Phone: (313)382-1270 or (800)438-2700
Fax: (313)382-2199
Store Location: M-F, 8:15-4.
Offers: Ceramic glazes, stains, brushes, music boxes, electrical wiring, clocks and lamp hardware.
Phone Orders: Yes.
Mail Orders: Yes.
Accepts: Discover, MasterCard, Visa

CREATIVE CORNER
P.O. Box 121
Canistota SD 57012
Contact: Nina Lambertz
Phone: (605)296-3261
Fax: (605)296-3261
Store Location: 241 Main St., Canistota SD 57012. M-F, 9-5; Sat, 9-1.
Offers: Over 3,000 items in bisque ware (fired and ready for you to paint or glaze). Includes vases, dishes, cups and canisters. Animal figures, such as deer, wolves, bears, bunnies, cats and dogs. Fish, such as tropical and bass; dolphins. Southwestern and Native American pieces. Holiday items for Christmas, Easter, Halloween and more. Many angels, unicorns, wizards, dragons, gargoyles and much more.
Catalog: $6.
Phone Orders: M-Sat.
Mail Orders: We ship UPS daily.
Discounts: Sells retail. Also wholesale to legitimate businesses.
Accepts: Discover, MasterCard, Visa

CREATIVE HOBBIES, INC.
900 Creek Rd.
Bellmawr NJ 08031
Contact: Ginny Rozzelle
Phone: (888)THE-KILN
Fax: (800)992-7675
E-mail: mail@creative-hobbies.com
Website: http://www.creative-hobbies.com
Offers: Ceramics and pottery supplies, bisque, clay, glazes, kilns, music boxes, clocks, lamp parts, lampshades and molds.
Catalog: 400 pages with color. $5 (refundable).
Phone Orders: M-F, 9-5 EST.
Mail Orders: 24-hour shipment, domestic or international.
Accepts: Discover, MasterCard, Visa

CRIDGE, INC.
P.O. Box 210
Morrisville PA 19067
Phone: (215)295-3667
Fax: (215)736-8634
Offers: Full line of porcelain jewelry blanks, plus ornaments, findings and inserts.
Catalog: Free.
Discounts: Quantity.

LOU DAVIS WHOLESALE
Dept. CS8
N3211 County Rd. H. N.
Lake Geneva WI 53147
Phone: (414)248-2000 or (800)748-7991
Offers: Brand-name craft and ceramic supplies, including music movements in more than 200 tunes, chalks, paints, spray finishes, airbrushes and compressors, clock movements, doll-making supplies, lamp parts and accessories, brushes, magnets, glitter, abrasives, adhesives and cleaning tools.
Catalog: $2 (refundable with order).
Accepts: Discover, MasterCard, Visa

DURALITE, INC.
P.O. Box 188
15 School St.
Riverton CT 06065
Phone: (860)379-3113
Fax: (860)379-5879
Offers: Rapid replacement coils and electric elements for all brands/types of kilns and furnaces, plus straight wire and continuous coil. Also offers switches, connectors and design services. Call or write for brochure and price list.
Discounts: Quantity.

E&T INDUSTRIES, INC.
516 Sea St.
Quincy MA 02196
Phone: (617)479-4107
Fax: (617)376-2533

Store Location: At above address. M-Th, 9-4 and 7-9; F, 9-2; Sat, 10-2. Call for summer hours.
Offers: Favor-Rite, Old Town and Daddy Molds. Africana and FashenHues paints.
Catalog: $6, mold catalog.

ENGELHARD CORP.
101 Wood Ave. S., CN-770
Iselin NJ 08830
Phone: (732)205-5000 or (800)631-9505
Fax: (732)632-9253
Offers: Hanovia overglaze products, including lusters, metallics, opal and mother-of-pearl (for ceramics, china and glass). Also offers Cerama-Pen gold or platinum applicator. Manufacturer. Contact your dealer; free technique sheets.

EVENHEAT KILN, INC.
6949 Legion Rd.
Caseville MI 48725
Contact: John Watson
Phone: (517)856-2281
Fax: (517)856-4040
E-mail: evenheat@avci.net
Website: www.evenheat-kiln.com
Store Location: At above address.
Offers: Manufacturer of electric hobby kilns and kiln accessories.
Catalog: Free.
Phone Orders: M-F, 8:30-5.
Mail Orders: Will ship US, Canada and international.
Discounts: Sells to distributors.
Accepts: MasterCard, Visa

FLORIDA CLAY ART CO.
Orlando-Sanford Airport
1645 Hangar Rd. #103
Sanford FL 32773
Contact: Carol
Phone: (407)330-1116 or (800)211-7713
Fax: (407)330-5058
E-mail: flclay@worldramp.net
Store Location: M,T,Th,F, 9-5; W, 9-1.
Offers: Tools, sponges, slip casting equipment, kilns, clay mixers, cork, pumps, rubber stoppers, stilts, posts, kitchen utensils (no handles), kitchen utensil handle, molds, bisque, hand-building tools, books and videos.
Catalog: Free. Monthly sales faxed.
Phone Orders: Yes.
Mail Orders: Yes. Generally UPS and filled within 48 hours.
Discounts: Quantity discounts on most merchandise.
Accepts: American Express, MasterCard, Visa, C.O.D.

FOREVER YOUNG ART & VIDEOS
(formerly AV Productions)
P.O. Box 99722
Troy MI 48099-9722
Contact: Lee Short
Phone: (248)740-0234

Fax: (248)524-2817
E-mail: artvideo@customnet.net
Website: www.artvideo.com
Offers: Videos: ceramic, doll making, jewelry, pottery and quilting. Ceramic cat pins, ceramic ornaments and cat poems.
Catalog: Free.
Phone Orders: Anytime.
Mail Orders: US, Canada and overseas.
Discounts: Sells wholesale to legitimate businesses.
Accepts: American Express, MasterCard, Visa

GEORGIES CERAMIC & CLAY CO., INC.
756 NE Lombard
Portland OR 97211
Contact: Stan Touneson
Phone: (503)283-1353
Fax: (503)283-1387
E-mail: info@georgies.com
Website: www.georgies.com
Offers: Pottery- and ceramic-making supplies, sculpture, glass fusing, candle making, enameling, dolls, stone and other 3-D arts.
Catalog: 208 pages.
Phone Orders: (800)999-2529.
Mail Orders: Yes.
Discounts: To all types of craft business, including home business.
Accepts: all major credit cards

GOLDLINE CERAMICS
3024 Gayle St.
Orange CA 92865
Contact: Bob Thompson
Phone: (714)637-2205
Store Location: At above address.
Offers: 1,500 personal name ceramic decals, hobo style in black. Extra common names. Name list $52. Prepayment required.
Mail Orders: 1-2 weeks.

HOLLAND MOLD, INC.
P.O. Box 5021
1040 Pennsylvania Ave.
Trenton NJ 08638
Phone: (609)392-7032
Fax: (609)394-0101
Offers: Molds including holiday items and sets, historical figures, wild animals, birds, eggs, steins, mugs, bowls, serving pieces, canisters, candlesticks, picture frames, plaques (marriage, birth, graduation and others), clocks, lamp bases, pedestals, bells, boxes, and lawn, garden and patio figures. Custom mold service available. Write for information.
Catalog: $7.
Discounts: Offered to those qualified. Schedule included in catalog.
Accepts: MasterCard, Visa

INSTAR BEAUTIFUL DECALS

P.O. Box 6609
124 Tices Lane
East Brunswick NJ 08816
Contact: Robert W. Engel
Phone: (732)238-0979
Fax: (800)975-4678
E-mail: instar@instar-usa.com
Website: www.instar-usa.com
Store Location: At above address. M-F, 9-5 EST.
Offers: Water-mount slide-off decals for crafts, glass and ceramics. Thousands of sizes. Highest order fill rate in the industry. Largest open stock decal provider in North America.
Catalog: $7 plus $3 p&h. Open stock, over 200 pages and in color. Graphics. Supplement available.
Phone Orders: M-F, 9-5 EST.
Mail Orders: Ship to US and Canada. Quick turnaround.
Discounts: 50% with 3 pieces of wholesale ID.
Accepts: American Express, Discover, MasterCard, Visa

JAY-KAY MOLDS

P.O. Box 2307
Quinlan TX 75474
Phone: (903)356-3416
Offers: Plaster molds for the ceramic industry, ranging from Southwest pieces to usable items.
Catalog: $6.
Discounts: Distributorships and other discounts available.

K-CERAMIC IMPORTS, INC.

732 Ballough Rd.
Daytona Beach FL 32114
Contact: John Koutouzis
Phone: (904)252-6530
Fax: (904)257-5486
Store Location: At above address.
Offers: Decals for ceramics, china, porcelain and tile. Synthetic sponges and natural sea sponges.
Catalog: Imported water-mount decals. Tile design.
Phone Orders: Yes.
Mail Orders: Yes.
Discounts: See catalog.
Accepts: MasterCard, Visa

KELLY'S CERAMICS, INC.

3016 Union Ave.
Pennsauken NJ 08109
Contact: Bertha S. Kelly
Phone: (609)665-4181
Fax: (609)665-4181
Store Location: At above address.
Offers: Molds, Gare products, greenware and bisque products, ceramic classes and seminars (Gare).
Mail Orders: Prepayment required.
Accepts: MasterCard, Visa

KEMPER ENTERPRISES, INC.

13595 12th St.
Chino CA 91710
Contact: Katie Munday
Phone: (800)388-5367 or (909)627-6191
Fax: (909)627-4008
E-mail: thetoolady@aol.com
Offers: Manufacturer and designer of tools for painting that include the Fluid Writer, Wipe-Out tool that erases mistakes, faux finishing tools and a spray gun cleaner set.
Catalog: Free. 70+ pages, color. Please send $1.50 for p&h.
Phone Orders: Customer service hours are M-F, 8-4:30 PST.
Mail Orders: Can expect order to ship within 2 days of receipt. Ship domestic and international through UPS.
Discounts: Sell wholesale to businesses. For account qualifications and status please contact.
Accepts: Discover, MasterCard, Visa, International Money Order, bank wire transfer in American dollars only

L&L KILN MANUFACTURING, INC.

6B Mt. Pleasant Dr.
Aston PA 19014
Contact: Denise Vance
Phone: (610)558-3899
Fax: (610)558-3698
E-mail: sales@hotkilns.com
Website: www.hotkilns.com
Store Locations: At above address. M-F, 8:30-5 EST.
Offers: Electric kilns for ceramics, pottery, glass and enameling. Kiln vents, program control.
Catalog: Free.
Phone Orders: M-F, 8:30-5 EST.
Mail Orders: Will ship anywhere.
Accepts: MasterCard, Visa

LAGUNA CLAY CO.

14400 Lomitas Ave.
City of Industry CA 91746
Contact: David Hoffman for information about becoming a distributor
Phone: (626)330-0631, ext. 229
Fax: (626)333-7694
E-mail: dave@lagunaclay.com
Store Locations: At above address. Locations in Denver CO (303)772-5398, Cambridge OH (614)439-4355, and Skaneateles NY (315)685-8378.
Offers: Line of ceramic supplies, including clays, glazes, deco products for screen, brush and decal printing. Also offers kilns, potter's wheels, videos and books. Consulting service available.
Catalog: $5 (schools no charge).
Phone Orders: Ask for order department.
Mail Orders: Yes.
Discounts: Volume purchases.

LAMP SPECIALTIES

P.O. Box 240
Westville NJ 08093-0240
Contact: George Strassner Jr.
Phone: (800)225-5526
Fax: (800)722-7061
E-mail: sales@lamp-specialties.com
Website: www.lamp-specialties.com
Offers: Sankyo windup music boxes, bank slots, mobile music boxes, clock movements, clock hands, clock numbers and faces, paintbrushes, Paasche airbrushes, electrical and lamp parts and supplies, ceramic and pottery supplies and equipment, and many various craft items, such as magnets, felt protection pads, stoppers, adhesives, display stands, plate stands and hangers, ornament caps, fountain pumps, lotion pumps and more.
Catalog: 240 pages. $5 (refundable).
Phone Orders: M-F, 9-5 EST.
Mail Orders: We ship worldwide. Orders outside of US require prepayment.
Discounts: Every item wholesale priced and discounted by quantity purchased.
Accepts: Discover, MasterCard, Visa

LILY POND PRODUCTS

351 W. Cromwell, Suite 105
Fresno CA 93711
Phone: (209)431-5003
Fax: (209)431-6718
Offers: Casting and mixing equipment, pour tables and pumps. Offers a complete line of equipment from the home hobbyist to the high-volume production studios, along with the "Big Puddle," the number one casting and mixing machine on the market. Complete line of interchangeable parts.
Catalog: Please write, call or fax for a free catalog and discount coupons.

MARYLAND CHINA CO.

54 Main St.
Reisterstown MD 21136
Phone: (410)833-5559
Fax: (410)833-1851
E-mail: mdchina@worldnet.att.net
Offers: Over 1,250 white porcelain blanks: tableware, giftware, novelty, souvenir items, white and gold banded dinnerware, coffee and beer mugs, promotional items, ashtrays and trivets, bells, plaques, desk accessories and others. Contact your dealer.

MAYCO COLORS

4077 Weaver Court S.
Hilliard OH 43026
Contact: Julie Ober
Phone: (614)876-1171
Fax: (614)876-9904
E-mail: info@maycocolors.com
Website: http://www.maycocolors.com
Offers: Ceramic colors and glazes for use on greenware or bisque. Full line of underglazes, lead-free glazes, crystal glazes, opaque stains and best-selling Stroke and Coat WonderGlaze for bisque. Also offer accessories, tools, sponges, brushes and molds. Manufacturer.
Catalog: $7.95. Color and mold.

MCRON CERAMIC MOLDS

2660 NE Seventh Ave.
Pompano Beach FL 33064
Phone: (954)784-7707
Fax: (954)784-7505
Offers: Ceramic molds, including McRon, Bil-Mar, Tesoro and Vicki's brands.
Catalog: $8, color (continental US only).
Accepts: Discover, MasterCard, Visa

MILE HI CERAMICS, INC.

77 Lipan St.
Denver CO 80223
Contact: Zen Z. Pool III
Phone: (303)825-4570
Fax: (303)825-6278
Store Location: At above address. M-F, 9-5.
Offers: Clay, ceramic and pottery supplies and equipment.
Catalog: 150 pages. $5.
Phone Orders: M-F, 9-5 MST.
Mail Orders: Will ship to US and Canada. Prepayment required. Allow 4 weeks for delivery.
Discounts: Sell wholesale to legitimate businesses.
Accepts: Discover, MasterCard, Visa

MINNESOTA CLAY USA

8001 Grand Ave. S.
Bloomington MN 55420
Contact: Bob Stryker
Phone: (612)884-9101 or (800)252-9872
Fax: (612)884-1820
E-mail: mnclayus@mm.com
Website: www.mm.com/mnclayus/
Store Location: At above address.
Offers: Clays including Rainbow Air-Dry Clay (no firing needed), clay bodies, stonewares and porcelains, glazes (liquid and dry), chemicals, stains, lusters, overglazes, plaster and pouring tables. Also offers kilns and kiln parts, the products of Creative Industry, Skutt, Cress, AMACO, Brent, Lehman, Ohaus and others.
Catalog: $5 (refundable with first order).
Phone Orders: Yes.
Mail Orders: Yes.
Discounts: Quantity; teachers and institutions; sells wholesale to legitimate businesses.
Accepts: American Express, MasterCard, Visa, school and institution purchase orders

MR. & MRS. OF DALLAS, INC.

8428 Hwy. 121 N.
Anna TX 75409
Contact: Mike McGuire

Phone: (800)878-7528
Fax: (972)423-2092
E-mail: mrandmrs@swbell.net
Website: www.paragon.com/mrandmrs
Store Location: At above address. M-F, 8-4:30.
Offers: China blanks, china paints, brushes, kilns, complete line of porcelain painting supplies, decals, glass lamps and ceramic bisque.
Catalog: China, bisque and decal. Free.
Phone Orders: Yes. During store hours.
Mail Orders: Yes. Domestic and international 48-hour processing.
Discounts: Yes.
Accepts: American Express, Discover, MasterCard, Visa

NATIONAL ARTCRAFT CO.

7996 Darrow Rd.
Twinsburg OH 44087
Phone: (888)937-2723
Fax: (800)292-4916
E-mail: nationalartcraft@worldnet.att.net
Website: www.nationalartcraft.com
Offers: A ceramic supplies catalog that shows ceramic and china paints, brushes, tools, studio equipment, cleaning and smoothing materials, kilns and firing equipment. A musical and clock movement catalog offers a wide selection of tunes and clock inserts. An electrical/lamp supply catalog and general craft catalog offer a range of craft supplies including glitters, miniature novelties, jewelry parts, cements, display items and more.
Catalog: Each (please specify) $1 (refundable).
Discounts: Quantity.
Accepts: Discover, MasterCard, Visa

OLYMPIC ENTERPRISES, INC.

715 McCartney Rd.
Youngstown OH 44505
Contact: Skevos A. Zembillas
Phone: (330)746-2726
Fax: (330)746-1156
Offers: Water-mount decal transfers: floral, angels, country designs, inspirational and border designs. Also carry a full line of artwork brushes.
Catalog: 198 pages of decals and brushes. $15 plus $3 p&h.
Phone Orders: M-F, 9-5 EST. Fax orders 24 hours a day.
Mail Orders: Ship to US, Canada and many other countries worldwide.
Discounts: Quantity discounts available.
Accepts: Discover, MasterCard, Visa

PARAGON INDUSTRIES, INC.

2011 S. Town E. Blvd.
Mesquite TX 75149-1122
Phone: (972)288-7557 or (800)876-4328
Fax: (972)222-0646
E-mail: paragonind@worldnet.att.net
Website: paragonweb.com
Offers: Full line of ceramic kilns, china painting kilns, heat-

treating and knife-making furnaces, glass-fused jewelry kilns and kiln accessories. Manufacturer. Sells to consumers only if there is no area dealer.
Catalog: Free.

PONY EXPRESS TRADING CO.

1011 S. Grant
Gallatin MO 64640-9746
Contact: Valerie Davis
Phone: (660)663-3747
Fax: (660)663-3748
Store Location: At above address.
Offers: Ceramic and craft supplies: music boxes, keywind, electronic, touch and bank. Electrical wiring: cords, sockets, nuts, washers and more. Mini quartz clock movements, clock numbers and bank stoppers. Ceramic firing supplies: cones and more. Ceramic mold trimmers, bands and straps. Duncan nonfired bisque stains, glazes, brushes, tools, Marx brushes and Kemper tools.
Catalog: Free upon request.
Phone Orders: M-Th, 9-5 CST.
Mail Orders: Ship UPS. Most orders shipped same day.
Discounts: Quantity based. See catalog for details.
Accepts: Discover, MasterCard, Visa

CAROL REINERT CERAMICS

1100 Grosser Rd.
Gilbertsville PA 19525
Contact: Carol Beidler
Phone: (610)367-4373
Fax: (610)367-4373
Store Location: At above address. M-Sat, 10-4 EST.
Offers: Ceramic molds by Dona's, Scioto, Nowell, Kimple, Clay Magic, Alberta, Doc Holliday and more. Manufacture Fairieland products, Fairy Princess molds and Budget Craft Products. Also carry Scioto, Kimple and Ceramichrome stains, Royal brushes, Glitter music boxes, electric supplies, plastic lights and many craft and ceramic products.
Catalog: $5 (refundable with $50 purchase).
Phone Orders: M-Sat, 10-4 EST.
Mail Orders: Ship by UPS. Prepaid. (4-8 weeks for check). By charge card 48 hours for in-stock items.
Discounts: Wholesale to legitimate businesses and professional crafters.
Accepts: American Express, MasterCard, Visa

RIVER VIEW MOLDS, INC.

2141 P Ave.
Williamsburg IA 52361
Contact: Dan or Frank
Phone: (319)668-9800
Fax: (319)668-9600
E-mail: rivervie@avalon.net
Store Location: At above address. M-F, 8-4:30.
Offers: Line of molds including holiday designs, figures and others.
Catalog: $7 plus p&h.

ROCKING B MANUFACTURING

3924 Camphor Ave.
Newbury Park CA 91320
Phone: (805)499-9336
Fax: (805)499-9336
Offers: Music boxes including Sankyo movement, mini, mobile, electronic Touch-Me, bank slot and Touch-Me with blinking lights, Waggie Arm and accordion sleeve movements. Accessories available include turntables, keys and extenders.
Catalog: Send SASE.
Discounts: Quantity; teachers and institutions; sells wholesale to legitimate businesses.

SCIOTO CERAMIC PRODUCTS, INC.

2455 Harrisburg Pike
Grove City OH 43123
Contact: P.J. Langdale, president, or Don Roullard, vice president
Phone: (614)871-0090
Fax: (614)871-8300
E-mail: info@sciotoceramics.com
Website: www.sciotoceramics.com
Offers: Molds, including classical, whimsical, contemporary, traditional, fantasy, holiday, Western and other motifs, plus cherubs and other angels, animals, fowl, figures, villages, crèches and Christmas ornaments. Also offers vases, planters, pots, pedestals, scenes, bird feeders, 2 chess sets, nonfire craft paint and brushes and others.
Catalog: $7 plus $3 p&h. Decorating guide: $5 plus $3 p&h.
Discounts: Sells wholesale to legitimate businesses.
Accepts: MasterCard, Visa

SCOTT PUBLICATIONS

30595 Eight Mile Rd.
Livonia MI 48152
Phone: (248)477-6650 or (800)458-8237
Fax: (248)477-6795
Offers: Instructional books, videos and magazines.
Catalog: Send SASE for list.
Discounts: Sells wholesale to legitimate businesses.

SOUTHERN OREGON POTTERY SUPPLY CO.

P.O. Box 15B
111 Talent Ave.
Talent OR 97540
Contact: Bill Morgan
Phone: (541)535-6700
Fax: (541)535-5929
Store Location: At above address. T-Sat, 10-5.
Offers: Kilns, wheels, glazes, tools, china paints, chemicals, plasters, books, equipment and more for schools, institutions, potters, ceramists, china painters and porcelain doll makers.
Catalog: Kiln brochure: free. Full catalog: $5 (refundable).
Phone Orders: T-Sat, 10-5. Fax orders 24 hours, 7 days.
Mail Orders: Ship to US and Canada, UPS and truck freight.
Discounts: On most equipment including kilns.
Accepts: Discover, MasterCard, Visa

STAR STILTS CO.

P.O. Box 367
Feasterville PA 19053
Phone: (215)357-1893
Fax: (215)953-8263
Offers: Stilts products including napkin ring, star tree, rods (setter for beads, buttons, trinkets and others), bell type, junior shelves, high stilts (5 sizes), element retaining stables and others. Contact your dealer.
Catalog: Write for free catalog.

SUGAR CREEK INDUSTRIES, INC.

P.O. Box 354
208 N. Main St.
Linden IN 47955
Contact: Tammy Tauscher
Phone: (765)339-4641
Fax: (765)339-4649
E-mail: scind@tctc.com
Website: http://www.tctc.com/scind
Offers: Slip-pouring mixing equipment for the ceramic industry. Spray booths, kilns and pouring and firing supplies. Fiberglass draining tables and tanks.
Catalog: Free.
Phone Orders: M-F, 7-3.
Mail Orders: Anywhere in the US and international. Prepayment required. UPS and truck shipments.
Discounts: We sell retail and wholesale. Discounts available to businesses.
Accepts: Discover, MasterCard, Visa

TAMPA BAY MOLD CO.

2724 22nd St. N.
St. Petersburg FL 33713
Phone: (813)823-3784
Fax: (813)821-6276
Offers: Original molds in a full line of traditional designs, bisque and technical sheets.
Catalog: $7.

TBR, INC.

824 Maxine NE
Albuquerque NM 87123
Phone: (505)292-0041 or (800)833-5408
Fax: (505)299-4425
Offers: Decals for many craft uses, including but not limited to ceramics, woodwork and candles. Other styles are available, but many are Southwestern and American Indian. Graphics available in English and Spanish. Porcelain blanks for jewelry and jewelry findings are also sold.
Catalog: $5.
Phone Orders: 24 hours.
Mail Orders: Orders shipped same or next business day.
Discounts: Listed in catalog.
Accepts: Discover, MasterCard, Visa, C.O.D.

WISE SCREENPRINT, INC.
1011 Valley St.
Dayton OH 45404
Contact: Cindy Sutter
Phone: (937)223-1573
Fax: (937)223-1115
Offers: Ceramic and glass decals, ready-to-decorate blank-ware.
Catalog: Free price list, color card and samples.
Phone Orders: Yes.
Mail Orders: Yes.
Accepts: American Express, Discover, MasterCard, Visa

YOZIE MOLD CO.
124 College Ave.
Dunbar PA 15431
Phone: (724)628-3693
Fax: (724)628-3693
Offers: Line of ceramic molds, designs include Art Deco, Judaic, dogs and others. Jewelry molds and findings also available.
Catalog: Color mold, $12; jewelry mold, $6.50.
Accepts: MasterCard, Visa

ZEMBILLAS SPONGE CO., INC.
P.O. Box 24
Campbell OH 44405
Phone: (216)755-1644
Fax: (216)755-0828
Offers: Mediterranean silk sponges in a variety of sizes, plus imported ceramic decals in a wide assortment of traditional motifs and Silver Falcon brushes.
Catalog: $7.50.

ZIP MANUFACTURING
13584 E. Manito Rd.
Pekin IL 61554
Phone: (309)346-7916
Offers: Zip porcelain and stoneware slips in 40 colors.
Catalog: Send SASE for price list.
Discounts: Quantity.

Clock Making

Also see Furniture Making & Upholstery; General Craft Supplies; Woodworking.

AMERICAN MINERAL GIFT
326 Steel Rd.
Feasterville PA 19053
Phone: (215)364-1114 or (800)706-0733
Fax: (215)953-5866
Offers: Miniquartz clock movements (3 shaft sizes). Jewelry eyeglass frame chains. Gift items.
Catalog: Free.
Discounts: Quantity.
Accepts: MasterCard, Visa

B&J ROCK SHOP, INC.
14744 Manchester Rd.
Ballwin MO 63011
Phone: (314)394-4567
Fax: (314)394-7109
Offers: Line of clock kits (clock movements with hands and numbers, polished/drilled agate clock faces and clear Lucite stands), desk clock kits and large models (with 5″ to 6½″ faces). Carries quartz clock movements—Seiko, battery with ⁵⁄₁₆″ or ¹¹⁄₁₆″ shaft (with hour, minute and second hands, hangers, hardware and numbers/dots).
Catalog: $3 (refundable).
Discounts: Quantity.

CLOCK N THINGS
147 Bullock Rd.
Foxworth MS 39483
Contact: James Hanberry
Phone: (601)736-8485
Store Location: At above address.
Offers: Clock motors, hands and numbers, clock faces, clock shapes, cypress wood slabs, high gloss finish (1:1 mix), pens, thermometers, plaques, foil prints and laser prints.
Catalog: Clock catalog, $1; color print catalog with over 750 subjects, $5 (credited on first order).
Phone Orders: 7 a.m.-9 p.m. CST.
Mail Orders: We ship UPS in US. Prepayment required. US Postal Service outside of the US. Orders are usually processed within 48 hours.
Discounts: Based on quantity.
Accepts: MasterCard, Visa, check, money order

CLOCK REPAIR CENTER
33 Boyd Dr.
Westbury NY 11590
Contact: Vincent Kazel
Phone: (516)997-4810
Fax: (516)373-4291
Offers: Clock movements, dials, numerals, clock hands.
Catalog: #200: 20-page brochure. Free. #210: Clock movements, repair parts, tools and supplies. 8½×11, 200 pages. $5.95.
Phone Orders: Yes.
Mail Orders: Yes.
Discounts: On quantity purchases.
Accepts: American Express, Discover, MasterCard, Visa

CREATIVE CLOCK
P.O. Box 565
357 High St.
Hanson MA 02341
Contact: Dan Re
Fax: (781)293-0057
Offers: Inexpensive quartz clock movements, battery only. Also carry all related clock building supplies except wood.
Catalog: $1 (refundable on first order).
Phone Orders: (800)293-2856.
Mail Orders: Ship daily UPS and parcel post.
Discounts: Sells to general public at wholesale prices.
Accepts: MasterCard, Visa

CREATIVE HOBBIES, INC.
900 Creek Rd.
Bellmawr NJ 08031
Contact: Ginny Rozzelle
Phone: (888)THE-KILN
Fax: (800)992-7675
E-mail: mail@creative-hobbies.com
Website: http://www.creative-hobbies.com
Offers: Ceramics and pottery supplies, bisque, clay, glazes, kilns, music boxes, clocks, lamp parts, lampshades and molds.
Catalog: 400 pages with color. $5 (refundable).
Phone Orders: M-F, 9-5 EST.
Mail Orders: 24-hour shipment, domestic or international.
Accepts: Discover, MasterCard, Visa

LOU DAVIS WHOLESALE
Dept. CS8
N3211 County Rd. H. N.
Lake Geneva WI 53147
Phone: (414)248-2000 or (800)748-7991
Offers: Brand-name craft and ceramic supplies, including

music movements in more than 200 tunes, chalks, paints, spray finishes, airbrushes and compressors, clock movements, doll-making supplies, lamp parts and accessories, brushes, magnets, glitter, abrasives, adhesives and cleaning tools.
Catalog: $2 (refundable with order).
Accepts: Discover, MasterCard, Visa

DECOR TIME PRODUCTS
P.O. Box 277698
Sacramento CA 95827-7698
Contact: Brent
Phone: (800)487-2524
Fax: (888)383-8982
Offers: Full line of clock parts, dials, quartz motors and accessories. Also carries epoxy, resin, pen sets and others.
Catalog: $1.
Phone Orders: Yes.
Mail Orders: At above address.
Discounts: 10% on first order.
Accepts: American Express, Discover, MasterCard, Visa

EMPEROR CLOCK, LLC
Dept. 6487
Emperor Industrial Park
Fairhope AL 36532
Phone: (334)928-2316
Offers: Clock kits, including grandfather, mantel and wall models in cherry or oak with solid brass West German movements and dials. Also carries furniture kits and assembled clocks.
Catalog: Color. $1.

KLOCKIT
Dept. CSS8
P.O. Box 636
Lake Geneva WI 53147
Phone: (800)556-2548
Fax: (414)248-9899
Offers: Clock kits (quartz or quartz Westminster chime movements), including wooden gears, shelf, schoolhouse or Alpine steeple models. Also carries wood blanks for clocks in various shapes, stitchery clocks, country wood kits (easy), desk clocks, wall clocks and jumbo watches. Grandfather, grandmother and cypress clocks, desk sets, contemporary wood/brass, time and weather, mantel, banjo/cloth, gallery, nautical, carriage, time zone, cottage, carriage/moving moon, 400-day crystal and wood and regulator types are also available. Parts available include chimes, hardware, fit-ups, movements, pendulums, wood shapes, brass nameplates, plus lamp items.
Catalog: Free. Full-color, 64 pages.
Accepts: Discover, MasterCard, Visa

KUEMPEL CHIME
21195 Minnetonka Blvd.
Excelsior MN 55331
Phone: (800)328-6445
Offers: Red-i-Kut traditional and contemporary clock kits, including grandfather, wall and mantel types of walnut, cherry or oak with German tabular bell and chime rod, one- and three-tune Westminster, Whittington and St. Michael styles. Brushed and polished brass clock pendulums and hand-painted moonwheels also available.
Catalog: $2.

MURRAY CLOCK CRAFT, LTD.
512 McNicoll Ave.
Willowdale, Ontario M2H 2E1
Canada
Phone: (416)499-4531
Offers: Clock plans and kits for grandfather, grandmother, wall and shelf models. Also carries battery, weight and spring-driven movements and dials.
Catalog: $2 (refundable).

N&N PLASTICS
11683 87th St. N.
Largo FL 33773
Contact: Angie
Phone: (813)397-8237
Fax: (813)397-8356
E-mail: manzana@sprnet.com
Offers: Manufacturer of plastic clock components: clock faces, numbers, corners and more. Also handle plastic alphabet letters in assorted styles and sizes.
Catalog: Free.
Phone Orders: M-F, 8-5 EST.
Mail Orders: Ships worldwide.
Discounts: Buy direct from manufacturer. $75 order minimum.
Accepts: MasterCard, Visa

TIME TECH WIRELESS COMMUNICATIONS, INC.
233 Philmont Ave.
Feasterville PA 19053
Contact: Ron Tashman
Phone: (215)354-1114
Fax: (215)953-5866
E-mail: clocksontherocks.com
Website: www.timetechwireless.com
Offers: Quartz clock movements, onyx clock faces, hands, numbers and clock accessories.
Catalog: Free.
Phone Orders: Yes.
Mail Orders: Yes.
Discounts: On large quantities.

Doll & Toy Making—Rigid

Also see Ceramics; Miniature Making, Miniatures & Doll-houses; Model Making; Woodworking; related categories.

AAA WEEFOKE EMPIRE
(formerly Weefoke Empire)
619 Fourth St.
Bremerton WA 98337-1411
Phone: (360)792-9293
Offers: Complete costume for your special dolls. Send SASE.
Phone Orders: Yes.
Mail Orders: Yes.
Discounts: By volume orders.

ADOPT-A-DOLL
1041 Lincoln Ave.
San Jose CA 95125
Contact: Jo Clausen
Phone: (408)298-3655
Fax: (408)298-8055
E-mail: clausen@pacbell.net
Store Location: At above address.
Offers: Doll supplies, greenware and bisque kits; accessories for Playhouse, Seeley, Global, Jean Nordquist, Kemper, Virginia La Vorgna, Connie Lee Finchum Patterns and Royal.
Phone Orders: Yes.
Mail Orders: Yes.
Discounts: Yes.
Accepts: Discover, MasterCard, Visa

AIM KILNS
350 SW Wake Robin
Corvallis OR 97333
Phone: (800)647-1624 or (800)222-5456 (in CA)
Offers: AIM Doll Kiln, 8″×8″×9″ deep, 120V, to cone 10 with kiln-sitter shutoff and infinite switch; an optional timer is available. Other kilns sizes 6″×6″ to 35″ diameter; automatic models; also shelves, cones and replacement parts.
Catalog: Free literature.
Discounts: Sells wholesale.

THE AMERICAN COASTER
7106 Lake Rd.
Montrose MI 48457
Phone: (810)639-7004
Offers: Early American coaster wagon kits and full-scale blueprints for farm and flat wagons, wheelbarrows, sleds, scooters and others. Wood and rubber wheel kits including Amish-made, steam bent handles and hounds; metal parts. Also offers completed unpainted wagons.
Catalog: Brochure. $1.

ANNE'S DOLL THINGS
2534 Munger Dr.
West Linn OR 97068
Contact: Anne Weeks
Phone: (503)656-9556
Fax: (503)655-7973
Store Location: At above address.
Offers: Hand glass craft doll eyes from England, all styles. Also offers doll teeth.
Catalog: Yes.
Phone Orders: Yes.
Mail Orders: Yes.
Accepts: MasterCard, Visa

BALDWIN FINE PORCELAIN
4886 Hercules, Suite H
El Paso TX 79904
Phone: (800)414-9876
Fax: (915)751-9821
Store Location: At above address. M-F, 8-4:30.
Offers: "Heirloom" doll-making kits for 9″-60″ dolls. Also carries supply packets (eyes, lashes, wigs, body patterns/stringing and other items).
Catalog: Send large SASE for list.
Discounts: Quantity.
Accepts: MasterCard, Visa

TOM BANWELL DESIGNS
16424 Gleko Rd.
Rough & Ready CA 95975
Phone: (530)432-1464
Fax: (530)432-5302
Offers: Instructional video, *The Art of Resin Dollmaking*. Rubber mold making and resin casting services.

BARBARA'S PLAYHOUSE
25377 Huntwood Ave.
Hayward CA 94544
Contact: Barbara Costa
Phone: (510)786-0068 or (510)785-1352
Fax: (510)786-6578 or (510)785-1354
Store Location: At above address.
Offers: Doll supplies and doll kits.
Catalog: $5.
Phone Orders: (800)799-1947 or (510)786-0668.
Mail Orders: Yes.

Discounts: Yes.
Accepts: American Express, Discover, MasterCard, Visa

BASS RIVER DOLLWORKS
P.O. Box 58
South Yarmouth MA 02664
Contact: Joseph or Louise Tierney
Phone: (508)394-0684
Offers: Originally designed doll molds.
Catalog: #10 SASE for brochure and discount information.
Phone Orders: Yes.
Mail Orders: Yes.
Discounts: Yes.
Accepts: MasterCard, Visa

BELL CERAMICS, INC.
P.O. Box 120127
Clermont FL 34712
Phone: (800)874-9025
Fax: (352)394-1270
E-mail: info@bellceramics.com
Website: www.bellceramics.com
Store Location: 197 Lake Minneola Dr., Clermont FL 34711.
M-F, 9-4.
Offers: Doll molds for over 200 modern and antique reproduction styles. Carries the Gold Marque Artist Series and others, plus porcelain and composition slip, dry and premixed china paints, wigs, patterns, eyes and other items.
Catalog: $8 by mail.
Phone Orders: Accepted M-F, 8-4 EST.
Accepts: MasterCard, Visa

BROWN HOUSE DOLLS
3200 N. Sand Lake Rd.
Allen MI 49227
Phone: (517)869-2833
Offers: Over 350 doll clothing pattern designs (in several sizes) including those of antique vintage, babies, toddlers and known dolls. Also carries doll accessories patterns.
Catalog: $2 ($3 foreign).
Accepts: Discover, MasterCard, Visa

BUNDLES OF LOVE
50 Southern Hills Lane
Calera AL 35040-4900
Contact: Joni or Chuck Morgan
Phone: (205)668-1119
Fax: (205)668-4266
Store Location: At above address. M-F, 9-5.
Offers: Soft-fire, bisque, painted and finished dolls. Also doll supplies, armatures, doll stands and more.
Catalog: $1.
Phone Orders: Yes.
Mail Orders: Will ship to US. Prepayment required. Allow 4-6 weeks for delivery.
Accepts: MasterCard, Visa, check, cashier's check, money order

CAS-NET CREATIONS
3417 Albantowne Way
Edgewood MD 21040
Contact: Nettie Schruhl
Phone: (410)671-9816
E-mail: casnet@erols.com
Store Location: At above address.
Offers: Soft-fired greenware, blanks, painted, assembled and fully finished miniature porcelain dolls. Some larger dolls also available. Kits to assemble hand-blown glass eyes and some wigs.
Catalog: #10 SASE.
Discounts: To legitimate businesses only.
Accepts: check, money order

CHICAGO LATEX PRODUCTS, INC.
P.O. Box 395
Crystal Lake IL 60039
Phone: (815)459-9680
Fax: (815)459-8560
Offers: Latex for molding, sculpture, mâché, casting, coatings and adhesives, including one-part natural or neoprene type, for figurines, displays, dolls and others. Call or write.

CHICK'S DOLL HATCHERY
3265A Industrial Dr.
Yuba City CA 95993
Contact: Lois Chick
Phone: (530)671-5639
Fax: (530)741-1065
E-mail: alchick@syix.com
Website: www.dollstuff.com
Store Location: Yuba City CA location, 10-6.
Offers: Vinyl doll and kits, porcelain doll, Dust-a-Way, Slip-a-Way and Strain-a-Way doll-making supplies. Accessories for 18″ doll, such as American Girl.
Catalog: Vinyl kit catalog. $2 (refundable on purchase).
Phone Orders: Yes.
Mail Orders: Yes.
Discounts: On quantity.
Accepts: American Express, Discover, MasterCard, Visa, check

COLLECTIBLE DOLL CO.
4216 Sixth NW
Seattle WA 98107
Contact: Jean Nordquist
Phone: (206)781-1963
Fax: (206)781-2258
E-mail: jean@jeannordquistdolls.com
Website: jeannordquistdolls.com
Store Location: At above address. M-F, 10-5; Sat, 10-2; closed T and Sun.
Offers: Over 300 molds, china paint, brushes, doll clothes, patterns, videos, wigs, glass eyes and much more.
Catalog: $9, set of 3.
Phone Orders: M-F, 9-5 PST.
Mail Orders: Ship worldwide. Prepayment required.

Discounts: For volume and to qualified dealers.
Accepts: MasterCard, Visa

CREATE AN HEIRLOOM
P.O. Box 480
West St.
Berlin MA 01503
Phone: (978)838-2130
Offers: Porcelain doll kits and accessories. Large variety of porcelain doll heads, including The Nativity Grouping, Three Wise Men, Victorian Carolers, Mr./Mrs. Claus, fairy sets, ornaments, heads, ballerina legs, angels, black angels and black Santa porcelain sets. Victorian, traditional smiling and Old World Santa sets.
Catalog: $1.
Discounts: Quantity.

CREATIVE PAPERCLAY CO., INC.
79 Daily Dr., Suite 101
Camarillo CA 93010
Contact: Michael Gerbasi
Phone: (805)484-6648
Fax: (805)484-8788
E-mail: webmaster@paperclay.com
Website: www.paperclay.com
Offers: Creative Paperclay, an air-hardening, lightweight material for doll heads and other parts. Also carries kits, molds and books.
Catalog: Yes.
Phone Orders: (800)899-5952.
Mail Orders: Yes.
Accepts: MasterCard, Visa

CR'S CRAFTS
P.O. Box 8-81CB
109 Fifth Ave. W.
Leland IA 50453
Phone: (515)567-3652
Fax: (515)567-3071
Website: www.crscraft.com
Store Location: At above address.
Offers: Extensive lines of doll-making supplies, including painted designer porcelain sets and heads, pre-sewn and composition bodies, patterns, wigs, hair, eyes and eyelashes. Mauerhan and Glorfix doll supplies, including collector quality vinyl dolls, vinyl and wool doll parts, and clay doll-making supplies. Carries fabrics, furniture, wicker, stands, clothing, shoes, accessories, patterns and books. Large selection of accessories for 18″ girl dolls.
Catalog: 148 pages. $2 US, $4 Canada (US funds) and $7 other countries (US funds).
Phone Orders: M-F, 8:30-3:30 CST.
Mail Orders: Will ship worldwide.
Discounts: Quantity and wholesale.
Accepts: Discover, MasterCard, Visa

LOU DAVIS WHOLESALE
Dept. CS8
N3211 County Rd. H. N.
Lake Geneva WI 53147
Phone: (414)248-2000 or (800)748-7991
Offers: Brand-name craft and ceramic supplies, including music movements in more than 200 tunes, chalks, paints, spray finishes, airbrushes and compressors, clock movements, doll-making supplies, lamp parts and accessories, brushes, magnets, glitter, abrasives, adhesives and cleaning tools.
Catalog: $2 (refundable with order).
Accepts: Discover, MasterCard, Visa

DEAR DOLLY
1602 Edgewater Dr.
Orlando FL 32804
Phone: (407)839-2041
Store Location: At above address.
Offers: Doll-making porcelain bisque and soft-fired.
Catalog: $3.50.

DIANA'S TREASURES, INC.
P.O. Box 206
219 E. Aspen
Fruita CO 81521
Phone: (970)858-7552
Fax: (970)858-3915
Store Location: At above address.
Offers: Vinyl doll kits including Michelle, Buttons, new Flower Face rag doll kits and others. Playhouse products. Doll clothes patterns. Also doll accessories, clothes and furniture. Call.
Discounts: Sells wholesale.
Accepts: MasterCard, Visa

DOLL ESSENTIALS
P.O. Box 969
705C Live Oak St.
Tarpon Springs FL 34688-0969
Contact: Suzanne Hazelbaker
Phone: (813)937-5561
Fax: (813)937-5561
E-mail: dollz@worldnet.att.net
Store Location: At above address. M-F, 10-5.
Offers: Doll clothes and vinyl and porcelain kits.
Catalog: $2 (refundable on first order).
Phone Orders: (800)937-5503. M-F, 8-5 EST.
Mail Orders: We ship prepaid, C.O.D. or credit card orders anywhere in the US. We ship orders to any other country by charging actual shipping charges and order to your credit card.
Discounts: Available to businesses.
Accepts: American Express, Discover, MasterCard, Visa

DOLL GALLERY, INC.
1137 Susan Rd.
Columbia SC 29210
Phone: (803)798-7044

Offers: Doll supplies for Playhouse, Kemper, Global, Seeley and others.
Catalog: Free.
Discounts: To hobbyists and retailers.

DOLL HAVEN

939 W. Main St.
Troy OH 45373
Contact: Tammy Sharpe
Phone: (937)339-9799
Fax: (937)339-1881
E-mail: dolls@nerg.com
Website: www2.nerg.com/dollhaven
Store Location: At above address. M-T, 10-8; W and Sat, 10-3; Th-F, 10-5.
Offers: Porcelain dolls, doll supplies and greenware, kits and custom-made dolls.
Catalog: Greenware log. Send SASE.
Phone Orders: During business hours or answering machine after hours.
Mail Orders: Ship anywhere. Prepayment required. Most orders shipped within 2 weeks; allow 6-8 weeks delivery.
Discounts: 20% to shop owners.
Accepts: MasterCard, Visa, check, money order

DOLL MAJIK

P.O. Box 56
Holmes PA 19043
Contact: Liz Halliday
Phone: (610)522-1704
Fax: (610)522-1704
E-mail: dollmajik@aol.com
Offers: Modern reproduction porcelain doll kits available. Soft-fire, bisque and painted kits. Distributor for Virginia LaVorgna paints and Real Eyes. All supplies to complete your doll are available.
Catalog: Upon request. $3 (refundable).
Phone Orders: M-F, 9:30-4:30 or you may leave a message.
Mail Orders: We ship internationally. Payment required before pouring.
Accepts: MasterCard, Visa, check, money order

DOLL SUPPLIES WAREHOUSE

6154 126th Ave. N.
Largo FL 33773
Contact: Gord Sercombe
Phone: (813)535-3655
Fax: (813)532-4485
Store Location: Warehouse, open aisle shopping.
Offers: Doll molds, porcelain slip, wigs, eyes, pates, eyelashes, patterns, tools, brushes and more. Also tights, stockings and shoes.
Catalog: From major suppliers.
Phone Orders: Yes.
Mail Orders: Yes.
Discounts: Dealer.
Accepts: Discover, MasterCard, Visa

THE DOLLMAKER

7533 Hickory Hills Dr.
Las Vegas NV 89130
Contact: Barbara Plaggemeyer
Phone: (702)655-1633 or (800)834-1411
Fax: (702)645-9617
E-mail: bplaggemey@aol.com
Website: Coming soon. Call.
Store Location: At above address by appointment.
Offers: Soft-fired greenware, porcelain doll kits, finished dolls, doll-making supplies, global wigs, Glastic realistic eyes.
Catalog: Listing of dolls on request.
Phone Orders: 7 a.m.-8 p.m. PST.
Mail Orders: US, Canada. Prepayment required. 100% guaranteed.
Accepts: American Express, Discover, MasterCard, Visa, check

THE DOLLMAKERS

505 S. Myrtle Ave.
Monrovia CA 91016
Phone: (626)357-1091
Store Location: At above address. Also 133 Yale Ave., Claremont CA 91711. (909)621-2878.
Offers: Complete line of doll supplies. Also offers finished dolls in clay, wax and porcelain. Bears also available. Holds classes. Send SASE.

DOLLSPART SUPPLY CO.

8000 Cooper Ave., Bldg. #28
Glendale NY 11385
Phone: (718)326-4587
Offers: Full and complete line of doll-making supplies, including kits for baby, fashion, ethnic and other dolls, plus doll parts, bodies, heads, hands, feet, eyes, wigs, ceramic supplies and paints, doll shoes, clothing, costumes, hats and stands. Also carries elastic cord rubber loops, doll sewing notions and trims.
Catalog: Free. Color.
Accepts: Discover, MasterCard, Visa

EUREKA DOLL CO.

P.O. Box 278
2395 Willow Breeze Rd.
Chino Valley AZ 86323
Contact: Dee Kemp Sybrandt
Phone: (520)636-2236
Fax: (520)636-2494
E-mail: dolls@eurekadollco.com
Website: www.eurekadollco.com
Store Location: At above address. Call for directions.
Offers: Supplies for all your doll-making needs. SEGLO from over 900 molds.
Catalog: Greenware list.
Phone Orders: M-F, 8-4 MST.
Mail Orders: Prepayment required. Allow 2-3 weeks for greenware orders. Will ship to US and Canada.

Discounts: Dealer discounts.
Accepts: MasterCard, Visa

THE FIBER STUDIO
P.O. Box 637 CSS
Henniker NH 03242
Phone: (603)428-7830
Offers: Lambskins for doll making—Tibetan, Lincoln, Kalgon and Pearl. Also offers mohair, wool, alpaca, flax and others.
Catalog: Send SASE for price list. Doll hair samples, $7.
Discounts: Sells wholesale.

FUN STUF
Dept. CS
P.O. Box 999
Yuma AZ 85366-0999
Offers: Line of porcelain and vinyl doll kits in a variety of sizes.
Catalog: $1, color.

GOLDENWEST MANUFACTURING, INC.
P.O. Box 1148
Cedar Ridge CA 95924
Contact: Roger Bodine
Phone: (530)272-1133
Fax: (530)272-1070
E-mail: goldenws@oro.net
Website: goldenwestmfg.com
Store Location: 13100 Grass Valley Ave,. Grass Valley CA 95945.
Offers: Casting resins, silicone rubber, fillers and miscellaneous supplies.
Catalog: Fast Cast.
Phone Orders: Yes.
Mail Orders: At P.O. Box.
Accepts: credit cards

HAMILTON EYE WAREHOUSE
P.O. Box 1258-MB
Moorpark CA 93021
Contact: Carol Hamilton
Phone: (805)529-5900
Fax: (805)529-2934
E-mail: hamilton@vcnet.com
Website: www.vcnet.com/hamilton
Offers: Solid glass paperweight eyes, hollow glass eyes and acrylic eyes. Available in 13 colors. Sizes 2mm to 30mm. Each pair matched. Bargains galore; stock-up time now.
Catalog: $1.
Phone Orders: Yes.
Mail Orders: Yes.
Discounts: Closeouts.
Accepts: MasterCard, Visa

HANDCRAFT DESIGNS
63 E. Broad St.
Hatfield PA 19440
Contact: Tony Kohn

Phone: (215)855-3022
Fax: (215)855-0184
Offers: Cernit modeling compound in 5 flesh tones and many colors. Also offers Crafty paper clay and LaDoll and Premier fine air-drying clays. Flumo air-drying casting slip, for use with plaster molds designed for porcelain and ceramic slips, is newest offering.
Catalog: Send #10 SASE with 55 cents postage.
Phone Orders: Yes.
Mail Orders: At above address. Include $6 p&h for orders $50-$99 wholesale.
Discounts: Wholesale to trade. $50 minimum.
Accepts: MasterCard, Visa

HELLO DOLLY
6550 Mobile Hwy.
Pensacola FL 32526
Contact: Glenda Martin
Phone: (850)944-3263
Fax: (850)944-7062
Store Location: At above address.
Offers: Doll-making supplies, greenware, doll wigs, doll clothes and doll repair.
Phone Orders: (800)438-7227.
Accepts: American Express, Discover, MasterCard, Visa

JUDITH HOWE, INC.
1240D N. Jefferson
Anaheim CA 92807
Contact: Judith Howe
Phone: (714)630-4677
Fax: (714)630-6938
E-mail: 4-winds@concentric.net
Store Location: At above address.
Offers: Porcelain eyes, doll stands, doll armatures and other doll items. We are also producing ceramic whirligigs.
Catalog: Free.
Phone Orders: Yes.
Mail Orders: Yes.
Discounts: To businesses only.
Accepts: MasterCard, Visa

KEMPER ENTERPRISES, INC.
13595 12th St.
Chino CA 91710
Contact: Katie Munday
Phone: (800)388-5367 or (909)627-6191
Fax: (909)627-4008
E-mail: thetoolady@aol.com
Offers: Manufacturer and designer of tools for painting that include the Fluid Writer, Wipe-Out tool that erases mistakes, faux finishing tools and a spray gun cleaner set.
Catalog: Free. 70+ pages, color. Please send $1.50 for p&h.
Phone Orders: Customer service hours are M-F, 8-4:30 PST.
Mail Orders: Can expect order to ship within 2 days of receipt. Ship domestic and international through UPS.
Discounts: Sell wholesale to businesses. For account qualifications and status please contact.

Accepts: Discover, MasterCard, Visa, International Money Order, bank wire transfer in American dollars only

LAND OF OZ DOLLS
(formerly Yesterday's Children)
1723 Portland Ave.
Savanna IL 61074
Phone: (815)273-3964
Fax: (815)273-4468
Offers: Doll supplies including wigs, eyes, eyelashes, stands and others. Carries patterns by Jean Nordquist and Yesterday's. Also carries Virginia LaVorgna china paints. Brands available include Playhouse, Kemper, Monique, Global, La Sioux, Seeley and Bell.
Catalog: $5.
Discounts: Sells wholesale.
Accepts: Discover, MasterCard, Visa

LAZY D DOLLS
608 127th St. S.
Tacoma WA 98444
Contact: Delores
Phone: (253)537-0063
Store Location: At above address.
Offers: Doll making classes, kits, bisque and finished dolls, as well as greenware.
Catalog: List with SASE.
Phone Orders: Yes.

LEGACY DOLLS, INC.
8340 Donal St.
Port Richey FL 34668
Contact: Steve
Phone: (813)848-6900
Website: http://people.delphi.com/legacy or http://www.web sampler.com/legacy
Store Location: At above address.
Offers: Molds porcelain, vinyl doll kits and doll supplies.
Catalog: Call.
Phone Orders: M-F, 9-4:30.
Mail Orders: Will ship anywhere.
Discounts: Call.
Accepts: MasterCard, Visa

LIFETIME CAREER SCHOOLS
Dept. CSS9918
101 Harrison St.
Archbald PA 18403
Phone: (717)876-6340 or (800)326-9221
Fax: (717)876-8179
Website: http://members.aol.com/lcslearn/lcsaol0.html
Offers: Home study diploma programs in landscaping, flower arranging and floristry, sewing/dressmaking, doll repair, secretarial, bookkeeping, cooking and small business management.
Catalog: Free.
Phone Orders: M-F, 8:30-5 EST.

Mail Orders: Will ship to any address.
Accepts: MasterCard, Visa, check, money order (no cash)

MA'S BODY SHOP
1628 Eifert Rd.
Holt MI 48842
Phone: (517)694-9022
Offers: Composition bodies for dolls—finished or straight from the mold, in a variety of sizes and types. Also repairs dolls.
Catalog: Send SASE for price list.

MASTER EYE BEVELER
10 Armstrong Rd.
Enfield CT 06082
Contact: Jackie Kemp
Phone: (860)749-0465
Fax: (860)749-4272
Store Location: Enfield CT location.
Offers: Eye beveling tools needed to make dolls. New china paint organizer tray holds 46 vials of china paint. You can add second and third tray to turn it into a lazy Susan. Also each tray holds 2 bottles of media and brushes. Brand new eye-sizing tool. When insterted into doll's eye it will stop at different millimeter sizes.
Catalog: Send SASE.
Phone Orders: Yes.
Mail Orders: P.O. Box 924, Enfield CT 06083-0924.
Discounts: Inquire.
Accepts: MasterCard, Visa, C.O.D., cash

MAYBELLE'S DOLLWORKS
140 Space Park Dr.
Nashville TN 37211
Phone: (615)831-0661
Store Location: At above address.
Offers: Doll supplies from Playhouse, Bell, Kemper, Monique, Global, Brown House, Sugar Creek, Royal and others. Carries Paragon kilns, plus armatures, pellets, tools, equipment and porcelain prop—in bulk or blanket.
Catalog: $7.50.
Discounts: Sells wholesale.
Accepts: American Express, Discover, MasterCard, Visa

JANICE NAIBERT
16590 Emory Lane
Rockville MD 20853
Phone: (301)774-9252
Fax: (301)924-1725
Offers: French human-hair doll wigs (for antique and contemporary dolls). Also carries leather shoes and cotton socks. Trims and accessories at wholesale only.
Catalog: Send large SASE for list.
Discounts: Trade.

ORIGINALS BY BEVERLY

P.O. Box 222
4157 E. Blood Rd.
Wales Center NY 14169
Contact: Beverly or Roger
Phone: (716)687-1009
Fax: (716)687-1009
E-mail: www.bdolls.com
Store Location: At above address.
Offers: Mold making for porcelain dolls and wax pouring. Also sculpting service.
Phone Orders: M-S, 9-6.
Mail Orders: Ship to US and Canada. 2-3 weeks for delivery. Prepayment or when project is finished.
Accepts: American Express, MasterCard, Visa

ORIGINALS BY ELAINE/PARKER-LEVI

901 Oak Hollow Place
Brandon FL 33510
Contact: Bobby
Phone: (813)654-0335 or (813)685-8791
Fax: (813)654-8490
Catalog: Large doll mold, $7. Miniature doll mold, $6.
Phone Orders: Yes.
Mail Orders: Yes.
Accepts: American Express, MasterCard, Visa, check

PAGE'S DOLLS

6969 L5 Lane
Escanaba MI 49829
Contact: Lillian Page
Phone: (906)786-6565
E-mail: ruthch@up.net
Website: http://www.deltami.org/dolls
Store Location: At above address. M-Sun, 9-7.
Offers: Doll greenware, doll kits, assembled dolls and doll supplies.
Catalog: Greenware list.
Phone Orders: Weekly.
Mail Orders: National and international. Prepayment required. Allow 4 weeks; SFGW kits, 8 weeks.
Discounts: 3 or more, 10%.
Accepts: American Express, Discover, MasterCard, Visa

PARKER'S ANGORAS AND MOHAIR

33534 State Hwy. 68
Redwood Falls MN 56283
Contact: Wanda or John Parker
Phone: (507)644-2489
Offers: Mohair (kid, yearling, adult) for doll crafters and handspinners. Raw (unwashed) and washed by the pound, also washed, combed and packaged by the ounce. 100% mohair roving and mohair with wool blends.
Catalog: Send #10 SASE and $1 for sample and price list.
Phone Orders: Yes.
Mail Orders: Will ship to US and Canada. Prepayment required. Allow up to three weeks for delivery.

Discounts: Sells wholesale to legitimate businesses.
Accepts: MasterCard, Visa, check, money order

ROSE PINKUL ORIGINALS

3541 Carmel Ave.
Irvine CA 92006
Contact: Rose Pinkul
Phone: (714)559-6874
Fax: (714)559-6804
E-mail: rpinkul@deltanet.com
Website: http://users.deltanet.com/~fpinkul
Offers: Plaster molds for making porcelain dolls, doll costume patterns, wigs and glass eyes.
Catalog: Yes.
Phone Orders: Yes.
Mail Orders: Yes.
Discounts: Seasonal.
Accepts: MasterCard, Visa

PIPPIN'S HOLLOW

7996 Darrow Rd.
Twinsburg OH 44087
Phone: (888)937-2723
Fax: (800)292-4916
E-mail: nationalartcraft@worldnet.att.net
Website: www.nationalartcraft.com
Offers: Porcelain doll kits, wigs, pates, wire frames, hookups and stringing items, wires, hooks and connectors. Also carries accessories, acrylic and animal eyes, whiskers, doll teeth, pellets, Friendly Plastic, fiberfill, plus baby sounds, criers and growlers. Stocks fabric and composition bodies, Cernit model compound, FIMO, Evenheat kilns, Kemper and Narco tools, Seeley China colors and kits. Cleaning items, adhesives, stands, music movements and parts, containers and display cases are also available.
Catalog: $2 (refundable).
Discounts: Quantity.
Accepts: Discover, MasterCard, Visa

PJ'S PORCELAIN DOLLS & SUPPLIES

2881 S. Broadway
Englewood CO 80110
Contact: Rose or Jean
Phone: (303)781-4223
Fax: (303)781-4223
Store Location: At above address. M, 10-5; T-Sat, 9-5.
Offers: Porcelain doll classes, full line doll-making supplies, Lee Middleton dolls, Apple Valley dolls and Boyds Bears.
Phone Orders: Yes.
Mail Orders: Yes.
Discounts: Yes.
Accepts: Discover, MasterCard, Visa, check, cash

PLUM CREEK DOLLMAKERS

647 Plum Creek Rd.
Bernville PA 19506
Contact: Helen Schaeffer
Phone: (610)488-6568

Fax: (610)488-0122
E-mail: dollmkrpc@aol.com
Website: http://www.plumcreekdolls.com
Store Location: At above address. M-T, 10-4; Sat, 10-2.
Offers: All doll-making supplies including porcelain, molds, china paint, brushes, wigs, acrylic and glass eyes, mohair, doll clothing, shoes, stockings, armatures, doll-making books, composition doll bodies, kilns, and doll furniture and accessories.
Catalog: $5.
Phone Orders: M-F, 10-5 EST.
Mail Orders: Ship worldwide. Prepayment US funds.
Accepts: Discover, MasterCard, Visa

ROMAN'S
9733 Palmetto Ave.
Fontana CA 92335
Phone: (909)823-1100
Offers: Doll-making molds, cloth bodies and patterns.
Catalog: Mold, $4.75; pattern, $4.75.
Accepts: Discover, MasterCard, Visa

SANDY'S DOLL WORLD
10301 W. State Rd. 32
Yorktown IN 47396
Contact: Sandy or Claude Deters
Phone: (765)759-7928
Store Location: At above address.
Offers: Vinyl doll kits, porcelain doll kits, clothes, shoes and socks.
Catalog: Vinyl doll kits. List of porcelain kits.
Phone Orders: M-F, 10-7 EST.
Mail Orders: US and Canada.
Discounts: Quantity discounts available.
Accepts: MasterCard, Visa

G. SCHOEPFER, INC.
460 Cook Hill Rd.
Cheshire CT 06410
Phone: (203)250-7794
Fax: (203)250-7796
Offers: Eyes for dolls, including round and oval paperweight, Glastic, Glastic Realistic and Lifetouch series eyes in full range of sizes and colors.
Catalog: Send SASE or call.

SCOTT PUBLICATIONS
30595 Eight Mile Rd.
Livonia MI 48152
Contact: Jeanette Foxe
Phone: (248)477-6650
Fax: (248)477-6795
E-mail: 104137.1254@compuserve.com
Store Location: At above address. 8-4.
Offers: Books and magazines for ceramics, doll making, doll collecting, miniatures and making soft dolls and animals.
Catalog: Free.
Phone Orders: (800)458-8237.

Mail Orders: Will ship internationally. Allow 10-12 weeks for delivery. US orders shipped via UPS.
Discounts: To our dealers of the magazines.
Accepts: Discover, MasterCard, Visa

DOREEN SINNETT TINY DOLLS AND MOLDS
P.O. Box 789
Paso Robles CA 93447-0789
Contact: Doreen Sinnett
Phone: (805)239-2048
Fax: (805)239-4821
Offers: Tiny doll-making molds and patterns. No doll over 6″ tall, and as small as 1½″.
Catalog: $4.50 postpaid. Color.
Phone Orders: Yes.
Mail Orders: At above address. Will ship international. Prepayment required.
Accepts: MasterCard, Visa

JEWEL SOMMARS
958 Cambridge Ave.
Sunnyvale CA 94087-1130
Contact: Jewel Sommars
Phone: (408)732-7177
Offers: Two videotapes: *Doll Making Technique* and *Delightful Dolls—Collecting and Creating*. Price each $49.95 ($5 p&h). Line of original dolls, "Jewel's Gems." Book, *Jewel's Dolls—A Photographic Journal* by Jewel Sommars. 130 pages, photographs, $14.95 ($5 p&h).
Catalog: "Jewel's Gems" brochure. List of collectible dolls for sale, $1 and SASE.
Discounts: Buy 2 videos, half price on 1.
Accepts: check, money order (no credit cards)

STANDARD DOLL SUPPLY HOUSE, INC.
23-83 31st St.
Long Island City NY 11105
Contact: Joan Henfield
Phone: (718)721-7787
Fax: (718)274-4231
Offers: Doll supplies, including china doll kits (old-fashioned, pincushion, character and *Gone With the Wind* characters), porcelain bisque kits (reproductions) and bisque doll heads and parts. Also carries body patterns, doll stands, accessories, eyes, wigs, magnifiers, patterns, books, notions, doll hangers, doll clothes, rack kits and other supplies. Offers vinyl undressed dolls and doll shoes.
Catalog: $3 (refundable).
Phone Orders: (800)543-6557.
Mail Orders: Yes.
Discounts: Quantity.
Accepts: American Express, MasterCard, Visa, check, money order

STONE'S STUFFING
500 Fitton Ave.
Hamilton OH 45015
Contact: Mary Stone

Phone: (513)887-7610
Fax: (513)887-7612
E-mail: mastone50@yahoo.com
Offers: Cloth bodies for porcelain dolls.
Catalog: $4.
Phone Orders: Yes.
Mail Orders: Yes.
Discounts: Wholesale and retail.
Accepts: American Express, Discover, MasterCard, Visa, check, money order, C.O.D.

TEAHAN MILLINERY STUDIO

Dept. CSS
4326 SE Woodstock Blvd., Suite 570
Portland OR 97206
Contact: Sandra Teahan
Phone: (503)653-7837
Fax: (503)653-7837
Offers: Specialty patterns and instruction for doll and teddy bear hats, including molded felt, formed buckram frame and stitched straw braid. Hat supplies: felt, straw braid, buckram, hat glue, hat wire, ribbon wire, hat molds and hat sizing.
Catalog: $3.50.
Mail Order: Prepayment required. Allow 6-8 weeks for delivery.
Accepts: check, money order

THE ULTIMATE COLLECTION, INC.

12773 W. Forest Hill Blvd., Suite 107
West Palm Beach FL 33414
Phone: (561)790-0137
Fax: (561)790-0179
Offers: Artist doll molds including baby heads—Sweetness (eyes open), Serenity (eyes closed), Hilary, Willow and Jess.
Catalog: $6.
Accepts: Discover, MasterCard, Visa

VICKI'S ORIGINAL DESIGNS, INC.

2100 E. 85th N.
Valley Center KS 67147
Contact: Vicki Hamilton
Phone: (316)838-9040
Fax: (316)755-0364
E-mail: vicki@vickis.com
Website: http://www.vickis.com
Store Location: At above address.

Offers: Doll molds, Lady Fashion or 300 patterns. One-year membership to Victorian Mercantile for $10.
Catalog: Pattern or doll catalog.
Phone Orders: Fax.
Mail Orders: P.O. Box 363, Valley Center KS 67147.
Discounts: 50% maximum.
Accepts: all bank cards, check, money order (no C.O.D.)

WEE WORLD OF DOLLS, INC.

112 W. Tarrant Rd.
Gardendale AL 35071
Phone: (205)631-9270
Store Location: At above address. M, T, Th and F, 9-4.
Offers: Porcelain doll kits and a line of supplies for antique and modern dolls by Playhouse, Seeley, Bell, Brown House, Monique and others.
Catalog: Send SASE for list.
Discounts: Sells wholesale.

THE WORLD OF MOHAIR

1007 Bower Rd.
West Harrison IN 47060
Contact: Sue Kneir
Phone: (812)637-3874
E-mail: sdkneir@aol.com
Website: http://members.aol.com/SDKneir/index.htm
Store Location: At above address.
Offers: Create your own doll wigs with our luxurious mohair and lamb. Washed curly locks in a variety of colors and styles. Also available are wefted hair, angora goat kits, elastic lace caps for doll heads and skin wigs.
Catalog: Free. SASE.
Phone Orders: Yes.
Mail Orders: Will ship to US and Canada.
Accepts: check, money order

YESTERDAY'S CHILDREN PATTERN COMPANY

413 Harvey St.
Des Plaines IL 60016
Phone: (847)635-3049
Offers: Over 350 easy-sew patterns for doll clothes, antique to country styles, for 8″-36″ dolls. Fabrics, notions and lace are also available.
Catalog: $4.
Discounts: Sells wholesale.

Fishing & Taxidermy

Also see General Craft Supplies; Nature Crafts; Outdoors & Outerwear.

THE ANGLERS ART
P.O. Box 148
Plainfield PA 17081
Phone: (717)243-9721
Fax: (717)243-8603
Offers: Full line of books on fly-fishing, including crafting of items and many others.
Catalog: Free.

ANGLER'S WORKSHOP
P.O. Box 1044
Woodland WA 98674
Phone: (360)225-9445
Fax: (360)255-8641
Offers: Rod-building and fly-tying kits, blanks, components, tying materials, rods, reels, lines, rod guides and tops and other fishing products.
Catalog: Write for free catalog, or send $1 for first-class mail.
Discounts: Sells wholesale to legitimate business.

EGGER'S
P.O. Box 1344
Cumming GA 30028
Contact: Gene Hansard
Phone: (770)887-8066
Fax: (770)889-8665
E-mail: hia@flash.net

Website: flytier.com
Store Location: 305 Atlanta Rd., Cumming GA 30040
Offers: Full line of fly tying and fly-fishing supplies.
Catalog: Check website.
Phone Orders: Yes.
Mail Orders: At P.O. Box.
Discounts: 10% first order.
Accepts: MasterCard, Visa

JANN'S NETCRAFT
P.O. Box 89
Maumee OH 43537
Phone: (419)868-8288
Offers: Materials/accessories for tackle building, including lure making, fly tying, rod building and net making.
Catalog: Free.

JERRY'S TACKLE
604 12th St.
Highland IL 62249
Phone: (800)500-6585
E-mail: jerrytck@fgi.net
Website: www.jerrystackle.com
Offers: Line of components for lures, jigs, feathers and fur for fly tying and rod building. Also offers KT products water-based paints and glitter finishes.
Catalog: Free.

MCKENZIE TAXIDERMY SUPPLY
P.O. Box 480
Granite Quarry NC 28072
Phone: (800)279-7985
Offers: Full line of taxidermy supplies, including deer and animal forms.
Catalog: Free.

Frames & Picture Framing

Also see Artist's Supplies, Graphics & Printing; General Craft Supplies; Woodworking; General Needlecraft Supplies; Quilting; other related categories.

AMERICAN FRAME CORP.

400 Tomahawk Dr.
Maumee OH 43537
Phone: (800)537-0944
Fax: (800)893-3898
E-mail: info@americanframe.com
Website: www.americanframe.com
Store Location: At above address. M-F, 9-4.
Offers: Laminated frame sections, metal frames, section pairs and custom cut frames. Also carries hardwood section frames, Plexiglas, matboards and foamcore.
Catalog: Free.
Accepts: American Express, Discover, MasterCard, Visa

DOCUMOUNTS FRAMING SERVICE, INC.

P.O. Box 26239
3709 W. First Ave.
Eugene OR 97402-0464
Contact: Guy Neville, general manager
Phone: (541)485-1704 or (800)769-5639
Fax: (541)686-1954
E-mail: documnts@documounts.com
Website: http://www.documounts.com/bargains
Store Location: At above address.
Offers: Retail outlet offers framing services for local customers.
Catalog: Call for free catalog.
Phone Orders: Yes.
Mail Orders: Check for total of order must be included before order can be processed.
Discounts: Volume discounts.

THE FLETCHER-TERRY CO.

65 Spring Lane
Farmington CT 06032
Phone: (800)843-3826
Offers: Picture-framing tools—FrameMaster stapler (fires flat points), FrameMate unit (flat framers, points or brads into molding), mat board cutters, glass and stained glass cutters. Call.

FRAME FIT CO.

P.O. Box 8926
Philadelphia PA 19135-0926
Contact: Steve Kress
Phone: (800)523-3693
Fax: (800)344-7010
E-mail: framefit@netaxs.com
Website: www.framefit.com
Store Location: 7353 Milnor St., Philadelphia PA 19136-4210.
Offers: Custom picture frames. Aluminum frames are available in 5 profiles and 22 colors. Elegant wood frames are available in 4 profiles and 6 shades. Evolution composite frames are available in a variety of 51 profiles and colors. Wood and evolution frames are available assembled or unassembled.
Catalog: Yes.
Phone Orders: Yes.
Discounts: Quantity.
Accepts: Discover, MasterCard, Visa, check, money order, C.O.D.

FRANKEN FRAMES

609 W. Walnut St.
Johnson City TN 37604
Phone: (423)926-8853 or (800)322-5899
Fax: (423)926-5123
E-mail: franken@usit.net
Website: www.frankenframes.com
Offers: Custom gallery-quality frames, linen liners, custom mats, hardware, canvases, stretcher bars, artist's materials and art supplies.
Catalog: Write or call.
Accepts: MasterCard, Visa, check, money order

GRAPHIK DIMENSIONS LTD.

2103 Brentwood St.
High Point NC 27263
Contact: Nancy Hoffman
Phone: (336)887-3700
Fax: (336)887-3773
E-mail: nhof@graphikdimensions.com
Website: www.graphikdimensions.com
Store Location: High Point NC location.
Offers: Picture frames in a full line of modern metals, lacquered styles and classic woods, plus frames with linen, burlap or suede liners. Other styles include rustic, traditional, contemporary, Oriental and European.
Catalog: Free. Color.
Phone Orders: (800)221-0262.
Accepts: Discover, MasterCard, Visa

THE METTLE CO.
Dept. K
P.O. Box 234
Middlesex NJ 08846
Contact: Tom Newton
Phone: (800)621-1329 or (732)805-9490
Fax: (732)764-0342
Offers: Custom cut aluminum and wood picture frames at wholesale prices.
Catalog: Free.
Phone Orders: Yes.
Mail Orders: Yes.
Discounts: Quantity.
Accepts: American Express, Discover, MasterCard, Visa

STU-ART
Dept. CSS
2045 Grand Ave.
Baldwin NY 11510
Phone: (516)546-5151

Offers: Mats and picture frames. Mats include conservation types, ready-mats and hand-cut beveled. Frames include aluminum, wood; frame sections, and preassembled aluminum and wood frames in a variety of sizes. Also carries plastic picture saver panels and shrink-wrap.
Catalog: Free.

WORLD FRAME CENTER
107 Maple St.
Denton TX 76201
Phone: (940)382-5556
Offers: Frames—traditional, ready-made types and sizes, plus gallery-style, ornately crafted frames, supplies and canvas.
Catalog: Free brochure and price list.

Furniture Making & Upholstery

Also see Basketry & Seat Weaving; Miniature Making, Miniatures & Dollhouses; Paints, Finishes & Adhesives; Woodworking; other related categories.

DESIGNER FURNITURE PLANS

P.O. Box 55
Neshanic Station NJ 08853
Phone: (908)469-6200
Offers: Furniture construction plans, including kids-size and other home furnishings.
Catalog: $2 for kids-sized furniture catalog. $3 for catalog of other home furnishings. $4.50 for both catalogs—includes 84 designs.

EMPEROR CLOCK, LLC

Dept. 6487
Emperor Industrial Park
Fairhope AL 36532
Phone: (334)928-2316
Offers: Clock kits, including grandfather, mantel and wall models in cherry or oak with solid brass West German movements and dials. Also carries furniture kits and assembled clocks.
Catalog: Color. $1.

FURNITURE DESIGNS, INC.

1827 Elmdale Ave.
Glenview IL 60025
Contact: Ernest A. Stranglen Jr.
Phone: (847)657-7526
Fax: (847)657-9262
Store Location: At above address. M-F, 9-5 CST.
Offers: More than 200 professionally designed full-size furniture plans including rolltop desks, dining tables, chairs, buffets, china hutches, curio cabinets, chests of drawers, dressers, beds, children's furniture, cradles, rocking horses, spinning wheels, gun cabinets, corner cabinets, Queen Anne lowboy and highboy, Morris chair and footrest, Adirondack and English garden furniture and more.

Catalog: $3.
Phone Orders: M-F, 9-5 CST; fax 24 hours a day.
Mail Orders: US, Canada and overseas.
Discounts: Teachers and schools; wholesale to businesses.
Accepts: MasterCard, Visa

QUALITY UPHOLSTERY

75 Diggs Blvd.
Warner Robins GA 31093
Contact: Fred Laumann
Phone: (912)922-8911
Fax: (912)953-7308
Store Location: At above address.
Offers: Upholstery instructional video by German craftsmen.

SHAKER WORKSHOPS

P.O. Box 8001
Ashburnham MA 01430
Phone: (800)840-9121
Fax: (978)827-9900
E-mail: shaker@shakerworkshops.com
Website: shakerworkshops.com
Store Location: 18 Mill Lane, Arlington MA 02174.
Offers: Shaker kits for rockers, dining chairs, tables, beds, pegboards and pegs. Also carries dolls, oval boxes and custom-made furniture.
Catalog: And tape samples, $1.
Accepts: American Express, Discover, MasterCard, Visa

V.U.E.

P.O. Box 128-CSS
El Verano CA 95433
Phone: (800)635-3493
Website: www.upholster.com
Store Location: 17421 Sonoma Hwy., El Verano CA 95476.
Offers: Instructional/training videos on upholstery, slipcovering and auto/marine recovering (car, truck and boat seats). Carries tools and upholstery supplies. Upholstery instruction on the Internet.
Catalog: Free brochure.
Discounts: Quantity.
Accepts: American Express, MasterCard, Visa

General Craft Supplies

Also see specific art/crafts chapters; Books & Booksellers; Publications; Associations.

Browse through this sourcebook for unexpected, unusual and often valuable items for your personal creative expression.

ALPEL PUBLISHING

P.O. Box 203-CSS
Chambly, Quebec J3L 4B3
Canada
Phone: (450)658-6205
Fax: (450)658-3514
Offers: *Catalogue of Canadian Catalogues*, a directory of 1,000 mail-order sources in 118 categories, including crafts, graphics, needlecrafts, woodworking and others. Also offers "Duplicate" reusable grid for enlarging miniature patterns, and sewing pattern books.
Catalog: Brochures and 20 sample patterns, $2.
Discounts: Teachers and institutions; sells wholesale to legitimate businesses and professionals.

AMERICAN ART CLAY CO., INC.

4717 W. 16th St.
Indianapolis IN 46222
Contact: Nancy Elliott
Phone: (317)244-6871 or (800)374-1600
Fax: (317)248-9300
E-mail: amacobrent@aol.com
Website: www.amaco.com
Offers: Craft supplies and modeling materials. Since 1919, AMACO has been a leading manufacturer of modeling clays, such as Permoplast, Plasti-i-clay, Marblex and Mexican; modeling materials, including Friendly Plastic, FIMO, polymer clay Millefiori Canes, Quilt Squares, Designer Squares, Sculptamold, Claycrete and Super Dough. Also Rub 'n Buff and Brush 'n Leaf metallic finishes, Batikit fabric dyes, Cotton Press hand-cast cotton paper products, and push molds for use with polymer clays.
Catalog: Free.
Phone Orders: M-F, 8-5 EST.
Mail Orders: Prepayment required. Will ship to US and Canada.
Discounts: Manufacturer—sells through distributors.
Accepts: Discover, MasterCard, Visa

THE ART STORE

935 Erie Blvd. E.
Syracuse NY 13210
Phone: (315)474-1000

Offers: Fiber arts/crafts supplies and equipment: Jacquard textile and silk paints, screen printing, marbling, FIMO, Sculpey, tie-dye, Procion dye, Jo Sonya and brushes.
Catalog: Complete list, $3.

DICK BLICK

Dept. CB
P.O. Box 1267
Galesburg IL 61402-1267
Phone: (309)343-6181
Offers: Full line of art/sculpture and other materials and equipment: soapstone, alabaster and stone sculpture tool sets. Modeling: instant papier-mâchés, Sculptamold, plastercraft gauze, plaster of Paris (and molds), Sculpey, FIMO and modeling clays. Clays: Mexican pottery, Marblex, Westwood ovencraft and others. Also offers Egyptian paste, earthenware and other kitchen-fired clays, plus glazes, ceramic and modeling tools/sets and aids.
Accepts: American Express, Discover, MasterCard, Visa

BOUTIQUE TRIMS, INC.

21200 Pontiac Trail
South Lyon MI 48178
Phone: (248)437-2017
Fax: (248)437-9436
E-mail: info@btcrafts.com
Website: www.btcrafts.com
Offers: AG and AS jewelry findings and charms, woodenware, paint and art supplies, silk flowers, floral supplies and dried materials. Also offers resin figures, papier-mâché and others.
Catalog: Metal findings, $3.
Discounts: Quantity; teachers, institutions and professionals.

BOYD'S

3511 Rushing Rd.
Augusta GA 30906
Contact: Patti Boyd
Phone: (706)798-3157
Fax: (706)560-2821
E-mail: homelight@aol.com
Website: members.aol.com/homelight/
Offers: Resin-It Crafting Instruction, including artwork on paper for jewelry, magnets and other items with resin surface and finishing.
Catalog: Formulas, booklet and Resin-It brochure/sample, $7.

BRIAN'S CRAFTS UNLIMITED

Dept. CSS
P.O. Box 731046
Ormond Beach, FL 32173-1046
Contact: Judy Oppenheimer
Phone: (904)672-2726
Fax: (904)760-9246
E-mail: bricrafts@aol.com
Offers: Doilies, muslin dolls and animals, ribbon roses, hats, glue guns, wood items, mini-brooms, hair clips, plastic fillable ornament, fused pearls, doll hair, bargain grab bags and more. Also we can special-order many items. We are the mail-order source for the following: Candle Magic, Wonder Bow supplies, Bedazzler studs and rhinestones, lap weaving.
Catalog: Sale flyers and brochures only. Send long SASE and specify interest.
Phone Orders: M-F, 9-6 EST.
Mail Orders: Shipped worldwide. Outside continental US must use credit card.
Discounts: Quantity discounts available.
Accepts: Discover, MasterCard, Visa

CHESTER BOOK CO.

4 Maple St.
Chester CT 06412
Contact: Lois Nadel
Phone: (860)526-9887
Fax: (860)526-9887
E-mail: office@chesterbookco.com
Website: office@chesterbookco.com
Offers: Line of quality books in variety of arts and crafts, including Japanese, African and other ethnic crafts; ceramics, fabric and fiber arts, dyeing, glass, jewelry making, metal working, paper crafting, furniture making and others.
Catalog: 44 pages. Free.
Phone Orders: (800)868-8515.
Mail Orders: Ships worldwide.
Accepts: MasterCard, Visa, check

CRAFT CATALOG

P.O. Box 1069
Reynoldsburg OH 43068
Contact: Farley Piper
Phone: (800)777-1442
Fax: (740)964-6212
E-mail: christy@craftwholesalers.com
Website: www.craftcatalog.com
Store Location: 2087 St. Rt. 256, Reynoldsburg OH 43068.
Offers: Paint, brushes, wood, Styrofoam, Polyfil, pom-poms, floral supplies, candle making, stencils, rub-ons, cookie cutters, hair, wood turnings, canvas, gifts, seasonal, clay, paper twist, Xmas, clock parts, wreaths and glue.
Catalog: Free.
Phone Orders: 24 hours.
Mail Orders: At P.O. Box.
Discounts: 20-50%.
Accepts: Discover, MasterCard, Visa, check

CRAFT KING, INC.

Dept. CSS2
P.O. Box 90637
Lakeland FL 33804
Contact: Customer Service Dept.
Phone: (888)CRAFTY-1
Fax: (941)648-2972
E-mail: craftking@gate.net
Store Location: 3033 Drane Field Rd., Lakeland FL 33811.
Offers: A wide range of discount craft supplies from many of the top manufacturers and importers. Dolls, miniatures, paints, wood, kits, beads and much, much more.
Catalog: Introductory catalog, 64 pages, free. Full catalog, 168 pages with first order. Also wholesale catalog to legitimate businesses.
Phone Orders: (800)769-9494. M-F, 8-7; Sat, 8:30-5 EST.
Mail Orders: Worldwide shipping.
Discounts: Everything discounted.
Accepts: Discover, MasterCard, Visa

CRAFT MAKERS OUTLET

3958 Linden Ave.
Dayton OH 45432
Contact: Rae Hinch
Phone: (937)252-7222
Fax: (937)252-5110
Store Location: West of Linden Avenue and Woodman Drive exit on Route 35. M-F, 10-8; Sat, 10-6; Sun, 12-5.
Offers: Variety of craft supplies: ribbon, lace, flowers, pom-poms, Styrofoam, paints, felt, plastic canvas, paper twist, candle wax, floating candles, feathers and chenille stems. Wedding supplies: guest books, champagne glasses, plastic bells, gloves and cake toppers.
Catalog: $2.
Phone Orders: (800)CRAFTS-5.
Accepts: American Express, Discover, MasterCard, Visa

CREATIVE CRAFT HOUSE

P.O. Box 2567
Bullhead City AZ 86430
Phone: (520)754-3300
Offers: Pinecone and seashell projects, plus other natural materials—pods, cones, foliages and Christmas materials. Also carries jewelry findings and parts, doll-making items, party and wedding favors, and animal and doll parts. Miniatures, beads, novelties, conchos, foil and mirrors are also available.
Catalog: $2, includes a bonus section of 37 pinecone and seasonal projects.
Discounts: Quantity.

CRYSBI CRAFTS, INC.

17514 S. Ave. 4 E
Yuma AZ 85365
Store Location: RR 3, High River, Alberta T1V 1N3 Canada
Offers: Craft supplies, including dried and preserved florals and moss, raffia, excelsior, wheats, grasses, flax, nests, wreaths, floral supplies and extensive silk flowers. Line of

baskets, wicker products and craft kits also available. Decorative items include laces, paper twist, doll hair, eyes, pompoms, bells, Styrofoam, buttons, ribbons, beads, magnets, birds, plush animals, hats, twists, chenille, glitter, felt, mop heads, doll furniture and more.

Catalog: Free.

Discounts: Quantity.

LOU DAVIS WHOLESALE

Dept. CS8
N3211 County Rd. H. N.
Lake Geneva WI 53147
Phone: (414)248-2000 or (800)748-7991
Offers: Brand-name craft and ceramic supplies, including music movements in more than 200 tunes, chalks, paints, spray finishes, airbrushes and compressors, clock movements, doll-making supplies, lamp parts and accessories, brushes, magnets, glitter, abrasives, adhesives and cleaning tools.
Catalog: $2 (refundable with order).
Accepts: Discover, MasterCard, Visa

DOVE BRUSH MANUFACTURING, INC.

280 Terrace Rd.
Tarpon Springs FL 34689
Contact: George N. Dovellos
Phone: (813)934-5283
Fax: (813)934-1142
E-mail: dove23@earthlink.net
Website: http://www.dovebrushes.com
Store Location: Tarpon Springs FL location.
Offers: Full art brush line covering doll making, ceramics, decorative painting, crafts and more; including "Mid-Night Dove" brushes and specialty brushes—½″ feather edge by Jill MacFarlane and others.
Catalog: $2.50 (nonrefundable).
Phone Orders: (800)334-3683.
Mail Orders: Prepaid orders only. Ship UPS.
Accepts: MasterCard, Visa, money order, C.O.D., cash

DOVER PUBLICATIONS, INC.

31 E. Second St.
Mineola NY 11501
Contact: Rhoda Dreifus, marketing manager
Phone: (516)294-7000, ext. 123
Store Location: 180 Varick St., Ninth Floor, New York NY 10004. Also 11 E. Second St., Mineola NY 11501.
Offers: Craft and needlecraft books. Carries a series of copyright-free design books, including clip art (holiday designs, borders, layout grids, old-fashioned animals, transportation, patriotic, sport, wedding, humorous, nautical and alphabets); designs from various eras, including Japanese, Chinese, Art Nouveau, Early Arabic and Mayan designs; stencil books; and folk designs. Also carries books on stained glass, calligraphy, costumes, art, silkscreen, bookbinding, paper, beads, jewelry, basketry, marionettes, leather, tole, miniatures and dollhouses. Needlecraft books on quilting, applique, knitting/

crochet, lace, many embroidery patterns, needlepoint and charted doll-making books.
Catalog: Write for free catalog.
Discounts: Check with marketing manager.

ENTERPRISE ART

Dept. 810
P.O. Box 2918
Largo FL 34649
Phone: (800)366-2218
Fax: (800)366-6121
E-mail: custserv@enterpriseart.com
Website: www.enterprisart.com
Offers: Line of craft kits, beads, jewelry-making supplies, doll products, angel-making parts, hard-to-find items, patterns and books.
Catalog: Basic supply catalog, $4.

GOODWIND'S KITES

3333 Wallingford Ave. N.
Seattle WA 98103
Contact: Retail: Doug Garza; Wholesale: Kathy Goodwind
Phone: (206)633-4780
Fax: (206)633-0301
E-mail: goodwind's@aol.com
Website: In the works.
Store Location: At above address. M-F, 10-6; Sat, 10-5; Sun, Noon-5 PST.
Offers: Kite crafting, banner-making and windsock-making supplies. *Goodwind's Ultimate Guide to Kitemaking Supplies and Parts* offers 20 years of sewing and building tips for kite, banner and windsock crafters. Printed patterns available with kits for high school sewing projects.
Catalog: Price list for all the goods offered in our guide.
Phone Orders: Accepted M-F, 10-6 PST.
Mail Orders: Will ship anywhere. Prepayment required.
Discounts: Sells wholesale to legitimate businesses.
Accepts: MasterCard, Visa with approval

GRANDLOVING

Dept. TCSS-GL
20 Birling Gap
Fairport NY 14450
Contact: Sue Johnson, coauthor
Phone: (716)223-4309
Fax: (716)223-4789
E-mail: 70671.321@compuserve.com
Website: http://world.std.com/~jcarlson/senior
Offers: *Grandloving: Making Memories With Your Grandchildren*, a new book, features over 200 innovative, inexpensive craft and activity ideas for grandparents to do with or mail to their grandchildren. Ideas from unique mother-in-law/daughter-in-law coauthors as well as over 300 families worldwide. 280 pages include illustrated projects as well as index and a guide to the best children's books and products.
Catalog: Flyer $1 and #10 SASE.
Phone Orders: Yes.
Mail Orders: Will ship worldwide. Personalized, autogra-

phed copies. Prepay by check or money order: $14.95 plus $3 p&h.

Discounts: Quantity: sells wholesale.
Accepts: check, money order, cash

HANG-EM HIGH FABRICS
1420 Yale Ave.
Richmond VA 23224
Phone: (804)233-6155
Offers: Kite kits, fabrics/materials: ripstop nylon, polyester and dacron. Carries adhesives, fiberglass and carbon spars, poles, webbing, dihedrals, line, fiberglass and aluminum couplings, caps, swivels, tapes, spools, eyelet tools and others.
Catalog: Free.

INTO THE WIND
1408 Pearl St.
Boulder CO 80302
Phone: (800)541-0314
Fax: (303)449-7315
Offers: Kite kits: Over 200 stunt and other kites. Carries kite-making supplies and tools, packs, wind meters, lighting systems, plus a full range of line, accessories and spare parts for sport (and other) kites.
Catalog: Free.

KELLY'S CRAFTS
4350 Wade Mill Rd.
Fairfield OH 45014
Phone: (800)796-5472 or (513)738-5566
Fax: (513)738-5568
Offers: Suncatchers, sand art fun mugs, buttons and miscellaneous activities.
Catalog: 200 pages for retail and distributors only.
Phone Orders: M-F, 8-5.
Discounts: Vary.
Accepts: MasterCard, Visa

KITE LINES
P.O. Box 466
Randallstown MD 21133
Contact: Valerie Govig
Phone: (410)922-1212
Fax: (410)922-4262
E-mail: kitelines@compuserve.com
Store Location: Visitors OK by appointment.
Offers: We have kite-crafting articles in every issue of *Kitelines* plus our bookstore offers kite-making books by mail order from all over the world.
Catalog: $5 for sample copy with bookstore.
Phone Orders: M-Sat, 10-10 EST.
Mail Orders: We ship to any country in the world.
Discounts: Retail only.
Accepts: American Express, MasterCard, Visa

JOE KUBERT ART & GRAPHIC SUPPLY
37A Myrtle Ave.
Dover NJ 07801
Phone: (973)328-3266

Fax: (973)328-7283
Store Location: At above address. M-F, 10-6; Sat, 9-4.
Offers: Artist's, cartoonist's, and graphic art materials, including boards, papers (art, parchments, drafting, etching, rag, others), paints, finger paints, brushes, palettes, pens, crayons, chalk, pencils, pastels, airbrushes, airbrush sets, calligraphy pens/inks, drafting materials/equipment and Pantographs. Also carries mat/paper cutters, projectors, easels, canvas, stretcher strips, graphic and printing supplies, frisket, grids, films, Letraset letters, tapes, film, waxers, light boxes, projectors, furniture, plus etching, block printing and silk-screen supplies and equipment, tools, knives and books.
Catalog: $4.

MAGEYE'S
(formerly MFD Enterprises, Inc.)
222 Sidney Baker S., Suite 202
Kerrville TX 78028
Contact: Kay Dechert
Phone: (800)210-6662
Fax: (830)896-6060
E-mail: sales@mageyes.com
Website: www.mageyes.com
Offers: Hands-free, head-mounted magnifier. It helps focus on the detail.
Catalog: Brochure.
Phone Orders: Yes.
Mail Orders: Prepayment required.
Discount: Sells wholesale.
Accepts: MasterCard, Visa

NATIONAL ARTCRAFT CO.
7996 Darrow Rd.
Twinsburg OH 44087
Phone: (888)937-2723
Fax: (800)292-4916
E-mail: nationalartcraft@worldnet.att.net
Website: ww.nationalartcraft.com
Offers: Three catalogs offer a broad range of hard-to-find craft products. A 112-page general craft catalog includes studio display items, cements and glues, jewelry parts, brushes, fountain pumps, doll glasses, novelty items, rhinestones, desk pens and miniatures. A 40-page musical/clock movement catalog includes a large selection of tunes and clock insert styles. Also offers a 32-page electrical/lamp catalog.
Catalog: $1 each.
Discounts: Quantity.

NANCY NEALE TYPECRAFT
P.O. Box 40
Roslyn NY 11576
Summer address: Steamboat Wharf Rd., Bernard ME 04612.
Fax: (207)244-5090 or (800)927-7469.
Phone: (516)612-7130
Fax: (516)621-7313 or (800)927-7469
E-mail: typenancy@aol.com
Website: www.acadia.net/typecraft/
Offers: Antique and old wood printing type (letters, num-

bers, punctuation, in 1″-5″ sizes, in a variety of styles). Most type is in English, some in German and Hebrew [inquire]; sold by 100-plus lots. Type can be used for printing, as ornaments, for collages, for nameplates, door knockers, inlaid wood patterns and more. Also carries old copper and zinc engravings, metal dingbats, printer's galleys, initials and others. Provides assistance and assembling instructions on request.

Catalog: Catalog and trial type order $10.

Accepts: MasterCard, Visa

SAX ARTS & CRAFTS

P.O. Box 510710
2405 S. Calhoun Rd.
New Berlin WI 53151
Phone: (414)784-6880

Offers: A variety of supplies (known brands), including a full line of weaving looms and aids, yarns, weaving kits, rug/craft yarns, embroidery/crewel threads, rug hook frames and aids, canvas, hoops, burlap and felt. Indian beading, beads, feathers, macrame, basketry and batik supplies, fabric paints, airbrush kits and inks, stencil films, trims, foam, stained glass kits, etching and beveled glass supplies and supplies for decoupage, jewelry making, leather, casting, plastics, wood and metal working are also available.

Catalog: $5 (refundable).

Discounts: Quantity; sells wholesale to legitimate businesses.

VIDEO LEARNING LIBRARY

(formerly Art Video Library)
5777 Azalea Dr.
Grants Pass OR 97526
Contact: Gail Newcomb
Phone: (541)479-7140
Fax: (541)476-8728
E-mail: vll@juno.com

Offers: Craft instructional videos available to members for sale or rent at low cost on payment of a yearly fee at low cost (rental can apply to purchase). Videos demonstrate paints, color, candy making, stencil, theorem, bronzing, soft-sculpture dolls, cake decorating, tole, stained glass, sculpting, plaster, water and other molds, bas relief, bronze casting, etching and engraving. Also offers videos on sewing basics, including knits, lingerie, jeans, embroidery, teddy bears and others.

Catalog: Free.

WIND UNDER YOUR WINGS

11046 W. Derby Ave.
Wauwatosa WI 53225
Phone: (414)461-3444

Offers: Stunt kite kits and spare parts including those for Shadow and Team Spirit models; includes carbon graphite spars and Carrington ripstop nylon sails.

Catalog: Write for brochure; send SASE for list.

Accepts: MasterCard, Visa

WINDSOKETS

3015 Quail Ave. N.
Golden Valley MN 55422
Contact: Ron Geldert
Phone: (612)529-6261 or (800)869-1333
Fax: (612)521-5518

Offers: Sourcing products, mainly wind-related items. I manufacture ¼″ delrin couplings, windsocks and accesories for the windsock industry, special mounting poles and specialty and custom windsocks and banners. I can source manufacturers, packagers and others.

Catalog: Separate flyer sheets.

Phone Orders: (800)869-1333.

Mail Orders: P.O. Box 22005, Minneapolis MN 55422.

Discounts: 2-10% net with approved credit; otherwise prepay or C.O.D.

Accepts: MasterCard, Visa

WOOD-N-CRAFTS, INC.

P.O. Box 140
405 N. Edgar St.
Lakeview MI 48850
Contact: Phillip Cole
Phone: (800)444-8075 or (517)352-8075
Fax: (517)352-6792
E-mail: info@wood-n-crafts.com
Website: www.wood-n-crafts.com

Store Location: Warehouse showroom at above address. M-F, 8:30-4:30 EST.

Offers: Wood turnings and cutouts, brass hardware, paints, beads, toy parts, stuffing, straw hats, wooden miniatures, floral supplies, raffia, excelsior, Spanish moss, chalkboards, glue, drywall and production screws, lazy Susan hardware and much, much more.

Catalog: Free with 10% off your first order.

Phone Orders: M-F, 8:30-4:30 EST.

Mail Orders: Will ship internationally: 40% for surface shipping outside US and Canada; free shipping on orders over $70 shipped within continental US.

Discounts: Sells wholesale to public.

Accepts: Discover, MasterCard, Visa, check, money order, C.O.D.

Glass Crafts & Stained Glass

Also see General Craft Supplies; Bead Crafts; Ceramics; other related categories.

ALICE'S STAINED GLASS (ASG)
Dept. CS
P.O. Box 552
Glendale AZ 85301
Contact: Alice or Tammy
Phone: (602)939-7260
Fax: (602)939-8044
Store Location: Call ahead for appointment.
Offers: Glass bead-making tools, supplies, videos and books; glass mosaic supplies and books; glass art-related supplies; handmade glass beads for the discriminating jeweler; and private bead-making classes.
Catalog: SASE for specific areas. 9,000-item "big book," $8 including postage.
Phone Orders: Yes.
Mail Orders: Worldwide shipping.
Discounts: Wholesale bead-making supplies to legitimate businesses.
Accepts: MasterCard, Visa (no C.O.D.)

C&R LOO, INC.
1085 Essex Ave.
Richmond CA 94801
Phone: (800)227-1780
Fax: (510)232-7810
E-mail: glass@crloo.com
Website: http://www.crloo.com
Store Location: M-F, 8:30-5.
Offers: The most extensive color selection in North America. Glassblowing color tools and supplies: Kugler Colors by Friederich, Q-Colors by Reichenbach, Wiesenthal, Zimmermann, Kevlar gloves, frit bowls, books and more. Fusing, lampworking and bead-making glass and supplies: Uroboros, Bullseye and Effetre (Moretti). Sheet glass, rods, cane, frits, powders and tubing. Dichroic glass for glassblowing, fusing and lampworking: sheet glass, rods, strips and patterns. Glass for Pate de Verre, mold materials, precious metal leaf, neon and more.
Catalog: Call for free catalog.
Phone Orders: Accepted M-F, 8:30-5.
Mail Orders: We ship worldwide. Free UPS shipping and $6 FedEx shipping upgrades for all overlay colors.
Accepts: Discover, MasterCard, Visa

COVINGTON ENGINEERING CORP.
P.O. Box 35
715 W. Colton Ave.
Redlands CA 92374
Phone: (909)793-6636
Offers: Glass machinery, including a glass beveling system, a 2-station unit with polisher, horizontal glass lap, sphere cutting cups and glass smoothing beveler. Also offers a glass lap kit, diamond mini-lap, arbors (for vertical glass units), belt sanders/polishers, web sanders, large sphere maker, cutter cups and supplies. Trim saws/cutters, arbors and accessories, lathes (engraver/cutter), Koolerant pumps, water and drain items are also available.
Catalog: Send SASE for list.

EASTERN ART GLASS
P.O. Box 9
Wyckoff NJ 07481
Phone: (201)847-0001
Offers: Glass etching and mirror removing kits and a glass engraving course. Carries rotary engraving power tools (to carve or engrave on glass, plastic, metal and wood). Supplies available include stencils, mirrors and slab glass. Glass etching and mirror decorating video course also available.
Catalog: $2.
Accepts: American Express, Discover, MasterCard, Visa

GLASS CRAFT, INC.
626 Moss St.
Golden CO 80401
Phone: (303)278-4670
Offers: Line of glassblowing equipment, tools, supplies and books.

HOTGLASS
213 S. Whisman Rd.
Mountain View CA 94041
Phone: (888)4HOTGLASS
Offers: Large selection of glass, tools and supplies for fusing and bead making. Also offers fusing, casting and bead-making kilns and Latticino machine.
Catalog: Free fusing or bead-making catalog.

HOUSTON STAINED GLASS SUPPLY
2002 Brittmore St.
Houston TX 77043
Contact: Neil Pickthall
Phone: (713)690-8844
Fax: (713)690-0008
E-mail: hsgs@aol.com
Website: http://www.hsgs.com

Store Location: M-F, 8-5.

Offers: Over 6,000 products for stained glass crafting, including 1,200 colors of glass and 800 beveled glass designs and shapes.

Catalog: Available annually.

Phone Orders: Yes.

Discounts: Sells wholesale to qualified customers.

Accepts: MasterCard, Visa

ED HOY'S INTERNATIONAL

(formerly Ed Hoy's Stained Glass Distributors)
1620 Frontenac Rd.
Naperville IL 60563
Phone: (630)420-0890
Website: http://www.edhoy.com
Offers: Glass crafting supplies, including glass bevels (shapes, clusters, color, mirror, panel and engraved), painted/fired shapes, gems, marbles, nuggets and jewels. Carries colored sheets including antiques, glashed, streakies, crackles, mirror, Oceana, textures, art, Bullseye, cathedral, Spectrum and others. Also carries scraps, fusing kilns, clay molds and supplies, fusing supplies and tools, plus fusible glass, fusing kits and projects, glass paints, brushes and stains. Tools available include circle and other cutters, pliers, shears, engravers, soldering irons, tools to bend foil, glass drills, burnishers, grinders, routers, belt sanders and saws. Also offers projectors, foil, came, channel, chemicals and lamp forms and bases. Contract dealers (retail stain glass stores).

Discounts: Sells wholesale only to legitimate businesses.

HUDSON GLASS CO., INC.

Dept. CS-8
219 N. Division St.
Peekskill NY 10566-2700
Phone: (800)413-2964 or (914)737-2124
Fax: (800)999-FAXIT or (914)737-4447
Store Location: At above address.
Offers: Stained glass supplies from Glastar, Inland, Morton, Worden, Reusche, Venture, Ungar, Weller, Fletcher, Armour, Bullseye, Kokomo, Carolyn Kyle and others. Carries glass fusing and etching supplies, mosaic supplies, stained and other types of glass, crystals, chemicals, foils, patterns, tools and equipment, electrical parts, box accessories, books and more.

Catalog: 144 pages. $5 ($3 refundable).

Phone Orders: M-F, 9-5; Sat, 9-4 EST.

Mail Orders: Will ship worldwide. Prepayment required. C.O.D. in US.

Discounts: Based on dollar volume. Sells wholesale to legitimate businesses.

Accepts: American Express, Discover, MasterCard, Visa

JAX CHEMICAL CO., INC.

78-11 267th St.
Floral Park NY 11004
Phone: (718)347-0057
Offers: Stained glass, lamps and lighting fixtures, hardware and Master Metal finishing solutions. Also offers antiques and statues. Chemicals and patinas to darken, clean and finish metals (lamp and lighting fixtures, hardware, jewelry, stained glass and furniture). Send SASE.

JURGEN INDUSTRIES, INC.

(formerly Jurgen Craft Products)
14700 172nd Dr. SE #1
Monroe WA 98272
Contact: Debra Hodge
Phone: (360)794-7886
Fax: (360)794-9825
E-mail: jurgen@jurgenindustries.com
Website: www.jurgenindustries.com
Offers: Glass stain paints: lacquer base and water base. Supplies to make simulated stain glass windows on glass or plastic. Quarts and gallons available.

Catalog: Available with color chart.

Phone Orders: Yes.

Mail Orders: Yes.

Accepts: prepayment C.O.D., credit terms available

CAROLYN KYLE ENTERPRISES, INC.

2840 E. Black Lake Blvd. SW
Olympia WA 98512
Contact: Marge Mix
Phone: (360)352-4427 or (800)428-7402
Fax: (360)943-3978
E-mail: ckepubs@aol.com
Website: www.artglassworld.com
Offers: Line of stained glass pattern books.

Catalog: Free.

Phone Orders: Yes.

Mail Orders: Yes.

Accepts: MasterCard, Visa

MEREDITH STAINED GLASS CENTER, INC.

(formerly The Stained Glass Superstore)
1115 East-West Hwy.
Silver Spring MD 20910
Contact: Jenna Meredith-Sanders
Phone: (800)966-6667
E-mail: stnglass@meredithglass.com
Website: www.meredithglass.com
Store Location: Silver Spring MD location.
Offers: Full line of stained glass and related supplies, tools and equipment. Lots of classes. Our full line is discounted and our website always features our latest sales and new products.

Catalog: 60 pages, color. Free.

Phone Orders: 7 days during business hours.

Mail Orders: Will ship anywhere. Order shipped same day if placed by 12 noon EST.

Discounts: Commercial accounts available to qualified stained glass or closely related business.

Accepts: American Express, Discover, MasterCard, Visa, check

MYTHICAL REFLECTIONS
360 N. Hwy. 17/92
Longwood FL 32750
Phone: (407)767-5510
Fax: (407)767-8830
E-mail: mythical@concentric.net
Offers: Stained glass, supplies, tools and equipment.
Catalog: Free.
Discounts: Monthly sales.

PARAGON INDUSTRIES, INC.
2011 S. Town E. Blvd.
Mesquite TX 75149
Phone: (800)876-4328 or (972)288-7557
Fax: (972)222-0646
E-mail: paragonind@worldnet.att.net
Website: paragonweb.com
Offers: Glass fusing kilns and digital temperature controller.
Catalog: Free.
Discounts: Sells wholesale to legitimate businesses.

PRAIRIE DESIGNS OF CALIFORNIA
P.O. Box 886
Brisbane CA 94005-0886
Contact: Dennis Casey
Phone: (415)468-5319
Fax: (415)468-6634
Offers: Full-size patterns and pattern books of stained glass windows and lamps designed by Frank Lloyd Wright. Came, glass, wood camp bases and lamp hardware also available.
Catalog: $2 (refundable with first order).
Mail Orders: Normally shipped same day received—worldwide.
Discounts: Available from wholesale distributors.

PREMIUM PRODUCTS OF LOUISIANA, INC.
dba Premium Glass Products and Premium Bevels
2006 Johnston St.
Lafayette LA 70503
Contact: Al Chauvin
Phone: (318)234-1642
Fax: (318)234-1646
Store Location: At above address.
Offers: Beveled glass and mirrored products of all shapes, sizes and colors. Custom beveling and mirror resilvering, tempering services and insulating glass.
Catalog: SASE.
Phone Orders: M-F, 7:30-5 CST.
Mail Orders: Will ship to US, Canada and Mexico. Prepayment required. Confimation of shipment at time of order.
Discounts: Wholesale to legitimate business.
Accepts: Discover, MasterCard, Visa

RAYER'S BEARDEN S.G. SUPPLY, INC.
6205 W. Kellogg
Wichita KS 67209
Phone: (800)228-4101
Store Location: At above address.

Offers: Full line of stained glass supplies for all levels, beginning to professional. Also offers Tiffany lamps, entryways and more. Classes and workshops available.
Catalog: Stained glass supplies.
Accepts: American Express, Discover, MasterCard, Visa

SAX ARTS & CRAFTS
P.O. Box 510710
2405 S. Calhoun Rd.
New Berlin WI 53151
Phone: (414)784-6880
Offers: A variety of supplies (known brands), including a full line of weaving looms and aids, yarns, weaving kits, rug/craft yarns, embroidery/crewel threads, rug hook frames and aids, canvas, hoops, burlap and felt. Indian beading, beads, feathers, macrame, basketry and batik supplies, fabric paints, airbrush kits and inks, stencil films, trims, foam, stained glass kits, etching and beveled glass supplies and supplies for decoupage, jewelry making, leather, casting, plastics, wood and metal working are also available.
Catalog: $5 (refundable).
Discounts: Quantity, sells wholesale to legitimate businesses.

UNITED ART GLASS, LTD.
1032 E. Ogden Ave. #128
Naperville IL 60563
Phone: (630)369-8168
Offers: Supplies/equipment including bevels, engraved, star, faceted, mirror, color, clusters, jewels, nuggets and marbles. Glass includes Bullseye, Chicago Art, Cotswold, Emaille, flashed, Flemish, antique Kokomo, Oceana, Waser, Wissmach, mirror, plate and others. Carries chemicals and tools, including 10 cutters, lead cames, shears, engravers, flexible shafts, glass drills, foiling machines, Foilomatic guide rollers and Glastar tools, Morton Surface systems (cutting shops), routers, saws, soldering irons and etching items. Metal lamp bases, fusing projects, fusing kilns, packs, equipment, Badger spray guns and paints. Kiln-firing items and patterns for lamp forms also available. Also offers repairs and restorations.
Catalog: $5.
Discounts: Quantity.

V.E.A.S. PRODUCTIONS
P.O. Box 278
Troy MI 48099
Phone: (248)584-2020 or (810)293-6931
Offers: Instructional video on Glass Erasing (a controlled form of sandblasting)—can also be used for wood, plastic or metal—program teaches techniques for professional results, for mirror decorating, monogramming and other projects, plus embellishing on glass. Also offers videos for gold leafing on glass.
Catalog: Send #10 SASE for free brochure.

WHITTEMORE-DURGIN
P.O. Box 2065
Hanover MA 02339
Phone: (781)871-1743 or (800)262-1790

Fax: (781)871-5597 or (800)786-3457

Website: www.penrose.com/glass

Store Location: 825 Market St., Rockland MA 02370. M, 8-8; T-F, 8-4:30; Sat, 8-12.

Offers: Stained glass, including French and German antique, cathedral types (in sheets and by the pound), antique, opalescent, clear beveled, jewels and others. Carries stained glass kits with tools, tool and supplies kits, Suncatcher kits, lampshade maker kits. Tools available include glass cutters, pliers, lead straighteners, soldering irons, glass grinders and accessories. Also offers lead came, copper foil, brass channel and banding, lamp parts, decorative chains, hinges, metal lamp bases, lead castings, patterns and books.

Catalog: $2.

Discounts: Quantity.

Jewelry Making & Lapidary

Also see General Craft Supplies; Bead Crafts; Native American & Frontier Crafts; Metalworking; Tools & Equipment; other related categories.

A.A. CLOUET
369 W. Fountain St.
Providence RI 02903
Contact: Ann Caldarone
Phone: (401)272-4100
Fax: (401)273-9758
Offers: Fasteners, ear nuts, clutch backs, clip pads, disks, guards, cushions, jewelers' staples, elastic barbs and others.
Catalog: Send SASE for list.

A&B JEWELS AND TOOLS
350 W. Grand River
Williamstown MI 48895
Contact: Jeff or Bill Gardiner
Phone: (517)655-4664
Fax: (517)655-4665
E-mail: tooline@voyager.net
Website: abtool.com
Store Location: At above address.
Offers: Bead cord, wire, needles, pliers, tweezers, bead boards, books, other beading tools, jewelry-making tools and supplies, lapidary tools and supplies, scales, gemological equipment and display items.
Catalog: Limited.
Phone Orders: Yes.
Mail Orders: Yes.
Discounts: Quantity.
Accepts: Discover, MasterCard, Visa

ACKLEY'S
3230 N. Stone Ave.
Colorado Springs CO 80907
Phone: (719)633-1153
Offers: Lapidary and silversmithing supplies and rough rock. Jewelry findings include ear wires, beads, chains and mountings.
Catalog: $1 (refundable).

ALMAR VIDEOS
(formerly A. Goodman)
P.O. Box 667
949 Beaumont Ave.
Beaumont CA 92223
Phone: (800)382-3237
Offers: Lapidary instruction videos covering lost wax cast-ing, meet-point faceting carving techniques, crystal and mineral energy, jewelry design, handcrafting, faceting, forming, plating, sphere making, emerald cutting, soldering, faceting, plus videos on opal, bead stringing, gemstone carving and lapidary basics.
Catalog: Send SASE for list.
Discounts: Sells wholesale to legitimate businesses.
Accepts: MasterCard, Visa

ALPHA SUPPLY, INC.
P.O. Box 2133
1225 Hollis St.
Bremerton WA 98310
Phone: (360)377-5629 or (800)257-4211
Offers: Over 15,000 items for casting, jewelry making, faceting, wax casting and display. Carries equipment for lapidary, beading, faceting and prospecting.
Catalog: Supply catalogs, $5.
Discounts: Quantity; institutions and professionals; sells wholesale to businesses.
Accepts: Discover, MasterCard, Visa

ALPINE CASTING CO.
3122 Karen Place
Colorado Springs CO 80901
Contact: Harry Hamill
Phone: (719)442-0709
Fax: (719)442-0711
Store Location: At above address.
Offers: Contract manufacturer of sterling, brass, bronze and pewter jewelry. The customer supplies the prototype and we do the rest. Mold making, casting and finishing.
Phone Orders: (800)365-2278.

AMAZON IMPORTS
P.O. Box 58
Williston Park NY 11596
Contact: Joe DeCristoforo
Phone: (800)888-GEMS
Fax: (516)741-9251
E-mail: amazonimpt@aol.com
Offers: Faceted gemstones: alexandrite, andalusite, beryls, topaz, sapphire, emeralds, tanzanite, amethysts, ametrine and tourmalines. Also sugilite rough and cabs.
Phone Orders: M-F, 9-5 EST.
Mail Orders: C.O.D. and/or prepayment required.
Discounts: Wholesale to legitimate business. Memo for retail jewelers and established customers.
Accepts: MasterCard, Visa

APACHE CANYON MINES

P.O. Box 530
West Camp, Turquoise Mountains
Baker CA 92309
Contact: Ed Nazelrod
Store Location: At above address.
Offers: World's finest gem-grade turquoise from our own Apache Canyon Mines—100% pure and not treated, extremely hard and strong; in rough, cut stones and drilled beads (nuggets). Completely guaranteed.
Catalog: Free price lists and information sheets. Sample packs for $20 (specify interest).
Mail Orders: Both retail and wholesale, foreign and domestic.
Discounts: Wholesale to the trade.
Accepts: check, money order, cash (no credit cards)

APL TRADER, INC.

P.O. Box 1900 RFU
New York NY 10185
Contact: Asha
Phone: (718)454-2954 or (800) 5APLTRA
Offers: Precious and semiprecious cut stones. Bead, cab and carvings.
Phone Orders: Yes.
Mail Orders: Yes.
Discounts: For wholesale buyers.

ARA IMPORTS

P.O. Box 41054
Brecksville OH 44141
Phone: (440)838-1372
Fax: (440)838-1367
Offers: Jewelry findings, including precious and semiprecious beads, plus pearls and corals.
Catalogs: Catalog and price list, $1.

ARE SUPPLY CO.

636 11th Ave. S.
Hopkins MN 55343
Phone: (800)763-4273 or (612)912-0982
Fax: (612)912-0981
Offers: A variety of craft metal in both sheet and wire. Findings and extensive line of tools and jewelry-making supplies.
Catalog: 225 pages. $5 (refundable on first purchase).

ART TECH CASTING CO.

P.O. Box 54
Scottsville NY 14546
Contact: Geoffrey
Phone: (800)419-9970
Fax: (716)889-9187
E-mail: arttech@concentric.net
Offers: Casting services—bronze, silver, gold, platinum, one-of-a-kind production. Mold making and model work also available.
Catalog: Informational brochure.
Phone Orders: Yes.

Mail Orders: Yes.
Accepts: American Express, MasterCard, Visa

ARTGEMS, INC.

7117 E. Third Ave., Suite 110
Scottsdale AZ 85251
Contact: Moon Shaikh
Phone: (602)951-0032
Fax: (602)991-1005
Store Location: At above address.
Offers: Gemstone beads, such as garnet, amethyst, tourmaline, citrine, moonstone, peridot, lapis, aquamarine, labradorite, opal, crystal quartz, smoky quartz, iolite, tanzanite, ruby, emerald, sapphire, apatite, fluorite and many more. Also tumbled chips, points, spheres, donuts, agate items and many varieties of pearls. Sterling silver, especially Nepali pendants.
Catalog: $5.
Phone Orders: Yes.
Mail Orders: Yes.
Accepts: American Express, Discover, MasterCard, Visa, check, money order, cash

ARTISTIC WIRE, LTD.

1210 Harrison Ave.
La Grange Park IL 60526
Contact: Sean O'Brien, Jack O'Brien or Kelly Steele
Phone: (630)530-7567
Fax: (630)530-7536
E-mail: artwire97@aol.com
Website: www.artistic/wire.com
Store Location: 752 N. Larch, Elmhurst IL 60126.
Offers: Wire.
Phone Orders: M-F, 8-5 CST.
Mail Orders: Worldwide, prepaid required, 4-6 weeks after receipt of order.
Discounts: Wholesale and retail.
Accepts: MasterCard, Visa

S. AXELROD CO.

7 W. 30th St.
New York NY 10001
Contact: Michael Axelrod
Phone: (212)594-3022
Fax: (212) 947-3787
Offers: Wholesale only. Minimum $100. Complete line jewelry findings, split key rings, earring parts, closures, neck chains, footage chains, charms, jump rings, pearls, lapidary parts, cages, screw eyes, bails, bead caps, bells, whistles, trimmings, leathercraft supplies, lanyard hooks, swivels, ball chains, rhinestones, acrylic jewels, sequins—everything.
Catalog: 160 pages, color. $10.
Mail Orders: Immediate delivery all items.
Discounts: All prices.
Accepts: MasterCard, Visa

B&J ROCK SHOP, INC.

14744 Manchester Rd.
Ballwin MO 63011
Contact: Julie Kepner
Phone: (314)394-4567
Fax: (314)394-7109
Store Location: At above address. M-Sat, 10-5.
Offers: Beads: Czech glass; gemstone; sterling, gold-filled 14K seed beads and Delicas; Bali, Thai and Indian silver; bone and horn; stringing supplies and books; and glass rods. Also cabochons and pendant, earring and bola settings. Quartz clock movements and agate clock faces.
Catalog: 50 pages. $3 (refundable).
Phone Orders: M-Sat, 10-5.
Mail Orders: Yes.
Discounts: Quantity.
Accepts: MasterCard, Visa

BEAD CREATIVE

5401 Sheridan Dr.
Williamsville NY 14221
Contact: Richard Alt
Phone: (716)626-4182
Fax: (716)626-4182
E-mail: ait116@aol.com
Website: www.snq.com/beadcreative
Store Location: M-F, 11-6 EST.
Offers: We carry Czech seed beads, tapanest Delicas and other beads—wood, bone, horn, glass, crystal, African, mirales and cloisonne. Also semiprecious, books, findings, Peruvian, ceramic and more.
Catalog: $3. 56 pages. Satisfaction guaranteed.
Phone Orders: (800)894-8058.
Mail Orders: At above address. M-F, 11-6 EST. No minimum.
Discounts: Quantity.
Accepts: American Express, Discover, MasterCard, Visa

BEADBOX, INC.

10135 E. Via Linda
Scottsdale AZ 85258
Phone: (800)BEADBOX
E-mail: beadbox@worldnet.att.net
Website: www.beadbox.com
Offers: Beads from 30 countries, exotics and unusuals, in a line of sizes/shapes, plus beading kits for jewelry and others.
Catalog: Color. $3.
Accepts: American Express, Discover, MasterCard, Visa

BOONE TRADING CO.

P.O. Box BB
562 Coyote Rd.
Brinnon WA 98320
Phone: (360)796-4330
Offers: Ivory carving and scrimshaw materials, including legal pre-embargo elephant ivory, walrus, fossil walrus, mammoth, hippo and warthog. Available in a variety of forms, including tusks, chunks, slabs, scrap, polished ivory jewelry and buckle blanks and beads. Also offers ivory carvings and scrimshaw, related books and tools, animal skulls, shark teeth, old trade beads, pearl shell and more.
Catalog: Send $1 for 48-page illustrated catalog.
Discounts: Sells wholesale to businesses.
Accepts: MasterCard, Visa

BOURGET BROS.

1636 11th St.
Santa Monica CA 90404
Phone: (800)828-3024
Fax: (800)607-2201
E-mail: borjay@worldnet.att.net
Website: www.bourgetbros.com
Store Location: At above address.
Offers: Lapidary/jewelry equipment/tools—full lines to cast, weld, drill, enamel, plate, engrave and others. Carries furnaces, saws, flexible shafts, magnifiers, files, torches, tumblers and metals (sterling silver, gold and gold-filled, copper in sheets, wires, channels, bezels and fancies). Also carries jewelry findings, wires, threads—full lines. Beads include turquoise, amber, gemstones, cabochons and synthetics. Stocks pearls, metal and sterling silver coil types, sterling silver button covers, chains, mounts and books.
Catalog: Tool/jewelry catalog; lapidary catalog.
Discounts: Quantity.
Accepts: MasterCard, Visa

COMMONS CRAFTS

P.O. Box 5012-CSS
Central Point OR 97502
Contact: Ann Commons
Phone: (541)664-1651 or (888)464-1651
Offers: The modern method of making arrowheads. Book and VHS, 55 minutes in color with instructions on making chipper board, preparing blanks and chipping arrowheads from 1/8″ to 17″ knife blades. Order blank includes prices of items needed.
Mail Orders: Will ship orders within 2 weeks to all states in US and Canada.
Accepts: check, money order

COPPER COYOTE BEADS, LTD.

9430 E. Golf Links #286-CSS
Tucson AZ 85730
Contact: Regina, office manager
Phone: (520)722-8440
Fax: (520)886-5214
E-mail: coyote@coppercoyote.com
Website: http://www.coppercoyote.com
Offers: Direct importer of Japanese seed beads sold wholesale only: Matsuno 6/O, 11/O and bugles, Miyuki 11/O and 14/O, Magatamas and Delicas. Czech pressed glass beads. Over 160 bead-related books sold retail and wholesale. Thread, needles, looms, Copper Coyote brand bead design graph paper.
Catalog: $2 each: retail book or wholesale bead with color sheets.

Phone Orders: Anytime.

Mail Orders: International. Prepayment or C.O.D.

Discounts: Sells wholesale to legitimate businesses. Resale number required.

Accepts: American Express, MasterCard, Visa

COVINGTON ENGINEERING CORP.

P.O. Box 35

Redlands CA 92373

Phone: (909)793-6636

Fax: (909)793-7641

E-mail: lapidary@discover.net

Store Location: 715 W. Colton Ave., Redlands CA 92374.

Offers: Lapidary/glass equipment, including lapidary machines (mills, carvers, combos, drum units, gem shops, grinders, slab saws, laps, sanders, sphere makers, tumblers and others), glass machines (bevelers, carving tools, coolerant systems, drills, engravers, laps, polishers, sanders, saws, smoothers, grinders and others), equipment/supplies (adhesives, beading items, dressers, drill bits, drums, Eastwing and jewelry tools), plus motors, templates and grinding wheels.

Catalog: Covington catalog.

Phone Orders: Yes.

Mail Orders: At P.O. Box.

Accepts: MasterCard, Visa

DENDRITICS, INC.

223 Crescent St.

Waltham MA 02154

Contact: Bill Brown

Phone: (800)437-9993

Fax: (781)893-5334

E-mail: bill@dendritics.com

Website: http://www.dendritics.com

Offers: Pocket portable electronic balances that weigh precious and semiprecious stones. Weigh 0 to 100 carats at .01 carat. Dimensions $5'' \times 3'' \times 1''$. Weight 8 ounces.

Catalog: Specification sheets.

Mail Orders: Sold through distributors.

DIAMOND PACIFIC TOOL CORP.

P.O. Box 1180

Barstow CA 92312-1180

Contact: Beth Pinnell

Phone: (800)253-2954

Fax: (760)255-1030

Store Location: 2620 W. Main St., Barstow CA 92311.

Offers: Jewelers' tools and supplies, diamond lapidary equipment, Foredom power tools, Eastwing tools, beading supplies, books and carving tools.

Catalog: Free. 108 pages.

Phone Orders: M-F, 8-5 PST.

Mail Orders: Will ship US and foreign countries. Prepayment required.

Discounts: Sells wholesale to qualified dealers. Call for information.

Accepts: American Express, Discover, MasterCard, Visa

DISCOUNT AGATE HOUSE

3401 N. Dodge Blvd.

Tucson AZ 85716

Contact: Bob Gary

Phone: (520)323-0781

Store Location: At above address. 9:30-5:30. Closed Sundays.

Offers: Cutting rocks from areas worldwide, lapidary machinery, accessories, sterling silver and smithing supplies and jewelry findings.

Catalog: Price list on rough rock. No catalog.

Discounts: Sells wholesale to legitimate businesses.

Accepts: Discover, MasterCard, Visa

EASTERN FINDINGS CORP.

19 W. 34th St.

New York NY 10001

Contact: Steven Posner, vice-president

Phone: (212)695-6640

Fax: (212)629-4018

E-mail: efc@easternfindings.com

Website: www.easternfindings.com

Store Location: At above address, 12th Floor.

Offers: Over 15,000 findings for the jewelry and craft industry. Includes charms, belt hooks, clasps, ear clips, beads, rings, filigree, ear wires, settings, end bars, keychains, neck chains, barrettes, hoops, neck bands, screw eyes, money clips, bar pins, caps, western collar tips, tie tacks, pierced post, clips and wire, bead boards, pliers and solder. Monthly specials.

Catalog: 160 pages. $10 (refundable with first order).

Phone Orders: (800)EFC-6640. Minimum order $25.

Mail Orders: Shipped within 48 hours via UPS. Open accounts to JBT rated 1 or 2; C.O.D. or request credit application.

Discounts: Quantity discounts available.

Accepts: MasterCard, Visa

ELOXITE CORP.

Dept. 40

806 Tenth St.

Wheatland WY 82201

Phone: (307)322-3050

Fax: (307)322-3055

Store Location: At above address.

Offers: Jewelry mountings—full line of buckles and inserts, bracelets, pendants, bolos, others, plus jewelry-making tools and supplies, 5 tumblers, clock parts and movements, display boxes, racks and earring displays. Beads include gemstone, seed and others. Books available.

Catalog: $1.

Discounts: Quantity; sells wholesale to legitimate businesses.

Accepts: MasterCard, Visa

ENGRAVING ARTS

P.O. Box 787
42400F N. Hwy. 101
Laytonville CA 95454
Contact: Clem Wilkes
Phone: (707)984-8203
Fax: (707)984-8045
Store Location: At above address. M-F, 8-5.
Offers: Custom branding irons for wood or leather, jewelry dies and stamps for embossing, coining, striking and more. Branding services and stamping services.
Catalog: Free brochure.
Mail Orders: We ship worldwide. Prepayment required outside US. Deposit required in US. 4-5 weeks for delivery.
Discounts: Only on multiple orders.
Accepts: check, money order

FAC-ETTE MANUFACTURING, INC.

P.O. Box 550
Wrightsville Beach NC 28480
Contact: R.R. Dobo
Phone: (910)256-9248
Fax: (910)256-9248
Store Location: 7110-AT Wrightsville Ave., Wilmington NC 28403.
Offers: Gem Master II faceting machine.
Catalog: Video and information package. Free.
Phone Orders: M-F, 8-4:30.
Mail Orders: Prepayment required.
Accepts: MasterCard, Visa

DAVID H. FELL & CO., INC.

6009 Bandini Blvd.
City of Commerce CA 90040
Contact: Ruth Fell Failer
Phone: (800)822-1996 or (213)722-9992
Fax: (213)722-6567
Website: http://mjsa.polygon.net/~10204
Store Location: Main office at above address. 8-4 PST. Also 550 S. Hill St., Suite 560, Los Angeles CA 90013. 9-5 PST.
Offers: Gold, silver and platinum sheet, wire, casing grain and solders. Refining services. Pattern sheet photo etched in copper, brass, stainless steel, silver and gold. Custom orders and low minimums.
Catalogs: Free products and services (including refining). Pattern sheet: 400 designs, $5 (refundable).
Phone Orders: M-F, 8-4 PST.
Mail Orders: Will ship US and Canada. Prepayment or C.O.D. Send refining to company address above.
Discounts: Quantity discounts on all products.
Accepts: MasterCard, Visa

FINISHING TOUCHES

2213 Deer Pass Trail
White Bear Lake MN 55110
Contact: Theresa Eckerson (612)653-7582 or Tracey Al-Hendi (612)739-3495
E-mail: ftouches01@aol.com

Offers: Clay beads, ceramic seed and glass beads, charms, jewelry-making supplies. Jewelry-making kits and other custom made crafts. Specializes in hair wrapping supplies and complete business start-up displays.
Catalog: 20 pages. Catalog with supplements, $4 (refundable with first order).
Phone Orders: (888)257-8478. M-F, 9-5 CST.
Mail Orders: Prepayment required. Allow 2-4 weeks for delivery.
Discounts: Sells wholesale to legitimate businesses.
Accepts: check, money order

FREI & BOREL

P.O. Box 796
126 Second St.
Oakland CA 94604
Contact: Hamid Rashidi
Phone: (510)832-0355 or (800)772-3456
Fax: (510)834-6217 or (800)900-3734
Website: www.frei.com
Store Location: 760 Market St., San Francisco CA 94102. (415)421-8133.
Offers: Tools and supplies, findings, watch materials, displays, Cristal cutting, chains, watchbands, jewelry items.
Catalog: Tools, findings, watch department and displays.
Phone Orders: Yes.
Mail Orders: At P.O. Box.
Accepts: American Express, MasterCard, Visa, request for credit application

GABRIEL'S

P.O. Box 222
Unionville OH 44088
Contact: Ray Gabriel
Phone: (800)359-5166
Fax: (440)428-5509
E-mail: ray@earthone.com
Website: http://www.xmission.com/~arts/gabriel/items.html
Offers: Jewelry-making and lapidary how-to videos for sale and rental by mail. Offers gemstone approvals for university and art center jewelry classes and sponsors a free jewelry design discussion group on the Internet. Unique-shaped gems including wedges, tongues and bullets. Serving jewelry designers since 1975.
Catalog: Free.
Phone Orders: 24 hours.
Mail Orders: At above address.
Discounts: 10% over $125; 20% over $250.
Accepts: MasterCard, Visa

THE GEMMARY

P.O. Box 2560
Fallbrook CA 92088
Phone: (619)728-3321
Offers: Out-of-print and rare books on gemology, jewelry (history and making), mineralogy and mining.
Catalog: $2.

GOLDEN HANDS PRESS

(formerly Art to Wear)
5 Crescent Pl. S. #2
St. Petersburg FL 33711
Contact: Bob Poris
Phone: (813)867-3711
Fax: (813)867-4211
Offers: 2 bead-stringing books: *Step-by-Step Bead Stringing* by Ruth F. Poris, $7.99+ shipping and *Advanced Beadwork* by Ruth F. Poris, $14.99+ shipping. Bead-stringing (jeweler's) tools such as pliers, tweezers, scissors, pin vises and awls. Also carries bead boards, needles, tips, crimps, tigertails, cable chains, foxtails, boullion wire, needle cards, silk cones, spool cord kits and jewelry findings. Beads include sterling, 14K, gold-filled types, semiprecious gemstone beads and freshwater pearls. Carries designer bead kits and books.
Phone Orders: M-F, 10-5 EST.
Mail Orders: Yes; prepayment.
Discounts: Depends on quantity for wholesalers, distributors, etc.
Accepts: MasterCard, Visa

GRIEGER'S

P.O. Box 93070
Pasadena CA 91109
Phone: (800)423-4181
Fax: (626)577-4751
Website: www.grieger.com
Offers: Jewelry-making/lapidary supplies, equipment, tools and accessories. Jewelry-making supplies include kits, display items (cases, boxes, trays and stands) and jewelry findings (in 14 karat, sterling silver, filled and others)—a full line—plus gemstone beads, baroque chip necklaces, chains, cabochons and stones (large variety—diamonds and pearls). Carries beading supplies and accessories. Also carries a full line of hand and power tools for lapidary, jewelry making, silversmithing and lost wax casting. Scales, casting metals, sterling silver sheet and wires, gold-filled and 14 karat wires, gold sheet and books are available.
Catalog: Free.
Discounts: Quantity; sells wholesale to legitimate businesses.
Accepts: American Express, Discover, MasterCard, Visa

GRYPHON CORP.

12417 Foothill Blvd.
Sylmar CA 91342
Phone: (818)890-7770
Offers: Diamond band saw (cuts glass, tile and minerals) and abrasive miter saw for cutting most metal up to ¾″ cross section. Manufacturer.
Catalog: Free.

HARDIES BEADS & JEWELRY

P.O. Box 1920
1270 W. Main St.
Quartzsite AZ 85346-1920
Contact: Steve, Brenda or Alice
Phone: (800)962-2775
Fax: (520)927-4814
E-mail: ahardies@redrivernet.com
Store Location: At above address. 8-5 MST.
Offers: Large selection of beads, findings and jewelry. Indian jewelry, gemstone jewelry, Austrian crystal jewelry, bead jewelry and Black Hills gold jewelry. We also offer a large selection of freshwater pearls. We do have books on beading, silversmithing, rocks and minerals, gemstones, gold finding and Arizona trails.
Catalog: $3 (refundable on first order).
Phone Orders: 7 days a week, 8-5 MST.
Mail Orders: We ship worldwide. Prepayment required.
Discounts: Wholesale and retail. See catalog.
Accepts: American Express, Discover, MasterCard, Visa

HEAVEN & EARTH

Rt. 1, Box 25
Marshfield VT 05658
Phone: (800)348-5155
Fax: (802)426-3441
E-mail: hevnerth@plainfield.bypass.com
Offers: Metaphysical gems and minerals, including moldavite, tanzanite, phenacite, sugilite, larimar, charoite, iolite, garnet, amethyst, opal and many others.
Catalog: Call or write for free catalog and periodic newsletter.

HONG KONG LAP.

2801 University Dr.
Coral Spring FL 33065
Contact: Mike Z.
Phone: (954)755-8777
Fax: (954)755-8780
Store Location: At above address.
Offers: Semiprecious stone beads in 100 colors and 100 or more different sizes and shapes.
Catalog: $3 (refundable with first order).
Phone Orders: Yes.
Mail Orders: Yes.
Discounts: As per catalog.
Accepts: MasterCard, Visa, check

HOUSE OF ONYX

The Aaron Bldg.
720 N. Main St.
Greenville KY 42345-1504
Contact: Fred Rowe III, president
Phone: (800)844-3100
Fax: (502)338-9605
E-mail: onyx@muhlon.com
Website: www.houseofonyx.com
Store Location: At above address.

Offers: Genuine gemstone beads, (loose), gold and silver chains and bead-stringing cord. Gemologists: appraisals and lab services.
Catalog: Monthly. Free.
Phone Orders: Yes.
Mail Orders: US only. Immediate shipments.
Discounts: 75% maximum.
Accepts: MasterCard, Visa, check, cash

INDIAN JEWELERS SUPPLY COMPANY
P.O. Box 1744
601 E. Coal Ave.
Gallup NM 87305-1774
Phone: (505)722-4451
Fax: (505)722-4172
Store Location: Gallup and Albuquerque NM locations.
Offers: Materials and tools for jewelers, knife makers, gunsmiths, bead stringers and others. Materials include sterling silver, karat golds, gold-filled and silver-filled, brass, copper, nickel, turquoise, coral, shell, malachite and fossil ivory. Tools by Grodbet, Kerr, Lortone, Crystalite, Raytech, Diamond Pacific, Dremel and Foredom.
Catalog: Set of 4 (metals, stones, findings and tools), $6 in the US.
Phone Orders: M-Sat, 8-5 MST.
Mail Orders: Will ship to just about anywhere—US postal service, UPS, ABF and Yellow Trucks.
Discounts: Price structures give automatic volume discounts.
Accepts: MasterCard, Visa, good check

KINGSLEY NORTH, INC.
P.O. Box 216
910 Brown St.
Norway MI 49870
Phone: (906)563-9228 or (800)338-9280
Fax: (906)563-7143
Store Location: At above address. M-F, 8-5; Sat 9-12.
Offers: Lapidary tools, equipment and supplies: diamond tools, saws, tumblers, soldering torches, gauges, cutters, gravers, pliers, screwdrivers, gripper and clamp, plus third hand, pickhammer, jewelry waxer kit, machine super kit, Flex-Shaft equipment, electroplating items and rolling mills. Gemstones include jaspers, quartz, agate, hematite, obsidian, others. Jewelry findings available include necklaces, earrings, ring and pendant mountings, bolos, chains and others.
Catalog: Free.
Discounts: 10-20% below list price.
Accepts: Discover, MasterCard, Visa

KRONA INTERNATIONAL
P.O. Box 9968
Colorado Springs CO 80932
Phone: (719)597-8779
Fax: (719)596-6980
Offers: Ruby, sapphire, emerald and other colored gems.
Catalog: Free lists.

LANEY CO.
6449 S. 209 E. Ave.
Broken Arrow OK 74014
Phone: (918)355-1955
Offers: Gold metal letter cutouts (computer/laser) in Old Timer and trophy styles. Wire available round and half, square, dome, rectangle, triangle, fancy and channel. Metal sheets, solders, fluxes, nickel pickle, leaves, bezel cups, ring shanks, beads, bolos, buckle backs and squash blossoms also available.
Catalog: Free.
Discounts: Quantity; teachers and institutions; sells wholesale to legitimate businesses.

LAPCRAFT, INC., U.S.A.
195 W. Olentangy St.
Powell OH 43065
Phone: (614)764-8993
Offers: Diamond tools—preforming/diamond grinding wheels, drilling/diamond drills, core drills, faceting/diamond discs, carving/diamond points, polishing/diamond powders.
Catalog: Free.

LJ BOOK & VIDEO SELLERS
60 Chestnut Ave., Suite 201
Devon PA 19333
Offers: Instructional videos on gemstone carving, glass bead making, beading, wire craft for beginners and advanced, design, jewelry finishing, soldering, metalsmithing and opal cutting.
Catalog: Call (800)676-4367.

LONNIE'S INC.
7155 E. Main St.
Mesa AZ 85207
Contact: Irene Huf
Phone: (602)832-2641
Fax: (602)985-6271
Store Location: At above address.
Offers: Lapidary supply, casting supply and jewelry supply. Gold and silver sheet and wire, stones, books and silver jewelry.
Catalog: Tool catalog, $5 (refundable). Silver jewelry catalog, $10 (refundable). Findings catalog free, lapidary catalog free.
Phone Orders: M-F, 8:30-5.
Mail Orders: Will ship UPS.
Accepts: Discover, MasterCard, Visa, check, money order

MARIS INTERNATIONAL
P.O. Box 2166
Germantown MD 20875
Contact: Shan Patty
Phone: (301)916-6787 or (800)847-9319
Fax: (301)540-6265
E-mail: gfzh62a@prodigy.com
Store Location: 19332 Churubuscola, Germantown MD 20874.

Offers: Wholesale and retail. Italian red corals, different shaped strings, cabochons, buttons, roses, round barrels, graduated strings, teardrops—hanging and heart-shaped, natural branches—polished and unpolished and more.
Catalog: Yes.
Phone Orders: Yes.
Mail Orders: Yes.
Accepts: MasterCard, Visa, check

MAXANT INDUSTRIES, INC.
Dept. W
P.O. Box 454
28 Harvard Rd.
Ayer MA 01432
Contact: Rick Thibault
Phone: (978)772-0576
Fax: (978)772-6365
E-mail: ric56@net1plus.com
Store Location: At above address. M-F, 8-4 EST.
Offers: Electrically heated water-jacketed stainless steel wax melting vats (includes pouring valves). Sizes range from 2-200 gallon capacity. Slab melting tanks, mixing and pouring tanks, as well as dipping tanks.
Catalog: Flyer. Send SASE.
Phone Orders: M-F, 8-4 EST.
Mail Orders: Ship nationwide and international. Prepayment required. Call for delivery time.
Accepts: MasterCard, Visa

METALLIFEROUS
34 W. 46th St.
New York NY 10036
Phone: (212)944-0909
Fax: (212)944-0644
Store Location: At above address. M-F, 8:30-6; Sat, 10-3.
Offers: Metals—titanium, bronze, fine silver, brass, copper, nickel silver, sterling silver, niobium, pewter and aluminum—sheet, wire, circles, rod, tube, stampings, machined parts, hoops, findings, solders and casting alloys. Carries enameling shapes and supplies, plus tools.
Catalog: 2 catalogs available: $4, base metals; $4, silver. $7.50 for both (nonrefundable).

MINNESOTA LAPIDARY SUPPLY CORP.
2825 Dupont Ave. S.
Minneapolis MN 55408
Phone: (612)872-7211
Fax: (612)871-1178
Offers: Lapidary equipment—rock cutting and polishing: Diamond saw blades, sanding belts and grinding wheels, diamond wheels and belts. Diamond products and tumbling grit.
Catalog: Free. Bonus coupons.
Discounts: Institutions; sells wholesale to legitimate businesses.

MORION CO.
32 Ransom Rd., Suite 10
Brighton MA 02135
Contact: Uriah Prichard

Phone: (617)787-4628 or (617)787-2133 or (617)536-6523
Fax: (617)787-4628 or (617) 787-2133
E-mail: morion@tiac.net
Store Location: At above address. M-F, 9-5 EST by appointment.
Offers: Laboratory-grown rough materials for faceting and carving: hydrothermal quartz large crystals (amethyst, citrine, green and blue); flame-fusion corundums (12 colors); flame-fusion spinels (16 colors); cubic zirconia (30 colors); yttrium-aluminium, garnet; Gallium-Gadolinium garnet; hydrothermal beryls (emerald, aquamarine and red); hydrothermal corundums; alexandrite; and opals.
Catalog: 5 pages. Free.
Phone Orders: M-F, 9-7 EST.
Mail Orders: Will ship around the world. Prepayment required. Allow 1 week for delivery.
Discounts: See our sale terms.
Accepts: MasterCard, Visa

MULTISTONE INTERNATIONAL, INC./STRAZBURG MINERAL GALLERY
135 S. Holliday St.
Strasburg VA 22657
Contact: Larry Hargrave, president or Cathy Gatling, office manager
Phone: (540)465-8777
Fax: (540)465-8773
E-mail: msinc@shentel.net
Website: www.angelfire.com/valmsigems/
Store Location: At above address.
Offers: Wholesale to trade only. Retail cut stones (cab and facets), cutting rough, mineral specimens, crystals, tumbled stones, rocks and wire wrap specimens.
Catalog: Cut stones, minerals and cutting rough.
Phone Orders: Yes.
Mail Orders: Yes.
Discounts: Yes.
Accepts: American Express, Discover, MasterCard, Visa

NGRAVER CO.
67 Wawecus Hill Rd. J.
Bozrah CT 06334
Phone: (860)823-1533
Offers: Hand-engraving, flexible shaft machines, gravers and liners, rotary handpieces, engravers blocks, chasing hammers, engravers pencils, electric etchers, graver sharpeners, sharpening stones, plus practice mediums, magnifiers, fixtures, punches, Florentine tools and others.
Catalog: $1 (refundable).

O'BRIEN MANUFACTURING
2081 Knowles Rd.
Medford OR 97501
Contact: John M. O'Brien
Phone: (541)775-2410
Fax: (541)732-0713
E-mail: obrien@grrtech.com
Website: obrienshowcases.com

Offers: Oak showcases, oak counter, wall cases and tabletop display of gallery quality.
Catalog: Free.
Phone Orders: Yes.
Mail Orders: Yes.

OPTIMAGEM
P.O. Box 1421
San Luis Obispo CA 93406
Phone: (800)543-5563
Fax: (805)544-6345
E-mail: optimagem@aol.com
Offers: Faceted and cabochon gemstones, including sapphire (colors), ruby, garnet, amethyst, topaz, tanzanite, tsavorite, aquamarine, citrine, peridot, opal and star sapphire. Also offers synthetic stones. Job cutting services available.
Catalog: Write for list.
Accepts: American Express, MasterCard, Visa

ORNAMENTAL RESOURCES, INC.
P.O. Box 3010
Idaho Springs CO 80452
Phone: (800)876-ORNA
Website: www.ornabead.com
Offers: Complete lines of glass beads, including faceted, cut, foiled, decorated, fancy, metal, ceramic, plastic, bone, stone, shell, bugles, pony and seed beads in all sizes. Collectors' beads, metal stampings, chains, appliqué materials, rhinestones, studs, sequins, glass jewels, tassels, buckles and buttons, Also offers beading tools and supplies and design assistance. $25 minimum order.
Catalog: $15 (with one year's supplements).

PARSER MINERALS CORP.
P.O. Box 1094
Danbury CT 06813
Phone: (203)744-6868
Offers: Rare and unusual gemstone cutting materials (rough): from Brazil—watermelon tourmaline, andalusite, jacobina amethyst, rutilated quartz, water clear topaz, rose quartz crystal and blue (indicolite) tourmaline. Others include rhodochrosite (Argentina), wine red garnet (India), Labradorite moonstone and apatite (Madagascar) and iolite (Tanzania). Diamonds.
Catalog: $2.

PRODUCT DEVELOPMENT INDUSTRIES, INC.
(formerly PDI, Inc.)
4500 E. Speedway Blvd., Suite 50
Tucson AZ 85712
Contact: Rodolfo Carballo
Phone: (800)238-2307
Fax: (520)881-2862
E-mail: carball@azstarnet.com
Website: http://fp.sedona.net/rodolfo
Offers: Dip and brush/pen 24 karat gold electroplating systems complete with all solutions and instructions. A clear acrylic protective coating system is also available.

Phone Orders: M-F, 8-5 MST.
Accepts: MasterCard, Visa

PIONEER GEM CORP.
P.O. Box 1513
Auburn WA 98071
Phone: (253)833-2760
Fax: (253)833-1418
Offers: Cabochons: opals, black opal, malachite, paua shell, jade, lapis, sapphires and others. Carries bulk bags mixed, plus faceted gemstones: citrine, amethyst, emerald, lapis, opal, ruby, sapphires, blue topaz and others.
Catalog: Catalog/price list, $5 (6 times yearly).
Phone Orders: (800)433-9590.
Discounts: Quantity; teachers and institutions; sells wholesale to legitimate businesses; large order discounts.

REACTIVE METALS STUDIO, INC.
P.O. Box 890
Clarkdale AZ 86324
Phone: (520)634-3434
Fax: (520)634-6734
Website: reactivemetals.com
Offers: Titanium, shakudo, shibuichi and mokume-gane sheet and wire. Also offers findings, fusion findings, beads, miniature nuts and bolts and Sparkie welders.
Catalog: Free.
Discounts: Quantity.

THE REFINER'S FIRE
P.O. Box 66612
Portland OR 97290
Contact: LeRoy Goertz
Phone: (503)775-5242
E-mail: lgoertz@teleport.com
Website: http://www.teleport.com/~lgoertz
Offers: The Coiling Gizmo. This is a hand-crank machine that coils wire onto wire. The Basic Plus model will coil about seven feet of wire. The Deluxe Model will coil about thirty feet of wire. Unusual jewelry and sculptures can be made with this coiled wire.
Catalog: Brochure available with #10 SASE.
Discounts: Sells wholesale to legitimate businesses.
Accepts: MasterCard, Visa

RIVIERA LAPIDARY
P.O. Box 40
366 N. Seventh St.
Riviera TX 78379-0040
Contact: Stan or Dorris
Phone: (512)296-3958
Fax: (512)296-3958
Store Location: At above address.
Offers: Gems and minerals, finished and rough, opal, amethyst, turquoise, jade, moonstone, agate, amber, garnet, aquamarine, star ruby, labradorite, drusy gems, crystals and others. Hundreds of different stones. Since 1976.
Catalog: 30 pages. $2.

Phone Orders: 8-8 CST.
Mail Orders: Worldwide. Prepayment required. 1 week or express delivery.
Discounts: Wholesale discounts offered.
Accepts: American Express, Discover, MasterCard, Visa

ROYAL FINDINGS, INC.
P.O. Box 92
301 W. Main St.
Chartley MA 02712
Contact: Andrew Harney or John Alves
Phone: (800)343-3343
Fax: (800)458-7423
Offers: Jewelry findings in gold, sterling, gold-filled and base metals. Also offering a full line of Mini Sparkie fusion welders.
Catalog: 24 pages of jewelry findings and fusion welders.
Phone Orders: 8-4:30 EST; voice mail after hours.
Mail Orders: Shipping worldwide using UPS or postal services.
Discounts: Published discounts for quantity.
Accepts: MasterCard, Visa, terms offered with credit references

SCOTTSDALE BEAD SUPPLY & IMPORTS, INC.
3625 N. Marshall Way
Scottsdale AZ 85251
Contact: Kelly or Mike Charveaux
Phone: (602)945-5988
Fax: (602)945-4248
Store Location: At above address.
Offers: Gemstone, Bali and Israeli silver, Czech beads, lampwork beads, Austrian xtal, dichroic beads and pendants and custom silver charms and pendants.
Catalog: Color. $5 (refundable on first order).
Phone Orders: $50 minimum order.
Mail Orders: $50 minimum order.
Discounts: Wholesale to qualified buyers.
Accepts: MasterCard, Visa

SHIPWRECK BEADS
2727 Westmoor Ct. SW
Olympia WA 98502
Phone: (360)754-2323
Fax: (360)754-2510
E-mail: sales@shipwreck-beads.com
Website: www.shipwreck-beads.com
Store Location: At above address.
Offers: Beads: Czech glass, gemstone, metallics, crystal, seed, wood, bone, buffalo horn, plastic, antique, trade and others, plus beading supplies and tools, jewelry findings and books.
Catalog: 108 pages, full color. $4.
Phone Orders: 7 days a week, 9-6 PST.
Discounts: Quantity; sells wholesale to legitimate businesses and professionals.
Accepts: Discover, MasterCard, Visa, net terms on approved credit

SILVER ARMADILLO
40 Westgate Pkwy.
Asheville NC 28806
Store Location: At above address.
Offers: Line of jewelry parts, beads, lapidary and rockhound equipment, minerals, others.
Catalog: Jewelers tool and supply catalog, $5 (refundable).

SPARKLING CITY GEMS
P.O. Box 905-CSS
Kingsville TX 78364
Phone: (512)296-3958
Fax: (512)296-3958
Offers: Precious and semiprecious gems, minerals and crystals, from alexandrite to zircon.
Catalog: 40-page gem list, $3.
Accepts: American Express, Discover, MasterCard, Visa

STARR GEMS, INC.
220 W. Drachman St.
Tucson AZ 85705
Phone: (520)882-8750 or (800)882-8750
Fax: (520)882-7947
Offers: Bulk silver and gold in sheets and wires. Jewelry findings and chains in silver and 14 karat gold, plus jewelry supplies and tools. Carries sterling concha stampings, E-Z Mount settings, beads and how-to books.
Catalog: $3.50.

STONE AGE INDUSTRIES
P.O. Box 383
Powell WY 82435
Phone: (307)754-4681 or (800)571-4681
Offers: Full line of Covington lapidary equipment, motors and commercial equipment, plus Eastwing tools, Foredom flexible shafts and brand tumblers. Carries gemstone rough and slaps from India, Brazil, Mexico, Africa and US and petrified palmwood, picture rock and others.
Catalog: $1.50.
Discounts: Quantity; sells wholesale to legitimate businesses.
Accepts: MasterCard, Visa

SUPPLIES 4 LESS
(formerly Craft Supplies 4 Less)
P.O. Box 93055
Las Vegas NV 89193-3055
Contact: Phyllis Leon
Phone: (702)263-1172
Fax: (702)896-9488
E-mail: art4less@anv.net
Offers: Glass beads from areas worldwide including grab bag assortments (crystal, antique, handmade, mosaic, trade and unusuals). Other beads include metal, plastic and acrylic. Carries jewelry findings, rhinestones, pewter and metal charms, beading supplies, FIMO, Sculpey, tools, adhesives, Friendly Plastic, kits and books.
Catalog: $4.

Mail Orders. Yes.
Discounts: Already discounted prices.
Accepts: check (3-week delay), money order, cash

T.B. HAGSTOZ & SON, INC.
709 Sansom St.
Philadelphia PA 19106
Phone: (800)922-1006
Fax: (215)922-7126
Offers: Metals: Gold, silver, gold-filled, platinum, pewter, copper, bronze, brass and nickel silver. Carries jewelry tools and equipment, waxes and accessories. Brands available include GFC, Vigor, Dremel, Foredom, Kerr and Af USA. Findings: 14 karat, sterling, gold-filled and base metals. Solders: Gold, silver, platinum and soft. Wire-wrapping and bead-stringing supplies are also available.
Catalog: $5 (refundable).
Accepts: MasterCard, Visa

TEXAS BEADS
(formerly Globe Union International, Inc.)
1237 American Pkwy.
Richardson TX 75081
Contact: Alfred Sher
Phone: (972)669-8181
Fax: (972)669-8639
E-mail: gubeads@dallas.net
Website: www.tx-beads.com
Offers: Gemstone beads and chips, including rose quartz, aventurine, jaspers, unakite, hematite, black quartz, onyx, dyed fossil, agate, tiger eye, carnelian, malachite, lapis, amethyst and others, plus color-treated quartz.

TRIPP'S MANUFACTURING
P.O. Box 1369
1406 Frontage Rd.
Socorro NM 87801
Phone: (800)545-7962
Fax: (505)835-2848
Offers: Jewelry-making supplies: Easy mounts in 14 karat gold and sterling including pendants, ladies' and men's rings in plain and fancy shapes, plus rings and other mountings. Line of chains: gold-filled, 14 karat, sterling silver and findings. Carries sterling castings, synthetic stones and natural faceted gemstones, including peridot, garnet, ruby and others.
Catalog: Free.
Discounts: Quantity.
Accepts: American Express, MasterCard, Visa

TRU-SQUARE METAL PRODUCTS/THUMLER'S TUMBLER
640 First St. S.W.
Auburn WA 98001
Contact: Al Thumler

Phone: (253)833-2310
Fax: (253)833-2349
Offers: Rock polishers and accessories. Abrasives and metal polishing media, choice of several models.
Catalog: Brochure and price list.
Phone Orders: (800)225-1017. M-F, 8-4:30 PST.
Mail Orders: Will ship UPS for C.O.D.
Accepts: American Express, Discover, MasterCard, Visa, money order, C.O.D

ULTRA TEC MFG., INC.
1025 E. Chestnut Ave.
Santa Ana CA 92701
Contact: Gus Munoz
Phone: (714)542-0608
Fax: (714)542-0627
E-mail: gus@ultratec-facet.com
Store Location: At above address. M-F, 8-5.
Offers: Ultra Tec faceting equipment—accessories and lapidary supplies for over 30 years.
Catalog: Free upon request.
Phone Orders: Available 24 hours—can leave message.
Mail Orders: Domestic and international.
Discounts: Authorized dealers only.
Accepts: MasterCard, Visa

THE WIRE WIZARD
P.O. Box 50312
Bellevue WA 98015-0312
Contact: Corrine Gurry
Phone: (425)644-1009
E-mail: beadlady@wolfenet.com
Website: www.wolfenet.com/~beadlady
Store Locations: Shows, expositions.
Offers: The original movable peg jewelry jig allows beginners to produce professional results quickly and easily. The kit includes heavy-duty metal jig base, 25 steel pegs, lots of instructions, patterns to learn with, wire to start out and spacers for large circumference turns. Good hand tools, too.
Phone Orders: (888)547-4447 anytime.
Mail Orders: Will ship worldwide.
Discounts: Wholesale to retail locations.
Accepts: American Express, Discover, MasterCard, Visa

ALAN ZANOTTI AFRICAN IMPORT COMPANY
20 Braunecker Rd.
Plymouth MA 02360
Phone: (508)746-8552
Offers: Ivory (legal from estates), bone material, fossil ivory, horns and skulls.
Catalog: Send SASE for list.

Leather Crafts

Also see General Craft Supplies; Native American & Frontier Crafts; Fabrics & Trims; other related categories.

BARTA HIDE CO.
888 Lakeville St.
Petaluma CA 94952
Contact: Andy, David or Connie
Phone: (707)762-2965 or (707)762-1088
Fax: (707)762-7013
Store Location: At above address.
Offers: Everything in the way of leather and hides.
Catalog: Price list.
Phone Orders: Yes.
Mail Orders: Worldwide.
Discounts: Depending on quantity.
Accepts: check, cash

THE BELT FACTORY
10754 N. Martineau Rd.
Elfrida AZ 85610-9041
Contact: Ellis L. Barnes
Phone: (520)642-3891
Fax: (520)642-3833
Offers: Precision stainless steel leather stamps. Fine saddle-making tools.

BERMAN LEATHER CO.
P.O. Box 1462
Boston MA 02205-1462
Contact: Robert S. Berman
Phone: (617)426-0870
Fax: (617)357-8564
Offers: Leather and leather-crafting supplies.
Catalog: $3 (refundable with first order).
Phone Orders: 24-hour answering service.
Mail Orders: Yes.
Discounts: Wholesale prices provided with tax resale number submitted with catalog request.
Accepts: MasterCard, Visa

HARVEY J. BOUTIN & SON
620 Doolittle Dr.
San Leandro CA 94577-1018
Contact: Patrick Malkassian
Phone: (510)569-6100
Fax: (510)569-6122
Offers: A wide selection of side leathers, full-upholstery hides, printed pig suede, deerskin and natural- and printed-hair calfskins.
Catalog: Master listing of stock monthly. Samples upon request.
Phone Orders: M-F, 9-5 PST. Worldwide shipments.
Discounts: Wholesale to businesses.
Accepts: MasterCard, Visa

C.S. OSBORNE & CO.
150 Jersey St.
Harrison NJ 07029
Phone: (973)483-3232
Fax: (973)484-3621
E-mail: cso@csosborne.com
Website: www.csosborne.com
Offers: Leather-crafting tools: snap setters (snaps), edgers, pliers, hot-glue guns, shoe and other hammers, punches, rawhide hammers and mallets, scratch compasses, nippers, creasers, gauges, gasket cutters, splitting machines, knives, shears, pincers, grommet dies (and grommets), hole cutters, awl hafts and awls, modeler tools, chisels, eyelet setters, space markers, embossing wheel carriages and needles. Also sail and palm thimbles and others. Manufacturer.
Catalog: Write for free catalog and name of nearest dealer.

CAMPBELL BOSWORTH MACHINERY CO.
720 N. Flagler Dr.
Fort Lauderdale FL 33304
Phone: (305)463-7910 or (800)327-9420
Offers: Leather machines and hand tools for splitting, plus airbrushes and compressors, overlocks, embossers, new/used and reconditioned machinery, heavy-duty sewing machines, hot stamping and cutout units and hand/kick presses. Line of hand tools includes punches, shears, measurers, cutters, modeling and edging tools, awls and others, plus jewels, rivets and snap setters.
Catalog: Free.

FEIBING COMPANY, INC.
516 S. Second St.
Milwaukee WI 53204
Phone: (414)271-5011 or (800)558-1033
Offers: Leather dyes: 27 colors (mixable/range of shades). Also carries paints and Rosolene finish. Manufacturer. Send SASE.

FERDCO CORP.

P.O. Box 261

107 S. C.D.A. Ave.

Harrison ID 83833

Contact: Cheryl Mathis

Phone: (208)689-3006 or (800)645-0197

Fax: (208)689-3008

Store Location: At above address.

Offers: Industrial sewing machine, new and used; technical help on industrial sewing machines; and needles, thread and parts for machines.

Catalog: Yes.

Phone Orders: (800)645-0197.

Mail Orders: At above address.

Accepts: MasterCard, Visa, lease purchase program

JOHN FONG EXOTIC LEATHER CO., INC.

1610 Hyde St.

San Francisco CA 94109

Contact: John Fong

Phone: (415)441-3519

Store Location: At above address. M-Sat, 12-5 PST.

Offers: Genuine reptile rare exotic leathers: alligator, anteater, elephant, hippo, frog, crocodile, python, anaconda, shark, stingray, guitarfish, ostrich and rattlesnake. Rawhide, ray skin, lizards, beaver tail and heavyweight kangaroo. Exotic scrap by the pound.

Catalog: $3 and double-stamped SAE.

Phone Orders: Yes.

Mail Orders: Yes.

Discounts: Please inquire.

Accepts: cashier's check, money order, credit with preapproval

HORWEEN LEATHER CO.

2015 N. Elston Ave.

Chicago IL 60614

Contact: John Culliton

Phone: (773)772-2026

Fax: (773)772-9235

Offers: Leathers: Chromexcel, Latigo, Waxed Flesh Chrxl (our version of Waxed French Calf), Horsefronts and Shell Cordovan.

Catalog: Call.

Phone Orders: Yes.

Mail Orders: At above address.

Accepts: MasterCard, Visa

THE LEATHER FACTORY, INC.

P.O. Box 50429

Fort Worth TX 76105

Phone: (800)433-3201

Store Location: Over 20 locations in the US and Canada.

Offers: A full line of leathers: garment, exotics, upholstery, moccasin, chap, saddle skirting and more. Carries a full line of leatherworking tools for the novice and professional, including a patented belt and strap embossing machine. Traditional and rubber-stamping leather kits, starter sets, moccasin kits, books, dyes, stains, finishes and scalers, adhesive, buckles, hardware and accessories.

Catalog: $3 (refundable with purchase).

Discounts: Schools, hospitals and institutions; sells wholesale to businesses.

LEATHER UNLIMITED CORP.

Dept. CS98

7155 Highway B.

Belgium WI 53004-0911

Contact: Joe O'Connell

Phone: (920)994-9464

Fax: (920)994-4099

Offers: A wide array of leather kits and finished products. Leather includes garment bag, splits, oak, deer, sheepskin, hair on hides, chamois and pieces. Leather findings include buckles, snaps, zippers, thread dies, dyes, belts, black powder, Indian lore, books, tanning kits, beads, conchos and more. Finished products include slippers, wallets, handbags, belts, cycle accessories, hats, cases, halters, dream catchers and more at wholesale prices.

Catalog: 92 pages. $2 (refundable).

Phone Orders: M-F, 7-4. Fax: 24 hours a day, 7 days a week.

Mail Orders: US, Canada, worldwide.

Discounts: Sells wholesale to legitimate businesses.

Accepts: Discover, MasterCard, Visa

MID-CONTINENT LEATHER SALES CO.

1539 S. Yale Ave.

Tulsa OK 74112

Phone: (800)926-2061

Offers: Leathers: saddle (skirting, latigo and others), rawhide, tooling (sides, strap sides, shoulders and others), plus chap and garment leathers (sides, splits and deerskin), lacing and stirrup leather. Carries conchos, snaps, grommets, inserting dies, buckles, rings, rigging plates, fasteners and zippers. Threads available include nylon and waxed linen. Also offers complete line of C.S. Osborne tools. Conditioners and finishes also available.

Catalog: $2 postage fee.

PILGRIM SHOE & SEWING MACHINE CO., INC.

21 Nightingale Ave.

Quincy MA 02169

Contact: Harris, Neal or Janice Feierstein

Phone: (617)786-8940 or (800)343-2202

Fax: (617)773-9012

E-mail: pilgrim.shoe.machine@worldnet.att.net

Website: www.pilgrimshoemachine.com

Store Location: At above address. M-F, 8-5.

Offers: New shoe machine parts and supplies, needles, thread, shoe and sewing machines and polishing and buffing wheels. Anything for shoes and leather machinery and parts.

Catalog: Free upon request.

Phone Orders: Yes.

Mail Orders: All over the world.

Discounts: Retail and wholesale.

Accepts: American Express, MasterCard, Visa, C.O.D.

POCAHONTAS LEATHER
P.O. Box 958
Yucca Valley CA 92286
Phone: (760)364-3510
Offers: Deer and elk skins (lots by the foot and up), tannery deep-Scotchgarded for water and soil resistance and pre-stretched for honest, usable footage.
Catalog: Send SASE for price list.

SAL'S LEATHER
P.O. Box 2190
101 S. Coombs, Suite F
Napa CA 94559
Contact: Sal Espinoza
Phone: (707)252-8000
Fax: (707)255-0648
Store Location: At above address.
Offers: Saddle leather, belting leather, tooling leather, chap leather, deerskin, lambskin, garment cowhide, pig suede, handbag leather and latigo leather.
Phone Orders: (707)252-8000 or (800)475-0155.
Mail Orders: P.O. Box 2190, Napa CA 94559.
Discounts: Volume.
Accepts: check (personal or company), C.O.D.

S-T LEATHER CO.
830 S. 17th St.
St. Louis MO 63103
Contact: Wendy Tinnin
Phone: (314)241-6009
Fax: (314)241-8428
Store Location: Locations in St. Louis MO and Columbus OH.
Offers: Supplies for leather crafters.
Catalog: Yes.
Phone Orders: (314)241-6009 or (800)381-5965.
Mail Orders: Yes.
Discounts: Quantity.
Accepts: MasterCard, Visa

TIPPMANN INDUSTRIAL PRODUCTS, INC.
3518 Adams Center Rd.
Fort Wayne IN 46806
Contact: Thomas Tippmann, general manager
Phone: (219)749-6022
Fax: (219)749-6619
Offers: Leather sewing machines and die press (clicker) manufacture. Sells to distributors, to dealers and direct.
Mail Orders: Yes.
Accepts: American Express, Discover, MasterCard, Visa

WEAVER LEATHER, INC.
P.O. Box 68
Mt. Hope OH 44660
Phone: (330)674-1782 or (800)WEAVER-1
Fax: (330)674-0030 or (800)6-WEAVER
Website: www.leathersupply.com
Offers: Leather hides: chap, suede, strap, skirting, harness, bridle, latigo and others. Hardware includes snaps, loops, rings, dees, buckles and others. Also carries leather crafting tools, thread, nylon webbing, poly rope, oils and dyes.
Catalog: Free.
Discounts: Quantity.

Metalworking

Also see Jewelry Making & Lapidary; Miniature Making, Miniatures & Dollhouses; Model Making; Sculpture & Modeling.

AMERICAN ART CLAY CO., INC.
4717 W. 16th St.
Indianapolis IN 46222
Contact: Nancy Elliott
Phone: (317)244-6871 or (800)374-1600
Fax: (317)248-9300
E-mail amacobrent@aol.com
Website: www.amaco.com
Offers: Metal enameling kilns (3), supplies, glass and metal enamel ceramic decorating colors.
Catalog: Free.
Phone Orders: M-F, 8-5 EST.
Mail Orders: Prepayment required. Will ship to US and Canada.
Discounts: Manufacturer—sells through distributors.
Accepts: Discover, MasterCard, Visa

COUNTRY ACCENTS
P.O. Box 437
Montoursville PA 17754
Contact: Marie C. Palotás
Phone: (717)478-4127
Fax: (717)478-2000
Offers: Made-to-order pierced metal panels in 18 different metals. Also sells tools, patterns and blank metal stock.
Catalog: $5.
Discounts: On quantity orders of standard-size finished panels only.
Accepts: MasterCard, Visa, check, money order

EAST WEST DYECOM, INC.
P.O. Box 12294
5238 Peters Creek Rd., Bldg. B
Roanoke VA 24024
Phone: (540)362-1489 or (800)407-6371
Fax: (540)362-7425 or (800)393-2660
E-mail: ewdc@rbnet.com
Website: http://www.roanoke.net/ewdc
Offers: Anodized aluminum: wire and wire shapes; sheets (solids, perforated and patterns); tubing (round and square); beads; rings, (1/8"-3/4"); chain; and other components. Available: dyes, inks, sealer and hand tools/supplies. Custom anodizing and dyeing service.
Catalog: Color. $5 (refundable on first order).
Phone Orders: M-F, 9-5 EST; 24-hour fax.

Mail Orders: Allow 4-6 weeks for delivery.
Discounts: Quantity; wholesale to business (minimum quantities apply).
Accepts: MasterCard, Visa

EDMUND SCIENTIFIC
101 E. Gloucester Pike
Barrington NJ 08007
Phone: (800)728-6999
Website: www.edsci.com
Offers: Technical and scientific products, including some for metalcrafting or useful aids: electroplating kits, 6 submersible pumps, compressors and over 20 small motors. Carries a wide array of miniature tools: Dremel Moto-Tools, pin vises, drills, hammers, jewelers' drill presses, mini-torches and table saws. Engravers' tools and wire benders. 30-plus magnifiers and loupes, diffraction grating and others also available.
Catalog: Write.

EXTRA SPECIAL PRODUCTS CORP.
P.O. Box 777
Greenville OH 45331
Phone: (937)548-9388 or (800)648-5945
Fax: (937)548-9580
Website: www.extraspecial.com
Offers: House of Copper line of die-cut copper shapes (to punch, bend, burnish, antique, paint and use as trims, window decorations, tree ornaments, candle trims, quilt templates, appliqué templates, wreath decorations and others) and a booklet with over 24 projects. Contact your dealer.
Catalog: Write.

MASTER MACHINIST VIDEOS
P.O. Box 4942
Akron OH 44310
Contact: David Burns
Phone: (800)988-0764
Offers: How-to instructional videos on the machine shop trades. We offer 3 videos. Tape 1: *Milling Machine*, 90 minutes; tape 2: *Engine Lathe*, 70 minutes; and tape 3: *Inspection Tools and Procedures*, 40 minutes. $29.95 each plus $3.95 p&h.
Phone Orders: Yes.
Discounts: All 3 tapes $79.95 plus $9.95 p&h.
Accepts: American Express, MasterCard, Visa, check, money order

NONFERROUS METALS CO.
P.O. Box 2595-CS
Waterbury CT 06723
Phone: (860)274-7255

Fax: (860)274-7202
Offers: Wire, including brass, copper, black annealed and galvanized, in a variety of gauges. Send SASE.

SCHLAIFER'S ENAMELING SUPPLIES

1012 Fair Oaks Ave. #170
South Pasadena CA 91030
Contact: Joan
Phone: (626)441-1127 or (800)525-5959
Fax: (626)441-1127
E-mail ses@kihakkt.jetcafe.org
Offers: Unleaded enamels and supplies for copper enameling, as well as copper shapes and bowls. Also 80-mesh glass for glass fusers, stain-glass painters and brass, stainless steel and aluminum enamelers. New 80-mesh Moretti Glass COE 104 for lampwork bead makers.
Catalog: Available upon request.
Phone Orders: Yes.
Mail Orders: Yes.
Accepts: Discover, MasterCard, Visa

SHELTECH

4207 Lead Ave. SE
Albuquerque NM 87108
Phone: (505)256-7073

Offers: Custom RT Stamping dies made of heat-treated tool steel for cutting parts from sheet metal. Blanking service with dies. Send SASE.

WOOD-MET SERVICES

Dept. CSS
3314 Shoff Circle
Peoria IL 61604
Phone: (306)637-9667
Offers: Over 700 plans to build home workshop machines/equipment for wood and metal work: universal clamping system, metal spinning, metal lathe, 9 woodturning chisels, miter arm for band saw and router, electric band sander, photographic equipment, air compressor, drill press items, router and band saw items, shop metal benders, welding and hand tools, fixtures, wood lathe items, sander with power feed, circular saw items, power rasps, 6 tools for grinding wheels, milling machine and metal shaper items. Investing cast equipment. Also offers circular saws, wood jointer, belt sander items and woodworkers' kits and sets.
Catalog: $1.
Discounts: Quantity; sells wholesale to legitimate businesses.

Miniature Making, Miniatures & Dollhouses

Also see Model Making; Paints, Finishes & Adhesives; Tools & Equipment; specific categories of interest.

JOAN ADAMS
2706 Sheridan Dr.
Sarasota FL 34239
Phone: (941)924-8185
Offers: Rug designs and completed rugs in punchneedle. Over 50 designs.
Catalog: $3.

AMERICAN CRAFT PRODUCTS
3150 State Line Rd.
North Bend OH 45052
Phone: (513)353-3390
E-mail: dees@one.net
Offers: Dollhouse windows and doors, ready to finish and install, scaled to fit standard dollhouse openings. Styles include tall Victorian, traditional, French and colonial. Both working and nonworking windows and ½″ scale available.
Catalog: $3.

THE COMPANY MOUSE
5050 Nicholson Lane
Rockville MD 20852
Contact: Sherry Needle
Phone: (301)881-5137
Fax: (301)983-9124
Store Location: At above address.
Offers: Dollhouses and everything necessary to build, decorate and electrify dollhouses. Everything for the dollhouse decorator and builder.
Phone Orders: Prepayment required. M-F, 11-6; Sat, 11-5.
Mail Orders: Prepayment required.
Accepts: MasterCard, Visa (not over phone)

CONCORD MINIATURES
1421 Pinewood St.
Rahway NJ 07065
Contact: Cecilia Schein or Gary Darwin
Phone: (800)888-0936
Fax: (732)382-8990
E-mail: cardinal.giftware@worldnet.att.net
Offers: Concord 1″ scale furniture and accessories with licensed product from Broyhill, The Lane Company, Robin Betterley, Museum of American Folk Art collection and Susanne Russo.
Catalog: 36 pages, full color. $7.50.
Phone Orders: Wholesale only. M-F, 8:30-5 EST.

Mail Orders: Wholesale only.
Discounts: Sells wholesale to legitimate businesses.
Accepts: MasterCard, Visa

DEE'S DELIGHTS, INC.
3150 State Line Rd.
North Bend OH 45052
Phone: (513)353-3390
E-mail: dees@one.net
Offers: FIMO modeling compound in a variety of colors (oven-bakes). Also offers more than 2,000 miniature and dollhouse-related items. Contact dealer, or send SASE for information.
Discounts: Sells wholesale to legitimate businesses.

DESIGN TECNICS MINIATURES
9548 Walmer
Overland Park KS 66212
Offers: House plans in 1″ scale and *Dollhouse Builders Handbook*. Also offers a 1920s cast-metal stove, refrigerator, modern tub and toilet in ¼″ scale. Available through Dollhouses and More.

DESIGNS BY JUDI
12202 Old 125
Scotland Neck NC 27874
Contact: Judy Arrington
Phone: (252)826-5483
E-mail: sndolls@3rddoor.com
Offers: Doll repair—all types except all cloth. Quality service. Reasonable prices. Owner of doll pays shipping. 10 years experience. Many happy customers. Doll clothes and patterns.
Catalog: Sash-a-Doll Clothes and patterns catalog: $3; miscellaneous doll clothes—patterns only: $3.
Mail Orders: Prepayment required.

DIAMOND "M" BRAND MOLD CO.
15W081 91st St.
Hinsdale IL 60521
Phone: (630)323-5691
Offers: 1″ scale miniature molds (poured in porcelain or ceramic) including 3-mold Victorian bath set (claw tub, pedestal sink and water-closet toilet). Other molds for tea sets, variety of pots, vases and country accessories, plus dolls and various items of furniture and fireplaces. Factory direct.
Catalog: $3.50 ($5 foreign).

DOLLHOUSES AND MORE

(formerly Miniature Lumber Shoppe)
812 Main St.
Grandview MO 64030
Contact: Carolyn Stephenson
Phone: (816)761-3999
Fax: (816)761-3999
Store Location: At above address. T-S, 10-5 CST.
Offers: Dollhouses and dollhouse items. Also manufacturer of windows, doors, moldings and miscellaneous components; publisher of dollhouse plans and handbook; and manufacturer of ¼" scale dollhouses.
Catalog: 1" scale products: $2. ¼" scale products: $2 (refundable).
Phone Orders: T-S, 10-5 CST.
Mail Orders: Will ship anywhere. Shipping added to order.
Discounts: Retail; wholesale to approved businesses.
Accepts: Discover, MasterCard, Visa

ENGLAND THINGS

15 Sullivan Farm
New Milford CT 06776
Phone: (860)350-4565
Offers: Line of miniature building kits, including houses, tollhouse, Victorian factory, clapboard shop and others. Also offers finished buildings.
Catalog: Brochures, $5 and large SASE.

FERN VASI DOLLS

P.O. Box 16164
Newport Beach CA 92659
Offers: Miniature kit, including 2" Raggedy Ann, Raggedy Andy, Christmas reindeer wall hanging and Mammy/Southern Belle "flip doll," $12.95 each. Add tax. $3 p&h. For further information send SASE.
Discounts: Buy 3, get 1 free. Also sells wholesale.

FERNWOOD MINIATURES

12730 Finlay Rd. NE
Silverton OR 97381
Phone: (503)873-2397
Offers: 1" scale miniature furniture kits of basswood, including Colonial, Early American, Shaker, Victorian, Empire, Craftman, Southwestern and country pieces. Offers dressers, stands, tables, chairs, desks, cabinets, beds, wardrobes and more.
Catalog: Send large SASE.

THE FIELDWOOD CO., INC.

P.O. Box 6
Chester VT 05143
Phone: (802)875-4127
Fax: (800)732-7894
Offers: "Precious Little Things" handcrafted scale miniature accessories, including food (artichokes in a pewter bowl, apples, baked goods, meats, vegetables in wicker basket, filled Mason jars, hand-blown glass and others). Also offers furnishings and accessories in 1", ½" and ¼" scales.

Catalog: 40 pages, color. $3.50 in US, $6.50 in Canada and abroad.
Phone Orders: Fax.
Discount: Sells wholesale.

HERITAGE MINIATURES

Dept. CSSP
44 Mountain Base Rd.
Goffstown NH 03045
Contact: Priscilla J. Gangi
Phone: (603)497-5041
Fax: (603)497-3094
E-mail: heritagemin@worldnet.att.net
Offers: Collector-quality dollhouse miniatures including porcelains, furniture, kitchenware and accesories. Authentic historic designs primarily 18th-19th century. Many items imported from England and Europe.
Catalog: Color. $5.
Phone Orders: Yes.
Mail Orders: Will ship worldwide.
Accepts: American Express, Discover, MasterCard, Visa

HOUSE OF CARON

10111 Larryln Dr.
Whittier CA 90603
Phone: (562)947-6753
Fax: (562)943-5103
Offers: Miniature doll molds by Parker-Levi, Keni, Paulette Stinson, Mystic, Theresa Glisson, Ayanna, Emanjay and House of Caron. Carries doll clothes patterns, books, dollmaking supplies, tools and accessories.
Catalog: Illustrated price lists, $3.
Discounts: Quantity.

INNOVATIVE PHOTOGRAPHY

1724 NW 36th
Lincoln City OR 97367
Phone: (541)994-9421
Offers: Framed miniature photos of Old Masters, impressionist and modern paintings by da Vinci, Rembrandt, Botticelli, van Gogh, Degas, Gainsborough, Picasso, Marin, Pollack and others, plus Gutmann babies, Eisley, C.B. Barber and J.W. Carries Victorian photos—framed or in folders, stereo-view cards, diplomas, certificates, postcards, color maps (US, world, states and antique), postcard and hanging display racks and others. Will do custom reduction of any photos.
Catalog: $3.

JANNA JOSEPH DESIGNS

P.O. Box 1262
Dunedin FL 34697
Contact: J. Joseph
Phone: (813)784-1877
Offers: Mini doll molds, how-to books and patterns.
Catalog: $5 (refundable with first mold order).
Phone Orders: Yes.
Mail Orders: Yes.

Discounts: Yes.
Accepts: US funds only

KARIN'S MINI GARDEN
2905 Ninth St. NW
Albuquerque NM 87107
Phone: (505)341-1709
Offers: Miniature garden items: variety of indoor and outdoor plants (in containers), cacti, succulents and arrangements, plus other realistic items.
Catalog: $3.50 (refundable).

KEMPER ENTERPRISES, INC.
13595 12th St.
Chino CA 91710
Contact: Katie Munday
Phone: (800)388-5367 or (909)627-6191
Fax: (909)627-4008
E-mail: thetoolady@aol.com
Offers: Manufacturer and designer of tools for painting that include the Fluid Writer, Wipe-Out tool that erases mistakes, faux finishing tools and a spray gun cleaner set.
Catalog: Free. 70+ pages, color. Please send $1.50 for p&h.
Phone Orders: Customer service hours are M-F, 8-4:30 PST.
Mail Orders: Can expect order to ship within 2 days of receipt. Ship domestic and international through UPS.
Discounts: Sell wholesale to businesses. For account qualifications and status please contact.
Accepts: Discover, MasterCard, Visa, International Money Order, bank wire transfer in American dollars only

KILKENNY MINIATURES
53-567 Kamehameha Hwy. #506
Punaluu HI 96717-9678
Contact: Jane Winston Kilkenny
Phone: (808)293-0522
E-mail: kilkennymini@hotmail.com
Website: In process. Ask via E-mail.
Offers: Original kits for 1″ scale romantic accessories and holiday items, including ultrafine glitter.
Catalog: Send long SASE for color catalog.
Mail Orders: Prepayment required.
Discounts: Sells wholesale to miniatures businesses.

KIMONA
3257 Cottman Ave.
Philadelphia PA 19149
Contact: Alma Luz Castro
Phone: (215)338-6790
Offers: Dress kits, Oriental wig kits, hair decorations/ornaments, pattern booklets and more.
Catalog: $2 with SASE.
Mail Orders: Please allow 6 weeks for special orders and other handcrafted items.
Discounts: On occasion. Not a wholesaler.
Accepts: check, money order

BETTY LAMPEN KNITTING BOOKS
2930 Jackson St.
San Francisco CA 94115-1007
Contact: Betty Lampen
Phone: (415)346-4673
Fax: (415)674-1114
E-mail: elampen@aol.com
Website: www.bettylampenknitbooks.com
Offers: 7 knitting books: *Miniature Sweaters, Miniature Pullovers, More Mini Sweater Designs, Sweaters for Teddy Bears, Teddy Bear Knits, Best Dressed Bears* and *Knitted Bears.*

LIGIA'S MINIATURES
(formerly Ligia Durstenfeld)
2315 Caracas St.
La Crescenta CA 91214
Contact: Ligia Durstenfeld
Phone: (818)248-8058
E-mail: jhhg@aol.com
Offers: Scale enameled miniatures, including bowls, Faberge eggs/silver, flower arrangements, other flowers, Oriental screens (enamel on copper) and others. Will custom enamel miniatures to specification.
Catalog: $4 (refundable).
Phone Orders: Yes.
Mail Orders: At above address.
Discounts: Some wholesale special discounts.

LITTLE GOODIES
P.O. Box 1004
Lewisville TX 75067
Contact: Diane Foster
Phone: (972)625-9303
Fax: (972)370-0290
E-mail: littlegoodies@riverstyx.com
Offers: Over 95 precut paper flower kits (1″ to 1′ scale): marigolds, hollyhocks, lilies of the valley, violets, lilies, carnations, irises, tulips, poppies, dandelions, rose bushes, ivy and others.
Catalog: $2 (refundable). International: free.
Mail Orders: US and international. Prepayment or credit card required. No postal money orders.
Discounts: Wholesale to legitimate businesses.
Accepts: MasterCard, Visa

LITTLE HOUSE OF MINIATURES ON CHELSEA LANE
622 Commercial
Waterloo IA 50701
Phone: (319)233-6506 or (319)234-3235
Store Location: At above address.
Offers: Over 30,000 miniature items, including dollhouse and furniture kits, dolls, wallpapers and other decorator components, electric wiring and building supplies and others.
Catalog: $20 (partially refundable).

LITTLE RED DOLL HOUSE
(formerly Little Red House at Beauvais Castle)
P.O. Box 4060
235 Harvard St.
Manchester NH 03108
Phone: (603)625-8944
Fax: (603)668-1474
Offers: Over 6,000 miniatures and accessories of known brands—furniture, figures, components and others. Specializes in dollhouse electrification.
Catalog: 300 pages. $5.
Accepts: MasterCard, Visa

MASTERPIECES IN MINIATURE
13083 Drummer Way
Grass Valley CA 95949
Contact: Ruth L. Mazur
Phone: (530)268-1429
Offers: Handcrafted, scaled miniatures in 1″, ½″ and ¼″ scales, including oil paintings, Peteco brass picture lights, artists' furniture and assorted household accessories. Instant Age weathering liquid for wood/painted surfaces also available. Also carries *Tips and Techniques for the Miniaturist* video.
Catalog: $3 (refundable with order).
Discounts: Sells wholesale to storefront shops.

MIDWEST CARRIAGE
P.O. Box 0024
Mentor OH 44060-0024
Contact: D. Justus
Phone: (440)257-9554
Fax: (440)209-8817
E-mail: mcarriage@aol.com
Store Location: Mentor OH location.
Offers: Horse-drawn vehicle plans, kits, books and accessories in miniature. Dollhouse furniture plans, books and how-to books.
Catalog: Yes.
Phone Orders: Yes.
Mail Orders: Yes.
Accepts: American Express, Discover, MasterCard, Visa

MINIATURE IMAGE
P.O. Box 465
Lawrenceburg IN 47025
Phone: (800)942-9076
E-mail: hmp@one.net
Website: miniatureimage.com
Offers: Scale dollhouses, dollhouse kits and basic building supplies, scale miniatures, including furniture kits and finished accessories, even hard-to-find items. Carries reference and how-to books and others.
Catalog: Full catalog, $30 (refundable).
Accepts: American Express, MasterCard, Visa

MINIATURE MAKER'S WORKSHOP
4515 N. Woodward Ave.
Royal Oak MI 48073
Phone: (248)549-0633
Fax: (248)258-0062
Store Location: At above address. T-Sat, 10-5.
Offers: Magic Mitre miniature mitering kit (for door, window and picture frames, other uses). Send SASE.

NORTHEASTERN SCALE MODELS, INC.
99 Cross St.
Methuen MA 01844
Contact: Nancy Oriol
Phone: (978)688-6019
Fax: (978)794-9104
E-mail: nesm@tiac.net
Website: www.nesm.com
Store Location: At above address.
Offers: Model-building materials, laser-cut trims and miniature kits. Also model railroad items and laser-cut kits.
Catalog: $1.50 (refundable with first order).
Phone Orders: Accepted for credit card orders.
Mail Orders: Accepted for credit card orders and prepaid orders (check or money order).
Discounts: To legitimate dealers, distributors and manufacturers.
Accepts: MasterCard, Visa

PAST CRAFTS PATTERNS
P.O. Box 16512
Alexandria VA 22302
Contact: Newbie Richardson
Phone: (703)684-0863
Fax: (703)684-0863
E-mail: easy4@juno.com
Offers: Historically accurate dolls' dress and miniature quilt plans and doll furniture woodworking plans for 14″, 16″, 18″ and American Girl dolls with detailed period notes for accurate period reproduction.
Catalog: $1.50.
Mail Orders: Will ship to Canada and US prepaid. Allow 10 days for delivery.
Discounts: Sells wholesale to legitimate businesses and home schoolers.
Accepts: check, money order

DON PERKINS MINIATURES
1708 59th St.
Des Moines IA 50322-6102
Contact: Don Perkins
Phone: (515)279-6639
Offers: White or natural 4-cord linen for miniature wicker work. White available in ½- or 1-pound spools. Natural available in 1-pound spools. Also 3-cord natural (for ½″ scale wicker) in ¼-pound spools. For further information, send SASE for price list.
Mail Orders: Yes.
Accepts: check, money order, cash

PORCELAIN BY DEL

41372 Yokum Rd.
Ponchatoula LA 70451
Contact: Del Mendoza
Phone: (504)386-6977
Offers: Porcelain dollhouse dolls.
Catalog: Price list. Send #10 SASE.

PUSSY CAT COMPANY

(formerly Gold and Betty Rimer)
515 Crystal Ave.
Findlay OH 45840
Contact: Betty Rimer
Phone: (419)423-3261
Store Location: At above address.
Offers: Dollhouse kits, furniture, foods, plants, carpets and all other accessories. Model plastic planes, cars, boats and R/C planes. Railroad trains, track, additional cars, engines and cabooses. We also have building components for all above and much more.
Catalog: Our dollhouse handcrafted furniture and accessories only.
Phone Orders: Yes.
Mail Orders: Prepaid.
Discounts: Wholesale to legitimate businesses only.
Accepts: Discover, MasterCard, Novus, Visa, other cards

BARBARA J. RAHEB

30132 Elizabeth Court
Agoura Hills CA 91301
Phone: (818)991-3109
Offers: Miniature books: over 350 selections of abridged and unabridged editions of well-known favorites, classics, reproduced antique books, masterpieces (professionally typeset, illustrated, hand-sewn, hardbound with titled decorative spines and cover designs stamped in 23 karat gold). Books are limited, numbered, fully readable editions in 1″ scale.
Catalog: Price list, $1.50.
Discounts: Sells wholesale.

REAL ADOBE BUILDING KITS

P.O. Box 1168
Nederland CO 80466
Contact: Zabet Freeman
Phone: (888)333-4073
E-mail: realadobe@yahoo.com
Offers: Adobe builder's kits. You can construct various adobe dollhouses, several Nativity creches, solar adobe home model, horno or any other adobe structure you can imagine (styles include mission, Sante Fe, fantasy, Pueblo, old European, Mideastern and Ol' West). The kits teach actual adobe construction skills. Kits include 1′ to ¾″ scale brick mold, wood pieces, adobe mix, plans, instructions and hardware. Priced $40-190. We also have access to miniature roof tiles, fire bricks and straw bales for realistic construction.
Catalog: Color brochure.

Mail Orders: Allow 6 weeks for delivery. Shipping charges $10-$25.
Accepts: check, money order

RONDEL WOOD PRODUCTS

63 U.S. Hwy. 1
Nobelboro ME 04555
Contact: Delly Schweighauser
Phone: (207)563-6693
Fax: (207)563-8769
Store Location: At above address.
Offers: Wood wagon and carriage kits in ¹⁄₁₂″ and ½″ scale: includes blueprints, cut pieces and components.
Catalog: Brochure, $3.

THE SIDE DOOR

P.O. Box 573
Dennisport MA 02639
Phone: (508)394-7715
Offers: Bisque dollhouse/doll kits, patterns, dressed dolls, trims, accessories.
Catalog: Illustrated brochure, $3.

SMALL HOUSES

8064 Columbia Rd.
Olmstead Falls OH 44138
Phone: (440)235-5051
Offers: Full line of dollhouses and components: furniture, wallpapers, carpet, building supplies and accessories.
Catalog: $29.95.

PHYLLIS STAFFORD

P.O. Box 157
Suffield CT 06078
Phone: (860)668-2391
Offers: Scale miniature carpet kits, including design reproductions (from 17th century) on 42 silk gauze mesh with DMC floss; also offers *Our Lady of Czestochowa* design kit. Has finished carpets.
Catalog: Send large SASE and $2.

RON STETKEWICZ

HCR 1, Box 61B
Cairo NY 12413
Contact: Ron Stetkewicz
Phone: (518)622-8311
Fax: (518)622-9247
E-mail: skhardware@aol.com
Website: www.ministuff.com
Offers: Miniature brass hardware: hinges, drawer pulls, lock plates, door knockers, door handles, doorknobs, drawer knobs, screens and notions and much more.
Catalog: $6.
Phone Orders: 7 days, 1-11.
Mail Orders: Will ship anywhere.
Accepts: MasterCard, Visa, check, money order

LINDA TAYLOR

2228 Leif Ave.

Muskegon MI 49441

Offers: Bears, cats and bunnies kits with illustrated step-by-step instructions, soft premarked fabric and more to make tiny stuffed animals with jointed arms and legs (only about 1″ tall when seated).

Catalog: Send long SASE for brochure.

TREE TREASURES

P.O. Box 1069

Bensalem PA 19020

Phone: (215)788-2818 or (800)251-7212

Fax: (215)788-6999

Store Location: Other location: 617 Rosa Ave., Croydon PA 19021.

Offers: Wooden cutouts, miniatures, turnings, beads, balls, wooden kits for kids, birdhouses, brass hinges, hardware, (screws, cup hooks, lazy Susan bearings and more), Forstne flat-bottom drill bits and wooden boxes.

Catalog: $2.

Phone Orders: M-F, 8-5 EST.

Mail Orders: At P.O. Box.

Accepts: MasterCard, Visa

W&D MINI HOMES

1005 Nota Dr.

Bloomington IN 47401

Phone: (812)332-2499

Offers: Native American scale miniatures (of clay, fiber, wood and more), including a variety of clothing, costumes, pottery, baskets, blankets, rugs, figures, paintings and others.

Catalog: Brochure, $1 and SASE (double postage).

WALDEN WOODS' DESIGNS

4604 Wilson Ave.

Signal Mountain TN 37377

Contact: Joan H. Thornbury

Phone: (423)517-0501

Fax: (423)517-0501

Offers: Collection of 60 counted cross-stitch kits including framed pictures, rugs, quilts and more.

Catalog: Color. $2 (refundable).

Phone Orders: Any day 8-8.

Mail Orders: Will ship anywhere. Prepaid orders. Allow 4 weeks for delivery.

Discounts: Wholesale orders accepted.

Accepts: check, money order

WARLING MINIATURES

22453 Covello St.

West Hills CA 91307

Phone: (818)340-9855

Fax: (818)999-6020

Offers: Miniatures (1″ and ½″) wicker furniture kits of Victorian to modern styles, including chairs, rockers, tables, sofas, baskets and others. Send large SASE.

PETER F. WESTCOTT

6256 N. 85th St.

Scottsdale AZ 85250

Phone: (602)956-1279

Offers: Furniture pattern books in 1″ scale, including Southwestern, mission, Shaker, Art Deco, Chippendale, modern and other styles. Send large SASE with two stamps.

Model Making—Aircraft

Also see Miniature Making, Miniatures & Dollhouses; Model Making—General; Model Making—Railroad; other related categories.

CARLSON ENGINE IMPORTS
814 E. Marconi Ave.
Phoenix AZ 85022
Offers: Glow and diesel model engines, including Aurora, AM, AME, CS, Cipolla, Elfin, Jin Shi, John, KMD MK-17, Letmo, Marz, MDC, Merco, Meteor, MVVS, MP Jet, Paw, Silver Swallow, Stas's, Pfeffer, Philtech and Rustler brands.
Catalog: 20 pages. $1.

EXECUFORM
(formerly Herrills Execuform)
P.O. Box 7853
Laguna Niguel CA 92607-2146
Contact: Mike or Maureen Herrill
Phone: (714)495-0705
Fax: (714)495-0705
Store Location: At above address.
Offers: 1/72 scale vacform kits, including Abrams, Beech, Bell, Canadair, Cessna, Consol, Convair, Curtiss, Douglas, Fairchild, Gen. Avia, Grumman, Howard, Hughes, Lockheed, Martin, North American, Northrop, Republic, Ryan, Seversky, Sikorsky, Spartan, Stinson, Timm, Vultee and Waco.
Catalog: Send $1 for profiles catalog.
Phone Orders: 24-hour ordering service.
Mail Orders: Ship prepaid worldwide per catalog data. Shipping overages refunded.
Discounts: Wholesale to legitimate businesses.
Accepts: no credit cards

INDOOR MODEL SUPPLY
P.O. Box 5311
Salem OR 97304
Contact: Lew Gitlow
Phone: (503)390-6350
Offers: Ultralight indoor-type En Pierance rubber-powered flying model kits, supplies and books; also gliders, helicopters and 13″ scale models. Also offers supplies, including indoor balsa, coverings, cements, winders and tools for model crafting.
Catalog: Illustrated. $2.

K&B MANUFACTURING
2100 College Dr.
Lake Havasu City AZ 86403
Phone: (520)453-3030

Fax: (520)453-3559
Offers: K & B model aircraft and marine engines, fuels, glow plugs, fiberglass cloth, super epoxy resin and primer, microballoon filler, ultrapoxy thinner and paints. Send SASE.

LENCRAFT
P.O. Box 770
Springville CA 93265
Offers: Aircraft kits, including hard-to-find models, decals and accessories by all WWI, Huma, Italeri, Matchbox, Pioneer, Vacuforms, Hasegawa, Model Decal, Xtra Color, Esoteric, Frog, Novo, Minicraft, REvell, KP, Falcon, Blue Rider, Fujimi, Airfix, Aeroclub, D.B. Conv., Meikraft, Heller and Rareplanes. Free search service for wanted kits.
Catalog: Send large SASE for list. Hot sheet mailing also available.

MIDWEST PRODUCTS CO., INC.
P.O. Box 564
400 S. Indiana St.
Hobart IN 46342
Contact: Customer service
Phone: (800)348-3497
Fax: (219)947-2347
E-mail: info@midwestproducts.com
Website: http://www.midwestproducts.com
Store Location: At above address.
Offers: Small dimensional, precision-cut wood for crafts, hobbies and students. Wood: balsa, basswood, walnut, mahogany, cherry, Sitka spruce, plywood, birch and Italian poplar. Wide selection of special shapes, moldings and scale lumber. Kits: model boat, aircraft, railroad bridges and educational. Other: railroad cork roadbed, boat and plane accessories and hobby paints. See your dealer or contact us for a catalog and the dealer nearest you.
Catalog: Free. Color.

OLD TIME PLAN SERVICE
P.O. Box 90310
San Jose CA 95109-3310
Contact: Al
Phone: (408)292-3382
Fax: (408)292-3323
Store Location: 253 N. Fourth St., San Jose CA 95112-5559.
Offers: Model airplane plans.
Catalog: 2 catalogs, $5 each: old-timer, nostalgia, radio control, rubber power and control line; flying scale.
Phone Orders: Yes.
Mail Orders: At P.O. Box.
Accepts: MasterCard, Visa

SIG MANUFACTURING CO., INC.

401-7 S. Front St.

Montezuma IA 50171

Phone: (515)623-5154

Fax: (515)623-3922

E-mail: flysig@netins.net

Offers: Model aircraft kits (balsa and plywood)—classic, biplanes, stunts, sports, multiwing, military, racers, trainers, gliders and others. Includes models for flying in confined area and for 2- to 9-channel radio equipment. Carries beginners' models and a variety of scale sizes. Also carries aircraft parts, kit plans, balsa, spruce, plywood, dowels, glues, wire, fuel, engines and metal sheets, including aluminum and brass. Also offers several weights of silk, silray, ply span tissue, nylon, polyester, plastic and flight foam. Stocks paints for foam, ARF models and casting materials, including resin, fiberglass and control lines. Services include vacuum molding, silkscreening, custom decals, laser cutting, wire bending, and composition and printing.

Catalog: $3, or contact a dealer.

Accepts: MasterCard, Visa

SUPERIOR BALSA & HOBBY SUPPLY

(formerly Superior Aircraft Materials)

12020 Centralia #G

Hawaiian Gardens CA 90716

Phone: (562)865-3220 or (800)488-9525

Offers: Balsa wood: sticks, wide sheets, "superlite," planks and others. Carries bargain balsa and birch plywood.

Catalog: Send SASE for price list.

UNIVERSAL HOVERCRAFT

P.O. Box 281

1204 Third St.

Cordova IL 61242

Offers: Plans for model hovercrafts, including air cushion vehicles that move inches above any surface, in a variety of types. Also offers full-size hovercraft plans.

Catalog: $2.

Model Making—General

Also see Miniature Making, Miniatures & Dollhouses; Model Making—Aircraft; Model Making—Railroad; other related categories.

A.J. FISHER, INC.
1002 Etowah Ave.
Royal Oak MI 48067
Phone: (248)541-0352
Offers: Model ship and yacht fittings to scratch build a competitive R/C model yacht in the 36/600, 1 meter, 50/800 or 10 rater class. Kits of Great Lakes and oceangoing vessels available, plus model-building plans and books.
Catalog: Illustrated. $3.

AE
(formerly Aerospace Composite Products)
14210 Doolittle Dr.
San Leandro CA 94577
Contact: Barbara Sparks
Phone: (510)352-2022
Fax: (510)352-2021
E-mail: info@acp-composites.com
Website: www.acp-composites.com
Store Location: At above address.
Offers: Composite materials: fiberglass, carbon fiber and Kevlar.
Catalog: Yes.
Phone Orders: Yes.
Mail Orders: Yes.
Discounts: Yes.
Accepts: all credit cards except Diners Club

APC HOBBIES
P.O. Box 122
Earlysville VA 22936
Phone: (804)973-2705
Offers: Model kits, including 2,000-plus old and out-of-production kits and new kits, including by Tamiya, Aoshima, Commanders ⅓₅, Mb ⅓₅₀, scale ships and Bandai ¼₄ and others.
Catalog: APC Full Line catalog, $4.50; old kit lists, $3 each.

APPLIED DESIGN CORP.
P.O. Box 3384
Torrance CA 90510
Contact: M. Nielson
Phone: (310)375-4120
Fax: (310)378-1590

Offers: Tools for model building, crafts and more: mini hand belt sander (adjustable tension), mini sandpaper strips, Mini-Glue Tips, T-bar aluminum sanding block (4½″, 11″, 22″), Ruff Stuff PSA sheet sandpaper (3 grits), mini compact hacksaw (10″ for wood, plastic and metal) and others.
Catalog: SASE or 75¢.
Phone Orders: Yes.
Mail Orders: Yes.
Discounts: 40% discount to dealers.
Accepts: check, money order

ERIC CLUTTON
913 Cedar Lane
Tullahoma TN 37388
Phone: (931)455-2256
Offers: P.A.W. diesels for model aircraft, 003-060, R/C and C/L. Also diesel fuel plus kits and plans for small R/C aircraft.
Catalog: Lists and information, $1.

FORMULA 1
5 Keane Ave.
Islington, Ontario M9B 2B6
Canada
Phone: (416)626-5781
Offers: Scale model classic racing and other cars by Tamiya, Fujimi, Hasegawa, Protar, Lemans Miniatures, Gunze, Modelers' and others.
Catalog: Free price list.
Accepts: American Express, MasterCard, Visa

GREAT PLANES MODEL DISTRIBUTORS COMPANY
P.O. Box 9021
2904 Research Rd.
Champaign IL 61826
Phone: (217)398-6300 or (800)637-7660
Fax: (217)398-1104
Offers: Model kits, including R/C cars, boats, airplanes, helicopters and accessories; model railroading, plastics, die-cast, roadracing and rockets. Tools, building supplies, activity crafts and science products also available. Carries publications, books and over 300 hobby lines, including the following brands: Great Planes (their own), Kyosho, O.S. Engines, Hobbico, Top Flight, U.S. AirCore, SuperTigre, DuraTrax, Heli-Max, DuraPlane, Dynaflite and OPS Engines. Call or write with inquiry.

I.H.S.
(formerly International Hobby Supply)
P.O. Box 426
Woodland Hills CA 91365
Contact: Steve Ginter
Phone: (818)886-0423
Fax: (818)886-2551
E-mail: plasticm@pacbell.net
Website: www.plasticmodels.com
Offers: Over 16,000 items, including a line of plastic model kits from most known manufacturers and a large selection of accessories, decals and books. Also offers science fiction items.
Catalog: 300 pages. $10 ($15 in Canada and Mexico).
Accepts: MasterCard, Visa, check

LIGHTSHEET SYSTEMS
319 Main Dunstable Rd.
Nashua NH 03062
Contact: Mike Emery
Phone: (603)595-7146
Fax: (603)595-7146
E-mail: trekfx@aol.com
Offers: Paper-thin electronic lighting film: neonlike white and blue lighting in dozens of standard sizes, which can be easily trimmed to size (even complex shapes). Ideal for models, props, miniatures, costumes and more. New for 1998: LightLine, 1.5 and 2.5mm diameter wirelike material based on LightSheet technology; flexible, holds its shape when bent and trims to any length. Supplier to TV/films: *Star Trek Deep Space Nine*, *Flubber* and many more.
Catalog: Free. Call or send SASE.
Phone Orders: C.O.D.
Mail Orders: Prepay with check or money order. Terms available to established clients.

MICRO-MARK
340-2449 Snyder Ave.
Berkeley Heights NJ 07922
Phone: (800)225-1066
Website: www.micromark.com
Offers: The most complete line of miniature, specialty and hard-to-find tools and supplies useful to hobbyists, miniaturists, crafters, jewelers and anyone else creating small objects and models. Our high-quality catalog shows more than 2,500 items, including miniature versions of power tools, which make difficult tasks go easy while providing excellent results. Normally, 98% of items are available from stock and shipped within 2 days after receipt of order.
Catalog: 80 pages. $1 ($2 outside US).
Accepts: American Express, MasterCard, Novus, Visa

NORTHEASTERN SCALE MODELS, INC.
99 Cross St.
Methuen MA 01844
Contact: Nancy Oriol
Phone: (978)688-6019

Fax: (978)794-9104
E-mail: nesm@tiac.net
Website: www.nesm.com
Store Location: At above address.
Offers: Model-building materials, laser-cut trims and miniature kits. Also model railroad items and laser-cut kits.
Catalog: $1.50 (refundable with first order).
Phone Orders: Accepted for credit card orders.
Mail Orders: Accepted for credit card orders and prepaid orders (check or money order).
Discounts: To legitimate dealers, distributors and manufacturers.
Accepts: MasterCard, Visa

OMNIMODELS
P.O. Box 708
Mahomet IL 61853-0708
Phone: (800)342-6464
Fax: (217)398-7731
Offers: OmniModels offers R/C car and airplane kits, plus parts, accessories, engines, radios and electronics by Dynaflite, Coverite, OmniModels, Sig Manufacturing, Trinity, Losi, Great Planes, Top Flight plus many other manufacturers.
Catalog: Free.
Phone Orders: Yes.
Mail Orders: At above address.
Accepts: Discover, MasterCard, Visa

PLASTRUCT, INC.
1020 S. Wallace Place
City of Industry CA 91748
Contact: Larry Patrick
Phone: (626)912-7016
Fax: (626)965-2036
E-mail: plastruct@aol.com
Offers: Scale plastic model parts for scratch model building. Over 3,500 products for model railroading, dollhouse, architectural and education.
Catalog: $5.
Phone Orders: 8-3.
Mail Orders: Yes.
Accepts: MasterCard, Visa

RESTORATION TRAIN PARTS
(formerly Chris Rossbach)
135 Richwood Dr.
Gloversville NY 12078
Contact: Chris Rossbach
Phone: (518)725-4446 (2-6 only, no night calls)
Offers: Large 1½" train parts catalog listing parts for standard, S and HO scale trains. Makes: Lionel, American Flyer, American Model Toy, Ives, Marx, Dorfan and Varney HO. Over 6,000 catalogs now sold. We stock over 20,000 parts, from small screws to carbon brushes, wheels and more. Minimum order is set at $35 less shipping.
Catalog: $18 prepaid.

RENÉ D. SERRAO
650 Ketch Harbour Rd.
Portuguese Cove, Nova Scotia B3V 1K1
Canada
Phone: (902)868-2954
Offers: Plans of America's Cup J Boats, ¾″ to 1′ scale; plans of America's Cup 12 metre, 1″ to 1′ scale. Plans of Canadian vessels including fishing boats and schooners.

SPAULDING TRADING AND SHIPPING
W290 County Rd. Q
Mindoro WI 54644
Phone: (608)857-3932
Fax: (608)857-3624
Offers: Model truck kits in 1/24 and 1/25 scales, current and discontinued kits, die-cast and plastic models, resin parts and truck books.
Catalog: $1.
Accepts: MasterCard, Visa

SPIVEY STORES-BERSTED HOBBY CRAFT
1303 Tuscaloosa Ave.
Birmingham AL 35211
Contact: Hal Spivey
Phone: (205)785-9690
Fax: (205)785-9692
Store Location: Western section.
Offers: Hobbies and trains, all sizes. Model airplanes, V/C and R/C, all types. Crafts, toys, 15,000 plaster molds—both 2nd and 3rd wax molds, wax, reed basket kits and birdhouse and bird feeder kits.
Catalog: Yes.
Phone Orders: Yes.
Mail Orders: Yes.
Discounts: Yes.
Accepts: all credit cards

TOWER HOBBIES
P.O. Box 9078
Champaign IL 61826
Phone: Order only: (800)637-4989; order assistance: (800)637-6050
Fax: (800)637-7303
Website: http://www.towerhobbies.com/
Offers: Tower offers over 10,000 R/C control products at the lowest possible prices for model cars, boats, airplanes, helicopters, engines and radios by over 300 manufacturers, including Tower Hobbies, Top Flight, O.S. Engines, Dura-Plane, Hobbico, Great Planes, U.S. Engines and SuperTigre.
Catalog: $3 or free with first order.
Phone Orders: Yes.
Mail Orders: At above address.
Accepts: Discover, MasterCard, Visa

VANTEC
460 Casa Real Placa
Nipomo CA 93444
Phone: (805)929-5055
Offers: R/C (18-channel) for boats, subs, robots, quarter scale, plus 6 servo channels for control surfaces, electric drive motors, proportional functions, and 8 momentary on-off functions for guns, torpedos, horns, cranes and sub diving pumps; has 4 key-on/key-off channels for lights and more.
Catalog: Specifications, $2.
Accepts: MasterCard, Visa

VINYLWRITE CUSTOM LETTERING
16043 Tulsa St.
Granada Hills CA 91344-5339
Contact: Cynthia
Phone: (818)363-7131
Fax: (818)363-7131
E-mail: vinylrt@relaypoint.net
Website: http://www.relaypoint.net/~vinylrt/
Offers: Custom lettering for model planes, boats and trains. Delivered prespaced and prealigned in premium cast vinyl only 2 mils thick. Choose from a wide array of type styles and colors in sizes ¼″-12″ in height. Information and sample available free for SASE (55¢). Custom scanning and cutting of your artwork also available.
Catalog: Free. Send #10 SASE (55¢).
Phone Orders: M-Th, 10-4 PST.
Mail Orders: Worldwide.
Accepts: check, money order

ZONA TOOL CO.
P.O. Box 502
Bethel CT 06801
Offers: Full line of razor saws, hand tools, pin vises and sawframes. Also Berna Assemblers Clamping System, which aids in the multiple clamping of model parts for assembly, gluing of miniatures and similar uses. Send SASE.
Discounts: Sells wholesale.

Model Making—Railroad

Also see Miniature Making, Miniatures & Dollhouses; Model Making—General; other related categories.

ASHLANDBARNS
990-CSS Butlercreek Rd.
Ashland OR 97520
Contact: Jay Wallace
Phone: (541)488-1541
Store Location: At above address.
Offers: Blueprints: 94 gorgeous barns, craft shops, garages with workshops, homes and hobby shops. Country styled.
Catalog: $5 (refunded with plan order).
Mail Orders: Yes.
Accepts: check, money order, cash

CABOOSE HOBBIES
500 S. Broadway
Denver CO 80209
Phone: (303)777-6766
Website: www.caboosehobbies.com
Offers: Model railroad items in all scales and gauges. Send SASE.

CENTRAL VALLEY
1203 Pike Lane
Oceano CA 93445
Phone: (805)489-8586
Offers: Model railroad kits in HO scale black, styrene plastic: Pratt truss bridges, single and double-track plate girder bridges, bridge tie sections, girders, fences, railings, steps, ladders, end beams and brake shoes (detailed).
Catalog: Contact dealer or send SASE.

DESIGN PRESERVATION MODELS
P.O. Box 66
Linn Creek MO 65052
Phone: (573)346-1234
Fax: (573)346-6700
Offers: Model kits, including buildings and other structures for towns and villages, and others.
Catalog: Color. $1.50 or 5 stamps.

GREEN FROG PRODUCTIONS LTD.
200 N. Cobb Pkwy., Suite 138
Marietta GA 30062
Contact: John M. Koch
Phone: (770)422-2220
Fax: (770)422-2467
E-mail: grnfrog@atl.mindspring.com
Website: http://www.greenfrog.com
Store Location: At above address.
Offers: Documentary subjects about railroading plus how-to about model railroading. All on video. Over 200 titles.
Catalog: Monthly issue.
Phone Orders: (800)227-1336.
Mail Orders: Will ship worldwide.
Discounts: Wholesale.
Accepts: American Express, Discover, MasterCard, Optima, Visa, check, money order

H&B PRECISION CARD MODELS
2026 Spring Branch Dr.
Vienna VA 22181
Phone: (703)281-0813
Fax: (703)281-0813
E-mail: 106022.2701@compuserve.com
Offers: Paper model kits for railroad buildings, in HO and N scale, including buildings, city blocks from German cities in N and Z scale, Australian HO and N scale model train accessories and others. Send #10 SASE.

LOCKWOOD PRODUCTS, INC.
5615 SW Willow Lane
Lake Oswego OR 97035
Contact: Cindy Lozeau
Phone: (503)635-8113
Fax: (503)635-2844
Website: www.thomasregister.com/loc-line
Offers: Loc-Line armature.
Catalog: Flyer available.
Discounts: Sells wholesale to legitimate businesses.

LOCOMOTIVE WORKSHOP
9 Rt. 520
Englishtown NJ 07726
Phone: (732)536-6873
Offers: Model railroad economy kits in O scale brass, plus scale and highrail. Also carries a wide range of O scale kits of Lobaugh and Loco Works parts for steam operation.
Catalog: Send large SASE for current newsletter.

DONALD B. MANLICK, MMR
2127 S. 11th St.
Manitowoc WI 54220-6513
Phone: (920)684-8688
Offers: Line of DM custom decals in HO, N, O and S scales. Send large SASE with double postage.

MINIATRONICS

561 Acorn St.
Deer Park NY 11729
Phone: (516)242-6464
Fax: (516)242-7796
Website: www.miniatronics.com
Offers: Electronics, including clear and colored incandescent lamps, micro mini connectors, blinker, flasher and standard LEDs, neonlike signs, power distribution blocks, terminal blocks, mini slide and toggle-type switches. Also miniature street and building lampposts and different types of lighting effects; flasher/beacons, incandescent flashers, strobes, and two-directional red warning light.
Catalog: $2 (refundable).
Accepts: American Express, Discover, MasterCard, Visa

NORTHEASTERN SCALE MODELS, INC.

99 Cross St.
Methuen MA 01844
Contact: Nancy Oriol
Phone: (978)688-6019
Fax: (978)794-9104
E-mail: nesm@tiac.net
Website: www.nesm.com
Store Location: At above address.
Offers: Model-building materials, laser-cut trims and miniature kits. Also model railroad items and laser-cut kits.
Catalog: $1.50 (refundable with first order).
Phone Orders: Accepted for credit card orders.
Mail Orders: Accepted for credit card orders and prepaid orders (check or money order).
Discounts: To legitimate dealers, distributors and manufacturers.
Accepts: MasterCard, Visa, check, money order

RAIL GRAPHICS

1183 N. Lancaster Circle
S. Elgin IL 60177
Phone: (847)742-5404
Fax: (847)742-5407
Offers: Custom decals from submitted artwork in sets for two model railroad cars; dimensional data for all eras; and computerized art and text services. Sizes for all scales. Send large SASE for free sample.

RAILS 'N SHAFTS

P.O. Box 300
Laurys Station PA 18059
Phone: (610)261-0133
Fax: (610)262-7962
Offers: Books on America's railroads, including B&O Steam, Canadian national railways, Chessie, C & NW power, Chicago's trains, Colorado rail, North Shore, diesel locomotive rosters, electric locomotive plans, Grand Trunk Western Guide to Tourist Railroads, Pennsylvania, Kansas City South-ern, Katy railroad, Lehigh and New England, MR Cyclopedia, Milwaukee electrics and rails, N&W, New York Central, Grand Central, Norfolk & Western, Old Dominion, passenger trains, cabooses, Mexican railroads, Red Arrow, St. Clair, Santa Fe Trails, Seaboard, Southern Pacific, trolleys, traction classics, Union Pacific and others.
Catalog: Send SASE.
Accepts: American Express, Discover, MasterCard, Visa

THE RED CABOOSE

23 W. 45th St. Downstairs
New York NY 10036
Contact: Allan Spitz
Phone: (212)575-0155
Fax: (212)575-0272
Store Location: At above address. M-F, 11-7; Sat, 11-6.
Offers: Model railroading equipment. Trains and their accessories in all scales and gauges, LGB to Z. American and European prototypes. Marklin specialists. Custom services: layout building, repairs and restorations. Airplane models: kits, die-cast, Herpa, Schabat, toy and model. Car models: plastic kits, Corgi, Schuco and die-cast. Military plastics. Scratch building supplies.
Phone Orders: Fax and phone order nationally and worldwide.
Mail Orders: Mail order nationally and worldwide.
Discounts: Retail sales.
Accepts: American Express, Discover, MasterCard, Visa, ATM, debit card

RESTORATION TRAIN PARTS

(formerly Chris Rossbach)
135 Richwood Dr.
Gloversville NY 12078
Contact: Chris Rossbach
Phone: (518)725-4446 (2-6 EST only, no night calls)
Offers: Large 1½″ train parts catalog listing parts for standard, S and HO scale trains. Makes: Lionel, American Flyer, American Model Toy, Ives, Marx, Dorfan and Varney HO. Over 6,000 catalogs now sold. We stock over 20,000 parts, from small screws to carbon brushes, wheels and more. Minimum order is set at $35 less shipping.
Catalog: $18 prepaid.

WOODLAND SCENICS

P.O. Box 98
Linn Creek MO 65052
Phone: (573)346-5555
Website: www.woodlandsenics.com
Offers: Model scenics, including turf and a variety of foilage and lichen in realistic colors. Carries decals—model graphics for letters, lines, numbers (any scale), dry transfers with authentic advertising, posters, signs and railroad heralds (full color).
Catalog: Contact your dealer or send 4 stamps for catalog.

Mold Crafts

Includes cake, candles, concrete, plaster, plastics. Also see Ceramics; Metalworking; Polymer Clay; Sculpture & Modeling; Paper Crafts & Papermaking; related categories.

AMERICAN ART CLAY CO., INC.
4717 W. 16th St.
Indianapolis IN 46222
Contact: Nancy Elliott
Phone: (317)244-6871 or (800)374-1600
Fax: (317)248-9300
E-mail: amacobrent@aol.com
Website: www.amaco.com
Offers: Craft supplies and modeling materials. Since 1919, AMACO has been a leading manufacturer of modeling clays, such as Permoplast, Plast-i-clay, Marblex and Mexican; modeling materials, including Friendly Plastic, FIMO, polymer clay Millefiori Canes, Quilt Squares, Designer Squares, Sculptamold, Claycrete and Super Dough. Also Rub 'n Buff and Brush 'n Leaf metallic finishes, Batikit fabric dyes, Cotton Press hand-cast cotton paper products, and push molds for use with polymer clays.
Catalog: Free.
Phone Orders: M-F, 8-5 EST.
Mail Orders: Prepayment required. Will ship to US and Canada.
Discounts: Manufacturer—sells through distributors.
Accepts: Discover, MasterCard, Visa

B&B HONEY FARM
Rt. 2, Box 245
Houston MN 55943
Contact: Bill or Robin
Phone: (507)896-3955
Fax: (507)896-4132
Store Location: Houston MN location.
Offers: Vast array of containers, glass and plastic for the herb, honey, candle and apple cider industries.
Catalog: Call for information.
Phone Orders: M-F, 7:30-5; Sat, 8-12 CST.
Mail Orders: Will ship UPS, parcel post or freight worldwide. Most orders shipped same day.
Discounts: Quantity discounts on all containers.
Accepts: MasterCard, Visa

THE BARKER CANDLE SUPPLY CO.
(formerly Barker Company)
15106 Tenth Ave. SW
Seattle WA 98166
Contact: Michelle Waye

Phone: (206)244-1835
Fax: (206)244-7334
E-mail: michelle@barkerco.com
Website: barkerco.com
Offers: Full line of candle-making supplies. Manufactures metal molds, over 100 sizes and shapes. Wax, additives, dyes, molds, equipment, beeswax, bayberry wax, books and more.
Catalog: Wholesale for businesses only.
Phone Orders: (800)543-0601.
Mail Orders: At above address.
Accepts: MasterCard, Visa

DICK BLICK
Dept. CB
P.O. Box 1267
Galesburg IL 61402-1267
Phone: (309)343-6181
Offers: Full line of art/sculpture and other materials and equipment: soapstone, alabaster, stone sculpture tool sets. Modeling: instant papier-mâchés, Sculptamold, plastercraft gauze, plaster of Paris (and molds), Sculpey, FIMO, modeling clays. Clays: Mexican pottery, Marblex, Westwood oven-craft, others. Also offers Egyptian paste, earthenware and other kitchen-fired clays, plus glazes, ceramic and modeling tools/sets and aids.
Accepts: American Express, Discover, MasterCard, Visa

BRUSHY MOUNTAIN BEE FARM, INC.
610 Bethany Church Rd.
Moravian Falls NC 28654
Contact: Sandy Forrest
Phone: (336)921-3640 or (800)233-7929
Fax: (336)921-2681
E-mail: sforrest@wilkes.net
Website: www.beeequipment.com
Store Location: Moravian Falls NC location.
Offers: Candle supplies, beeswax, soap-making supplies, molds, mead (wine) making equipment and beekeeping supplies.
Catalog: 76 pages, b&w and color. Free.
Phone Orders: (800)233-9729. M-F, 8:30-5 EST.
Mail Orders: Yes. Prepaid required. 2 weeks delivery time.
Discounts: Quantity discounts on some items.
Accepts: Discover, MasterCard, Visa

CANDLECHEM CO.
P.O. Box 705
32 Thayer Circle
Randolph MA 02368
Contact: Arnie Galina
Phone: (781)963-4161

Fax: (781)963-3440
E-mail: candlechem@aol.com
Website: www.alcasoft.com/candlechem
Store Location: 56 Intervale St., Brockton MA 02402.
Offers: Candle-making supplies, scents, dyes, pigments, waxes, wax additives, molds and wicking.
Catalog: $3.
Phone Orders: M-Sat, 9-5.
Mail Orders: Will ship to US and Canada. Foreign orders accepted.

THE CANDLE SHOP OF SQUIRES STREET SQUARE

52 Courtland St.
Rockford MI 49341
Contact: Pete Charnley
Phone: (616)866-4260
Store Location: At above address. M-S, 10:30-5:30.
Offers: Complete line of candle-making supplies.
Accepts: MasterCard, Visa

CASTINGS

P.O. Box 298
Eastsound WA 98245
Phone: (360)376-3266
Fax: (360)376-3280
Offers: Casting equipment and supplies for creating toy soldiers, Civil War figures/horses, cannons and weapons, cowboys, Indians and cavalrymen, plus action soldiers of WWI and WWII, aircraft, medieval horses/riders, Napoleonic foot soldiers, artillery and riders/horses. Also offers a German marching band mold, carousel molds, chess set molds (fantasy, Waterloo and King Richard's Court) and winter village molds (carolers, Santa, snowman, skaters, boy and girl on sleds and streetlamp). Carries paint kits for mold sets, complete introductory starter kits, casting metals and instruction booklets. Small vulcanizer for silicone rubber mold making from a master in an hour in the kitchen oven. Also RTV mold-making materials.
Catalog: Product information, $1.
Discounts: Quantity.

CASTOLITE

4915 Dean
Woodstock IL 60098
Phone: (815)338-4670
Offers: Liquid plastics for casting, coating, fiberglassing, reproducing and embedding, plus additives and fillers.
Catalog: $3.

CEMENTEX LATEX CORP.

121 Varick St.
New York NY 10013
Phone: (212)741-1770 or (800)782-9056
Fax: (212)627-2770
Offers: Natural latex molding compounds: high solids type with medium viscosity (brushable or sprayable) to cast plaster, Portland cement and some waxes; also carries a prevulcanized type. Stocks latex for casting hollow articles (pour into plaster mold—when used with filler, very hard articles may be obtained), plus 2-part RTV polysulfide rubber for flexible molds (pourable for casting plaster, cement and others). Manufactures and compounds natural and synthetic latex materials. Send SASE.

CHICAGO LATEX PRODUCTS, INC.

P.O. Box 395
Crystal Lake IL 60039
Phone: (815)459-9680
Fax: (815)459-8560
Offers: Latex for molding, sculpture, mâché, casting, coatings and adhesives, including 1-part natural or neoprene type, for figurines, displays, dolls and others. Call or write.

COOKIE MOLD CARVER

P.O. Box 25
Belleville IL 62222
Phone: (618)233-7689
Offers: Carved wooden molds for creating "edible art." Over 100 designs. Includes springerle presses, cookie/butter stamps and personalized birth and anniversary plaques.
Catalog: $2 (refundable).

CREATIVE PAPERCLAY CO., INC.

79 Daily Dr., Suite 101
Camarillo CA 93010
Contact: Michael Gerbasi
Phone: (805)484-6648
Fax: (805)484-8788
E-mail: webmaster@paperclay.com
Website: www.paperclay.com
Offers: Paperclay modeling material, molds for masks, doll heads and others, plus kits and books.
Catalog: Yes.
Phone Orders: (800)899-5952.
Mail Orders: Yes.
Accepts: MasterCard, Visa

GLORYBEE, INC.

120 N. Seneca Rd.
Eugene OR 97402
Contact: Shannon Arch
Phone: (800)456-7923
Fax: (541)689-9692
E-mail: sales@glorybee.com
Website: www.glorybee.com
Store Location: At above address. M-F, 9-5.
Offers: Complete line of candle- and soap-making supplies, including beeswax, paraffin, molds, wicking, candleholders, color chips, candle and soap fragrances, glycerin soap, soap-making oils, essential oils, books and lots more.
Catalog: 48 pages, color. Free.
Phone Orders: M-F, 8-5 PST.
Mail Orders: Ship in the US and internationally. Prepayment required. Allow 2-3 weeks for delivery.
Discounts: Sells wholesale to legitimate businesses.
Accepts: Discover, MasterCard, Visa

HONEYWAX/CANDLE-FLEX MOLDS

501 S. First St.

Hackensack MN 56452

Contact: Shawn Osburnsen

Phone: (800)880-7694, ext. 101

Fax: (218)675-6156

E-mail: honeywax@mannlakeltd.com

Website: http://www.mannlakeltd.com

Store Location: Showroom in Hackensack MN.

Offers: Easy-to-use, extremely detailed, long-lasting molds for candle making, plaster and soap making. Wax crystals in 6 colors and 100% beeswax, wicking and how-to books.

Catalog: Full color, wholesale and retail. Free.

Phone Orders: Yes. 24-hour service.

Mail Orders: At above address. Will ship worldwide.

Discounts: Wholesale available.

Accepts: Discover, MasterCard, Visa

KEMPER ENTERPRISES, INC.

(formerly Kemper Manufacturing Co.)

13595 12th St.

Chino CA 91710

Contact: Katie Munday

Phone: (800)388-5367 or (909)627-6191

Fax: (909)627-4008

E-mail: thetoolady@aol.com

Offers: Offers cake and candy-making decorator sets. Tools: flower and leaf cutting, rollers, mini ribbon sculpting, detail carving, bud-setter, others.

Catalog: Free. 70+ pages, color. Please send $1.50 for p&h.

Phone Orders: Customer service hours are M-F, 8-4:30 PST.

Mail Orders: Can expect order to ship within 2 days of receipt. Ship domestic and international through UPS.

Discounts: Sell wholesale to businesses. For account qualifications and status please contact.

Accepts: Discover, MasterCard, Visa, International Money Order, bank wire transfer in American dollars only

KATHRYN LUNA

24796 Sunstar Ln.

Dana Point CA 92629

Offers: Molds for casting/crafting beeswax, chalkware, chocolate or papier-mâché; available in antique replica and other holiday designs.

Catalog: $3 (refundable).

MAXANT INDUSTRIES

Dept. CDT

P.O. Box 454

Ayer MA 01432

Phone: (978)772-0576

Fax: (978)772-6365

Offers: Candle-making tanks, including double-wall water jacketed, electrically heated for pouring into molds or for dipping. Send SASE.

POURETTE MANUFACTURING CO.

P.O. Box 17056

1418 NW 53rd

Seattle WA 98107

Contact: Carol Behme or Mike Kouacs

Phone: (206)789-3188, ext. 14 or 17

Fax: (206)789-3640

E-mail: pourette@aol.com

Website: www.pourette.com

Store Location: Seattle WA location.

Offers: Full line of candle-making supplies, including metal, plastic, specialty and other molds, waxes, scents, colors, additives, glass containers and books.

Catalog: Free.

Phone Orders: Yes.

Mail Orders: Yes.

Discounts: 40% wholesale.

Accepts: American Express, MasterCard, Visa, check, money order, cash

THE SOAP SALOON

5710 Auburn Blvd., Suite 6

Sacramento CA 95841

Phone: (916)334-4894

Fax: (916)334-4897

Store Location: At above address.

Offers: Soap and candle supplies for the handmade soap and candle maker. Molds—soap and candle—oils, fragrances, books and videos. Ready-made glycerin soap, lotions and bubble bath ready to scent and color.

Catalog: $2.

Phone Orders: M-F, 8-5 PST.

Mail Orders: UPS and postal shipped daily.

Discounts: Volume.

Accepts: American Express, MasterCard, Visa

SPIVEY STORES-BERSTED HOBBY CRAFT

1303 Tuscaloosa Ave.

Birmingham AL 35211

Contact: Hal Spivey

Phone: (205)785-9690

Fax: (205)785-9692

Store Location: Western section.

Offers: Hobbies and trains, all sizes. Model airplanes, V/C and R/C, all types. Crafts, toys, 15,000 plaster molds—both 2nd and 3rd wax molds, wax, reed basket kits and birdhouse and bird feeder kits.

Catalog: Yes.

Phone Orders: Yes.

Mail Orders: Yes.

Discounts: Yes.

Accepts: all credit cards

SWEET CELEBRATIONS

P.O. Box 39426

Edina MN 55439

Phone: (800)328-6722

Offers: Line of cake- and candy-making molds, tools, pans, accessories, ornaments and books.

Catalog: $2.

VACUUM FORM

272 Morgan Hill Dr.
Lake Orion MI 48360
Contact: Doug Walsh
Phone: (248)391-2974
Fax: (248)391-8290
Offers: Construction plans and parts for larger vacuum form-ing machines. Build a machine yourself and save 80% off the cost of new equipment with the same performance. Construction plans for 2×2, 2×3 and 2×4 foot machines (sheet size). These are commercial-duty machines suitable for production or prototypes.

Catalog: Free brochure.

Phone Orders: 8-6 EST.

Mail Orders: Will ship anywhere.

Discounts: Will discount to dealers for resale.

Accepts: MasterCard, Visa, C.O.D.

Native American & Frontier Crafts

Also see Basketry & Seat Weaving; Bead Crafts; Leather Crafts; General Needlecraft Supplies.

ADVANCE CANVAS DESIGN
(formerly Earthworks)
33 N. Uncompahgre Ave.
Montrose CO 81401
Contact: Emma Kigar
Phone: (970)240-2111 or (800)288-3190
Fax: (970)240-2146
E-mail: advance@frontier.net
Website: www.advancecanvas.com
Store Location: At above address.
Offers: Authentic Native American tipis, playhouse tipis and yurts.
Catalog: Color, 12 pages. $2.
Phone Orders: M-F, 8-5 MST.
Mail Orders: Ships worldwide.
Discounts: To authorized dealers.
Accepts: American Express, MasterCard, Visa

BUFFALO TIPI POLE CO.
99 Raven Ridge
Sandpoint ID 83864
Contact: Dave
Phone: (208)263-6953
Fax: (208)265-2096
Offers: Native American tipis and reproduction items.
Catalog: $2.
Phone Orders: Yes.
Mail Orders: Yes.
Accepts: MasterCard, Visa

CHARLES A. CASPER
Rt. 1, Box 379
May TX 76857
Contact: Charles A. Casper
Phone: (915)643-2388
Store Location: At above address.
Offers: Native American peace pipe kits and peace pipe bowl molds (ceramic). Wooden stems.
Catalog: Send five 32¢ stamps.
Mail Orders: Will ship to US.
Discounts: 35% off list.

CRAZY CROW TRADING POST
P.O. Box 847
Pottsboro TX 75076
Phone: (903)786-2330

Fax: (903)786-9059
Offers: Beads, bone hairpipe, chevrons, tin cones, tacks and nails. Also offers knife blades and knife-making supplies, mandellas, rosettes, beaded strips and shawl fringes. Kits including breastplates, chokers, war bonnets, moccasins, bead looms, shawls, bustles, knives, fans and roaches, all with illustrated instructions. Native American clothing patterns, accessories, hats, war bonnets, porky roaches, sinew, claws, teeth, quills, hides and furs, feathers, broadcloth, German silver work and 18th and 19th century clothing also available.
Catalog: $3.
Discounts: Quantity.

EAGLE FEATHER TRADING POST
168 W. 12th St.
Ogden UT 84404
Phone: (801)393-3991
Fax: (801)745-0903
E-mail: eglcrafts@aol.com
Store Location: At above address. M-Sat, 9-6.
Offers: Native American craft supplies and kits, including single feather, beaded pouch, 17 chokers, 4 headdresses, bustles, necklaces, bandoliers, breastplates, bell sets and medicine pouches. Authentic clothing patterns are available for war shirts, frontiersmen's shirts, leather dresses and others. Beads available include bugle, striped pony and large holed beads; faceted glass and plastic, tile, loose and strung seed and trade beads. Conchos, tin cones and cowrie shells also available. Stocks scissors and glue, punches, awls, cutters, chisels, buckle blanks, fringes, blankets and books.
Catalog: 144 pages, color. $4.
Discounts: Quantity; teachers and institutions; sells wholesale to legitimate businesses.
Accepts: Discover, MasterCard, Visa

GREY OWL INDIAN CRAFT CO., INC.
P.O. Box 340468
13205 Merrick Blvd.
Jamaica NY 11434
Phone: (718)341-4000
Store Location: At above address.
Offers: Over 4,000 Native American and craft items, including costume kits and parts (roaches, headdresses and others), beading and beads (trade, seed, cut beads, crow, pony and brass), bone hairpipes, elk teeth, tin cones, feathers, shawl fringe, leathers (cowhide and others), furs, bones, skins, animal parts, blankets, videos and books.
Catalog: $3.
Discounts: Quantity; teachers and institutions; sells wholesale to businesses.
Accepts: American Express, Discover, MasterCard, Visa

PANTHER PRIMITIVES

P.O. Box 32-55

Normantown WV 25267

Phone: (304)462-7718

Offers: Tipi poles, lacing pins, instruction books (also ready-made items for store booths), waterproof canvas and cottons by the yard, frontier clothing kits and patterns, bead kits, plus beads, looms and supplies. Stocks bone choker kits, 15 flags (historical), tinware, oak kegs, wood buckets, metal tinder-boxes, candle molds, quills, quillwork kits and finished items.

Catalog: $2 (refundable).

Discounts: Sells wholesale to legitimate businesses.

Accepts: Discover, MasterCard, Visa

SAX ARTS & CRAFTS

P.O. Box 510710

2405 S. Calhoun Rd.

New Berlin WI 53151

Phone: (414)784-6880

Offers: Artist's supplies (known brands), including a full line of weaving looms and aids, yarns, weaving kits, rug/craft yarns, embroidery/crewel threads, rug hook frames and aids, canvas, hoops, burlap and felt. Indian beading, beads, feathers, macrame, basketry and batik supplies, fabric paints, airbrush kits and inks, stencil films, trims, foam, stained glass kits, etching and beveled glass supplies and supplies for decoupage, jewelry making, leather, casting, plastics, wood and metal working are also available.

Catalog: $5 (refundable).

Discounts: Quantity, sells wholesale to legitimate businesses.

STORMCLOUD TRADING CO.

725 Snelling Ave. N.

St. Paul MN 55104

Contact: Sandi Graves

Phone: (612)645-0343

Fax: (612)645-5745

E-mail: beadstorm@aol.com

Website: Under construction.

Store Location: At above address.

Offers: A large variety of beads and other craft supplies.

Catalog: Over 100 pages. $5 (refundable).

Phone Orders: Yes.

Mail Orders: Yes.

Discounts: 10% for professional discounts, 15-30% for quantities.

Accepts: Discover, MasterCard, Visa, check prepaid, C.O.D.

SWEET MEDICINE

P.O. Box 30128

Phoenix AZ 85046

Phone: (602)443-1127

Fax: (602)443-4337

Offers: Feathers, leather, beads, crystals, animal bones gourds, Pendleton blankets and more.

Catalog: Call or send $3.

Discounts: Sells wholesale to legitimate businesses.

VEON CREATIONS

3565 State Rd. V

DeSoto MO 63020

Contact: Char or Veon

Phone: (314)586-5377

Fax: (314)586-5377

E-mail: veonbds@jcn1.com

Website: www.jcn1.com/veonbds

Store Location: At above address. M-F, 11-7 CST.

Offers: Beads, beadworking supplies, jewelry findings, bead and crafts how-to books, American Indian heritage books and Indian craft supplies. *Creative Beaded Earrings*, Volumes 1-4 (retail and wholesale).

Catalog: Bead & Supplies, $4. Book, $4.

Phone Orders: M-F, 11-7 CST.

Mail Orders: Will ship to US and Canada. Prepaid required.

Discounts: Bulk discounts on beads. Wholesale Creative Beaded Earrings, Volumes 1-4.

Accepts: MasterCard, Visa, check, money order

WAKEDA TRADING POST

P.O. Box 19146

Sacramento CA 95819

Phone: (916)485-9838

E-mail: wakeda@pacbell.net

Offers: Native American crafts and garment patterns for authentic, Early American fur hats, shirts, pants, leggings, breechclouts, dresses, capotes, coats and accessories. Costume kits include chokers, war bonnets, quillwork, moccasins, fans, hair roaches, breechclouts. Carries shawls and metallic fringes, trade cloths, wool, calico, blankets, beads (seed, pony, iris, luster, crow, tile and others), bead supplies, looms, mirrors, brass nails, tin cones, buckles, metal spots and bells. Naturals available include sweet grass, ropes, sage, gourds and cedar. Also carries hides and furs including sheep, beaver, coyote, red fox and ermine, plus tails. Carries leathers for garment buckskins, thongs, straps, rawhide and latigo. Porcupine quills and teeth are also available.

Catalog: $2.

Discounts: Quantity; sometimes sells wholesale to legitimate businesses.

Accepts: MasterCard, Visa

Nature Crafts

Also see General Craft Supplies; Basketry & Seat Weaving; Miniature Making, Miniatures & Dollhouses; Model Making; Fabrics & Trims; other related categories.

ANGEL'S EARTH NATURAL PRODUCT INGREDIENTS
1633 Scheffer Ave.
St. Paul MN 55116
Contact: M. Miron
Phone: (612)698-3601
Fax: (612)398-3636
E-mail: a-earth@pconline.com
Website: Coming soon.
Offers: Soap, toiletries, cosmetic, candle and fragrancing ingredients, including essential/fragrance/vegetable/infused oils, colorants and micas, waxes, clays, herbs, salts, gums/resins and preservatives. Also packaging and labels, molds, kits, supplies, books, blank incense sticks, diffusers, herbal salves, gifts and more.
Catalog: Retail, $3; wholesale, $3 and business ID.
Phone Orders: Yes.
Mail Orders: Generally US and Canada. Overseas special arrangement.
Discounts: Write or E-mail for bulk quantity purchases.
Accepts: check, money order, C.O.D.

THE AROMATIC PLANT PROJECT
219 Carl St.
San Francisco CA 94117
Contact: Jeanne Rose
Phone: (415)564-7685
Fax: (415)564-6799
Offers: Essential oils and pure, fresh hydrosols.
Catalog: $2.50. 24 pages with newsletter on the latest info in aromatherapy.
Phone Orders: 24 hours.
Mail Orders: Yes.
Discounts: Up to 40% wholesale discount.
Accepts: MasterCard, Visa

ATLANTIC SPICE CO.
P.O. Box 205
North Truro MA 02652
Phone: (800)316-7965
Fax: (508)487-2550
Website: www.atlanticspice.com
Offers: Full line of herbs, spices and potpourri ingredients.
Catalog: Free.
Discounts: Quantity; sells wholesale.

DOROTHY BIDDLE SERVICE
348 Greeley Lake Rd.
Greeley PA 18425
Phone: (717)226-3239
Fax: (717)226-0349
Offers: Flower drying/arranging supplies/equipment: preservatives, floral clays, foam, picks, pins, wires, tapes, snips, flower presses, holders, beach pebbles, marble chips, moss, adhesives and silica gel. Also carries garden tools, accessories and books.
Catalog: 50¢.
Discounts: Quantity; teachers and institutions; sells wholesale to legitimate businesses.

CADILLAC MOUNTAIN FARM
4481 Porter Gulch Rd.
Aptos CA 95003
Phone: (408)476-9595
Offers: Dried flowers, herbs, exotics and supplies.
Catalog: Send SASE for list.
Discounts: Sells wholesale.

THE CANING SHOP
Dept. CSS
926 Gilman St.
Berkeley CA 94710
Phone: (800)544-3373
Fax: (510)527-7718
Website: http://www.caning.com
Store Location: At above address.
Offers: *The Complete Book of Gourd Craft*, a guide to gourd crafting that includes 22 projects, 55 techniques and 300 designs. Also includes color photographs of the work of over 120 contemporary artists and covers wood burning, carving, inlay and painting techniques. Carries a full line of basketry materials. Send SASE.
Accepts: MasterCard, Visa

EVERLASTINGS
20220 US 6
Milford IN 46542
Phone: (219)831-5763
Offers: Line of dried flowers, preserved greens and ferns in bunches. Also carries heather ti trees, hydrangea and peonies.
Catalog: Send SASE for price list. Does not offer shipping.

THE GINGER TREE
Dept. CSS
P.O. Box 595
Brooksville FL 34605-0595
Contact: Kathleen Meskil

Phone: (352)796-3201
Fax: (352)796-3201
Offers: Full line of potpourri and aromatherapy supplies, flowers, spices, fixatives, fragrance and essential oils, pourable resins, carrier oils and unscented bath and baby products. Also some packaging supplies, books and information sheets.
Catalog: $2. Contains much information.
Phone Orders: M-F, 10-7; Sat, 12-5 EST.
Mail Orders: Shipping to US; Canadian and foreign orders charge or advance arrangements.
Discounts: Wholesale to businesses; please send tax ID.
Accepts: Discover, MasterCard, Visa

GINGHAM 'N SPICE, LTD.

P.O. Box 88C
Gardenville PA 18926
Contact: Nancy Booth
Phone: (215)348-3595
Fax: (215)348-8021
E-mail: victoria@exsites-ltd.com
Website: http://www.exsites-ltd.com/mysweetvictoria
Offers: Fragrance and essential oils, carrier oils, rose and orange flower waters, beeswax, unscented lotion and bath gels, potpourri materials, bottles and storage containers and 2 books—*Scentsatious: 95 Recipes for Fragrance* and *Perfumes, Splashes and Colognes: How to Make, Wear and Select Fragrances.*
Catalog: $2 (refundable with purchase). Request fragrance and crafting catalog.
Phone Orders: Yes.
Mail Orders: At above address.
Accepts: MasterCard, Visa

HERBALLY YOURS, LTD.

P.O. Box 3074
Kamloops, British Columbia V2C 6B7
Canada
Phone: (250)554-4344
Fax: (250)554-4331
Offers: Full line of oils, including essential, specialty and fragrance types. Also offers muslin drawstring bags and gift items.

HOFFMAN HATCHERY

P.O. Box 129
Gratz PA 17030
Phone: (717)365-3694
Offers: Eggs (blown): goose, duck and turkey.
Catalog: Send SASE for price list.

J&T IMPORTS DRIED FLOWERS

143 S. Cedros Ave.
Solana Beach CA 92075
Contact: Joe Zucken
Phone: (619)481-9781
Fax: (619)481-0776
E-mail: j&timports@sd.znet.com
Website: www.driedflowers.com

Store Location: At above address.
Offers: Dried/preserved flowers/naturals. We carry over 250 dried and preserved flowers. Featuring recycling fountains. Also carry ribbons, silks and floral supplies.
Phone Orders: Yes.
Mail Orders: We ship UPS and US postal service.
Discounts: Quantity; teachers and institutions. Wholesale.
Accepts: Discover, MasterCard, Visa, check

LILY OF THE VALLEY

3969 Fox Ave.
Minerva OH 44657
Phone: (303)862-3920
Store Location: At above address.
Offers: Over 740 species of herbal plants, dried herbs—perennials, scented species, everlastings, rare and unusuals (including passion vine and carob) and others.
Catalog: Plant and product list, $1 (refundable).
Discounts: Quantity; sells wholesale to legitimate businesses.

MAKING THYME HERB SHOPPE

(formerly Herb Shoppe)
199 Madison Ave., Shop #2
Greenwood IN 46142
Contact: Deborah A. Wilson
Phone: (317)889-4395
Fax: (317)535-5833
E-mail: dwilson9600@aol.com
Store Location: At above address.
Offers: Bulk herbs, potpourri supplies, bulk teas, essential oils and herb bunch wreaths.
Catalog: $3 (refundable on first order).
Phone Orders: (317)889-4395. M-F.
Mail Orders: Ship to US and Canada. Prepayment. Allow 6-8 weeks for delivery.
Accepts: MasterCard, Visa

MCFADDEN'S VINES & WREATHS

330 Grindstaff Rd.
Butler TN 37640
Contact: Betty, Joe or Tammy McFadden
Phone: (423)768-2472
Store Location: At address above.
Offers: Unusual creations in appalachian "Curly Q" grapevine, brier, log moss and honeysuckle. Original flaired birch, hearts, ovals, round wreaths, evergreens and cones. Special orders considered. Satisfaction guaranteed.
Catalog: $1 or call above number.
Phone Orders: M-Sat, 7 a.m.-8 p.m. EST.
Mail Orders: Retail anywhere ASAP. No minimum.
Accepts: prepayment, C.O.D.

A MOMENT IN TIME BOTANICALS, INC.

6102 Avenida Encinas, Suite M
Carlsbad CA 92009
Contact: Kristin Sipe
Phone: (760)930-3456

Fax: (760)930-3455
E-mail: sales@momentintime.com
Store Location: 5600 Avenida Encinas #33, Carlsbad CA. M-F, 7-3:30 PST.
Offers: Kiln-dried, glycerin-preserved and freeze-dried flowers, foliages and fuits. Offered in bulk or consumer packs.
Catalog: Free.
Phone Orders: 7 days, 24 hours.
Mail Orders: Ship worldwide. Allow 1 week for delivery.
Discounts: Sell wholesale to legitimate businesses.
Accepts: American Express, Diners Club, Discover, Master-Card, Visa, C.O.D.

MOUNTAIN FARMS, INC.

307 Number Nine Rd.
Fairview NC 28730
Contact: Nancy Herbst
Phone: (800)628-4709
Fax: (800)393-3646
E-mail: mountainfarms@mindspring.com
Website: mountainfarms.home.mindspring.com
Offers: A complete line of dried and preserved flowers, roses, foliages, herbs, cones and pods for the floral trade.
Catalog: 32 pages, color. Free. Wholesale only, please.
Phone Orders: M-F, 9-5 EST.
Mail Orders: Will ship US. Prepayment required. Ships same day.
Accepts: American Express, Discover, MasterCard, Visa

NATURE'S HERB CO.

1010 46th St.
Emeryville CA 94608
Phone: (510)601-0700
Offers: Over 350 bulk spices and herbs, plus potpourri ingredients in bulk quantities; all products milled and blended in-house. Also has bulk teas and powdered botanicals, bulk gelatin capsules, and packaged teas and spices.
Catalog: Write or call for free catalog.
Discounts: Sells wholesale to businesses with resale license.

NATURE'S HOLLER

15739 Old Lowery Rd. N.
Omaha AR 72662
Contact: Michele or Mark Head
Phone: (870)426-5489
Store Location: At above address.
Offers: Naturals, wood crafts, decorated wreaths, arches, birdhouses and supplies.
Catalog: $2 ($1 refundable).
Phone Orders: M-F, 7-7 CST. C.O.D. first-time orders.
Mail Orders: Yes.
Discounts: 5-30%.
Accepts: check, money order, C.O.D.

NORTHWIND PUBLICATIONS

(formerly Northwind Farm Publications)
439 Ponderosa Way
Jemez Springs NM 87025-8036
Contact: Paula Oliver

Phone: (505)829-3448
Fax: (505)829-3449
E-mail: herbbiz@aol.com
Offers: We publish *The Business of Herbs*, a bimonthly journal for herb growers and serious herb enthusiasts. Cover all aspects of herb growing and marketing, including ornamental herbs, dried flowers, fragrant plants and culinary herbs. $24 (US) or $30 (Canada). Also publish *The Herb Resource Directory* with over 1,100 sources and resources for herb growers, crafters and designers.
Catalog: SASE (33¢).
Mail Orders: Yes.

OAK RIDGE FARMS

P.O. Box 28
Basking Ridge NJ 07920
Contact: Kate Ahrens
Phone: (908)766-2772
Fax: (908)953-9070
E-mail: oakridg@ix.netcom.com
Website: www.oakridgefarms.com
Offers: Dried flowers, herbs, ferns, fillers and preserved foliages. Full selection of finishing touches for floral design. Wreath and swag bases of every description. Wholesale prices to buyers of all sizes.
Catalog: Fully illustrated. Free.
Phone Orders: M-Sat, 9-5 EST or leave message for return call.
Mail Orders: Shipping worldwide.
Discounts: Large orders receive additional discounts.
Accepts: all major credit cards

OUR NEST EGG

205 S. Fifth
Mapleton, IA 51034
Phone: (712)882-1940
Offers: Natural eggs: ostrich, rhea, emu, goose and duck. Egg decorating materials: line of pearl and metal ornaments/findings. Tools: markers, cutters, drills and marker-units. Supplies: braids, ribbons, rhinestones, mirrors, adhesives, finishes, miniatures, hinges, hinge rings, brass tubes and rods. Carries 65-plus egg stands and books.
Catalog: $4.

PRIDE'S FARM

RR 2, Box 389
Lebanon ME 04027
Contact: Peggy Pride
Phone: (207)324-7167
Fax: (207)324-7167
E-mail: pfarm@gwi.net
Offers: Pressed flowers. Excellent quality guaranteed. Approximately 25 different flowers and foliage.
Catalog: B&w, free; color, $3.
Phone Orders: Yes.
Mail Orders: Will ship to US and Canada. Prepayment required.

Discounts: Sell wholesale; send certificate.
Accepts: check, money order

RAIN SHADOW LABS
P.O. Box 1125
Scappoose OR 97056
Contact: Customer service.
Phone: (800)543-9133
Fax: (503)543-3416
Website: www.raincountry.com
Offers: Manufacturers of natural-base bath, body and home fragrance products, lotions, spa crystals, glycerine soaps and more. Available in bulk and private label. Order stock products or custom. A wide assortment of choices to add to your own product base or expand your own line.
Catalog: Call for free catalog.
Phone Orders: Yes.
Discounts: Sells wholesale to businesses.
Accepts: American Express, Discovery, MasterCard, Visa

RAVEN'S NEST HERBALS
P.O. Box 370
Duluth GA 30096
Contact: Terry Cochran
Phone: (770)242-3901
Fax: (770)582-9879
E-mail: ravens@mindspring.com
Website: http://www.atl.mindspring.com/~ravens/rnest.htm
Offers: Herbs, spices, teas, extracts, fragrance and essential oils, henna, incense, pet products, gifts, bath products, theramune products, books and potpourri.
Catalog: Both wholesale and retail, $1.50 (refundable with order). 24 pages.
Phone Orders: 7 days a week, 9 a.m.-10 p.m. EST.
Mail Orders: At above address. Will ship internationally. Average 2-3 weeks delivery.
Discounts: On bulk orders. Free shipping on orders over $300.
Accepts: MasterCard, Visa, check, money order

SAN FRANCISCO HERB CO.
250 14th St.
San Francisco CA 94103
Contact: Neil Hanscomb
Phone: (415)861-7174
Fax: (415)861-4440
E-mail: comments@sfherb.com
Website: www.sfherb.com
Store Location: At above address.
Offers: Wholesale to the public for 25 years. Herbs, spices, tea, spice blends, potpourri ingredients and essential and fragrance oils.
Catalog: Free. 35 potpourri recipes included.
Phone Orders: 9-5 PST.
Mail Orders: Will ship worldwide.

Discounts: 5-pound and 25-pound discounts; freight allowance available.
Accepts: Discover, MasterCard, Visa

THE SEASHELL CO.
1104 East St.
Cape May NJ 08204
Contact: Ellie Stotz or Nanette Berg
Phone: (609)898-4466
Fax: (609)898-1460
E-mail: seashells@algorithms.com
Website: www.algorithms.com/users/seashells
Offers: Seashells, seashell jewelry and related items.
Catalog: 20 pages, full color. $2.
Phone Orders: M-F, 9-5 EST.
Mail Orders: Will ship worldwide. Prepayment required.
Discounts: To legitimate businesses.
Accepts: American Express, MasterCard, Visa

SHADY SIDE HERB FARM
P.O. Box 190459
Hungry Horse MT 59919
Contact: Amy Hinman-Shade
Phone: (406)387-4184
Fax: (406)387-4184
E-mail: herbfarm@digisys.net
Website: http://www.montanaweb.com/gardens/
Store Location: Coram MT location. T-Sat, 10-6 (June-Aug).
Offers: Montana-made gifts, soap-making supplies, essential oils, dried flowers and instruction.
Mail Orders: Will ship US and Canada. Please allow 4-6 weeks delivery.
Discounts: Wholesale discount to verified businesses.
Accepts: Discover, MasterCard, Visa, check, cash

THE SHELL FACTORY
2787 N. Tamiami Trail
North Ft. Myers FL 33908
Contact: Teri Karp
Phone: (888)4-SHELLS
Fax: (888)SHELLS-1
E-mail: shellfac@earthlink.net
Website: www.shellfactory.com
Store Location: At above address.
Offers: Millions of shells, packaged or individual; shell craft kits; shell craft instruction books; and unfinished resin products, such as stepping stones and garden critters.
Catalog: Free.
Phone Orders: (888)4-SHELLS, ext. 12.
Accepts: all major credit cards, C.O.D., net 30 with approved credit

SIMPLY DE-VINE
654 Kendall Rd.
Cave Junction OR 97523
Contact: Meri Gerber

Phone: (541)592-3752
Fax: (541)592-4424
Store Location: At above address (Foris Winery).
Offers: Grapevine wreaths: teardrops, heart, oval, matted back and others. Carries baskets, bundles and cane wreaths. Manufacturer. Special orders service.
Phone Orders: M-F, 8-5 PST.
Mail Orders: In the US. Allow 1-3 weeks for delivery.
Discounts: Wholesale.
Accepts: MasterCard, Visa

SUNFEATHER NATURAL SOAP CO.

1551 State Hwy. 72
Potsdam NY 13676
Phone: (315)265-3648
Fax: (315)265-2902
Offers: Soap-making kits, bulk soaps, supplies and books.
Catalog: Color. $2.

TOM THUMB WORKSHOPS

P.O. Box 357
14100 Lankford Hwy.
Mappsville VA 23407
Phone: (757)824-3507
Store Location: At above address.
Offers: Dried flowers, including herbs on stems, cockscomb, hydrangeas, lavender, pepper berries, tallow berries and mini-rosebuds. Cones and pods, including hemlock, bakuli, cedar, eucalyputus, lotus and nigella. Potpourri, including blackberry, royal lavendar, woods, roses and others. How-to literature for bath salts, lotions and creams. Plastic bags, cellophane and cloth bags, boxes, lotion bottles and cream jars. Mosses, wreaths, raffia and wire. Full line of herbs, spices and essential and fragance oils. Books.
Catalog: Free.
Discounts: Quantity.
Accepts: MasterCard, Visa

THE ULTIMATE HERB & SPICE SHOPPE

P.O. Box 395
203 Azalea
Duenweg MO 64841
Contact: Tina or Karen Ashworth
Phone: (417)782-0457
Fax: (417)782-7733

E-mail: herbshoppe@talleytech.com
Store Location: At above address.
Offers: Over 700 bulk herbs and spices, bulk teas and potpourris, botanical craft items in bulk, and oils and other supplies.
Catalog: $2 retail; $1 wholesale. Oils only.
Phone Orders: T-Sat, 10-6 CST.
Mail Orders: We will ship to US and Canada. Prepayment required; otherwise, C.O.D. Allow 1-2 weeks for delivery.
Discounts: Sell wholesale to legitimate businesses.

VAL'S NATURALS

3435 Pinedale Dr.
Lakeland FL 33811
Phone: (941)648-2320
Offers: Dried miniature roses, pepper berries and other naturals.
Catalog: Free catalog and price list.
Discounts: Sells wholesale.

WEST MOUNTAIN GOURD FARM

P.O. Box 1049
Gilmer TX 75644
Phone: (903)734-5204
Offers: Gourds in a wide range of shapes and sizes, cleaned and ready to paint or craft.
Catalog: $3.

WOODCREEK FARMS, INC.

12419 Jerry City Rd.
Cygnet OH 43413
Contact: Sales staff
Phone (800)664-1630
Fax: (419)655-2224
E-mail: woodcreek@wcnet.org
Website: www.woodcreekfarms.com
Store Location: At above address. M-F, 9-5 EST.
Offers: Dried flowers, herbs, wreaths, swags, assorted supplies, baskets and wall mounts. Everlasting dried flowers and herbs in plug trays. Live plants for spring planting.
Catalog: Free.
Phone Orders: M-F, 9-5 EST.
Mail Orders: UPS or mail. US or Canada. Prepayment to Canada. Short delivery time.
Discounts: We only sell wholesale; tax number needed.
Accepts: Discover, MasterCard, Visa

Paints, Finishes & Adhesives

Also see Artist's Supplies, Graphics & Printing; Tole & Decorative Crafts; other categories throughout the book.

ART ESSENTIALS OF NEW YORK, LTD.
3 Cross St.
Suffern NY 10901
Phone: (800)283-5323
Offers: Gold leaf, genuine and composition, sheets and rolls (22 and 23 karat patent, 22 and 23 karat glass type, white gold, French pale gold, lemon gold, gold metal or composition types). Also offers silver leaf. Supplies: gilding size and gilding knife, burnishing clay, and other tools and brushes. Carries technical books.
Catalog: Free.
Discounts: Quantity; teachers, institutions and professionals.

BENBOW CHEMICAL PACKAGING, INC.
935 E. Hiawatha Blvd.
Syracuse NY 13208
Phone: (315)474-8236
Fax: (315)478-1307
Offers: Fezandie & Sperrle dry pigments for artist's colors.
Catalog: Free price list.

CRESCENT BRONZE POWDER CO., INC.
3400 N. Avondale Ave.
Chicago IL 60618-5432
Contact: Monte Lazarus
Phone: (773)539-2441
Fax: (773)539-1131
Offers: Metallic pigment colors (112) including 86 metallics (28 gold shades), 14 pearlescent, 11 fluorescent and 1 phosphorescent. Metallic paints and lacquers, plus glitters, diamond dust, beads, bronzing liquids (heat resistant) epoxy-coated foil glitters, concrete finishes, aluminum paints, primers, clears, sealers and screen ink colors.
Catalog: Contact a dealer or request free color cards. Also price lists.
Phone Orders: M-F, 8-4 CST.
Mail Orders: Will ship to US and Canada. Prepayment for opening order.
Discounts: Sells wholesale to legitimate businesses.
Accepts: no credit cards

DELTA TECHNICAL COATINGS, INC.
2550 Pellissier Place
Whittier CA 90601-1505
Contact: Delta Customer Service Dept.
Phone: (562)695-7969 or (800)423-4135
Fax: (562)695-5157
E-mail: deltacrafts@aol.com
Offers: Ceramcoat acrylic paints, Air-Dry PermEnamel paints, stencils and transfers, Cherished Memories Stencils and Acid-Free Photo-Safe Paints, Stencil Magic stencils, stencil paint cremes and accessories and Fabric Paints.

GOLD LEAF & METALLIC POWDERS
74 Trinity Place, Suite 1200
New York NY 10006
Contact: Steve Martinez
Phone: (212)267-4900 or (800)322-0323
Fax: (212)608-4245
Store Location: At above address.
Offers: Imitation gold, German and Chinese, aluminum and copper leaf, real gold leaf, 22 and 23 karat and more. Beginners' gilder's kits.
Catalog: Send $2.
Phone Orders: Yes.
Mail Orders: Will ship to US and international.
Discounts: Wholesale.
Accepts: MasterCard, Visa, check, C.O.D., cash

SAX ARTS & CRAFTS
P.O. Box 510710
2405 S. Calhoun Rd.
New Berlin WI 53151
Phone: (414)784-6880
Offers: Artists' supplies (known brands), including paints, brushes, palette knives, boxes, organizers, trays, markers and pens. Also carries sumi supplies, airbrush kits/accessories and compressors, paints, inks, canvas, stretchers, tools, easels, boards, plus a full line of papers, boards, mats and cutters. Also offers frames, framing tools and supplies, knives, scissors, adhesives, paper cutters, waxers, glue guns, tapes, punches and pencils. Carries artists' aids such as mannequins and models. Drafting items, calligraphy and lettering tools, light boxes, mounting presses, film projectors, photography supplies, magnifier lamps and furniture are also available. Stocks block printing supplies and presses, etching and screenprinting items/kits, T-shirt printing machines, photo and speed screen supplies, videos (art and craft), filmstrips and books.
Catalog: $5 (refundable).
Discounts: Quantity; wholesale to legitimate resellers.
Accepts: American Express, Discover, MasterCard, Visa

SEPP LEAF PRODUCTS, INC.
381 Park Ave. S.
New York NY 10016
Contact: Peter Sepp

Phone: (212)683-2840
Fax: (212)725-0308
E-mail: sales@seppleaf.com
Website: seppleaf.com
Store Location: Showroom for trade at above address. M-F, 9-5.
Offers: The Sepp Gilding Workshop series of kits and a full range of genuine gold, silver and metal leaf, plus gilding supplies and tools. Liberon fine-finishing and restoration products, mica powders and Mixol tinting pastes complement the comprehensive group of products offered. Products sold wholesale to manufacturers, distributors and trade. Retail sales best serviced by local distributors.

Catalog: Available on request.
Phone Orders: M-F, 9-5.
Mail Orders: UPS shipping to trade, manufacturers and distributors.
Discounts: Wholesale distributor.
Accepts: American Express, MasterCard, Visa

U.S. BRONZE POWDERS, INC.
P.O. Box 31
408 Rt. 202
Flemington NJ 08822-0031
Phone: (908)782-5454
Offers: Aluminum, bronze and copper metallic pigments. Call our customer service department at (800)544-0186.

Paper Crafts & Papermaking

Also see General Craft Supplies; Artist's Supplies, Graphics & Printing; other categories throughout the book.

BEE PAPER CO.
P.O. Box 2366
Wayne NJ 07474
Offers: Aquabee plotter paper—for check plots, charts, graphs and more, available in grades from economy bond to 100% rag vellum. Sold by sheets or rolls or cut to specifications. Send SASE.

CANOY STUDIO
8570 NW Marshall
Portland OR 97229
Contact: Patrece Canoy
Phone: (503)292-6205
Fax: (503)291-1151
Store Location: At above address.
Offers: Processed paper pulp.
Catalog: Product flyer/order sheet.
Phone Orders: (503)292-6205 or (888)260-4889.
Mail Orders: At above address.
Discounts: Wholesale (art supply stores).
Accepts: check, money order

COLLAGE STUDIO
P.O. Box 3455
Sunriver OR 97707
Contact: Deborah Sprague
Phone: (541)593-6041
E-mail: paperfibe@aol.com
Website: http://members.aol.com/paperfibe/collage.html
Offers: Decorative and handmade papers, collage packs and kits, papermaking supplies, including moulds, deckles, cotton linter, Pearl-ex and more.
Catalog: Catalog with paper samples, $3. Collage grab bag with catalog, $10.
Phone Orders: 7 days, 24 hours.
Mail Orders: US and Canada.
Accepts: MasterCard, Visa, check, money order

COLOPHON BOOK ARTS SUPPLY
36 Ryan St. SE
Lacey WA 98503
Phone: (360)459-2940
Fax: (360)459-2945
Website: www.thegrid.net/colophon
Offers: Supplies and books for hand bookbinding, suminagashi and traditional paper marbling.

Catalog: $2 each.
Accepts: MasterCard, Visa

GOLD'S ARTWORKS, INC.
2100 N. Pine St.
Lumberton NC 28358
Phone: (800)356-2306
Offers: Line of papermaking products, including kits, molds, deckles, cotton pulp and pigments.
Catalog: Free.

GOOD STAMPS—STAMP GOODS
30901 Timberline Rd.
Willits CA 95490
Contact: Emmy Good
Phone: (707)459-9124
Fax: (707)459-5021
E-mail: gssg@pacific.net.com
Website: www.rubberstampgoods.com
Store Location: 56 Main St., Willits CA 95490.
Offers: Rubber stamps and supplies. The new Zig Zag greeting card. *A-Z: A Good Guide to Rubber Stamping* (activities and projects for using stamps in the classroom or home school).
Catalog: Catalog 6.5, $4.
Phone Orders: (800)637-6401.
Mail Orders: At Timberline Rd. address.
Accepts: American Express, Discover, MasterCard, Visa

GREEN SNEAKERS, INC.
P.O. Box 614
Bel Air MD 21014
Contact: Nick Romer
E-mail: nromer6844@aol.com
Offers: Kreate-A-Lope envelope maker and Kreate-A-Bag gift bag-making system.
Catalog: Send #10 SASE.

JACKSON STUDIO
3124 Sandage Ave.
Ft. Worth TX 76109
Contact: Sally Jackson or Len Lipsky
Phone: (817)923-9433
Fax: (817)923-9433
E-mail: serifm@fastlane.net
Store Location: At above address.
Offers: Book presses, flat file plans, marbled paper, handmade books, calligraphy and custom and Renaissance invitations.
Phone Orders: Yes.
Mail Orders: At above address.
Accepts: check, cash

LAKE CITY CRAFT CO.

Dept. 440
P.O. Box 2009
Nixa MO 65714
Phone: (417)725-8444
Fax: (417)725-8448
Website: www.quilling.com
Offers: Complete quilling line: paper, books, kits and tools.
Catalog: Color. $2 p&h.
Phone Orders: 8-4 CST.
Discounts: Sells wholesale to legitimate businesses.
Accepts: MasterCard, check, money order

LOOSE ENDS

P.O. Box 20310
Keizer OR 97307
Contact: Sandi Reinke
Phone: (503)390-7457
Fax: (503)390-4724
E-mail: info@4loosends.com
Website: www.4loosends.com
Offers: Handmade papers, blank journals, recycled papers, fragment collage kits, paper parts (handmade paper assortments), decorative fabric paper and botanical ribbons, organic textiles, dried florals, botanicals, shells, mosses and fossil leaves.
Catalog: 192 pages, color. $5.
Phone Orders: Ask for Clayton or Sarah.
Mail Orders: Ask for wholesale or retail price list.

GREG MARKIM, INC.

P.O. Box 13245
Milwaukee WI 53213
Contact: Kim Schiedermayer
Phone: (414)453-1480 or (800)453-1485
Fax: (414)453-1495
Offers: Arnold Grummer's EASY Paper-Making kits and supplies. Kits for home and classroom use; cotton linters; Double Deckle project templates, books, videos, skeleton leaves, botanicals and metallic dusts and sprinkles for papermaking.
Catalog: Send request and two first class stamps.
Phone Orders: (800)453-1485.
Mail Orders: At above address.
Discounts: For wholesale only. Send photocopy of business license and credit sheet. $100 minimum.
Accepts: MasterCard, Visa, check, money order

LEE S. MCDONALD, INC.

P.O. Box 264
523 Medford St.
Charlestown MA 02129
Contact: Emily Aydelott
Phone: (617)242-2505 or (888)627-2737
Fax: (617)242-8825
E-mail: mcpaper@aol.com
Offers: Hand papermaking supplies.
Catalog: Free.

Phone Orders: (888)627-2737.
Mail Orders: At above address.
Discounts: Wholesale discounts for resale stores.
Accepts: American Express, Discover, MasterCard, Visa, 2% net 30

MIZ BEARS CREATIONS

(formerly Simply Elegant Designs)
2248 Obispo Ave. #206
Signal Hill CA 90806
Contact: Nancy Long
Phone: (562)498-7168
Fax: (562)494-6795
E-mail: mizbearsakanancylong@worldnet.att.net
Store Location: At above address.
Offers: Craft and needlework pattern books, complete line of DMC floss, Papernayan Persian yarns, Erica Wilson Persian yarns, craft kits, memorybook cutouts, precut quilt designs, quilling papers and supplies. Paper-snipping patterns and designs as well as kits.
Catalog: $2 (refundable with first order).
Phone Orders: M-S, 9-6 PST.
Mail Orders: Will ship to Canada. All orders shipped within 24 hours of receipt. US Postal Service Priority or UPS ground.
Discounts: Wholesale to legitimate businesses.
Accepts: Discover, MasterCard, Visa, money order in US funds

JOHN NEAL, BOOKSELLER

1833 Spring Garden St.
Greensboro NC 27403
Phone: (336)272-6139 or (800)369-9598
Fax: (336)272-9015
Website: www.johnnealbooks.com
Offers: Book-arts books on bookbinding, paper crafting, calligraphy, lettering, layouts, marbling and others. Also offers supplies, including calligraphy and other pens and lettering, brushes, inks, gouache, gold leaf, fine papers, tools and light boxes.
Catalog: Free.
Discounts: Runs sales.

ORIGAMI USA

15 W. 77th St.
New York NY 10024-5192
Phone: (212)769-5635
Fax: (212)769-5668
Website: www.origami-usa.org
Offers: Origami books and instructional videos; a full range of origami papers from around the world.
Catalog: Write for a free catalog.
Accepts: MasterCard, Visa

PAPER ARTS MILL & STUDIO

930 W. 23rd St., Suite 16
Tempe AZ 85282-1820
Contact: C. Grey
Phone: (602)966-1998
Fax: (602)966-2628
E-mail: c.grey@paperarts.com
Website: www.paperarts.com
Store Location: At above address. T-Sat, 10-5:30.
Offers: Handmade, exotic, decorative, acid-free, Oriental and fine art papers from around the world. Paper swatches are available. Papermaking supplies, casting kits, on-site paper mill, linter, chemicals, moulds and deckles, made-to-order pulp, workshops and books. Bookbinding, tools, board, glue, headband, bone folders, linen cord, screw posts, eyelets and punches. Creative invitations, vellum envelopes and paper, wax and seals, custom embossers and custom stone chops personalized. Collage supplies, innovative gifts, deckled rulers and deckled scissors. Gift certificates.
Catalog: 40 pages. $2 (includes shipping). Fax or E-mail.
Mail Orders: Will ship to Canada and the US. No C.O.D. To insure accuracy, we accept only written orders by mail, fax or E-mail.
Discounts: Coupons sent to customers on our mailing list.
Accepts: American Express, MasterCard, Visa

QUILL-IT

P.O. Box 1304-CSS
Elmhurst IL 60126
Phone: (630)834-5371
Offers: Quilling papers (full line of colors and widths), kits, tools, fringers, miniature containers, shadow box and other frames and books.
Catalog: $1 (refundable).

SAX ARTS & CRAFTS

P.O. Box 510710
New Berlin WI 53151
Contact: Judy Nagel
Phone: (414)785-8494
Fax: (414)785-8418
E-mail: saxarts@execpc.com
Website: http://www.saxarts.com
Offers: Arts/crafts supplies. Papermaking: kits, vat, molds, felts, cotton linters, unbleached abaca pulp, methylcellulose and retention aid (for colors). Papers (in known brands): drawing, construction (regular and large), sulphite, Color Kraft, backgrounds, plus plates, bags, Origami packs and papers; features include fadeless colors, corrugation, borders, doilies, precut puzzle sheets, fluorescents, gummed, neons, flint, cellophanes (and colors), crepe and streamers, metallics, tissue (and pomps squares kits), Mod Podge art paper tape, velour, printing types and etching. Offers 11 rice papers—3 pads, 2 assortments—plus boards, scratchboards and books.
Catalog: $5 (refundable).
Discounts: Quantity; teachers and institutions; sells wholesale to businesses with retail licenses.
Accepts: American Express, Discover, MasterCard, Visa

STICKER PLANET

10736 Jefferson Blvd. #503
Culver City CA 90230
Contact: Customer service
Phone: (800)557-8678 (US) or (310)204-7060 (international)
Fax: (800)537-2260 (US) or (310)204-7072 (international)
E-mail: mail@stickerplanet.com
Website: www.stickerplanet.com
Store Location: Locations in Los Angeles and Santa Monica CA. Call for addresses and hours.
Offers: Santa Monica location features full line of scrapbooking supplies and rubber stamps. Both stores feature thousands of stickers. Mail-order catalog shows over 350 acid-free, high-quality sticker designs by famous manufacturers, for crafters and hobbyists.
Catalog: High quality, full color, 68 pages. $5 (refundable). Package includes 50 project ideas, how-to guide to sticker art, reusable storage pouch, plus free periodic catalog supplement mailings.
Phone Orders: M-F, 7-7; Sat-Sun, 8-3 PST.
Mail Orders: Will ship to US and international (additional fee). Prepayment required. Allow 1 week within US. No minimum order required.
Discounts: Volume and multiple-sticker discounts available. Will also sell wholesale to legitimate businesses.
Accepts: Discover, MasterCard, Visa, check, money order

TWINROCKER HANDMADE PAPER

P.O. Box 413
100 E. Third St.
Brookston IN 47923
Contact: Kathryn Clark
Phone: (765)563-3119
Fax: (765)563-8946
E-mail: twinrock@twinrocker.com
Website: www.twinrocker.com
Store Location: At above address.
Offers: Papermaking and bookbinding supplies: pulps, pigments, fibers, moulds, books, glues and others. Handmade papers for watercolor, drawing, printmaking, watercolor, stationery and invitations. Sizes from 3×4 up to 34×48 in all shapes and thicknesses. Swatch set of 65 papers, $20.
Catalog: Free papermaking supply catalog. Paper swatch set, $20.
Phone Orders: M-F, 8-5:30 EST.
Mail Orders: Everywhere in the world.
Discounts: Quantity discounts.
Accepts: all credit cards, C.O.D., prepayment

Photography

Also see Artist's Supplies, Graphics & Printing; other related categories.

AAA CAMERA EXCHANGE, INC.

43 Seventh Ave.
New York NY 10011
Contact: Sol Stein
Phone: (212)242-5800
Fax: (212)675-3957
Offers: Camera outfits: beginner—with camera, lens, film, tripod, gadget bag, strap and flash; Dream Kit and Deluxe SLR outfits—with choice/selection of cameras (Canon, Minolta, Fujica, Pentax, Olympus, Ricoh or Yashica). Cameras—these brands and also Chinon, Mamiya, Konica and others. ID cameras: Polaroids, Shackman and Beatti. Lenses: Leitz, Minox, Nikon, Minolta, Canon, Sigma, Soligor, Tamron and others.
Catalog: Send SASE or call for list.
Accepts: American Express, MasterCard, Visa

A&I CAMERA CLASSICS, LTD.

2 World Financial Center
New York NY 10281
Phone: (800)786-4695
Fax: (212)786-0825
Store Location: At above address.
Offers: Cameras/equipment: Canon, Nikon, Olympus, Pentax, Konica, Minolta, Yashica, Leica, Polaroid and others. Books, collectible cameras from Alpa to Zeiss available.
Catalog: Send SASE for list.
Accepts: American Express, Discover, MasterCard, Visa

B&H PHOTO-VIDEO

420 Ninth Ave.
New York NY 10001
Contact: Photo: J.J.; video/audio: Brent
Phone: (212)444-6600 or (800)947-9950
Fax: (212)239-7770
E-mail: webmaster@bhphotovideo.com (or visit website for topic-specific E-mail addresses)
Website: www.bhphotovideo.com
Store Location: At above address. M-Th, 9-7; Fri, 9-1; Sun, 10-5.
Offers: Photo, video, professional audio and electronic imaging equipment and accessories at extremely competitive prices. All brands in stock. Prices quoted over the phone.
Catalog: Yes.
Phone Orders: During store hours above.

Mail Orders: Shipped in USA and worldwide.
Discounts: Yes.
Accepts: American Express, Discover, MasterCard, Visa

BENDER PHOTOGRAPHIC, INC.

19691 Beaver Valley Rd.
Leavenworth WA 98826
Contact: Jay Bender
Phone: (509)763-2626
Fax: (509)763-1043
E-mail: info@benderphoto.com
Website: http://www.benderphoto.com
Offers: 4×5 and 8×10 view camera kits and accessories. Also pinhole photography kits and cameras.
Catalog: 16 pages. Free.
Phone Orders: (800)776-3199. M-S, 8 a.m.-9 p.m. PST.
Mail Orders: At above address. Prepayment required. Will ship anywhere. See website for rates.
Accepts: Discover, MasterCard, Visa, check, money order

BROMWELL MARKETING

3 Allegheny Center #111
Pittsburgh PA 15212
Phone: (412)321-4118
Offers: Cameras, equipment and supplies for large format: view cameras, lenses, tripods and a full line of accessories and specialty items.
Catalog: Free.

CALUMET PHOTOGRAPHIC

890 Supreme Dr.
Bensenville IL 60106
Phone: (800)CALUMET
Fax: (630)860-7105
Offers: Line of wet-side and dry-side darkroom items, including those manufactured by the company and other brands—Zone IV, Gravity Works and more; for any size darkroom.
Catalog: $5.

CAMBRIDGE CAMERA EXCHANGE, INC.

119 W. 17th St.
New York NY 10011
Phone: (212)675-8600
E-mail: cambridgecamera@juno.com
Website: cambridgeny.com
Offers: Cameras and equipment in known brands: Agfa-Gevaert, Bronica, Cambron, Canon, Casio, Chinon, Exakta, Fuji, Hasselblad, Kodak, Konica, Leica, Lindenblatt, Mamiya, Praktica, Ricoh, Rollei, Topcon, Vivitar, Contax/Yashica, Polaroid and Passport. Other imaging equipment, plus 4×5

and 8 × 10 cameras. Stocks lenses, flashes, exposure meters, tripods, darkroom equipment and used cameras.
Catalog: Free.
Discounts: Sells wholesale.
Accepts: American Express, Diners Club, Discover, Master-Card, Visa

VERONICA CASS, INC.

(formerly VC Photographic Art Supplies)
7506 New Jersey Ave.
Hudson FL 34667-3263
Phone: (813)863-2738
Fax: (813)862-3567
E-mail: veronicacassinc@worldnet.att.net
Store Location: At above address.
Offers: Photographic retouching and enhancements products, including b&w and color for negative and print. Materials include dyes, oils, acrylics, pencils, brushes and airbrushing. Books and videotapes. Classes available.
Catalog: Supply and school catalog available.
Phone Orders: Yes.
Mail Orders: Yes.
Accepts: American Express, Discover, MasterCard, Visa

CPM, INC.

10830 Sanden Dr.
Dallas TX 75238
Phone: (214)349-9799
Fax: (214)503-1557
Offers: Darkroom equipment, including water pressure and temperature controls, filters, faucets, sinks and drains, cabinets, exhaust and air-cleaning units. Also safelights, blackout material, studio prop-posing stools and tables, backdrops and supports, accessories and more.
Catalog: Delta 1 catalog available.

DORAN ENTERPRISES

2779 S. 34th St.
Milwaukee WI 53215
Phone: (414)645-0109
Fax: (414)645-1744
Offers: Over 100 models of darkroom products, including sheet and roll film processors, agitator, washers, safelights, fans and louvers, easels, dryers, cutters, rollers, trays, film tanks, accessories and more.
Catalog: Free.

FRANKLIN DISTRIBUTORS CORP.

P.O. Box 320
Denville NJ 07834
Contact: Alan Gill
Phone: (973)267-2710
Fax: (888)663-1643
Offers: Line of archival storage materials for slide, negative and print storage including Perma-Saf pages of polypropylene for file cabinets with hanging bars that insert into channels or punching for binders.
Catalog: Archival materials catalog.

Phone Orders: Yes.
Discounts: 10% discount for those who mention this publication.
Accepts: MasterCard, Visa, check, C.O.D

FUJI PHOTO FILM U.S.A., INC.

555 Taxter Rd.
Elmsford NY 10523
Phone: (914)789-8100
Website: www.fujifilm.com
Offers: Fuji film and cameras in a variety of sizes/types. For further information, contact dealer, call (800)800-FUJI or visit website.

MINOLTA CORP.

101 Williams Dr.
Ramsey NJ 07446
Phone: (201)825-4000
Website: minoltausa.com
Offers: Film cameras, digital cameras, binoculars, accessory lenses, photographic meters, 35mm and Advanced Photo System film, scanners and other consumer products and business equipment.

THE NEW WALL STREET CAMERA

(formerly Wall Street Camera)
82 Wall St.
New York NY 10005
Contact: Andy
Phone: (212)344-0011
Fax: (212)425-5999
Website: www.wallstreetcamera.com
Offers: Camera equipment by Bronica, Hasselblad, Rollei, Pentax, Mamiya, Canon and Leica. Press/view cameras: Omega, Contax, Nikon and Sinar. Also offers lenses and light meters (known brands), plus zoom outfits by Olympus and Minolta. Video camcorders and darkroom outfits (enlarger plus accessories) also available. Allows trade-ins of cameras for new models. Call.
Discounts: Below list prices.
Accepts: American Express, MasterCard, Visa

NEW YORK INSTITUTE OF PHOTOGRAPHY

211 E. 43rd St.
New York NY 10017
Phone: (212)867-8260
Website: www.nyip.com
Offers: Photography home study course—30-lesson program covering both the basics and advanced, professional aspects of photography. Includes a mini-course in video techniques, with training materials, cassette tape communication, and individual attention and constructive criticism to enhance learning.
Catalog: Free *Career Guide* and catalog. (800)336-NYIP.

NIKON, INC.
Consumer Relations
19601 Hamilton Ave.
Torrance CA 90502
Phone: (310)516-7124
Fax: (310)719-9782
Website: www.nikonusa.com
Offers: Photographic equipment, including the F5 camera, which shoots 8 perfectly auto focused frames per second and uses a 1,005-segment color-sensitive exposure system. Also, other cameras, lenses and accessories from Nikon's world-renowned total imaging system. In addition, digital cameras, film scanners, optics and equipment for industry and the life sciences, eyewear, binoculars, scopes, underwater imaging equipment and instruments for surveyors and eye doctors. For more information, contact your Nikon dealer.
Catalog: Call for Nikon Consumer Product Guide.

PHOTOGRAPHER'S EDGE, INC.
855-C Garden of the Gods Rd.
Colorado Springs CO 80907
Phone: (800)550-9254
Fax: (800)964-1246
Store Location: At above address. M-F, 8:30-4:30.
Offers: Do-it-yourself greeting cards for nature photographers. For personal use, gifts or a business opportunity.
Catalog: Free catalog and samples upon request.
Phone Orders: M-F, 8-5 MST.
Mail Orders: No C.O.D. Allow up to 2½ weeks delivery time.
Discounts: Pricing structure allows for discounts with volume per order.
Accepts: Discover, MasterCard, Visa, check, money order

PHOTOGRAPHERS FORMULARY
P.O. Box 950
Condon MT 59826
Contact: Lynn Wilson
Phone: (800)922-5255
Fax: (406)754-2896
E-mail: formulary@montana.com
Website: http://www.photoformulary.com
Store Location: HC 31 Box 89, Condon MT 59826.
Offers: Full and complete line of photographic chemicals for processing and printing. Cyanotype and Van Dyke kits for transfer of negative images onto fabric. Blue and brown printing on fabric using negatives. Family heirlooms are made with these processes.
Catalog: Yes.
Mail Orders: Yes.
Discounts: For large quantity—to be determined. We do have dealer programs.
Accepts: all major credit cards

THE PIERCE CO.
9801 Nicollet
Minneapolis MN 55420
Phone: (612)884-1991 or (800)338-9801
Website: www.pierce-artery.com
Offers: Photography studio products: painted backgrounds (25 including scenics), photography supplies, photo albums and mounts, drapes, printed forms, poly bags, toys and others.
Catalog: Free.

PNTA (PACIFIC NORTHWEST THEATRE ASSOCIATES)
333 Westlake Ave. N.
Seattle WA 98109
Phone: (206)622-7850 or (800)622-7850
Fax: (206)628-3162
E-mail: sales@pnta.com
Website: www.pnta.com
Store Location: At above address.
Offers: Full line of theatre, stage and studio supplies, including scenic paints, fabrics, hardware, books and materials. Thermoplastics, including nontoxic, workable fabric-form, sheets and pellets for modeling and free-form sculpture are also available. Colors include gold leaf, bronzing powders, fiber dyes, fluorescents and others. We also carry makeup material and tools, books on making theatre props, masks, scenic design, lighting and more.
Catalog: Free. 104 pages.
Phone Orders: M-F, 9-6; Sat, 11-5.
Mail Orders: Prepayment required. Same-day shipping on most orders placed by 1 p.m.
Accepts: MasterCard, Visa, P.O. on approved credit

SHOOTERS OF USA LAB
P.O. Box 8640
Rolling Meadows IL 60008
Contact: Nick Patec
Phone: (847)934-2000
Fax: (847)934-2008
Website: www.shooterslab.com
Offers: 20 × 30 custom enlargements $9.98 from any size negative.
Catalog: 16 pages for mail order.
Phone Orders: (847)956-1010. M-F, 9-6.
Discounts: Maximum 40% professional photographers.
Accepts: MasterCard, Visa

THOMAS INSTRUMENT CO., INC.
1313 Belleview Ave.
Charlottesville VA 22901
Phone: (804)977-8150
Fax: (804)977-8151
Offers: Duplex Super Safelight, a darkroom light with monochromatic light source and special filters to give soft light. Others. Contact dealer, or call/write for details.

Polymer Clay

Also see General Craft Supplies; Jewelry Making & Lapidary; Mold Crafts.

AMERICAN ART CLAY CO., INC.
4717 W. 16th St.
Indianapolis IN 46222
Contact: Nancy Elliott
Phone: (317)244-6871 or (800)374-1600
Fax: (317)248-9300
E-mail: amacobrent@aol.com
Website: www.amaco.com
Offers: Craft supplies and modeling materials. Since 1919, AMACO has been a leading manufacturer of modeling clays, such as Permoplast, Plast-i-clay, Marblex and Mexican; modeling materials, including Friendly Plastic, FIMO, polymer clay Millefiori Canes, Quilt Squares, Designer Squares, Sculptamold, Claycrete and Super Dough. Also Rub 'n Buff and Brush 'n Leaf metallic finishes, Batikit fabric dyes, Cotton Press hand-cast cotton paper products, and push molds for use with polymer clays.
Catalog: Free.
Phone Orders: M-F, 8-5 EST.
Mail Orders: Prepayment required. Will ship to US and Canada.
Discounts: Manufacturer—sells through distributors.
Accepts: Discover, MasterCard, Visa

THE ART STORE
935 Erie Blvd. E.
Syracuse NY 13210
Phone: (315)474-1000
Offers: Fiber arts/crafts supplies and equipment: Jacquard textile and silk paints, screen printing, marbling, FIMO, Sculpey, tie-dye, Procion dye, Jo Sonya and brushes.
Catalog: Complete list, $3.

DICK BLICK
Dept. CB
P.O. Box 1267
Galesburg IL 61402-1267
Phone: (309)343-6181
Offers: Full line of art/sculpture and other materials and equipment: soapstone, alabaster and stone sculpture tool sets. Modeling: instant papier-mâchés, Sculptamold, plastercraft gauze, plaster of Paris (and molds), Sculpey, FIMO and modeling clays. Clays: Mexican pottery, Marblex, Westwood ovencraft and others. Also offers Egyptian paste, earthenware and other kitchen-fired clays, plus glazes, ceramic and modeling tools/sets and aids.
Accepts: American Express, Discover, MasterCard, Visa

GAMEPLAN VIDEOS
(formerly Gameplan/Abstract Change)
2233 McKinley Ave.
Berkeley CA 94703
Phone: (510)843-9969
Offers: Videos on polymer clay crafting.

KEMPER ENTERPRISES, INC.
13595 12th St.
Chino CA 91710
Contact: Katie Munday
Phone: (800)388-5367 or (909)627-6191
Fax: (909)627-4008
E-mail: thetoolady@aol.com
Offers: Imaginaries There Is No Limit, a new product line for children that includes the "Too Much Fun" klay pen kits and storybook finger puppet kits, which develop imagination. Designer and manufacturer of clay and paint tools for children, including the art notebook and tools for polymer clay, including the klay gun and pattern cutters. Distributes Cernit, the hardest baking polymer clay with new "natures colors" and "metallics."
Catalog: Free. 70+ pages, color. $1.50 for p&h.
Phone Orders: Customer service hours are M-F, 8-4:30 PST.
Mail Orders: Can expect order to ship within 2 days of receipt. Ship domestic and international through UPS.
Discounts: Sell wholesale to businesses. For account qualifications and status please contact.
Accepts: Discover, MasterCard, Visa, International Money Order, bank wire transfer in American dollars only

POLYFORM PRODUCTS COMPANY, INC.
1901 Estes Ave.
Elk Grove Village IL 60007
Contact: Jan Walcott
Phone: (847)427-0020
Fax: (847)427-0426
Website: www.sculpey.com
Offers: Polymer clays, kits, multi-packs, glazes and diluents.
Catalog: Free. 12 pages, color.
Phone Orders: M-F, 8-5 CST.
Mail Orders: Will ship to US and internationally.
Discounts: Sells wholesale to legitimate distributors.
Accepts: MasterCard, Visa

Rubber Stamping & Stamp Making

Also see General Craft Supplies; Artist's Supplies, Graphic & Printing; Paints, Finishes & Adhesives; Paper Crafts & Papermaking; Fabric Decorating; Scrapbooking.

A.I.P.
P.O. Box 163 TCB
West Orange NJ 07052
Contact: Joan-Marie or Mary Ann
Phone: (973)736-8023
Fax: (973)736-0440
E-mail: aipsvips@aol.com
Store Location: 516 Pleasant Valley Way, West Orange NJ 07052. Call for hours. Open Saturdays.
Offers: Original art rubber stamp line, custom stamps, accessories and matchbook notepads.
Catalog: $3 for A.I.P.'s-V.I.P.'s original stamps only and some accessories.
Phone Orders: M-F, 9-5 EST. Minimum order required.
Mail Orders: USA only. No C.O.D. Shipped in 5-7 working days.
Discounts: Only to retail storefronts.
Accepts: MasterCard, Visa, check, money order

À LA ART STAMPCRAFTERS
37500 N. Industrial Pkwy.
Willoughby OH 44094
Contact: Bruce Powell
Phone: (440)942-7885
Fax: (440)942-7888
E-mail: alaart@en.com
Store Location: At above address. M-F, 8-5.
Offers: Manufactures art rubber stamps. Sells wholesale and mail-order retail.
Catalog: $4.50 (refundable).
Phone Orders: M-F, 8-5 EST.
Mail Orders: Shipped worldwide in 48 hours.
Discounts: Sell wholesale to qualified accounts.
Accepts: MasterCard, Visa

A.T.A.P. MARKING PRODUCTS
435 N. Union Blvd.
Colorado Springs CO 80909
Contact: Larry Liska
Phone: (719)636-1020 or (719)636-1021
Fax: (719)636-2051
Store Location: At above address.
Offers: Rubber stamps, art stamps, laser engraving and campaign and school buttons in 3 sizes (1¼, 2½ and 3). Full color

transfer on cloth, coffee cups and photo stamps (a stamp made from a picture, picture is returned).
Catalog: Art stamp catalog, $5.
Phone Orders: Prepayment is needed.
Mail Orders: With payment.
Discounts: Wholesale large orders.
Accepts: MasterCard, Visa

ALEXTAMPING RUBBER STAMP ART
P.O. Box 742
Soulsbyville CA 95372
Contact: Karen Canto
Phone: (209)533-1834
Fax: (209)533-1746
E-mail: alext@mlode.com
Offers: Rubber stamp art—original designs and accessories.
Catalog: $3.
Phone Orders: M-S, 9-6 PST.
Mail Orders: Will ship to US and Canada.
Discounts: Wholesale to store owners.
Accepts: Discover, MasterCard, Visa

AMPERSAND PRESS
750 Lake St.
Port Townsend WA 98368
Contact: Amy Mook
Phone: (360)379-5187
Fax: (360)379-0324
E-mail: mooburg@olympus.net
Website: www.ampersandpress.com
Offers: Rubber stamps: wildlife animals and garden-themed images.
Catalog: Free. 10 pages.
Phone Orders: M-F, 9-5 PST.
Mail Orders: Prepayment required. Will ship anywhere. Orders shipped in 24 hours.
Discounts: Wholesale to legitimate businesses.
Accepts: American Express, MasterCard, Visa

ANNE-MADE DESIGNS
P.O. Box 697-S
214 Union St.
Erwin TN 37650
Contact: Anne Olney, owner
Phone: (423)743-8596
Store Location: At above address. Call for appointment.
Offers: 9,230 rubber stamp designs available both mounted and unmounted. Limited supplies of stamp pads, embossing powders and mounting cushion. Custom-made stamps available. May 1998 marked our 25th anniversary selling rubber stamps by mail.

Catalog: 258 pages. $8.50 prepaid, with free 3×5 card of unmounted stamps.
Phone Orders: Wholesale only; net 30 days.
Mail Orders: Yes.
Discounts: Wholesale orders to stamp and gift stores.
Accepts: check, money order, cash (no credit cards)

ANN-TICIPATIONS
6852 Pacific Ave., Suite D
Stockton CA 95207
Contact: Ann Stevenson
Phone: (209)952-5538
Fax: (800)809-5054
E-mail: ann-t@concentric.net
Offers: We offer a wide variety of top-quality rubber stamps that are very interactive. Hand-stamped samples that help increase and promote sales are available to retail stores.
Catalog: $5.
Phone Orders: Yes.
Mail Orders: Yes.
Accepts: MasterCard, Visa, check, net 30 available with credit approval

THE ANTIQUARIAN'S IMPRESSIONS
475 N. 1075 W.
Angola IN 46703
Contact: Bobbie Likens
E-mail: bdlikens@locl.net
Offers: Catalog of rubber stamps, mostly old-fashioned images in a variety of themes.
Catalog: $3 (nonrefundable).
Mail Orders: Prepayment required. No wholesale.
Accepts: MasterCard, Visa, check

ART GONE WILD!
3110 Payne Ave.
Cleveland OH 44114
Contact: Margaret Hamge or Ted Cutts
Phone: (800)945-3980
Fax: (888)401-2979
E-mail: artgwild@aol.com
Offers: Stamp manufacturer.
Catalog: $6. 140 pages, full color (refund with $30 purchase).
Phone Orders: Yes.
Mail Orders: Yes.
Accepts: American Express, Discover, MasterCard, Visa, check, money order

ART IMPRESSIONS
6079 Trail Ave. NE
Keizer OR 97303
Contact: Pauline (retail) or Betty (wholesale)
Phone: (800)393-2014
Fax: (503)393-7956
Store Location: At above address. M-Sat, 9:30-6.
Offers: All artistic rubber stamps and related supplies. Over 100 companies. Factory seconds on Art Impressions stamps. Unmounted Art Impressions stamps.
Catalog: $4.50, or free with current business license.
Phone Orders: Not retail.
Mail Orders: Not retail.
Accepts: Discover, MasterCard, Visa

THE ARTIST STAMPS
1535 N. Niagara St.
Burbank CA 91505-1653
Contact: Pat Spinoso
Phone: (818)845-6704
Fax: (818)563-2762
E-mail: theartiststps@theartiststamps.com
Website: www.theartiststamps.com
Offers: Wholesale and retail. Sample cards sent with wholesale order.
Catalog: $3 US, $4 overseas and Canada.
Phone Orders: Fax orders anytime; phone 8-8 PST.
Mail Orders: Allow 2 weeks for delivery. Free shipping with prepaid $200 wholesale orders.
Accepts: American Express, MasterCard, Visa

ARTISTIC STAMP EXCHANGE (A.S.E.)
5580 Havana St. #3A
Denver CO 80239
Contact: Gary Walker
Phone: (303)371-1260
Fax: (303)371-0675
E-mail: stamperII@suna.com
Offers: Rubber stamps, stamp pads, trophies, plaques, art markers, embossing powders, engraving, glitter, scissors and other numerous art accessories along with custom laser-cut items and labels.
Catalog: $7 plus p&h.
Phone Orders: Yes.
Mail Orders: At above address.
Discounts: Wholesale order by request.
Accepts: Discover, MasterCard, Visa

BARTHOLOMEW'S INK RUBBER STAMPS
P.O. Box 359
Warner NH 03278
Contact: Sandy Bartholomew
Phone: (603)456-2056
Fax: (603)456-2056
E-mail: beezink@conknet.com
Offers: Mystery-themed original rubber stamps and accessories.
Catalog: $3.
Phone Orders: Fax orders accepted anytime.
Mail Orders: Will ship anywhere on earth.
Discounts: Sells wholesale to storefronts.
Accepts: MasterCard, Visa, check, money order

BIZZARRO RUBBER STAMPS

P.O. Box 292
Greenville RI 02828
Contact: Doreen Tirocchi
Phone: (401)231-8777
Fax: (401)231-4770
E-mail: bizzaroinc@earthlink.net
Website: http://www.newenglandcrafts.com/bizzaro/bizindex.htm
Offers: Design rubber stamps: sports figures, map of US, alphabet stamp sets and others. Supplies include embossing powders and rainbow stamp pads. Also offers *How to Use Rubber Stamps* books.
Catalog: $3.
Phone Orders: M-F, 9-4 EST.
Mail Orders: US, Canada, UK, Europe, Japan and some Middle East and Asia.
Discounts: Wholesale to businesses.
Accepts: MasterCard, Visa

BLACKBERRY CREEK

9477 W. 9505
Covington IN 47932
Contact: Pat Huffman
Phone: (765)693-4571
E-mail: patony@localline.com
Offers: Crafters' hangtags, business cards, custom tags, rubber stamps and patterns.
Catalog: 24 pages, plus supplement. $2 (refundable).
Phone Orders: Evenings and weekends.
Mail Orders: Will ship to Canada and overseas (with credit card orders).
Discounts: Wholesale to businesses, include copy of retail license with catalog request.
Accepts: MasterCard, Visa, check, money order

CAT DANCING DESIGN

P.O. Box 369
Gilroy CA 95021-0369
Contact: Cathy Marshall
Offers: Artistic rubber stamps and Memories ink pads. We offer rubber stamps mounted on wood or unmounted at half the price.
Catalog: $3 (refundable with $20 purchase).
Mail Orders: Prepayment required. Allow 2-4 weeks for delivery.
Discounts: Sells wholesale to legitimate businesses.

CeMe

647 Canyon View Rd.
Bozeman MT 59715
Contact: Roma (406)585-9118 or Sindi (801)782-7497
E-mail: byerly@imt.net (Roma) or haslerw@jcave.com (Sindi)
Offers: Mounted or unmounted stamps that are deeply etched for quality images. Low-cost embossing powders.
Catalog: $3 (refundable).

Mail Orders: Prepaid. Allow 2-3 weeks delivery. US or Canada.
Discounts: For stamp of the month, big orders and wholesale to businesses with resale license.

CLĀCRITTER DESIGNS

White Rabbit Ridge
575 Plainview Rd.
Wimberley TX 78676-9614
Contact: Leslie Falteisek
Phone: (830)833-2585
Fax: (830)833-2585
Store Location: At above address.
Offers: Realistically drawn animal rubber stamps and address stamps. Also custom work. Dogs, cats, horses, cattle, sheep, goats, pigs and wild animals from fin to fur.
Catalog: 36 pages. $2 (refundable).
Phone Orders: With follow-up payment.
Mail Orders: Ship worldwide.
Discounts: 50% wholesale; 30% breed clubs.
Accepts: check, money order

CLASSIC STATUS STAMP CO.

205 Stover Rd.
Charlevoix MI 49720
Contact: Steve Toornman
Phone: (616)547-9784
Fax: (616)547-9784
E-mail: rclassic@freeway.net
Website: www.classicstatus.com
Offers: World's largest collection of auto and motorcycle stamps. American road nostalgia stamps, reptile stamps and others.
Catalog: $3.
Phone Orders: Yes.
Mail Orders: Yes.
Discounts: Wholesale 50%.
Accepts: MasterCard, Visa

A COUNTRY WELCOME

P.O. Box 128
Sweet Home OR 97386
Contact: Vicki Sele or Kirsten Offutt
Phone: (541)367-3986
E-mail: kv@acountrywelcome.com
Store Location: At above address.
Offers: Rubber stamps, mounted and unmounted, and supplies. We are an angel company.
Catalog: $3 (refundable with minimum $20 first order).
Phone Orders: M-F, 9-5 PST.
Mail Orders: We ship to US and international. Prepayment required.
Discounts: Sells wholesale to businesses.
Accepts: MasterCard, Visa

CRAFT STAMPS

P.O. Box 681
Oak Lawn IL 60454
Contact: Donna Jackson

Phone: (773)585-6918
Fax: (773)582-2244
E-mail: craftstamp@aol.com
Offers: Rubber art stamps for all types of stamping and craft projects. Also stamps designed for scrapbooks and memory albums.
Catalog: $4 (refundable on first order).
Phone Orders: Yes.
Mail Orders: Yes.
Discounts: Wholesale with proper identification. Will refer to a retailer when available in customer's location.
Accepts: MasterCard, Visa

CRAFTSMAN RUBBER STAMPS

2650 Chuckanut St.
Eugene OR 97408-7330
Contact: Alan Wagner
Phone: (541)345-4226
Fax: (541)345-4336
E-mail: crftsman@cyberis.net
Store Location: At above address.
Offers: Over 600 art stamp designs, both mounted and un-mounted. Specializing in stamps for card makers. Angel company with no use restrictions. Also stamp pads and embossing powders. Stamps custom made for any application as well.
Catalog: $2 (refundable).
Phone Orders: M-F, 10-6 PST.
Mail Orders: Ship worldwide. Prepayment required. Allow 6-8 weeks for delivery.
Discounts: Wholesale with proof of business entity (craft related).
Accepts: Discover, MasterCard, Visa

THE DISCOVERY STAMP COMPANY

8510 174th Ave. KPS
Longbranch WA 98351
Contact: Barb or Dave
Phone: (253)884-1772 or (800)780-1940
Fax: (253)884-9130
E-mail: stamp@blarg.net.
Website: http://www.blarg.net/~stamp/
Offers: Rubber stamps with nature and wildlife designs, rubber stamp supplies such as ink pads, embossing powders, heat guns, foil, flocking, Static Magic and more. We also make stamps from customers' artwork for them to sell.
Catalog: Retail catalog, $3 (refundable with first purchase).
Phone Orders: M-F, 9-5 PST.
Mail Orders: Prepayment required.
Discounts: We sell wholesale to qualified buyers.
Accepts: MasterCard, Visa

D.J. INKERS

P.O. Box 1509
Sherwood OR 97140
Contact: Lana Davis
Phone: (800)325-4890
Fax: (503)625-9785
E-mail: lana@djinkers.com
Website: www.djinkers.com
Offers: Rubber art stamps and accessories, computer clip art, gift line of ready-made products, acid-free designer paper, stickers and clip art books.
Catalog: 85 pages, full color. $5 (refundable with order).
Phone Orders: 8-5, voice mail 24 hours.
Mail Orders: Ship UPS same day.
Accepts: MasterCard, Visa, check, money order, school purchase order

DOUBLE D RUBBER STAMPS, INC.

P.O. Box 1
Olivia MN 56277
Phone: (320)523-1522
E-mail: doubled@midstate.tds.net
Website: www.doubledstamps.com
Offers: Sign language alphabet rubber stamps and over 900 other designs.
Catalog: 2 catalogs, $5 (refundable).
Discounts: Wholesale; send copy of resale permit or license.
Accepts: Discover, MasterCard, Visa

DREAMLINK

P.O. Box 8028
Woodland CA 95776-8028
Contact: Chris or Jeff
Phone: (530)661-1221
E-mail: jduncan@mother.com
Offers: Unique and all original decorative rubber stamps. Designs include hearts, stars, celestial and more. Also included is our popular greetings grab bag which is 5 sheets of uncut rubber with over 150 words/phrases to make your own personalized greeting cards. Also available are 2 supplements to the original greetings grab bag.
Catalog: $2 (refundable).
Phone Orders: No credit cards.
Mail Orders: Yes.
Accepts: check, money order (US funds only)

ECCENTRICKS

P.O. Box 1789
189 S. East End Ave.
Pomona CA 91766-1789
Contact: Pat Ziegler
Phone: (800)XTRICKS or (800)987-4257
Fax: (800)548-0839
E-mail: eccentricks@worldnet.att.net or xtricks@aol.com
Website: www.eccentricks.com
Offers: Rubber art stamps—just for the fun of it! Eccen-Tricks stamps are divided into 11 fun theme categories full of characters, scenery and plenty of doo-dad elements perfect for scrapbookers.
Catalog: 200 pages, free to legitimate businesses, otherwise $3.50.
Phone Orders: M-F, 9-4 PST (credit cards only).
Mail Orders: Yes.
Discounts: Wholesale to legitimate businesses.
Accepts: Discover, MasterCard, Visa, check

EMBOSSING ARTS CO.

P.O. Box 439
31961 Rolland Dr.
Tangent OR 97389
Contact: Wilma Cooper
Phone: (541)928-9898
Fax: (541)928-9977
E-mail: wilma@embossingarts.com
Website: www.embossingarts.com
Store Location: At above address.
Offers: Original line of art stamps, embossing supplies, brass stencils, exotic papers and blank cards and envelopes.
Catalog: 137 pages, color. $5 (refundable).
Phone Orders: M-F, 8:30-5 PST.
Mail Orders: Domestic and international.
Discounts: Sells wholesale to legitimate businesses.
Accepts: MasterCard, Visa

EUREKA! STAMPS

442 Breesport
San Antonio TX 78216
Contact: Pamela King
Phone: (210)979-8200
Fax: (210)979-8383
E-mail: eureka4him@aol.com
Offers: High-quality rubber stamps of a unique, whimsical style. Accessory items also available: embossing powders, flocking and specialty papers.
Catalog: Over 700 images in over 95 pages.
Phone Orders: M-F, 8:30-4:30.
Mail Orders: Will ship anywhere.
Discounts: Will sell wholesale to legitimate businesses after receipt of business license.
Accepts: MasterCard, Visa, check, C.O.D., net 30 after approved

EXPRESSIONS OF YOU

5412 93rd Dr. SE
Snohomish WA 98290
Contact: Susan Lee
Phone: (360)568-1295
Fax: (360)568-1295
Offers: Rubber stamps and memory album supplies, such as stamps, pads, markers, paper, embossing, supplies, binders, protective sheets, decorative scissors, stickers, patterned papers, circle cutters, punches, journals, photo corners, glues, templates, die-cuts, stencils and sealing wax. A wide variety of styles to choose from. Hints and tips throughout.
Catalog: 90 pages. $5 ($5 refundable coupon).
Phone Orders: M-F, 10-5 PST.
Mail Orders: Will ship to US, Canada and overseas at actual costs. Allow 3-4 weeks US.
Discounts: Coupons and sales in quarterly newsletter.
Accepts: MasterCard, Visa, check

FOG ISLAND RUBBER STAMPS, INC.

10020 Main St., Suite 544
Bellevue WA 98004
Phone: (425)688-0447
Fax: (425)453-2178
Offers: Wholesale/retail rubber stamp catalog. Over 400 original and funny designs. Our specialty is ''people'' stamps.
Catalog: $2.
Mail Orders: Prepayment required.
Discounts: Sells wholesale to legitimate businesses.

FREEHAND STAMPS

P.O. Box 5213
Santa Barbara CA 93150
Contact: Marilyn Wilke
Phone: (805)565-9908
Fax: (805)565-9908
E-mail: frhndstmps@aol.com
Website: Under construction.
Offers: Handcrafted art rubber stamps. All designs are original artwork.
Catalog: $2 (refundable with order).
Mail Orders: Will ship in US and international.
Accepts: check, money order

GENESIS RUBBERSTAMPS

P.O. Box 2673
Anniston AL 36202
Contact: Margaret Tarleton
Phone: (256)236-7787
Fax: (256)235-2107
E-mail: genesisrs@aol.com
Offers: Cats, horses, birds, teachers' stamps, creative stamps and border stamps.
Catalog: $2 (refundable). Free catalog sampler.

GOOD STAMPS—STAMP GOODS

30901 Timberline Rd.
Willits CA 95490
Contact: Emmy Good
Phone: (707)459-9124
Fax: (707)459-5021
E-mail: gssg@pacific.net
Website: www.rubberstampgoods.com
Store Location: 56 S. Main St., Willits CA 95490.
Offers: Rubber stamps—over 3,000—holidays, all 50 states, African, J. Bloch's Egyptian, sports, dance, drama, floral, fauna and esoterica. New Zig Zag card.
Catalog: #6½, $4.
Phone Orders: Yes.
Mail Orders: Yes.
Discounts: US and retail.
Accepts: American Express, Discover, MasterCard, Visa

GRAPHIC RUBBER STAMP CO.

P.O. Box 255
N. Hollywood CA 91601
Phone: (818)899-5050
Fax: (818)899-5051
Store Locations: Other location: 12734 Brandford St., Unit 19, Arleta CA 91331.
Offers: Rubber stamp designs: circus, sheep, photographic, castles, borders, people, telephones, bicycles, flowers, Hollywood, dancers, sports, trees, animals, fantasy, quotations, alphabets, transportation, Native American, spiritual, cartoons and others. Also offers embossing powders (kit available) and techniques video.
Catalog: Catalog displaying 900 stamps, $4.
Discounts: Quantity; sells wholesale to legitimate businesses.

HER RUBBER-STAMPS FOR WILD WOMEN

P.O. Box 21004
Eugene OR 97402
Contact: Ellen Radcliffe
Phone: (541)726-7034
Offers: Rubber stamps, unmounted rubber stamps, stamp pads and grab bags.
Catalog: $2.50 (refundable).
Mail Orders: Will ship anywhere. Prepayment required. Allow 3-4 weeks delivery.
Discounts: Wholesale to businesses.
Accepts: MasterCard, Visa

HOLLY BERRY HOUSE ORIGINALS

P.O. Box 8109
Colorado Springs CO 80933-8109
Contact: Kathy Read
Phone: (719)636-2752
Fax: (719)636-2765
E-mail: hbho@juno.com
Store Location: 2409 W. Colorado Ave., Unit C, Colorado Springs CO 89094-3021.
Offers: Original design rubber art stamps with prints, porcelain pieces, wood shapes and stencils to match.
Catalog: $5. Wholesale packet available.
Phone Orders: (800)735-2752.
Mail Orders: At P.O. Box.
Accepts: American Express, Discover, MasterCard, Visa

HOT OFF THE PRESS, INC.

1250 NW Third Ave.
Canby OR 97013
Contact: Customer service
Phone: (503)266-9102
Fax: (503)266-8749
E-mail: hotp@earthlink.net
Website: http://www.hotp.com
Offers: Over 300 craft instruction books on everything from kids' craft home decor, memory albums and more. Paper Pizazz patterned papers for scrapbooking, punch-outs, cards

with pizazz and many more scrapbook and card-making accessories.
Catalog: 48 pages, full color. $2.
Phone Orders: M-F, 8:30-5 PST. Voice mail is returned.
Mail Orders: Will ship anywhere. Prepayment required. Allow 4-8 weeks for delivery.
Discounts: Sells wholesale to legitimate businesses.
Accepts: MasterCard, Visa

HOT POTATOES

2805 Columbine Place
Nashville TN 37204
Contact: Mary
Phone: (615)269-8002
Fax: (615)269-8004
E-mail: mary@hotpotatoes.com
Website: hotpotatoes.com
Offers: We have deeply etched rubber stamps for fabric, paper and home decor. Our stamps are famous for embossing on velvet.
Catalog: $5.
Phone Orders: M-F, 9-5 CST.
Mail Orders: Yes.
Discounts: Wholesale to actual storefronts only.
Accepts: Discover, MasterCard, Visa, check

IMPRESSIVE STAMPS

P.O. Box 2464
Sandy VT 84091
Phone: (801)255-5208 or (888)A-INK-PAD
Fax: (801)568-1621
Store Location: 9176 S. 300 W. #6, Sandy VT 84070.
Offers: Decorative rubber stamps by 11 artists, and related supplies.
Catalog: $6 and $1.50 p&h.
Phone Orders: Fax.
Mail Orders: At P.O. Box.
Accepts: Discover, MasterCard, Visa

INKADINKADO

60 Cummings Park
Woburn MA 01801
Phone: (781)938-6100
Fax: (781)938-5585
E-mail: sales@inkadinkado.com
Website: http://www.inkadinkado.com
Offers: Rubber stamps, paper products and unusual craft items.
Catalog: Write or call for free catalog.

INKERS-A-WAY

P.O. Box 2425
Sebastopol CA 95473
Offers: Original art rubber stamps, mounted and unmounted, including scene building, memory book, cartoonlike images of people, kids, animals, cars, trucks and planes. Also offers people/occupations as well as postal, address and message frames. Interactive sets featuring foreground to horizon depth

of streets, parks, toy trains and the ocean. Movie theater and holiday themes and stamps designed for laminating are also available.

Catalog: $3 (refundable).
Discounts: Inquire regarding wholesale.
Accepts: American Express, Discover, MasterCard, Visa

INNOVATIONS

P.O. Box 890100
Temecula CA 92589-0100
Contact: Surra Hublik
Phone: (888)CRAFT34
Fax: (888)CRAFT35
Offers: Supplies for making memory scrapbook albums. Carries the entire line of items (rubber stamps, specialty paper and more) from the following companies: All Night Media, American Traditional Stencils, Azadi, Clearsnap (Colorbox, Paintbox2, Petal Point and others), Hero, Holly Pond Hill, Personal Stamp Exchange, Rubber Stampede, Stampendous and Tsukineko (Fabrico, Kaleidacolor, Encore and others). Papermaking kits and supplies from Arnold Grummer, specialty glues for the Floral Pro Crafty Magic Melt Glue Gun with palm feed grip, Risso Print Goco, cross-stitch kits, embroidery kits, Faster Plaster from Plaid, Dimensional Magic from Plaid, stencils and kits from Delta for making your memory scrapbook albums and loads more.
Catalog: Over 150 pages, b&w and full color. $3 (refundable with first order).
Phone Orders: M-F, 9-5 PST. If using a credit card, you can fax orders 24 hours a day, 7 days a week.
Mail Orders: Yes.
Accepts: American Express, Discover, MasterCard, Visa

JACKSON MARKING PRODUCTS CO., INC.

Brownsville Rd.
Mt. Vernon IL 62864
Contact: Tom Jackson
Phone: (800)STAMP-CALL
Fax: (800)STAMP-FAX
E-mail: jmpco@rubber-stamp.com
Website: www.rubber-stamp.com
Offers: Rubber stamp-making equipment: precision rubber stamp presses, hand press and stamp die-cutting machines, and hot stamping and laminating equipment. Also offers mount strip (6 styles), matrix board, stamp gum, cushions, pads and inks, solutions, self-inkers, racks, 64 typestyles and handles. Services: photo engraving of artwork, matrix board molding and rubber die molding.
Catalog: Free brochure.
Discounts: Quantity.

JD IMPRESSIONS

P.O. Box 26895
Fresno CA 93729-6895
Contact: Donna Kohler
Phone: (209)276-1633
Fax: (209)276-1416
Offers: Rubber stamp line includes project stamps for woven hearts, cornucopias, baskets, boxes and party stamps. Also photo mounting corner stamps and frame stamps.
Catalog: $4. Includes coupon for free grab bag when placing first order.
Phone Orders: M-F, 8-6 PST.
Mail Orders: US and Canada.
Discounts: Wholesale to rubber stamp stores and gift stores.
Accepts: MasterCard, Visa

JUDI-KINS RUBBER STAMPS

17803 S. Harvard
Gardena CA 90248
Phone: (310)515-1115
Fax: (310)323-6619
Offers: A diverse collection of original rubber stamp designs: big backgrounds, cubes (4 images on a block of wood), Asian, Celtic and other cultural designs. An exclusive line of premium embossing powders and exceptional paper products.
Catalog: $5.
Phone Orders: M-F, 9-5 PST.
Discounts: Wholesale to legitimate businesses.
Accepts: American Express, Discover, JCB, MasterCard, Visa

JUST IMAGINE

P.O. Box 18312
Anaheim CA 92817-8312
Contact: Susan
Phone: (714)693-0464
Fax: (714)693-0464
E-mail: justimajn@aol.com
Offers: Retail—free embossing powder. We manufacture art rubber stamps.
Catalog: Retail and wholesale.
Phone Orders: Yes.
Mail Orders: Yes.

KALLIGRAPHIKA

P.O. Box 501
Maumee OH 43537
Contact: Sherri Chekal
Phone: (419)874-5448
Fax: (419)874-5448
E-mail: sschekal@compuserve.com
Website: http://ourworld.compuserve.com/homepages/sschekal
Offers: Medieval-, Renaissance- and fantasy-designed rubber stamps. Over 900 designs. Mounted and unmounted stamps. Some neat supplies too for stampers.
Catalog: Over 100 pages. $3 (refundable).
Phone Orders: Yes.
Mail Orders: Yes.
Discounts: Sell wholesale to legitimate businesses.
Accepts: MasterCard, Visa, check, money order

KATIE'S CLOSET

7150 N. 58th Ave.
Glendale AZ 85301
Contact: Katie Crow
Phone: (602)937-3750
Fax: (602)435-9387
E-mail: kcrow@goodnet.com
Store Location: At above address.
Offers: Rubber art stamps, papers, inks, markers, colored pencils and other accessories associated with rubber stamping and paper arts.
Phone Orders: M-Sat, 10-6. Fax 24 hours a day.
Mail Orders: Prepaid. Allow 4-6 weeks.
Accepts: American Express, MasterCard, Visa

KNOCK ON WOOD

3300 Lehigh St., South Mall
Allentown PA 18103
Contact: Deb Golden
Phone: (610)791-0616
Fax: (610)791-2632
Store Location: At above address. M-Sat, 10-9; Sun 12-5.
Offers: Thousands of rubber stamps and accessories and paper products used in the craft of rubber stamping. Free in-store demos. Retail only.
Catalog: 225-page Personal Stamp Exchange (PSX) catalog with free project guide.
Phone Orders: (800)STAMP-21.
Mail Orders: Carry complete line of PSX stamps and accessories. Mail order for PSX. Prepayment required. Ship 1-3 weeks.
Discounts: Discount card given to all customers.
Accepts: Discover, MasterCard, Visa

L.A. STAMPWORKS

P.O. Box 2329
North Hollywood CA 91610-0329
Contact: Donna DiMarco
Phone: (818)761-8757
Fax: (818)761-0973
E-mail: stampworks@aol.com
Website: www.stampworks.com
Offers: Art stamps for the hobbyist. Over 1,000 images in catalog. Exclusive distributors of all Popeye and friends stamps.
Catalog: $5. 124 pages.
Phone Orders: Yes.
Mail Orders: Worldwide.
Discounts: To legitimate wholesale buyers.
Accepts: MasterCard, Visa

LADY & THE STAMP

P.O. Box 6815
Chandler AZ 85246-6815
Contact: Lynn M. Marble, owner/artist
Phone: (602)961-0273
E-mail: ladylynn@getnet.com
Website: www.getnet.com/~ladylynn

Store Location: Chandler AZ location. (Call for appointment/directions.)
Offers: Art rubber stamps with personality. Deeply etched images and sayings available mounted on the finest hourglass maple, or unmounted available for half price. Wood blocks and cushion also available.
Catalog: $3.50 (refundable).
Phone Orders: Accepted for quicker turnaround.
Mail Orders: Prepayment required. Will ship to US and Canada and overseas.
Discounts: Wholesale available with license. Retail: buy 4 get 1 free.
Accepts: check, money order

LASTING IMPRESSIONS

217 Greenwood Ave.
Bethel CT 06801
Phone: (203)792-3740
Fax: (203)743-4389
E-mail: rubermania@aol.com
Store Location: At above address. M-F, 10-6; Sat, 10-5.
Offers: Original rubber stamps in floral, holiday, nature, household and miscellaneous designs. Also offers Rubber Mania Monthly, the Rubber Stamp of the Month Club. For more info on club, send SASE.
Catalog: $2.
Phone Orders: During normal business hours.
Mail Orders: Prepay. Ship to US only.
Discounts: Wholesale to storefronts.
Accepts: Discover, MasterCard, Visa

LEIGH'S WISHING WELL

931 University Ave. #305
Honolulu HI 96826
Contact: Leigh Sturgeon
Phone: (808)941-4440
Fax: (808)955-6437
E-mail: lww@leighswishingwell.com
Website: http://leighswishingwell.com
Offers: CD-ROM computer clip art, CD-ROM craft publications and CD-ROM scrapbooking and cross-stitching patterns.
Catalog: Send #10 SASE with 55¢ stamp attached.
Mail Orders: US and Canada. Prepayment required. Allow 4-6 weeks for delivery.
Discounts: Sells wholesale to legitimate businesses.
Accepts: check, money order

LIQUID NEON

5130 E. Charleston Blvd., Suite 5-52
Las Vegas NV 89122
Contact: Karen LaPratt
Phone: (702)641-7142
Fax: (702)641-7001
Offers: Rubber stamps, foil, glue, E-Z Airbrushing.
Catalog: Color, 24 pages and insert for $3.
Phone Orders: M-F, 8-5 PST.
Mail Orders: Retail orders accompanied by payment.

Wholesale orders: minimum first order $150, subsequent order $75.

Accepts: check, money order

LORIE'S RUBBER MADNESS

19175 Palm Vista
Yorba Linda CA 92886
Contact: Lorie Gorden
Phone: (714)777-8228
Fax: (714)970-0376
E-mail: lrm@scvnet.com
Website: www.stampsrus.com
Offers: Offering discount stamps and supplies from over 25 stamp companies and suppliers. We also carry and discount scrapbook supplies and stickers.
Catalog: Yes.
Phone Orders: Yes.
Mail Orders: Yes.
Discounts: 30% standard on everything.
Accepts: MasterCard, Visa

LOVE YOU TO BITS

P.O. Box 5748
Redwood City CA 94063
Phone: (415)367-1177
Offers: Over 1,000 original rubber stamp designs: whimsical holiday motifs, quotes and signs, Christian stamps, stamps in Spanish, animals, flowers, cartoon creatures and others.
Catalog: $7.
Discounts: Sells wholesale.

LOVING LITTLE RUBBER STAMPS

P.O. Box 384
Newburyport MA 01950
Phone: (978)465-9954
Offers: Over 1,500 rubber stamp designs—originals and oldies: special occasion, holiday, quotes, people, money, food, seashore, ecology, buildings, sports, animals, vintage motifs, hands, borders, signs and others.
Catalog: $2.

MAINE STREET STAMPS

P.O. Box 14
Kingfield ME 04947
Contact: Jenny
Phone: (207)265-2500
E-mail: stamps@opdag.com
Website: www.opdag.com/ms.html
Offers: Rubber stamps. Designs include angels and fairies, Victorian, flowers, holidays and more.
Catalog: 40 pages. $2 (refundable).
Phone Orders: Yes.
Accepts: MasterCard, Visa

MEER IMAGE CRAFT

P.O. Box 112
Arcata CA 95518
Contact: Steven
Phone: (707)822-4338

Fax: (707)822-5985
E-mail: meer@humboldt1.com
Website: www.humboldt1.com/~meer
Offers: Original art rubber stamps. Themes include natural, fantasy, nudes, scenery and insects. Stamps are available unmounted for half price.
Catalog: Over 300 images. $2.
Phone Orders: Toll-free order line: (800)757-1717. Messages returned promptly.
Mail Orders: First class mail or airmail to anywhere on the planet.
Discounts: Wholesale to storefront businesses.
Accepts: MasterCard, Visa, check, money order (US funds)

LOUIS MELIND CO.

P.O. Box 1112
Skokie IL 60076-8112
Phone: (847)581-2500
Fax: (800)782-2542
Offers: Raw materials for businesses that make rubber stamps. Art stamp-making supplies, including stamp gum, wood and plastic mounts in popular hourglass shape, cushion, adhesive and matrix; vulcanizer and indexing ink. Production of rubber dies from artwork—submit samples and quantities for quote (must be original artwork or licensed for your use). Stationery seals and embossers with custom or stock artwork.
Catalog: Call or write for free catalog (Mention *Crafts Supply Sourcebook*).
Discounts: Quantity.
Accepts: American Express, MasterCard, Visa

MOE WUBBA

P.O. Box 1445
San Luis Obispo CA 93406
Contact: Susan Burdick
Phone: (805)547-1MOE
Fax: (805)547-1663
E-mail: moewubba@aol.com
Offers: Classic images, hand-carved originals, illustrations by Emily Mills and Swirly Stamps by Moe Wubba.
Catalog: $4 (refundable).
Phone Orders: Accepted: M-F, 10-3 PST.
Mail Orders: Prepaid to US, Canada and international (shipping costs are doubled for international orders).
Discounts: Wholesale to retail storefronts.
Accepts: American Express, Discover, MasterCard, Visa

MOUNT RUBBERMORE

P.O. Box 93136
Southlake TX 76092
Contact: Customer service representative
Phone: (817)491-3136
Fax: (817)491-3133
E-mail: cs@mountrubbermore.com
Website: www.mountrubbermore.com
Offers: Custom stamp manufacturing from your art. Our original art stamps mounted on wood, diamond mount acrylic or unmounted. Diamond Mount'n Grid, 35 Stick-Stamp-

Store, Xyron manufacturer's representative and manufacturing supplies from presses to colored art on labels for stamps.
Catalog: $5 (refundable with order).
Phone Orders: M-F, 9-5 CST.
Mail Orders: Will ship to US and international. Prepayment required. Allow 6 weeks delivery. International—credit cards only.
Discounts: Wholesale available.
Accepts: American Express, Discover, MasterCard, Visa

MUSEUM OF MODERN RUBBER
2457 Hyperion Ave.
Los Angeles, CA 90027
Contact: Jane Beard
Phone: (213) 662-1133
Fax: (213)668-4911
Offers: Wood-mounted rubber stamps in a broad range of images, including art masterpieces, people, sayings, background patterns and project-oriented stamps.
Catalog: $4.
Phone Orders: M-F, 10-5 PST.
Mail Orders: Yes.
Discounts: Sells wholesale.
Accepts: MasterCard, Visa

MY SENTIMENTS EXACTLY!
4695 Centauri Rd., Suite 100
Colorado Springs CO 80919
Contact: Amy Kennedy
Phone: (719)522-1101
Fax: (719)522-0797
E-mail: info@sentiments.com
Website: www.sentiments.com
Offers: Over 800 sentiment-only rubber stamps: prose, poems, quotes, quips and others.
Catalog: 80 pages. $6 (refundable).
Phone Orders: Yes.
Mail Orders: Yes.
Accepts: American Express, Discover, MasterCard, Visa

NAME BRAND & RIGHTEOUS RUBBER STAMPS
(formerly Name Brand)
P.O. Box 34245
Bethesda MD 20827
Contact: L. Abrams
Phone: (301)299-3062
Fax: (301)299-3063
E-mail: namebrand@erols.com
Offers: Calligraphic rubber stamps—over 1,000 names, inspirational expressions, greetings, holidays and custom stamps.
Catalog: 50 pages. $4 (refundable).
Phone Orders: M-F, 9-5 EST.
Mail Orders: Prepayment or credit card required. Will ship anywhere.
Discounts: Wholesale to legitimate businesses.
Accepts: MasterCard, Visa

NEMA INK/STUDIO C STAMPS
P.O. Box 210930
Nashville TN 37221-0930
Contact: Cheryl Nemanich
E-mail: nemaink@aol.com
Offers: Deep-etched rubber art stamps, mounted and unmounted. Retail and wholesale. Unmounted half price. $2 shipping on unmounted stamps. Wide range of subjects. Many images hand-carved.
Catalog: $2 (US funds only).
Mail Orders: Prepayment required. Fast delivery.
Discounts: Wholesale to storefronts only. Prepaid. No unmounted.

NON SEQUITUR RUBBER STAMPS
P.O. Box 5836
Pasadena TX 77508-5836
Contact: Lisette Cannedy
Phone: (713)475-9009
Fax: (713)475-9506
E-mail: nonsequitur@nonsequiturstamps.com
Website: http://www.nonsequiturstamps.com
Offers: HALOS mounts, Rollatag and Artistic rubber stamps.
Catalog: $4, with partial refund.
Mail Orders: Yes.
Accepts: MasterCard, Visa, check, cash

OCTOPUS INK
P.O. Box 715
Kent WA 98035
Contact: K.S. McKenzie
Phone: (253)854-1804
Offers: Rubber art stamps, mostly with a marine theme. Images include both fantasy and realism (mermaids, people, beach, ocean, sea life and more). 2 collectible alphabet sets. Also offer unmounted rubber dies and supplies for mounting stamps (scissors, cushion and cling vinyl).
Catalog: Over 700 images. $5 (refundable).
Mail Orders: Will ship to US and Canada.
Discounts: No wholesale.
Accepts: check, money order

100 PROOF PRESS
P.O. Box 299
Athens OH 45701
Contact: Ann Moneypenny
Phone: (740)594-2315
Fax: (740)594-2516
Offers: Finely crafted rubber art stamps, specializing in finely detailed, realistic images.
Catalog: 104 pages with over 3,000 images. $4 (refundable).
Phone Orders: M-F, 9-3 EST.
Mail Orders: Anywhere on the globe.
Discounts: No wholesale at this time.
Accepts: MasterCard, Visa, check

PAINTED TURTLE STUDIO

362 Second St. Pike, Suite 171
Southampton PA 18966
Phone: (215)745-5029
Fax: (215)745-7322
E-mail: painturtle@aol.com
Website: Coming soon. E-mail us for URL.
Offers: Painted Turtle Studio line of original and antique art rubber stamps—mounted and unmounted—Victoria Papers, Atlantic Papers, 3D Crystal Lacquer, HALOS stamp-mounting system, stampable wood boxes and cutouts, clear envelopes, project kits and clocks for stamp projects.
Catalog: $2 (refundable).
Phone Orders: M-Sat, 9-6 EST. Fax credit card orders anytime.
Mail Orders: Will ship worldwide, prepaid in US funds.
Discounts: Wholesale prices for Painted Turtle Studio mounted stamps, project kits, Victoria Papers and Atlantic Papers to legitimate businesses. Provide copy of business license.
Accepts: Discover, MasterCard, Visa, check, money order

PAPER PARACHUTE

P.O. Box 91385
Portland OR 97291-0385
Contact: Agi Werner or Vikkie Leonardo
Offers: Unmounted rubber stamps. Variety of styles.
Catalog: Retail catalog, $4.95. 132 pages with tips. Wholesale catalog coming soon.
Mail Orders: Will ship to US and Canada. For international shipments please send for shipping rates. 2-6 week delivery. Prepayment.
Accepts: check

PIPE DREAMS

Dept. CSS
P.O. Box 275
Erving MA 01344
Phone: (978)544-7334
Fax: (978)544-0191
Offers: Graphic rubber stamps, including Victorian, teacher, country, angels, names, holiday and other subjects.
Catalog: Send large SASE for list of subjects.
Discounts: 10% discount with mention of the *Crafts Supply Sourcebook*. Wholesale available to qualified businesses.

POSH IMPRESSIONS

875 E. Birch St.
Brea CA 92821
Phone: (714)529-9933
Store Location: Other Address: 4708 Barranka Pkwy., Irvine CA 92604. (714)651-1145.
Offers: Exclusive rubber stamps of over 40,000 images, plus sticker rolls and unlimited accessories. Also offers classes, plus instructional materials from Dee Gruenig.
Catalog: $5.
Discounts: Sells wholesale; lifetime 10% discount through 500 Club.

PRINT KRAFT

3109 Mandigo
Portage MI 49002-7573
Contact: Patty Sulcs
Phone: (616)649-3175
Fax: (616)649-3175
E-mail: printkraft@aol.com
Offers: Mounted, unmounted, wholesale, retail. Embossing powders, cardstock and miracle tape.
Catalog: $3 (refundable with first order). Over 500 designs.
Phone Orders: M-F, 9-9.
Mail Orders: Will ship to US, Canada. Overseas by credit card only. P&h at our cost.
Discounts: Wholesale to storefronts only.
Accepts: MasterCard, Visa

PRINT PLAY

P.O. Box 4252
Portland OR 97208
Phone: (503)697-0915
Fax: (503)675-0536
Offers: Individual words rubber stamp collection to help children learn to read and write. Also offers a wide selection of animal and bird tracks.
Catalog: Send SASE for free catalog.

RED HOT RUBBER, INC.

363 W. Glade Rd.
Palatine IL 60067
Phone: (847)991-6700
E-mail: msredhott@aol.com
Offers: Line of rubber stamps, including foods, animals, birthday, western, Halloween, Valentine's Day, Easter, Christmas, greetings and others. Unmounted stamps also available.
Catalog: $3 (refundable).
Discounts: Sells wholesale.

RICH AND (ALMOST) FAMOUS RUBBER STAMPS

681 Skyline Rd.
Ventura CA 93003
Contact: Lynne Estrada or Terry Lombardi
Phone: (805)644-3991
Fax: (805)644-3991
E-mail: raafstamps@aol.com
Offers: Rubber stamps, mounted and unmounted. Photo journaling stamps and scrapbooking stamps as well as a full line of images for all types of stamping.
Catalog: $5.
Mail Orders: Retail and wholesale orders accepted. Must be prepaid by check or money order or C.O.D.
Discounts: Wholesale.
Accepts: check, cash

ROSEBUD RUBBER STAMPS, INC.

3550 El Ferrol
Bridgeton MO 63044
Contact: Mary or Paul Kyburz

Phone: (314)298-0250
Fax: (314)739-8477
E-mail: rosebudrs@aol.com
Offers: Artistic rubber stamps, including Christian designs and sayings, Southwestern, floral, holiday and baby designs.
Catalog: $4 (refundable).
Phone Orders: 24-hour fax.
Mail Orders: Will ship to US and Canada. Prepayment required. Allow 3-4 weeks for delivery.
Discounts: Sells wholesale; send copy of resale/tax license.
Accepts: Discover, MasterCard, Visa

RUBBER DUCK STAMP CO.

P.O. Box 416
Medford OR 97501
Phone: (541)734-7390
Offers: Rubber stamps, including ducks, rabbits, teddy bears, Easter baskets, flowers and others. Assorted die-cuts. Supplies: pads, inks and wood blocks.
Catalog: *Ducklog*, $2.50 (half refundable).
Discounts: Sells wholesale.

THE RUBBER FARM

P.O. Box 501
Maumee OH 43551
Contact: Sherri Chekal
Phone: (419)874-5448
Fax: (419)874-5448
E-mail: sschekal@compuserve.com
Website: http://ourworld.compuserve.com/homepages/sschekal
Offers: Realistic farm and country rubber stamps, unmounted and mounted.
Catalog: 60 pages. $2 (refundable).
Phone Orders: Yes.
Mail Orders: Yes.
Discounts: Occasionally. Wholesale available.
Accepts: MasterCard, Visa, check, money order, cash

RUBBER POET & YES! PIGS CAN FLY

P.O. Box 218-CS
Rockville UT 84763
Contact: Barry
Phone: (435)772-3441
Fax: (800)906-POET
E-mail: rubrpoet@infowest.com
Website: www.wyoming.com/~cavenewt/pigs/
Offers: Petroglyphs, nature, southwest cactus, fabric designs, fantasy and art deco women, from the ridiculous to the sublime. Pithy quotes of John Muir and Edward Abbey.
Catalog: 4th edition, 700-image Rubber Poet; 92 pages, $3 (refundable). Yes! Pigs Can Fly catalog of 400 images, $3. Both catalogs, $5.
Phone Orders: Yes.
Mail Orders: Will ship to foreign addresses. Foreign fax: (435)772-3464.
Discounts: Wholesale to storefronts only.
Accepts: MasterCard, Visa

RUBBER RAILROAD STAMP WORKS

1320 NW Northrup St.
Portland OR 97209
Contact: Lance Petersen
Phone: (503)226-9895
Store Location: At above address. T-F, 11-6. Sat, 11-5.
Offers: Rubber stamps on railroads and railroading.
Catalog: $3.
Phone Orders: T-Sat, 11-5 PST.
Mail Orders: Ship via US postal service. Prepayment required. Allow 4-6 weeks.
Discounts: Sell wholesale to retail stores.
Accepts: MasterCard, Visa

RUBBER STAMP RANCH

4204 Lead Ave. SE
Albuquerque NM 87108
Contact: Hollis Hedlund
Phone: (505)255-3305
Fax: (505)255-0295
Store Location: At above address.
Offers: Display of the stamps we make plus stamping accessories.
Catalog: Free.
Phone Orders: (800)728-9762.
Mail Orders: Retail and wholesale.
Accepts: MasterCard, Visa

RUBBER STAMPS OF AMERICA

P.O. Box 567
25 Warner Center Rd.
Saxtons River VT 05154
Contact: Laurie Indenbaum
Phone: (802)869-2622
Fax: (802)869-2262
Website: www.stampusa.com
Offers: A unique line of graphic rubber stamps. Over 1,000 designs: wildlife, alphabets, people, holidays, ethnic, fifties, nature, travel and cosmos. High-quality stamps manufactured in Vermont.
Catalog: 45 pages. $2.50 (refundable).
Phone Orders: M-F, 9-4; Sat, 10-4.
Mail Orders: Ship anywhere. Prepayment required.
Discounts: Wholesale to legitimate retailers.
Accepts: American Express, Discover, MasterCard, Visa

SONOMA STAMP CO.

#25 Kentucky St.
Petaluma CA 94952
Contact: Kim Hanson
Phone: (707)766-8810
Fax: (707)766-8795
Store Location: At above address. M-Sat, 10-5; Sun, 12-4.
Offers: Rubber stamps and accessories. We represent retail mail order for Hero Arts and Personal Stamp Exchange.
Catalog: Represent catalogs for Hero Arts and Personal Stamp Exchange.

Phone Orders: (800)336-4242. M-Sat, 10-5; Sun, 12-4. Fax orders accepted 24 hours a day.
Mail Orders: Worldwide. For international orders we only charge for shipping and insurance, not for handling.
Discounts: Domestic stamp club.
Accepts: MasterCard, Visa, check, money order

STAMP ANTONIO
1931 NW Military Hwy.
San Antonio TX 78213
Contact: Carrie Edelmann
Phone: (210)342-6217
Fax: (210)342-6218
E-mail: santonio1@aol.com
Store Location: At above address. M-Sat, 10-6; Th, 10-7.
Offers: Retail only store. We carry over 100 different stamp companies and a large selection of art supplies and accessories. Packaged and per sheet papers. Largest stamp selection in the Southwest.
Catalog: Stamp Antonio designs only. $1.
Accepts: Discover, MasterCard, Visa

STAMP DIEGO
2650 Jamacha Rd., Suite 139
El Cajon CA 92019
Contact: Jenny Griffiths
Phone: (619)670-4782 or (800)845-2312
Fax: (619)670-4782
E-mail: stampdiego@aol.com
Store Location: Other location: Seaport Village, 803B W. Harbor Dr., San Diego CA 92101. M-F, 9-7; Sat, 10-5; Sun, 12-4.
Offers: Rubber stamps and scrapbooking.
Catalog: Stamp Diego catalog for $4 (refunded with purchase). 160-page Stampendous catalog for $8 (free stamp with purchase). Personal Stamp Exchange catalog $12 (includes free how-to book). Bonus package: buy all 3 catalogs for $22 (includes free stamp and $5 rebate with first order).
Phone Orders. Yes.
Mail Orders: Will ship around the world. Prepayment required. Allow 2-3 weeks for delivery.
Discounts: Preferred customer card.
Accepts: American Express, Discover, MasterCard, Visa, check

STAMP OASIS
5000 W. Oakey Blvd. #D-14
Las Vegas NV 89102
Contact: Pat
Phone: (702)880-8886
Fax: (702)880-8887
E-mail: jimmf@stampoasis.com
Website: stampoasis.com
Store Location: 4750 W. Sahara Ave., Las Vegas NV 89102.
Offers: Over 30,000 fun rubber stamps from over 150 companies. Knowledgeable and helpful staff. Demos on the spot. Open 7 days.
Catalog: $5. Has over 900 original designs.

Phone Orders: Yes. M-F, 9-4 PST.
Mail Orders: Ship within 1 week. Wholesale to legitimate business.
Accepts: all credit cards

STAMP OF EXCELLENCE, INC.
1105 Main St.
Canon City CO 81212
Phone: (719)275-8422
Fax: (719)275-7950
Store Location: At above address.
Offers: Line of rubber stamps including special occasion (designs and quotes): holiday, birthday, baby, bridal, party, Valentine's and springtime flowers. Other subjects include angels and spiritual quotes, kitchen, mail, "frames," classroom, notecard, Oriental, Native American, cosmic, fantasy, scenic, animals and others. Full line unmounted. Full line of supplies.
Catalog: $3. Angel flyer, $1.
Discounts: Quantity; sells wholesale to legitimate businesses.
Accepts: American Express, Discover, MasterCard, Visa

STAMP OUT CUTE
7084 N. Cedar #137
Fresno CA 93720
Contact: Sonny or Linda
Phone: (408)445-8671
Website: Soon.
Catalog: $3.
Mail Orders: $2.50 minimum, p&h.
Discounts: Grab bags $10 (minimum $40 value).
Accepts: check, money order

STAMP THYME
201 S. State St.
Lockport IL 60441
Contact: Marilyn Ellison
Phone: (800)STAMP93 or (815)836-8180
Fax: (815)838-4424, Attn.: Norm
E-mail: marilynell@aol.com
Store Location: At above address. M-F, 11-6; Th, 11-8; Sat, 10-5.
Offers: Thousands of artistic rubber stamps and a complete line of accessories, books and videos.
Catalog: Stampendous, PSX and others.
Phone Orders: Yes.
Mail Orders: Yes.
Discounts: Few.
Accepts: Discover, Visa, check, money order

STAMP YOUR ART OUT
9225 S. Orange Blossom Trail
Orlando FL 32837
Contact: Bert or Judy Hayslett
Phone: (407)816-0037
Fax: (407)816-4428
Store Location: At above address. M-Sat, 10-6. Sun, 12-4.

Offers: Over 50,000 "fun" rubber stamps (largest selection in America). Also stencils, light tables, oil sticks, photo album and scrapbooking supplies, craft magazines and videotapes. Fabric stamping supplies and huge selection of stickers (Mrs. Grossman, Mr. Grossman, Stickopotamus, Mary Englebreit, Melissa Neufield, Frances Meyer and Paper House).
Catalog: Stampendous, $8; Hero Arts, $10; Personal Stamp Exchange, $12.
Phone Orders: Accepted with credit card.
Mail Orders: Yes.
Discounts: No wholesale.
Accepts: American Express, Diners Club, Discover, MasterCard, Visa, check, money order

STAMPA ROSA

320 Tesconi Circle, Suite N
Santa Rosa CA 95401
Contact: Patricia McPhee
Phone: (707)570-0763 or (800)554-5755
Fax: (707)570-0868
E-mail: stamparosa@aol.com
Website: http://www.homezone.com/stamparosa
Store Location: 2322 Midway Dr., Santa Rosa CA 95404. (707)527-8267.
Offers: Stamp pads, brush markers, colored pencil, paper, all scrapbook material, rubber stamps, die-cut machine, stickers, trinkets, glitter and embossing powder.
Catalog: House Mouse, $6; Marna, $6; Stampa Rosa, $6.
Phone Orders: Yes.
Mail Orders: At company address above.
Accepts: Discover, MasterCard, Visa

STAMPAMANIA

(formerly Victoria Christie Designs)
Willow Tree Plaza
1045 11th St.
Lakeport CA 95453
Contact: Victoria Christie
Phone: (707)263-0688
Store Location: Northern California shores and Clear Lake locations.
Offers: 1,200 square feet of rubber stamps. Art stamps from over 150 companies custom made from your artwork. Address, signature, endorsement stamps, classes, workshop, kids kamp, full line of accessories and video for rental. Stampers paradise at the lake.
Catalog: Yes.
Phone Orders: Yes.
Mail Orders: Yes.
Accepts: MasterCard, Visa

STAMPIN' AND SCRAPPIN'

5610 District Blvd., Suite 107
Bakersfield CA 93313
Contact: Michelle
Phone: (805)397-0202 or (800)810-0772
Fax: (805)665-9005
E-mail: sales@stampinscrappin.com

Website: www.stampinscrappin.com
Store Location: At above address.
Offers: Rubber stamping and scrapbooking products, classes, contests and more.
Catalog: On-line catalog, plus a printable catalog.
Phone Orders: 24 hours a day.
Mail Orders: Will ship anywhere in the world. Most orders are shipped within 24 hours.
Discounts: Various store and on-line sales.
Accepts: American Express, MasterCard, Visa, check, money order

STAMPIN AROUND

2027 196th St. SW, Suite R-2
Lynnwood WA 98036
Contact: Carl
Phone: (425)744-1993
Fax: (425)744-1890
E-mail: iluv2stamp@aol.com
Store Location: Lynnwood WA location.
Offers: Rubber stamps and rubber stamp art supplies, stencils, scrapbooking, supplies, exotic papers and more.
Phone Orders: Yes.
Mail Orders: Yes.
Accepts: American Express, Discover, MasterCard, Visa

THE STAMPIN' PLACE

P.O. Box 43
Big Lake MN 55309
Contact: Rhea
Phone: (800)634-3717 or (612)263-6646
Fax: (800)634-3718 or (612)263-6463
E-mail: info@stampin.com
Website: www.stampin.com
Store Location: Locations in Big Lake, Golden Valley and Roseville MN.
Offers: Over 2,000 images. Rubber art stamps, custom stamps and accessories for stamping. Brass stencils, scrapbooking supplies and accessories.
Catalog: Available free with order of $20, or $3 refundable.
Phone Orders: Yes.
Mail Orders: At P.O. Box.
Discounts: Artie's Stamp Club: 15% discount after first $100 spent.
Accepts: Discover, MasterCard, Visa

STAMPINGTON & CO.

22992 Mill Creek, Suite B
Laguna Hills CA 92653
Contact: Kellene Giloff
Phone: (714)380-7318
Fax: (714)380-9355
E-mail somersetad@aol.com
Offers: Classic art and country rubber art stamps; *Somerset Studio* magazine featuring full-color samples and techniques for art stamping, calligraphy, and paper crafting; and *Stampers' Sampler* magazine featuring more than 125 full-color samples of rubber art stamping in every issue.

Catalog: Catalog/idea book, $13.95; includes $5 gift certificate.
Phone Orders: M-F, 9-5 PST.
Mail Orders: Domestic and international; prepayment required. Allow 3-6 weeks for delivery.
Discounts: Wholesale to storefront businesses.
Accepts: MasterCard, Visa

STAMPINKS UNLIMITED
P.O. Box 97
Shortsville, NY 14548-0097
Contact: Robin Allen
Fax: (716)289-3177
E-mail: stampink@eznet.net
Website: http://www.home.eznet.net/~stampink
Offers: Over 1,000 artistic rubber stamps from 25 different artists. Catalog contains carousel animal designs and a complete carousel alphabet; blue willow teapots, plates and bowls; a full line of authentic international doll costume stamps; and many unique calligraphy stamps. Carries mail art, slogans, stars, hearts, postoids, fortunes and even a fortune cookie. All of the stamps are made with maple handles and high-quality gum rubber. Turnaround on most orders is 1 day.
Catalog: Latest 54-page catalog, $3.
Mail Orders: Will ship worldwide. Prepayment required.
Discounts: Sells wholesale. Unmounted at half price.
Accepts: check drawn on US bank, money order

STAMPOURRI!
P.O. Box 3434
La Habra CA 90632
Contact: Gretchen Stevens
Phone: (714)526-1644
Fax: (714)526-4344
Website: http://www.localmall.com/stampourri
Store Location: 231 E. Imperial Hwy., Suite 240, Fullerton CA 92835. M-F, 9-3.
Offers: Country folk art, 3D window, potting table, gardening, inspirational, paper packs and colored pencils.
Catalog: Volume 6, $5. Wholesale and retail.
Phone Orders: (888)80-STAMP.
Mail Orders: Yes.
Accepts: MasterCard, Visa

JIM STEPHAN'S RUBBER ART INK
P.O. Box 5603
Redwood City CA 94063
Contact: Jim Stephan
Phone: (650)364-5696
Fax: (650)364-5696
E-mail: jimstamper@aol.com
Offers: Rubber stamps, rainbow pads and mounting supplies.
Catalog: 30 pages. $3 (refundable).
Phone Orders: M-F, 8-4 PST.
Mail Orders: Outside US is shipped at cost charged to MasterCard or Visa. US is flat fee $3 per order.
Accepts: MasterCard, Visa

STEWART STAMPS
P.O. Box 38
White Lake WI 54491
Contact: Leslie Stewart
Phone: (715)882-3510 or (715)276-6998
Fax: (715)276-6998
E-mail: stewstamps@aol.com
Website: Pending.
Store Location: Birchwood Gallery, Lakewood, WI.
Offers: Unique and original rubber art stamps, including hand-carved images by Leslie Stewart, free-form designs by Dori Chinn (DC Afterhours) and Indigenous Inspirations by James Merritt.
Catalog: $3 (refundable); free to wholesale with copy of retail license.
Phone Orders: (715)276-6998. 10-5 CST except Tuesdays.
Mail Orders: Prepayment required. Allow 1-2 weeks. Most orders shipped within 48 hours.
Discounts: Sells wholesale to legitimate storefront businesses.
Accepts: Discover, MasterCard, Visa

STICKER PLANET
10736 Jefferson Blvd. #503
Culver City CA 90230
Contact: Customer service
Phone: (800)557-8678 (US) or (310)204-7060 (international)
Fax: (800)537-2260 (US) or (310)204-7072 (international)
E-mail: mail@stickerplanet.com
Website: www.stickerplanet.com
Store Location: Locations in Los Angeles and Santa Monica CA. Call for addresses and hours.
Offers: Santa Monica location features full line of scrapbooking supplies and rubber stamps. Both stores feature thousands of stickers. Mail-order catalog shows over 350 acid-free, high-quality sticker designs by famous manufacturers, for crafters and hobbyists.
Catalog: High quality, full color, 68 pages. $5 (refundable). Package includes 50 project ideas, how-to guide to sticker art, reusable storage pouch, plus free periodic catalog supplement mailings.
Phone Orders: M-F, 7-7; Sat-Sun, 8-3 PST.
Mail Orders: Will ship to US and international (additional fee). Prepayment required. Allow 1 week within US. No minimum order required.
Discounts: Volume and multiple-sticker discounts available. Will also sell wholesale to legitimate businesses.
Accepts: Discover, MasterCard, Visa, check, money order

TATTERED BEAR & BUNDLES OF BUNNIES
P.O. Box 63
Eastlake CO 80614
Contact: Ali or Fred
Phone: (303)457-0361
Offers: Artist available for art and/or custom design work. Design licensing available. Rubber stamps, mounted and un-

mounted, 17 different limited edition signed and numbered 8 × 10 prints of bunnies and bears.
Catalog: Rubber stamp catalog, $3; mail to above address.
Mail Orders: At above address.
Discounts: Offered periodically.
Accepts: check, money order for fastest delivery

THIRD COAST RUBBER STAMPS

P.O. Box 66665
Houston TX 77266
Contact: V. Settle
Phone: (713)522-8348
Fax: (713)522-8348
E-mail: thirdcoast@mail.com
Website: http://www.thirdcoastrs.com
Offers: Top-quality unmounted art rubber stamps
Catalog: $4 (refundable with order). Over 1,000 images. Something for all tastes.
Phone Orders: Yes.
Mail Orders: International.
Discounts: Frequent sales—check website.
Accepts: American Express, MasterCard, Visa

TICKLED INK

116 Ridge Rd.
Albert Lea MN 56007
Contact: Darcy Netzer
Phone: (507)373-4965
E-mail: ddnetzer@smig.net
Offers: Original design artistic rubber stamps.
Catalog: $1.50 (refundable with order).
Mail Orders: Will ship to US and Canada. Prepayment required. Allow 1 month for delivery.
Discounts: Will sell wholesale to legitimate businesses.

TOOMUCHFUN RUBBERSTAMPS

2200 Coolidge Rd., Suite 14
East Lansing MI 48823
Phone: (517)351-2030
Fax: (517)347-1465
Store Location: At above address. M-F, 10-9; Sat, 10-6.
Offers: Rubber stamp motifs, including special occasions and holidays. Also Toomuchfun exclusives such as folios, box stamps and or-bits.
Catalog: Check with your local retailer for our mini catalogs and project guides, or call toll-free for more information.
Discounts: $3 shipping; free over $50 purchase within continental US.
Accepts: Discover, MasterCard, Visa

TOUCHÉ RUBBER STAMPS

1827 16½ St. NW
Rochester MN 55901
Contact: Susan Tollers
Phone: (507)288-2317
Fax: (507)286-1428
E-mail dfvt74b@prodigy.com
Offers: Artistic rubber stamps; inspirational verses, seasonal and everyday. Accessories: stamp pads, embossing powder and cards.
Catalog: 96 pages. $4 (refundable with minimum order).
Phone Orders: M-F, 10-5 CST.
Mail Orders: To US. Foreign orders shipped at cost. Allow 2-6 weeks for delivery.
Discounts: Wholesale with valid documentation.
Accepts: MasterCard, Visa

THE WRITE TYPE

5424-10 Sunol Blvd., Suite 268
Pleasanton CA 94566
Contact: Laura Bonnel
Phone: (925)417-7567
Fax: (925)462-8837
E-mail: thewritype@aol.com
Offers: Memory supplies, scrapbooking products and craft supplies. Rubber stamps and stamping supplies.
Catalog: 32 pages. $3 (refundable on first purchase).
Phone Orders: M-F, 10-4 PST.
Mail Orders: Prepayment required. Will ship 7-10 working days.
Discounts: Retail only; discounted prices.
Accepts: MasterCard, Visa

ZUM GALI GALI RUBBER STAMPS

P.O. Box 610187
Newton Highlands, MA 02161-0187
Contact: Arlene or Dean Bandes
Phone: (617)965-1268
Fax: (617)965-6158
E-mail: zgg@world.std.com
Offers: Original artwork, including pattern, Judaica, New England, lighthouses, whimsical animals, birds, eraser carved images, sports, strong graphic design, architecture and postoids. Also carries interactive sets, including Design Your Own Jerusalem, bicycle kit and Cubist guitar set. Unmounted stamps also available.
Catalog: 40 pages. $3 (refundable).
Mail Orders: Prepayment required.
Discounts: Sells wholesale; nonprofit organizations.

Scientific Supplies & Equipment

Also see Tools & Equipment—Multipurpose; Associations; Publications.

ADVANCE SCIENTIFIC & CHEMICAL, INC.
2345 SW 34th St.
Ft. Lauderdale FL 33312
Contact: Alan
Phone: (954)327-0900 or (800)524-2436
Fax: (954)327-0903
E-mail: sales@advance-scientific.com
Website: http://www.advance-scientific.com
Store Location: At above address.
Offers: Distributor of small and bulk quantities of chemicals, lab glassware and instruments, microscopes and supplies. Also offers education science kits and reference materials.
Catalog: 240 pages. $5 (refundable).
Phone Orders: M-F, 8:30-6 EST.
Mail Orders: Prepayment required.
Accepts: all credit cards, company check, money order

AMERICAN SCIENCE & SURPLUS
3605 Howard St.
Skokie IL 60076
Contact: Scott McCausland
Phone: (847)982-0874
Fax: (847)982-0881
E-mail: scott@sciplus.com
Website: www.sciplus.com
Store Location: Locations in Chicago IL (3) and Milwaukee WI.
Offers: Thousands of craft and educational supplies, kits and components: tools, strange materials, motors, lab glassware and instruments, brushes, office supplies, electrical components, magnets, lenses, mirrors, toys and novelties.
Catalog: 64-96 pages. Free.
Phone Orders: (847)982-0870; M-F, 8-5 CST. Fax: (800)934-0722.
Mail Orders: US and territory shipments only.

Discounts: Most items 50% or more off regular retail.
Accepts: Discover, MasterCard, Visa, check, money order

EDMUND SCIENTIFIC
101 E. Gloucester Pike
Barrington NJ 08007
Contact: Bob Sheairs (advertising only)
Phone: (609)574-3488, ext. 6844
Fax: (609)573-6262
E-mail: sheairs@edsci.com
Website: www.edsci.com
Store Location: Barrington NJ location.
Offers: Something for every science enthusiast! Kits for mini hot-air balloons, steam engines, magnifiers, positioning equipment, specialty tools, telescopes and accessories, plastic bottles, light guides and specialty lighting. Jewelers' items and more.
Catalog: Scientifics. Free. 4-color.
Phone Orders: (800)728-6999.
Mail Orders: At above address.
Discounts: Volume discounts.
Accepts: American Express, Diners Club, Discover, MasterCard, Optima, Visa, check

PYROTEK, INC.
P.O. Box 300
Sweet Valley PA 18656
Contact: Joe Meeko
Phone: (717)256-3087
Fax: (717)256-3087
E-mail: pyrotek@epix.net
Website: Developing right now.
Offers: Hobby and experimenters' chemicals, glassware, how-to books and videos, rocketry supplies, potassium perchlorate, potassium chlorate, nitrates, magnesium, aluminum, titanium powders, hobby fuse, lab acids—hundreds of items. Make your own rocket motors and homemade fuels.
Catalog: $2.
Phone Orders: Yes.
Mail Orders: Yes.
Discounts: Bulk.
Accepts: MasterCard, Visa

Scrapbooking

Also see Artist's Supplies, Graphics & Printing; General Craft Supplies; Paper Crafts & Papermaking; Photography; Rubber Stamping & Stamp Making.

ACCU-CUT SYSTEMS
1035 E. Dodge St.
Fremont NE 68026
Contact: C.J. Ludwig
Phone: (800)288-1670 or (402)721-4134
Fax: (800)369-1332 or (402)721-5778
E-mail: cj@accucut.com
Website: www.accucut.com
Offers: The Mark III and Mark IV Roller Cutting Machine and more than 1,400 dies. They are used to cut shapes for scrapbook pages, greeting cards, home decorations and other craft projects.
Catalog: Call (800)288-1670 for free catalog and nearest retailer.
Phone Orders: (800)288-1670.
Mail Orders: Yes.
Discounts: Call.
Accepts: American Express, Discover, MasterCard, Visa

MARIE BROWNING CREATES
P.O. Box 224
Brentwood Bay, British Columbia V8M 1R3
Canada
Contact: Marie Browning, CPD, SCD
Phone: (250)652-3143
Fax: (250)652-3143
Website: Under construction.
Store Location: Brentwood Bay, British Columbia location.
Offers: Pergamano supplies (parchment craft): complete catalog of all parchment-crafting tools, paper, books, patterns, video classes and workshops available. Will travel and teach.
Catalog: $1 (refundable).
Phone Orders: Yes (machine).
Mail Orders: Will ship to US and Canada by surface post. Allow 6 weeks for delivery.
Accepts: Visa

CALCOLA, INC.
P.O. Box 60326, Apt. 325
Houston TX 77205
Contact: Oscar af Strom
Phone: (011-525)308-1575
Fax: (011-525)308-1575
E-mail: afstrom@mail.comunnet.com.mx
Store Location: Mexico City, Mexico location.
Offers: Material for do-it-yourself decals (stickers and iron-ons).
Catalog: Yes.
Phone Orders: From known customers.
Mail Orders: Will ship from Houston. Prepayment required (US check or money order).
Discounts: We are members of HIA and offer 50% to retailers for orders of $100 and 50%/30% for wholesalers for orders of $500.

CHRISTY CRAFTS, INC.
P.O. Box 492
Hinsdale IL 60521
Contact: Betty Christy
Phone: (630)323-6505
Offers: Crafts of the 1800s: paper cutting, iron-on silhouettes, mini memory collage boxes, quilling supplies (books and papers and tools) and wooden ornaments to paint.
Catalog: $1. 12 pages.
Phone Orders: Yes.
Mail Orders: Retail and dealer.

CRAFT CASTLE
732 Mono Way
Sonora CA 95370
Contact: Darlene Drummond, owner
Phone: (209)533-1935
Fax: (209)533-3061
E-mail: craftcas@mlode.com
Website: www.craftcastle.com
Store Location: Sonora CA location. M-Sat, 9-6; Sun, 12-5.
Offers: Needlecraft, fine arts, crafts—paints, wood, stencils and memory album—floral and jewelry supplies.
Phone Orders: With credit card plus p&h.
Accepts: major credit cards, personal check, money order

CRAFT STAMPS
P.O. Box 6B1
Oak Lawn IL 60454
Contact: Donna Jackson
Phone: (773)585-6918
Fax: (773)582-2244
E-mail: craftstamp@aol.com
Offers: Rubber art stamps for all types of stamping and craft projects. Also stamps designed for scrapbooks and memory albums.
Catalog: $4 (refundable on first order).
Phone Orders: Yes. (Will refer to a retailer when available in customer's location.)
Mail Orders: Yes.

Discounts: Wholesale with proper identification.
Accepts: MasterCard, Visa

CREATIVE XPRESS!!
295 W. Center
Provo UT 84601-4430
Contact: Jason Frederick
Phone: (800)563-8679
Fax: (801)373-1446
E-mail: catalog@creativexpress.com
Website: www.creativexpress.com
Store Location: At above address.
Offers: Provo craft products. Scrapbook and tole painting supplies, paper, templates, stencils, clip art, instruction books, wood, art supplies, stickers, rub-ons and much more.
Catalog: 48 pages, color. Free.
Phone Orders: M-F, 8-8; Sat, 9-5 MST.
Mail Orders: We ship anywhere in the world. Usually takes 7-10 working days.
Discounts: Many promotions and coupons.
Accepts: Discover, MasterCard, Visa

CUT IT UP
4543 Orange Grove Ave.
Sacramento CA 95841
Contact: Tom or Vicky Breslin
Phone: (916)482-2288
Fax: (916)482-1331
E-mail: tamara@scrapramento.com
Website: http://www.scrapramento.com/
Store Location: Howe 'Bout Arden, 2100 Arden Way, Suite 105, Sacramento CA 95825.
Catalog: Yes.
Phone Orders: Yes.
Mail Orders: Yes.
Accepts: MasterCard, Visa

D.J. INKERS
P.O. Box 1509
Sherwood OR 97140
Contact: Lana Davis
Phone: (800)325-4890
Fax: (503)625-9785
E-mail: lana@djinkers.com
Website: www.djinkers.com
Offers: Rubber art stamps and accessories, computer clip art, gift line of ready-made products, acid-free designer paper, stickers and clip art books.
Catalog: 85 pages, full color. $5 (refundable with order).
Phone Orders: 8-5; voice mail 24 hours.
Mail Orders: Ship UPS same day.
Accepts: MasterCard, Visa, check, money order, school purchase order

DESIGN A CARD
P.O. Box 5314
Englewood FL 34224
Contact: Pat Blevins

Phone: (941)475-1121
Fax: (941)475-2773
Offers: Award-winning, quality tools for the paper arts. Art Deckle, the stainless ruler with the wavy edge—quickly tear a natural, uncut edge on all paper. Use Nouveau Corner Design Templates, made of thick Mylar, to trace or emboss (no light table required) exquisite shapes and designs on edges of paper.
Catalog: $1.
Phone Orders: Yes.
Mail Orders: Yes.
Discounts: Wholesale information sent on request.
Accepts: MasterCard, Visa

ELLISON CRAFT & DESIGN
25862 Commercentre Dr.
Lake Forest CA 92630-8804
Contact: Customer service
Phone: (800)253-2238
Fax: (888)270-1200
E-mail: info@ellison.com
Website: www.ellison.com
Offers: Hand-operated die-cutting machines and over 1,000 dies. Custom die work available. Idea books and videos and special materials to use in machines.
Catalog: Free 100-page catalog to retailers and professional crafters. Call for a retailer near you.
Phone Orders: M-F, 8-4 PST.
Mail Orders: See ordering information in our catalog.
Discounts: Offers vary.
Accepts: MasterCard, Novus, Visa

EXPRESSIONS OF YOU
5412 93rd Dr. SE
Snohomish WA 98290
Contact: Susan Lee
Phone: (360)568-1295
Fax: (360)568-1295
Offers: Rubber stamps and memory album supplies, such as stamps, pads, markers, paper, embossing, supplies, binders, protective sheets, decorative scissors, stickers, patterned papers, circle cutters, punches, journals, photo corners, glues, templates, die-cuts, stencils and sealing wax. A wide variety of styles to choose from. Hints and tips throughout.
Catalog: 90 pages. $5 ($5 refundable coupon).
Phone Orders: M-F, 10-5 PST.
Mail Orders: Will ship to US, Canada and overseas at actual costs. Allow 3-4 weeks US.
Discounts: Coupons and sales in quarterly newsletter.
Accepts: MasterCard, Visa, check

GENESIS RUBBERSTAMPS
P.O. Box 2673
Anniston AL 36202
Contact: Margaret Tarleton
Phone: (256)236-7787
Fax: (256)235-2107
E-mail: genesisrs@aol.com

Offers: Cats, horses, birds, teachers' stamps, creative stamps and border stamps.

Catalog: $2 (refundable). Free catalog sampler.

GIGGLINS MEMORY CRAFTS

9229 Via Segovia
New Port Richey FL 34655
Contact: Paula Padovano
Phone: (813)372-7486
Fax: (813)372-7486
E-mail lauranne@gte.net
Website: http://home1.gte.net/lauranne/gigglins.html
Offers: Scrapbook supplies, acid-free papers, stickers, albums, templates, pens and our very own u-cuts and headliners.
Catalog: $1 for catalog and sample.
Mail Orders: Will ship to US and Canada. Payment required. Allow 4-6 weeks for delivery.
Accepts: check, money order

GLOBAL DESIGNS, INC.

301 16th Ave. SE
Waseca MN 56093
Contact: Bill Steffan
Phone: (507)835-8009
Fax: (507)835-8541
E-mail: bill@vikingpub.com
Offers: CD-ROMs of decorative click art for PC and Mac. About 200 designs for greeting cards, photo albums, stationery and craft items on each CD. 5 titles available.
Catalog: Free for asking.
Phone Orders: 8:30-5 CST.
Mail Orders: Worldwide.
Discounts: To distributors and retailers.
Accepts: American Express, MasterCard, Visa

GREEN SNEAKERS, INC.

P.O. Box 614
Bel Air MD 21014
Contact: Nick Romer
E-mail: nromer6844@aol.com
Offers: Kreate-a-Lope envelope maker and Kreate-a-Bag gift bag-making system.
Catalog: Send #10 SASE.

HANDMADE SCRAPS

3807 Whispering Lane
Falls Church VA 22041
Contact: Alex Bishop
Phone: (703)256-5149
Fax: (703)256-5149
Offers: Specialty memory book pages and paper shapes.
Phone Orders: Yes.
Mail Orders: At above address.
Discounts: Wholesale and retail.
Accepts: check, money order

HOT OFF THE PRESS, INC.

1250 NW Third Ave.
Canby OR 97013
Contact: Customer service department
Phone: (503)266-9102
Fax: (503)266-8749
E-mail: hotp@earthlink.net
Website: www.hotp.com
Offers: Craft idea and instruction books, covering kids' crafts, floral design, polymer clay, bridal crafts, memory albums and more. Manufactures Paper Pizazz, acid-free, lignin-free decorative papers for scrapbooking. Also manufactures Cards with Pizazz patterned card stock as well as a variety of scrapbooking and card-making accessories.
Catalog: 43 pages, color. $2.
Phone Orders: 8:30-5 PST; voice mail messages are also returned.
Mail Orders: Ships anywhere. Prepayment required (in US dollars). Allow 4-6 weeks for delivery.
Discounts: Sells wholesale to legitimate businesses.
Accepts: MasterCard, Visa

INNOVATIONS

P.O. Box 890100
Temecula CA 92589-0100
Contact: Surra Hublik
Phone: (888)CRAFT34
Fax: (888)CRAFT35
Offers: Supplies for making memory scrapbook albums. Carries the entire line of items (rubber stamps, specialty paper and more) from the following companies: All Night Media, American Traditional Stencils, Azadi, Clearsnap (Colorbox, Paintbox2, Petal Point and others), Hero, Holly Pond Hill, Personal Stamp Exchange, Rubber Stampede, Stampendous and Tsukineko (Fabrico, Kaleidacolor, Encore and others). Papermaking kits and supplies from Arnold Grummer, specialty glues for the Floral Pro Crafty Magic Melt Glue Gun with palm feed grip, Risso Print Goco, cross-stitch kits, embroidery kits, Faster Plaster from Plaid, Dimensional Magic from Plaid, stencils and kits from Delta for making your memory scrapbook albums and loads more.
Catalog: Over 150 pages, b&w and full color. $3 (refundable with first order).
Phone Orders: M-F, 9-5 PST. If using a credit card, you can fax orders 24 hours a day, 7 days a week.
Mail Orders: Yes.
Accepts: American Express, Discover, MasterCard, Visa

KOZY MEMORIES

6006 Marsh Hawk Court
Elk Grove CA 95758
Contact: Debbie
Phone: (916)683-5090
Fax: (916)684-8730
E-mail: mkozisek@softcom.net
Store Location: Showroom open by appointment only.

Offers: Quality scrapbook supplies for less. Will also do special orders.

Catalog: $2 (refundable with order).

Phone Orders: Yes.

Mail Orders: Yes.

Accepts: American Express, MasterCard, Visa, personal check, money order

MICROFLEUR USA

1281 Kimmerling Rd. #5-265

Gardnerville NV 89410

Contact: Janine Primrose

Phone: (888)88FLEUR

Fax: (702)265-5571

Offers: 2 sizes of Microfleur/microwave flower press/drier. 5″ square (regular), 9″ square (maximum). Presses and dries flowers in microwave in minutes.

Phone Orders: M-F, 9-5 PST.

Mail Orders: Will ship US, prepayment required. Allow 1-2 weeks for delivery.

Discounts: Sells wholesale to legitimate businesses.

Accepts: MasterCard, Visa

MRS. V.A.'S PHOTO DESIGNS

P.O. Box 7173

Prospect CT 06712

Contact: Pamela Van Allen

Phone: (203)723-5484

Fax: (203)723-6961

E-mail: mrsvaphoto@aol.com

Offers: Albums for photos and scrapbooking, binders, 8½×11 and 12×12 border and background papers, scrapbook kits, card stock, page protectors, stencils, rulers, adhesives, paper punches, stickers, die-cut shapes, pens, markers, Cropper Hopper products and software for scrapbooking.

Catalog: Full color. $3 (refundable with $3 coupon).

Phone Orders: M-F, 12-5; Sat, 10-5 EST.

Mail Orders: Will ship to US.

Accepts: MasterCard, Visa

NATURE'S PAPER

P.O. Box 416

Ft. Jones CA 96032

Contact: Lynn Wright or Rich Frank

Phone: (800)542-4025

Fax: (530)468-5715

E-mail: treefree@sisqtel.net

Website: www.naturespaper.com

Store Location: 11959 Main St., Ft. Jones CA 96053.

Offers: Over 200 parent sheets (22×30) handmade paper—all tree free—social and letter-size stationery and envelopes. Journals, writing sets and a host of other tree-free handmade paper products.

Catalog: 153-page swatch book; 5×7 sheets hand-bound in sugarcane paper. $19.95.

Phone Orders: M-F, 9-5 PST.

Mail Orders: All orders are shipped within 2 days of receipt.

Discounts: Wholesale to storefronts and home-based businesses with licenses.

Accepts: MasterCard, Visa

ONE HEART . . . ONE MIND, LLC

10608 Widmer

Lenexa KS 66215

Contact: Becki Speakman

Phone: (913)498-3690

Fax: (913)498-0166

E-mail: freshfunky@earthlink.net

Offers: Fresh and Funky stencils to fit design needs. Mini stencils and large stencils available in assorted sizes of checks, stripes, swirls, squiggles, dots, stars and hearts. Multiuse stencils in 34 designs for frames, memory albums, stationery, cards and more.

Catalog: $3.

Phone Orders: M-F, 9-4 CST.

Mail Orders: Prepayment required.

Discounts: Wholesale.

Accepts: MasterCard, Visa

OPTIC GRAPHICS, INC.

101 Dover Rd.

Glen Burnie MD 21060

Contact: Donna Korper

Phone: (800)638-7107

Fax: (410)760-4082

E-mail opticinc@erols.com

Offers: Memory book kits, post-bound albums and D-ring memory book binders.

Catalog: Free upon request.

Phone Orders: For trade only. M-F, 9-5 EST.

Accepts: MasterCard, Visa, credit terms for qualified trade only

RICH AND (ALMOST) FAMOUS RUBBER STAMPS

681 Skyline Rd.

Ventura CA 93003

Contact: Lynne Estrada or Terry Lombardi

Phone: (805)644-3991

Fax: (805)644-3991

E-mail: raafstamps@aol.com

Offers: Rubber stamps, mounted and unmounted. Photo journaling stamps and scrapbooking stamps as well as a full line of images for all types of stamping.

Catalog: $5.

Mail Orders: Retail and wholesale orders accepted. Must be prepaid by check or money order or C.O.D.

Discounts: Wholesale.

Accepts: check, cash

ROCKY MOUNTAIN CRAFT

540 E. 500 N

American Fork UT 84003

Contact: Erline Lindberg, owner

Phone: (800)270-9130

Fax: (801)756-0577

E-mail: castellan@rmcraft.com
Website: www.rmcraft.com
Offers: Complete line of scrapbook supplies; 30% off retail. Includes binders, sheet protectors, glues and mounts, rulers, photo frames, paper tools and scissors. Acid-free card stock, pens, pencils, markers; pattern paper, stickers and stationery by the sheet. Kits, die-cut, stencils, craft punches, books and clip art.
Catalog: Color. $3 (refundable with order).
Phone Orders: 10-6 MST.
Mail Orders: Yes. Ship all over the world.
Discounts: Sales every week.
Accepts: Discover, MasterCard, Visa, check, money order

SCRAPBOOK WORLD

(formerly Merit Albums, Inc.)
19444 Business Center Dr.
Northridge CA 91324
Contact: Violet Bosak
Phone: (818)886-5100
Fax: (818)886-5425
Website: http://www.quikpages.com/m/merit
Store Location: At above address. M-S, 10-5:30
Offers: Scrapbooks, photo albums, stickers, templates, scissors, corner rounders, pens, glue sticks, circle cutter, paper trimmers, theme papers and more.
Phone Orders: M-F, 8-3 PST.
Mail Orders: Ship throughout US and Canada.
Accepts: American Express, Discover, MasterCard, Visa, C.O.D.

SCRAPBOOKS 'N MORE

5769 Westcreek
Ft. Worth TX 76133
Contact: Denise Tolman
Phone: (817)294-4600
Fax: (817)294-2526
E-mail: starmstr@ix.netcom.com
Website: www.scrapbooksnmore.com
Store Location: At above address.
Offers: Supplies for scrapbooks: albums, page protectors, pens, stickers, die-cuts, adhesives, 12×12 pattern and solid paper, $8\frac{1}{2} \times 11$ pattern and solid paper, templates, rulers and pens.
Catalog: Yes.
Phone Orders: Yes.
Mail Orders: Yes.
Discounts: Yes.
Accepts: Discover, MasterCard, Visa

SCRAPPERS UNLIMITED

P.O. Box 337
Eureka MO 63025-0337
Contact: Tami Pfeil
Fax: (314)938-5182 or (800)898-9969
E-mail: info@scrappers.com
Website: Coming soon.
Offers: Scrappers Unlimited is your alternative resource of

scrapbooking tools and supplies from these popular companies: Webway, 3L, Tombow, Canson, Fiskars, Black-Cat, Sakura, Eksuccess, Zig, Stickopotamus, Cut-It-Up, Scrap-Ease, DJ Inkers, Making Memories and more.
Catalog: 16-page, full-color retail catalog.
Phone Orders: Toll-free fax order line.
Mail Orders: Will ship to US and Canada. Prepayment required.
Accepts: MasterCard, Visa, check, money order

STAMP YOUR ART OUT

9225 S. Orange Blossom Trail
Orlando FL 32837
Contact: Bert or Judy Hayslett
Phone: (407)816-0037
Fax: (407)816-4428
Store Location: At above address. M-Sat, 10-6; Sun, 12-4.
Offers: Over 50,000 "fun" rubber stamps (largest selection in America). Also stencils, light tables, oil sticks, photo album and scrapbooking supplies, craft magazines and videotapes. Fabric stamping supplies and huge selection of stickers (Mrs. Grossman, Mr. Grossman, Stickopotamus, Mary Englebreit, Melissa Neufield, Frances Meyer and Paper House).
Catalog: Stampendous, $8; Hero Arts, $10; Personal Stamp Exchange, $12.
Phone Orders: Accepted with credit card.
Mail Orders: Yes.
Discounts: No wholesale.
Accepts: American Express, Diners Club, Discover, MasterCard, Visa, check, money order

STAMPIN' AND SCRAPPIN'

5610 District Blvd., Suite 107
Bakersfield CA 93313
Contact: Michelle
Phone: (805)397-0202 or (800)810-0772
Fax: (805)665-9005
E-mail: sales@stampinscrappin.com
Website: www.stampinscrappin.com
Store Location: At above address.
Offers: Rubber stamping and scrapbooking products, classes, contests and more.
Catalog: On-line catalog, plus a printable catalog.
Phone Orders: 24 hours a day.
Mail Orders: Will ship anywhere in the world. Orders are shipped within 24 hours.
Discounts: Various store and on-line sales.
Accepts: American Express, MasterCard, Visa, check, money order

STAMPIN AROUND

2027 196th St. SW, Suite R-2
Lynnwood WA 98036
Contact: Carl
Phone: (425)744-1993
Fax: (425)744-1890
E-mail: luv2stamp@aol.com
Store Location: Lynnwood WA location.

Offers: Rubber stamps and rubber stamp art supplies, stencils, scrapbooking supplies, exotic papers and more.
Phone Orders: Yes.
Mail Orders: Yes.
Accepts: American Express, Discover, MasterCard, Visa

STAMPINGTON & CO.
22992 Mill Creek, Suite B
Laguna Hills CA 92653
Contact: Kellene Giloff
Phone: (714)380-7318
Fax: (714)380-9355
E-mail somersetad@aol.com
Offers: Classic art and country rubber art stamps; *Somerset Studio* magazine featuring full-color samples and techniques for art stamping, calligraphy, and paper crafting; and *Stampers' Sampler* magazine featuring more than 125 full-color samples of rubber art stamping in every issue.
Catalog: Catalog/idea book, $13.95; includes $5 gift certificate.
Phone Orders: M-F, 9-5 PST.
Mail Orders: Domestic and international; prepayment required. Allow 3-6 weeks for delivery.
Discounts: Wholesale to storefront businesses.
Accepts: MasterCard, Visa

STICKER PLANET
10736 Jefferson Blvd. #503
Culver City CA 90230
Contact: Customer service
Phone: (800)557-8678 (US) or (310)204-7060 (international)
Fax: (800)537-2260 (US) or (310)204-7072 (international)
E-mail: mail@stickerplanet.com
Website: www.stickerplanet.com
Store Location: Locations in Los Angeles and Santa Monica CA. Call for addresses and hours.
Offers: Santa Monica location features full line of scrapbooking supplies and rubber stamps. Both stores feature thousand of stickers. Mail-order catalog shows over 350 acid-free, high-quality sticker designs by famous manufacturers, for crafters and hobbyists.
Catalog: High quality, full color, 68 pages. $5 (refundable). Package includes 50 project ideas, how-to guide to sticker art, reusable storage pouch, plus free periodic catalog supplement mailings.
Phone Orders: M-F, 7-7; Sat-Sun, 8-3 PST.
Mail Orders: Will ship to US and international (additional fee). Prepayment required. Allow 1 week within US. No minimum order required.
Discounts: Volume and multiple-sticker discounts available. Will also sell wholesale to legitimate businesses.
Accepts: Discover, MasterCard, Visa, check, money order

WIMPOLE STREET CREATIONS
419 W. 500 S.
Bountiful UT 84010
Contact: Jeen Brown
Phone: (801)298-0504
Fax: (801)298-1333
E-mail: wimpole@xmission.com
Website: www.wimpolestreet.com
Store Location: At above address.
Offers: Battenburg, crochet and dyed lace, dolls, home decor, pattern books, holiday, ready-made gifts, wearables, baby items and wedding/celebrations. Products available in bulk and kits.
Catalog: Annual; call for information.
Phone Orders: (801)298-0504 or (800)765-0504 (orders only).
Mail Orders: Yes.
Discounts: Sell wholesale to business with resale tax ID number.
Accepts: MasterCard, Visa, check, cash

THE WRITE TYPE
5424-10 Sunol Blvd., Suite 268
Pleasanton CA 94566
Contact: Laura Bonnel
Phone: (925)417-7567
Fax: (925)462-8837
E-mail: thewritype@aol.com
Offers: Memory supplies, scrapbooking products and craft supplies. Rubber stamps and stamping supplies.
Catalog: 32 pages. $3 (refundable on first purchase).
Phone Orders: M-F, 10-4 PST.
Mail Orders: Prepayment required. Will ship 7-10 working days.
Discounts: Retail only; discounted prices.
Accepts: MasterCard, Visa

Sculpture & Modeling

Also see Ceramics; Metalworking; Mold Crafts; Woodworking.

AMERICAN ART CLAY CO., INC.
4717 W. 16th St.
Indianapolis IN 46222
Contact: Nancy Elliott
Phone: (317)244-6871 or (800)374-1600
Fax: (317)248-9300
E-mail: amacobrent@aol.com
Website: www.amaco.com
Offers: Craft supplies and modeling materials. Since 1919, AMACO has been a leading manufacturer of modeling clays, such as Permoplast, Plast-i-clay, Marblex and Mexican; modeling materials, including Friendly Plastic, FIMO, polymer clay Millefiori Canes, Quilt Squares, Designer Squares, Sculptamold, Claycrete and SuperDough. Also Rub 'n Buff and Brush 'n Leaf metallic finishes, Batikit fabric dyes, Cotton Press hand-cast cotton paper products, and push molds for use with polymer clays.
Catalog: Free.
Phone Orders: M-F, 8-5 EST.
Mail Orders: Prepayment required. Will ship to US and Canada.
Discounts: Manufacturer—sells through distributors.
Accepts: Discover, MasterCard, Visa

DICK BLICK
Dept. CB
P.O. Box 1267
Galesburg IL 61402-1267
Phone: (309)343-6181
Offers: Full line of art/sculpture and other materials and equipment: soapstone, alabaster and stone sculpture tool sets. Modeling: instant papier-mâchés, Sculptamold, plastercraft gauze, plaster of Paris (and molds), Sculpey, FIMO and modeling clays. Clays: Mexican pottery, Marblex, Westwood ovencraft and others. Also offers Egyptian paste, earthenware and other kitchen-fired clays, plus glazes, ceramic and modeling tools/sets and aids.
Accepts: American Express, Discover, MasterCard, Visa

CLAY FACTORY OF ESCONDIDO
P.O. Box 460598
Escondido CA 92046-0598
Contact: Howard or Marie Segal
Phone: (760)741-3242
Fax: (760)741-5436
E-mail: clayfactoryinc@clayfactoryinc.com
Website: www.clayfactoryinc.com
Store Location: 750 N. Citracado Pkwy. #23, Escondido CA 92029. M-F, 9-5.
Offers: Premo Sculpey, Super Sculpey, Sculpey III, Granitex, ElastiClay, Cernit, Pearl Powders, Kemper tools and videos by Marie Segal, Maureen Carlson, Tory Hughes and Donna Kato.
Catalog: Yes.
Phone Orders: Yes.
Mail Orders: Yes.
Discounts: Retail and wholesale.
Accepts: MasterCard, Visa

THE COMPLEAT SCULPTOR
90 Van Dam St.
New York NY 10013
Contact: Bill Thompsen
Phone: (212)243-6074
Fax: (212)243-6374
E-mail: tcs@sculpt.com
Website: http//:www.sculpt.com
Store Location: New York NY location.
Offers: One-stop shopping for all of your sculpting needs. The world's largest selection of stone, wood, clay, molding and casting materials. We also provide backup services, mold-making/casting, finishing and mounting, show installation and photography.
Catalog: Free upon request. 108 pages.
Phone Orders: M-Sat, 9-6; T, 9-8.
Mail Orders: We ship UPS, domestic and international. Surcharges for next day and second-day air and C.O.D.
Accepts: American Express, MasterCard, Visa

DESIGN CONSULTING SERVICE
41355 Covelo Rd.
Willits CA 95490
Phone: (707)984-8394
Offers: Low shrink wax for electroplated molds. Also offers custom rooting of vinyl heads. Call or write.

DODD: DISCOUNT MARBLE & GRANITE
P.O. Box 2721
North Hill CA 91393
Phone: (818)891-1909 or (800)2-SCULPT
Offers: Stones for sculpting, including marble, granite, alabaster, limestone, sandstone, onyx, soapstone, steatite, serpentine, travertine, lapis, sodalite and others, to 5 tons. Tools include chisels, mallets, rasps, rifflers, turning pins, grinding machines, discs and burrs, bits, diamond saws and others. Supplies include bases, polishing compounds, epoxies and others. Videos and books also available.

Catalog: Free list; request in writing only.
Discounts: Quantity buyers, schools and professional groups and trade.

DURHAM

P.O. Box 804
Des Moines IA 50304
Phone: (515)243-0491
Offers: Durham's Rock Hard Water Putty: molds, carves, sculpts, models or casts (no firing). Available at hardware, paint and home center stores nationwide.
Catalog: Send large SASE for handcraft booklet.

THE ROBERT FIDA SCULPTURE STUDIO

1100 Storey Blvd.
Cheyenne WY 82009
Phone: (888)635-5056
Offers: *The Sculptor's Studio* video series with Robert Fida covers mold making and casting, including casting with concrete, plaster, hydrostone, hydrocal, pewter, bronze, pecan shell, marble. Also covers gold leafing, finishing techniques for concrete and plaster, shrinking castings, marketing for the visual artist and other topics.
Catalog: Call for brochure.

GAMEPLAN VIDEOS

(formerly Gameplan Artranch)
2233 McKinley Ave.
Berkeley CA 94703
Phone: (510)843-9969
Offers: Instructional videos on working with polymer clay, including a foundation course and surface techniques, mokume gane, embellishments, molds/stamps/tools, and recreating materials, including lapis, bone, ivory, jade, amber and coral.
Catalog: Free.

KEMPER ENTERPRISES, INC.

13595 12th St.
Chino CA 91710
Contact: Katie Munday
Phone: (800)388-5367 or (909)627-6191
Fax: (909)627-4008
E-mail: thetoolady@aol.com
Offers: Manufacturer and designer of tools for polymer clay, including the Klay Gun and pattern cutters. Distributes Cernit, the hardest baking polymer clay with new "nature's colors" and "metallics." Carries Imaginaries There Is No Limit, a new product line for children that includes the "too much fun" klay pen kits and storybook finger puppet kits, which develop imagination. Designer and manufacturer of clay and paint tools for children, including the Art Notebook.
Catalog: Free. 70+ pages, color. $1.50 for p&h.
Mail Orders: Can expect order to ship within 2 days of receipt. Ship domestic and international through UPS.
Phone Orders: Customer service hours are M-F, 8-4:30 PST.

Discount: Sell wholesale to businesses. For account qualifications and status, please contact.
Accepts: Discover, MasterCard, Visa, International Money Order, bank wire transfer in American dollars only

MONTOYA/MAS INTERNATIONAL, INC.

435 Southern Blvd.
West Palm Beach FL 33405
Phone: (407)832-4401
Store Location: At above address.
Offers: Carving stones (imported), line of marble bases (many sizes/colors), over 1,600 sculpture tools (including hard-to-find), clays and waxes. Services available include art foundry, casting, mounting, repairs and restoration. Complete selection of fine art supplies.
Catalog: $3.
Discounts: Quantity; teachers and institutions; sells wholesale to legitimate businesses.

STEATITE OF SOUTHERN OREGON, INC.

2891 Elk Lane
Grants Pass OR 97527
Contact: John or Beverly Pugh
Phone: (541)479-3646
Fax: (541)479-3646
Store Location: At above address. M-F, 8-5.
Offers: Multicolored soapstone and black and dark green chlorite from our mines. Other colored soapstone from the western states. Basic Soapstone Carving Booklet. All soapstone is thoroughly tested and is asbestos free. Other soft stones include numerous colors of alabaster, anhydrite and catlinite. Harder stones include marble in a variety of colors, limestone and travertine. Complete line of sculpting tools and supplies by Trow and Holden, Alpha Professional tools and many other companies.
Catalog: Free introductory packet.
Phone Orders: M-F, 7-6 PST.
Mail Orders: Ship throughout US and Canada. New accounts prepaid please. 2-3 weeks for delivery.
Discounts: Wholesale to legitimate businesses.
Accepts: Discover, MasterCard, Visa

TROW AND HOLDEN CO., INC.

P.O. Box 475
45-57 S. Main St.
Barre VT 05641
Contact: Lauren LaMorte
Phone: (800)451-4349
Fax: (802)476-7025
E-mail: trowco@aol.com
Offers: Line of stone sculpting and cutting tools: 5 pneumatic carving tools, pneumatic stone carving sets, soft stone hand-carving sets, mallets, carbide tip chisels, rippers, chisels (machine, splitter, cleanup, double blade, marble lettering, 4-point, 9-point, marble tooth and cutting types) and carver's and other drills.
Catalog: Free.

Tole & Decorative Crafts

Also see General Craft Supplies; Artist's Supplies, Graphics & Printing; Miniature Making, Miniatures & Dollhouses; Paints, Finishes & Adhesives; Fabric Decorating; other related categories.

ACCENTS IN PINE
Dept. BCS8
P.O. Box 7387
Gonic NH 03839
Contact: P.G. Olds
Phone: (603)332-4579
Fax: (603)332-4579
E-mail: accents@ttlc.net
Website: http://ttlc.net/accents/
Offers: Woodcraft plans and patterns. Huge assortment of popular designs. Over 1,500 full-size patterns for yard, holiday, country projects, gifts, toys and more.
Catalog: Illustrated, sample pattern included. $2.
Phone Orders: 24-hour voice mail.
Mail Orders: Will ship anywhere. Prepayment required (US funds).
Discounts: Quantity discounts available to everyone.
Accepts: MasterCard, Visa

ADVENTURES IN CRAFTS
Yorkville Station
P.O. Box 6058
New York NY 10128
Phone: (212)410-9793
Fax: (212)410-9793
Offers: Decoupage products, including prints (animals, flowers, Oriental, Godey's Ladies, Anton Pieck and others) and b&w prints (botanicals, borders, birds and animals) and decoupage kits designed by Dee Davis. Also offers wood products, including boxes, lap desks, tables and more. Gilding supplies available include Dutch metal gold/silver leaf. Carries hardware, papers, decoupage scissors, brayer, burnisher, tools, finishes and books of prints. Basic textbook *Decoupage Paper Cutouts for Decorations and Pleasure* by Dee Davis, $19.95 plus $4.95 p&h.
Catalog: $3.50.

THE ARTIST'S CLUB
P.O. Box 8930
Vancouver, WA 98668
Phone: (800)845-6507
Offers: Tole painting/country home unpainted wood decorations, including Christmas ornaments and decorations, spring bunnies, watering cans and others. Also offers painting projects, paints, brushes, tools and instruction books.
Catalog: Free.
Accepts: American Express, Discover, JCB, MasterCard, Visa

B&B PUBLISHING, INC.
P.O. Box 420268
Kissimmee FL 34742
Phone: (407)870-2121
Offers: How-to decorative painting videos and books by Maureen McNaughton and Linda Wise.
Catalog: Free brochure.
Discounts: Sells wholesale to legitimate businesses.

BARCLAY LEAF IMPORTS, INC.
21 Wilson Terrace
Elizabeth NJ 07208
Phone: (908)353-5522
Fax: (908)353-5525
Offers: Gold leaf, including introductory packages and line of professional supplies. Also offers metal leaf. Send SASE.

THE BOX CO.
(formerly White Pine Designs, Inc.)
3877 Christytown Rd.
Story City IA 50248
Contact: Jennifer
Phone: (515)733-5086
Fax: (515)733-5086
Offers: Raw wood Shaker band boxes. Handcrafted from quality birch wood.
Mail Orders: Worldwide.
Discounts: Wholesale and distributor.
Accepts: MasterCard, Visa, check

BRIDGEWATER SCROLLWORKS
47318 Mountain Ash Blvd.
Osage MN 56570
Contact: Terry LaFleur
Phone: (218)573-3094
Offers: Wood cutouts—over 1,000 shapes, including hearts, animals, flowers, figures and others. Custom cutting service.
Catalog: Catalog temporarily out of print as we fill your custom orders.
Discounts: Quantity.
Accepts: Discover, MasterCard, Visa

CAPE COD COOPERAGE
1150 Queen Anne Rd.
Chatham MA 02633
Phone: (508)432-0788

Fax: (508)430-0317
Store Location: Cape Cod MA location.
Offers: Barrel staves—sanded, ready-to-decorate/paint—and slates in all shapes and sizes.
Catalog: Send SASE for list.
Phone Orders: Yes.
Mail Orders: Yes.
Discounts: Wholesale.
Accepts: MasterCard, Visa, check, C.O.D.

CRAFTERS STOREHOUSE

(formerly Rainbow Woods)
1480 Bells Ferry Rd.
Marietta GA 30066
Phone: (800)423-2762
Fax: (770)499-9191
Website: crafterstorehouse.com
Offers: Unfinished wood turnings, shapes and cutouts, including dowels, wheels, pegs, hearts, stars and a full line of wooden shapes. A complete assortment of hardware, jewelry findings and paints are available.
Catalog: Free.
Phone Orders: Yes.
Mail Orders: At above address.
Accepts: Discover, MasterCard, Visa

CRAFTS JUST FOR YOU

2030 Clinton Ave.
Alameda CA 94501
Phone: (800)272-3848
Fax: (510)521-4789
Offers: Over 6,000 products in lines of paints, brushes, pre-cut wood, stencils, tole books and more.
Catalog: $5.

CUPBOARD DISTRIBUTING

P.O. Box 148CSS
119 Miami St.
Urbana OH 43078
Phone: (937)652-3338
Fax: (937)652-3398
E-mail: cupboard@foryou.net
Website: www.foryou.net/~cupboard
Store Location: At above address. M-F, 9-5; Sat, 10-4. Open to public.
Offers: Quality unfinished wood shapes, turnings and surfaces, such as birdhouses, gardening supplies, fences, chunky shapes, hearts, stars, buttons, spools, beads, miniatures, eggs, fruit, candlesticks, pegs, dowels, knobs, wheels and axles, spindles, finials, plugs and Christmas ornaments. Also craft items, paints, brushes, stains, varnishes, stencils, hardware, jewelry findings and custom cutting available.
Catalog: $2 (refundable).
Phone Orders: M-F, 8-5; Sat, 10-4 EST.
Mail Orders: Most orders shipped within 24 hours. Prepayment required.
Accepts: Discover, MasterCard, Visa

CUSTOM WOOD CUT-OUTS UNLIMITED

P.O. Box 518
Massillon OH 44648-0518
Contact: David Harting
Phone: (330)832-2919
Fax: (330)832-2919
Offers: Wood items for tole and decorative painters. Also will do custom wood cutting.
Catalog: $2 (refundable).
Phone Orders: Yes.
Mail Orders: Yes.
Discounts: Yes.
Accepts: MasterCard, Visa

DECORATIVE ARTS STUDIO

P.O. Box 227
Main St.
Danby VT 05739
Contact: Zilda McKinstry
Phone: (802)293-5775
Fax: (802)293-5775
Store Location: At above address.
Offers: Professional-quality stencils, brushes, paints and related supplies. Stencil styles include Early American, Victorian, Art Deco, arts and crafts and contemporary. Master stenciler on staff to answer technical questions. Classes also available.
Catalog: $4.
Phone Orders: M-F, 9:30-5:30.
Mail Orders: Orders shipped within 48 hours to US and Canada.
Discounts: Dealer terms available.
Accepts: check, money order, C.O.D.

DESIGNS BY BENTWOOD, INC.

P.O. Box 1676
Thomasville GA 31799
Phone: (912)226-1223
Offers: Bentwood products for painting, including boxes—pie, bonnet, bride's, cheese, tine, purse, paint, pantry and others. Also offers scoops, piggins, sifter, wastebaskets and canisters.

DUX' DEKES DECOY CO.

1356 North Rd.
Greenwich NY 12834
Phone: (518)692-7703 or (800)553-4725
Offers: Over 100 patterns of carved decoy blanks, including swan, goose, duck, loon, shorebirds and wading blanks (miniature to full-size white pine or basswood). Also offers cork decoy kits and paint kits for usable hunting decoys. Write or call.
Discounts: Sells wholesale.
Accepts: MasterCard, Visa

THE ELBRIDGE CO.

6110 Merriam Lane
Merriam KS 66203
Contact: David Tannahill

Phone: (913)384-6188 or (888)384-4401 (US and Canada)
Fax: (913)384-6268
Store Location: At above address.
Offers: Wooden lampshades available in a variety of shapes, including round, square, rectangle, octagon and oval. Expertly crafted and ready for your finish of paint or stain.
Catalog: Free.
Phone Orders: Yes.
Mail Orders: Will ship UPS or US mail overseas.
Discounts: Wholesale and retail.
Accepts: MasterCard, Visa

FLORA & CO. MULTIMEDIA

P.O. Box 8263
Albuquerque NM 87198
Contact: Jan Flora
Phone: (505)255-9988
Fax: (505)255-9988
E-mail: crafts@floraco.com
Website: floraco.com
Offers: Silkscreen instruction video, adapted to the home workshop, demonstrating techniques for reproducing patterns on fabric, wood, paper, plastics and other flat surfaces; a workbook is included. Also puppet making. Send SASE.
Phone Orders: Fax 24 hours a day.
Mail Orders: Immediate shipment.
Accepts: American Express, Discover, MasterCard, Visa

CHAROLETTE FORD TRUNKS

P.O. Box 536
14 S. Haney
Spearman TX 79081
Contact: Tammy Benton or Charolette Ford
Phone: (806)659-3027 or (800)553-2649
Fax: (806)659-5614
E-mail: trunks@charolettefordtrunks.com
Website: www.charolettefordtrunks.com
Store Location: At above address. M-F, 8:30-4 CST.
Offers: Trunks, wooden boxes, how-to books and videos, catalog, deco prints, cowhides, wooden western boxes and window frames and old windowpanes decorated.
Catalog: 60 pages. $2.
Phone Orders: (800)553-2649.
Mail Orders: P.O. Box 536, Spearman TX 79081.
Discounts: Over $100, 10% off. 25 or more videos, $9.95.
Accepts: American Express, Discover, MasterCard, Visa, check, money order

THE GATSONIAN DETAIL

RR 2, Box 48
Chillicothe MO 64601
Phone: (660)646-0015
Offers: Pecan resin ready-to-paint figurines, including angels, Santas, bears, bunnies, ornaments, villages and others.
Catalog: 40 pages, color. $4.

GODIN ART, INC.

352 German School Rd.
RR 1
Paris, Ontario N3L 3E1
Canada
Contact: Jessica or Pat Godin
Phone: (519)448-1244
Fax: (519)448-1302
E-mail: godinart@networx.on.ca
Offers: Cast waterfowl carvings including life-size drakes (canvas back, bufflehead, blue-winged teal, green-winged teal and wigeon) by Pat Godin. Also offers blending brushes, waterfowl pattern books and instructional videos. Call or write.
Catalog: Flyers available.
Phone Orders: M-S, 9-5 EST.
Mail Orders: We ship anywhere.
Discounts: Wholesale.
Accepts: Visa

GOLD LEAF & METALLIC POWDERS

74 Trinity Place, Suite 1200
New York NY 10006
Contact: Steve Martinez
Phone: (212)267-4900 or (800)322-0323
Fax: (212)608-4245
Store Location: At above address.
Offers: Genuine and composition gold leaf in a variety of karats and shades. Plus silver, palladium, copper and aluminum leaf. Supplies for patinating and gilding. Restoration aids. Gold leaf kits for the novice.
Catalog: $2.
Phone Orders: Yes.
Mail Orders: Will ship to US and international.
Discounts: Wholesale.
Accepts: MasterCard, Visa, check, C.O.D., cash

THE GREAT WALL DECORATOR STENCILS

881 Lockhaven Dr.
Los Altos CA 94024
Contact: Lorraine A. Hereld
Phone: (650)969-2766
Fax: (650)969-2766
Store Location: Studio at above address.
Offers: Designers specializing in stencil designs for children's rooms.
Catalog: Color. $4.
Phone Orders: M-F, 9-5 PST. Fax anytime.
Mail Orders: To US and Canada.
Discounts: Sell wholesale or retail.

HERITAGE SAW CO.

11225 Sixth St. E.
St. Petersburg FL 33706
Phone: (813)367-7557
Offers: Line of miniature steel saws, aluminum skillets and irons for tole painting.

Catalog: $2.
Discounts: Sells wholesale.

HOME CRAFT EXPRESS, INC.
P.O. Box 24890
San Jose CA 95154
Phone: (800)301-7377
Fax: (800)528-4193
Offers: Decorative painting products, including paints, brushes and supplies by Delta, Jo Sonja, Loew Cornell, DecoArt, Robert Simmons, Blair Satin Tole, Designs From the Heart, White Lightning and others. Also offers papier maché items, painting videos and books.
Catalog: Free.

J&R INDUSTRIES, INC.
P.O. Box 4221
Shawnee Mission KS 66204
Contact: Kathy Whalen
Phone: (913)362-6667 or (800)999-9513 or (888)83-CRAFT
Fax: (913)362-7421
Offers: Complete line of papier-mâché, paints, brushes, stains, sealers, varnishes, wood products (plaques, cutouts, shapes and boxes), wire forms (angel wings, hangers, quilt hangers, paintable slate shapes and barrel staves), paintable watches, clock parts, musical movements, Dremel tools, X-Acto blades, jewelry findings and resin figures.
Catalog: Papier-mâché, free. General supply, $3 (refundable with order).
Phone Orders: M-F, 8-5.
Mail Orders: Will ship anywhere, f.o.b. our dock in Shawnee Mission KS.
Discounts: Sells wholesale to legitimate businesses only.
Accepts: MasterCard, Visa, prepaid, C.O.D., 1% 10 net 30 on approved credit

JENNINGS DECOY CO.
601 Franklin Ave. NE
St. Cloud MN 56304
Phone: (320)253-2253
Fax: (320)253-9537
Offers: Over 1,400 products for carvers: basswood, tupelo, butternut cutouts and cutout kits—wildfowl, Santas and others. Also offers eyes, other accessories, patterns, cork decoy kits and books.
Catalog: Free.

KEMPER ENTERPRISES, INC.
13595 12th St.
Chino CA 91710
Contact: Katie Munday
Phone: (800)388-5367 or (909)627-6191
Fax: (909)627-4008
E-mail: thetoolady@aol.com
Offers: Designer and manufacturer of tools for embossing and stenciling. Look for our new Rubit tool.
Catalog: Free. 70+ pages, color. $1.50 for p&h.
Phone Orders: M-F, 8-4:30 PST.

Mail Orders: Can expect order to ship within 2 days of receipt. Ship domestic and international through UPS.
Discounts: Sell wholesale to businesses. For account qualifications and status please contact.
Accepts: Discover, MasterCard, Visa, International Money Order, bank wire transfer in American dollars only

LADYBUG COTTAGE
9339 Rosedale Hwy., Suite F
Bakersfield CA 93312
Contact: Shirley Vance
Phone: (805)588-8798
Fax: (805)589-5103*51
Store Location: At above address.
Offers: Classes, cut wood and pattern packets. Silk floral sales and design. Blended crafts for sale.
Catalog: Single page brochure.
Phone Orders: Yes.
Accepts: Discover, MasterCard, Visa

THE MAGIC BRUSH, INC.
P.O. Box 530
Portal AZ 85632
Contact: Sherry C. Nelson
Phone: (520)558-2285
Fax: (520)558-2285
Store Location: 3 Creek Rd., Portal AZ 85632
Offers: Pattern/instruction books for decorative painting, by Sherry C. Nelson, MDA, including how to paint realistic birds, butterflies and animals on wood, reverse glass or canvas; carries design/pattern packets.
Catalog: Yes.
Phone Orders: Yes.
Mail Orders: Yes.
Accepts: MasterCard, Visa

MANOR HOUSE DESIGN
85 Great Lake Dr.
Annapolis MD 21403-3725
Phone: (410)268-9782
Fax: (410)268-9782
Offers: Precut stencils (Mylar, acetate) of wreaths, potted flowers, topiaries, tabletop, trompe l'oeil, bird cages and others—detailed cut. Precut stencils for wall murals. No stencil patterns.
Catalog: $5.
Discounts: Sells wholesale to legitimate businesses.
Accepts: MasterCard, Visa

MARILYN'S DECORATIVE ARTS STUDIO
1763 S. Leyden
Denver CO 80224
Contact: Marilyn Corners
Phone: (303)758-8266
Fax: (303)757-5516
E-mail: marilyn@mdas.com
Website: www.mdas.com
Store Location: At above address. Hours by appointment.

Offers: Pattern packets for furniture, clothing and luggage. Designs to paint. Full-size patterns, complete instructions and photos. Also a book of stroke word designs to decorate baby things.
Catalog: Can be printed from website.
Phone Orders: Leave message on voice mail.
Mail Orders: 24-hour turnaround.
Discounts: 40% on orders 12 or more/3 of a kind.
Accepts: MasterCard, Visa, check, money order

POSITIVELY COUNTRY/ORNAMENTS UNLIMITED

(formerly Ornaments Unlimited)
7416 Bay Shore Dr. W. 190
Muskego WI 53150
Phone: (800)762-3556
Fax: (414)679-1578
Offers: Birch ply cutout ornaments and others, in ⅛" or ¼" birch plywood. Custom cutting service for original patterns. Call or write.
Discounts: Sells wholesale. Distributor prices available.

ROYAL DESIGN STUDIO

2504 Transporation Ave., Suite H
National City CA 91950
Contact: Melanie Royals
Phone: (619)477-3559, orders (800)747-9767
Fax: (619)477-8193
E-mail: royaldesign@aol.com
Website: www.fauxfx.com/royaldesign.html
Store Location: At above address, by appointment.
Offers: Precut designer stencils for trompe l'oeil, murals, borders and focal points. Instructional videos and workshops.
Catalog: 40 pages, full color, redeem with order.
Phone Orders: Yes.
Mail Orders: Ships to US and abroad. Prepayment required.
Discounts: Wholesale to storefronts. Professional discount available.
Accepts: American Express, MasterCard, Visa

S&G, INC.

P.O. Box 805
Howell MI 48844
Phone: (517)546-9240
Fax: (517)546-9720
Offers: Line of wind chimes, preprimed and ready-to-print metal in four sizes. Also offers wind chime patterns. Call or send SASE.
Discounts: Sells wholesale to dealers.

SANDEEN'S SCANDINAVIAN ART, GIFTS & NEEDLECRAFT

1315 White Bear Ave.
St. Paul MN 55106
Contact: Gail R. Sandeen
Phone: (612)776-7012
Store Location: At above address.
Offers: Tole-painting and folk art supplies, including wood items, paints, patterns and instructional books. Also offers

Norwegian rosemaling, Swedish Dala painting and Bavarian Bauernmalerei.
Catalog: $3 (refundable). Also offers a free giftware catalog.
Phone Orders: Yes.
Mail Orders: Yes.
Accepts: American Express, MasterCard, Visa

JACKIE SHAW STUDIO

13306 Edgemont Rd.
Smithsburg MD 21783
Phone: (301)824-7592
Offers: 100 videos/books, including *View It 'N Do It* decorative painting lessons by Jackie Shaw, Ardi Hansen, Nancy Michael, Sherry Gunter and others. Subjects include angels, wildflowers, birds/butterflies, animals, simple strokes and faux finishes. Pattern books include subjects such as folk art, wood, fabric painting, tin punch, stenciling and others. Also carries brushes and kits. Contact your dealer.
Catalog: $1.
Discounts: Sells wholesale to legitimate businesses.

SIMS DESIGN

24 Tower Cres.
Barrie, Ontario L4N 2V2
Canada
Contact: Order desk
Phone: (705)725-0152
Fax: (705)725-8637
E-mail: sims@drlogick.com
Offers: Laser-cut stencils: The Sims Collection specializes in wispy, romantic designs, faux architectural details and trompe l'oeil. Designs include whimsical fairies, a 64" potted tree and garden birdhouse with fluttering birds. Brush on a gently aged look with old block, columns and a hole in the wall that lets the sky shine through.
Catalog: 12 pages, color. $3 (refundable).
Phone Orders: 7 days a week, 24 hours a day.
Mail Orders: Will ship worldwide. Prepayment required.
Discounts: Legitimate wholesale inquiries welcome.
Accepts: MasterCard, Visa, International Money Orders

STENART STENCILS

P.O. Box 114
24 Jefferson Ave.
Pitman NJ 08071
Contact: Aimee Burgin
Phone: (609)589-9857
Fax: (609)582-0004
E-mail: stenart@snip.net
Offers: Delightful collection of 395 precut quality stencils for home decor and crafts. Florals, country, garden and mural themes, mini stencils and more! Easy-to-use stenciling sponges and stencil paint also available.
Catalog: 64 pages. $4.95 (refundable).
Mail Orders: Yes.
Discounts: Wholesale and professional crafters to legitimate businesses.
Accepts: MasterCard, Visa

STENCIL EASE INTERNATIONAL, LLC

P.O. Box 1127
7 Center Rd. W.
Old Saybrook CT 06475
Contact: Brian Greenho
Phone: (800)334-1776
Fax: (860)395-0166
E-mail: stencile@snet.net
Website: www.stencilease.com
Offers: Laser-cut home decor stencils, Spill-Proof dry solid stencil paints, stencil brushes, antique bronzing stencils, garden delight stencils, brass stencils, decorator stamps, acrylic glaze paints, Japan paint colors, Fabtex paints, Rub 'n Buff paints, how-to books and videos.
Catalog: 75 pages, over 250 designs; call (800)334-1776 for nearest dealer.
Phone Orders: Yes.
Mail Orders: Yes.
Discounts: Wholesale only.
Accepts: American Express, MasterCard, Visa

STENCIL HOUSE OF N.H., INC.

P.O. Box 16109
Hooksett NH 03106
Phone: (603)625-1716
Offers: Over 230 stencils (from Mylar) designs: reproductions, children's, florals, traditional and others—for hard surfaces and fabrics. Also offers Paintstiks, acrylics, stencil adhesives, brushes, cleaners and floor cloths. Services include custom designing and stenciling information.
Catalog: $4 (refundable).
Phone Orders: (800)622-9416.
Discounts: Sells wholesale to legitimate businesses.

STENCILS BY NANCY

15219 Stuebner Airline #5
Houston TX 77069
Contact: Nancy Tribolet
Phone: (281)893-2227
Fax: (281)893-6733
E-mail: stennan@aol.com
Store Location: At above address. M-F, 10-5; Sat, 10-4.
Offers: Stencils, paints, brushes and related supplies. Teaches classes. Custom stenciling.
Catalog: 16 pages, full color. $5.
Phone Orders: M-Sat, 8-7 CST.
Mail Orders: Will ship to US, Canada, Mexico and worldwide. Prepayment required.
Discounts: Wholesale to legitimate businesses.
Accepts: American Express, MasterCard, Visa

STONE BRIDGE COLLECTION

2 Mill St.
Pakenham, Ontario K0A 2X0
Canada
Contact: Laurie Sattler
Phone: (613)624-5080
Fax: (613)624-5081
E-mail: lsattler@stonebridgecoll.com
Website: www.stonebridgecoll.com
Offers: Check our Internet site for on-line newsletter "Techniques." On-line shopping available. We are the largest distributor of decorative art pattern packets (featuring over 1,000 packets from top artists). Quality wood pieces, decoys, tinware, painting supplies and baskets.
Catalog: $3, US; $4, Canadian.
Phone Orders: (800)ART-TOLE. M-F, 9-5 EST.
Mail Orders: Will ship internationally. Prepayment required. Friendly service. Other location: 4411 Bee Ridge Rd., Suite 256, Sarasota FL 34233.
Discounts: Wholesale to legitimate businesses.
Accepts: MasterCard, Visa

SURMA

11 E. Seventh St.
New York, NY 10003
Phone: (212)477-0729
Fax: (212)473-0439
Offers: Line of Ukranian egg decorating kits, dyes and other supplies. Also candle-making supplies, including 100% pure beeswax and paraffin.
Catalog: Free.

SWISS MUSIC BOX, LTD.

Dept. CSS
P.O. Box 26063
Shawnee Mission KS 66225-6063
Contact: Elaine Kieffer
Phone: (800)255-0676
Offers: Swiss and Japanese musical mechanisms, wood patterns and unpainted boxes.
Catalog: Brochure.
Phone Orders: M-F, 10-5; Sat, 10-2 CST.
Mail Orders: Prepayment. Allow 2-5 days for shipment.
Accepts: American Express, Discover, MasterCard, Visa

TREE TREASURES

P.O. Box 1069
Bensalem PA 19020
Phone: (215)788-2818 or (800)251-7212
Fax: (215)788-6999
Store Location: Other location: 617 Rosa Ave., Croydon PA 19021.
Offers: Wooden cutouts, miniatures, turnings, beads, balls, wooden kits for kids, birdhouses, brass hinges, hardware (screws, cup hooks, lazy Susan bearings and more), Forstner flat-bottom drill bits and wooden boxes.
Catalog: $2.
Phone Orders: M-F, 8-5 EST.
Mail Orders: At P.O. Box.
Accepts: MasterCard, Visa

VESTERHEIM NORWEGIAN-AMERICAN MUSEUM

P.O. Box 379
502 W. Water St.
Decorah IA 52101
Contact: Donna Bergan

Phone: (319)382-9682
Fax: (319)382-8828
E-mail: vesterheim@vesterheim.com
Website: www.vesterheim.com
Store Location: At above address; Main Street of business area, 7 days a week.
Offers: Woodenware, paints, brushes and instruction books for rosemaling. Norwegian and Scandinavian interest books and gifts.
Catalog: Rosemaler's Supplies Catalog and gift shop and Heritage Books fliers. Free.
Phone Orders: (800)979-3346.
Mail Orders: P.O. Box 379, Decorah IA 52101.
Discounts: Membership—10%.
Accepts: all major credit cards

VIKING FOLK ART PUBLICATIONS, INC.
301 16th Ave. SE
Waseca MN 56093
Contact: Jan Draheim
Phone: (507)835-8009
Fax: (507)835-8541
E-mail: bill@vikingpub.com
Website: www.viking-publications.com
Offers: Decorative painting instructional books. Wide range of subject matter from American, Norwegian, Russian, Bavarian and Spanish to Japanese folk art. Also available home decor, florals and landscape on canvas. High-quality color photos with well-written instructions and patterns.
Catalog: Available for asking.
Phone Orders: 8:30-5 CST.
Mail Orders: Ship worldwide.
Discounts: To distributors and legitimate retailers.
Accepts: American Express, MasterCard, Visa

VIKING WOODCRAFTS, INC.
1317 Eighth St. SE
Waseca MN 56093
Phone: (507)835-8043
Fax: (507)835-3895
Offers: Ready-to-paint decorative items, including wood items, ash baskets, metal shapes and others. Also carries Jo Sonja paints, accessories and more.
Catalog: Over 500 pages.

WOOD TO PAINT
P.O. Box 70
Mound MN 55364
Offers: Line of precut wood kits. Also offer stenciling and painting supplies, hardware items and books.
Catalog: $2.
Accepts: Discover, MasterCard, Visa

THE WOODEN HEART
182 Carden Dr.
Elizabethton TN 37643
Contact: Janice Miller
Phone: (423)543-5602
E-mail: wheart@perffered.com
Offers: New book titled *Season in Time*, 52 pages on wooden furniture, fabric and more. Book offers detail linework instructions, excellent photos and designs. Retails for $11.95. Pattern packets available.
Catalog: Send 2 stamps. Free.
Phone Orders: M-F, 9-6 EST.
Mail Orders: Will ship to US. All orders prepaid.
Discounts: To shops and home studios.

WOODEN MEMORIES
Rt. 1 Box 87
Bear Lake PA 16402
Contact: Ken Williams
Phone: (814)489-3002
Fax: (814)489-0222
E-mail: woodmem@penn.com
Website: http://c1web.com/woodmem
Store Location: Lottsville PA location.
Offers: Woodworking, tole painting and decorative painting patterns, ready-to-assemble and ready-to-paint kits.
Catalog: 100 plans and kits for woodworking and painting.
Phone Orders: M-Sat, 8-6 EST.
Mail Orders: Ship worldwide.
Discounts: Wholesale to resale businesses.
Accepts: American Express, Discover, MasterCard, Visa

ZIM'S, INC.
4370 S. 300 West
Salt Lake City UT 84107
Phone: (801)268-2505
Fax: (801)268-9859
E-mail: nanae@interserv.com
Website: Soon.
Store Location: At above address.
Offers: Unique wood figures, birdhouses, nutcrackers and a huge variety of exclusive wood products. We stock 73,000 various art and craft items from our creative wood line to doll parts, art supplies, basic craft products, naturals, stitchery, instruction books and much more.
Catalog: Over 700 pages. $10 (refundable).
Phone Orders: (800)453-6420.
Mail Orders: At above address. Worldwide.
Discounts: Wholesale, distributor and direct import.
Accepts: American Express, Discover, MasterCard, Visa, (American Express not valid for wholesale purchases)

Tools & Equipment—Multipurpose

Also see specific arts, crafts and needlecrafts categories.

ARTOGRAPH, INC.
2838 Vicksburg Lane N.
Minneapolis MN 55447
Phone: (612)553-1112
Offers: Artograph opaque projectors (transfers, enlarges or reduces photos, designs or patterns for tracing), including compact models and others plus floor stands. Manufacturer. New Lightracer light box with conveniently slanted 10 × 12 illuminated surface for tracing patterns, designs, stenciling and more. Contact your dealer, or write.

BLUE RIDGE MACHINERY & TOOLS, INC.
P.O. Box 536
Hurricane WV 25526
Phone: (304)562-3538
Fax: (304)562-5311
Offers: Machinery/tools, including lathes, milling machines and hand and power tools by Unimat, Compact, Maximat, Myford, Sherline, Atlas, Jet and many other manufacturers. Also offers machine shop supplies and accessories.
Catalog: Free.
Discounts: Sells wholesale to legitimate businesses.

BRANDMARK
462 Carthage Dr.
Beavercreek OH 45434
Phone: (937)426-6843 or (800)323-2570
Fax: (937)426-9722
Offers: Branding irons in solid brass, with convenient torch heating. The first line of each brand reads "Handcrafted by" and is followed by a custom-made second line of 20 letters and spaces maximum. The brands feature ¼″ letters with line borders. Also offers an electric model. Send SASE for details.
Accepts: American Express, Discover, MasterCard, Visa

THE DAN-SIG CO.
P.O. Box 2141
Memphis TN 38101
Phone: (901)525-8464
Offers: Dazor line of magnifier lamps in a variety of styles and types, including floating arm pedestal and a floating arm model on rollers. Also offers replacement lamps and bulbs. Contact your dealer, or send SASE. Send phone number in query.

DREMEL
4915 21st St.
Racine WI 53406
Phone: (414)554-1390
Fax: (414)554-7654
Website: http://dremel.com
Offers: Power tools, attachments and accessories, including redesigned MultiPro high-speed rotary tools, Flex-Shaft attachments and drill presses, plus 2-speed scroll saws, disc/belt sanders, engravers, attachments and over 165 bits. Manufacturer.
Catalog: Free. Book of over 175 uses, free.

THE FOREDOM ELECTRIC CO.
16 Stony Hill Rd.
Bethel CT 06801
Phone: (203)792-8622
Offers: Flexible shaft rotary power tools, 21 handpieces and accessories tools to cut, grind, buff, polish, sand and deburr. Also offers bench lathes (variable speeds), handpiece holders, and power tools and accessories for crafts and jewelry making. Manufacturer.
Catalog: Contact your dealer or write for free catalog.

HARBOR FREIGHT TOOLS
P.O. Box 6010
3491 Mission Oaks Blvd.
Camarillo CA 93012
Phone: (800)423-2567
Fax: (800)905-5220
Website: http://www.harborfreight.com
Store Location: At above address.
Offers: Full line of power and hand tools, equipment and accessories by American Tool, Black & Decker, DeWALT, Campbell-Hausfeld, Chicago Pneumatic, Homelite, Makita, Milwaukee, Porter-Cable, Ryobi, JB Power and many more. Also offer outdoor maintenance, automotive, compressors, shop equipment, pumps, generators and welding equipment.
Catalog: 56 pages, color.
Phone Orders: 24 hours a day, 7 days a week. Can also fax.
Mail Orders: See shipping information in catalog.
Accepts: American Express, Discover, MasterCard, Visa

HERITAGE SAW CO.
11225 Sixth St. E.
St Petersburg FL 33706
Phone: (813)367-7557
Offers: Line of miniature steel saws, aluminum skillets and irons for tole painting.
Catalog: $2.
Discounts: Sells wholesale.

HTC

332 E. Lincoln
P.O. Box 839
Royal Oak MI 48068-0839
Phone: (800)624-2027
Offers: Mobile machine bases (shop on wheels) as well as many other space-saving workshop accessories for all your stationary and bench-top power tools.
Catalog: Call for your free catalog.

MINI-VAC

634 E. Colorado St.
Glendale CA 91205
Contact: Erik Miglins
Phone: (818)244-6777
Fax: (818)244-5858
Store Location: At above address.
Offers: Miniature vacuum cleaner—Mini-Vac—the world's smallest vacuum cleaner for cleaning your valuable models, miniatures, dollhouses, figurines, sewing machines, computers, arts, crafts and more.
Phone Orders: M-F, 9-6 PST.
Mail Orders: Will ship to US and Canada. Prepayment required.
Discounts: Sells wholesale to legitimate businesses.
Accepts: American Express, Discover, MasterCard, Visa

PARAGRAPHICS CORP.

1455 W. Center St.
Orem UT 84057
Phone: (801)225-8300 or (800)624-7415
Offers: Paragrave hi-tech engraving system (with thin, ultra-high-speed drill in Parapak). It engraves glass, metal, wood and other hard surfaces. Also offers high-pressure sandblasting system, with easy-to-use stencil system that works on virtually any hard surface. Demonstration video available. Send SASE.
Accepts: Discover, MasterCard, Visa

REX GRAPHIC SUPPLY

P.O. Box 6626
Raritan Center
Edison NJ 08818-6626
Contact: Ron Thomas
Phone: (732)613-8777
Fax: (732)390-8065
E-mail: ront@home.com
Offers: Complete line of drafting engineering, graphic art and school/office supplies. Featuring The Creator graphic arts table, the original True Angle, Hyglo 6-in-1 rotary craft punch, The Ring Pen and Craft Cuts decorative-edged scissors.
Catalog: Free.
Phone Orders: M-F, 9-5 EST.
Mail Orders: Prepayment required. Allow 2-4 weeks for delivery. Other Location: P.O. Box 24238, Tempe AZ 85285. Phone: (602)968-6475 or (800)821-7125; fax: (602)921-9266.
Discounts: Sells wholesale to trade.
Accepts: MasterCard, Visa

TOOL CRIB OF THE NORTH

1603 12th Ave. N.
Grand Forks ND 58203
Contact: Lori Bakken
Phone: (701)780-2882
Fax: (701)746-2869
E-mail: bakken@corpcomm.net
Website: www.toolcribofthenorth.com
Store Location: Locations in Grand Forks, Fargo, Minot and Bismarck ND and Duluth MN.
Offers: Power tools by DeWALT, Delta, Jet, Milwaukee, Porter-Cable, Bosch, Makita, Freud, Powermatic, Panasonic, Ryobi, Black & Decker, Performax and others.
Catalog: 108 pages. Free.
Phone Orders: (800)358-3096.
Discounts: All products discounted at 40% off list price.
Accepts: Discover, MasterCard, Visa

Wood Carving

Also see General Craft Supplies; Doll & Toy Making—Rigid; Furniture Making & Upholstery; Frames & Picture Framing; Woodworking; other related categories.

CAPE FORGE
P.O. Box 987
Burlington VT 05402-0987
Contact: Karyn dePunte
Phone: (802)244-7010
Fax: (802)244-1168
E-mail: mike@capeforge.com
Website: www.capeforge.com
Offers: Traditional hand-forged wood carving tools. A complete line of carving knives, chisels, drawknives, palm tools, bent blades, micro tools and custom work.
Catalog: $1.
Phone Orders: Leave message if no answer and someone will get back to you shortly.
Mail Orders: Ship anywhere. Allow 3-6 weeks delivery.
Discounts: Quantity discounts available. Wholesalers welcome.
Accepts: Discover, MasterCard, Visa, personal check

DECOY AND WOOD CARVING SUPPLIES
201-12 St. Anne St.
St. Albert, Alberta T8N 4E2
Canada
Contact: Alan K. Spiller
Phone: (888)458-7086
Fax: (888)458-7086
Store Location: At above address. T-Sat, 11-5.
Offers: Woodburning tools, books and patterns, hand carving tools, type/bosswood blanks, study bills, study cable, glass eyes and molded feet, study casts, paints and brushes, power tools and accessories, decorative finished decoys and classes for beginners or experienced carvers.
Catalog: 22 pages, b&w. $2 Canadian.
Phone Orders: 24 hours per day.
Mail Orders: Will ship anywhere. Prepayment required.
Discounts: Will sell wholesale to businesses.
Accepts: MasterCard, Visa

FALLS RUN WOODCARVING
9395 Falls Rd.
Girard PA 16417
Contact: David W. Bennett, president
Phone: (814)734-3690 or (800)524-9077
Fax: (814)734-2435

E-mail: dbennett@erie.net
Website: www.fallsrun.com
Offers: Wood carving tools: Flexcut chisels and mallet tools and accessories. Manufacturer of wood carving tools. Dealers worldwide; call or check website.
Catalog: On request.
Phone Orders: Yes.
Mail Orders: Worldwide. Call for details.
Discounts: Wholesale to dealers.
Accepts: MasterCard, Visa

GILMER WOOD CO.
2211 NW St. Helens Rd.
Portland OR 97210
Phone: (503)274-1271
Fax: (503)274-9839
Offers: Over 100 species of rare and exotic woods in logs, planks and squares. Also offers turning, cutlery and musical instrument woods.
Catalog: $2.

THE HELICONIA PRESS, INC.
P.O. Box 200
Clayton, Ontario K0A 1P0
Canada
Contact: William Whiting
Phone: (613)256-7300
Fax: (613)256-7532
E-mail: info@natureartists.com
Website: www.natureartists.com/heliconia/
Offers: Carving aids (bird carving), including instructional and pattern books, and paintable casting and videos.
Catalog: List of products available upon request.
Phone Orders: Accepted, but first-time orders prepaid.
Mail Orders: Will ship anywhere surface post. Allow 2-3 weeks in US and Canada.
Discounts: Sell wholesale to legitimate businesses (prepaid first orders).
Accepts: check, money order

HOT TOOLS
P.O. Box 615
24 Tioga Way
Marblehead MA 01945
Contact: Debra Rhodes
Phone: (781)639-1000
Fax: (781)631-8887
E-mail: mmn@mmnewman.com
Website: mmnewman.com
Store Location: At above address.

Offers: Woodburning tools, hot knife, library marker, lacquer burn-in knife and stencilmaker.
Catalog: 10-page flyer.
Phone Orders: M-F, 9-5 EST.
Mail Orders: Yes.
Accepts: MasterCard, Visa

CHRISTIAN J. HUMMUL CO.

P.O. Box 1093
11001-A York Rd.
Hunt Valley MD 21030
Contact: Raymond M. Zajac
Phone: (410)771-0144
Fax: (410)771-9332
E-mail: rzajac@bcpl.net
Website: http://www.bcpl.net/~rzajac/index.html
Store Location: At above address.
Offers: Wood carving and woodburning (pyrography) supplies. Over 1,600 bird and animal patterns, books, videos, power and hand carving tools, basswood, glass eyes, cast pewter bird feet, airbrush, artist paint brushes and acrylic and alkyd paints.
Catalog: 64 pages. Free.
Phone Orders: (800)762-0235.
Mail Orders: P.O. Box 1093, Hunt Valley MD 21030.
Discounts: Over 600 items in catalog discounted from list price.
Accepts: Discover, MasterCard, Visa

J.H. KLINE CARVING SHOP

P.O. Box 445
Forge Hill Rd.
Manchester PA 17345
Phone: (717)266-3501
Offers: Over 1,400 patterns of precut wood blanks, Foredom tools, glass eyes, woodburning units, bits, carvers, sanders, abrasives, cast bills and feet.
Catalog: $1 (refundable).

JANTZ SUPPLY

P.O. Box 584-CS
Davis OK 73030
Phone: (800)351-8900
Offers: Knife-making supplies, including over 100 blades and blade kits (with handle material, fittings and instructions). Also offers tools (by Dremel, Baldor, Starrett and others), abrasives and polishing equipment.
Catalog: $3.
Accepts: Discover, MasterCard, Visa

JENNINGS DECOY CO.

601 Franklin Ave. NE
St. Cloud MN 56304
Phone: (320)253-2253
Fax: (320)253-9537
Offers: Over 1,400 products for carvers: basswood, tupelo, butternut cutouts and cutout kits—wildfowl, Santas and oth-

ers. Also offers eyes, other accessories, patterns, cork decoy kits and books.
Catalog: Free.

JERRY'S

9536 W. 7-Mile Rd.
Northville MI 48167
Contact: Jerry Davis
Phone: (734)348-0492
Offers: Decoy supplies: tools, materials and literature.
Catalog: Yes.
Phone Orders: Yes.
Mail Orders: Yes.
Accepts: check

MDI WOODCARVERS SUPPLY

228 Main St.
Bar Harbor ME 04609
Phone: (800)866-5728
Offers: Selection of both traditional hand carving tools and complete selection of power carving supplies. Write.
Accepts: Discover, MasterCard, Visa

MOUNTAIN WOODCARVERS, INC.

P.O. Box 3485
150 E. Riverside Dr.
Estes Park CO 80517
Phone: (970)586-8678
Fax: (970)586-5500
Store Location: At above address. M-Sat, 10-5; Sun, 12-5.
Offers: Hand carving tools from Austria, Germany, Switzerland and the US, including power carvers and woodburners. Extensive selection of wood carving books and videos. US distributor for Precarvaustria roughouts. Also many basswood roughouts, including animals, people, fish and more. Bird feet, glass eyes and basswood blanks. Wood carving classes and seminars.
Catalog: $2.
Phone Orders: M-Sat, 10-5; Sun, 12-5.
Mail Orders: Worldwide.
Accepts: major credit cards

PROTECTIVE SPECIALTIES DEVELOPMENT GROUP

Dept CSS5
P.O. Box 39060
Philadelphia PA 19136
Contact: Ed Allen, order control
Phone: (215)331-0242
Fax: (215)331-0242, T-Sat, 9-4
E-mail: prospecial@earthlink.net
Website: http://home.earthlink.net/~prospecial
Offers: Wood-carvers' dust elimination tool, Vac-U-Shield, other power carver equipment, new inventions for the industry and dog grooming equipment, specializing in cutting-edge unique products, such as: Clippin' Sling, CaddyPillar, Klip Klot and grooming instruction book recommended by NDGA and SPCA.
Catalog: $1 (refundable first order).

Phone Orders: Accepted from D&B rated stores after first paid order.
Mail Orders: Prepayment required for all areas. Will ship overseas.
Discounts: Wholesales some products purchased in quantity.
Accepts: check, postal money orders, cash

RAM PRODUCTS, INC.
5 Elkins Rd.
East Brunswick NJ 08816
Contact: Aaron Kudrowitz
Phone: (732)651-5500
Fax: (732)651-6688
E-mail: ramprodinc@mcione.com
Store Location: At above address. M-F, 8:30-5:30.
Offers: Assorted styles of electric wood-carving drill sets.
Catalog: 4-page color catalog. No charge.
Phone Orders: M-F, 8:30-5:30 EST.
Mail Orders: Will ship to US and Canada.
Accepts: American Express, Discover, MasterCard, Visa

RAZERTIP INDUSTRIES
P.O. Box 1258
Martensville, Saskatchewan S0K 2T0
Canada
Contact: Cam Merkle
Phone: (306)931-0889
Fax: (306)242-6119
E-mail: razertip@sk.sympatico.ca
Website: http://www3.sk.sympatico.ca/razertip/
Store Location: Hwy. 12 N., Martensville, Saskatchewan S0K 2T0 Canada. Call first for directions.
Offers: Very fine detail burner for wood, leather, plastic, wax, gourds and more. Over 200 pen and tip styles available. Also manufactures Razaire modular portable dust control systems for hobbyists and home workshops. Bird carving and artist supplies also available.
Catalog: Free. 32 pages, b&w.
Phone Orders: M-F, 9-5 CST.
Mail Orders: Will ship anywhere. Prepayment required.
Discounts: Wholesale to authorized dealers.
Accepts: American Express, MasterCard, Visa

G. SCHOEPFER, INC.
460 Cook Hill Rd.
Cheshire CT 06410
Contact: Dave Pagano
Phone: (203)250-7794
Fax: (203)250-7796
Offers: Eyes for all purposes—dolls, teddy bears, decoys, birds, fish, small figures and sculptures—glass and plastic.
Catalog: Free. Send SASE.
Phone Orders: (800)875-6939.

SCULPTURE HOUSE, INC.
100 Camp Meeting Ave.
Skillman NJ 08558
Contact: Chris

Phone: (609)466-2986
Fax: (609)466-2450
Website: www.sculpturehouse.com
Store Location: At above address.
Offers: Sculpturing tools and materials.
Catalog: 80 pages. $4.
Phone Orders: M-F, 9-4 EST.
Mail Orders: Will ship worldwide.
Discounts: Wholesale to legitimate dealers.
Accepts: MasterCard, Visa

SUGAR PINE WOODCARVING SUPPLIES
P.O. Box 859
315 W. Sherman
Lebanon OR 97355
Contact: Customer service
Phone: (541)451-1538
Fax: (541)451-5455
E-mail: rmi@dnc.net
Store Location: At above address.
Offers: Complete line of wood-carving supplies.
Catalog: Free on request.
Phone Orders: (800)452-2783.
Mail Orders: P.O. Box 859, Lebanon OR 97355.
Accepts: Discover, MasterCard, Visa, C.O.D.

ULTRA SPEED PRODUCTS
18500 E. Aschoff
Zigzag OR 97049
Contact: Bill Vogel or Diana DeChand
Phone: (503)622-4387
Fax: (503)622-3252 or (503)622-6329
E-mail: ultraspeed@email.com
Website: www.mornet.com/ultraspeed
Offers: Wood carving supplies.
Phone Orders: Anytime.
Mail Orders: Will ship anywhere. Ship UPS. Allow 5-6 working days. Prepayment required.
Accepts: all major credit cards

WILDLIFE CARVINGS AND SUPPLIES
1301 Halleck's Rd. E.
RR 3
Brockville, Ontario K6V 5T3
Canada
Contact: Les Boszormeny
Phone: (613)342-0088
Fax: (613)342-0088
E-mail: wildlife@cybertap.com
Website: http://www.cybertap.com/wildlife/
Store Location: At above address.
Offers: Wood carving and art supplies, tupelo and basswood. Foredom, NSK, ruby and diamond cutters, silver brushes, books, study casts and bills and imported German glass eyes. Also quality handcrafted wildlife wood carvings, retail or wholesale.
Catalog: 30 pages. $3 (refundable).
Phone Orders: 7 days a week.

Mail Orders: 7 days a week. Prepayment required. Shipped with 24 hours.
Discounts: On volume glass eye orders and wholesale carvings.
Accepts: Visa, money order

WOOD CARVERS SUPPLY, INC.

P.O. Box 7500
Englewood FL 34295-7500
Contact: Timothy Effrem
Phone: (941)698-0123
Fax: (941)698-0329
Offers: Discover the joy and relaxation of wood carving. Order our superb color, 76-page catalog with over 2,000 items, including hand and power carving tools, books, knives and much more.
Catalog: 76 pages, color. Send $2 for a 2-year subscription.
Phone Orders: 24 hours a day every day.
Mail Orders: Will ship anyplace worldwide. Prepaid required. Allow 7 working days for delivery.
Discounts: Carving Club discounts available.
Accepts: American Express, Discover, MasterCard, Visa, check

WOOD N' THINGS, INC.

601 E. 44th St. #3
Boise ID 83714
Phone: (208)375-9663 or (800)365-4613

E-mail: kathleen@carvingsupplies.com
Website: http://www.carvingsupplies.com
Offers: Carving supplies by Foredom and Auto Mach, including gouges, burners, knives, glass eyes, woods and over 300 books.
Catalog: Free.
Accepts: American Express, Discover, MasterCard, Visa

WOODCHIPS CARVING SUPPLIES, LTD.

8521 Eastlake Dr.
Burnaby, British Columbia V5A 4T7
Canada
Contact: Cliff Steele
Phone: (604)421-1101
Fax: (604)421-1052
E-mail: cliff4wood@aol.com
Website: www.lionsgate.com/webtown/woodchips
Store Location: At above address. M-F, 8-4:30.
Offers: Woods, books, hand and power tools, eyes, knives, gouges by Pfiel and Flexcut, ADZ and many other wood carving supplies. Also stock many patterns listed in catalog and on Internet.
Catalog: $2. Approximately 80 pages.
Phone Orders: Yes.
Mail Orders: Yes.
Discounts: Retail only.
Accepts: MasterCard, Visa

Woodworking

Also see General Craft Supplies; Doll & Toy Making—Rigid; Furniture Making & Upholstery; Frames & Picture Framing; Tools & Equipment; Wood Carving; related categories.

ADAMS WOOD PRODUCTS, LTD., L.P.
974 Forest Dr.
Morristown TN 37814
Contact: David J. Adams
Phone: (423)587-2942
Fax: (423)586-2188
Offers: Solid wood Queen Anne legs, table bases and table legs. Complete chair and table kits in oak, cherry, maple, walnut and mahogany. In stock. No minimum.
Catalog: Free.
Phone Orders: Yes.
Mail Orders: At above address.
Discounts: Per catalog.
Accepts: Discover, MasterCard, Visa

ADVANCED MACHINERY
P.O. Box 312
New Castle DE 19720
Phone: (800)322-2226
Offers: Full line of scroll saw blades, accessories and improvements for almost any scroll saw, plus Hegner precision scroll saws. Also offers Apollo paint spray systems and Plano glue press. Write.

WILLIAM ALDEN CO.
27 Stuart St.
Boston MA 02116
Phone: (800)249-8665 or (617)426-3430 (outside US)
Offers: Power tools and equipment, including Hitachi, DeWALT, Porter-Cable, Delta and others.
Catalog: Free.

BADGER HARDWOOD OF WISCONSIN, LTD.
N. 1517 Hwy. 14
Walworth WI 53184
Phone: (414)275-1162 or (800)252-2373
Fax: (414)275-9855
E-mail: badgerwood@badgerwood.com
Website: www.badgerwood.com
Offers: Aromatic cedar, ash, aspen, basswood, birch, butternut, cherry, mahogany, hickory, hackberry, hard and soft maple, nothern white pine, poplar, red elm, red oak quartersawn, red and white oak, walnut and others.
Catalog: Free.

Discounts: Special prices on 20 b.f. bulk packs of lumber.
Accepts: MasterCard, Visa

BOGERT & HOPPER, INC.
P.O. Box 119
Northport NY 11768
Phone: (516)261-6173 or (800)338-9938
Offers: Wood parts: wheels, axles, Shaker pegs, candle cups, dowels and others. Please call.

BURL TREE
3527 Broadway St.
Eureka CA 95503
Phone: (707)442-1319 or (800)785-BURL
Offers: Burlwoods: redwood, maple, buckeye, manzanita, madrone, oak, myrtle, walnut, rhododendron, yew and nutmeg; size or thickness for any/all uses. Call.
Discounts: Sells wholesale, based on quantity.

CARTER PRODUCTS CO., INC.
437 Spring St. NE
Grand Rapids MI 49503
Contact: Customer service
Phone: (616)451-2928
Fax: (616)451-4330
E-mail: sales@carterproducts.com
Website: www.carterproducts.com
Offers: Delta (Rockwell) 14″ and 20″ band saw guide conversion kits plus other kits for Jet 14″ and 20″, Grizzly 16″ and 18″, General 15″, Powermatic 14″, SCM S45 Mini-Max 18″, Davis & Wells 20″, Centauro, Grob, Meber and other saws 14″ wheel diameter and larger. Also available bandsaw tires in sizes 10″-42″ and tire adhesive. We are a manufacturer and sell through 800 retail dealers in the US.
Catalog: For saws listed above.
Phone Orders: M-F, 8-5 EST.
Mail Orders: Prepayment required. Call for total charges including shipping.
Discounts: Sells wholesale to authorized Carter dealers.
Accepts: no credit cards

CASEY'S WOOD PRODUCTS
P.O. Box 365
Woolwich ME 04579
Phone: (800)45-CASEY
Offers: Factory seconds woodenware: Shaker pegs, beanpot candle cups (by 100-plus lots), turnings, dowels and novelties in first and second quality. Hardware includes small hinges, screws, lazy Susan bearings and others.
Catalog: $1.

CERTAINLY WOOD

11753 Big Tree Rd.
East Aurora NY 14052
Phone: (716)655-0206
Fax: (716)655-3446
Offers: Fine wood veneers in a variety of species. Also offers custom plywood and exotic hardwoods.
Catalog: Free.

COLONIAL HARDWOODS, INC.

7953 Cameron Brown Court
Springfield VA 22153
Contact: Marie Otmar
Phone: (703)451-9217
Fax: (703)451-0186
Store Location: At above address.
Offers: Over 120 species of lumber custom cut to size—burls, woodworking supplies and veneers.
Catalog: Send SASE.
Phone Orders: (800)466-5451. M-Sat, 9-5.
Mail Orders: Yes.
Accepts: Discover, MasterCard, Visa

ALBERT CONSTANTINE & SON, INC.

2050 Eastchester Rd.
Bronx NY 10461
Contact: Glenn Docherty
Phone: (718)792-1600 or (800)223-8087
Fax: (718)792-2110
E-mail: grd99wodoc@aol.com
Website: www.constantines.com
Store Location: Location in Bronx NY and Ft. Lauderdale FL.
Offers: Woodworking/veneering supplies: kits, 80-plus veneers, veneering tools, marquetry kits, Optivisor, pantograph, chisels, mallets, drawknives, carving tools, woodburners, planes, spokeshaves, scrapers, sharpeners, saws, cutters, measurers and rasps. Also offers joiners, routers, doweling units, planers, sanders, sprayers, engravers, gilding supplies, stains, finishes, furniture plans (full-size), carving and decoy kits. Tools: knives, vises, router bits, nailers and woodturning tools. Materials: lumber and turning blocks. Carries clock parts, dollhouse/furniture kits, model kits, toy parts, upholstery tools/supplies, cane, webbing, guitar/dulcimer parts and woods, lamp parts, workbenches and books.
Catalog: Free. 128 pages.
Phone Orders: M-F, 7:30-5:30; Sat, 8-4.
Accepts: all major credit cards

CRAFTERS MART

P.O. Box 2342-CS
Greeley CO 80632
Phone Orders: (970)351-0676
Offers: Wood parts/shapes, including turnings (Shaker pegs, candle cups and balls), wheels, door harp tuning pens, clapper balls, plus harp wire, hangers and others.
Catalog: $2 (refundable).

CUSTOM WOOD CUT-OUTS UNLIMITED

P.O. Box 518
Massillon OH 44648-0518
Contact: David Harting
Phone: (330)832-2919
Fax: (330)832-2919
Offers: Wood items for tole and decorative painters. Also will do custom wood cutting.
Catalog: $2 (refundable).
Phone Orders: Yes.
Mail Orders: Yes.
Discounts: Yes.
Accepts: MasterCard, Visa

DOUGLAS WOOD PRODUCTS, INC.

P.O. Box 25245
Greenville SC 29616
Phone: (864)289-9533
Fax: (864)288-0926
Store Location: Greenville SC location.
Offers: Accessories for Shopsmith, Total Shop and Master Shop. Also manufacture air filters and dust collection.
Catalog: Free. 24 pages.
Phone Orders: M-F, 8-6 EST.
Discounts: Wholesale or retail.
Accepts: Discover, MasterCard, Visa

DREMEL

4915 21st St.
Racine WI 53406
Contact: Peggy A. Brunet
Phone: (414)554-1390
Fax: (414)554-7654
Website: http://dremel.com
Offers: Power tools, attachments and accessories, including redesigned MultiPro high-speed rotary tools, Flex-Shaft attachments and drill presses, plus 2-speed scroll saws, disc/belt sanders, engravers, attachments and over 165 bits. Manufacturer. Call (800)437-3635 for a dealer near you.
Catalog: Free. Book of over 175 uses, free.

E.C. MITCHELL CO., INC.

P.O. Box 607
88 Boston St.
Middleton MA 01949
Contact: Michael D. Kelly, president
Phone: (978)774-1191
Fax: (978) 774-2494
Website: Available in near future.
Store Location: At above address.
Offers: We sell and manufacture abrasive cords and tapes (used to deburr). Sample accurate flexible sanding/abrasive cords and more.
Catalog: Brochures available.
Phone Orders: We ship from our facility f.o.b. Middleton MA.
Mail Orders: Same as phone orders.

Discounts: Discount schedule on price list.
Accepts: no credit cards; terms net 30 days cash

EAGLE AMERICA CORP.

P.O. Box 1099
Chardon OH 44024
Phone: (800)872-2511
Offers: Largest selection of American-made router bits, saw blades, cutting tools, router accessories and thousands of woodworking helpers.
Catalog: Request free catalog.
Discounts: Volume discount on selected items. See catalog for specials.
Accepts: Discover, MasterCard, Visa

ECON-ABRASIVES, INC.

P.O. Box 1628
4900 Preston Rd.
Frisco TX 75034
Contact: Sales department
Phone: (800)367-4101
Fax: (972)377-2248
Store Location: Frisco TX location.
Offers: Coated abrasive products, including belts, sheets, discs, rolls and assorted woodworking products. We custom make abrasive belts any size in any grit. We stock router bits, wood putty finishing supplies and hundreds of other products.
Catalog: 30 pages. Free.
Phone Orders: Yes.
Mail Orders: Ship US, Canada and Puerto Rico.
Accepts: Discover, MasterCard, Visa, C.O.D.

FROG TOOL CO., LTD.

2169 Illinois Rt. 26
Dixon IL 61021
Phone: (800)648-1270
Offers: Hand woodworking tools: German carving, Swedish carving, hammers, screwdrivers, Japanese sharpening items, doweling jigs, bevelers, cutters, drills, measuring items, planes, drawknives, spokeshaves, musical instrument tools, saws, veneering/turning tools, vises, woodburning tools, lathes, dowels, table hardware, sanding items, log cabin tools and finishes. Also offers books on woodworking and finishing materials.
Catalog: $5.
Discounts: Quantity; sells wholesale to legitimate businesses.
Accepts: MasterCard, Visa

GARRETT WADE CO., INC.

161 Avenue of the Americas
New York NY 10013
Phone: (212)807-1757 or (800)221-2942
Offers: Full line of woodworking hand tools, including the new advanced precision honing guide (sets micro bevels), "blind nailer" tool (like a positioning jig), scrapers with prepared edges for longer use, multiangle aluminum gauges, band saw blades (including $\frac{1}{16}''$ narrow, in raker style, and "cabinetmaker's special" skip-tooth and unset raker) and other scroll and cabinet styles. Also offers saw-setting gauges, gap-filling glue and other common and unique hand tools.
Catalog: Free.

GRIZZLY INDUSTRIAL, INC.

(formerly Grizzly Imports, Inc.)
2406 Reach Rd.
Williamsport, PA 17701
Phone: (717)326-3806 or (800)523-4777
Offers: Shop equipment: sanders (drum, combo and others), saws (heavy-duty, band and others), planers, jointers, shapers, dust collectors and others. Write or call.
Mail Orders: Other location: P.O. Box 2069, Bellingham WA 98227. (360)647-0801.
Accepts: Discover, MasterCard, Visa

HOME TOPS

(formerly Home Lumber Co.)
499 Whitewater St.
Whitewater WI 53190
Contact: Geoff Hale
Phone: (800)262-5482
Fax: (414)473-6908
E-mail: tooltime@idcnet.com
Website: www.homelumbercom.com
Offers: Decorative wood fence post tops in extra large unique designs. Woodworking tools/equipment by Bosch, DeWALT, Makita, Bostitch, Ryobi and others.
Catalog: Send SASE.
Phone Orders: M-F, 8-6 EST.
Mail Orders: Worldwide.
Discounts: Volume prices and approved wholesale.
Accepts: Discover, MasterCard, Visa

HOOD FINISHING PRODUCTS, INC.

61 Berry St.
Somerset NJ 08873
Phone: (800)229-0934
Fax: (732)254-6063
Website: www.hoodfinishing.com
Offers: Line of products for wood finishing and refinishing from surface preparation to wood care.
Catalog: Free.

HORTON BRASSES

P.O. Box 120
Nooks Hill Rd.
Cromwell CT 06416
Phone: (860)635-4400
Offers: Full line of cabinet and furniture hardware for homes and antiques, including handles, knobs, latches, hinges and slides in many styles (brass, antiqued and others).
Catalog: $4.

HOWEE'S, INC.
2220 S. Prosperity Ave.
Joplin MO 64801
Phone: (417)623-0656
Offers: Wood turnings, including wheels, pegs, spindles, candle cups, knobs, rings, spools, fruits, hearts, finials, boxes, smokestacks, miniatures, beads, bells, buckets, dolls, bowling pins, dowels. Also offers hardware, hinges, scroll saw blades, sanding and clock making supplies.
Catalog: Free.
Discounts: Quantity; sells wholesale.

HTC
P.O. Box 839
332 E. Lincoln
Royal Oak, MI 48068-0839
Phone: (800)624-2027
Offers: Mobile machine bases (shop on wheels) as well as many other space-saving workshop accessories for all your stationary and bench-top power tools.
Catalog: Call for your free catalog.

HYDROCOTE CO., INC.
P.O. Box 160
Tennent NJ 07763
Contact: Joan Goldberg
Phone: (800)229-4937 or (732)257-4344
Fax: (732)254-6063
Offers: Full line of water-based, enviornmentally safe products for wood finishing and refinishing.
Catalog: Free.
Phone Orders: (800)229-4937. M-F, 8-5 EST.
Discounts: Sells wholesale to distributors.
Accepts: Discover, MasterCard, Visa, C.O.D.

KAYNE & SON CUSTOM HARDWARE, INC.
100 Daniel Ridge Rd.
Candler NC 28715
Contact: Steve Kayne
Phone: (828)667-8868 or (828)665-1988
Fax: (828)665-8303
E-mail: kaynehdwc@ioa.com
Store Location: Gallery: M-T, 8:30-5:30; F-Sun, by appointment.
Offers: Builders/household/gate hardware, strap hinges, thumb latch sets, locks, fireplace tools and equipment, hand-forged and cast brass/bronze hardware finished black, antiqued and polished. Reproductions and restoration/repairs. Metalsmithing/blacksmithing tools, including anvils, air hammers, swage blocks, hammers, tongs, cones and more.
Catalog: $5. Free blacksmithing tools catalog.
Phone Orders: 7 days, 7:30 a.m.-11 p.m.
Accepts: MasterCard, Visa

THE LETTERMEN CO., LLC
34-279 Linda Way
Cathedral City CA 92234
Contact: Michael or David Saks
Phone: (760)328-8310
Fax: (760)328-8310
Store Location: At above address. 7 days a week, 9-5.
Offers: 3-D custom-cut letters and logos. Foamboard, plastic, Sintra and wood products available with anodized metallic laminates as well as plastic laminates.
Catalog: Samples and sample cases available for nominal fees.
Phone Orders: 7 days a week, 24 hours a day.
Mail Orders: Will ship to US and Canada. Prepayment required. Allow 3-4 weeks for delivery.
Discounts: Wholesale to the trades.
Accepts: certified check, company check

MAFELL NORTH AMERICA, INC.
80 Earhart Dr., Unit 9
Williamsville NY 14221
Contact: Dennis Hambruch
Phone: (716)626-9303
Fax: (716)626-9304
E-mail: mafell@msn.com
Website: http://www.mafell.de
Store Location: At above address. 8-4:30 EST.
Offers: Portable woodworking machinery from Germany that includes 3 portable table saws and 2 combination jointer/planers. We also offer other portable machinery for working with large timbers and glue-laminated beams.
Phone Orders: M-F, 8-4:30 or leave message
Mail Orders: Ship worldwide. Prepayment required. Delivery usually from stock.
Accepts: MasterCard, Visa

MANNY'S WOODWORKERS PLACE
555 Broadway St.
Lexington KY 40508
Phone: (606)255-5444
Offers: Woodworking books and videos on a variety of topics, including wood turning, carving, carpentry, and furniture making, toy making and others.
Catalog: $2.

MANZANITA DECORATIVE WOOD
1554 Round Potrero Rd.
Potrero CA 91963-0111
Contact: Jack Reider
Phone: (619)478-5849
Fax: (619)478-5130
Store Location: At above address (warehouse). By appointment.
Offers: Manzanita and buckeye burls, banksia cones and Australian hardwood turning squares. Imported direct.
Catalog: Color product sheet with wholesale or retail price sheet.
Discounts: Sells wholesale and retail.
Accepts: MasterCard, Visa

MAPLEWOOD CRAFTS

1 Maplewood Dr.
Hazleton PA 18201-9798
Contact: Pam Beber, vice-president of sales
Phone: (800)899-0134
Fax: (717)384-2500
Store Location: Outlet store for discontinued or overstock merchandise. At above address. W-Sat, 10-4.
Offers: Beads, needlecraft, puzzles, ceramics, beaded crafts, memory album miscellaneous, plastic canvas, dollhouses, latch hook, glass etching, woodworking supplies and glues.
Catalog: 80 pages, color.
Phone Orders: M-F, 7:30 a.m.-11 p.m.; Sat, 8:30-5 EST.
Mail Orders: Ships worldwide. All orders shipped in 24 hours from 100,000 sq. ft. warehouse.
Discount: Sells wholesale to retail outlets. Minimum wholesale order $125.
Accepts: American Express, Discover, MasterCard, Visa

MASTERCRAFT PLANS

P.O. Box 5100
Kent WA 98064
Offers: Patterns (full-size) in packets: jigsaw items, birdhouses, shelves, windmills, tool houses, donkeys with carts, garden furniture, gifts and novelties, country crafts, variety designs and others.
Catalog: Send SASE.

MEISEL HARDWARE SPECIALTIES

P.O. Box 70
Mound MN 55364
Phone: (612)479-2138
Offers: Over 850 woodworking project plans, including country, storage and outdoor furniture; kitchen items, intarsia, child's furniture and toys, lamps, music boxes, holiday cutouts, bird feeders and houses, and lawn ornaments; wood turnings and parts. Hardware available includes wind chime tubing, parts for music boxes and others.
Catalog: $2.
Accepts: MasterCard, Visa

MLCS-ROUTER BITS & PROFESSIONAL WOODWORKING PRODUCTS

(formerly MLCS, Ltd.)
P.O. Box 4053
Rydal PA 19046
Contact: M. Levy
Phone: (800)533-9298
Fax: (215)938-5070
E-mail: sawdust@mlcswoodworking.com
Website: www.mlcswoodworking.com
Store Location: 2381 Philmont Ave., Huntingdon Valley PA 19006.
Offers: Woodworking machines, tools, supplies and hobby center.
Catalog: Yes.
Phone Orders: (800)533-9298.

Mail Orders: At P.O. Box.
Accepts: American Express, Discover, MasterCard, Visa

OAK LEAF WOOD 'N SUPPLIES

210 N. Main
Moweaqua IL 62550
Phone: (217)768-3202
Offers: Line of bowl blanks and spindle stock in domestic and exotic woods, woodcraft supplies and tools. Call or write.

PERFORMAX PRODUCTS, INC.

12257 Nicollet Ave. S.
Burnsville MN 55337
Contact: Sales
Phone: (800)334-4910 or (612)895-9922
Fax: (612)895-5485
Offers: Drum sanders from 16"-50". Offers the versatility to sand from rough sawn to finish material in minutes. Virtually eliminates hand sanding. Sand as short as 2¼". Sand detailed fretwork without breaking or rounding over. Owned and recommended by Dirk Boehman. A must for the shop. A professional finish at a hobbyist price.

PORTA-NAILS, INC.

P.O. Box 1257
Wilmington NC 28402
Contact: Jerry Coleman
Phone: (800)634-9281
Fax: (910)763-8650
E-mail: pni@wilmington.net
Website: porta-nails.com
Offers: Woodworking machines: dowel mate, ring master, panel template, router arc attachment, router mate, universal router table and others.
Phone Orders: M-F, 7:30-5 EST.
Mail Orders: Will ship to US and Canada. Prepayment requested. Allow 1-6 weeks for delivery.
Accepts: MasterCard, Visa

PRICE CUTTER, INC.

P.O. Box 1100
Chardon OH 44024
Phone: (888)288-2487
Offers: High quality with lowest prices. Saw blades, books, router bits and woodworking accessories.
Catalog: Free.
Discounts: See catalog for special offers.
Accepts: American Express, Discover, MasterCard, Visa

R.B. INDUSTRIES, INC.

P.O. Box 369
1801 Vine St.
Harrisonville MO 64701
Phone: (816)884-3534 or (800)487-2623
Fax: (816)884-2463
E-mail: info@rbiwoodtools.com
Website: www.rbiwoodtools.com
Store Location: At above address. M-F, 8-5; Sat, 9-2.
Offers: RBI Hawk line of scroll saws, including beginner

and professional models. Also offers wood, scroll saw blades and pattern books.

Catalog: Free information kit available.

Phone Orders: (800)487-2623. M-Th, 8-8; F, 8-5; Sat, 9-2.

Mail Orders: P.O. Box 369, Harrisonville MO 64701. Ships US and Canada. Prepayment required. 10-14 days delivery.

Accepts: American Express, Discover, MasterCard, RBI credit card, Visa

SAX ARTS & CRAFTS

P.O. Box 510710

2405 Calhoun Rd.

New Berlin WI 53151

Phone: (414)784-6880

Offers: A variety of supplies (known brands), including a full line of weaving looms and aids, yarns, weaving kits, rug/craft yarns, embroidery/crewel threads, rug hook frames and aids, canvas, hoops, burlap and felt. Native American beading, beads, feathers, macrame, basketry and batik supplies, fabric paints, airbrush kits and inks, stencil films, trims, foam, stained glass kits, etching and beveled glass supplies and supplies for decoupage, jewelry making, leather, casting, plastics, wood and metalworking are also available.

Catalog: $5 (refundable).

Discounts: Quantity, sells wholesale to legitimate businesses.

7 CORNERS HARDWARE/TOOLS ON SALE

216 W. 7th St.

St. Paul MN 55102

Contact: Chris Johnson

Phone: (800)328-0457

Fax: (612)224-8263

E-mail: sevencornr@aol.com

Website: www.7cornershdwe.com

Store Location: At above address.

Offers: Great power and hand tool selection featuring free freight and America's lowest tool prices.

Catalog: 520 pages. Free.

Phone Orders: M-F, 7-5:30; Sat, 8-1 CST.

Mail Orders: Freight free in 48 states.

Accepts: American Express, Discover, MasterCard, Visa, check, money order, purchase orders from schools, municipalities and government

SUN DESIGNS

P.O. Box 6

Oconomowoc WI 53066

Phone: (414)567-4255

Offers: Design plan books for 55 gazebos (mix-and-match designs for railings, fascia and more), birdhouses/feeders, toys, backyard structures, cupolas and bridges, and privies. Construction plans, all designs. Send SASE.

Discounts: Sells wholesale to legitimate businesses.

Accepts: MasterCard, Visa

TOOL CRIB OF THE NORTH

1603 12th Ave. N.

Grand Forks ND 58203

Contact: Lori Bakken

Phone: (701)780-2882

Fax: (701)746-2869

E-mail: bakken@cerpcomm.net

Website: www.toolcribofthenorth.com

Store Location: Locations in Grand Forks, Fargo, Minot and Bismarck ND and Duluth MN.

Offers: Power tools by DeWALT, Delta, Jet, Milwaukee, Porter-Cable, Bosch, Makita, Freud, Powermatic, Panasonic, Ryobi, Black & Decker, Performax and others.

Cable: 108 pages. Free.

Phone Orders: (800)358-3096.

Mail Orders: (800)358-3096.

Discounts: All product discounted at 40% off list price.

Accepts: Discover, MasterCard, Visa

TOOL FACTORY OUTLET

P.O. Box 461

Rt. 17M

Goshen NY 10924

Contact: Barton Schineller, vice president

Phone: (914)294-7900

Fax: (914)294-1211

Offers: Power tools and equipment by Bosch, Porter-Cable, Milwaukee, DeWALT, Bostitch, Makita, Ryobi, Delta, Duo-Fast, Dremel and others. Call or write.

Catalog: 12 pages. Free.

Phone Orders: M-F, 7-6; Th, 7-7; Sat, 8-5.

Mail Orders: Yes.

Accepts: American Express, Discover, MasterCard, Visa

TREMONT NAIL CO.

8 Elm St.

P.O. Box 111

Wareham MA 02571

Phone: (800)842-0560

Offers: Old-fashioned steel-cut nails, 20 types from old patterns: rosehead, wrought-head and others.

Catalog: Free.

Discounts: Quantity; teachers and institutions; sells wholesale to legitimate businesses and professionals.

TREND-LINES, INC.

135 American Legion Hwy.

Revere MA 02151

Phone: (800)767-9999

Offers: Over 3,000 woodworking tools: saws, routers, planers, bands, jointers, grinders, drills, planer jointers, sanders, mortisers, drill presses, laminate sitters, trimmers, Dremel tools and others. Accessories: sawhorses, supports, airbrushes, nail/spray guns, sandblasters, vises, measuring and carving/turning tools and router bits. Also offers wood sign layout kit, dollhouse kits, project plans, turning items, folding table legs, metal wheels, cedar liners/blocks and finishes.

Catalog: Free.
Accepts: Discover, MasterCard, Visa

VAUGHN & BUSHNELL MANUFACTURING CO.

11414 Maple Ave.
Hebron IL 60034
Phone: (815)648-2446
Offers: Vaughn hand tools, including hammers, picks and axes. Contact dealer, or send SASE.

VEGA ENTERPRISES, INC.

Rt. 3, Box 193
Decatur IL 62526
Phone: (800)222-8342
Offers: Woodworking tools/equipment: saw fences—professional, utility, radial, mitre and others. Lathe duplicators—2 models; lathes—bench, heavy and bowl. Also offers sanders, tenon jigs, mitre gauges, stock feed systems and mobile bases. Call or write.

STEVE WALL LUMBER CO.

P.O. Box 287
Mayodan NC 27027
Contact: Steve Wall
Phone: (336)427-0637 or (800)633-4062
Fax: (336)427-7588
E-mail: wallwood@netmcr.com
Website: www.walllumber.com
Store Location: 544 River Rd., Mayodan NC 27027-8195. At Hwy. 220 bypass.
Offers: Hardwood lumber, exotic lumber, thin lumber for crafts, hardwood plywood and Baltic birch plywood. Shipped by UPS or truck.
Catalog: $1.
Phone Orders: (800)633-4062.
Mail Orders: At P.O. Box.
Accepts: Discover, MasterCard, Visa

WILKE MACHINERY CO.

3230 Susquehanna Trail
York PA 17402
Contact: Curtis Wilke
Phone: (717)764-5000 or (800)235-2100
Fax: (717)764-3778
Website: www.wilkemach.com
Store Location: York PA location.
Offers: Bridgewood woodworking machinery, including shapers, planers, jointers, table saws, band saws and others.
Catalog: Free. 1998 woodworking and metalworking machinery catalog.
Phone Orders: (800)235-2100.
Mail Orders: At above address.

WOODARTIST

P.O. Box 80003
Charleston SC 29416-0003
Contact: W.P. Wachter
Phone: (805)571-4728

Fax: (805)571-6603
Offers: Antique birdhouse plans over 100 years old.

WOODCRAFT SUPPLY CORP.

P.O. Box 1686
210 Wood County Industrial Park
Parkersburg WV 26102
Phone: (800)225-1153
Website: www.woodcraft.com
Offers: Woodworking tools: sculptors'/carving, punches, adzes, hooks, rasps, files, rifflers, and measuring and layout tools/equipment. Also offers planes, vises, framing tools/equipment, plus tools to dowel, turn, log build, do marquetry and veneering. Carries branding irons and power tools by Dremel, Delta and Foredom. Specialty: planes, vises, saws, miters and clamps. Also carries glass domes and inserts, clock parts, musical movements, hardware, wood, plans and books.
Catalog: Free.
Discounts: Quantity; teachers and institutions.
Accepts: American Express, Discover, MasterCard, Optima, Visa

WOODCRAFTS AND SUPPLIES

405 E. Indiana St.
Oblong IL 62449
Contact: Carole Jones
Phone: (618)592-4907
Fax: (618)592-4902
E-mail: herb5@frs-1.com
Website: www.weshop.com/woodcrafts/
Store Location: At above address. M-Th, 9-4; F, 9-3 CST.
Offers: Woodworking and craft supplies, hardware, pegs, dowels, hearts, band saw blades, glue, miniatures and candle cups, wholesale and retail.
Catalog: Free.
Phone: (800)592-4907. M-F, 9-4 CST.
Mail Orders: Ship worldwide, usually within 24 hours.
Discounts: Wholesale, quantity discounts.
Accepts: American Express, Discover, MasterCard, Visa

WOODEN MEMORIES

Rt. 1 Box 87
Bear Lake PA 16402
Contact: Ken Williams
Phone: (814)489-3002
Fax: (814)489-0222
E-mail: woodmem@penn.com
Website: http://c1web.com/woodmem
Store Location: Lottsville PA location.
Offers: Woodworking, tole painting and decorative painting patterns, ready-to-assemble and ready-to-paint kits.
Catalog: 100 plans and kits for woodworking and painting.
Phone Orders: M-Sat, 8-6 EST.
Mail Orders: Ship worldwide.
Discounts: Wholesale to resale businesses.
Accepts: American Express, Discover, MasterCard, Visa

WOOD-PLY LUMBER CORP.

100 Bennington Ave.

Freeport NY 11520

Phone: (516)378-2612 or (800)354-9002

Fax: (516)376-0345

Offers: Over 80 species of exotic/domestic hardwoods including lumber, plywood, paper and foil-backed veneers, bowl blanks, burls, turning blocks and squares, tabletop and clock slabs, alabaster and soapstone. Wood and stone carving tools and wood finishes are also available.

Catalog: Send SASE for list.

WOODWORKER'S BOOK CLUB

P.O. Box 12171

Cincinnati OH 45212-0171

Phone: (513)531-8250

Offers: Each month brings a free issue of the club newsletter, describing the main selection and up to 100 more how-to and reference books for woodworkers. Members have 10 days to decide. Write for latest membership joining offer. Three books for $10 with no obligation to buy another is the current offer. Call for information.

WOODWORKER'S SUPPLY, INC.

1108 N. Glenn Rd.

Casper WY 82601

Phone: (800)645-9292

Fax: (800)853-9663

E-mail: info@woodworker.com

Store Location: At above address. Also locations in Albuquerque NM, Graham NC and Seabrook NH. M-F, 7:30-5:30; Sat, 9-3; Sun, 11-3.

Offers: Woodworking machinery: routers, borers, saws, shapers, scrolls, planers, sanders, pantographs, plus woodturning items, cedar lining and veneers, Bosch power tools, laminates, trimmers, drills and router. Porter-Cable routers and others. Also offers hardware, lights, cutters, drawer slides, lock sets, folding table legs, latches, hinges, doweling tools/aids, picture framing guns and Framemate items (miter box, clamps and others). Carries a full line of routers and other bits, plus edge banding systems, joining machines and drill presses.

Catalog: Free. 156 pages, 4 color.

Phone Orders: Yes.

Mail Orders: Worldwide shipment. Typically 3 days or less in contiguous US.

Discounts: Wholesale available to bona fide businesses.

Accepts: Discover, MasterCard, Visa, check, money order

WOODWORKS

4521 Anderson Blvd.

Fort Worth TX 76117

Phone: (800)722-0311 or (817)581-5230

Fax: (817)581-5235

Store Location: At above address.

Offers: Largest selection of American-made wood turnings. Cutouts: angels, apples, animals, Christmas, geometrics and more. Also offer beads, spools, balls, blocks, pegs, cups, wheels and many hard-to-find accessories.

Catalog: 64 pages, color. Free.

Phone Orders: 8:30-5 CST.

Mail Orders: Ship all over world. Orders shipped within 24-48 hours. Foreign customers please inquire about freight policy.

Discounts: All wholesale prices. Free freight at $50.

Accepts: Discover, MasterCard, Visa, check, money order, C.O.D.

Needlecrafts, Sewing & Fiber Arts

Batik & Dyeing

Also see Artist's Supplies, Graphics & Printing; Fabric Decorating; Fabrics & Trims; General Needlecraft Supplies; Rug Making; Spinning & Weaving; other related categories.

ALASKA DYEWORKS
300 W. Swanson #106
Wasilla AK 99654
Contact: Victoria Barnett or Brandee Brashear
Phone: (907)373-6562
Fax: (907)373-6562
E-mail: akdye@akdye.com
Website: www.akdye.com
Store Location: At above address.
Offers: High-quality hand-dyed 100% cotton fabrics. Hand-dyed silk ribbons for embroidery. Procion dye and dyeing supplies. A starter tie-dye kit complete with everything needed, except clothing, for the beginner. Hand-dyed cotton clothing.
Catalog: Swatch book (10 pages) available for $15 (plus p&h) or free with $100 purchase or combined purchases.
Phone Orders: (800)478-1755.
Mail Orders: At above address.
Discounts: We do offer a guild discount. Please call to confirm.
Accepts: American Express, MasterCard, Visa, check, money order, credit applications

ALJO MANUFACTURING CO.
81-83 Franklin St.
New York NY 10013
Contact: Herb Schiffrin or Robin Hull
Phone: (212)226-2878
Fax: (212)274-9616
Store Location: At above address. M-F, 8:30-6. All products available.
Offers: Dyes for cotton and rayon (direct dyes); silk, wool and nylon (acid dyes); acetate, nylon, spandex and acrylic (disperse dyes); cotton and rayon (vat dyes); cotton, rayon, and silk (fibre-reactive cold process).
Catalog: Free with directions for use and application of above dyes.
Phone Orders: Ship within 24 hours.
Mail Orders: Ship within 24 hours.
Discounts: According to quantity.
Accepts: MasterCard, Visa

AMERICAN ART CLAY CO., INC.
4717 W. 16th St.
Indianapolis IN 46222
Contact: Nancy Elliott
Phone: (317)244-6871 or (800)374-1600
Fax: (317)248-9300
E-mail: amacobrent@aol.com
Website: www.amaco.com
Offers: Craft supplies and modeling materials. Since 1919, AMACO has been a leading manufacturer of modeling clays, such as Permoplast, Plast-i-clay, Marblex and Mexican; modeling materials, including Friendly Plastic, FIMO, polymer clay Millefiori Canes, Quilt Squares, Designer Squares, Sculptamold, Claycrete and Super Dough. Also Rub 'n Buff and Brush 'n Leaf metallic finishes, Batikit fabric dyes, Cotton Press hand-cast cotton paper products, and push molds for use with polymer clays.
Catalog: Free.
Phone Orders: M-F, 8-5 EST.
Mail Orders: Prepayment required. Will ship to US and Canada.
Discounts: Manufacturer—sells through distributors.
Accepts: Discover, MasterCard, Visa

BATIKS ETCETERA
411 Pine St.
Fort Mill SC 29715
Contact: Jan Smiley
Phone: (800)BATIKS-ETC or (800)228-4573 or (803)547-4299
Fax: (803)802-3877
E-mail: batiks@cetlink.net
Website: www.batiks.com
Offers: The most complete selection of batik fabrics available worldwide. Indonesian, Indian and African fabrics. Cottons and rayons. Handwoven fabrics, patterns, books, cotton and wool batting and more.
Catalog: Sample swatches, $5.
Phone Orders: M-F, 10-6 EST.
Mail Orders: Ship internationally and nationally. Prepayment required.
Accepts: American Express, MasterCard, Visa

DHARMA TRADING CO.
P.O. Box 150916
San Rafael CA 94915
Phone: (800)542-5227
Fax: (415)456-8747
E-mail: catalog@dharmatrading.com
Website: www.dharmatrading.com

Store Location: 1604 Fourth St., San Rafael CA 94901.
Offers: Complete line of fiber art supplies: dyes for natural fabrics (including 200 colors of Procion), Resist and Discharge products, paints and supplies for silk, marbling, tie-dye, batik, printing, stamping, hand painting and stenciling, as well as kits and how-to books. White clothing blanks and accessories in cotton and silk, as well as cotton, rayon, silk and hemp fabrics for dyeing. Tools, fabric markers, transfer paper and lots more.
Catalog: Free. 120 pages.
Phone Orders: M-F, 8-5 PST.
Mail Orders: Prepay or credit card. E-mail orders.
Discounts: Quantity.
Accepts: Discover, MasterCard, Visa

G&K CRAFT INDUSTRIES
P.O. Box 38
Somerset MA 02726
Phone: (800)GKCRAFT or (508)676-3883
Fax: (508)676-3980
Offers: Reactive dyes for cotton, linen, rayon and silk: PRO MX & H. Acid dyes for wool, silk and nylon: Country Classics and PRO WashFast. Carries PROfab Textile Inks, Marbling Colors and many Pebeo products: Setasilk, Setacolor, Pebeo Soie and Setaskrib+ markers. Also offers numerous dye and fabric paint kits and store displays, as well as resist supplies/tools, waxes and workroom and safety supplies.
Catalog: Free.
Phone Orders: M-F, 8:30-5 EST.
Mail Orders: Will ship internationally.
Discounts: Wholesale for resale only.
Accepts: MasterCard, Visa

PRO CHEMICAL & DYE
P.O. Box 14
Somerset MA 02726
Phone: (800)2-BUY-DYE (orders and catalog) or (508)676-3838 (technical assistance)
Fax: (508)676-3980
E-mail: pro-chemical@worldnet.att.net
Website: www.prochemical.com
Offers: Reactive dyes for cotton, linen, rayon and silk: PRO MX & H and Sabracron F. Acid dyes for wool, silk and nylon: WashFast, Kiton, Sabraset and One Shot. Also offers Disperse dyes for polyester, Direct dyes and Synthetic Indigo. Carries PROfab Textile Inks, Pure Color Concentrates, Marbling Colors and many Pebeo products: Setacolor, Setasilk, Pebeo Soie, water- and solvent-based gutta and Setaskrib+ markers. We also offer paint and dye kits, discharge and resist supplies/tools, waxes and workroom and safety supplies. Our in-house lab offers color-matching services and technical advice while our clasroom offers visting artist workshops year-round.
Catalog: Free.
Phone Orders: M-F, 8:30-5 EST.
Mail Orders: Will ship internationally.
Discounts: Quantity discounts.
Accepts: MasterCard, Visa

RUPERT, GIBBON & SPIDER, INC./JACQUARD PRODUCTS
P.O. Box 425
Healdsburg CA 95448
Phone: (707)433-9577 or (800)442-0455
Offers: Over 50 silk and cotton fabrics, imported silk and cotton scarves. Manufactures Jacquard line of paints and dyes for fabrics; complete line of books and accessories. Also offers Jacquard wood products, easels, frames and stitchery items.
Catalog: Free, referrals to nearest store.
Discounts: Quantity; sells wholesale to legitimate businesses.

SAX ARTS & CRAFTS
P.O. Box 510710
2405 S. Calhoun Rd.
New Berlin WI 53151
Phone: (414)784-6880
Offers: A variety of supplies (known brands), including a full line of weaving looms and aids, yarns, weaving kits, rug/craft yarns, embroidery/crewel threads, rug hook frames and aids, canvas, hoops, burlap and felt. Native American beading, beads, feathers, macrame, basketry and batik supplies, fabric paints, airbrush kits and inks, stencil films, trims, foam, stained glass kits, etching and beveled glass supplies and supplies for decoupage, jewelry making, leather, casting, plastics, wood and metalworking are also available.
Catalog: $5 (refundable).
Discounts: Quantity, wholesale to legitimate resellers.

TEXTILE COLORS
(formerly Ivy Imports, Inc.)
P.O. Box 887
Riverdale MD 20738
Phone: (301)474-7347
Fax: (301)441-2395
Offers: Instructional videos, kits, and books on silk painting, dyeing and related subjects. Also offers services, including fabric finishing, hemming, tie making and custom screening of designs. Books include *The Complete Book of Silk Painting* and *Creative Silk Painting* (silk painting as a fine art) by Diane Tuckman and Jan Janas (North Light Books).
Catalog: $3.
Discounts: Sells wholesale to businesses.

Clothing & Accessories

Also see Costumes—Ethnic, Historic, Special Occasion; Doll, Toy & Clothes Making—Soft; Fabrics & Trims; Outdoors & Outerwear; Sewing; other related categories.

ALPEL PUBLISHING
P.O. Box 203-CSS
Chambly, Quebec J3L 4B3
Canada
Phone: (450)658-6205
Offers: Patterns/instruction books, including *Easy Sewing for Infants* (with 70 patterns), *Easy Sewing for Children* (75 patterns for 3- to 10-year-olds), *Easy Sewing for Adults* (78 patterns) and *Easy Halloween Costumes for Children* (60 costumes for 3- to 12-year-olds) all for $16.10. Halloween book includes ideas and patterns for accessories and mini-patterns. Duplicut vinyl grid sheets for enlarging patterns are also available. Also offers *Hey Kids, Let's Make Gifts* ($17.50) and *Catalog of Canadian Catalogs* ($16.95).
Catalog: 20 sample patterns, $5.
Discounts: Quantity.

B&B'S BLUEPRINTS
P.O. Box 1043
Sugar Land TX 77487-1043
Contact: Alva Winston
Phone: (281)545-9545
Offers: Sewing patterns primarily for children, with some patterns for mother and daughter. Patterns are versatile to allow for many different embellishments. Most patterns include several style variations such as collars, pant length, sleeve length and cuffs. All sizes are in one pattern. Sizing is ample to allow for the fit children like today.
Catalog: 20 pages. No charge. Send #10 SASE.
Phone Orders: M-F, 8-6 CST, or leave message 24 hours.
Mail Orders: Will ship to US, Canada. Prepayment required. Shipped next day.
Discounts: Sells wholesale to legitimate businesses.
Accepts: MasterCard, Visa, check, money order

CHARTRU ENTERPRISE
P.O. Box 177
Platteville CO 80651-0177
Contact: Charlene "Charlie" Casson
Phone: (970)785-0562
Store Location: 507-A Main St., Platteville CO 80651.
Offers: All occasion wallet pattern (with checkbook holder, license pocket, credit card section and coin purse). Also offers accessories and patterns.
Catalog: Yes.

CLOTHING DESIGNS BY LA FRED
4200 Park Blvd., Suite 102
Oakland CA 94602
Contact: Fred Blocbaum
Phone: (510)893-6811
Fax: (510)893-6811
Offers: Pattern line featuring elegant classic clothing with a contemporary twist.
Catalog: Brochure.
Phone Orders: Yes.
Mail Orders: At above address.
Accepts: American Express, Discover, MasterCard, Visa

COCHENILLE DESIGN STUDIO
243 N. Hwy. 101 #11
Solana Beach CA 92075
Contact: Susan Lazear
Phone: (619)259-1698
Fax: (619)259-3746
E-mail: info@cochenille.com
Website: www.cochenille.com
Offers: Computer software programs: Stitch Painter used for gridded crafts—beading, knitting, cross-stitch, weaving and more; and Garment Styler, a charting and shaping program that allows you to create a pattern for sewing or knitting. Also available are various books and videos.
Catalog: $1.
Phone Orders: M-T, 9:30-4 PST.
Mail Orders: Prepayment required. Allow 2 weeks for delivery.
Discounts: Dealers only.
Accepts: MasterCard, Visa

COLOR ME PATTERNS
P.O. Box 1909
Kerrville TX 78029-1909
Contact: Henry Stevenson
Phone: (830)367-2514
Fax: (830)367-4203
Offers: Specialty patterns for clothing, quilts and crafts. Also some hand-dyed and painted fabrics.
Catalog: Yes.
Phone Orders: Yes.
Mail Orders: Yes.
Accepts: MasterCard, Visa, check, money order, cash

COSTUMERS QUARTERLY

2400 E. Colonial Dr., Suite 28-7
Orlando FL 32803
Contact: Danny Veal
Phone: (407)898-3646
Fax: (407)894-8818
E-mail: glitzflash@aol.com
Store Location: At above address.
Offers: Everything a costume maker would want or need. Hundreds of fabrics, trims, notions, wigs, hats and feathers, all available at a flip of the page. We have rhinestones, sequins, petticoats, gloves, millinery supplies and much more.
Catalog: 18 pages. $2.
Phone Orders: Accepted during business hours.
Mail Orders: Will mail to US, Canada and Puerto Rico.
Accepts: American Express, MasterCard, Visa

CREATE-A-TIE

1816 Aberdeen Ave. NE
Renton WA 98056
Phone: (425)226-0937
Offers: Clip-on tie and bow tie patterns in children's through adult sizes (includes 3 tie clips and full-size pattern) and tie clips. Send SASE.
Discounts: Quantity; sells wholesale to legitimate businesses.

DABL'S PERETTE'S AFRICAN BEAD GALLERY

P.O. Box 711
1257 Washington Blvd.
Detroit MI 48226
Contact: Olayame Dabl's
Phone: (313)964-4247
Fax: (313)964-4281
Store Location: At above address. M-Sat, 12-9.
Offers: Perhaps Michigan's largest selection of African beads, textiles and carvings. Thousands of rare, old and new items. Traditional masks, jewelry, figures and metal. Beads from the 1600s, 1700s, 1800s and 1900s.
Catalog: 48 pages, 8½×11, b&w. $5 p&h.
Phone Orders: (800)530-6830. M-F, 12-5.
Mail Orders: Will ship anywhere, C.O.D. and prepayment.
Discounts: Retail and wholesale. ID required.
Accepts: check, money order, C.O.D.

D.L. DESIGNS HAT PATTERNS

P.O. Box 1382
Studio City CA 91604
Contact: Deborah Ambrosino
E-mail: d.l.hatpatterns@aol.com
Offers: Modern and historical hat patterns for men and women. Patterns are full-size, fully illustrated with step-by-step instructions and offer a list of millinery suppliers. Each pattern is a condensed millinery course for all skill levels.
Catalog: 13 pages. $1 (refundable).
Discounts: Wholesale (minimum 10-pattern order).
Accepts: US currency only

DOS DE TEJAS PATTERNS

P.O. Box 1636
Sherman TX 75091
Contact: Stan Odam
Phone: (903)893-0064
Fax: (903)893-0064
Website: www.dosdetejas.com
Offers: Over 40 fashion patterns sized 6-24, instructional videos of classes, complete garment kits, sueded rayon fabric, sewers' and quilters' T-shirts, Charlatan button kits. Consult your local independent dealer for the pattern of the month.
Catalog: $2.
Phone Orders: (800)8-TEJAS-8.
Mail Orders: At above address.
Accepts: MasterCard, Visa

EILEEN'S DESIGN STUDIO

4503 Bacon School Rd.
St. Joseph MI 49085
Contact: Eileen Chapman
Phone: (800)279-4443 or (616)429-1876
Fax: (616)429-1876
E-mail: eds@parrett.net
Website: www.eileensdesignstudio.com
Offers: Wearable art (quilt related) patterns and books, paper piecing patterns and books, totes on wheels and Amish Heritage Collection.
Catalog: Free. Send large SASE.
Phone Orders: M-F, 9-6 EST.
Mail Orders: Check catalog or website.
Discounts: Sells wholesale to legitimate businesses.
Accepts: MasterCard, Visa

ÉLAN PATTERN CO.

Dept. C
534 Sandalwood Dr.
El Cajon CA 92021
Contact: Cynthia Elam
Phone: (619)442-1167
E-mail: sewelan@adnc.com
Offers: Bra patterns in regular and plus sizes, bra kits in colors and white, bra-making supplies and pattern weights.
Catalog: $1.50. Color swatches, $1.
Phone Orders: (888)739-3526.
Mail Orders: Ship worldwide.
Discounts: Wholesale to retailers only.
Accepts: MasterCard, Visa, check, money order

FASHION BLUEPRINTS

2191 Blossom Valley Dr.
San Jose CA 95124
Phone: (408)356-5291
Offers: Classic ethnic clothing patterns—over 30 designs in blueprint format, multisize, for women, men, children—some fashionable today. Patterns include wrap dresses, tunics, pants, jackets, vests, tops, robes, shirts, coats and others—with Oriental, Far Eastern, African, Mexican and European

origins. Early American patterns that adapt to today: prairie skirt, gown, apron and shirts.

Catalog: $2.

Discounts: Sells wholesale to businesses.

GHEE'S

2620 Centenary Blvd. #2-250

Shreveport LA 71104

Contact: Linda McGhee

Phone: (318)226-1701

Fax: (318)226-1781

E-mail: ghees@softdisk.com

Website: www.ghees.com

Offers: Handbag-making supplies: metal frames in a variety of sizes and shapes, magnetic closures, chains, handbag accessories, handbag and vest patterns, notions and award-winning books: *Spiraling Schemes and Chromatics*, *More . . . Texture With Textiles*, *Texture With Textiles* and also *A Companion Project Book*. The books are on fabric manipulation.

Catalog: $1.

Phone Orders: M-F, 9-5 CST.

Mail Orders: Will ship to US and Canada.

Accepts: MasterCard, Visa

GRANDE PATTERN CO.

2095 E. Madison Ave.

El Cajon CA 92019

Contact: Sherry McDowell

Phone: (619)441-1412

Offers: Men's clothing patterns to size 8XL, pattern weights and other sewing notions.

Catalog: Brochure, $1.

Mail Orders: Prepayment required. Will ship anywhere.

Discounts: Dealers welcome.

Accepts: check, money order

GREAT COPY PATTERNS

4901 Washington Ave.

Racine WI 53408

Contact: Ruthann Spiegelhoff

Phone: (414)632-2660

Fax: (414)632-0152

Store Location: At above address. M and W, 10-9; T, Th-Sat, 10-5.

Offers: Great Copy patterns, *Polarfleece Pizzazz* book, *More Polarfleece Pizzazz* book. Fabrics and stretch-and-sew patterns.

Catalog: Free. Great Copy Brochure.

Phone Orders: Accepted M-Sat.

Mail Orders: Will ship to US and Canada.

Accepts: Discover, MasterCard, Visa

KAY GUILES DESIGNS

P.O. Box 855

Petal MS 39465

Contact: Kay Guiles

Phone: (601)582-8312

E-mail: kguiles@aol.com

Offers: Unique line of classic girls' patterns with related books and smocking plates.

Catalog: Brochure free with SASE.

Phone Orders: Yes.

Mail Orders: Yes.

Discounts: Wholesale to legitimate businesses.

Accepts: MasterCard, Visa

JEAN HARDY PATTERNS

2151 La Cuesta Dr.

Santa Ana CA 92705

Phone: (714)544-1608

Website: www.antelope.com/jeanharpat

Offers: Men's and women's riding clothes patterns for English, Western and saddle seat riding.

Catalog: $1.

HARRIET'S TCS

P.O. Box 1363

Winchester VA 22604-1363

Contact: Harriet A. Engler

Phone: (540)667-2541

Fax: (540)722-4618

Website: www.harriet's.com

Store Location: By appointment.

Offers: Over 200 vintage patterns for men, women and children. XL sizes available. Circa 1300-1945. 8 styles of hoops, corsets, boning, fabric, 100% polished cotton and silks. Rental packages for all ages, $125-200 range (you supply the body). Parasols, fans, gloves, men's silk ties, vintage tails and more.

Catalog: With color photos, $12.

Phone Orders: 4-6 EST.

Mail Orders: Yes.

Discounts: Patterns/wholesale in quantity only.

Accepts: American Express, Discover, MasterCard, Visa

HESSON COLLECTABLES

1261 S. Lloyd

Lombard IL 60148

Phone: (630)627-3298

Offers: Mail-order catalogs of 1900-96, including Sears, Montgomery Ward, J.C. Penney, Alden and Spiegel's.

Catalog: List of more than 2,000 catalogs, $4.

THE KWIK-SEW PATTERN CO., INC.

3000 Washington Ave. N.

Minneapolis MN 55411-1699

Contact: Diana Bade

Phone: (612)521-7651

Fax: (612)521-1662

E-mail: info@kwiksew.com
Website: www.kwiksew.com
Offers: Over 850 patterns for the entire family. The largest selection of swimwear, actionwear and lingerie.
Mail Orders: See your dealer, or send SASE for information.

LACELAND
P.O. Box 820849
Houston TX 77282
Phone: (281)983-5223
Offers: Laces and bridal laces and motifs; swimsuits and lingerie patterns. Also offers fabrics, including Lycra, tricot, stretch laces and others. Underwires, bra cups and others also available.

ELIZABETH LEE DESIGNS
P.O. Box 696
Bluebell UT 84007
Contact: Mary Bird
Phone: (800)449-3350
Fax: (435)454-3450
E-mail: eldesign@ubtanet.com
Website: elizabethlee.com
Store Location: Altamont UT location.
Offers: Fashion patterns for nursing moms. Buy 4 patterns, get 1 free. Sunrise Design patterns at great prices.
Catalog: 40 pages, b&w. Free.
Phone Orders: (435)454-3350. M-F, 8:30-3 MST.
Mail Orders: Ships all over world with prepayment.
Discounts: Retail only.
Accepts: American Express, Discover, MasterCard, Visa

LOGAN KITS
Rt. 3, Box 380
Double Springs AL 35553
Contact: Evelyn Logan
Phone: (205)486-7732
Fax: (205)480-0070
Store Location: At above address. Require appointment.
Offers: Cotton velour, thermal, underwires, lingerie kits, pounds and yard goods, tricot, cotton Lycra, spandex, lace, elastic, interlock, plaids, jersey, fleece, collars, thread, towels, Sew Lovely patterns and rib and free pattern.
Catalog: 28 pages. $1.50.
Mail Orders: Prepayment required.
Discounts: Quantity; sells wholesale.
Accepts: no credit cards

MARY WALES LOOMIS
1487 Parrott Dr.
San Mateo CA 94402
Contact: Mary Wales Loomis
Phone: (650)345-8012
Fax: (650)345-3206
E-mail: shoes@dnai.com
Website: www.marywalesloomis.com
Offers: Book: *Make Your Own Shoes.*

Phone Orders: Yes.
Mail Orders: At above address.
Discounts: Discounts to wholesalers depending on amount of order.
Accepts: MasterCard, Visa

NEW YORK FELT, INC.
107 Court St., Suite 171
Watertown NY 13601
Contact: Todd Badalato
Phone: (800)635-3267
Fax: (315)788-4807
E-mail: nyfelt@gisco.net
Offers: Wool and synthetic felts for display, craft, decorative and novelty. Die-cutting and trimming.
Catalog: Information kits and swatch cards.
Phone Orders: Yes.
Mail Orders: Will ship to US and Canada.
Discounts: Wholesale prices.
Accepts: MasterCard, Visa, C.O.D.

NEW YORK THEATRICAL SUPPLY, INC.
263 W. 38th St., Store #3
New York NY 10018
Contact: Kumar
Phone: (212)840-3120
Fax: (212)840-3159
Store Location: At above address.
Offers: All kinds of Lycra-spandex, fur, feathers, stretch velvet, rayon velvet, holographics materials, Feather St. Vynol, slinky, chiffons, satin, sparkle, organza, stretch lace and more.
Catalog: 16 pages. $20.
Phone Orders: M-F, 9-6:30; Sat, 10-5.
Mail Orders: Ship via UPS.
Discounts: Wholesale and retail.
Accepts: major credit cards

PAW PRINTS
19618 Canyon Dr.
Granite Falls WA 98252
Contact: Dana Bontrager
Phone: (360)691-4293
Fax: (360)691-4293
E-mail: dana@purrfection.com
Website: www.purrfection.com
Offers: Artistic garment patterns. Multisize from XS to 5XL.
Catalog: B&w. $1; free with order.
Phone Orders: M-Sat, 9-7 PST.
Mail Orders: Domestic and international.
Discounts: Wholesale to businesses.
Accepts: MasterCard, Visa

PREEMIE-YUMS
2260 Gibson Woods Court NW
Salem OR 97304
Contact: Lisa Purkerson

Phone: (503)370-9279
Fax: (503)370-9279
Offers: Preemie patterns, ready-wear and related items for infants 4-6 pounds. Many items we carry also work for dolls.
Catalog: Send $1.50 and 32¢ postage stamp for brochure.
Phone Orders: M-F, 9-5 PST.
Discounts: Available to wholesale or hospital accounts.
Accepts: MasterCard, Visa

SAF-T-POCKETS

822 NW Murray Blvd., Suite 163
Portland OR 97229
Contact: Jo Reimer
Phone: (503)643-1968
Fax: (503)643-0764
E-mail: joreimer@easystreet.com
Offers: Jacket, vest and coat patterns featuring lots of secure, hidden pockets for travel safety and convenience.
Catalog: Send #10 SASE.
Phone Orders: M-F, 9-6 PST.
Mail Orders: Will ship to Canada. Prepay with US funds.
Discounts: Wholesale to qualified shops.
Accepts: MasterCard, Visa

SEW SASSY FABRICS

900 Bob Wallace #124
Huntsville AL 35801
Contact: Catherine Montgomery
Phone: (256)536-4405 (M-F, 10-5 CST)
Fax: (256)536-5488
E-mail: catherine@sewsassy.com
Website: www.sewsassy.com
Offers: Lingerie materials, including tricot with matching lace elastics, slip straps, all over stretch lace, charmeuse, re-embroidered lace and lightweight knits; bra accessories and power knit for girdles and bras. Lycra and Hologram Lycra in solids, prints, linings, sheer, cotton types and stretch velvet. Line of patterns from Stretch & Sew and Kwik-Sew.
Catalog: $2; $3 out of US (US funds).
Mail Orders: Out of country, MasterCard or Visa only.
Discounts: Quantity prices.
Accepts: MasterCard, Visa

SEWBABY

313 N. Mattis Ave., Suite 116
Champaign IL 61821
Contact: Ann Brodsky
Phone: (217)398-1440 or (800)249-1907
Fax: (217)398-6340
E-mail: sewbaby@sewbaby.com
Website: www.sewbaby.com

Store Location: Champaign IL location.
Offers: Childrens' fabrics, unique patterns, snaps, novelty buttons, lace and bows. Fabric Club $10/year for 5 swatch mailings.
Catalog: Free.
Phone Orders: (800)249-1907.
Mail Orders: Yes.
Discounts: Coupons in catalog and Fabric Club.
Accepts: Discover, MasterCard, Visa, check, money order

SEWGRAND PATTERNS

185-9040 Blundell Rd. #272
Richmond, British Columbia V6Y 1K3
Canada
Contact: Corinne Cordoni
Phone: (604)274-3276
Fax: (604)274-3274
E-mail: corinne@sewgrand.com
Website: www.sewgrand.com
Store Location: Other location: P.O. Box 8019, 1160 Yew Ave., BIN 21, Blaine WA 98231.
Offers: Home sewing patterns, specializing in fashion and lifestyle clothing designs for plus sizes.
Catalog: $2 (refundable).
Phone Orders: (800)252-8872. M-F, 9-5 PST.
Mail Orders: Will sell wholesale to businesses. Minimum order applies.
Accepts: American Express, MasterCard, Visa

SUITABILITY

P.O. Box 3244
Chico CA 95927
Phone: (800)207-0256
Website: http://www.Suitability.com
Offers: Equestrian clothing and horse equipment patterns, including Western duster and others.
Catalog: Free.

SUITABLES

P.O. Box 17601
San Antonio TX 78217
Offers: Instructions for no-sew fabric-covered shoes and fabric-covered belts, $5. Send SASE for details.

THE THREAD BARE PATTERN CO.

P.O. Box 1484
Havelock NC 28532
Phone: (919)447-4081
Fax: (800)4-PATTERN
E-mail: patterns@costalnet.com
Offers: Whimsical wearable art patterns, including jackets and vests.

Costumes—Ethnic, Historic, Special Occasion

Also see Clothing & Accessories; Doll, Toy & Clothes Making—Soft; Fabrics & Trims; other related categories.

ALPEL PUBLISHING
P.O. Box 203-CSS
Chambly, Quebec J3L 4B3
Canada
Phone: (450)658-6205
Fax: (450)658-3514
Offers: Easy-Sew pattern book: children's traditional costumes (3- to 12-year-olds) and pirates, Peter Pan, robots and others; includes accessories and patterns to be enlarged. Makeup and wigs are also covered. Carries Duplicut wipe-clean, vinyl grid sheets for pattern enlargement.
Catalog: Free brochure with sample infant's pattern, $1.

ALTERYEARS
3749 E. Colorado Blvd.
Pasadena CA 91107
Phone: (626)585-2994
Fax: (626)432-4530
E-mail: 72437.674@compuserve.com
Website: www.alteryears.com
Offers: Over 1,400 historical, ethnic and specialty patterns from 48 companies. Also sells over 200 hard-to-find supplies and accessories, complete corsetry supplies, millinery, hoops and bustles, gloves, panniers, clasps and others, and nearly 1,000 costume reference books.
Catalog: $5, fourth class; $8, Priority.

AMAZON DRYGOODS
2218 E. 11th St.
Davenport IA 52803
Phone: (319)322-6800 or (800)798-7979
Fax: (319)322-4003
Offers: Nineteenth-century-inspired products: Over 1,200 historic/ethnic clothes patterns from 1390 to 1950, with emphasis on the 1800s—coats, cloaks, hats, bonnets, gowns, suits, corsets, lingerie, underwear, formal clothes, everyday, work outfits and military uniforms (sizes for most patterns: ladies' 6 to 44-plus, men's 32 to 48-plus). Supplies: hoop wire, boning, stays, ostrich feathers, specialty fabrics (including fancies), uniform wools, tradecloth and veilings. Native American/frontier patterns available.
Catalog: General catalog, $3. Shoe catalog, $5. Pattern catalog, $7. Drapery catalog, $2.
Accepts: American Express, Discover, MasterCard, Visa

ARON'S
8974 E. Huntington Dr.
San Gabriel CA 91775
Phone: (626)285-8544
Offers: Line of square dance and western clothing patterns and accessories. 32 colors of western snaps.
Catalog: Western patterns and square dance patterns catalog, $2.

BAER FABRICS
515 E. Market St.
Louisville KY 40202
Phone: (502)569-7010 or (800)769-7776
Fax: (502)582-2331
Offers: Special bridal collection of fabrics, including taffetas, satins, chiffons, organzas, nettings and laces in a range of colors, plus trims, notions and supplies. Also offers prom and evening wear collection. Also sells Ultrasuede, Ultrasuede light and Ultraleather in 75 colors. Personal shopper service.
Catalog: Bridal collection sample set (#11525), $10. Prom and evening wear collection sample set (#12525), $6. Ultrasuede and Ultraleather sample set (#01525), $9.50. Notions and trims catalog, $3.
Discounts: Quantity; teachers, institutions and businesses.

BUCKAROO BOBBINS
P.O. Box 1168
Chino Valley AZ 86323
Phone: (520)636-1885
Offers: Clothing patterns of authentic vintage western style.
Catalog: $2.

DOERING DESIGNS
68935 233rd St.
Dassel MN 55325
Offers: Selection of Scandinavian costume patterns—women's, men's and children's multisize; 14″ and 18″ dolls. Braid and pewter also available.
Catalog: $2.

FABRIC DEPOT
P.O. Box 1556
Sugar Land TX 77487-1556
Contact: Susan Stacy
Phone: (281)933-8800
Fax: (281)933-8800
Offers: Lycras, notions, patterns and bridal lace. Fabrics and patterns for swimsuits, lingerie, skating, drill team and dance costumes. A fantastic selection of Lycras, powernets, glistenets, tricots, trims, notions, underwires and bra cups.

Catalog: Regular catalog, $2. Color samples, $2. Bridal catalog, $2.
Phone Orders: M-F, 9-5 EST.
Mail Orders: Same day shipping. Shipped by UPS ground. UPS 1 and 2 day delivery available with extra charge. Priority mail also available.
Discounts: Quantity discounts are 20-50%.
Accepts: Discover, MasterCard, Visa

FOLKWEAR
67 Broadway
Asheville NC 28801
Contact: Kate Mathews
Phone: (704)236-9730 or (800)284-3388
Fax: (704)236-2869
E-mail: larkmail@larkbooks.com
Website: www.larkbooks.com
Offers: Sewing patterns adapted from traditional ethnic costumes and vintage fashions from around the world. Multisize patterns for men, women and children include complete sewing instructions, historical lore and information about traditional embellishment techniques. Available from Folkwear headquarters and Folkwear dealers all over.
Catalog: Free.
Phone Orders: US (800)284-3388, anytime; outside US (704)236-9730, M-F, 8:30-5:30 EST.
Discounts: Wholesale to dealers only.
Accepts: American Express, Discover, MasterCard, Visa

HARPAGON
P.O. Box 161125
Rocky River OH 44116
Contact: Claudia Lynch
Phone: (440)333-3143
Fax: (440)333-5974
E-mail: idoveils@aol.com
Website: http://members.aol.com/idoveils/harpagon.html
Offers: Wedding-related sewing and craft books. Publishers of *"I Do" Veils—So Can You!*
Catalog: Brochure of wedding-related sewing and craft books.
Phone Orders: (800)295-0586 orders only; answer by voice mail.
Mail Orders: Worldwide shipping.
Discounts: Quantity wholesaling available to retailers.
Accepts: MasterCard, Visa, check, money order

HARPER HOUSE
P.O. Box 39
Williamstown PA 17098
Contact: D. Glosek
Phone: (717)647-7807
Fax: (717)647-2480
E-mail: harperh@epix.net
Website: www.longago.com
Offers: Vintage sewing patterns—medieval through 1900s. Sewing tools and large book selection.
Catalog: $7 fee charged for catalog. Free with website order.

Phone Orders: Yes.
Mail Orders: Yes.
Discounts: None.
Accepts: American Express, MasterCard, Visa

HARRIET'S TCS
P.O. Box 1363
Winchester VA 22604-1363
Contact: Harriet A. Engler
Phone: (540)667-2541
Fax: (540)722-4618
Website: www.harriet's.com
Store Location: By appointment.
Offers: Over 200 vintage patterns for men, women and children. XL sizes available. Circa 1300-1945. 8 styles of hoops, corsets, boning, fabric, 100% polished cotton and silks. Rental packages for all ages, $125-200 range (you supply the body). Parasols, fans, gloves, men's silk ties, vintage tails and more.
Catalog: With color photos, $12.
Phone Orders: 4-6 EST.
Mail Orders: Yes.
Discounts: Patterns/wholesale in quantity only.
Accepts: American Express, Discover, MasterCard, Visa

MEDIEVAL MISCELLANEA
6530 Spring Valley Dr.
Alexandria VA 22312
Phone: (703)642-1740
Fax: (703)642-1740
Offers: Period patterns for garments of the medieval era—a variety of male and female styles, headgear and others. Also rents and sells period Pavilions. Write or call.
Discounts: Sells wholesale.

NEWARK DRESSMAKER SUPPLY
Dept. CSS
P.O. Box 20730
Lehigh Valley PA 18002
Contact: Lucy W. Perusse
Phone: (610)837-7500 or (800)736-6783
Fax: (610)837-9115
Offers: Sewing, bridal and craft supplies, aids and fabrics. Bridal supplies include pearl buttons, looping, hair boning, appliqués, bubbles, plastic combs, pearls, veils and fabrics (laces, satins, moire, organza, espirit, denim, cotton, nylon net, tulle and illusion). Utility fabrics of silver cloth, diaper and flannel. Also offers pressing items, fabric paints, zippers, plastic beads, pearls, doll accessories and patterns.
Catalog: Free.
Phone Orders: Request larger catalog for total products.
Mail Orders: Will ship to Canada.
Discounts: Quantity. Sells wholesale. Orders over $50 receive 10% discount.
Accepts: MasterCard, Novus, Visa

PAST PATTERNS

217 S. Fifth St.
Richmond IN 47374
Contact: Saundra Ros Autman
Phone:(765)962-3333
Fax: (765)962-3773
E-mail: pastpat@thepoint.net
Website: http://www.thepoint.net/~pastpat/
Store Location: At above address.
Offers: All that is in catalog.
Catalog: 32 pages. $4.
Phone Orders: M-F, 10-4.
Mail Orders: Yes.
Accepts: Discover, MasterCard, Visa

PATTERNS OF HISTORY

816 State St., Suite CS
Madison WI 53706
Phone: (608)264-6428
Offers: Patterns for garments of the nineteenth century, including gowns in a variety of styles.
Catalog: Send for free brochure.

PEGEE OF WILLIAMSBURG—PATTERNS FROM HISTORIE

P.O. Box 127
Williamsburg VA 23187-0127
Contact: Pegee Miller
Phone: (757)220-2722
Offers: Historic patterns, including 1776 ladies' dress, girls' dress, ladies' cloak, men's and boys' shirt, breeches and waistcoat, men's military/civilian coat, Scarlett O'Hara's Barbecue Party Dress, hoop skirt and Green Velveteen Portieres Dress, Bonnie's blue riding habit and others. Patterns are replicas of the original, with detailed instructions and illustrations.
Catalog: Brochure, $2.50.
Phone Orders: With credit card.
Mail Orders: Yes.
Accepts: American Express, Discover, MasterCard, Visa

PIECES OF OLDE

824 W. 36th St.
Baltimore MD 21211
Contact: Nancy Wertheimer
Phone: (410)466-4984 or (410)366-4949 (store)
Fax: (410)466-9326
E-mail: world@ix.netcom.com
Website: www.piecesofolde.com
Store Location: At above address. Th-F, 10-7; Sat, 10-6; Sun, 12-4; or by appointment or chance.
Offers: Vintage 1940s fabrics by the yard and other old fabrics, vintage buttons—bakelite; lace—old; patterns; urban artifacts; corbels, columns and grates.
Catalog: On-line.
Phone Orders: (410)466-4984.
Mail Orders: P.O. Box 65130, Baltimore MD 21209.

Discounts: Wholesale discounts.
Accepts: American Express, MasterCard, Visa

R.L. SHEP

P.O. Box 2706
Fort Bragg CA 95437
Phone: (707)964-8662
Offers: Out-of-print books on textiles and costumes. Also carries reprints of Edwardian and Victorian titles for accurate reproduction of period clothing and other use.
Catalog: Free brochure.
Discounts: Sells wholesale to legitimate businesses.

ROCKING HORSE FARM

P.O. Box 608-C
North Jackson OH 44451
Offers: Over 90 historic and vintage clothing patterns for medieval period and 1740 to 1950.
Catalog: Pattern catalog, $3.
Accepts: check, money order

ROSEBAR TEXTILE CO., INC.

93 Entin Rd.
Clifton NJ 07014
Phone: (201)777-0078 or (800)631-8573
Fax: (973)777-0246
Offers: Fabrics, including satins, taffetas, sheers, lamés, jacquards, velvets, flocking, prints, novelties and linings. Supplies and accessories, box, ribbon, tabletop, elegant craft and bridal and evening wear fabrics. Send SASE for details.

MURIELLE ROY & CO.

67 Platts Mill Rd.
Naugatuck CT 06770
Phone: (203)729-0480
Fax: (203)720-2101
Offers: Fabrics and trims for performers, including Lycras, chiffons, silks, laces, stretch sheer, mesh, velvets, satin and foil. Also offers glitter and metallic Lycra, feathers, sequins, beaded fringe and others.
Catalog: $4.
Accepts: American Express, Discover, MasterCard, Visa

THE WHOLE COSTUMER'S CATALOGUE

P.O. Box 207M
2860 Main St.
Beallsville PA 15313
Phone: (724)632-3242
Offers: A directory of costume resources for craftspeople, costumers, fiber artists and sewers, including a shopping guide to New York, Los Angeles and Philadelphia, books and periodicals, organizations and a wide range of source listings for historical and ethnic clothing and accessories. Also lists fabrics, trims, casting materials, paints and dyes, tools, patterns and many others.
Catalog: 14th edition, April 1, 1998. Price: $20 (includes shipping).

Doll, Toy & Clothes Making—Soft

Also see Doll & Toy Making—Rigid; Miniature Making, Miniatures & Dollhouses; Fabrics & Trims; Knitting & Crochet; other related categories.

AIRTEX CONSUMER PRODUCTS
150 Industrial Park Blvd.
Cokato MN 55321
Contact: Marty Fitzloff
Phone: (320)286-2696
Fax: (320)286-2428
E-mail: airtex@cmgate.com
Website: www.airtex.com
Store Location: Manufacturing plant is in Cokato MN (wholesale only).
Offers: Complete line of filling products, polyester fiberfill, quilt batting, pillow forms and foam and cotton quilt batting.
Catalog: (800)851-8887.
Phone Orders: (800)851-8887.
Mail Orders: Call for freight charges and send check to Industrial Park Blvd. address.
Discounts: (800)851-8887. Call for volume pricing.
Accepts: MasterCard, Visa, C.O.D., prepaid net 30 upon credit approval

ALL CREATURES STUFFED AND SMALL
4865 Saratoga Ave., Suite 201
San Diego CA 92107
Contact: Allen Strommer or Michelle Strommer (design artist)
Phone: (619)523-4228
Fax: (619)523-5358
E-mail: acssbear@aol.com
Offers: Kits and patterns for miniature teddy bears and other animals. Finished products handmade by the artist available by special order.
Catalog: $3.
Phone Orders: M-F, 9-5 PST.
Mail Orders: We ship all over the world within 24 hours.
Discounts: Wholesale, inquiries welcome.
Accepts: MasterCard, Visa

ANIMAL CRACKERS PATTERN CO.
1404 Peyton Rd.
Los Lunas NM 87031
Contact: Patricia Hanson
Phone: (505)865-7218
Fax: (505)865-6272
Store Location: At above address. M-F, 10-5.

Offers: Patterns, kits, mohair, glass eyes, joints and other supplies to create collector quality bears and other stuffed animals.
Catalog: 40 pages. $2.
Phone Orders: M-F, 9-9 MST. 24-hour answering machine.
Mail Orders: Usually within 48 hours, worldwide.
Discounts: Wholesale patterns. Minimum 3 patterns of one kind (or $25) plus tax.
Accepts: MasterCard, Visa

ATLANTA PUFFECTIONS
P.O. Box 13524
Atlanta GA 30324
Phone: (404)262-7437
Offers: Over 75 soft doll, animal patterns including Puff Ima Doorstop Mouse, Nanny and the Twins and others. Supplies (to support patterns).
Catalog: 16-page newsletter, including at least 3 free patterns, $2.
Discounts: Sells wholesale to legitimate businesses.

BASICALLY BEARS
825 Seventh St. SE
Oelwein IA 50662
Contact: Mary Ellen Brandt
Phone: (319)283-3748
Fax: (319)283-3748
E-mail: bfltd@trxinc.com
Website: http://www.freeyellow.com/members/maryelle/index.html
Offers: Antique shoe buttons, bears from recycled fur, custom orders from your fur, band instruments made into lamps and sterling and silver plate silverware made into jewelry.
Catalog: Pictures of bears only.
Phone Orders: Yes.
Mail Orders: At above address. Allow 6-8 weeks for one bear and 2-3 months for more. Immediate shipping on shoe button orders that are prepaid.
Discounts: Wholesale prices on bears to shop owners; none on shoe buttons.
Accepts: MasterCard, Visa, international checks

BEMIDJI WOOLEN MILLS
P.O. Box 277
Bemidji MN 56619-0277
Contact: Bill Batchelder
Phone: (218)751-5166 or (888)751-5166
Fax: (218)751-4659
Website: www.bemidjiwool.com
Store Location: 301 Irvine Ave. NW, Bemidji MN 56601.
Offers: Rockford Red Heel socks, 100% wool yarns, 100%

wool roving, 100% wool quilt batting, 100% polyester batting and stuffing, and wool fabric for craft work and sewing.
Catalog: *The Wool Street Journal.*
Phone Orders: (888)751-5166.
Mail Orders: At P.O. Box.
Accepts: American Express, Discover, MasterCard, Visa, check

BY DIANE
1126 Ivon Ave.
Endicott NY 13760
Phone: (607)754-0391
Offers: Fuzzy Friends toy kits/patterns including teddy bears, sea creatures, other wild and domestic animals and hand puppet kits/patterns. Also offers animal eyes, noses and joint sets, glass eyes, armatures and furs.
Catalog: $3.
Discounts: Quantity; teachers and institutions; sells wholesale to legitimate businesses.

CASEY DOLLS
1930 Blairsville Hwy.
Murphy NC 28906
Contact: Jackie Casey
Phone: (704)837-4114
E-mail: caseyj@dnet.net
Website: http://www.caseydolls.com
Store Location: At above address (Old Cupboard General Store).
Offers: Patterns for cloth dolls: (1) 16½″ Butterfly Lady patterns, $11 (postage paid) in US; and (2) Casey's hand turning kit (includes brass turning tools), $11 (postage paid) in US.
Mail Orders: At above address.
Accepts: check, money order (no credit cards)

A CHILD'S DREAM
2990 Linden Dr.
Boulder CO 80304
Contact: Holly Colangelo
Phone: (303)442-0437
Fax: (303)443-4923
E-mail: todream@earthlink.net
Store Location: At above address.
Offers: 100% wool felt in 30 colors, plant-dyed fabrics, silks, dolls and doll supplies, natural handwork supplies, puppetry kits, storytelling materials to nurture a child's sense for life and imagination.
Catalog: 40 pages. Free.
Phone Orders: Yes.
Mail Orders: Will ship worldwide.
Discounts: When applicable.
Accepts: MasterCard, Visa

CLOSE KNIT PRESS/TE CORP.
P.O. Box 1500
Campton NH 03223-1500
Contact: Linn Downs
Phone: (603)726-4700

Fax: (603)726-8818
E-mail: dolls@tecorp.com
Website: http://www.tecorp.com
Offers: Hand-knit, machine-knit and crochet patterns for 18″ modern dolls and 15″ baby dolls, as well as bears and bunnies.
Catalog: Free brochure.
Phone Orders: Yes.
Mail Orders: Anywhere.
Discounts: Wholesale to legitimate businesses.
Accepts: American Express, MasterCard, Visa

CR'S CRAFTS
P.O. Box 8-81 CB
109 Fifth Ave. W.
Leland IA 50453
Phone: (515)567-3652
Fax: (515)567-3071
Website: www.crscraft.com
Store Location: At above address (showroom). M-F, 8:30-3:30 CST.
Offers: Doll, bear and animal patterns, kits and supplies: doll heads and hands. Animal parts, fabrics, fur fabrics, mohair, eyes, noses, joints, armatures, stuffing, music boxes, wings, wigs and hair. Also offers doll and bear clothing, clothing patterns, stands, miniatures, hats, shoes, socks, glasses and doll furniture. Large selection of items for 18″ girl dolls.
Catalog: 148 pages. $2 ($4 Canada, $7 other countries—US funds).
Phone Orders: M-F, 8:30-3:30 CST.
Mail Orders: Ship worldwide. Prepayment required. Most orders shipped same day.
Discounts: Quantity and wholesale.
Accepts: Discover, MasterCard, Visa

DISCO JOINTS & TEDDIES
32 Old Carriage Court
Kitchner, Ontario N2P 1V3
Canada
Contact: Karen Meadows
Phone: (519)895-0579
Fax: (519)895-2835
E-mail: chris70@golden.net
Catalog: Price list, free.
Phone Orders: Yes.
Mail Orders: All products for mail order.
Accepts: Visa, check, money order

THE DOLLHOUSE FACTORY
P.O. Box 456
157 Main St.
Lebanon NJ 08833
Phone: (908)236-6404
Offers: Full line of name-brand dollhouses and supplies—needlework, wood, lighting, components, accessories, wallpapers, furniture, moldings, hardware and masonry. Kits and tools also available.
Catalog: $5.50.

DONNA'S DOLLS, CLOTH DOLLS WITH TIES TO THE PAST

212 Melrose #201

Liberty MO 64068

Contact: Donna Root

Phone: (816)792-2036

Offers: I sell patterns for 16-25″ cloth dolls. Designs are for dolls dressed in historically accurate 1800s clothing, including a boy doll wearing a 1900 suit. Also featured are patterns for a doll and 5 different outfits to make for her. The 16″ dolls are a boy and girl that have bendable arms and legs to sit on a shelf or small chair. All designs are original.

Catalog: Color. $3.

Mail Orders: Accepted from individuals and shops.

Discounts: Legitimate shops please write for wholesale price list.

Accepts: money order, US funds (no charge cards)

EDINBURGH IMPORTS, INC.

P.O. Box 340

Newbury Park CA 91319-0340

Contact: Ron or Elke Block

Phone: (805)376-1700

Fax: (805)376-1711

E-mail: rblock@edinburgh.com

Website: www.edinburgh.com

Store Location: 1121 Lawrence Dr., Newbury Park CA 91320.

Offers: 900 imported mohair, alpaca and wool, plus fabrics, books, over 250 patterns and kits 1½″-4½′ and all the supplies for making stuffed animals and teddy bears.

Catalog: 32 pages, with inserts and monthly specials flyer.

Phone Orders: (800)334-6274 or (805)376-1700. M-F, 8:30-5 PST.

Mail Orders: At P.O. Box. Will ship worldwide.

Discounts: Quantity discounts. Wholesale where applicable.

Accepts: Discover, MasterCard, Visa

THE ENCHANTED ATTIC

Rt. 5, Box 165AAA

Oakview Addition

El Dorado Springs MO 64744

Contact: Barb Spencer

Phone: (417)876-5131

Fax: (417)876-3671

E-mail: jspen@getonthe.net

Offers: 44 original cloth doll patterns for various size lady, children, animal, holiday and ethnic dolls, with their clothing. 2 books of traceable faces, with mix-and-match facial features for creating other doll faces, and 1 book of hairstyles with instructions and illustrations are also available.

Catalog: Send $2 for foldout brochure.

Mail Orders: Yes.

Discounts: Sells wholesale.

Accepts: check, cash

ENDANGERED SPECIES

231 Islamorada Lane

Naples FL 34114-8405

Contact: Pat Martin

Store Location: At above address.

Offers: Original patterns for soft sculpture animals or pillows: Pokey Bear, Rita Rhino, Fat Cat, Tina Tiger, Peter Parrot, Bessy Bovine, Elvis Eagle, Troy Carousel, Horse Head, E.T., Superman, Lydia Lizard, Diana Dinosaur and new pattern Olivia Ostrich. Send $6 per pattern; $2 extra for custom requests not already offered and large SASE. Patterns show front and back views.

Catalog: Photos.

Mail Orders: At above address.

Accepts: check, money order

E Z POSE FLEXIBLE DOLL BODIES

P.O. Box 97

250 Copper Ave.

Crestone CO 81131

Contact: Sandi Patterson

Phone: (719)256-4235

Fax: (719)256-4209

E-mail: cspatt@fone.net

Offers: Flexible urethane foam doll bodies 8-30″ tall.

Phone Orders: Yes.

Mail Orders: US, Canada and Europe. Prepayment required.

Discounts: Doll shop discounts.

Accepts: all major credit cards

FAIRFIELD PROCESSING CORP.

P.O. Box 1157

Danbury CT 06813-1157

Phone: (800)243-0989

Fax: (203)792-9710

E-mail: ffld.prcssng.corp@snet.net

Website: www.poly-fil.com

Offers: Fairfield Processing Corporation manufactures a complete line of high-quality products for the home sewing, quilt and craft industries. Poly-fil, Soft Touch and Crafters Choice brand fiberfill, batting and pillow form products are easy to use, available in many sizes and unconditionally guaranteed. New products include quilt pattern books, bumper batting and a chair cushion insert. Poly-fil is internationally available and accepted as the brand of excellence.

Catalog: Free.

Phone Orders: M-F, 8-5 EST.

Discounts: Sells wholesale to companies with tax ID number; 2-carton minimum.

Accepts: MasterCard, Visa

FAMILIAR CO.

229 Sergeant Ave.

Ft. Thomas KY 41075

Contact: Jesse Chandler

Phone: (606)781-2297

E-mail: mkaplan@one.net

Website: http://w3.one.net/~mkaplan/familiar.htm

Offers: One-of-a-kind cloth dolls, fiber art pieces, original doll patterns and doll-making and fiber art classes, workshops and seminars.
Catalog: $2.
Mail Orders: Will ship. Prepayment required. Allow 4-6 weeks for delivery.
Discounts: Sells wholesale to legitimate businesses.

FANCYWORK AND FASHION

4728 Dodge St.
Duluth MN 55804
Phone: (800)365-5257
Offers: Several doll costuming pattern books for 18″ vinyl and porcelain dolls. Authors of *The Best Doll Clothes Book*.
Catalog: Call or write for free brochure.
Accepts: MasterCard, Visa

FIBERS & MORE

P.O. Box 636
Camas WA 98607
Phone: (800)584-0711
E-mail: mail@fiberconnections.com
Website: http://www.fiberconnections.com
Offers: Doll hair, in a full range of styles. Also offers knit and handweaving kits.
Catalog: Doll hair catalog, $4.75, with 135 yarn/fiber samples.
Accepts: MasterCard, Visa

FLEECE & UNICORN YARNS & FIBERS

Rt. 5, Box 368
Stillwater OK 74074
Contact: Barbara Muret
Phone: (405)377-7105
E-mail muret@cowboy.net
Website: www.cowboy.net/~muret
Offers: Doll-hair yarns and fibers, embellishment, yarns and knitting, crochet and weaving yarns. Hand-spinning and weaving equipment. Designer garments.
Catalog: Free.
Phone Orders: Yes.
Mail Orders: Will ship international.
Discounts: Bulk quantities available.
Accepts: MasterCard, Visa, check, C.O.D.

FLORA & CO. MULTIMEDIA

P.O. Box 4263
Albuquerque NM 87198
Contact: Jan Flora
Phone: (505)255-9988
Fax: (505)255-9988
E-mail: crafts@floraco.com
Website: floraco.com
Offers: Silkscreen instruction video, adapted to the home workshop, demonstrating techniques for reproducing patterns on fabric, wood, paper, plastics and other flat surfaces; a workbook is included. Also puppet making. Send SASE.
Phone Orders: 24 hours.

Mail Orders: Immediate shipment.
Accepts: American Express, Discover, MasterCard, Visa

GOLDEN FUN SOFT TOY SUPPLIES

P.O. Box 3324
Danville CA 94506
Contact: Renee Raponi
Phone: (925)648-0146
Fax: (925)648-0146
Offers: All supplies to make soft toys: patterns, eyes, noses, joints, music, squeakers, rattles, books, kits, fur and more.
Catalog: $1.
Phone Orders: Yes.
Mail Orders: Yes.
Discounts: Quantity discounts.
Accepts: American Express, Discover, MasterCard, Visa

SALLY GOODSPEED

2318 N. Charles St.
Baltimore MD 21218
Phone: (410)235-6736
Offers: Reprints of 1900-40 embroidery, quilt and paint designs; over 600 Sunbonnet Babies and Colonial Ladies, many from Corbett's Primer; and Dolly Dingle, Kewpies, Greenaway, Cabot and McKim. Also offers 1920s Boudoir Doll patterns.
Catalog: $2.95.
Mail Orders: Yes.

HEARTFELT

995 E. Otero Ave.
Littleton CO 80122
Contact: Bev or Mike Hurley
Phone: (303)795-1264
Offers: Pressed felt doll kits with 3-D molded felt mask. Felt body material, pattern instructions and leg, arm and neck joints. Kit can be ordered with 1 pound painted or unpainted mask. Costume pattern and wig available separately.
Catalog: Send SASE for brochure.
Discounts: Sells wholesale.

HENRY'S ATTIC

5 Mercury Ave.
Monroe NY 10950-9736
Contact: Samira Galler
Phone: (914)783-3930
Fax: (914)782-2548
Offers: Undyed natural fiber yarns and fibers. Also dyed brushed mohair yarn. Yarns suitable for hand dyeing, hand knitting, hand weaving and doll hair. Fibers (wool, alpaca, flax, and mohair) suitable for hand spinning and doll hair.
Catalog: Sample set, $20.
Phone Orders: M-F, 9-6 EST.
Discounts: Sells wholesale only to legitimate businesses.

HERITAGE MINIATURES

Dept. CSSL
44 Mountain Base Rd.
Goffstown NH 03045
Contact: Priscilla J. Gangi
Phone: (603)497-5041
Fax: (603)497-3094
E-mail: heritagemin@worldnet.att.net
Offers: Supplies for doll sewing and miniaturists. Beautiful silks, European lace and trim, antique beads, silk ribbon, silk ribbon embroidery supplies, gemstones, feathers, silk thread, kits, patterns, instruction books and videos and much more.
Catalog: $3 (refundable).
Phone Orders: Yes.
Mail Orders: Will ship worldwide.
Discounts: Quantity discounts.
Accepts: American Express, Discover, MasterCard, Visa

INTERCAL TRADING GROUP

1760 Monrovia, Suite A-17
Costa Mesa CA 92627
Contact: Carole Cook
Phone: (714)645-9396
Fax: (714)645-5471
E-mail: kjeld@intercaltg.com
Website: http://www.intercaltg.com/
Store Location: At above address. M-F, 8-4 by appointment.
Offers: Mohair and teddy bear makings supplies. Intercal Trading is a direct importer of English and German mohairs. We also offer other teddy bear supplies, including glass eyes, wool felt and jointing systems as well as patterns and kits for teddy bear making.
Catalog: Domestic, 3 first-class stamps.
Phone Orders: M-F, 8-4.
Mail Orders: At above address.
Accepts: MasterCard, Visa

JOAN JANSEN

Dept. CSS
P.O. Box 85
Monterey Park CA 91754
Contact: Joan Jansen
Offers: Catalog of original cloth doll patterns plus a free 12″ beanbag Santa pattern. All patterns are full-size and are completely illustrated, teaching patterns.
Catalog: $1 (refundable with first order).
Mail Orders: Yes.
Accepts: check (US funds only), US postal order

JAY GEE DESIGNS

1963 Weslemkoon Lake Rd.
Gilmour, Ontario K0L 1W0
Canada
Contact: Joyce Gee
Phone: (613)474-2826
Store Location: At above address.
Offers: Patterns for cloth dolls. Medieval, sixteenth through nineteenth centuries. Topsy-Turvey and others. Also completed dolls.
Catalog: $3 (refundable).
Mail Orders: US, Canada and overseas.
Discounts: On some designs at year-end.
Accepts: check (no C.O.D.)

THE KEZI WORKS

P.O. Box 17631
Portland OR 97217
Contact: Jane Smithe
Phone: (503)286-9385
Fax: (503)285-6303
E-mail: keziworks@earthlink.net
Website: www.thekeziworks.com
Offers: Premier cloth doll patterns by famous doll artist/designer Kezi Matthews.
Catalog: B&w. $1; free with order.
Phone Orders: 9:30-4:30 PST.
Mail Orders: Ship worldwide. Prepayment required.
Discounts: Retail mail order.
Accepts: MasterCard, Visa

THE LACEMAKER

4602 Mahoning Ave. NW, Suite C
Warren OH 44483
Contact: Tracy Jackson
Phone: (330)847-6535 or (800)747-2220
Fax: (330)847-8456
E-mail: taj@grapevinenet.com
Website: www.lacemakerusa.com
Store Location: Warren OH location.
Offers: Supplies for bobbin lace, tatting, knit or crochet lace, needlepoint and bobbins, threads, shuttles and painted canvases.
Catalog: $5.
Phone Orders: M-F, 10-5 EST.
Mail Orders: Anywhere.
Discounts: Small wholesale line.
Accepts: MasterCard, Visa

SALLY LAMPI/SALLY & FRIENDS

2261 Beckham Way
Hayward CA 94541
Contact: Sally
Phone: (510)886-1943
Offers: Cloth doll patterns.
Catalog: Yes.
Phone Orders: Yes.
Mail Orders: Yes.

LITTLE JOYS

5114 Point Fosdick Dr. NW #E292
Gig Harbor WA 98335
Contact: Joy Chambers
Phone: (253)853-5182
Fax: (253)853-5185
Offers: Natural fiber Waldorf-inspired dolls in various eth-

nicity, styles and sizes. Doll-making kits and supplies, such as 100% cotton skin tone knit in 6 colors, mohair and bouclé yarns. Also offers doll-making workshops nationwide.
Catalog: Color. $2 (refunded with first order).
Phone Orders: M-S, 9-5 PST.
Mail Orders: Will ship anywhere. Prepayment required. Allow 2-4 weeks for delivery.
Discounts: Quantity price list.
Accepts: check, money order

LITTLE OLD LADY ORIGINALS/ELINOR PEACE BAILEY
1779 East Ave.
Hayward CA 94541
Contact: Elinor, Gary or Beth
Phone: (510)582-2702
Fax: (510)581-2967
Store Location: At above address.
Offers: Doll patterns, books and tools.
Catalog: Yes.
Phone Orders: Yes.
Mail Orders: Yes.
Accepts: check, money order

MIMI'S BOOKS & PATTERN FOR THE SERIOUS DOLLMAKER
P.O. Box 662
300 Nancy Dr.
Point Pleasant NJ 08742
Contact: Mimi or Jim Winer
Phone: (732)899-0804
Fax: (732)714-9306
E-mail: mimi@mimidolls.com
Website: www.mimidolls.com
Offers: Books, patterns and videos for serious doll making. All media.
Catalog: Free.
Phone Orders: Yes.
Mail Orders: At above address.
Discounts: Wholesale and retail and discounts for doll clubs.
Accepts: MasterCard, Visa, check, postal money orders

NANC
P.O. Box 1552
Westport WA 98595
Contact: Nancy Eichenberger
Phone: (360)268-9759
Fax: (360)268-6014
E-mail: nancdesigns@olynet.com
Store Location: 214 Grand Army, Westport WA 98595.
Offers: Original and unique doll patterns and sculpted doll heads. Also available through catalog. Doll classes available also.
Catalog: $2 (refundable with order).
Mail Orders: From catalog. Ship US and Canada.
Discounts: Wholesale.
Accepts: check, money order

ONE & ONLY CREATIONS
P.O. Box 2730
Napa CA 94558
Contact: Jil N. McDaniel
Phone: (800)262-6768
Fax: (916)663-4541
Website: www.oneandonlycreations.com
Offers: A variety of high-quality doll hair—makers of Curly Hair, Mini-Curl, Wavy Wool, Royal Fleece, Lil Loopies, Bumples, and Wavy Hair. Also iron-on doll faces and porcelain doll faces.
Catalog: Free. Full color.
Phone Orders: M-F, 8-4:30 PST.
Mail Orders: Will ship anywhere. Prepayment required. Orders shipped in 48 hours.
Discounts: Sells wholesale to retail outlets only.
Accepts: MasterCard, Visa, check

PAST CRAFTS PATTERNS
P.O. Box 16512
Alexandria VA 22302
Contact: Newbie Richardson
Phone: (703)684-0863
Fax: (703)684-0863
E-mail: easy4@juno.com
Offers: Historically accurate dolls' dress and miniature quilt plans and doll furniture woodworking plans for 14″, 16″, 18″ and American Girl dolls with detailed period notes for accurate period reproductions.
Catalog: $1.50.
Mail Orders: Will ship to Canada and US prepaid. Allow 10 days for delivery.
Discounts: Sells wholesale to legitimate businesses and home schoolers.
Accepts: check, money order

ELISE PEEPLES DOLLS
23403 NE 92nd Ave.
Battle Ground WA 98604
Contact: Elise Peeples
Phone: (360)687-1827
E-mail: beel@ix.netcom.com
Offers: Unique cloth doll patterns. Doll-making doll clubs and shops may inquire about classes.
Catalog: $1.

PG'S ENCHANTED DOLLS & THE DOLL HOSPITAL
4360 W. Oakland Park Blvd. #CC
Ft. Lauderdale FL 33313
Contact: Gloria Centi
Phone: (954)739-9030
Fax: (954)714-9597
E-mail: gcenti@ix.netcom.com
Website: www.pgsdolls.com
Store Location: At above address. T-Sat, 10-5.
Offers: Doll accessories, eyes, wigs, hats, jewelry, shoes, socks and clothes. Bear joints, mohair, bear kits, doll kits, stands, display cases, Dolly Dustless, trunks and suitcases.

Sculpting and cleaning tools, neck buttons, elastic cord, S-hooks and plastic ties. Doll and fabric cleaning solutions. Custom doll and bear clothes.
Catalog: Doll: color, $5. Bear: $2.
Phone Orders: 24-hour answering machine.
Mail Orders: Shipped Priority Mail with insurance or UPS.
Discounts: Wholesale with application.
Accepts: American Express, Discover, MasterCard, Visa

PMC DESIGNS
P.O. Box 720463
San Diego CA 92172-0463
Contact: Patti Medaris Culea
Phone: (619)484-5118
Fax: (619)484-5122
E-mail: pmcdesigns@aol.com
Website: www.pmcdesigns.com
Offers: Patterns for cloth dolls, turning and stuffing tools and lucet (for making cords/braids). One-of-a-kind cloth dolls. Teaching and speaking. Doll patterns are whimsical in nature.
Catalog: Full color. $2.50.
Phone Orders: M-F, 11-6 PST.
Mail Orders: Will ship to anywhere. Prepayment is required. Allow 2 weeks for delivery.
Discounts: Wholesale to businesses.
Accepts: MasterCard, Visa

BEVERLY POWERS
P.O. Box 13
South Lyon MI 48178
Offers: Over 1,700 antique and commercial out-of-print patterns for doll wardrobes, old cloth dolls and animals.
Catalog: $5.

PUPPET MASTER PRODUCTION
6334 N. Glenn
Fresno CA 93704-1530
Contact: Jack E. Fisette
Phone: (209)439-3132
Store Location: At above address. M-Sat, 9-6.
Offers: How-to videos. Puppet Making, Puppet Workshops, Creative Classes and more. For schools, churches, colleges, fairs, businesses and teachers. For fun and profit. Also make dolls and animals with two faces for profit and other dolls.
Catalog: To receive free catalog, send SASE.
Phone Orders: No telephone orders.
Mail Orders: Will ship within US only. Prepayment required.
Discounts: To churches, schools and others.
Accepts: check, money order, cashier's check

PUTNAM CO., INC.
P.O. Box 310
810 Wisconsin St.
Walworth WI 53184
Contact: Betty Ann Lasley
Phone: (800)338-4776 or (414)275-2104
Fax: (414)275-6509

E-mail: putnam@genevaonline.com
Offers: High-quality line of quilt batting, fiberfill and pillow forms. Brand names, special edition and soft shapes. Creator of Faces of the World colored fiberfills for ethnic doll making. Product available at leading craft and sewing stores through Herrschners catalog and Nancy's Notions.
Catalog: Send $1 and SASE for free instruction sheets.
Phone Orders: Yes.

THE QUILTING B
224 Second St. SE
Cedar Rapids IA 52401
Phone: (319)363-1643
Offers: Line of over 35 textured yarns and fibers for Santa beards and doll hair. Send SASE.

ROPER
P.O. Box 34922
Richmond VA 23234
Contact: Lynda K. Roper
Phone: (804)271-7541
E-mail: roperc@erols.com
Offers: Knit-doll clothes pattern booklets for popular dolls.
Catalog: Send SASE for listing.
Mail Orders: To US and Canada. Prepayment required. Orders mailed within 24 hours when possible.
Accepts: check, money order (no credit cards)

S.O. DOLLIGHTFUL DOLLS (SANJEAN ORIGINALS)
109 Lake Stephen Lane
Blythewood SC 29016
Contact: Sandra Blake
Phone: (803)786-6904
E-mail: griot@worldnet.att.net
Offers: Ethnic dolls (porcelain, cloth and synthetic clay) and doll patterns. Commissions available.
Catalog: Brochure of patterns available.
Mail Orders: Prepayment required. 4-6 weeks.

SEW SPECIAL
Dept. CS
P.O. Box 276646
Sacramento CA 95827
Phone: (916)361-2086
Offers: Over 100 original patterns for dolls and holiday decorations in country themes. Also offers hard-to-find supplies, including doll body fabric, hair products, bulk buttons, wooden spools and embellishments.
Catalog: $2.
Discounts: Sells wholesale.

SEWSWEET DOLLS FROM CAROLEE CREATIONS
Dept. SG
787 Industrial Dr.
Elmhurst IL 60126-1141
Phone: (630)530-7175
Fax: (630)530-8489
E-mail: sewsweetdl@aol.com
Website: www.caroleecreations.com

Offers: Full line of unique, easy-to-sew cloth doll and animal patterns including the sought-after "Time Out or Pouter." Also delightful children and toddlers, dancing dolls, soft-sculpture, jointed, poseable, sports, dress-me, life-size babies and toddlers, delightful teddy bears and cats—even a moose! Hard-to-find doll-making supplies, including HairMaster hair loom, hairstyle book, display cases, books, custom body fabric and hair-making materials and more.
Catalog: Color. $2.
Mail Orders: Yes.
Accepts: Discover, MasterCard, Visa

SHARIN-A-LITTLE-BIT
3315 Monier Circle, Suite 2
Rancho Cordova CA 95742
Contact: Sharon Sharp
Phone: (916)851-0170
Fax: (916)851-1721
E-mail: sharinalb@juno.com
Website: www.skiens.com/sharinalb.htm
Offers: Doll patterns and wood kits, Raflets curly raffia, doll supplies and doll bodies.
Catalog: $3 (free with purchase).
Phone Orders: 9-4 PST.
Mail Orders: Yes.
Discounts: Wholesale terms.
Accepts: American Express, MasterCard, Visa, check, money order

SHIRLEY ANN GIFTS
1139 Autumn St.
Roseville MN 55113
Contact: Shirley Lentsch
Phone: (612)488-2368
E-mail: surelyican@aol.com
Offers: Original, fun and unique. Over 80 patterns for bears and other collectible critters, including Golliwogs.
Catalog: $3.
Mail Orders: Payment with order.
Discounts: Free pattern with a $35 order.

SMALLWORKS
10465 NW Lee Court
Portland OR 97229
Contact: Melinda Small Paterson
Phone: (503)203-6787
E-mail: melinda@smallwork.com
Website: http://www.smallwork.com
Offers: Patterns for cloth dolls and creatures from mythology, such as dragon, Pegasus and others. Miniature fairies in porcelain.
Catalog: B&w flyer. Send double-stamped, preaddressed envelope.
Phone Orders: M-F, 9-5 PST.
Mail Orders: Will ship to US, Canada and international. Prepayment required. 1 month delivery on international.
Discounts: Sells wholesale patterns to legitimate businesses.
Accepts: MasterCard, Visa

SOMETHING SPECIAL
502 N. Canal
Carlsbad NM 88220
Contact: Jeanne or Gayle
Phone: (505)885-4666 or (800)272-6992
E-mail: alladin@carlsbadnm.com
Store Location: At above address.
Offers: Southwestern speciality items in home decorating. Porcelain dolls and doll kits; some supplies.
Catalog: In process. Send SASE for doll list.
Phone Orders: (800)272-6992.
Mail Orders: At above address.
Discounts: Wholesale to storefronts.
Accepts: MasterCard, Visa

SPARE BEAR PARTS
P.O. Box 56
Interlochen MI 49643
Contact: Linda or Gordon Mead
Phone: (616)276-7915
Fax: (616)276-7921
E-mail: sales@sparebear.com
Website: www.sparebear.com
Offers: Teddy bear making supplies: US and imported synthetic plush, mohair plush, glass and plastic eyes, growlers and music boxes, teddy joints, paw pad materials, stuffing and patterns. Mini-bear making supplies too.
Catalog: Annual, $2. Newsletters, free.
Phone Orders: Yes.
Mail Orders: P.O. Box 56C, Interlochen MI 49643.
Discounts: Quantity discount.
Accepts: Discover, MasterCard, Visa

SPRINGTIME DESIGN
3000 Topley Ave.
Las Cruces NM 80005
Offers: Line of animal and doll patterns, including Joy Angel and others.
Catalog: Pattern catalog, $1 and large SASE.

STANDARD DOLL SUPPLY HOUSE, INC.
23-83 31st St.
Long Island City NY 11105
Contact: Joan Henfield
Phone: (718)721-7787
Fax: (718)274-4231
Website: catalogcity.com
Offers: Doll-making supplies, including doll parts, body patterns (8″-36″), shoes, socks, hats, stands, doll clothes patterns, hangers, sewing notions (small zippers, buttons and snaps) and sewing aids. Mini zippers and buttons, tags, bags, magnifiers and books are also available. Carries porcelain and other dolls and porcelain and china doll kits. Also supplies for popular 18″ dolls.
Catalog: $3 (refundable).
Phone Orders: (800)543-6557.
Mail Orders: At above address.
Discounts: Quantity discounts allowed.

Accepts: American Express, MasterCard, Visa, check, money order

TEDDY TOGS

P.O. Box 9563

Bend OR 97708-9563

Contact: Elizabeth S. Mabry

Phone: (541)382-7959

Fax: (541)388-9254

Offers: Original design knitting patterns for teddy bear clothes, sweaters, hats, pants, etc. Sizes for 16-18″ bears, some 6-8″.

Catalog: Color sheet of all available patterns.

Phone Orders: M-F, 9-4 PST.

Mail Orders: Will send US and Canada.

Discounts: Wholesale to shops.

Accepts: check, money order

UNICORN STUDIOS

424 Blount Ave.

Knoxville TN 37920

Contact: Amy Holston

Phone: (423)573-1863

Fax: (423)573-0451

E-mail: ehj1125351@aol.com

Website: www.tmox.com/unicorn

Offers: Musical accessories and musical movements, electronic sounds, project books and instruction books.

Catalog: (800)874-5317. $1.

Phone Orders: M-F, 9-1 EST.

Mail Orders: Will ship to US and Canada. Allow 2-3 weeks for delivery.

Accepts: MasterCard, Visa

KATE WEBSTER COMPANY

Dept. CS98

18 Railroad Ave.

Rockport MA 01966

Contact: Helene Rowell

Phone: (978)546-6462

Fax: (978)546-6466

Offers: Doll costuming supplies, doll and teddy bear jewelry and accessories, plus buckles, buttons, parasol and purse frames and fairy wings. Numerous items for 16-20″ play dolls.

Catalog: 40 pages. $3.

Phone Orders: Yes.

Mail Orders: Yes.

Discounts: Quantity.

Accepts: Discover, MasterCard, Visa

Embroidery & Cross-Stitch

Also see Bead Crafts; General Needlecraft Supplies; Miniature Making, Miniatures & Dollhouses; Needlepoint; Quilting; Sewing; other related categories.

ARTISAN DESIGN

P.O. Box 2433
Broken Arrow OK 74012
Phone: (800)747-8263
Fax: (918)258-7298
E-mail: artdes3192@aol.com
Website: www.artisandesign.com
Offers: Gazelle floor stand, Elan tabletop/lapstand with accessories, Lokscroll scroll frames in variety of sizes and a Stitcher's Box for carrying supplies.
Catalog: Free brochure and price list.
Phone Orders: M-Th, 8-5; F, 8-2 CST.
Mail Orders: Prepay required.
Accepts: MasterCard, Visa, check, money order

AUNT EFFIE'S HEIRLOOMS

P.O. Box 55374
Madison WI 53705
Contact: Brenna Berdine Hopkins
Phone: E-mail us for update
Fax: E-mail us for update
E-mail: aunteffie@ibm.net
Offers: Vintage embroidery patterns from romantic flower baskets to whimsical kitchen helpers. Sunbonnet Babies to Crinoline Ladies. Redwork, stamped "penny squares," dolls, quilt blocks, dresser sets, day of the week towels, layettes, crib quilts and lots more. "Hope Chest" pattern-of-the-month club. Kits designed especially for kids to embroider, plus nursery books and motifs for little tea linens. Authentic embroidery patterns from 1880s-1940s for re-creating genuine linens from collectible eras, or combining into new creations to match your decor. Easy to embroider. A unique resource for anyone who loves embroidery, from romantic to whimsical.
Catalog: $3 (includes subscription to *Fancywork Times*, our biannual newsletter for art needlework enthusiasts).
Phone Orders: Yes.
Mail Orders: Ship to US, Canada and international. Prepayment in US funds required. International readers please write for specifics.
Discounts: Various offers throughout the year.
Accepts: check, money order in US funds only

CANTERBURY DESIGNS, INC.

P.O. Box 204060
Martinez GA 30917
Phone: (706)860-1674
Fax: (706)860-9614
Offers: Over 80 cross-stitch books and leaflets: original and reproduced samplers, scenes, miniatures, holiday motifs, baby, florals, quilts, borders and others.
Catalog: Call or write for color brochure, $3.
Discounts: Teachers and institutions; sells wholesale to legitimate businesses.

COMPUCRAFTS

P.O. Box 6326
Lincoln Center MA 01773
Contact: David L. Natwig
Phone: (800)263-0045 or (978)263-8007
Fax: (978)264-0619
E-mail: compucraft@aol.com
Website: www.compucrafts.com
Store Location: At above address.
Offers: Cross-stitch design software for Windows and Macintosh to create designs manually or automatically from any color picture.
Catalog: 10 pages, color. Free.
Phone Orders: M-F, 8-5.
Mail Orders: Free shipping to US and Canada; $12 international air mail.
Discounts: Wholesale discounts in quantities of 2 or more.
Accepts: MasterCard, Visa, check (US funds drawn on US bank)

CRAFTS BY DONNA

P.O. Box 1456
Costa Mesa CA 92628-1456
Contact: Donna Friebertshauser
Phone: (714)545-8567
Fax: (714)545-8567
E-mail: dsignsbydf@aol.com
Offers: Complete line of rayon (Brazilian) threads, battenberg lace tapes, 1/16" polyester ribbon, 4mm (1/8") silk luster ribbon. Original designs and kits for dimensional (Brazilian) embroidery, trapunto, ribbon embroidery, battenberg lace, blackwork and other counted thread techniques.
Catalog: $2 (includes special offer coupon).
Phone Orders: Yes.
Mail Orders: Yes.
Discounts: Retail and wholesale.

CRAFTSMEN'S STUDIO

2727 Ring Rd.
Greensboro NC 27405-5129
Contact: Russell Sockwell
Phone: (336)621-4994
Fax: (336)621-4992
E-mail: craftsmens@aol.com
Website: http://www.needlearts.com
Offers: Craftsmen's Studio specializes in simple patterns for duplicate stitch on our unique line of sweaters. All accessories used in our designs are available from us. We also carry the full line of Zweigart needlework fabrics, canvases and premade items.
Catalog: $3. Includes designs.
Phone Orders: (800)234-2808. M-F, 9-5:30.
Mail Orders: Typically ship within 24 hours.
Accepts: MasterCard, Visa

CROSS STITCH A MEMORY BY TWILIGHT DESIGNS

(formerly Twilight Designs)
Dept. CSS
2051 Robinwood Dr.
Algonquin IL 60102
Contact: Stephanie Coriale
Phone: (847)854-9367
E-mail: coriales@ix.netcom.com
Website: pw2.netcom.com/~coriales/twilight/index.html
Offers: Cross-stitch a memory. Custom cross-stitch patterns and kits from photographs and artwork. Includes color DMC chart and symbols only chart of almost any size. Send photo, desired size of finished project, cloth count and any special instructions (cropping, background removal or others) and $24.95 and $3 p&h. Return photo with pattern in 4-6 weeks. Call with special requests.
Mail Orders: Please call for additional information.
Accepts: check, money order (made out to Stephanie Coriale).

DANDELION

18749 Spooks Hill Rd.
Parkton MD 21120
Contact: Karen P. Cohn
Phone: (410)329-8020
E-mail: kpcohn@aol.com
Store Location: At above address. By appointment only.
Offers: Books, kits and supplies for contemporary stumpwork designs for embroidery, appliqué and crazy quilting. Vintage needlework tools and books. Classes. Baltimore album-style and primitive appliqué patterns for quilters.
Catalog: Color. $3.
Phone Orders: Call for color choices, requests, updates and available vintage books and tools.
Mail Orders: Foreign orders in US dollars. Prepaid.
Discounts: Sells wholesale to legitimate businesses.
Accepts: check, money order

DAVIS COMPUTER SERVICES, INC.

P.O. Box 750141
New Orleans LA 70715
Contact: Ken Davis
Phone: (800)231-3480 or (504)899-9706
E-mail: kdavisjr@worldnet.att.net
Website: www.easygrapher.com
Offers: EasyGrapher computer programs for designing needlework graphs, including cross-stitch, needlepoint, bargello, hardanger and plastic canvas. Converts pictures into cross-stitch graphs. Available for Windows 3.1 or 95.
Catalog: Brochure available.
Phone Orders: M-F, 9-4 CST.
Mail Orders: Will ship anywhere. Prepayment required.
Discounts: Sells wholesale to legitimate businesses.
Accepts: American Express, MasterCard, Visa

THE ESSAMPLAINE

4126 44th St.
Red Deer, Alberta T4N 1H2
Canada
Contact: Margriet Hogue
Phone: (403)347-3574
Fax: (403)347-4047
Offers: Reproduction sample kits and charts as well as books on samples.
Catalog: $3.
Phone Orders: Yes.
Mail Orders: Yes.
Discounts: Retail or wholesale to the trade.
Accepts: MasterCard, Visa

FANCYWORK

P.O. Box 130
2708 Slaterville Rd.
Slaterville Springs NY 14881
E-mail: fancywork@clarityconnect.com
Website: http://www.clarityconnect.com/webpages/fancy work/fancywork.htm
Offers: 10,000 cross-stitch books—most all design categories: country, classic, contemporary, holiday motif, men, women, children, babies, whimsical, Oriental, Western, nautical, Early American, flowers, wild and domestic animals, scenes, geometrics and many others in mini to large sizes. Accessories for cross-stitch are also available.
Catalog: Catalog/sample newsletter, $2.

FIREFLY EMBROIDERIES

P.O. Box 304
Davisburg MI 48350
Phone: (800)447-6218
E-mail: ffbead@mich.com
Offers: Beaded embroidery kits with glass beads, sequins, pattern, needles and fabric in a variety of designs for clothing, jewelry and accessories. Also offers Pinzazz beaded stickpin kits and Razzmatazz beaded barrette kits. Luminette beaded lampshade kits.
Catalog: $2.

5 T'S EMBROIDERY SUPPLY

P.O. Box 484
Macedon NY 14502
Phone: (315)986-8434
Fax: (315) 986-8436
E-mail: ask5ts@webtv.net
Website: www.5ts.com
Offers: Line of machine embroidery supplies, including threads, backings, scissors and nippers, denim shirts, needles and other notions.
Catalog: Call or write for free catalog.
Accepts: Discover, MasterCard, Visa

HANDS ON

4721 Magazine St.
New Orleans LA 70115
Contact: Gaby Kety or Mimi Smith
Phone: (504)899-4327
E-mail: milmsmith@aol.com
Website: http://www.needlearts.com
Store Location: At above address.
Offers: Lessons in embroidery by mail.
Catalog: List of lessons offered.
Discounts: Group rates.
Accepts: MasterCard, Visa

HH DESIGNS

P.O. Box 231
1474 N. Point Village Center
Reston VA 20194
Offers: Line of candlewick (colonial needlecraft) pillow kits—simple embroidery stitches in a variety of designs.
Catalog: $2.

INTERNATIONAL HOUSE OF BUNKA, INC.

19 Tulane Crescent
Don Mills, Ontario M3A 2B9
Canada
Contact: Kathy Haney
Phone: (416)445-1875
Fax: (416)444-6705
E-mail: bunka@idirect.com
Store Location: At above address. M-F, 9-5; evenings and weekends by appointment.
Offers: Japanese bunka embroidery kits, punch needles, Tokyo rayon threads, accessories, supplies, teach yourself starter kits, instructions and custom framing service. Mail-order service and lessons by certified instructors.
Catalog: HOBI-Tokyo catalog, $14.95.
Phone Orders: M-Sat, 9 a.m.-11 p.m.
Mail Orders: Anywhere. Prepayment required for new customers.
Discounts: Sell wholesale and retail.
Accepts: Visa, check, money order

JUST NEEDLIN'

611 NE Woods Chapel
Lee's Summit MO 64064
Phone: (816)246-5102

Offers: Cross-stitch fabrics: Aida (colors), Anne, Damask, Davos, Fiddlers, Floba, Jobelan, Klostern, Linda, linens and others. Also offers Balger, threads by Weeks Dye Works, the Caron Collection, Gentle Art and all Mill Hill products, DMC Rayon Floss, DMC Flower Thread and more. Carries perforated papers, projects (with inserts), hoops, scroll frames, magnifiers and other aids, and over 1,800 design chart booklets.
Catalog: $4 (refundable).

KNIGHT'S THREAD EXPRESS

75 McIntire Rd.
New Gloucester ME 04260
Contact: Yvette Knight
Phone: (888)826-1519
E-mail: yvettek@ibm.net
Website: http://www.threadexpress.com
Offers: Hand embroidery threads (for cross-stitch, hardanger, crewel, silk ribbon, canvas work, quilting and heirloom sewing) from DMC, Alyce Schroth, Anchor, YLI and Krewik. Includes cottons, silks, wools, metallics and specialties. Fabrics, accessories and books. Catalog with complete number and color listings; free samples.
Catalog: $1 (refundable with first order).
Phone Orders: M-Sat, 8-6 EST.
Mail Orders: Require prepayment. Will ship US and Canada.
Discounts: EGA members, 10%.
Accepts: MasterCard, Visa, check

MARY JANE'S CROSS 'N STITCH, INC.

1948 Keim Court
Naperville IL 60565
Contact: Carol Witte
Phone: (630)355-0071
Fax: (630)355-0396
E-mail: ybrm80b@prodigy.com
Website: maryjanes.com
Offers: Over 1,200 stitchery books, leaflets and charts. An extensive line of cross-stitch fabrics, accessories, fibers and floss.
Catalog: $7.50 ($5 refundable).
Phone Orders: M-F, 7-3 CST.
Mail Orders: Ship worldwide.
Accepts: Discover, MasterCard, Visa

MASTERSTITCH DESIGNS, INC.

P.O. Box 60164
Renton WA 98058-3164
Contact: Tim or Sheri Plumlee
Phone: (425)235-5779
Fax: (425)235-5668
E-mail: tim8849@masterstitch.com
Website: www.masterstitch.com or www.pixelstitch.com
Offers: We sell software for designing cross-stitch patterns. The main feature of the software is for a person to take one of her personal pictures, clip art or any other picture that has been put into the computer and use PixelStitch to convert that picture to DMC floss colors and then print out a chart.
Catalog: Informatonal flyer available. Slide show demo is

also available for $5. The $5 will apply toward the purchase of PixelStitch (by phone or mail). Slide show demo is free when downloaded from our website.

Phone Orders: (800)673-2324.

Mail Orders: At above address.

Accepts: American Express, Discover, MasterCard, Visa, check, money order

ANNE POWELL, LTD.

P.O. Box 3060

Stuart FL 34995

Phone: (407)287-3007

E-mail: apowell@annepowellltd.com

Website: http://www.annepowellltd.com

Offers: Counted cross-stitch charts, kits, Glenshee linen, Solingen embroidery scissors, plus antique sewing tools, informative books and gift items for needlecrafters.

Catalog: $5.

Discounts: Sells wholesale to legitimate businesses.

RIBBONWORKS PUBLICATIONS

P.O. Box 345

Gladewater TX 75647

Contact: Brenda Kennebeck or Sheila Hadley

Phone: (903)845-4000

Fax: (903)636-5778

E-mail: ribbontalk@aol.com

Website: http://members.aol.com/ribbontalk

Offers: Silk ribbon embroidery books and kits published by our company and other supplies, such as ribbon, scissors and needles. All your embroidery needs.

Catalog: 8 pages, color. Free.

Phone Orders: (903)845-5000. M-F, 8-5 CST.

Mail Orders: At above address. Will ship to US and Canada. 4-6 weeks delivery.

Discounts: Wholesales to legitimate businesses.

Accepts: MasterCard, Visa, check, money order (US currency only)

ROBISON-ANTON TEXTILE CO.

P.O. Box 159

Fairview NJ 07022

Phone: (201)941-0500 or (800)932-0250

Offers: Super Luster embroidery floss on 1.25-lb. cones of 6-strand mercerized cotton; available in 335 colors. Specializes in cones for kit manufacturers. Contact your dealer, or send SASE.

SANDEEN'S SCANDINAVIAN ART, GIFTS & NEEDLECRAFT

1315 White Bear Ave.

St. Paul MN 55106

Contact: Gail R. Sandeen

Phone: (612)776-7012

Store Location: At above address.

Offers: Swedish, Norwegian and Danish embroidery/handcraft supplies: kits, hardanger supplies, brackets and others. Also offers a giftware catalog at no charge.

Catalog: $2 (refundable on your first order).

Phone Orders: Yes.

Mail Orders: Yes.

Accepts: American Express, MasterCard, Visa

SAX ARTS & CRAFTS

P.O. Box 510710

2405 S. Calhoun Rd.

New Berlin WI 53151

Phone: (414)784-6880

Offers: A variety of supplies (known brands), including a full line of weaving looms and aids, yarns, weaving kits, rug/craft yarns, embroidery/crewel threads, rug hook frames and aids, canvas, hoops, burlap, felt. Native American beading, beads, feathers, macrame, basketry and batik supplies, fabric paints, airbrush kits and inks, stencil films, trims, foam, stained glass kits, etching and beveled glass supplies and supplies for decoupage, jewelry making, leather, casting, plastics, wood and metalworking are also available.

Catalog: $5 (refundable).

Discounts: Quantity; sells wholesale to legitimate businesses.

SEW ORIGINAL NEEDLEART

6439 Ming Ave. #A

Bakersfield CA 93309

Contact: Sharon E. Wainwright

Phone: (805)832-9276

Fax: (805)832-0597

E-mail: sew6439@aol.com

Store Location: Sagepointe Shopping Center at Ming Avenue and Ashe Road.

Offers: Excellent selection of evenweave fabrics, including hand-dyed linens. Also variety of fibers, including full line of DMC floss, Perle Cotton, Rayon Floss and Flower Thread. Also overdyed fibers, metallics and more. Outstanding collection of books/charts always featuring the newest. Selected kits, including Shepherd's Bush.

Phone Orders: M-Sat, 10-5:30 PST.

Mail Orders: Most happy to accommodate mail orders via UPS or first-class shipping.

Accepts: American Express, Discover, MasterCard, Visa, personal check

THE STRAWBERRY SAMPLER

#7 Olde Ridge Village

Chadds Ford PA 19317

Phone: (610)459-8580 or (800)634-6106

Fax: (610)361-8528

E-mail: shop@strawberrysampler.com

Website: www.strawberrysampler.com

Store Location: Olde Ridge Village, 1 mile south of Route 1 at Route 202 and Ridge Road. M-Sat, 10-5; Th, 10-8.

Offers: Cross-stitch designs, including samplers, florals and animals, Oriental, Danish, holiday motifs, house and home, friends and family, Shepherd's Bush, Prairie Schooler, Lizzie Kate, Lavender & Lace, Miribilia and many exclusive designs. Hundreds of different fabrics, fibers, accessories and frames (including our exclusive line of handcrafted frames).

Custom cross-stitch framing and hand-carved mats. Classes for all levels. New website catalog offering on-line ordering and E-mail.

Catalog: B&w print catalog (quarterly), $5 (refundable).
Mail Orders: Yes.
Accepts: MasterCard, Visa

STRINGS 'N THINGS
1228 Blossom Terrace
Boiling Springs PA 17007
Phone: (717)258-6022
Offers: Threads: Marlitt, silk, metallic, wool, tatting, embroidery/tapestry cottons, cutwork, Pearl cotton, DMC and Baroque (and other) crochet cottons, Persian wool, Balger filaments and braid. Send SASE.
Discounts: Quantity.

THUMBELINA NEEDLEWORK SHOP
P.O. Box 1065
1685 Copenhagen Dr.
Solvang CA 93464
Contact: Brenda Knudsen
Phone: (805)688-4136 or (800)789-4136
Fax: (805)688-4136, 5:30 p.m.-9 a.m. PST.
E-mail: info@thumbelina.com
Website: http://www.thumbelina.com/
Store Location: At above address.
Offers: Publications and kits from Denmark including Oehlmschlager, Eva Rosentand, Danish Handcraft Guild and Permin. Full line of kits from major American needlework companies. Needlepoint canvases from Margo, SEG and Royal Paris Fabrics, canvas, DMC cottons and wools for needlepoint and counted cross-stitch. Tatting books and supplies and collectors thimbles. Bellpull hardware.
Catalog: Supply list upon request (emphasizes Danish items).

Phone Orders: M-F, 9-5 PST.
Mail Orders: Will ship to US, Canada, Europe, Middle East, Pacific Rim, Australia, New Zealand, Africa and South America.
Accepts: American Express, Discover, MasterCard, Visa

VERY VICTORIAN NOTIONS
P.O. Box 18985
Denver CO 80218
Contact: Holly van Kleeck
Phone: (303)393-8377
Fax: (303)393-8357
E-mail: vvnotions@aol.com
Offers: Silk ribbons, French wired ribbons, books, patterns, videos, kits, crazy quilt supplies—buttons charms, fabrics, laces and embroidery threads—silk, rayon and metallics. Framecraft items.
Catalog: 32 pages with photos. $3.
Phone Orders: Fax orders preferred, voice mail available 24 hours for phone orders.
Mail Orders: Will ship international.
Accepts: MasterCard, Visa

THE YARN BASKET
150 Falling Spring Rd.
Chambersburg PA 17201
Contact: Sue Sollenberger
Phone: (717)263-3236
Store Location: I-81, exit 6 and Route PA 30, behind Shoney's.
Offers: Knitting and crochet yarns, patterns and accessories. Needlepoint yarns and accessories. Cross-stitch, ribbon embroidery and crewel classes.
Phone Orders: (888)YRN-BSKT.
Mail Orders: Will ship UPS, Priority Mail and regular mail.
Accepts: Discover, MasterCard, Visa

Fabric Decorating

Also see Bead Crafts; General Needlecraft Supplies; Batik & Dyeing; Embroidery & Cross-Stitch; Fabrics & Trims; Sewing.

A.T.A.P. MARKING PRODUCTS

435 N. Union Blvd.
Colorado Springs CO 80909
Contact: Larry Liska
Phone: (719)636-1020 or (719)636-1021
Fax: (719)636-2051
Store Location: At above address.
Offers: Rubber stamps, art stamps, laser engraving campaign and school buttons in 3 sizes (1¼, 2½ and 3), full color transfer on cloth, coffee cups and photo stamps (a stamp made from a picture—picture is returned).
Catalog: Art stamp catalog, $5.
Phone Orders: Prepayment is needed.
Mail Orders: With payment.
Discounts: Wholesale large orders.
Accepts: MasterCard, Visa

THE ART STORE

935 Erie Blvd. E.
Syracuse NY 13210
Phone: (315)474-1000
Offers: Fiber arts/crafts supplies and equipment: Jacquard textile and silk paints, screen printing, marbling, FIMO, Sculpey, tie-dye, Procion dye, Jo Sonya and brushes.
Catalog: Complete list, $3.

ARTISTICALLY INCLINED SPORTSWEAR, INC.

1480 Terrell Mill Rd. #110
Marietta GA 30067
Contact: Marla Broderson
Phone: (770)980-9100
Fax: (770)980-1350
E-mail: marlalynnb@aol.com
Offers: "Blank" and embellished fashions for decorating, including denim shirts, vests, blazers and dresses, 50/50 knit pants sets in 12 colors. Children's, one size, plus size and S-XXL in denim.
Catalog: Free. Specialize in professional crafters.
Phone Orders: M-F, 9-5 EST.
Mail Orders: Ship within 24 hours.
Discounts: Volume to wholesale businesses.
Accepts: Discover, MasterCard, Visa, C.O.D.

BLUEPRINTS-PRINTABLE

1400-A Marsten Rd.
Burlingame CA 94010-2422
Contact: Barbara Hewitt
Phone: (800)356-0445
Fax: (650)348-2888
Offers: Blueprinting DESIGN & PRINT kits: T-shirts, squares, yardage (cotton sheeting, silks and rayon) ready to print in sunlight and rinse in water. Accessory blanks and yardage for surface design. Book: *Blueprints on Fabric*.
Catalog: Free.
Phone Orders: (800)356-0445.
Mail Orders: At above address.
Discounts: Wholesale.
Accepts: Discover, MasterCard, Visa

BY JUPITER!

7162 N. 58th Ave.
Glendale AZ 85301
Contact: Marian or Deanne
Phone: (602)931-2658
Fax: (602)931-2704
Store Location: Historic Catlin Court in Old Town Glendale.
Offers: Over 1,700 brass charms and castings. Also available in antique silver and antique gold plated finishes. Great for jewelry, embellishing frames, bottles, clothing, ribbon embroidery, memory albums, art stamping projects and more.
Catalog: $5, actual-size pictures of each charm/finding.
Phone Orders: M-Sat, 9-5.
Mail Orders: No prepayments please; use credit card.
Discounts: Wholesale available to bona fide business with proper ID.
Accepts: American Express, Discover, MasterCard, Visa

DHARMA TRADING CO.

P.O. Box 150916
San Rafael CA 94915
Phone: (800)542-5227
Fax: (415)456-8747
E-mail: catalog@dharmatrading.com
Website: www.dharmatrading.com
Store Location: 1604 Fourth St., San Rafael CA 94901.
Offers: Complete line of fiber art supplies: dyes for natural fabrics (including 100 colors of Procion), Resist and Discharge products, paints and supplies for silk, marbling, tie-dye, batik, printing, stamping, hand painting and stenciling, as well as kits and how-to books. White clothing blanks and accessories in cotton and silk, as well as cotton, rayon, silk and helm fabrics for dyeing. Tools, fabric markers, transfer paper and lots more.

Catalog: Free. 120 pages.
Phone Orders: M-F, 8-5 PST.
Mail Orders: Prepay or credit card. E-mail orders.
Discounts: Quantity.
Accepts: Discover, MasterCard, Visa

EXTRA SPECIAL PRODUCTS CORP.

P.O. Box 777
Greenville OH 45331
Phone: (937)548-9388 or (800)648-5945
Fax: (937)548-9580
Website: www.extraspecial.com
Offers: House of Copper line of die-cut copper shapes (to punch, bend, burnish, antique, paint and use as trims, window decorations, tree ornaments, candle trims, quilt templates, appliqué templates, wreath decorations and others) and a booklet with over 24 projects.
Catalog: Contact your dealer, or write.

FIREFLY EMBROIDERIES

P.O. Box 304
Davisburg MI 48350
Phone: (800)447-6218
E-mail: ffbead@mich.com
Offers: Beaded embroidery kits with glass beads, sequins, pattern, needles and fabric in a variety of designs for clothing, jewelry and accessories. Also offers Pinzazz beaded stickpin kits and Razzmatazz beaded barrette kits and Luminette beaded lampshade kits.
Catalog: $2.

FLORA & CO. MULTIMEDIA

P.O. Box 8263
Albuquerque NM 87198
Contact: Jan Flora
Phone: (505)255-9988
Fax: (505)255-9988
E-mail: crafts@floraco.com
Website: floraco.com
Offers: Silkscreen printing video adapted to the home workshop, demonstrating techniques for reproducing patterns on fabric, wood, paper, plastics and other flat surfaces; a workbook is included. Also puppet making.
Phone Orders: 24 hours.
Mail Orders: Immediate shipment.
Accepts: American Express, Discover, MasterCard, Visa

G&K CRAFT INDUSTRIES

P.O. Box 38
Somerset MA 02726
Phone: (800)GKCRAFT or (508)676-3883
Fax: (508)676-3980
Offers: Reactive dyes for cotton, linen, rayon and silk: PRO MS & H. Acid dyes for wool, silk and nylon: Country Classics and PRO WashFast. Carries PROfab Textile Inks, Marbling Colors and many Pebeo products: Setasilk, Setacolor, Pebeo Soie and Setaskrib+ markers. We also offer numerous dye and fabric paint kits and store displays, as well as resist supplies/tools, waxes and workroom and safety supplies.
Catalog: Free.
Phone Orders: M-F, 8:30-5 EST.
Mail Orders: Will ship internationally.
Discounts: Wholesale for resale only.
Accepts: MasterCard, Visa

GRAMMA'S GRAPHICS, INC.

Dept. TCSS-P8
20 Birling Gap
Fairport NY 14450
Phone: (716)223-4309
Fax: (716)223-4789
E-mail: 70671.321@compuserve.com
Website: http://www.frontiernet.net/~bubblink/donnelly/
Offers: Fabric and paper "Sun Print" kits—fabric images created by printing photo negatives, objects, stencils or cutouts on material treated with a light-sensitive solution; sun exposure turns prints blue. Designs are permanent and washable. Also offers untreated cotton print cloth by the yard, refill kits, assembly instructions for heirloom portrait quilt and sun print pillows, toning instructions for changing the blue to other colors and source to make line or halftone negatives. School/group sun kits for notecards and gift tags.
Catalog: Brochure, $1 and large SASE.
Mail Orders: Will ship worldwide.
Discounts: Quantity. Sells wholesale.
Accepts: check, money order (US funds)

IMAGINATION STATION

P.O. Box 2157
White City OR 97503
Phone: (800)338-3857
Offers: Photographs transferred to fabric: b&w, color and sepia. Enlarges and reduces, customized to order (photos returned).
Catalog: Free brochure.
Accepts: MasterCard, Visa

MALLERY PRESS

4206 Sheraton Dr.
Flint MI 48532-3557
Contact: Ami Simms
Phone: (800)278-4824
Fax: (810)230-1516
E-mail: amisimms@aol.com
Website: http://quilt.com/amisimms
Offers: Books on quilt making and Photos-To-Fabric transfer paper and supplies. Wholesale and retail.
Catalog: Send long SASE.
Phone Orders: (800)-A-STITCH. Will ship worldwide.
Mail Orders: Prepayment required.
Accepts: MasterCard, Visa

MARILYN'S DECORATIVE ARTS STUDIO

1763 S. Leyden
Denver CO 80224
Contact: Marilyn Corners

Phone: (303)758-8266
Fax: (303)755-5516
E-mail: marilyn@mdas.com
Website: www.mdas.com
Store Location: At above address. Hours by appointment.
Offers: Pattern packets for furniture, clothing and luggage, designs to paint. Full-size patterns, complete instructions and photos. Also a book of stroke word designs to decorate baby things.
Catalog: Can be printed from website.
Phone Orders: Yes. Leave message on voice mail.
Mail Orders: 24-hour turnaround.
Discounts: 40% on orders of 12 or more/3 of a kind.
Accepts: MasterCard, Visa, check, money order

PENTEL OF AMERICA, LTD.

2805 Columbia St.
Torrance CA 90503
Contact: Janet Quan
Phone: (800)421-1419
Fax: (310)320-4036
E-mail: pr@pentel.com
Website: www.pentel.com
Offers: Fabric Fun pastel dye sticks. Also offers artist's oil pastels, watercolors, pens and automatic pens, adhesives.
Catalog: Informational only.

PHOTOGRAPHERS FORMULARY

P.O. Box 950
Condon MT 59826
Contact: Lynn Wilson
Phone: (800)922-5255
Fax: (406)754-2896
E-mail: formulary@montana.com
Website: htpp://www.montana.com/formulary/index.html
Store Location: Condon MT location.
Offers: Chemical kits to make images on fabric, paper and more; heirlooms on material for quilts, wall hangers and others.
Catalog: Yes.
Phone Orders: Yes.
Mail Orders: Yes.
Discounts: 10% new customer. Volume discounts.
Accepts: all major credit cards

PRO CHEMICAL & DYE

P.O. Box 14
Somerset MA 02726
Phone: (800)2-BUY-DYE (orders and catalog) or (508)676-3838 (technical assistance)
Fax: (508)676-3980
E-mail: pro-chemical@worldnet.att.net.
Website: www.prochemical.com
Offers: Reactive dyes for cotton, linen, rayon and silk: PRO MX & H, and Sabracron F. Acid dyes for wool, silk and nylon: WashFast, Kiton, Sabraset and One Shot. Also offers

Disperse dyes for polyester, Direct dyes and Synthetic Indigo. Carries PROfab Textile Inks, Pure Color Concentrates, Marbling Colors and many Pebeo products: Setacolor, Setasilk, Pebeo Soie, water- and solvent-kits, discharge and resist supplies/tools, waxes and workroom and safety supplies. Our inhouse lab offers color-matching services and technical advice while our classroom offers visiting artist workshops year-round.
Catalog: Free.
Phone Orders: M-F, 8:30-5 EST.
Mail Orders: Will ship internationally.
Discounts: Quantity discounts.
Accepts: MasterCard, Visa

QUALIN INTERNATIONAL, INC.

P.O. Box 31145
San Francisco CA 94131
Phone: (415)333-8500
Fax: (415)282-8789
Offers: Silk fabrics (also blanks, scarves and others) of natural white, plus silk painting supplies.
Catalog: Send SASE.

RUBBER POET & YES! PIGS CAN FLY

P.O. Box 218
Rockville UT 84763
Contact: Barry Sochat
Phone: (435)772-3441
Fax: (435)777-3464
E-mail: rubrpoet@infowest.com
Website: www.wyoming.com/~cavenewt/pigs/
Offers: Retail and wholesale rubbers stamps, Magic Cling backing, Superstick backing for unmounted stamps, and acrylic handle sets. We offer noncute, gorgeous Art Deco designs, nature, petroglyphs, fabric designs and pithy quotes, women images and science fiction.
Catalog: Rubber Poet (92 pages, b&w, 700 images): $3. Yes! Pigs Can Fly (16 pages, b&w, 450 images): $3. Both catalogs: $5 (refundable with first order).
Phone Orders: Daytime hours.
Mail Orders: At above address. 1-2 week delivery time. Will ship foreign orders air mail.
Discounts: Wholesale to legitimate storefronts only.
Accepts: MasterCard, Visa (foreign orders must arrange payment in US dollars)

SILKPAINT CORP.

P.O. Box 18
Waldron MO 64092
Phone: (816)891-7774
Fax: (816)891-7775
E-mail: art@silkpaint.com
Website: www.silkpaint.com
Offers: The AirPen for drawing fine lines with paint, resist, ceramic glazes and glue; Paper-Etch Dissolving Gel, Fiber-

Etch Fabric Remover, Silkpaint! brand resist, and Silkpaint! kits.

Catalog: Free.

Discounts: Sells products in quantities at wholesale to legitimate businesses.

Accepts: MasterCard, Visa

SOHO SOUTH

P.O. Box 1324

Cullman AL 35056-1324

Contact: Diana Douglass Jones

Phone: (205)739-6114

Fax: (205)734-6759

E-mail: soho@airnet.net

Offers: Czech glass beads, Japanese Delicas, gemstone beads and beading tools, supplies and books. Also sterling silver findings.

Catalog: $3.

Phone Orders: M-F, 9-5 CST.

Mail Orders: Yes. Showroom by appointment only.

Discounts: Quantity discounts.

Accepts: Discover, MasterCard, Visa, check

TEXTILE COLORS

P.O. Box 887

Riverdale MD 20738

Phone: (301)474-7347

E-mail: pointsilk@aol.com

Offers: FabricArts all-fabric paints and mediums, dyes, sample and other painting kits. Also offers silk and wool fabrics and silk scarves. Carries tools, brushes, accessories, chemicals, cleaners, videos and books.

Catalog: Call or write.

Discounts: Quantity; teachers, institutions and professionals.

ULTRA TREASURES BY COLLINS CREATIONS

(formerly Collins Creations)

510 FM 416

Streetman TX 75859-4056

Contact: Dorothy Collins

Phone: (903)599-2648

Fax: (903)599-4058

E-mail: ultra@ultratreasures.com

Website: www.ultratreasures.com

Store Location: At above address. M-F, 9-7 CST.

Offers: Appliqué and ultrasuede cutwork patterns. Also offers ultrasuede by piece and by yardage. Quilt-Pro software for quilters.

Catalog: Yes.

Phone Orders: No minimum order.

Mail Orders: No minimum order.

Discounts: Wholesale.

Accepts: Discover, MasterCard, Visa ($10 minimum charge)

WEB OF THREAD

1410 Broadway

Paducah KY 42001

Contact: Sharee Dawn Roberts

Phone: (502)575-9700

Fax: (502)575-0904

Website: www.suncompsvc.com/webofthread

Store Location: At above address.

Offers: Specialty threads and ribbons.

Catalog: $3, or free with first order.

Mail Orders: Yes.

Discounts: Yes.

Accepts: Discover, MasterCard, Visa

WHAT'S NEW, LTD.

3716 E. Main St.

Mesa AZ 85205

Contact: George Gerber

Phone: (602)830-4581

Fax: (602)832-2928

Offers: Scrap-ease scrapbook products, calendars, fabric appliqué, felt doll kits, ornament kits, wooden angel kits and more.

Phone Orders: (602)830-4581. M-F, 7:30-4:30 MST.

Discounts: Wholesale to legitimate businesses only.

Fabrics & Trims

Also see most other categories in Section II.

ARISE, INC.
6925 Willow St. NW
Washington DC 20012
Contact: Jeff Craig
Phone: (202)291-0770
Fax: (202)291-2073
E-mail: arisedc@aol.com
Website: www.arisedc.com/arise
Store Location: Washington DC location.
Offers: Indonesian and Indian fabrics; vintage Japanese kimono; new Japanese yukata; women's clothing lines; kasuri clothing, accessories and home decor items; Philippine baskets and furntiure; and Japanese furniture and antiques.
Catalog: For wholesale only.
Phone Orders: M-F, 10-6 EST.
Discounts: Given to legitimate wholesale companies.

BAER FABRICS
515 E. Market St.
Louisville KY 40202
Phone: (502)569-7010 or (800)769-7776
Fax: (502)582-2331
Offers: Special bridal collection of fabrics, including taffetas, satins, chiffons, organzas, nettings and laces in a range of colors, plus trims, notions and supplies. Also offers prom and evening wear collection. Also sells Ultrasuede, Ultrasuede light and Ultraleather in 75 colors. Personal shopper service.
Catalog: Bridal collection sample set (#11525), $10. Prom and evening wear collection sample set (#12525), $6. Ultrasuede and Ultraleather sample set (#01525), $9.50. Notions and trims catalog, $3.
Discounts: Quantity; teachers, institutions and businesses.

SONYA LEE BARRINGTON
837 47th Ave.
San Francisco CA 94121
Phone: (415)221-6510
Offers: Hand-dyed cotton fabrics, including over 300 solids and a variety of patterns. Call for appointment to see fabrics (studio only).
Catalog: Swatches, $5.
Mail Orders: Yes.
Accepts: MasterCard, Visa

BATIKS ETCETERA
411 Pine St.
Fort Mill SC 29715
Contact: Jan Smiley
Phone: (800)BATIKS-ETC or (800)228-4573 or (803)547-4299
Fax: (803)802-3877
E-mail: batiks@cetlink.net
Website: www.batiks.com
Offers: The most complete selection of batik fabrics available worldwide. Indonesian, Indian and African fabrics. Cottons and rayons. Handwoven fabrics, patterns, books, cotton and wool batting and more.
Catalog: Sample swatches, $5.
Phone Orders: M-F, 10-6 EST.
Mail Orders: Ship internationally and nationally. Prepayment required.
Accepts: American Express, MasterCard, Visa

THE BELT & BUTTON CONNECTION, INC.
120 Jersey Ave.
New Brunswick NJ 08901
Contact: Shari Aronoff
Phone: (732)448-0600
Fax: (732)448-0631
E-mail: info@beltbutton.com
Website: http://www.beltbutton.com
Store Location: At above address. M-F, 8:30-4:30.
Offers: We manufacture custom belts and buttons. Also available: rhinestone, pearl and combination buttons, rhinestone buckles, rhinestone zippers, leather, suede and patent leather. If you don't see it, call us.
Catalog: Multipage brochure. Free.
Phone Orders: Yes.
Mail Orders: Prepayment required. 10 workings maximum.
Discounts: Wholesale orders.

THE BINDING STITCH
8 Taunton Ave.
Dennis MA 02638
Contact: Marcia Brown
Phone: (508)385-2444
Fax: (508)385-2444
E-mail: bstitch@capecod.net
Website: www.bindingstitch.com
Store Location: At above address. M-F, 9:30-3:30.
Offers: Dressmaker cotton velveteens (71 colors), needlepoint finishing services, full anchor fibers and blocking kits.
Catalog: Swatch cards, $10.
Accepts: MasterCard, Visa

BLYTHE DESIGNS

P.O. Box 17506-CS
Seattle WA 98107
Contact: Giselle Blythe
Phone: (206)789-6772
Fax: (206)789-6772
Offers: Fabulous feline fabrics! Cat-print fabrics for quilting, clothing and more.
Catalog: Send SASE for current information.
Phone Orders: Fax or leave a message.
Mail Orders: Worldwide.
Discounts: Inquire on letterhead for business discount.
Accepts: MasterCard, Visa, check, money order

BRITEX-BY-MAIL

146 Geary St.
San Francisco CA 94108
Phone: (415)392-2910
Store Location: At above address. M-W, F and Sat, 9:30-6; Th, 9:30-8.
Offers: Fashion fabrics in a variety of domestic/imported cottons, blends, silks, linens, rayons, woolens, knits, spandex and others. Swatch service available. Specify needs, describing garment/yardage and fiber wanted, price restrictions; for personal consultation include $5.
Accepts: American Express, MasterCard, Visa

SAWYER BROOK DISTINCTIVE FABRICS

P.O. Box 1800
Clinton MA 01510
Phone: (978)368-3133
E-mail: sbdf@ultranet.com
Website: www.ultranet.com/~sbdf
Offers: Collections of imported and domestic fabrics—cotton, silk, linen, wool and rayon coordinated for color and texture. Unique line of specialty buttons chosen to coordinate with the fabrics. Staffed by fabric specialists. Send SASE for samples.
Accepts: MasterCard, Visa

CINEMA LEATHERS, INC.

9555 Owensmouth Ave. #1
Chatsworth CA 91311
Contact: Arline Winkler
Phone: (818)772-4600
Fax: (818)772-1134
E-mail: cnmalthrs@aol.com
Website: //www.cinema-leathers.com
Store Location: At above address. M-F, 9-4.
Offers: Garment leathers, including suedes and napa—lamb, pig, cow, novelties and foils.
Discounts: For quantity orders.

COASTAL BUTTON & TRIM, INC.

P.O. Box 285
Monrovia MD 21770-0285
Contact: Beth Kindermann or Marian Tvorek
Phone: (301)874-5568 or (800)632-8632
Fax: (301)874-5586
E-mail: sales@coastalbutton.com
Website: www.coastalbutton.com
Offers: Buttons and craft supplies.
Catalog: Free.
Phone Orders: M-F, 10-4 EST.
Mail Orders: Will ship to US only via UPS or USPS.
Discounts: Wholesale prices at 50 pounds of buttons.
Accepts: MasterCard, Visa, check

CODE FELT, LTD.

P.O. Box 130
Perth, Ontario K7H 3E3
Canada
Contact: Anwer Omar
Phone: (800)782-5763 (Canada) or (800)635-3267 (US)
Fax: (613)264-0261
E-mail: codefelt@superaje.com
Website: http://www.superaje.com/~codefelt
Store Location: At above address.
Offers: Felt—pressed wool, synthetic, burlap and vinyl.
Catalog: Shade cards, $3 (refundable).
Phone Orders: M-F, 8:30-4:30 EST.
Mail Orders: Will ship across Canada or US promptly.
Discounts: Quantity. Teachers and institutions.
Accepts: MasterCard, Visa

D'ANTON LEATHER CO.

5530 Vincent Ave. N.E.
West Branch IA 52358
Phone: (319)643-2568
Offers: Full line of luxury garment leathers: suedes, smooth and fun types in a variety of colors, textures and finishes.
Catalog: $2 and SASE.
Discounts: Quantity. Sells retail and wholesale.

DELICATE STITCHES BY SYLVIA

2913 N. Wild Mountain Rd.
Tulsa OK 74127
Contact: Sylvia Fooshee
Phone: (918)245-5998
E-mail: sewnsyl@aol.com
Store Location: Home-based business at above address.
Offers: Smocking and heirloom sewing supplies. Patterns for smocking and heirloom sewing, smocking plates, fabrics, laces, threads, books and bimonthly newsletter.
Catalog: 50 pages. $8.
Phone Orders: (800)471-2697. T-Sat, 9-3 CST.
Mail Orders: Yes.
Discounts: Retail sales only. Discounts available on large quantity purchases.
Accepts: Discover, MasterCard, Visa

EVENING STAR DESIGNS

200 Merrimack St., Suite 401
Haverhill MA 01830
Contact: Carolyn S. Cibik or Valerie Kelley
Phone: (978)372-3473 or (800)666-3562

Fax: (978)372-6535
E-mail: evening.star.designs@worldnet.att.net
Website: http://home.att.net/~evening.star.design
Offers: Crazy quilting supplies: fancy fabrics, lace, trim, ribbon, embroidery threads, silk ribbon, metallic, braid and ribbon, beads, (glass, mother-of-pearl, semiprecious stone, porcelain, crystal and more), buttons, books, patterns and kits.
Catalog: $3.
Phone Orders: Yes.
Mail Orders: At above address.
Accepts: MasterCard, Visa, check, money order

FABRIC GALLERY

146 W. Grand River
Williamston MI 48895
Phone: (517)655-4573
Store Location: At above address. M-Sat, 10-5; Th, 10-8.
Offers: Fashion fabrics: imported/domestic silks, wools and cottons. Line of buttons and others. Swatches service, silk, wool gabardine or cotton shirtings, each $4, or all three for $10.

FAMOUS LABELS FABRIC OUTLET SWATCH CLUB

1849 Pioneer Pike E.
Springfield OR 97477
Contact: Marylyn Minney or Pam Halford
Phone: (541)747-4670
Fax: (541)747-0121
Store Location: At above address.
Offers: Club plan—members join with yearly $16 fee. Receive mailer every 6-8 weeks of swatches of designer sportswear and activewear fabrics, including rayons, cottons, jerseys, wovens and Lycras.
Phone Orders: Yes.
Mail Orders: Yes.
Discounts: Yes.
Accepts: Discover, MasterCard, Visa

FANCIFULS, INC.

P.O. Box 76
Killawog NY 13794
Contact: Donna or Vince Pedini
Phone: (607)849-6870
Fax: (607)849-6870
E-mail: fancifuls@clarityconnect.com
Website: www.fancifulsinc.com
Offers: Over 3,000 different designs of raw brass charms and embellishments. No minimum order.
Catalog: Over 90 pages. $5 (refunded with first order of $30 or more).
Phone Orders: M-F, 9-5 EST.
Mail Orders: Will ship to Canada and foreign.
Accepts: MasterCard, Visa

FASHION FABRICS CLUB

10490 Baur Blvd.
St. Louis MO 63132
Phone: (800)468-0602

Offers: Club plan. Members join with yearly fee and receive monthly swatch kits of designer fabrics, including Blassport, Liz Claiborne, Villager, Herman Geist, Leslie Fay, Koret, Jones N.Y., Evan Picone, Polo and others. Membership, $4.95. (US only).
Accepts: MasterCard, Visa

FIELD'S FABRICS

1695 44th SE
Grand Rapids MI 49508
Phone: (616)455-4570
Fax: (616)455-1052
E-mail: fields@12k.com
Website: www.fieldsfabrics.com
Store Location: At above address. M-Sat, 9-9.
Offers: Everything from Ultrasuede to broadcloth, Microfiber, silks, woolens, metallics, brocades, satin, knits, gabardine, cotton prints, felt, fur, velvet, denim, camouflage, equestrian prints, Lycras, uniform fabrics and much more. Plus notions and sewing tools.
Accepts: American Express, Discover, MasterCard, Visa

GLOBAL VILLAGE IMPORTS

3439 NE Sandy Blvd. #263
Portland OR 97232
Phone: (503)236-9245
Fax: (503)233-0827
Website: www.globalfabric.com/~gvi
Offers: Line of hand-loomed ikat cottons from Mayan weavers in bright colors and exotic designs.
Catalog: Swatch pack, $5; international customers, $7.50 (US funds).
Discounts: Sells wholesale.

GREAT AMERICAN SEWING FACTORY

Dept. CS
8 Croton Dam Rd.
Ossining NY 10562-2822
Contact: Michael or Vita
Phone: (914)941-7444
Offers: Sewing trims, including laces (eyelet, cotton cluny, flat and ruffled and double- and triple-ruffled laces), ribbons (satin and grosgrain), elastics, Velcro, appliqués, ricrac, ribbon roses, pearls and many other trims.
Catalog: $1.
Phone Orders: M-F, 9-7 EST.
Mail Orders: Prepayment required. Allow 2 weeks for delivery.
Discounts: Quantity discounts available.
Accepts: MasterCard, Visa, check

MAUREEN GREESON & CO.

510 Ellington Rd.
South Windsor CT 06074
Contact: Maureen Greeson
Phone: (860)528-8168
Store Location: At above address. Hours by appointment.
Offers: Swiss batiste, silks, ribbons, laces and trims (new

and antique), kits, miscellaneous sewing supplies, doll supplies and our own leather doll shoes and kits.
Catalog: Series of newsletters. Send SASE for your first.
Phone Orders: Accepted M-F, 10-4 EST.
Mail Orders: Will ship to US and Canada. Allow 6-8 weeks for delivery.
Discounts: Great savings in each newsletter.
Accepts: American Express, MasterCard, Visa

H.E. GOLDBERG & CO., INC.
9050 Martin Luther King Jr. Way S.
Seattle WA 98118
Fax: (206)722-0435
Offers: Tanned furs and skins: large/small quantities—fox, beaver, mink, calfskin, lambskin, muskrat, raccoon, rabbit skin, opossum, reindeer, ermine and others.
Catalog: Price list, $1.
Accepts: MasterCard, Visa

HERMES LEATHER
45 W. 34th St., Room 1108
New York NY 10001
Phone: (212)947-1153
Fax: (212)967-2701
E-mail: hermesleather@worldnet.att.net
Website: hermesleather.com
Store Location: At above address. M-F, 8-5.
Offers: Line of garment leathers/suedes; hides, pig suede, cabretta and others. Custom colors available.
Catalog: Send SASE for swatch card.
Discounts: Sells wholesale to legitimate businesses.

JEHLOR FANTASY FABRICS
730 Andover Park W.
Seattle WA 98188
Phone: (206)575-8250
Fax: (206)575-8250
Website: www.adnetmk.com/jehlor
Store Location: At above address. M-Sat, 10-6; Sun, 1-5.
Offers: Specialty fabrics: sequined and beaded fabrics, "cracked ice," metallics, brocades, lamés, satins, chiffons, Lycra, stretch satin and nude sheers. Trims: rhinestones, glass beads and jewels, sequins, appliqués/trims, fringe, feathers and others.
Catalog: $5.
Discounts: Quantity.

KATHRYN'S LACE
P.O. Box 71
Ottumwa IA 52501
Contact: Kathryn Gettings
Phone: (515)684-7920
Fax: (515)684-7920
E-mail: kimp@lisco.net
Offers: Swiss batiste, English netting, organdy velvet, Swiss embroideries, French Val Laces, French tatting laces, Venice lace, embroidered cotton netting, English laces, organza lace trims and alençon with and without pearls and sequins. Alen-

çon and overall lace, organza overall lace and Venise lace overall.
Catalog: $5.
Phone Orders: Yes.
Mail Orders: Yes.
Accepts: no credit cards

L.P. THUR FABRICS
126 W. 23rd St.
New York NY 10011
Phone: (212)243-4913
Fax: (212)243-4913
E-mail: l.p.thur.fabrics@prodigy.net
Store Location: At above address. M-F, 9:30-5:30; W, 9:30-7; Sat-Sun, 12-5.
Offers: Velvets, lamé, silks, tapestries, solid cottons, cotton prints, canvas, vinyl, felt, tulle, satin, taffeta, muslin, sheers, cheesecloth, wool, fleece, corduroy, ribbon, elastic, Velcro, buttons and others. Wholesale and retail. Call or write for further details.

LACE HEAVEN, INC.
P.O. Box 50150
2524 Dauphin Island Pkwy.
Mobile AL 36605
Contact: Patricia Puckett
Phone: (334)478-5644
Fax: (334)450-0489
Store Location: At above address.
Offers: Fabrics: lace, lycra, velour, tricots, stretch lace, T-shirt knits, flannels and others. Also offers lace inserts, trims and notions.
Catalog: $3 (refundable).
Phone Orders: (800)478-5645. M-S, 10-4.
Mail Orders: No C.O.D.s
Discounts: Quantity.
Accepts: Discover, MasterCard, Visa, check, money order

LE FILET LINENS & LACES
610 Locust St.
Oak Harbor OH 43449
Contact: Mayetta Bradbury
Phone: (800)818-5495
Fax: (419)898-1369
Offers: Battenberg and crocheted doilies, trims, edgings, vests, collars, inserts, umbrellas, picture frames and boxes, stiffened Battenberg and crocheted items, porcelain dolls, craft books and supplies. Also kits and supplies to make battenberg lace by hand.
Catalog: 60 pages. $3 (includes many crafting suggestions).
Phone Orders: M-F, 10-5; Sat, 10-1 EST.
Mail Orders: Prepayment required. Orders are shipped promptly.
Discounts: Quantity discounts.
Accepts: MasterCard, Visa

THE LEATHER FACTORY, INC.

P.O. Box 50429
3847 E. Loop 820
Fort Worth TX 76105
Phone: (800)433-3201
Offers: Leather skins for garment making: cowhide, deerskin, elk, rabbit, thin velvet suedes and others. Lining leathers: kip, pigskin and others. Exotic leathers: python, cobra, embossed splits in alligator lizard and ostrich grains.
Catalog: $3.

LEATHER UNLIMITED CORP.

Dept. CS98
7155 Hwy. B
Belgium WI 53004-0911
Contact: Joe O'Connell
Phone: (920)994-9464
Fax: (920)994-4099
Offers: A wide array of leather, kits and finished products. Leather includes garment bag, splits, oak, deer, sheepskin, hair on hides, chamois and pieces. Leather findings include buckles, snaps, zippers, thread, dies, dyes, belts, black powder, Indian lore, books, tanning kits, beads, conchos and more. Finished products include slippers, wallets, handbags, belts, cycle accessories, hats, cases, halters, dream catchers and more at wholesale prices.
Catalog: 92 pages. $2 (refundable).
Phone Orders: M-F, 7-4. Fax: 24 hours, 7 days a week.
Mail Orders: US, Canada and worldwide.
Discounts: Sells wholesale to legitimate businesses.
Accepts: Discover, MasterCard, Visa

LINDA'S—YOUR ULTRASUEDE SPECIALIST

24 Main St.
Norwich, Ontario N0J 1P0
Canada
Contact: Linda Janden Borre
Phone: (519)863-2887
Fax: (519)424-2655
E-mail: lindas@oxford.net
Website: www.oxford.net/~lindas
Store Location: At above address.
Offers: UltraSuede. Regular and light and Ultraleather yardage and squares. Also related patterns, notions and books.
Catalog: Swatches, $5.
Phone Orders: M-Sat, 9-5:30 EST.
Mail Orders: Worldwide.
Discounts: Available with volume.
Accepts: MasterCard, Visa

LUCHI YARNS INTERNATIONAL

1055 Paramount Pkwy., Unit E
Batavia IL 60510
Contact: David Lu
Phone: (630)761-9674
Fax: (630)761-9675
E-mail: lysilk@aol.com
Store Location: At above address.

Offers: Silk scarves, silk fabrics, silk yarn and fiber for fiber artists.
Catalog: Brochure.
Phone Orders: 24 hours.
Mail Orders: Will ship to US and Canada.
Accepts: MasterCard, Visa

SYLVIA MACNEIL

2325 Main St.
West Barnstable MA 02668
Phone: (508)362-3875
Offers: Antique fabrics (1860-1900): silk taffeta, faille, cottons, woolens and others.
Catalog: Send SASE for list.

THE MATERIAL WORLD

5700 Monroe St.
Sylvania OH 43560
Contact: Sandra Wagner
Phone: (419)885-5416
Store Location: At above address. M-F 10:30-6; Sat, 10-5.
Offers: Line of quality fashion fabrics—imported and domestic silks, wools, cottons, blends and others; coordinated selections from areas worldwide.
Catalog: Send $12 to receive collection or swatches 4 times a year.
Phone Orders: M-Sat, 11-5.
Mail Orders: Will ship to US and Canada within 48 hours.
Accepts: MasterCard, Visa, check, money order

MICHIKO'S CREATIONS

P.O. Box 4313
Napa CA 94558
Contact: Michiko Somerville
Phone: (707)224-8546
Fax: (707)224-2246
E-mail: michiko@michikoscreations.com
Website: http://www.michikoscreations.com
Offers: Specialize in Ultrasuede brand fabrics in yardage, a wide variety of sampler packages and original easy-to-make project kits.
Catalog: Available color information, free. Color card with 120 swatches, $10.
Phone Orders: M-F, 9-5 PST.
Mail Orders: Will ship to US, Canada, Japan and Australia. Will be shipped within 3 working days by air mail.
Discounts: Quantity discount is available for business customer.
Accepts: MasterCard, Visa, check, money order, C.O.D.

MILL END STORE

12155 SW Broadway
Beaverton OR 97005
Phone: (503)646-3000
Store Location: 9701 SE McLoughlin Blvd., Portland OR 97222. Phone: (503)786-1234. Fax: (503)786-2022
Offers: Fabrics, including imported cottons, wools and silks; outerwear fabrics, including nylon, packcloth, fleece, rain-

wear, knits and ribbing. Also offers bridal, drapery and upholstery fabrics, polyesters, velvets, velveteen, laces and trims. Patterns, notions, yarns and needlework items also available.
Catalog: Send SASE for brochure or with inquiry.

MONTEREY, INC.
1725 E. Delavan Dr.
Janesville WI 53546
Contact: Susie Potter
Phone: (608)754-8309 or (800)432-9959
Fax: (608)757-3312
Website: www.montereyoutlet.com
Offers: Synthetic furs: shags, shearling, plush, toy animal types, closeouts and remnants. Also offers stuffings.
Catalog: Send for free brochure or $5 for sample package.
Phone Orders: $25 minimum; C.O.D., $100 minimum.
Mail Orders: $25 minimum.

NATIONAL NONWOVENS
P.O. Box 150
Easthampton MA 01027
Contact: Customer service, ext. 213
Phone: (800)333-3469 or (413)527-3445
Fax: (413)527-0456
E-mail: nanonwovens@aol.com
Website: www.textileshow.com
Offers: Washable 100% acrylic felt, various blends of wool-felt by the bolt, square or special felt shapes, with or without pressure-sensitive backing. Custom color matching and die-cutting capabilities.
Catalog: Color cards available.
Phone Orders: M-F, 8-5 EST.
Mail Orders: $200 minimum order.

CAMELA NITSCHKE RIBBONRY
119 Louisiana Ave.
Perrysburg OH 43551
Phone: (419)872-0073
Offers: French ribbons, including reproductions of seventeenth- and eighteenth-century styles; flower and ornament ribbon kits; instructional videos on holiday ornaments and flowers. Also carries handcrafted bridal accessories.
Catalog: Call for free information brochure.

NUSTYLE QUILTING FRAME CO., SUPPLIES
P.O.Box 61
Hwy. 52 W.
Stover MO 65078
Contact: Ruth Williams
Phone: (573)377-2244 or (800)821-7490
Fax: (573)377-2833
Store Location: 290 W. Fourth, Hwy. 52 W.
Offers: Long arm quilting machines and frames; hand quilting frames, different styles; large rolls Dacron and cotton-batt; Dacron thread for machine quilting and regular sewing, all colors; quilting books; all type of patterns for clothing, crafts, quilt rulers, cutting boards, cutters; all types of no-

tions; full line of embroidery blocks and threads; over 4,000 bolts of fabrics, name brands.
Catalog: Yes.
Phone Orders: Yes.
Mail Orders: Ship nationwide including Canada, AK and HI.
Discounts: Yes.
Accepts: Discover, MasterCard, Visa

OPPENHEIM'S
P.O. Box 29
120 E. Main St.
North Manchester IN 46962
Phone: (219)982-6848 or (800)461-6728
Fax: (219)982-6557
Store Location: At above address. M-F, 9-5.
Offers: Fabrics (including irregulars): linen-look and many other cottons, knits, satins, polyester and polycottons, calicos, rug weavers' scraps, faux fur, needlecraft and bridal fabrics, taffetas, muslin netting and cheesecloth. Specialty fabrics: wool remnants, Ultrasuede scraps and Christmas. Also offers trims, stamped goods and quilt blocks, pillow forms, upholstery squares, "thermal suede" lining, rubber sheeting, poly doll cloth, wool mattress pads, polyfill and trims. Carries cut/sew and other sewing projects, plus remnants and package bargains.
Catalog: Write or call.
Accepts: Discover, MasterCard, Visa

ORIENTAL SILK CO.
8377 Beverly Blvd.
Los Angeles CA 90048
Contact: Ken Wong
Phone: (213)651-2323
Fax: (213)651-2323
Store Location: At above address. M-Sat, 9-6.
Offers: Finest imported silks, woolens, porcelains, hand embroideries and linens from China and the Orient. Incredible color selection.
Catalog: Price list is available.
Phone Orders: Yes.
Mail Orders: Prepayment required. Ship UPS.
Discounts: Wholesale discount 10% with resale number.
Accepts: MasterCard, Visa, check, money order

ORNAMENTAL RESOURCES, INC.
P.O. Box 3010
Idaho Springs CO 80452
Phone: (800)876-ORNA
Website: ornabead.com
Offers: Complete lines of glass beads, including faceted, cut, foiled, decorated, fancy, metal, ceramic, plastic, bone, stone, shell, bugles, pony and seed beads in all sizes. Collectors' beads, metal stampings, chains, appliqué materials, rhinestones, studs, sequins, glass jewels, tassels, buckles and buttons. Also offers beading tools and supplies and design assistance. $25 minimum order.
Catalog: $15 (with one year's supplements).

PERFECT PALETTE FABRIC CLUB

313 N. Mattis Ave., Suite 116
Champaign IL 61821
Contact: Ann Brodsky
Phone: (217)398-1440 or (888)887-9080
Fax: (217)398-6340
Store Location: Champaign IL location.
Offers: Women's apparel fabric by mail. Dyed to match knits, ribbing, plus coordinating fabrics. Kwik Sew and Stretch & Sew patterns. Fabric Club membership: $12/year for 4 issues of swatches.
Catalog: $3.
Phone Orders: (888)887-9080.
Mail Orders: Yes.
Discounts: Coupons in each issue.
Accepts: Discover, MasterCard, Visa, check, money order

PHILIPS-BOYNE CORP.

135 Rome St.
Farmingdale NY 11735
Contact: Customer service
Phone: (516)755-1230
Fax: (516)755-1259
Offers: Fine shirtings: woven fabrics, imported/domestic in cottons, silks, blends and novelties. Also offers yarn dyed in stripes, checks and plaids. Wholesale only.
Catalog: Sample package, $3 (refundable).
Accepts: American Express, Discover, MasterCard, Visa

QUALIN INTERNATIONAL, INC.

P.O. Box 31145
San Francisco CA 94131
Phone: (415)333-8500
Fax: (415)282-8789
Offers: Silk fabrics (also blanks, scarves and others) of natural white, plus silk painting supplies.
Catalog: Send SASE.

THE RIBBON FACTORY OUTLET

P.O. Box 405
600 N. Brown St.
Titusville PA 16354
Contact: Carol Steinbuhler
Phone: (814)827-6431
Fax: (814)827-4191
E-mail: ribbon@tbscc.com
Website: http://www.ribbonfactory.com
Store Location: At above address. M-F, 10-4 EST.
Offers: High-quality woven edge ribbon: satins, grosgrains, picot and wire-edge ribbon; machine-tied bows, and custom hot cutting. Sample packs available for $2. Christmas ribbon available year-round. Call for satin overrun specials.
Catalog: 16 pages, full color. $2.
Phone Orders: M-F, 9-5 EST. Fax accepted 24 hours a day.
Mail Orders: All orders shipped in 24-48 hours.
Discounts: Quantity discounts: 500-1,999 yards, 10%;

2,000-4,999 yards, 20%; 5,000-19,999 yards, 30%; over 20,000 yards, 35% discount.
Accepts: MasterCard, Visa

SANDY'S LACE & TRIMS

7417 N. Knoxville
Peoria IL 61614
Contact: Sandy Staker
Phone: (309)689-1943
Fax: (309)689-1942
E-mail: sandys.lace.trims@juno.com
Offers: Fine-quality cotton antique and new laces, silk ribbon, trims, bunka, crystals, watch cases, stencilers, brass accessories, findings, miniature kits, fabrics, silks, wools and wide selection of mini prints. Silk satin ribbon and beads for the miniature world, doll world, silk ribbon embroidery and other hobby projects.
Catalog: 54 pages. $3.
Phone Orders: Any time.
Mail Orders: Ship anywhere in the world.
Discounts: See Sandy's Victorian Trims for wholesale catalog.
Accepts: MasterCard, Visa, check (drawn on US bank)

SEW FABULOUS FABRICS

P.O. Box 742
3470 W. Coldwater Rd.
Mt. Morris MI 48458
Contact: Jeffie Johnson
Phone: (810)789-3948
Fax: (810)789-2621
E-mail: wgjj@kode.net
Website: www.americanquilts.com/african
Store Location: Home-based mail-order company. Home visits by appointment.
Offers: Authentic African fabrics. 100% cotton. Several pre-cut packages available containing quarter yards, "fat quarter," half yard, full yard cuts, sampler package. Swatch book available featuring hundreds of 8×8 swatches, cottons, rayon, polyesters and more. Handmade "mudcloth" (bogolanfini) panels. "Roclon" muslin, quilter's dream 100% cotton batting, foundation pattern, African inspired appliqué patterns, books about quilters, misc. items.
Catalog: $5 (refundable).
Phone Orders: Not accepted at this time.
Mail Orders: Will ship to US and Canada. Prepayment required. Allow 30 days delivery.
Accepts: check, money order

SILKS 'N' SUCH

8224 E. Virginia Ave.
Scottsdale AZ 85257
Contact: Stell Pries
Phone: (602)947-5018
Store Location: At above address.
Offers: Swiss Nelona batiste, Swiss cotton pique, cotton organdy, velvet and velveteen, silk organza, cotton organdy, China silk, Thai silk, taffeta, brocade, French laces, Swiss

embroideries and imported trims, French wire-edge ribbon and silk ribbon $\frac{1}{16}$-$1\frac{1}{4}''$, old laces and feathers, buttons and clothes.

Catalog: $3. Lists all merchandise.
Phone Orders: Yes.
Mail Orders: Yes.
Accepts: check, cash

SUCH-A-DEAL LACE & TRIM
3515 Sunrise Blvd. #18-S
Rancho Cordova CA 95742
Phone: (916)635-LACE or (800)368-3186
Fax: (916)635-4655
E-mail: laces@such-a-deal.com
Website: such-a-deal.com
Store Location: At above address. M-F, 9-6; Sat, 9-4.
Offers: Wholesale distributor of ruffle lace, fat lace, ribbon, satin roses, braids, gimps, venise, eyelet, battenberg, cluny, pearls, doilies, metallic braid and more.
Catalog: $3 (refundable with order).
Accepts: American Express, MasterCard, Visa ($50 minimum order)

SUPER SILK, INC.
P.O. Box 527596
Flushing NY 11352
Contact: Customer service
Phone: (800)432-7455 or (718)886-2606
Fax: (718)886-2657
Offers: Silk fabric, dupioni shantung, silk charmeuse, silk chiffon, China silk, silk linen, silk organza, silk taffeta, silk organza metallic plain and crinkle, silk tussah, duchess satin and more.
Catalog: Available upon request, complete sample set of silk fabric, $18.
Phone Orders: M-F, 9-7 EST.
Mail Orders: Will ship to US and Canada.
Discounts: According to yardage.
Accepts: American Express, Discover, MasterCard, Visa

TESTFABRICS, INC.
P.O. Box 26
415 Delaware Ave.
West Pittston PA 18643
Phone: (717)603-0432
Fax: (717)603-0433
E-mail: testfabric@aol.com
Offers: Fabrics made from the commercially available fibers that are prepared for printing, dyeing, painting or treating with other topical finishes. A collection of textile materials for textile and object conservation, painting restoration, exhibit building and design and storage facilities.
Catalog: Free.
Phone Orders: M-F, 8-5 EST.
Mail Orders: Orders shipped via UPS generally; by other carriers by request.
Discounts: Prices break according to quantity.
Accepts: American Express, MasterCard, Visa

TINSEL TRADING CO.
47 W. 38th St.
New York NY 10018
Contact: Marcia Ceppos
Phone: (212)730-1030
Fax: (212)768-8823
E-mail: tinseltrading@juno.com
Store Location: At above address.
Offers: Trims, fringes, vintage flowers, vintage metallic trims, cords, tassels and vintage buttons.
Catalog: Video, $15.
Phone Orders: Yes.
Mail Orders: US, Canada and international.
Discounts: Retail and wholesale.

ULTRAMOUSE, LTD.
3433 Bennington Court
Bloomfield Hills MI 48301
Contact: Alice Ann Kilgore
Phone: (248)646-8712
Offers: Ultrasuede in 9×12 pieces in many bright colors—your choice. Also appliqué patterns and books on appliqué.
Catalog: $2.
Phone Orders: (800)225-1887.
Mail Orders: At above address.
Accepts: MasterCard, Visa

THE UNIQUE SPOOL
407 Corte Majorca
Vacaville CA 95688
Contact: Roberta Dent
Phone: (707)448-1538
Fax: (707)447-5161
E-mail: spool@uniquespool.com
Website: www.uniquespool.com
Offers: African fabrics, Australian prints, African Fabric Club, ethnic patterns, notions and gifts.
Catalog: Send #10 SASE (2 stamps).
Phone Orders: Yes.
Mail Orders: Domestic and overseas.
Discounts: Wholesale; minimum requirements.
Accepts: American Express, Discover, MasterCard, Visa

General Needlecraft Supplies

Also see General Craft Supplies and specific categories in Section II.

BUFFALO BATT & FELT
3307 Walden Ave.
Depew NY 14043
Phone: (716)683-4100
Offers: Superfluff polyester stuffing available in bags and bulk rolls. Also available are premium and standard pillow inserts in a variety of sizes. Also offer quilt batts in sizes crib through king in lofts up to 2″.
Catalog: Brochure and swatches, $1 (refundable).
Discounts: Wholesale prices with quantity.

COUNTRY NEEDLEWORKS, INC.
584 Chicago Dr.
Jenison MI 49428
Contact: Cheryl Van Haitsma or Barb Langerak
Phone: (616)457-9410
Fax: (616)457-9510
Store Location: At above address.
Offers: Cross-stitch, quilting, yarns and threads, framing, stamps and accessories, memory books and accessories, giftware.
Phone Orders: Yes. M-Sat, 9:30-9.
Mail Orders: Yes.
Discounts: Schools and churches, quilt and embroiderers' guilds.
Accepts: American Express, Discover, MasterCard, Visa, debit

CRAFTS BY DONNA
P.O. Box 1456
Costa Mesa CA 92628-1456
Contact: Donna Friebertshauser
Phone: (714)545-8567
Fax: (714)545-8567
E-mail: dsignsbydf@aol.com
Offers: Complete line of rayon (Brazilian) threads, battenberg lace tapes, 1/16″ polyester ribbon, 4mm (1/8″) silk luster ribbon. Original designs and kits for dimensional (Brazililan) embroidery, trapunto, ribbon embroidery, battenberg lace, blackwork and other counted thread techniques.
Catalog: $2 (includes special offer coupon).
Phone Orders: Yes.
Mail Orders: Yes.
Discounts: Retail and wholesale.

CREATIVE CRAFT HOUSE
P.O. Box 2567
Bullhead City AZ 86430
Offers: Line of trims: braids in a variety of styles and widths, plastic and other beads, rhinestones and naturals.
Catalog: 80 pages. $2. Includes pinecone and seashell projects.

CUMBERLAND YARN SHOP
51 Birchwood Lane #11
Crossville TN 38555
Contact: Jean Marr
Phone: (931)707-1026
Fax: (931)707-1026
E-mail: cdjjmarr@usit.net
Store Location: At above address. T-F, 10-5; Sat, 10-2.
Offers: Specializes in natural fibers—wool, cotton, blends, mohair. Classes. Special orders. Needles by Addi Turbo, Susan Bates, Brittany Clover.
Phone Orders: T-F, 10-5; Sat, 10-2.
Mail Orders: Will ship to US, Canada.
Accepts: Discover, MasterCard, Visa

ELANN FIBRE COMPANY
Box 771
Cranbrook, British Columbia V1C 4J5
Canada
Contact: Ann Cannon-Brown
Phone: (250)426-0616
Fax: (250)426-0618
E-mail: elann@cyberlink.bc.ca
Website: http://www.elann.com
Store Location: Box 257, Eureka MT 59917-0257.
Offers: Yarns, books, patterns, tools and accessories for knitters and other natural fibre lovers.
Catalog: Downloadable version at the website.
Phone Orders: M-Th, 9-2 MST.
Mail Orders: Will ship to US, Canada and overseas. Prepayment required.
Discounts: Frequent purchasers plan.
Accepts: Discover, MasterCard, Visa

FAIRFIELD PROCESSING CORP.
P.O. Box 1157
Danbury CT 06813-1157
Phone: (800)243-0989
Fax: (203)792-9710
E-mail: ffld.prcssng.corp@snet.net
Website: www.poly-fil.com
Offers: Fairfield Processing Corporation manufactures a complete line of high-quality products for the home sewing,

quilt and craft industries. Poly-fil, Soft Touch and Crafters Choice brand fiberfill, batting and pillow form products are easy to use, available in many sizes and unconditionally guaranteed. New products include quilt pattern books, bumper batting and a chair cushion insert. Poly-fil is internationally available and accepted as the brand of excellence.

Catalog: Free. Call.

Phone Orders: M-F, 8-5 EST.

Discounts: Sells wholesale to companies with tax ID number; 2-carton minimum.

Accepts: MasterCard, Visa

THE GOLDEN NEEDLE

509 E. Park Ave.

Libertyville IL 60048

Contact: Elizabeth Redleaf

Phone: (847)549-7579

Fax: (847)549-7589

Store Location: At above address. T-F, 10-5:30; Th, 10-8; Sat, 10-5.

Offers: Needlepoint and counted cross-stitch classes, hand-painted canvases, over 100 lines of thread and custom finishing. Ask about stitcher reward program.

Catalog: Write for free newsletter.

Phone Orders: T-Sat, 10-5 CST.

Mail Orders: Prepayment required.

Accepts: American Express, MasterCard, Visa

HANDWORKS

7181 Batesville Rd.

Afton VA 22920

Phone: (800)346-2004

Offers: Line of children's sewing projects, knitting baskets and others. Natural materials.

Catalog: Send SASE for list.

HERRSCHNERS

2800 Hoover Rd.

Stevens Point WI 54492-0001

Contact: Customer order department

Phone: (800)441-0838

Fax: (715)341-2250

Website: www.herrschners.com

Store Location: At above address. Open 7 days a week.

Offers: Quality counted cross-stitch, needlepoint, embroidery, crewel, quilting, latch hook, plastic canvas, kits and accessories. Features Zweigart fabrics, Kreinik threads, complete line of DMC products and large selection of Red Heart and specialty yarns, thread, patterns and supplies. Also offers stamped table linens and pillowcases, holiday crafts, painting and beaded crafts and many hard-to-find and exclusive items.

Catalog: Free. Color.

Phone Orders: 24 hours a day, 7 days a week.

Mail Orders: Will ship to US and Canada. Rush delivery and gift delivery available.

Discounts: Look for our weekly specials on our website.

Accepts: American Express, Discover, MasterCard, Visa

HIGH COUNTRY WEST NEEDLEWORK SHOP

114 N. San Francisco St., Suite 201

Flagstaff AZ 86001

Phone: (520)779-2900 or (800)847-6020

Offers: Hand-painted canvases by many of the top canvas artists. Also offers custom designing, as well as its own design line. Many Southwestern pieces are also produced. Fibers, fibers, fibers. Woolmasters, Medici, Appleton and its own fiber lines, including Felicity's Garden, a 50% silk and 50% Australian wool. Silks, beads, crystals and more.

Catalog: Subscription, $4.

Accepts: MasterCard, Visa

IDENT-IFY LABEL CORP.

P.O. Box 140204

Brooklyn NY 11214-0204

Contact: Anthony

Phone: (718)436-3126

Fax: (718)436-9302

E-mail: identify01@aol.com

Offers: Personalized printed clothing labels, name tapes, woven labels, custom-printed labels with your logo and sewing notions.

Catalog: $1 (refundable with first order).

Phone Orders: (888)60-LABEL.

Mail Orders: Will ship anywhere in the world.

Catalog: Free brochure.

Discounts: Quantity and institutional.

Accepts: MasterCard, Visa, check, money order

INTERWEAVE PRESS

201 E. 4th St.

Loveland CO 80537

Phone: (800)645-3675

Fax: (970)667-8317

Offers: Needlecraft books: weaving titles and patterns, dyeing, spinning, textiles, yarn guide, knitting, sweaters, care of spinning wheels.

Catalog: Contact dealer.

Discounts: Sells wholesale to legitimate businesses.

LACIS

3163 Adeline St.

Berkeley CA 94703

Phone: (510)843-7178

Fax: (510)843-5018

Store Location: Separate retail store and gallery at 2982 Adeline St., Berkeley CA 94703.

Offers: Extensive threads, ribbons and supplies for lace making, embroidery and costume. Lace making tools, sew-on purse frames, tatting shuttles and reproduction tools, tassel forms, DMC Floche and other cotton threads, EdMar Brazilian embroidery and Japanese Bunka threads. Selection of period images on silks and other fabrics. Also publisher of over 60 books on needlework and costume and 3,000 titles on textiles and costume in English and foreign languages. Photo transfer service (images or documents to fabric) also available.

Catalog: $5.
Discounts: Wholesale available to needlework industry.

THE LAVENDER ROSE
P.O. Box 1365
Snohomish WA 98291-1365
Contact: M. Windsor Vest
Phone: (360)568-0867
E-mail: lavrose@gte.net
Website: http://home1.gte.net/lavrose/index.htm
Offers: Patterns and kits for Berlin work, blackwork, cutwork, drawnwork and lace making. All original designs. Also reprints of actual designs of the late 1800s.
Catalog: $2.
Phone Orders: Yes.
Mail Orders: Primarily mail order.
Accepts: no credit cards

LE FILET LINENS & LACES
610 Locust St.
Oak Harbor OH 43449
Contact: Mayetta Bradbury
Phone: (800)818-5495
Fax: (419)898-1369
Offers: Battenberg and crocheted doilies, trims, edgings, vests, collars, inserts, umbrellas, picture frames and boxes, stiffened battenberg and crocheted items, porcelain dolls. Craft books and supplies. Also kits and supplies to make battenberg lace by hand.
Catalog: 60 pages. $3 (includes many crafting suggestions).
Phone Orders: M-F, 10-5; Sat, 10-1 EST.
Mail Orders: Prepayment required. Orders are shipped promptly.
Discounts: Quantity discounts.
Accepts: MasterCard, Visa

THE MAGIC NEEDLE OF LIMERICK, MAINE
RR 2, Box 172
Limerick ME 04048
E-mail: jmmichlr@gwi.net
Offers: Crazy Quilting patterns, materials and packages. Silk ribbon patterns and supplies. Dover iron-on transfer books, foundation fabrics, a dyeing kit, punchneedle set and assorted other items. Swatch club specializes in high quality trims, threads and fabrics.
Catalog: $2. The Magic Needle Swatch Club is a bimonthly subscription service that is $8 for one year (6 issues).
Mail Orders: At above address.
Discounts: Swatch Club purchases are discounted.
Accepts: MasterCard, Visa

MAPLEWOOD CRAFTS
1 Maplewood Dr.
Hazleton PA 18201-9798
Contact: Pam Beber, vice-president of sales
Phone: (800)899-0134
Fax: (717)384-2500
Store Location: Outlet store for discontinued or overstock

merchandise. At above address. W-Sat, 10-4.
Offers: Beads, needlecraft, puzzles, ceramics, beaded crafts, memory album miscellaneous, plastic canvas, dollhouses, latch hook, glass etching, woodworking supplies and glues.
Catalog: 80 pages, color.
Phone Orders: M-F, 7:30 a.m.-11 p.m.; Sat, 8:30-5 EST.
Mail Orders: Ships worldwide. All orders shipped in 24 hours from 100,000 sq. ft. warehouse.
Discount: Sells wholesale to retail outlets. Minimum wholesale order $125.
Accepts: American Express, Discover, MasterCard, Visa

MARY MAXIM, INC.
P.O. Box 5019
2001 Holland Ave.
Port Huron MI 48061-5019
Phone: (810)987-2000 or (800)962-9504
Offers: Kits: quilting, cross-stitch, crewel, embroidery and others. Also offers cloth doll supplies, notions, sewing aids, threads, quilting frames and stands, holiday items, stencils, batting and fiberfill, pillow forms and other supplies, plus yarn kits and supplies, plastic canvas needlepoint kits, and beaded craft kits.
Catalog: Free. 72-page color.

NANCY'S NOTIONS
P.O. Box 683
Beaver Dam WI 53916-0683
Contact: Kathleen Hasson
Phone: (920)887-0391 or (800)833-0690
Fax: (920)887-2183 or (800)255-8119
Website: http://www.nancysnotions.com
Store Location: 333 Beichl Ave., Beaver Dam WI 53916. M-F, 9-5; W, 9-8; Sat, 9-4.
Offers: A source for unique sewing and quilting supplies and accessories, including thread for any type of plain or decorative stitching, specialty presser feet, hundreds of handy notions, important machine care tools, practical serger products and beautiful fabrics, plus educational videos and references from the Sewing With Nancy public television program. Nancy's Notions offers value priced products, staff-tested quality, guaranteed satisfaction, knowledgeable and friendly customer service and speedy delivery.
Catalog: Free.
Phone Orders: (800)833-0690.
Mail Orders: At P.O. Box.
Discounts: Sewing professionals, please call for details.
Accepts: Discover, MasterCard, Visa

NEWARK DRESSMAKER SUPPLY
Dept. CSS
P.O. Box 20730
Lehigh Valley PA 18002
Phone: (610)837-7500 or (800)736-6783
Fax: (610)837-9115
Offers: Needlecraft/sewing items. Threads: Swiss Metrosene, machine rayon, silk, Coats & Clark, elastic, cotton, upholstery, metallics, ribbon floss, overlocks and stretch nylon.

Also offers zippers (including doll-size), buckles, bow-tie clips, silk and dry flowers, ribbons, over 50 laces, metallics, bindings, tapes, elastics and buttons. Carries fabrics, appliqués, scissors, cutters, bridal items, veiling, flowers and others. Doll items: heads, eyes, stands and others. Also carries stencils, adhesives, paints and beads.

Catalog: Free.

Discounts: Quantity. Sells wholesale. Orders over $50 receive a 10% discount.

Accepts: Discover, MasterCard, Visa

NUSTYLE QUILTING FRAME CO., SUPPLIES

P.O. Box 61

Hwy. 52 W.

Stover MO 65078

Contact: Ruth Williams

Phone: (573)377-2244 or (800)821-7490

Fax: (573)377-2833

Store Location: 290 W. Fourth, Hwy. 52 W.

Offers: Long arm quilting machines and frames; hand quilting frames, different styles; large rolls Dacron and cotton-batt; Dacron thread for machine quilting and regular sewing, all colors; quilting books; all type of patterns for clothing, crafts, quilt rulers, cutting boards, cutters; all types of notions; full line of embroidery blocks and threads; over 4,000 bolts of fabrics, name brands.

Catalog: Yes.

Phone Orders: Yes.

Mail Orders: Ships nationwide, including Canada, AK and HI.

Discounts: Yes.

Accepts: Discover, MasterCard, Visa

PEDDLER'S WAGON

P.O. Box 109 CS

Lamar MO 64759-0109

Phone: (417)682-3734

Offers: Out-of-print preowned needlework and quilting books and magazines. Mail order only.

Catalog: Free book search. Send large SASE with inquiry. Next 3 catalogs in each category, $3 (refundable).

PERSONAL THREADS BOUTIQUE

8025 W. Dodge Rd.

Omaha NE 68114-3413

Contact: Carolyn Lewis

Phone: (402)391-7733

Fax: (402)391-0039

E-mail: carolyn@personalthreads.com

Website: http://www.personalthreads.com

Store Location: At above address. M-F, 9-6; Sat, 9-3 CST.

Offers: The finest knitting, weaving and needlecraft supplies. Hand-dyed wools, hand-painted needlepoint canvases, yarns, flosses, needles and crochet hooks, pattern books and looms. Colinette Tank; Dale, Plymouth, Annabell Fox, Amy Blatt, Caron, Classic Elite, Gloria Tracy, Prism, Nore, Muench and many more. On-line searchable catalog.

Catalog: Free quarterly newsletter/catalog (must be requested in writing).

Phone Orders: (800)306-7733. M-F, 9-6; Sat, 9-3 CST.

Mail Orders: Use form in catalog, or order on-line.

Discounts: Annual New Year's sale, 12/26-1/15, 20% off all merchandise.

Accepts: American Express, MasterCard, Visa

PILLOWS-N-PICTURES

P.O. Box 3438

Peoria IL 61612

Contact: Terry Rose

Phone: (800)297-1072 or (309)243-7157

Fax: (309)243-7157

E-mail: pillows-n-pictures@juno.com

Website: In the works.

Store Location: 12213 N. Woodcrest, Room F, Dunlap IL 61525. Other location: 3457 N. University, Suite 220, Peoria IL 61604.

Offers: Custom finishing, stitching, design, decorative home sewing, needlework supplies and kits, cross-stitch, embroidery, crewel, needlepoint, stumpwork, gold work and more. Antique reproduction needlework fabrics, handcrafted gifts, stumpwork box collection, gifts, custom-painted pet portraits, preowned book list and newsletter 2-3 times yearly.

Catalog: Yearly, $3 (nonrefundable). Free brochure.

Phone Orders: M-Sat, 9-6 CST.

Mail Orders: Will ship worldwide. Prepayment required. Allow 4-8 weeks for delivery.

Discounts: Wholesale to legitimate businesses. Frequent sales for retail.

Accepts: check, money order (US dollars, drawn on US banks)

SAX ARTS & CRAFTS

P.O. Box 510710

2405 Calhoun Rd.

New Berlin WI 53151

Phone: (414)784-6880

Offers: A variety of supplies (known brands), including a full line of weaving looms and aids, yarns, weaving kits, rug/craft yarns, embroidery/crewel threads, rug hook frames and aids, canvas, hoops, burlap and felt. Native American beading, beads, feathers, macrame, basketry and batik supplies, fabric paints, airbrush kits and inks, stencil films, trims, foam, stained glass kits, etching and beveled glass supplies and supplies for decoupage, jewelry making, leather, casting, plastics, wood and metalworking are also available.

Catalog: $5 (refundable).

Discounts: Quantity, sells wholesale to legitimate businesses.

SOURCE MARKETING, LTD.

600 E. 9th St.

Michigan City IN 46360

Phone: (219)873-1000

Fax: (219)872-9003

Offers: GlissenGloss metallic threads: subdued, antique,

shimmer or multi-ply sparkly metallics in a variety of colors for needlepoint, plastic canvas and cross-stitch.
Catalog: $1.
Accepts: MasterCard, Visa

STEMMER HOUSE PUBLISHERS, INC.
2627 Caves Rd.
Owings Mills MD 21117-2919
Contact: Barbara Holdridge
Phone: (410)363-3690
Fax: (410)363-8459
E-mail: stemmerhousepublishers@erols.com
Website: www.stemmer.com
Offers: The International Design Library: books featuring authentic designs of nearly every period and culture, from African to Victorian. Covers are in full color; interior designs are rendered in b&w fine line.
Catalog: 16 pages, illustrated.
Phone Orders: (800)676-7511.
Mail Orders: At above address. Shipments made throughout the world. Prepayment required. Allow 4-6 weeks for delivery.
Discounts: 1-4, 20%; 5-24, 42%; 25-99, 43%; 100-300, 44% to wholesale businesses.
Accepts: American Express, MasterCard, Visa

STUDIO WORD PROCESSING, LTD.
5010-50 Ave.
Camrose, Alberta T4V 0S5
Canada
Contact: Lois Larson
Phone: (403)672-5887
Fax: (403)672-9570
E-mail: swp@ccinet.ab.ca
Website: http://www.studioword.com
Store Location: At above address. M-F, 9-5:30; Sat, 9:30-12.
Offers: Software Directory for Fiber Artists, which details features and sources of 275-plus computer programs for weaving, knitting, quilting, sewing and needlework. Directory also includes artist profiles and sample printouts.
Catalog: 2-page flyer lists directory and computer training manuals.
Phone Orders: M-F, 9-5:30; Sat 9:30-12.
Mail Orders: Ship anywhere.
Discounts: Wholesale available.
Accepts: MasterCard, Visa

SUSAN'S FIBERSHOP
N250 Hwy. A
Columbus WI 53925
Contact: Susan McFarland
Phone: (920)623-4237
Fax: (920)623-0120
E-mail: susanfiber@internetwis.com
Store Location: Columbus WI location.
Offers: Books and classes. Spinning, weaving, knitting, crochet and glass fusing. Equipment for the above related items.
Catalog: Coming soon.

Phone Orders: (888)603-4237.
Mail Orders: Yes.
Accepts: American Express, Discover, MasterCard, Visa

TAYLOR'S CUTAWAYS & STUFF
2802 E. Washington St.
Urbana IL 61802-4660
E-mail: tcutaway@sprynet.com
Website: http://home.sprynet.com/sprynet/tcutaway
Offers: Fabric remnants sold by the pound: satin, velvet, cottons, velour, silk, polyester, fur, felt and others. Inexpensive soft toy patterns, precut shapes, calico, squares, lace, trims, buttons, doll and animal parts, eyes, potpourri fragrances, iron-on transfer books and quilting and crochet patterns. Empty teabaglets for packaging your own teas and coffee. Save by buying direct.
Catalog: $1.

THUMBELINA NEEDLEWORK
P.O. Box 1065
1685 Copenhagen Dr.
Solvang CA 93464
Contact: Brenda Knudsen
Phone: (805)688-4136 or (800)789-4136
Fax: (805)688-4136, 5:30 p.m.-9 a.m. PST
E-mail: info@thumbelina.com
Website: http://www.thumbelina.com/
Store Location: At above address.
Offers: Publications and kits from Denmark, including Oehlenschlager, Eva Rosentand, Danish Handcraft Guild and Permin. Full line of kits from major American needlework companies. Needlepoint canvases from Margot. SEG and Royal Paris. Fabrics, canvas, DMC cottons and wools for needlepoint and counted cross-stitch. Tatting books and supplies and collectors' thimbles. Bellpull hardware.
Catalog: Supply list upon request (emphasizes Danish items).
Phone Orders: M-F, 9-5 PST.
Mail Orders: Will ship to US, Canada, Europe, Middle East, Pacific Rim, Australia, New Zealand, Africa and South America.
Accepts: American Express, Discover, MasterCard, Visa

THE UNIQUE SPOOL
407 Corte Majorca
Vacaville CA 95688
Offers: African fabrics: cotton yardage, swatches and Australian fabrics. Also offers patterns for African wildlife vest (appliqué), Christmas quilt, wall hangings, placemats, caftans, long vest, yo-yo vest, skirts, cloth doll patterns and Christmas patterns. Tube threads and spool insert also available. Send SASE.

WELLSPRING GALLERY
P.O. Box 64429
Los Angeles CA 90064
Phone: (310)441-4204
Website: www.wellspringgallery.com

Offers: Line of art supplies and books for fiber artists.

Catalog: Call or send for color catalog.

WOODEN PORCH BOOKS

Rt. 1, Box 262

Middlebourne WV 26149

Phone: (304)386-4434

Fax: (304)386-4868

E-mail: woodenpo@interloc.com

Offers: Used and out-of-print books (fiber art and related categories): fashion, costume, sewing and dressmaking—garments, pattern design, historic ethnic costumes, fabric design, children's and tailoring. Needlework: beaded bags, embroidery, lace making, crochet, knitting, quilting, dyeing, needlepoint, smocking and others.

Catalog: Send $3 for next three catalogs: weaving, spinning and dyeing.

YLI CORP.

161 W. Main St.

Rock Hill SC 29730

Phone: (800)296-8139

Offers: Silk embroidery products, including ribbons in 185 colors, thread, floss, kits, patterns, needles and silk ribbon, embroidery videos and books. Also offers serging threads, including Wooly Nylon, Candleight metallic yarn, Pearl Crown Rayon, Designer-6, Jean Stitch and Success; metallic, monofilament and lingerie/bobbin thread. 100% cotton quilting thread.

Home Decorating

Also see most other categories where home accessories are listed.

A B C HOME DECORATIVE DISCOUNT FABRICS
126 W. 23rd St.
New York NY 10011
Phone: (212)414-1416
Fax: (212)243-4913
Store Location: At above address. M-F, 9:30-5:30; W, 9:30-7; Sat-Sun, 12-5.
Offers: Line of unique hard-to-find tapestries, upholstery, draperies, wall coverings and window treatments. All major brands carried. At huge discount prices! Plus closeouts. Custom reupholstery done. Call for further information.
Phone Orders: Yes.
Discounts: Wholesale and retail.
Accepts: MasterCard, Visa

DOBRY ENTERPRESS
Dept. CSSB
P.O. Box 112
Severna Park MD 21146
Phone: (410)437-0297
Fax: (410)937-9200
Offers: Instruction books on custom draperies, cloud shades, no-sew drapery swags and jabots.
Catalog: Free literature.
Discounts: Quantity; teachers and institutions; sells wholesale to legitimate businesses.
Accepts: Discover, MasterCard, Visa

ELECTRICAL CONNECTIONS, INC.
3704 Friendsview Dr.
Greensboro NC 27410
Contact: John Porter
Phone: (800)741-7329
Fax: (336)665-1705
E-mail: jporter176@aol.com
Offers: Lamp-making supplies, lamp cords, fiber drip candle covers, sockets, glass globes, lightbulbs, basket adapters, Mason jar lid adapters and many hard-to-find items.
Catalog: Free upon request.
Phone Orders: 24 hours a day, 7 days a week, 365 days a year.
Mail Orders: Will ship to US and Canada.
Discounts: Sells wholesale to legitimate business.
Accepts: MasterCard, Visa, C.O.D., net 30 with approved credit

FABRIC CENTER
P.O. Box 8212
484 Electric Ave.
Fitchburg MA 01420
Phone: (508)343-4402
Fax: (508)343-8139
Offers: Full line of home decorating fabrics.
Catalog: Free brochure. Catalog, $3.

FAIRFIELD PROCESSING CORP.
P.O. Box 1157
Danbury CT 06813-1157
Phone: (800)243-0989
Fax: (203)792-9710
E-mail: ffld.prcssng.corp@snet.net
Website: www.poly-fil.com
Offers: Fairfield Processing Corporation manufactures a complete line of high-quality products for the home sewing, quilt and craft industries. Poly-fil, Soft Touch and Crafters Choice brand fiberfill, batting and pillow form products are easy to use, available in many sizes and unconditionally guaranteed. New products include quilt pattern books, bumper batting and a chair cushion insert. Poly-fil is internationally available and accepted as the brand of excellence.
Catalog: Free.
Phone Orders: M-F, 8-5 EST.
Discounts: Sells wholesale to companies with tax ID number; 2-carton minimum.
Accepts: MasterCard, Visa

HANCOCK'S OF PADUCAH
(formerly Hancock Fabrics)
3841 Hinkleville Rd.
Paducah KY 42001
Contact: Justin Hancock
Phone: (800)845-8723
Store Location: Near Interstate 24, exit 4. Hwy. 60.
Offers: America's largest stock of quilting fabrics and notions. Also home decorating fabrics, drapery and upholstery fabrics. Store known worldwide. If you want fabric, this is the number one store in America to shop.
Catalog: Quilting fabric and home decorating.
Phone Orders: Yes.
Discounts: To legitimate business and full bolts.
Accepts: Discover, MasterCard, Visa

HOMESPUN FABRICS & DRAPERIES
P.O. Box 4315-CSS
Thousand Oaks CA 91359
Phone: (805)495-6392
Fax: (805)495-6392

E-mail: widefabric@aol.com
Website: http://members.aol.com/widefabric
Offers: 10-foot wide cotton fabrics—textured, washable and nontoxic. For seamless draperies, wall coverings, upholstery, slipcovers, tablecloths, bedspreads, crafts and more.
Catalog: Planning kit and fabric samples, $2.
Phone Orders: Yes.
Mail Orders: Prepayment required. Allow 7-10 business days for delivery.
Discounts: Factory pricing.
Accepts: MasterCard, Visa

INSTANT INTERIORS
P.O. Box 1793
Eugene OR 97440
Phone: (541)689-4608
Offers: Instant decoration how-to booklets: *Bed Covers, Easiest Furniture Covers, Fabric Space Makers, Table Toppings, Lampshades, Quickest Curtains* and *Pillows and Cushions.*
Catalog: Contact your dealer, or send SASE for catalog sheets.

THE LAMP SHOP
P.O. Box 3606
Concord NH 03302
Phone: (603)224-1603
Offers: Line of lampshade-making supplies and instruction books.
Catalog: $3.
Discounts: Sells wholesale.

MARLENE'S DECORATOR FABRICS
Dept. 2J
301 Beech St.
Hackensack NJ 07601
Contact: Kelly
Phone: (201)843-0844
Offers: Marlene's Decorator Fabrics has been selling upholstery, slipcovers and drapery goods since 1946, and can save you up to 60% on the list prices of fabrics by Ametex, Anju, Artmark, Paul Barrow, Berger, Covington, Greeff, Kasmir, Kaufman, Kravet, Ralph Lauren, Sanderson, Stout, Stroheim & Roman, Waverly/Schumacher Wesco and many others. Write or call for a price quote, or send SASE with a sample if you're not sure of the maufacturer or pattern. Specify the yardage needed and whether you're interested in upholstery, drapery or other decorator fabric.
Catalog: Free brochure. Send SASE.
Phone Orders: Minimum order is 4 yards retail, 15 yards wholesale.
Mail Orders: Prepayment required. Allow 3-4 weeks for delivery.
Discounts: 25-50% off.
Accepts: American Express, MasterCard, Visa, money order

ROLLERWALL, INC.
P.O. Box 757
Silver Spring MD 20918
Phone: (301)680-2510
Fax: (301)680-2513
E-mail: sales@rollerwall.com
Website: http://www.rollerwall.com
Offers: Embossed stencil rollers for wall patterns (florals, traditional, colonial and contemporary designs).
Catalog: Send for free information.

SHEFFIELD SCHOOL OF INTERIOR DESIGN
211 E. 43rd St.
New York NY 10017
Contact: Michael Baron
Phone: (212)661-7270, ext. 215
Fax: (212)867-8122
E-mail: sheff@mail.idt.net
Website: www.sheffield.edu
Store Location: At above address. M-F, 9-5.
Offers: Correspondence course in interior design. Videotapes, audiotapes and individual critique on audiotape by professional NY interior designers.
Catalog: Free.
Phone Orders: (800)445-7279. 24 hours.
Mail Orders: At above address.

SOUTHWEST DECORATIVES
191 Big Horn Ridge NE
Albuquerque NM 87122
Contact: Mary-Jo McCarthy
Phone: (505)856-9585
Fax: (505)856-7270
E-mail: swd@swdecoratives.com
Website: http://www.swdecoratives.com
Offers: Quilting, appliqué, clothing and craft patterns and kits, all with a Southwest theme. Also Southwest Christmas accessories, chile pepper lights, electric luminarias, cookie cutters and tree skirt and boot patterns and kits.
Catalog: 24 pages, b&w. $3.
Phone Orders: M-Sun, 9-9.
Mail Orders: We ship worldwide. We accept only US funds, credit cards only on international sales.
Discounts: Wholesale to quilt shops.
Accepts: MasterCard, Visa

VIKING FOLK ART PUBLICATIONS, INC.
301 16th Ave. SE
Waseca MN 56093
Contact: Jan Draheim
Phone: (507)835-8009
Fax: (507)835-8541
E-mail: bill@vikingpub.com
Website: www.viking-publications.com
Offers: Decorative painting instructional books. Wide range of subject matter from American, Norwegian, Russian, Bavarian and Spanish to Japanese folk art. Also available home decor, florals and landscape on canvas. High-quality color photos with well-written instructions and patterns.
Catalog: Available for asking.
Phone Orders: 8:30-5 CST.
Mail Orders: Ship worldwide.

Discounts: To distributors and legitimate retailers.
Accepts: American Express, MasterCard, Visa

THE WARM CO.
(formerly Warm Products, Inc.)
954 E. Union St.
Seattle WA 98122
Contact: Brandy Fisher
Phone: (800)234-9276
Fax: (206)320-0974
E-mail: brandy@warmcompany.com
Website: www.warmcompany.com
Offers: Warm Window insulated fabric, with 4 layers quilted together for energy saving. Warm & Natural needled cotton batting for quilts, crafts and wearable art, Steam-A-Seam fabric fusing web and soft and bright, needled polyester batting.
Catalog: Brochures and pricing available.

Discounts: Available for quantity wholesale orders.
Accepts: MasterCard, Visa

WITH HEART & HAND
258 Dedham St.
Norfolk MA 02056
Contact: Diane or Loretta
Phone: (508)384-5740
Fax: (508)384-5740
Store Location: Norfolk MA location.
Offers: Home furnishings: gifts, gourmet foods, cards, fabric, lighting and pottery.
Catalog: $5. Catalog and swatches, $12.
Phone Orders: Yes.
Mail Orders: At above address.
Discounts: Trade discount—fabric only.
Accepts: American Express, Discover, MasterCard, Visa

Knitting & Crochet

Also see General Needlecraft Supplies; Rug Making; Spinning & Weaving; Yarns; other related categories.

ALDEA'S ALMAR VIDEOS
(formerly Aldea's)
P.O. Box 667
Beaumont CA 92223
Phone: (909)845-5825
Offers: Machine knitting instructional videos by Alvina Murdaugh covering basics, converting hand to machine knitting, techniques, maintenance, tips, ribber techniques and gifts. Also offers a variety of clothing titles (coats, sweaters, dresses, skirts, pants and others).
Catalog: Send SASE for list.
Discounts: Sells wholesale.
Accepts: MasterCard, Visa

ALL BRANDS SEWING MACHINES
9789 Florida Blvd.
Baton Rouge LA 70815
Phone: (504)923-1285 or (800)SEWSERG
Fax: (800)866-1261 or (504)923-1261
E-mail sewserg@aol.com
Website: www.allbrands.com
Offers: Knitting machines: Brother, Knitking, Studio Singer, Elna Toyota Knitcraft and Bond/Baby Knit/Simplicity Bulkys. Also offers all machine accessories. Service contracts available. Sewing, embroidery and serger machines.
Catalog: Send SASE for brochures (specify product interest and price level).
Accepts: American Express, Discover, MasterCard, Visa

ANNIE'S ATTIC
1 Annie Lane
Big Sandy TX 75755
Contact: Customer service department
Phone: (903)636-4303 or (800)AT-ANNIE
Fax: (800)882-6643
E-mail: Coming soon.
Website: Coming soon.
Store Location: The Needlecraft Outlet, 701 W. Broadway, Big Sandy TX. M-F, 9-5; Sat, 10-5; Sun, 1-5.
Offers: Crochet kits/patterns: afghans, scarves/hats, slippers, buttons, bows, jewelry, rugs, doilies, bath and flower sets, potholders, layette items, baby outfits, sweaters, collars, fashion and other doll clothes, toys, baskets, others. Also offers plastic canvas kits, yarns, knitting and canvas accessories and instructional videos.

Catalog: Free. 40 pages.
Phone Orders: (800)LV-ANNIE.
Mail Orders: At Annie Lane address.
Discounts: Sells wholesale. Quantity discounts.
Accepts: American Express, Discover, MasterCard, Visa

ARKY ARKY CREATIONS
4300 Ashe Rd. #102
Bakersfield CA 93313
Contact: Kathy Sasser
Phone: (805)397-5488
Store Location: At above address.
Offers: Yarn, patterns, knitting and crochet supplies. We offer our own design series called the Crumpet and Tea Collection. A must for every knitter!
Catalog: Free brochure with #10 SASE.
Phone Orders: T-Sat, 10-3 PST.
Mail Orders: Will ship to US. Prepayment required. Allow 2-3 weeks for delivery.
Accepts: MasterCard, Visa

AUNTIE KNITS, INC.
212 Rock Rd.
Glen Rock NJ 07452-1707
Contact: Joyce
Phone: (201)447-1331
Store Location: At above address. T-F, 10-5:30; Sat, 11-5.
Offers: Yarns, old favorites and new by major companies. Special children's patterns, too!
Catalog: Flyers for children's sweaters.
Phone Orders: Yes.
Mail Orders: Will ship anywhere in US.
Accepts: American Express, Discover, MasterCard, Visa

BAGLADY PRESS, LLC
P.O. Box 2409
Evergreen CO 80437-2409
Contact: Jeff Williams
Phone: (303)670-2177
Fax: (303)670-2179
E-mail: baglady@baglady.com
Website: www.baglady.com
Offers: Beaded bag series of books, fine European purse frames, beads, #8 perle cotton thread, sizes 00-000000 knitting needles, fabric bag designs and charm.
Catalog: Free.
Phone Orders: (888)222-4523. M-F, 9-6.
Mail Orders: Retail orders. P&h, $5 per order US and Canada. US orders sent by Priority Mail.
Discounts: Wholesale discounts available to retail stores.
Accepts: MasterCard, Visa

BARE HILL STUDIOS/FIBER LOFT

P.O. Box 327
Rt. 111 (Post Office Bldg.)
Harvard MA 01451
Contact: Reba Maisel
Phone: (800)874-YARN
Fax: (978)456-8480
Store Location: At above address.
Offers: Natural fiber yarns for machine/hand crochet/knitting and weaving: Rowan, Tahki, Elite, Sirdar, Noro, Jaeger, Reynolds and more. Also offers mill ends and exotic fibers (silks, angoras and ribbons).
Catalog: Yarn samples, $5.25. Additional exotic fibers, ribbon, $2.75.
Phone Orders: Yes.
Mail Orders: At above address.
Discounts: Quantity discount.
Accepts: Discover, MasterCard, Visa, check

BARKIM, LTD.

47 W. Polk St., Suite 100
Chicago IL 60605
Phone: (773)548-2211 or (888)548-2211
Fax: (773)624-3380
E-mail: barkimltd@aol.com
Website: www.barkim.com
Offers: Yarns from New England, Canada, Norway and Iceland. Also offers Guernsey wool (England), Rowan kits and yarns, Shetland and Aran yarns and Jo Sharp yarn. Carries mini kits and other patterns.
Catalog: Catalog and yarn samples, $4 (refundable); send SASE for newsletter.
Accepts: American Express, Discover, MasterCard, Visa

CARA L. BERNHAUSER PRESENTS "TOMORROW'S HEIRLOOMS"

33-S Buckmanville Rd.
Newtown PA 18940
Contact: Cara
Phone: (215)598-7070
E-mail: caramark@dplus.net
Website: http://www.dplus.net/caramark/home.html
Store Location: At above address. By appointment only.
Offers: Passap, Brother, Bond, Studio and Knitking knitting machines. All your knitting supplies. Over 1,000 books in stock. Also videos, yarn and unique gadgets.
Catalog: Some information sheets for specific machine, book and video lists. Please see website for complete details.
Phone Orders: (800)813-6469. M-Sun, 7-7 EST. Leave a message if you miss me.
Mail Orders: We ship within 2 days from stock, 2 weeks for most special orders. E-mail requests most welcome! Call or fax credit card information (800)813-6469. We will keep on file for future E-mail/fax orders, if requested.
Discounts: We offer 10% to everyone on most items. Designers and production knitters contact me for details.

Accepts: Bravo, Discover, MasterCard, Novus, Visa, check (ship after check clears)

ANN C. BUSHFIELD

P.O. Box 187
Romney IN 47981
Offers: Preowned books: crochet, knitting and other needle-crafts.
Catalog: 100+ page list. $3 (refundable).

BUSYBODY'S

385 Lancaster Ave.
Haverford PA 19041
Contact: Jane Macan
Phone: (610)649-9477
Fax: (610)649-9477
Store Location: At above address. M-Sat, 10-4; closed Sat in June, July and August.
Catalog: Newsletter only.
Phone Orders: Yes.
Mail Orders: Yes.
Discounts: Yes.
Accepts: all major credit cards

CAROLINA HOMESPUN

190 Eastridge Rd.
Ridgeway VA 24148
Contact: Merike Saarniit, owner
Phone: (540)957-1174
Fax: (540)957-2644
E-mail: carolina_homespun@msn.com
Store Location: At above address. By appointment only.
Offers: Spinning, weaving, knitting, fibercrafting equipment and supplies including spinning wheels, looms, dyes, fibers, yarns, books, videos. Merike teaches workshops at the sheep farm and on the road.
Catalog: $2.
Phone Orders: Anytime (leave message if calling after hours).
Mail Orders: UPS shipper. Will ship anywhere.
Discounts: Some wholesale to legitimate businesses.
Accepts: American Express, Discover, MasterCard, Visa

CATHERINE KNITS

544 77th St.
Brooklyn NY 11209-3308
Contact: Catherine M. Conrad, president/owner
Phone: (718)836-6439
E-mail: tcs.conlol@worldnet.att.net
Website: http://www.angelfire.com/ny/catherineknits/index
.html
Offers: Robert Powell Lace shawl kits, Hazel Carter Lace shawl kits and other kits. Bamboo, ebony, rosewood, birch and addi needles. State-of-the-art knitting accessories. Classic and contemporary books.
Catalog: Free or $3 annual subscription.
Phone Orders: Yes.
Mail Orders: Yes.

Accepts: MasterCard, Visa, check, money order (payable in US dollars)

CHARLES PUBLISHING

P.O. Box 577
Weatherford TX 76086
Offers: Over 300 crochet, sewing and needlepoint patterns, including known characters and creatures, Roadrunner, Coyote, Country Bunny, King Lion, football player, cheerleader, dinosaurs and others.
Catalog: Send SASE for complete list.

COTTAGE CREATIONS

At the Farm on Deer Creek
Carpenter IA 50426-0070
Contact: Carol A. Anderson
Phone: (515)324-1280
Offers: Knitting patterns.
Catalog: Send large SASE for brochure.
Phone Orders: Yes.
Mail Orders: US, Canada and overseas.
Discounts: Yarn shops or catalogs.
Accepts: MasterCard, Visa, check, cash

COTTON CLOUDS

5176 S. 14th Ave.
Safford AZ 85546
Contact: Irene Schmoller
Phone: (800)322-7888
Fax: (520)428-6630
E-mail: cottonclouds@az.org
Website: cottonclouds.com
Store Location: Safford AZ location.
Offers: Cotton and cotton blend yarns as well as rayon chenille yarns. Cotton spinning fibers and spinning wheels, knitting machines, books and exclusively designed kits.
Catalog: $6.50 ($5 refundable).
Phone Orders: M-F, 8-3.
Mail Orders: Yes.
Discounts: Bulk discounts. Weekly specials.
Accepts: MasterCard, Visa

CREATIVE HANDCRAFTS

79 Elm St.
Danvers MA 01923
Phone: (978) 774-7770
Offers: Hand knitting yarns—variety of types and odd lots. Also offers books and Ashford wheels.

CUSTOM KNITS & MANUFACTURING

Rt. 1, Box 16
Lake Park MN 56554
Contact: Dorothy A. Rosman
Phone: (218)238-5882
Fax: (218)238-5882
E-mail: cknitmfg@tekstar.com
Website: www.cknitmfg.com
Store Location: Call for directions.
Offers: Many different yarn trees, G-Carriage Monitor and many other items from the machine knitter.
Catalog: Free.
Phone Orders: (800)726-4084. M-Sat, 8-6 CST.
Mail Orders: Ship as soon as possible.
Discounts: Wholesale to retailers.
Accepts: MasterCard, Visa

DESIGNS BY CYNTHIA WISE

122 Scoville Hill Rd.
Harwinton CT 06791
Contact: Cynthia Wise
Phone: (860)485-9489
Fax: (860)485-9489
E-mail: cynthia.yanok@snet.net
Website: http://pages.cthome.net/cynthiawisedesigns/
Store Location: At above address.
Offers: Natural fiber yarns, kits and original designs by Cynthia Wise. Clover bamboo needles and natural buttons.
Catalog: Catalog and color card, $2.
Mail Orders: Prepayment.
Accepts: check, money order

DIMITY

389 Dewey St.
Churchville NY 14428
Phone: (716)293-1468
E-mail: dimity@aol.com
Offers: Knitting machines by Brother, Knitking and Studio. Accessories, yarn and books also available. DesignaKnit dealer.
Catalog: Send SASE for mini catalog or E-mail.

DOLLETTES-N-THINGS

P.O. Box 1005
Herndon VA 20172-1005
Contact: Annette Roennow
Phone: (703)476-0632
Fax: (703)476-0632
E-mail: aroennow@dollette.com
Website: http://www.dollette.com
Offers: Knitting patterns for dolls, toys and bears. (Some kits are available.)
Catalog: $3.
Phone Orders: Yes.
Mail Orders: Yes.
Accepts: MasterCard, Visa

ECONO-CRAFT

280 N. Palermo Rd.
Palermo ME 04354-7102
Contact: Donna Paradis
Phone: (207)993-2774
Store Location: At above address.
Offers: Cotton spandex yarn for the knitting machine along with other closeout yarns. Also carries patterns and books.
Catalog: Brochure available. Send #10 SASE.
Phone Orders: M-Sat, 9-6 EST.
Mail Orders: To all countries.

Discounts: Quantity discounts.
Accepts: MasterCard, Visa

ELEGANT STITCHES

14125 S. Dixie Hwy., Suite H
Miami FL 33176
Contact: Jeanne Dykstra
Phone: (305)232-4005
E-mail: elegantst@aol.com
Website: http://members.aol.com/eleganst/
Store Location: At above address. Store hours vary with season. Please call ahead.
Offers: Yarns for knit and crochet: wools, cotton, acrylic, blend and hand-dyes. Wide selection of patterns and books. Classes for various levels of knitting, crochet and embroidery.
Catalog: Printout of website.
Phone Orders: During store hours.
Mail Orders: Anywhere in the world.
Accepts: MasterCard, Visa

THE FIBER STUDIO

P.O. Box 637 CSS
9 Foster Hill Rd.
Henniker NH 03242
Website: http://wwwconknet.com/fiberstudio
Offers: Natural yarns and equipment for knitting and crocheting (also for weaving and spinning) with cottons, wools and mohairs. Also offers closeout yarns.
Catalog: 60 yarn samples, $5; Equipment catalog, $1.
Discounts: Quantity.
Accepts: MasterCard, Visa

THE FIFTH STITCH

300 Clinton St.
Defiance OH 43512
Contact: Ellen Upp
Phone: (419)782-0991
E-mail: alelupp@defnet.com
Store Location: At above address. At corner of Second St.
Offers: Domestic and imported yarns from major manufacturers, Amy Blatt, Paton's, Tahki, Berroco, Wendy, Sirdar and many others.
Phone Orders: Yes.
Mail Orders: Yes.
Accepts: Discover, MasterCard, Visa

FINGERLAKES WOOLEN MILL

1193 Stewarts Corners Rd.
Genoa NY 13071
Phone: (800)441-WOOL
E-mail: yarn@fingerlakes-yarns.com
Website: http://www.fingerlakes-yarns.com
Offers: Fingerlake yarns: wools, angora/wool, silk/wool blends, brushed mohair and Unspun in 23 colors. Sock, stocking and sweater kits. Fulled kits for felting (hats, mittens, socks, tams and backpacks), spinning kits and roving and sheep pins also available.

Catalog: $4 for samples.
Discounts: Sells wholesale to yarn stores and professional designers.

FRY DESIGNS

515 NW Wide Ave.
Roseburg OR 97470
Offers: Over 250 original plastic-canvas needlepoint patterns: tissue box covers (Indians, animals, birds, flowers, lighthouse, snowmobile and others), toothpick holders (covered bridge, motor home, school, Dutch-windmill and others) and samplers (wedding, graduation, holidays and others). Over 75 original crochet patterns: tissue box covers (outhouse, barn, house, mailbox, church, doghouse and others) and 12″ pillows (ladybug, goose, Christmas and others).
Catalog: Send SASE for free lists.

GOSSAMER THREADS & MORE

575 Fourth Ave.
Durango CO 81301
Phone: (970)247-2822
Offers: Knitting yarns: wools, linens, cottons, silks, alpaca and cashmere, plus lace knitting items, including some hard to find. Send SASE.
Accepts: MasterCard, Visa

GRAND VIEW COUNTRY STORE

US Rt. 2
Randolph NH 03570
Phone: (800)898-5715 or (603)466-5715
Offers: Hundreds of yarns, original knitting kits and patterns. Also offers a line of wool yarn from our own sheep. Holds "Weekend Knit-Ins."
Catalog: Call or write for newsletter containing a free pattern. $3 one-time charge (free after ordering).

THE HILL KNITTERY, INC.

10720 Yonge St.
Richmond Hill, Ontario L4C 3C9
Canada
Contact: Bev Nimon
Phone: (905)770-4341
Fax: (905)770-8701
E-mail: dnimon@idirect.com
Store Location: M-Sat, 10-6.
Offers: Wide range of imported natural fiber yarns, patterns and books and accessories. Excellent lessons and workshops provided.
Phone Orders: Yes.
Mail Orders: We will ship Canada or US on prepaid orders.
Accepts: Interac, MasterCard, Visa

IDLE HANDS

P.O. Box 761
Walpole MA 02081
Contact: Lisa McFetridge
Phone: (508)359-5432
E-mail: lisagmc@aol.com
Offers: Infant, children, adult and doll knitting patterns.

Catalog: Current color flyers available.
Phone Orders: M-S, 8-8 EST.
Mail Orders: Will ship to US and Canada. US funds only.
Discounts: Wholesale only. Volume and prepayment discounts available.
Accepts: check

IMAGIKNIT 2000

3493 Bayou Rd.
Rt. 3
Orillia, Ontario L3V 6H3
Canada
Contact: Ruth Humphreys
Phone: (705)689-8676 or (800)318-9426
Fax: (705)689-9851
E-mail: imagiknit@muskoka.net
Website: www.muskoka.net/~imagiknit
Store Location: At above address. Th-Sat mornings.
Offers: Quality yarn books and needles and kits: Rowan, Koigu, Mission Falls, Patons and Imagiknit designs.
Catalog: Newsletter twice a year.
Phone Orders: (800)318-9426.
Mail Orders: Ship anywhere in Canada and US by post.
Discounts: To order by E-mail and knitting guild members.
Accepts: MasterCard, Visa

JANKNITS

1500 Cohagen Rd.
Ingomar MT 59039
Contact: Janet Mysse
Phone: (406)354-6621
Fax: (406)354-6721
E-mail: janknits@midrivers.com
Website: montanaroundup.com
Offers: Line of knitting books by Janet Mysse, including *Affordable Furs*, featuring working with fur and leather. Also *The Classics*, *Fisherman Knits*, and *Cabbage Soup* for soft sculptured dolls. A line of yarns is also available. Send SASE.
Phone Orders: Yes.
Mail Orders: Yes.
Discounts: Sells wholesale.
Accepts: MasterCard, Visa

KNIT KNACK SHOP, INC.

Rt. 3, Box 104
Peru IN 46970
Contact: Harold or Charlene Shafer
Phone: (765)985-3164
Fax: (888)648-3902
E-mail: knitshop@netusal.net
Website: www.knitknackshop.com
Store Location: Peru IN location.
Offers: Machine knitting yarns, knitting machines, Hague Linkens, machine knitting books and machine knitting assembly.
Catalog: Books and yarns.
Phone Orders: M-F.
Mail Orders: Priority Mail and UPS.

Discounts: Sells wholesale in some items.
Accepts: Discover, MasterCard, Visa

KNIT 'N KNEEDLE

722 W. Center
Duncanville TX 75116-4568
Contact: Judi Anne Murphy
Phone: (972)296-4008
Fax: (972)298-1944
E-mail: knk1944@aol.com
Website: http://members.aol.com/knk1944
Offers: Complete line of hand/machine yarns, supplies and accessories. Also crochet, cross-stitch and latch hook supplies. Classes in all areas of knitting/crochet.
Catalog: In progress. In addition to a quarterly newsletter (we have a monthly E-newsletter).
Phone Orders: Yes.
Mail Orders: Yes.
Discounts: TKGA or knitting/crochet guilds.
Accepts: American Express, Discover, MasterCard, Visa

KNITTING TRADITIONS

P.O. Box 421
Delta PA 17314
Contact: Beth Brown-Reinsel
Phone: (717)456-7950
E-mail: knittradit@aol.com
Website: http://members.aol.com/knittradit
Offers: British-made yarns, patterns, books, knitting accessories and kits.
Catalog: Catalog and yarn samples, $5.
Phone Orders: M-F, 9-5 EST.
Mail Orders: Will ship to US and Canada. Prepayment required.
Accepts: Discover, MasterCard, Visa

KRUH KNITS, MERCHANTS TO THE MACHINE KNITTER

P.O. Box 1587
Avon CT 06001
Phone: (860)651-4353
Offers: Knitting machines and machine accessories, computer programs, videotapes and electronic patterns. Also offers finishing tools, furniture, lamps, aids, videos, yarn winders, motors, gauge helps, punch cards, ravel cords and sewing aids. Carries a full line of yarns. Offers Frequent Buyer's Club and Video Rental Club.
Catalog: 168 pages. $5. Includes discount coupons.

JEAN LAMPE-DESIGNS IN FIBERS

1293 NW Wall St. #1501
Bend OR 97701
Offers: Luxury hand-spun yarns for socks and sweaters: Snug Buggies knit kits for children's slippers; minifulling boards for felting. Also offers custom-made, mini-yarn swifts of cherry wood.
Catalog: Send #10 SASE.

LION BRAND YARN CO.

34 W. 15th St.
New York NY 10011
Contact: Ilana Rabinowitz
Phone: (212)243-8995
Fax: (212)627-8154
E-mail: lionyarn@aol.com
Website: www.lionbrand.com
Offers: Yarn, needles, hooks, kits and accessories.
Catalog: (800)258-9276.
Phone Orders: (800)258-9276.
Mail Orders: At above address.
Discounts: Sells wholesale to legitimate businesses.
Accepts: MasterCard, Visa, check, money order

THE MANNINGS

P.O. Box 687
East Berlin PA 17316
Contact: Carol J. Woolcock
Phone: (717)624-2223
E-mail: mannings@sun-link.com
Website: http://www.the-mannings.com
Store Location: 1132 Green Ridge Rd., East Berlin PA 17316.
Offers: Yarns of most major manufacturers, mill ends and books. Also offers spinning and weaving products, knitting yarns, books and needles.
Catalog: Catalog and yarn style card, $2.50.
Phone Orders: M-F, 9-4:30 EST.
Mail Orders: Ship worldwide. Prepayment required.
Accepts: Discover, MasterCard, Visa

MIZ BEARS CREATIONS

2248 Obispo Ave. #206
Signal Hill CA 90806
Contact: Nancy Long
Phone: (562)498-7168 or (800)774-9988
Fax: (562)494-6795
E-mail: mizbearsakanancylong@worldnet.att.net
Store Location: At above address. M-F, 9-6 PST.
Offers: Complete line of Patarnayan Persian yarn in twist braids, Red Heart precut rug yarn, knit patterns, crochet patterns, complete clover needle assortments, DMC Floss, Erica Wilson Persian yarns, assorted hand-painted canvas and afghan kits (knit and crochet).
Catalog: $2 (refundable).
Phone Orders: M-F, 9-6 PST.
Mail Orders: Will ship to US, Canada and US territories. Prepayment required at time of order. Allow 4-7 days for shipping.
Discounts: Wholesale to legitimate business with proper identification.
Accepts: Discover, MasterCard, Visa

MOUNTAIN COLORS YARN

P.O. Box 156
Corvallis MT 59828
Contact: Leslie Taylor

Phone: (406)777-3377
Fax: (406)777-7313
E-mail: redfox@bitterroot.net
Store Location: 4072 Eastside Hwy., Stevensville MT 59870. In the Creamery Bldg.
Offers: Hand-painted yarns, including multicolored wool, mohair and novelty in 26 different colors. Patterns and kits for assorted sweaters, vests, socks, hats, mittens and more.
Catalog: Free. Catalog and color cards, $7.
Phone Orders: M-F, 9-3.
Mail Orders: Ship to US and Canada.
Discounts: Sell wholesale to legitimate businesses.
Accepts: MasterCard, Visa

N.S.D. PRODUCTS

P.O. Box 880
Brandon MS 39043
Phone: (601)825-6831 or (800)514-9210
Offers: Camel crochet (uses crochet hooks but looks like knitting)—wooden hooks, needles, instruction patterns and books.
Catalog: Free catalog request line. Call (800)524-9210.
Discounts: Sells wholesale.
Accepts: Discover, MasterCard, Visa

THE NEEDLE ARTS BOOK SHOPPE

95 Watch Hill Rd.
King City, Ontario L7B 1K1
Canada
Contact: Marsha White
Phone: (905)833-3745
Fax: (905)833-9069 or (888)860-3338
E-mail: needles@interlog.com
Website: http://www.interlog.com/~needles
Offers: Specializing in knitting books: traditional, ethnic, designer knits, reference and instruction.
Catalog: 28-page pamphlet, free.
Phone Orders: M-F, 9-5 EST.
Mail Orders: Ship to US and Canada plus international.
Accepts: Visa

NORDIC FIBER ARTS

4 Cutts Rd.
Durham NH 03824
Contact: Debbie Gremlitz
Phone: (603)868-1196
Fax: Coming soon.
E-mail: Coming soon.
Website: Future plans.
Offers: Largest selection of Norwegian Rauma yarns in US. Novi knitting needles from Norway, imported pewter buttons and clasps, embroidered bands, books, gifts and accessories. Traditional and original designs.
Catalog: Free.
Phone Orders: M-Sat, 9-9 EST.
Mail Orders: Will ship to Canada and other countries. Orders shipped within 24 hours of receipt.

Accepts: MasterCard, Visa, check, money order, cash (all in US funds)

PATTERNWORKS

P.O. Box 1690
Poughkeepsie NY 12601
Contact: Linda Skolnik
Phone: (914)462-8000
Fax: (914)462-8074
E-mail: knit@patternworks.com
Website: www.patternworks.com
Store Location: 36A Southgate Dr., Poughkeepsie NY 12601 (¼ mile off Rt. 9).
Offers: World's largest selection of knitting supplies—yarns, tools, books, software and videos. Also buttons, needlepoint, tatting and spinning supplies.
Catalog: 96 pages, full color.
Phone Orders: (800)438-5464.
Mail Orders: At P.O. Box.
Accepts: American Express, Discover, MasterCard, Visa

RAM WOOLS

143 Smith St.
Winnipeg, Manitoba R3C 1J5
Canada
Contact: I. Gaspard
Phone: (204)942-2797
Fax: (204)947-0024
E-mail: ram@gaspard.ca
Website: http://www.gaspard.ca/ramwools.htm
Store Location: At above address. 10-5:30 M-Sat.
Offers: Retail yarn sales, kits, patterns, books and all hand-knitting related accessories. Classes, workshops, fashion shows, ready-made handknit sweaters. Catalog sales.
Catalog: 40 pages, full color. Free twice a year.
Phone Orders: (800)263-8002. M-Sat, 10-4:30.
Mail Orders: Yes. Ship within Canada and US.
Discounts: Special promotions will be advertised.
Accepts: MasterCard, Visa, check (prepayment)

RHEA DESIGN

1503 First Concession
Athelstan, Quebec J0S 1A0
Canada
Contact: Susan Ostrovsky or Robert Wilson
Phone: (450)264-2089
Fax: (450)264-2089
E-mail: rhea@rocler.qc.ca
Website: http://www.rocler.qc.ca/rhea
Offers: Select mohair yarns and knitting kits.
Catalog: Knitting kits. Mohair yarn and patterns.
Phone Orders: Yes.
Mail Orders: Will ship to US and Canada.
Discounts: Wholesale orders with discounts available.
Accepts: MasterCard, Visa

ROCLITH CREATIONS

HC 30, Box 4A
Arthur WV 26816
Phone: (800)240-5484
Offers: Keyto Knitlite knitting machine light, adjustable clamp-on, with triphosphor fluorescent tube the length of machine with output the equivalent to a 250W incandescent bulb. Call or send SASE.

SALT SPRING ISLAND FIBRE STUDIOS

121 Mountain Rd.
Salt Spring Island, British Columbia V0K 1T8
Canada
Contact: Mary Padden or Pat Daniel
Phone: (250)653-4033
Fax: (250)537-9930
E-mail: susanb@islandnet.com
Website: Under construction.
Store Location: 7 studios on Salt Spring. Call to arrange visit.
Offers: Alpaca, mohair, llama wool yarns, raw fleece and rovings. Also knitting patterns, tools and knit kits. Custom spinning, dyeing and weaving.
Catalog: $4.
Phone Orders: M-F, 9-5 PST.
Mail Orders: Will ship anywhere the post goes. Allow 6 weeks for delivery.
Accepts: MasterCard, money order

SCHOOL PRODUCTS CO., INC.

1201 Broadway
New York NY 10001
Contact: Berta Karapetyan
Phone: (212)679-3516
Fax: (212)679-3519
E-mail: berta@schoolproducts.com
Website: www.schoolproducts.com
Store Location: At above address. Between 28th and 29th Streets.
Offers: Knitting machines, yarns, weaving looms, books, videos and knitting software.
Catalog: Hand knitting and hand weaving, $2.
Phone Orders: (800)847-4127.
Mail Orders: School products. At above address.
Discounts: Students.
Accepts: American Express, MasterCard, Visa

SCHOOLHOUSE PRESS

6899 Cary Bluff
Pittsville WI 54466
Contact: Meg Swansen
Phone: (715)884-2799
Fax: (715)884-2829
Offers: Books, wool, videos, needles, buttons and scores of items for hand knitters. Since 1959.
Catalog: $5 for samples of 13 types of wool plus catalog.
Phone Orders: (800)YOU-KNIT.
Mail Orders: At above address.

Discounts: To wholesalers.
Accepts: Discover, MasterCard, Visa

SEW-KNIT DISTRIBUTORS
9789 Florida St.
Baton Rouge LA 70815
Phone: (504)923-1260 or (800)BUY-KNIT
Fax: (800)866-1261 or (504)923-1261
E-mail: sewserg@aol.com
Website: www.sewserg.com
Offers: Knitting machines and accessories by Brother, Knitking and Studio Singer. Also offers videotapes, ribbers, winders, hobbies, laces, hand punches, transfers, strippers, tools, bed extensions, Dazor lamp, tilt stand metal, Sussman irons, Jiffy steamers, Baby Lock sergers, Read pleaters and Stanley pleaters. Carries dress forms and blocking cloth.
Catalog: Send SASE for accessory price lists and product brochures. On-line catalog.
Accepts: American Express, Discover, MasterCard, Visa

SHELRIDGE FARM
RR 2
Ariss, Ontario N0B 1B0
Canada
Contact: Buffy Taylor
Phone: (519)846-9662
E-mail: btaylor@shelridge.com
Website: http://www.shelridge.com
Store Location: At above address.
Offers: Wool, wool/cotton and wool/silk knitting yarns, custom designed knitting kits, turbo knitting needles and accessories, books, sheep paraphernalia.
Catalog: See website.
Phone Orders: Anytime.
Mail Orders: Will ship anywhere.
Accepts: MasterCard, Visa

SHIRLEY'S DIST.
(formerly By Shirley McKibben)
3720 Hood Court
Turlock CA 95382
Contact: Shirley McKibben
Phone: (209)668-0550
Store Location: At above address.
Offers: Machine knitting instructional videos by Shirley McKibben (5) and others, including repair for Toyota machines.
Catalog: Send SASE for list.

SHIRRÉT
P.O. Box 1338-CSS
Madison CT 06443
Contact: Lady McCrady
Phone: (888)4-SHIRRET
Fax: (203)245-7935
E-mail: info@shirret.com
Website: www.shirret.com
Offers: Shirrét combines shirring and crochet to make luxurious museum-quality rugs with rich colors and patterns. Recycled fabrics—old clothes—are cut easily and look like new when gathered on a needle and double-crocheted row upon row. *The Art of Shirrét* book of easy directions and patterns is available, as are the special Shirrét needle, Shirrét cord, marking gauge and pins, spindle, labels and starting fabric. Video available for groups.
Catalog: Big color poster with 13 Shirrét rugs, $1. Free price list.
Phone Orders: Yes.
Mail Orders: We ship worldwide. See price list.
Discounts: Wholesale available to teachers and shops.
Accepts: MasterCard, Visa, check, money order

SKACEL COLLECTION, INC.
P.O. Box 88110
Seattle WA 98138-2110
Phone: (253)854-2710
Fax: (253)854-2571
Offers: Fine European knitting yarns, crochet yarn, Peter Gregory knitting patterns and the Addi Turbo needles.
Phone Orders: M-F, 7:30-5 PST.
Mail Oders: US and Canada.
Discounts: We sell wholesale only (no retail) to legitimate businesses.
Accepts: MasterCard, Visa

SPIN CRAFT
P.O. Box 327
Salmon ID 83467
Contact: Connie Delaney
Phone: (208)756-3076
Fax: (208)756-3076
E-mail: spincraft@aol.com
Store Location: 300 Monroe St., Salmon ID 83467.
Offers: Knitting, crochet and weaving patterns for hand-spun or exotic yarns. Knit-to-Fit patterns include easy calculations for any size from any yarn.
Catalog: Free. Call.
Mail Orders: At P.O. Box. Quick response.
Discounts: Buy 5 patterns, get 1 free.
Accepts: check, money order

STEPHANIE'S STUDIO & YARN
1637 Appian Rd.
Bybee TN 37713
Contact: Bill or Stephanie Widmann
Phone: (423)623-1986 or (800)323-9411
Fax: (423)623-9565
E-mail: yarn@planetc.com
Website: http://members.aol.com/dsgneryarn
Store Location: At above address. M-F, 8:30-5.
Offers: Cone yarns for machine knitting, weaving, crocheting, hand knitting and crafts. Also acrylics, cottons, blends and metallic yarns. Stephanie's Yarn Club $14 a year. Receive yarn sample catalog, patterns, quarterly newsletter, 5% off regular prices, sales and toll-free number.
Catalog: Stephanie's Yarn Club includes catalog.

Phone Orders: Yes.
Mail Orders: Ship UPS.
Discounts: Below wholesale prices every day. Sales often.
Accepts: Discover, MasterCard, Visa, check, money order

TD CREATIONS
421 Horn Ave. S.
Moorhead MN 56560
Phone: (218)236-7987
Offers: Crochet patterns for 15″ doll bodies and 15″ fashion dolls: old-fashioned dresses and matching hats in ruffled, striped, hoop or straight styles with a lacy look.
Catalog: Send SASE for list.
Accepts: MasterCard, Visa

TESS' DESIGNER YARNS
33 Strawberry Point
Stenben ME 04680
Phone: (207)546-2483 or (800)321-TESS
Offers: Designer yarns and silk fabrics, including crepe de chine, china and broadcloth silk, raw, suede charmeuse and dyed-to-match yarns. Send SASE for information.

THREE KITTENS YARN SHOPPE
805 Sibley Memorial Hwy.
St. Paul MN 55118
Contact: Karen
Phone: (651)457-4969 or (800)489-4969
Store Location: Diamond Jim's Mall, at above address.
Offers: Complete selection of yarns, patterns, needles, notions, hand-painted needlepoint canvases. Rainbow Gallery, Caron Collection Overdyed from Needle Necessities, DMC, fiskers, blank canvas, patterns, counted cross-stitch books, linens, finishing accessories, Hardanger, Brazilian embroidery, tatting supplies, huck weaving.
Catalog: 20 pages. No charge.
Phone Orders: M-Sat, regular hours.
Mail Orders: Prepayment required. Will ship anywhere.
Accepts: Discover, MasterCard, Visa

BONNIE TRIOLA YARNS
343 E. Gore Rd.
Erie PA 16509
Contact: Bonnie Triola
Phone: (814)825-7821
Fax: (814)824-5418
E-mail: btriola@moose.erie.net
Website: http://moose.erie.net/~btriola
Offers: Cone yarn for machine knitters, weavers and crafters. Wholesale and retail. Specializes in high-quality designer closeouts at fantastic prices.
Catalog: $10.
Phone Orders: Yes.
Mail Orders: Yes.
Discounts: Yes.
Accepts: MasterCard, Visa, check

THE WEAVER'S LOFT
P.O. Box 13
308 S. Pennsylvania Ave.
Centre Hall PA 16828
Contact: Molly Mahaffy
Phone: (800)693-7242 or (814)364-1433
E-mail: yarnshop@aol.com
Website: www.shopsite.com/yarnshop
Store Location: At above address. T-Sat, 10-6.
Offers: Full line of knitting and weaving yarns and equipment. Also spinning supplies.
Catalog: Free. $18 yarn sample set (partially refundable).
Phone Orders: T-Sat, 10-6 EST.
Mail Orders: Both domestic and foreign. Orders mailed within 3 days.
Discounts: Wholesales Ann Grout drop spindles and Jamieson & Smith Shetland wool to legitimate shops.
Accepts: Discover, MasterCard, Visa

WHIPPLETREE YARN & GIFTS
3504 Chicago Dr.
Hudsonville MI 49426
Phone: (616)664-4487
Offers: Wide variety of yarns. Also books and supplies for knitters and crocheters.

THE WOOL CONNECTION
34 E. Main St.
Avon CT 06001
Contact: Phyllis
Phone: (860)678-1710
Fax: (860)677-7039
E-mail: wool@tiac.net
Website: woolconnection.com
Store Location: At above address.
Offers: Yarns, books, buttons, kids' craft kits, oriental rug making and needlepoint—complete finishing for needlepoint.
Catalog: 36 pages, full color.
Phone Orders: (800)933-9665.
Mail Orders: At above address.
Accepts: Discover, MasterCard, Visa

THE WOOLY WEST
1417 S. 1100 E.
Salt Lake City UT 84105
Contact: Nancy Bush
Phone: (801)487-9378
E-mail: woolywest@sisna.com
Store Location: At above address. M-S, 10-6.
Offers: Fine selection of natural fiber for knitters. Also patterns, needles, buttons and other accessories for knitting.
Catalog: Yes.
Phone Orders: M-S, 10-6 MST.
Mail Orders: Yes.
Accepts: American Express, MasterCard, Visa

YARN BARN

930 Massachusetts St.
Lawrence KS 66044
Contact: Susan Bateman
Phone: (785)842-4333 or (800)468-0035
Fax: (785)842-0794
E-mail: yarnbarn@idir.net.
Website: www.yarnbarn-ks.com
Store Location: At above address. 7 days a week.
Offers: Large selection of knitting and weaving yarns with supplies and equipment to cover those areas as well as spinning and dyeing, rug braiding and needlepoint. Hundreds of books covering most textile arts. Over 180 videos on same.
Catalog: 3 free options: (1) knitting and crochet (2) spinning equipment and (3) videos.
Phone Orders: (800)468-0035. M-Sat, 9:30-5:30 CST.
Mail Orders: Any location. Prepayment please.
Discounts: Quantity discounts on yarns and fibers. Looms and spinning wheels competitively priced.
Accepts: Discover, MasterCard, Visa, check, money order

THE YARN BASKET

150 Falling Spring Rd.
Chambersburg PA 17201
Contact: Sue Sollenberger
Phone: (717)263-3236
Store Location: I-81, exit 6 and Rt. 30, behind Shoney's.
Offers: Knitting and crochet yarns, patterns and accessories. Needlepoint yarns and accessories. Cross-stitch, ribbon embroidery and crewel classes.
Phone Orders: (888)YRN-BSKT.
Mail Orders: Will ship UPS, Priority Mail and regular mail.
Accepts: Discover, MasterCard, Visa

YARN EXPRESSIONS

7914 S. Memorial Pkwy.
Huntsville AL 35802
Contact: Meg Manning
Phone: (256)881-0260
Fax: (256)880-8269
E-mail: knit@yarnexpressions.com
Website: www.yarnexpressions.com
Store Location: Village Center on South Memorial Parkway, between Byrd Spring Rd. and Charlotte Dr.
Offers: Wide selection of materials for hand knitters and crocheters.
Catalog: Quarterly newsletter available, free.
Phone Orders: (800)283-8409.
Mail Orders: Will ship to US and Canada. Credit card or prepayment by check required.
Accepts: Discover, MasterCard, Visa, check

YARN-IT-ALL

1487 Sumneytown Pike
Lansdale PA 19446
Phone: (215)362-3300
Fax: (215)412-3656
Store Location: At above address. Call for appointment.
Offers: Brother knitting machines—electronic fine needle, bulky punch card and all accessories. Also offers Brother stands/tables and accessories. Yarns: Sunray, Mayflower, JaggerSpun, Bramwell, Phentex, Millor and others. Videos, patterns and books are also available.
Catalog: Free.
Discounts: Quantity.
Accepts: MasterCard, Visa

THE YARN SHOP AND FIBRES

549 Main St.
Laconia NH 03246
Contact: Ellen or Ely
Phone: (603)528-1221 or (800)375-1221
E-mail: yarnshop@cyberportal.net
Website: www.cyberportal.net/yarnshop
Store Location: At above address.
Offers: Full range of yarns, classes, books, spinning equipment and supplies, cross-stitch charts, floss and fabric.
Phone Orders: Yes.
Mail Orders: Yes.
Accepts: American Express, Discover, MasterCard, Visa

Knotting

Also see General Needlecraft Supplies; Knitting & Crochet; Yarns; other related categories.

ALCON BRAID

(formerly Al Con Enterprises)
P.O. Box 429
Hickory NC 28603
Phone: (800)523-4371
Fax: (704)328-1700
E-mail: sandra@griffinshine.com
Offers: Alcon Brand macrame braid/cord—full line of colors (3.5mm and 6/8mm). Also offers patterns, splicing kit and handy hooks.
Catalog: Free catalog and sample.
Discounts: Quantity. Sells wholesale.

BEGGAR'S LACE, INC.

P.O. Box 481223
Denver CO 80248
Contact: Joan Kehrer
Phone: (303)233-2600
Fax: (303)235-0356
E-mail: lacelady@rmii.com
Store Location: By appointment only.
Offers: Supplies to make lace: shuttles, bobbins, fine threads, books, needles and more.
Catalog: $2 (refundable).
Phone Orders: Yes.
Mail Orders: Yes.
Accepts: Discover, MasterCard, Visa, check, money order

BRIAN'S CRAFTS UNLIMITED

Dept. CSS
P.O. Box 731046
Ormond Beach FL 32173-1046
Contact: Judy Oppenheimer
Phone: (904)672-2726
Fax: (904)760-9246
E-mail: bricrafts@aol.com
Offers: Doilies, muslin dolls and animals, ribbon roses, hats, glue guns, wood items, mini brooms, hair clips, plastic fillable ornaments, fused pearls, doll hair, bargain grab bags and more. Also we can special order many items. We are the mail-order source for the following: Candle Magic, Wonder Bow supplies, Bedazzler studs and rhinestones and Lap Weaving Looms.
Catalog: Sale flyers and brochures only. Send long SASE and specify interest (outside US send $1).

Phone Orders: M-F, 9-6 EST.
Mail Orders: Shipped worldwide. Outside continental US must use credit card.
Discounts: Quantity discounts available.
Accepts: Discover, MasterCard, Visa

HOUSE OF CRAFTS & STUFF, INC.

5157 Gall Blvd.
Zephyrhills FL 33541
Contact: Harold J. Pile Jr.
Phone: (813)782-0223
Fax: (813)780-8700
Store Location: At above address.
Offers: Beads, books, macrame, styrofoam, art supplies, doll supplies, needle supplies, plastic canvas, jewelry supplies, chenille, paints and all the basics.
Catalog: $2.
Phone Orders: Yes.
Mail Orders: At above address.
Accepts: MasterCard, Visa

THE LAVENDER ROSE

P.O. Box 1365
Snohomish WA 98291-1365
Contact: M. Windsor Vest
Phone: (360)568-0867
E-mail: lavrose@gte.net
Website: http://home1.gte.net/lavrose/index.htm
Offers: Patterns and kits for Berlin work, blackwork, cutwork, drawn work and lace making. All original designs. Also reprints of actual designs of late 1800s.
Catalog: $2.
Phone Orders: Yes.
Mail Orders: Primarily mail order.
Accepts: no credit cards

LE FILET LINENS & LACES

610 Locust St.
Oak Harbor OH 43449
Contact: Mayetta Bradbury
Phone: (800)818-5495
Fax: (419)898-1369
Offers: Battenberg and crocheted doilies, trims, edgings, vests, collars, inserts, umbrellas, picture frames and boxes. Stiffened battenberg and crocheted items. Porcelain dolls, craft books and supplies. Also kits and supplies to make battenberg lace by hand.
Catalog: 60 pages. $3 (includes many crafting suggestions).
Phone Orders: M-F, 10-5; Sat, 10-1 EST.
Mail Orders: Prepayment required. Orders are shipped promptly.

Discounts: Quantity discounts.
Accepts: MasterCard, Visa

MOONRISE
2804 Fretz Valley Rd.
Perkasie PA 18944-4033
Contact: Sandy Terp
Phone: (215)795-0345
Fax: (215)795-0345
E-mail: sandy_at_moonrise@juno.com
Store Location: At above address.
Offers: Hand knitting books, tools, design work; kits, thread and yarn for lace knitting.
Catalog: 8 pages, b&w. No charge.
Phone Orders: Must be established customer or prepay.
Mail Orders: Anywhere if payment made as below. Orders go out same week.
Discounts: Most books. Wholesale only on self-published books (30%).
Accepts: check, US money order, international postal money order, no foreign check, no credit cards

THE OHIO HEMPERY, INC.
P.O. Box 18
Guysville OH 45736
Contact: D. Daniels
Phone: (800)BUY-HEMP
Fax: (740)662-6445
E-mail: hempery@hempery.com
Website: www.hempery.com
Offers: Hemp products, including twine, webbing rope, fabric, paper, raw fiber materials, oils, seeds, books, accessories, clothing and others.
Catalog: Free retail catalog.
Phone Orders: M-F, 8-8; Sat, 9-5 EST.
Mail Orders: Standard UPS ground unless otherwise requested. All orders prepaid. Most orders shipped within 24 hours of receipt.
Discounts: Wholesale prices are available to legitimate retailers who present a valid tax ID number, vendor license number or tax exemption form.
Accepts: all major credit cards

SAX ARTS & CRAFTS
P.O. Box 510710
2405 S. Calhoun Rd.
New Berlin WI 53151
Phone: (414)784-6880

Offers: A variety of supplies (known brands), including a full line of weaving looms and aids, yarns, weaving kits, rug/craft yarns, embroidery/crewel threads, rug hook frames and aids, canvas hoops, burlap and felt. Native American beading, beads, feathers, macrame, basketry and batik supplies, fabric paints, airbrush kits and inks, stencil films, trims, foam, stained glass kits, etching and beveled glass supplies and supplies for decoupage, jewelry making, leather, casting, plastics, wood and metalworking are also available.
Catalog: $5 (refundable).
Discounts: Quantity; sells wholesale to legitimate businesses.

TEXTILE ENTERPRISES, INC.
P.O. Box 154
216 Main St.
Whitesburg GA 30185
Phone: (404)834-2094
Store Location: At above address.
Offers: Dried and painted floral products, Spanish moss, excelsior, wreaths and others. Floral supplies: foams, wires, tapes and pins. Natural materials: variety of cones, pods, lotus and grapevine. Wreaths: statice, twig, wheat, wood bases, gypsophilia and others. Bells, beads, novelties, baskets, macrame cord, craft cords and supplies.
Discounts: Quantity; sells wholesale to legitimate businesses.

VICTORIAN VIDEO
930 Massachusetts
Lawrence KS 66044
Contact: Susan Bateman
Phone: (785)842-4333 or (800)848-0284
Fax: (785)842-0794
E-mail: yarnbarn@idir.net
Website: www.victorianvid.com
Store Location: At above address.
Offers: Over 180 instructional videos on weaving, spinning, dyeing, knitting, crochet, beadwork, rug making, quilting, sewing, lace making and more.
Catalog: Free.
Phone Orders: (800)848-0284. M-Sat, 9-5:30 CST.
Mail Orders: Prepayment required. Prompt shipping.
Discounts: Sells wholesale to legitimate businesses.
Accepts: Discover, MasterCard, Visa, check, money order

Needlepoint

Also see General Needlecraft Supplies; Embroidery & Cross-Stitch; Yarns; other related categories.

ARTS ARRAY
P.O. Box 546
Cottage Grove OR 97424
Contact: Hal Wagner
Phone: (541)942-8070
Offers: Line of European "tapestries" (hand-silkscreened color on Penelope double-weave) and kits: over 500 motifs by Royal Paris, Tapex, Margot Seg, Rico and others in traditional and classic designs—religious, Renaissance, florals, wildlife, seasonal, masterpieces, whimsical subjects and others. Also offers petit point kits (over 26) in classic designs.
Catalog: $2.
Phone Orders: Yes.
Mail Orders: Yes.

CAMUS INTERNATIONAL
222 Gulf Rd., Suite 606
Lansing NY 14882
Contact: Agnes M. Bonick
Phone: (607)533-7124
Fax: (607)533-7130
Offers: Your source for Celtic stitchery kits, including Tartan point pillow kits in over 300 tartans, cross-stitch and needlepoint kits from the British Isles.
Catalog: $2 (refundable).
Phone Orders: 24 hours. Leave message.
Mail Orders: Will ship worldwide.
Discounts: Wholesale accounts welcome.
Accepts: MasterCard, Visa

GITTA'S CHARTED PETIT POINT
271 Lakeshore Rd. E.
Port Credit, Ontario L5G 1G8
Canada
Phone: (905)274-7189
Fax: (905)274-2194
Offers: Needlepoint/petit point (and cross-stitch) charts/kits in over 62 traditional motifs: scenes, Victorian, Renaissance, Inuit children, florals, fowl and others. Fabrics: linens and others. Brand-name threads: wool and cottons. Also offers canvases, silk gauze and custom needlework framing.
Catalog: $5.
Discounts: Teachers and institutions; sells wholesale to businesses.

HEDGEHOG HANDWORKS
P.O. Box 45384
Westchester CA 90045
Contact: Joady Gorelick
Phone: (888)670-6040 or (310)670-6040
Offers: Silk threads, real metal threads, linen thread, cotton thread, metallics, pailettes, linen fabric, silk gauze, fancy tools and accessories. Books on: embroidery, historic costume, textiles and millinery. Corset-making supplies, hoopwire and silk ribbon embroidery supplies.
Catalog: Over 90 pages. $5 (refundable with $30 order).
Phone Orders: M-F, 9-5 PST.
Mail Orders: Will ship anywhere in the world.
Accepts: MasterCard, Visa

THE LAVENDER ROSE
P.O. Box 1365
Snohomish WA 98291-1365
Contact: M. Windsor Vest
Phone: (360)568-0867
E-mail: lavrose@gte.net
Website: http://home1.gte.net/lavrose/index.htm
Offers: Patterns and kits for Berlin work, blackwork, cutwork, drawn work and lace making. All original designs. Also reprints of actual designs of late 1800s.
Catalog: $2.
Phone Orders: Yes.
Mail Orders: Primarily mail order.
Accepts: no credit cards

JEAN MCINTOSH, LTD.
P.O. Box 232
Pembina ND 58271
Phone: (204)786-1634
Fax: (204)774-4159
Store Location: Other location: 1115 Empress St., Winnipeg, Manitoba R3E 3H1 Canada. M-F, 9-5.
Offers: Needlepoint and petit point kits and charts: traditional and classic designs in a wide range of motifs, including florals, scenic tapestries and others. Also offers cross-stitch materials.
Catalog: 35 pages, color. $5.
Phone Orders: (800)665-1361. 24 hours.
Mail Orders: Will ship to US and Canada. Prepayment required. Allow 6-8 weeks for delivery.
Discounts: Sells wholesale to legitimate businesses.
Accepts: MasterCard, Visa

WINDSONG YARN & NEEDLE ARTS
149 W. Michigan Ave.
Marshall MI 49068
Contact: Cathy Davis
Phone: (616)789-1210
Store Location: Historic downtown Marshall.
Offers: Hand-knitting yarns and supplies, needlepoint canvas, hand-painted designs, charts and threads.
Catalog: Yes.
Phone Orders: (888)789-8585.
Mail Orders: Yes.
Discounts: Yes.
Accepts: MasterCard, Visa, check

THE YARN BASKET
150 Falling Spring Rd.
Chambersburg PA 17201
Contact: Sue Sollenberger
Phone: (717)263-3236
Store Location: I-81, exit 6 and Route 30, behind Shoney's.
Offers: Knitting and crochet yarns, patterns and accessories. Needlepoint yarns and accessories. Cross-stitch, ribbon embroidery and crewel classes.
Phone Orders: (888)YRN-BSKT.
Mail Orders: Will ship UPS, Priority Mail and regular mail.
Accepts: Discover, MasterCard, Visa

Outdoors & Outerwear

Also see Clothing & Accessories; Fabrics & Trims; Knitting & Crochet; Quilting; Sewing; other specific categories.

BEACON FABRICS & NOTIONS

(formerly Marine Sewing)
6801 Gulfport Blvd.
St. Petersburg FL 33707
Phone: (813)345-6994 or (800)713-8157
Fax: (813)347-1424
Offers: Line of outdoor fabrics: canvas, vinyls, others (for boating/camping and outdoor items). Also offers notions for outdoor-fabric sewing.

FROSTLINE KITS

2525 River Rd.
Grand Junction CO 81505
Phone: (970)241-0155
E-mail: seweasy@frostlinekits.com
Offers: Precut outerwear kits (coats, jackets, baby wear and others) for adults and children: robes, comforters and others—ready to sew.
Catalog: Write.
Accepts: American Express, Discover, MasterCard, Visa

THE GREEN PEPPER

1285 River Rd.
Eugene OR 97404
Contact: Arlene Haislip or Susan Downs
Phone: (541)689-3292
Fax: (541)689-3591
Offers: 85 outerwear clothing patterns for adults and children, including suits, pants, jackets, tops, mittens, booties, vests and others. Also offers patterns for carriers/equipment, including garment and other bags, fanny pack, sleeping bag quilts, ponchos, horse blanket and windsocks. Fabrics also available, including nylon/Lycra, waterproof and water-repellent selections. Polartec fleece, insulations, heavy ribbing and Neoprene. Also offers YKK zippers, buckles, hooks, hardware, webbing and thread.
Catalog: Yes.
Phone Orders: Yes.
Mail Orders: Yes.
Discounts: Yes.
Accepts: MasterCard, Visa

HANG-EM HIGH FABRICS

1420 Yale Ave.
Richmond VA 23224
Phone: (804)233-6155
Fax: (804)233-6155
E-mail: tmarvin@erols.com
Website: www.citystar.com/hang-em-high
Offers: Fabrics: ripstop nylons, polyesters for kites, banners and flags. Supplies: webbing, repair tapes, swivels, rods and tubes (fiberglass and carbon), kite fittings, eyelet tools and more.
Catalog: Free.

KARLIN OF QUAKERTOWN

420 E. Broad St.
Quakertown PA 18951-1756
Contact: Stuart R. Scott
Phone: (800)828-7798
Fax: (215)536-1906
E-mail: scottyflag@enter.net
Offers: All flag banner-making supplies. Fade-and-spray resistant nylon fabric in 39 colors. 60″ width, 1/4 yard-plus purchase. 600 decorative flag patterns in stock, full-size and garden. Poles, brackets, thread, needles and appliqué scissors.
Catalog: $2 (refundable with first order).
Discounts: Quantity.

OUTDOOR WILDERNESS FABRICS, INC.

16415 N. Midland Blvd.
Nampa ID 83687
Contact: Betty Levis
Phone: (208)466-1602
Fax: (208)463-4622
E-mail: www.owfinc@lesbois.com
Website: owfinc.com
Store Location: At above address.
Offers: Outdoor fabrics: Polartec, Ultrex, Taslan, Supplex, Ballistics and Cordura. Also offers insulations, No-See-Um Mesh, hardware and other supplies.
Catalog: Free. Sample, $5.
Phone Orders: (800)693-7467.
Discounts: Retail, wholesale and quantity pricing.
Accepts: Discover, MasterCard, Visa

QUEST OUTFITTERS

619 Cattlemen Rd.
Sarasota FL 34232
Phone: (941)378-1620
Offers: Line of outdoor fabrics, including Polartec, Ultrex Thinsulate, Cordura, pack cloth, Supplex and more. Also offers wear and gear patterns, fasteners, zippers and other hardware, as well as stretch binding for use on fleece fabrics.
Catalog: Free.
Accepts: MasterCard, Visa

RAIN SHED

707 NW 11th St.
Corvallis OR 97330
Phone: (541)753-8900
Store Location: At above address. Hours: T-Sat, 9:30-5:30.
Offers: Outerwear patterns/kits/supplies. Brand patterns by Kwik-Sew, Burda, Green Pepper, Stretch'N Sew, Suitability and Travel Pals. Patterns: parkas, pants, vests, jackets, coveralls, suits, gaiters, caps, nightshirts, rompers, robes, swimsuits, riding outfits, totes, caddies, comforters and windsocks. Luggage: daypacks, cases and bags (ski, duffle, flight, diaper and thermal bottle). Fabrics: coated/uncoated nylons and Supplex, Polartec fleece, Cordura, vinyls, packcloth, waterproof/breatheables, wicking knits, mesh, fleece, Lycra, blends/cottons, camouflage and insulations. Also offers reflective tapes, webbings, cords, repair tapes, Velcro, notions, tools (snaps/setters, eyelets, hot tips, cutters and scissors) and hardware.
Catalog: $1.
Accepts: Discover, MasterCard, Visa

SEATTLE FABRICS

8702 Aurora Ave. N.
Seattle WA 98103
Phone: (206)525-0670
Fax: (206)525-0779
Offers: Outdoor/recreational fabrics: Ultrex, Gore-Tex, Lycra, taffeta, ripstop, oxford, packcloth, Cordura, Sunbrella, Textilene, closed cell foam, mosquito netting, heat-seal packcloth and others. Also offers hardware, sewing notions and webbing. Custom orders.
Catalog: Price list, $3 (refundable).

SHARLAINE'S FABRIC WAREHOUSE

(formerly Sharlaine Products)
104 Washington St.
Auburn ME 04210
Contact: Kelly Anear, general manager
Phone: (207)784-7151
Fax: (207)784-2200
E-mail: kelly@fabricwarehouse.com
Website: www.fabricwarehouse.com
Store Location: At above address.
Offers: Full line of sewing supplies and notions, including outdoor and marine fabrics.
Catalog: $2 (refundable with first order).
Phone Orders: Call or E-mail.
Mail Orders: P.O. Box 1365, Auburn ME 04211.
Discounts: Wholesale to legitimate businesses; need tax number and FID.
Accepts: Discover, MasterCard, Visa (no C.O.D.)

TIMBERLINE SEWING KITS

P.O. Box 126-CS
Pittsfield NH 03263
Phone: (603)435-8888
Offers: Outerwear kits: jackets, vests, parkas, foot mittens and gaiters. Luggage kits: cargo bags, travel bags, totes, bike bags and log carrier. Comforter kits also available. Fabrics: nylons, Cordura, taffeta, ripstop and water-repellent types. Also offers goose and duck down.
Catalog: Brochure, $1. Fabrics list on request.
Discounts: Teachers and institutions.

WEATHER OR NOT FABRICS & FINDINGS CO.

2845 Pacific Blvd. SW
Albany OR 97321
Contact: Paula Connashan
Phone: (541)924-1446
Fax: (541)924-1446
E-mail: weatherornot@proaxis.com
Website: www.proaxis.com/~weatherornot
Store Location: At above address. M-F, 9-6; Sat, 10-5.
Offers: Fabrics for working and playing outside. Polartec, Supplex knits and wovens. Coolmax, Ultrex, Cordura, sport zippers, hardware, etc., camo fabrics in all styles, Solarweave sun protective fabric for clothing.
Catalog: $2.
Phone Orders: Yes.
Mail Orders: Yes.
Discounts: Yes.
Accepts: American Express, MasterCard, Visa

WY'EAST FABRICS

P.O. Box 7328
2895 Val Pak Rd. NE
Salem OR 97303
Contact: Steve Eck
Phone: (503)364-8419
Fax: (503)391-8057
E-mail: info@wyeastfabrics.com
Website: www.wyeastfabrics.com
Store Location: At above address.
Offers: Full-service supplier of outdoor fabrics including Polartec fleece, Ultrex, Cordura, patterns, webbing and much more. Offers 4 ways to order, including phone, fax, mail and on-line ordering using a secure server.
Catalog: On-line. Hard-copy catalog available for $2.
Phone Orders: Yes.
Mail Orders: Yes.
Discounts: Occasional sales.
Accepts: MasterCard, Visa, check

Quilting

Also see General Needlecraft Supplies; Fabrics & Trims; Sewing; other related categories.

AIRTEX CONSUMER PRODUCTS
150 Industrial Park Blvd.
Cokato MN 55321
Contact: Marty Fitzloff
Phone: (320)286-2696
Fax: (320)286-2428
E-mail: airtex@cmgate.com
Website: www.airtex.com
Store Location: Manufacturing plant is in Cokato MN (wholesale only).
Offers: Complete line of filling products, polyester fiberfill, quilt batting, pillow forms and foam and cotton quilt batting.
Catalog: (800)851-8887.
Phone Orders: (800)851-8887.
Mail Orders: Call for freight charges and send check to above address.
Discounts: Call (800)851-8887 for volume pricing.
Accepts: MasterCard, Visa, prepaid net 30 upon credit approval

ART-IN-A-PINCH QUILT HANGERS
6549 Keystone Rd.
Milaca MN 56353
Contact: Shelley
Phone: (888)369-4500
Fax: (320)983-2151
Offers: Art-In-A-Pinch wooden hangers are quick, safe and beautiful. Also hangs rugs, weavings and more. 9 standard sizes plus custom orders accepted.
Catalog: Send or call for free brochure.
Accepts: Discover, MasterCard, Visa

AYOLA PATCHWORK
P.O. Box 2061
Fairfield IA 52556
Contact: Jane Lourds
Phone: (515)472-8705
Offers: Quilting charm squares 4″.
Mail Orders: $5 for 50 4″ charm squares.
Accepts: check, cash

CARDWELL SPILLER DYEWORKS
(formerly Spiller Dyeworks)
2524 Pine Bluff Rd.
Colorado Springs CO 80909-1316
Contact: Cardwell Spiller

Phone: (719)471-7161
Fax: (719)471-7161
Offers: Wholesale and retail source of hand-dyed fabrics. Base fabrics include pima cotton, linen, silk, rayon challis and rayon/silk velvet. Offer 34 standard colors. We also do custom work. Single and multiple colors available. Retail—no order too small. Wholesale—$100 minimum.
Catalog: Ordering information, color card and usable samples. $5, US; $7, international.
Phone Orders: Always happy to talk, but all orders must be prepaid.
Mail Orders: Will ship anywhere. All orders prepaid. Allow 2-6 weeks.
Discounts: 20% off first retail order; free p&h on all retail orders to US.
Accepts: check, money order (US and international)

THE CALICO CAT
204 E. Main
Auburn WA 98002
Phone: (800)908-0885
E-mail: calicocat@mci2000.com
Offers: Block-Of-The-Month fabric kits; for a sampler quilt members pay modest fee and receive "makes 12″ block" fabric monthly; in Christmas, pastel and cozy flannel. Newsletter available. Call or send SASE.

COCHENILLE DESIGN STUDIO
P.O. Box 4276
Encinitas CA 92023
Contact: Susan Lazear
Phone: (619)259-1698
Fax: (619)259-3746
E-mail: info@cochenille.com
Website: www.cochenille.com
Offers: Computer software for multiple crafts. Stitch Painter: grid design software. Garment Styler: garment design sewing patterns and knitting instruction. Books and design aids.
Catalog: $1.
Phone Orders: Yes.
Mail Orders: Yes.
Accepts: MasterCard, Visa, check, cash

COLONIAL PATTERNS
340 W. Fifth St.
Kansas City MO 64105
Phone: (816)471-3313
Fax: (816)842-1969
Offers: Aunt Martha's transfer patterns, ballpoint tube paint, flour sack towels, pillowcases, quilt kits and quilt design

books. Also offers "Uncle Bud's Yard Buddies" wood patterns. See your dealer, or write.

CONNECTING THREADS
P.O. Box 8940
Vancouver WA 98668
Phone: (800)574-6454
Fax: (360)260-8877
Offers: Extensive collection of quilt patterns and instruction books. Quilting tools, threads, notions, cutters, markers, batting hoops and frames.
Catalog: Free. Call or write.

THE COTTON PATCH
1025 Brown Ave.
Lafayette CA 94549
Phone: (800)835-4418
Offers: Wide range of cotton prints and solid fabrics, including authentic African and Japanese cotton. Sulky rayon and metallic threads and silk ribbon; quilting and sewing notions, patterns and 500 quilt-related and sewing books also available.
Catalog: Catalog and fabric swatches, $8 ($5 refundable).

CROSLEY-GRIFFITH PUBLISHING COMPANY, INC.
1321 Broad St.
Grinnell IA 50112
Contact: Steve Bennett
Phone: (515)236-4854
Fax: (515)236-4854
E-mail: crosgriff@aol.com
Website: http://quilt.com/judym
Offers: Quilt books by Judy Martin, including *The Block Book*, *Judy Martin's Ultimate Rotary Cutting Reference* and *Pieced Borders* (with Marsha McCloskey.) Also Judy Martin's Ultimate Rotary Tools.
Catalog: Available upon request.
Discounts: Regular wholesale discounts apply to legitimate resellers.
Accepts: MasterCard, Visa

EXTRA SPECIAL PRODUCTS CORP.
P.O. Box 777
Greenville OH 45331
Phone: (937)548-9388 or (800)648-5945
Fax: (937)548-9580
Website: www.extraspecial.com
Offers: House of Copper line of die-cut copper shapes (to punch, bend, burnish, antique, paint and use as trims, window decorations, tree ornaments, candle trims, quilt templates, appliqué templates, wreath decorations and others) and a booklet with over 24 projects.
Catalog: See your dealer, or write.

FABRIC DEPOT, INC.
700 SE 122nd Ave.
Portland OR 97233
Phone: (503)252-9530
Fax: (503)252-9556

E-mail: fabricdepot@worldnet.att.net
Website: www.fabricdepot.com
Store Location: At above address. M-F, 9-9; Sat, 9-7; Sun, 10-7.
Offers: Full-line fabric store from A to Z. Porcelain dolls and supplies, beds, Lara Craft wood products, quilting supplies and stitchery.
Phone Orders: (800)392-3376.
Mail Orders: Will ship to US and Canada. Prepayment or C.O.D.
Discounts: Wholesale discounts offered. Mimimum: full box notions, full bolt fabric. No dollar minimum.
Accepts: American Express, Discover, MasterCard, Visa

FABRIC SHACK
P.O. Box 517
99 S. Marvin Ln.
Waynesville OH 45068
Contact: Maxine Young
Phone: (513)897-0092
Fax: (513)897-7176
E-mail: info@fabricshack.com
Website: www.fabricshack.com
Store Location: At above address.
Offers: Up-to-date thousands of home's fun, unusual and select better-quality quilting and fabrics. Books, notions, home decor tapestries and laces, as well as better name brands in decor in chintz and others.
Phone Orders: Yes.
Mail Orders: Yes.
Discounts: As always in our reasonable prices.
Accepts: Discover, MasterCard, Visa

FAIRFIELD PROCESSING CORP.
P.O. Box 1157
Danbury CT 06813-1157
Phone: (800)243-0989
Fax: (203)792-9710
E-mail: ffld.prcssng.corp@snet.net
Website: www.poly-fil.com
Offers: Fairfield Processing Corporation manufactures a complete line of high-quality products for the home sewing, quilt and craft industries. Poly-fil, Soft Touch and Crafters Choice brand fiberfill, batting and pillow form products are easy to use, available in many sizes and unconditionally guaranteed. New products include quilt pattern books, bumper batting and a chair cushion insert. Poly-fil is internationally available and accepted as the brand of excellence.
Catalog: Free. Call.
Phone Orders: M-F, 8-5 EST.
Discounts: Sells wholesale to companies with tax ID number, 2-carton minimum.
Accepts: MasterCard, Visa

THE GIBBS CO.
606 Sixth St. NE
Canton OH 44702
Contact: Elane Young

Phone: (330)455-5344 or (800)775-4427
Fax: (330)455-3051
Offers: Gibbs quilting, embroidery and framing hoops in oak, hickory and poplar. Also offers basketry supplies.
Catalog: Quilt and basketry hoops; please specify.
Discounts: Quantity; teachers, institutions and professionals; sells wholesale to legitimate businesses.

GINGER'S NEEDLEWORKS
P.O. Box 92047
Lafayette LA 70509-2047
Contact: (318)232-7847
Fax: (318)232-7847
E-mail: quilts@1america.net
Store Location: 905 E. Gloria Switch Rd., Lafayette LA 70507-2619.
Offers: Fabric packages, books, patterns and many designer fabrics.
Catalog: $1.
Phone Orders: Yes.
Mail Orders: At P.O. Box.
Accepts: American Express, Discover, MasterCard, Visa

SALLY GOODSPEED
2318 N. Charles St.
Baltimore MD 21218
Phone: (410)235-6736
Offers: Reprints of 1900-40 embroidery, quilt and paint designs. Over 600 Sunbonnet Babies and Colonial Ladies, many from Corbett's Primer. Dolly Dingle, Kewpies, Greenaway, Cabot and McKim. Also 1920s Boudoir Doll patterns.
Catalog: $2.95.
Mail Orders: Yes.

CHRIS HANNER & COMPANY
3687 Coldwater Lane
Snellville GA 30039
Phone: (770)981-9550 or (800)533-7259
Fax: (770)981-3572
E-mail: hanner@mindspring.com
Offers: Unique new quilting thimble "My Favorite Thimble."
Phone Orders: Yes.
Mail Orders: Yes.
Discounts: Wholesale and retail.

HAPCO PRODUCTS/MULBERRY SILK & THINGS
P.O. Box 150
210 N. Central
Rocheport MO 65279
Contact: Alice Snyder
Phone: (573)698-2102
Fax: (573)698-2102
E-mail: silkbatt@aol.com
Store Location: At above address.
Offers: Quilting notions: needles, thimbles and silk batting—the all-natural, soft, elegant batting for clothes as well as quilts.

Catalog: Send SASE.
Phone Orders: Yes.
Mail Orders: Yes.
Discounts: Sells wholesale to legitimate business.
Accepts: American Express, Discover, MasterCard, Visa, check, money order, cash

HINTERBERG DESIGN, INC.
2805 E. Progress Dr.
West Bend WI 53095
Phone: (800)443-5800
Fax: (414)338-3852
E-mail: info@hinterberg.com
Website: hinterberg.com
Store Location: Factory showroom at above address.
Offers: Quilting frames, hoops and display racks.
Catalog: Free color brochures on all products.
Phone Orders: M-S, 8-5 CST.
Mail Orders: At above address.
Accepts: American Express, Discover, MasterCard, Visa

I LOVE QUILTING BOOK CLUB
1507 Dana Ave.
Cincinnati OH 45207
Contact: Mary Dacres, editor
Phone: (513)531-2690
Fax: (513)531-4744
Offers: About every 4 weeks a free issue of the club catalog and newsletter, describing the main selection book, several alternates and dozens of other book offerings including hard-to-find tools and gadgets, videos and more—all at a discount price.

J.D. SERVICES
340½ S. Redlands Rd.
Grand Junction CO 81503
Contact: Jack Dierberger
Phone: (800)835-7817
E-mail: j.d.services@americanquilts.com
Website: http://www.americanquilts.com/jdservices
Store Location: At above address.
Offers: Custom templates for the quilter made from their patterns. Also will cut templates for publishers of quilting books in large quantities or other plastic products, all made from acrylic plastic.
Catalog: On request.
Phone Orders: 8-6 MST.
Mail Orders: Will mail to US and Canada. Prepayment required.
Discounts: On quantity amounts.
Accepts: check, money order

JASMINE HEIRLOOMS
500 Fairview Dr.
Greenville SC 29609
Phone: (800)736-7326
Offers: Heirloom-quality frames and hoops suitable for quilting, rug hooking and needlework. Hoops are available

on floor stands, lap stands or just plain. Budget-model floor frame also available. Porcelain thimbles for both top and underhand protection. Additional complementary items, such as quilt rack for floor and wall, and caddy for floor frame.

Catalog: Call for free brochure, 24 hours a day, 7 days a week.

Phone Orders: M-F, 9:30-5 EST.

Mail Orders: We ship worldwide.

Discounts: Available only to established shops and catalog houses.

Accepts: American Express, Discover, MasterCard, Visa

KEEPSAKE QUILTING

P.O. Box 1618

Route 25B

Centre Harbor NH 03226

Offers: Quilting supplies: Patterns, books, stencils, a variety of aids, fabric medleys, quilting kits, over 600 cotton swatches (solids, plaids, patterns, textures and others), specialty fabric assortments, batting and muslin.

Catalog: Free. 128 pages, color. Call (800)865-9458.

KEN QUILT MANUFACTURING CO.

113 Pattie St.

Wichita KS 67211

Phone: (316)262-3438

Fax: (316)262-3455

Offers: Professional model quilting machines, variable speed to full 3,500 RPM; four-way quilting operations.

Catalog: Send stamp for literature and prices.

Accepts: Discover, MasterCard, Visa

THE KIRK COLLECTION

1513 Military Ave.

Omaha NE 68111-3924

Contact: Nancy T. Kirk

Phone: (402)551-0386 or (800)398-2542

Fax: (800)960-8335 or (402)551-0971

E-mail: kirkcoll@aol.com

Website: http://www.kirkcollection.com

Store Location: At above address. T-Sat, 10-5, or by appointment.

Offers: Antique and reproduction fabrics, antique lace, crazy quilt fabrics and trims, cigarette silks, natural fiber batting (cotton, wool and silk), feed sacks, antique quilts, tops and blocks and fabrics for historic doll costuming. Also monthly fabric clubs.

Catalog: Free.

Phone Orders: Yes.

Mail Orders: We ship worldwide. Orders generally shipped within 48 hours.

Accepts: American Express, Discover, JCB, MasterCard, Visa

LA MAISON PIQUEE

P.O. Box 1891

Milwaukee WI 53201-1891

Contact: Kathleen L. Briggs or Adeline L.F. Briggs, designer in residence

Phone: (414)332-4590

Offers: Quilt pattern sets: French quilting directions and French quilting crafts projects. Example: Wisconsin idea quilt, commissioned by Wisconsin Arts Board jointly with American Revolution Bicentennial Commission, preserves nineteenth-century Wisconsin versions of popular American patchwork patterns.

Catalog: Pattern list describes sampler quilt pattern sets and more.

Mail Orders: Yes.

Discounts: Teachers and other quilt outlets, such as retail stores.

Accepts: check, money order

LITTLE BY LITTLE

P.O. Box 2017

Burleson TX 76097-2017

Contact: Barbara Loe

Phone: (817)295-4416

Store Location: 206 Hoover Rd., Burleson TX 76028. Visits arranged.

Offers: Mail order; always free shipping; quality top-line 100% cotton for quilting. Specializing in customer service. Moda fabrics, including 80 colors of Moda Marble Solids. Also carry homespuns by Red Wagon and Mission Valley, prints, and seasonals. Quilt books and notions. Order packets of 4″ square samples that are labeled; you then order by the swatch number. Fat quarters; yardage.

Catalog: Typed 3-page information sheets called "brochure." Free.

Phone Orders: M-Sat, 8 a.m.-11 p.m. CST.

Mail Orders: Our specialty, as owner and her daughter are homebound most of the time. We cater to our mail-order customers as friends.

Discounts: Free shipping. Free birthday club with any purchase (free fat quarters or choice on birthday).

Accepts: American Express, Discover, MasterCard, Visa, check, money order

VICTORIA LOUISE, MERCERS

P.O. Box 266

Jefferson MD 21755

Contact: Diane Stull

Phone: (301)473-4140

E-mail: stull@fred.net

Website: http://www.fred.net/stull/victoria.html

Offers: Historical patterns and kits, bonnet forms and fine fabrics, including silk taffeta, dupioni, organza, plain and embroidered organdies and silk and cotton tulle. Real laces, fancy ribbons and trims, notions, conservation supplies and antique and vintage items.

Catalog: 55 pages. $5.

Phone Orders: M-F, 9-5 EST.

Mail Orders: Will ship to US and Canada.

Discounts: Wholesale to legitimate businesses.

Accepts: American Express, Discover, check, money order

MAIN STREET BY MAIL
7548 Main St.
Sykesville MD 21784
Contact: Kim
Phone: (410)795-7904 or (800)791-9609
Fax: (410)549-2512
Offers: Quality knit fabrics to include interlocks, rib, Lycra cotton solids, jerseys, pointelles, novelty knits, outerwear fleece. Notions carried include: Stretch & Sew elastic and notions, Snap Source snaps, Kwik Sew books and patterns, Stretch & Sew patterns and other notions designed for knits.
Catalog: $4 with complete swatch set.
Phone Orders: M-F, 10-6; Sat, 10-5.
Mail Orders: At above address. Ship to APO, US, Canada within 24 hours.
Accepts: American Express, Discover, MasterCard, Visa, check, money order

MATERIALS UNLIMITED
P.O. Box 449
Glide OR 97443
Contact: Susan Flury (541)496-3897 or Donnabelle Jones (541)496-3398
Store Location: 288 Helms Rd., Idleyld Park OR 97447.
Offers: Precut quilt kits for pillows and table runners, baby quilts, wall hangings; twin, reg., king and queen sizes. Also finished quilts.
Catalog: $2.50.
Phone Orders: Yes.
Mail Orders: Shipped worldwide.
Accepts: MasterCard, Visa

MOUNTAIN MIST
100 Williams St.
Cincinnati OH 45215
Phone: (513)948-5276 or (800)345-7150
E-mail: stearns@fuse.net
Website: http://www.palaver.com/mountainmist/
Offers: Cotton and polyester quilt batting, cotton-covered pillow forms and polyester stuffing. Line of quilt patterns with templates in florals, inspirational and other designs. Manufacturer. Contact your dealer, or send SASE.

NUSTYLE QUILTING FRAME CO., SUPPLIES
P.O.Box 61
Hwy. 52 W.
Stover MO 65078
Contact: Ruth Williams
Phone: (573)377-2244 or (800)821-7490
Fax: (573)377-2833
Store Location: 290 W. 4th, Hwy. 52 W., Stover MO 65078.
Offers: Long arm quilting machines and frames; hand quilting frames, different styles; large rolls Dacron and cotton-batt; Dacron thread for machine quilting and regular sewing, all colors; quilting books; all type of patterns for clothing, crafts, quilt rulers, cutting boards, cutters; all types of notions; full line of embroidery blocks and threads; over 4,000 bolts of fabrics, name brands.

Catalog: Yes.
Phone Orders: Yes.
Mail Orders: Ship nationwide including Canada, AK and HI.
Discounts: Yes.
Accepts: Discover, MasterCard, Visa

PAPER PIECES
P.O. Box 2931
Redmond WA 98073-2931
Contact: Tess Herlan
Phone: (425)867-1537 or (800)337-1537
Fax: (425)556-4849
Offers: Precut papers for English (hand) paper, piece quilt-making, patterns, books, kits and notions for hand piecing.
Catalog: Full color.
Phone Orders: Yes.
Mail Orders: Yes.
Accepts: MasterCard, Visa

QUILT-BOOKS-USA
P.O. Box 171
Stevensville MI 49127
Contact: Nikki Tittle
Phone: (888)QUILT-BK or (616)429-1760
Fax: (616)429-1876
E-mail: tittle@parrett.net
Website: www.quilt-books-usa.com
Offers: Over 17,000 quilt books, Willitt's Amish Heritage Collection and totes on wheels.
Catalog: $3.
Phone Orders: M-F, 9-6 EST.
Mail Orders: Free shipping on US orders. International: actual is added.
Accepts: MasterCard, Visa

QUILTERS' RESOURCE, INC.
P.O. Box 148850
Chicago IL 60614
Contact: Bonnie Benson
Phone: (773)278-5695
Fax: (773)278-1348
E-mail: qripatch@aol.com
Offers: Quilting and needle art supplies and French wire-edged ribbons. Distributor of books and magazines from Japan, Australia and England.
Catalog: 500 pages. $15.
Phone Orders: M-F, 8:30-5 CST.
Mail Orders: Will ship worldwide.
Discounts: Sells wholesale to retail stores only.
Accepts: MasterCard, Visa

QUILTING BOOKS UNLIMITED
1911 W. Wilson
Batavia IL 60510
Phone: (630)406-0237
Fax: (630)406-0237
Store Location: At above address.

Offers: Approximately 2,000 quilting book titles—classic, contemporary and other motifs for quilts, clothing and home accessories; covers a variety of techniques/methods. Also offers sewing notions and over 2,000 bolts of 100% cotton fabrics.
Catalog: Catalog of books, $2.
Discounts: Quantity.

QUILTWORK PATCHES
209 SW Second St.
Corvallis OR 97333
Phone: (541)752-4820
Offers: Large selection of 100% cotton fabrics, including precut assortments. Squares and coordinated fat quarter bundles. Also supplies, books, patterns and a Designer Fabric Club. Friendly, knowledgeable sales staff.
Catalog: Free brochure.

THE QUILTWORKS
1055 E. 79th St.
Minneapolis MN 55420-1460
Contact: Harry Bornstein, president
Phone: (612)854-1460 or (800)328-1850
Fax: (612)854-7254
E-mail: hbornstein@r-and-z.com
Website: http://www.r-and-z.com
Offers: Quilting fabrics: Concord, Marcus, Wamsutta, Peter Pan, Bernartex, Hoffman, Dan River, Mission Valley, RJR, South Seas and VIP. Full line of supplies. Contact a dealer.
Discounts: Sells wholesale.

ST. PETER WOOLEN MILL
101 W. Broadway
St. Peter MN 56082
Phone: (507)931-3734
Fax: (507)931-9040
E-mail: spwoolen@prairie.lakes.com
Website: www.woolenmill.com
Store Location: At above address. M,T,W and F, 9-5:30; Th, 9-8; Sat, 9-5; Sun, 12-4.
Offers: Nature's Comforts wool batting and custom wool, recarding service. Also makes comforter, pillow and mattress pads.
Catalog: Free brochure.
Discounts: Sells wholesale.
Accepts: American Express, Discover, MasterCard, Visa

JUDY SPEEZAK QUILTS
425 Fifth Ave.
Brooklyn NY 11215
Contact: Judy Speezak
Phone: (718)369-3513

Offers: Authentic feedsack cottons, prewashed 6″ squares, 25-piece assortments.
Mail Orders: Mail orders only. Prepayment required.
Accepts: check, money order (US funds only)

THE STITCHIN' POST
P.O. Box 280
311 W. Cascade
Sisters OR 97759
Contact: Lawry Thorn
Phone: (541)549-6061
Fax: (541)549-1922
E-mail: stitchin@empnet.com
Website: www.stitchinpost.com
Store Location: At above address. 9-5 PST, 7 days a week.
Offers: Quilt shop.
Phone Orders: 9-5 PST. Also fax or E-mail.
Accepts: MasterCard, Visa

TONI'S TREASURES
480 N. Third W.
Rigby ID 83442
Contact: Toni Smith
Phone: (208)745-6703
Website: srv.net
Store Location: At above address.
Offers: Complete line of paper piecing quilt patterns, retail and wholesale.
Catalog: 16 pages, b&w with color insert. $1.
Phone Orders: (800)397-1684.
Mail Orders: Will ship to Canada and US. Prepayment required on retail.
Discounts: Wholesale to shop owners.
Accepts: MasterCard, Visa

VICTORIAN PLEASURES
#1, 4610-45 St.
Olds, Alberta T4H 1A1
Canada
Contact: Betty Caskey
Phone: (403)556-3999 or (888)362-7455
Fax: (403)556-1686
E-mail: silkworm@telvsplanet.net
Website: www.victorianpleasures.com
Store Location: At above address.
Offers: Crazy quilting and silk ribbon supplies, including books, kits and fabrics.
Catalog: 32 pages.
Phone Orders: (888)362-7455.
Mail Orders: To US and Canada. Prepaid. Allow 4-6 weeks for delivery.
Accepts: MasterCard, Visa, check, money order

Rug Making

Also see General Needlecraft Supplies; Knitting & Crochet; Spinning & Weaving; Yarns; other related categories.

ANDERSON HANDCRAFTED PRODUCTS

18962 McKays Cove Lane
Leonardtown MD 20650
Phone: (301)994-2262
Offers: Models of rug-hooking frames made from beautiful hardwood and fully adjustable (height/angle); floor model (#95) and ultralight portable (#85) (postpaid).
Catalog: Send SASE for further descriptive literature.

THE BASICS AND BEYOND

1429 Raven Hill Rd.
Mechanicsburg PA 17055
Contact: Jacalyn Krewson
Phone: (717)697-0096
E-mail: hookbasics@aol.com
Offers: Educational journal for traditional rug hookers. It is 16-22 pages in length and is published quarterly. Complimentary issue available for $2 to cover p&h. Subscription rates (subject to change) are: continental US, $15; Canada, $18 (US funds); and elsewhere, $25 (US funds).
Phone Orders: M-F, 8-5 EST.
Mail Orders: At above address.
Accepts: check, money order (US funds)

PATSY BECKER

P.O. Box 1050
South Orleans MA 02662
Phone: (508)240-0346
Offers: Line of Patsy rug-hooking designs in whimsical/folk art style motifs.
Catalog: $5.

NANCY BLAIR: TOMORROW'S HEIRLOOMS

11310 Prairie
Allendale MI 49401
Phone: (616)895-6378
Offers: Rug-hooking supplies, including wools/tweeds in wide range of colors, dyed wool, kits, dyes, cutters, frames, bindings and hooks. Also offers ready-to-cover footstool of finished or unfinished oak.
Catalog: Send $3.
Discounts: Sells wholesale.

BRAID-AID FABRICS

466 Washington St.
Pembroke MA 02359
Contact: Douglas McAloney
Phone: (781)826-6091
Fax: (781)826-6610
Store Location: At above address.
Offers: Rug-hooking and rug-braiding supplies. For hooking: 6 types of backing, hooks, cutters, frame, books, stamped patterns, dyes, kits and woolens. For braiding: woolens, books, kits, Braid-Aids, Braidkin, Braid-Klamp and lacing thread.
Catalog: 100 pages, 8½×11, color. $7.
Phone Orders: M-Sat, 10-5.
Mail Orders: Ship anywhere. Fast delivery.
Discounts: Sells to teachers and wholesale.
Accepts: MasterCard, Visa

BURLAP 'N RAGS

52 Courtland St.
Rockford MI 49341
Phone: (616)866-4260
Store Location: At above address. Open daily year-round.
Offers: Complete line of rug-hooking supplies and small kits.
Catalog: SASE for flyer of primitive kits and a price list of supplies.

BY THE DOOR HOOKED RUGS

RR 5
Amherst, Nova Scotia B4H 3Y3
Canada
Contact: Deanne Fitzpatrick
Phone: (902)667-0560
Fax: (902)667-0560
E-mail: nstn4704@fox.nstn.ca
Website: http://fox.nstn.ca/~nstn4704/home/
Store Loction: Amherst Nova Scotia location.
Offers: One-of-a-kind hooked rugs, wholesale/retail rug-hooking kits (primitive).
Catalog: $2. $20 with sample kit.
Phone Orders: Yes.
Mail Orders: Yes.
Discounts: 50% on wholesale orders.
Accepts: MasterCard, Visa

COLORS BY MARYANNE

10 Oak Point
Wrentham MA 02093
Contact: Maryanne Lincoln
Phone: (508)384-8188
E-mail: 10217.1402@compuserve.com
Offers: Collections of dyed wool samples and formulas for rug hookers and dyers. Custom-dyed wools for rug-hooking lectures and dye demos. Seminar on color and dyeing.

Phone Orders: All reasonable hours, even weekends.

Mail Orders: P&h will be added to all orders. US and Canada. US funds only, please.

Discounts: Teachers extended courtesy discounts.

Accepts: check, money order, postal money order (no credit cards)

LINDA RAE COUGHLIN

P.O. Box 4616

Warren NJ 07059

Contact: Linda Rae Coughlin

Phone: (908)647-8100

Store Location: At above address.

Offers: Rug restoration, 3-D rug hooking kits and patterns, workshops and photography of artwork, rug and others.

Catalog: $3.

Phone Orders: With prepayment.

Mail Orders: Prepayment required.

Discounts: Call for information.

Accepts: check, money order

COUNTRY BRAID HOUSE

462 Main St.

Tilton NH 03276

Contact: Jan Jurta

Phone: (603)286-4511

Fax: (603)286-4155

E-mail: info@countrybraidhouse.com

Website: www.countrybraidhouse.com

Store Location: At above address. M-F, 9-5; Sat, 9-4.

Offers: Rug-braiding kits and supplies, wool by the yard and remnant wool by the pound.

Catalog: Free brochure.

Phone Orders: M-F, 9-5; Sat, 9-4.

Mail Orders: Will ship to US and Canada. Prepayment required. 2-4 weeks.

Accepts: Discover, MasterCard, Visa

COX ENTERPRISES—RUG BRAIDING WITH VERNA

Rt. 2, Box 245

Verona Island ME 04416

Contact: Verna Cox

Phone: (207)469-6402

Fax: (207)469-6243

E-mail: braider@mint.net

Website: www.mint.net/rugsbyverna

Offers: Rug braiding: videos, manual, equipment and mill end wool.

Catalog: Free.

Phone Orders: 8-5 daily.

Mail Orders: Will ship anywhere. Prepayment required.

Discounts: Available to distributors and retail outlets.

Accepts: MasterCard, Visa

THE CRAFTY EWE

P.O. Box 1603

Bonners Ferry ID 83805

Contact: Signe Nickerson

Phone: (208)267-5062

Fax: (208)267-5062

Offers: Australian locker hooking supplies: locker hooks, spiral-bound book, canvas, kits and carded wool. Wholesale and retail pricing.

Catalog: Send SASE for price list.

Phone Orders: Yes.

Mail Orders: Yes.

Discounts: Wholesale pricing upon written request.

Accepts: MasterCard, Visa (for additional 50¢ per order)

DIFRANZA DESIGNS

25 Bow St.

North Reading MA 01864

Phone: (978)664-2034

Offers: Hooked rug patterns/kits (burlap and precut wool fabrics): traditional and contemporary designs (for brick covers, tapestries, chair seats and pillows), including unusuals, florals, special occasion/personalized, New England motifs and others.

Catalog: $5.

Discounts: Teachers; sells wholesale to legitimate businesses.

THE DORR MILL STORE

P.O. Box 88

Guild NH 03754

Contact: Terry Dorr

Phone: (603)863-1197

E-mail: dorrmillstore@sugar-river.net

Store Location: At above address. M-Sat, 9-5.

Offers: Wool fabric (exclusive decorator colors for hooking, braiding and quilting) and tweeds. Also offers hooking kits in a variety of traditional designs.

Catalog: Free supply list or send $3 for color card set.

Phone Orders: M-Sat, 9-5.

Mail Orders: Can ship anywhere.

Discounts: Teachers or shop owners.

Accepts: Discover, MasterCard, Visa

DRAKE'S WOOL

P.O. Box 281

586 Rappahannock Dr.

White Stone VA 22578

Contact: Nancy Drake

Phone: (804)435-8808

Fax: (804)436-8808

Store Location: At above address. M-F, 10-4:30, Sat 10-2. Winter hours: call.

Offers: Rooms full of wool! Traditional rug-hooking supplies and primitive patterns and kits, cutters, books, hooks, Puritan frames, stands, linen, monk's cloth, premium burlap, dyes, scissors and more.

Catalog: Flyer. $2.

Phone Orders: Yes. M-Sat, 10-4:30.

Mail Orders: Will ship UPS or postal service within 1-3 weeks.

Accepts: MasterCard, Visa

EHB DESIGNS

132 Rosedale Valley Rd.
Toronto, Ontario M4W 1P7
Canada
Contact: Liz Ballentine
Phone: (416)964-0634
Fax: (416)964-0634
E-mail: Soon.
Store Location: At above address.
Offers: Acid dyes for wool, silk, mohair, angora, nylon yarn or fabric. Also offers fiber-reactive dyes for cotton, linen, rayon and basketry materials and auxiliary chemicals and instructions for dye, paint and print work. Cotton quilt fabric, silk and wool merino yarns and hand-dyed and hand-painted yarns also available. Also offers technical assistance.
Catalog: Free.
Phone Orders: M-F, 8:30-6:30 EST.
Mail Orders: Will ship worldwide.
Discounts: Wholesale to schools, theater groups, guilds and professional fibre artists.

HARRY M. FRASER CO.

433 Duggins Rd.
Stoneville NC 27048
Phone: (336)573-9830
Fax: (336)573-3545
Offers: Supplies for hooking and braiding. Wool fabric by the yard or pound, plus others. Also offers rug hooks, braiding sets, cloth slitting machines and others.
Catalog: Patterns and supplies catalog, $6. Free price list.

FREDERICKSBURG RUGS

P.O. Box 649
Fredericksburg TX 78624
Contact: Laurice Heath
Phone: (830)997-6083
Store Location: Summer 1998 plus B&B on location.
Offers: Specializes in rug-hooking kits and classes, including a complete line of rug-hooking supplies for traditional and primitive rug hooking with wool fabric. Holds 3-day rug-hooking retreats for beginners in an Old World environment.
Catalog: $4. Instructional 40-page color kit brochures and retreat schedules.
Phone Orders: Yes.
Mail Orders: Yes.
Accepts: American Express, MasterCard, Visa, check

GINNY'S GEMS

5167 Robinhood Dr.
Willoughby OH 44094
Phone: (216)951-1311
Offers: Full line of patterns (burlap and monk's cloth) for hooked rugs: Navajo, other Indian and Southwestern designs (kachinas, pottery, symbolic and others), Oriental and Eastern patterns. Dry dyes and dye formula books available.
Catalog: $5.50.

Discounts: Teachers and institutions; sells wholesale to legitimate businesses.
Accepts: MasterCard, Visa

HANDS ACROSS TIME RUG HOOKING STUDIO

RR 1
Pugwashjunction, Nova Scotia B0K 1M0
Canada
Contact: Sarah Ladd
Phone: (902)257-2267
Fax: (902)257-2267
Store Location: 2526 Fountain Rd., Middleboro, Nova Scotia B0K 1M0 Canada.
Offers: Rug-hooking supplies for the beginner and experienced hooker. Custom-dyed wool, unique patterns, kits, hooks, cloth strippers, dyeing supplies, books and more. Ongoing workshops for the beginner and experienced.
Catalog: $4 (Canadian).
Phone Orders: Accepted M-F, 9-4 AST.
Mail Orders: Will ship anywhere. Allow 4-6 weeks. Prepayment required on special orders.
Discounts: 15% teachers's discount on orders over $50. Wholesale inquiries welcome.
Accepts: Visa (add 4% service charge), US exchange rate: 1.25%

HARTMAN'S HOOK

7240 Mystic Dr.
Hudson OH 44236
Contact: Cindy Hartman
Phone: (330)653-9730
Fax: (330)528-0742
E-mail: Changing.
Offers: Traditional primitive rug hooking: custom rugs, kits, lessons, supplies—the Hartman Hook (brass and ewe wool, made in Ireland)—wool (as is and dyed), backing, patterns, frames and cutters.
Catalog: $5 for color pictures and supply list.
Accepts: MasterCard, Visa

HIGHLAND HEART HOOKERY

23 Chartwell Lane
Halifax, Nova Scotia B3M 3S7
Canada
Contact: Anne or Doug Rankin
Phone: (902)445-4644
Fax: (902)445-4644
E-mail: aq288@ccn.cs.dal.ca
Store Location: At above address.
Offers: Rug-hooking supplies, patterns, kits, frames, hand-dyed wools, other rug-hooking supplies.
Catalog: Available September 1998.
Phone Orders: Yes.
Mail Orders: Will ship to US and Canada.
Discounts: Sell wholesale to legitimate businesses. Discounts to teachers.
Accepts: Visa—retail only

THE HOOK NOOK

1 Morgan Rd.
Flemington NJ 08822
Phone: (908)806-8083
Offers: Lib Callaway Collection of rug-hooking patterns. Also classes and supplies.
Catalog: $6.

I.W. DESIGNS

513 Clemson Dr.
Pittsburgh PA 15243
Contact: Sandra Brown
Phone: (412)279-4373
E-mail: sand25176@aol.com
Website: i_w_designs.com
Offers: Rug-hooking frame: the Pittsburgh Crafting Frame, which folds for travel; folds to 2″ high and fits in book bag; gripper strip design.
Catalog: See website.
Phone Orders: Yes.
Mail Orders: At above address.
Discounts: On quantity orders.
Accepts: personal check

JACQUELINE DESIGNS

237 Pine Point Rd.
Scarborough ME 04074
Phone: (207)883-5403
Website: http://www.rughookersnetwork.com
Offers: Rug-hooking patterns in traditional and primitive designs (on cotton, homespun, linen, wool and burlap with precut wool strips): florals, fruits, pictorals, scenics, Christmas motifs and others. Also offers bliss cutters, wool yardage, custom-dyed swatches, precut stripettes, frames (Puritan and hoops), custom designing and workshops. New book: *Leaves, Flowers and Scrolls* and others.
Catalog: Catalog, $8 postpaid. Instructor booklet, $14.95 prepaid.
Discounts: Teachers and institutions; sells wholesale to legitimate businesses.

LIZIANA CREATIONS

770 Blue Hills Ave.
Bloomfield CT 06002
Contact: Diana O'Brien
Phone: (860)243-8955 or (860)289-0430
Fax: (860)242-9919
E-mail: diana@ntplx.net
Website: www.liziana.com
Store Location: At above address. M,T,F, 10-4:30; 1st Sat, 9-4.
Offers: Traditional rug-hooking supplies, equipment and lessons; patterns; wool: dyed and off the bolt; kits; hook-ins and programs presented throughout the year. Custom designing service available.
Catalog: $3.
Phone Orders: Yes.

Mail Orders: US and Canada. Prepayment by check or money order. Allow 4 weeks delivery.
Discounts: Available to teachers upon receipt of legitimate references.
Accepts: no credit cards

MANDY'S WOOL SHED

24 W. Wind Rd.
West Gardiner ME 04345
Phone: (207)582-5059
Offers: Wool fabric (for hooking, braiding and weaving): tweeds, plaids, solids in pastels and white wool.
Catalog: Samples set (100), $3.
Discounts: Quantity.

MORTON HOUSE PRIMITIVES

9860 Crestwood Terrace
Eden Prairie MN 55347
Phone: (612)936-0966
Offers: Primitive rug-hooking designs printed on monk's cloth, rug warp or linen.
Catalog: $4.50 prepaid.
Discounts: Teachers and shops.

THE MOUNTAIN HANDCRAFTS CO.

3 Van Buren St.
Eureka Springs AR 72632
Contact: Diane Gay
Phone: (501)253-4965
Fax: (501)253-2143
E-mail: davidgay@ipa.net
Website: www.eureka-net.com/handcraft
Store Location: At above address. 9-8 during season.
Offers: Primitive rug-hooking supplies, including kits, patterns, a variety of hooks, books, magazines and a very large selection of recycled and overdyed wools.
Catalog: Price list, free for asking (and on-line).
Phone Orders: Yes.
Mail Orders: Yes.
Accepts: American Express, Discover, MasterCard, Visa

PAT MOYER

308 W. Main St.
Terre Hill PA 17581
Contact: Pat Moyer
Phone: (717)445-6263
Store Location: Terre Hill PA location.
Offers: Designs by Pay Moyer. Patterns for hooked rugs, all styles and sizes. Catalog/workbook. Dial-a-Harmony color wheel makes color selection easy; harmonious color combinations shown on dials.
Catalog: Send SASE for details.
Phone Orders: Yes.
Mail Orders: Yes.
Discounts: To teachers only.
Accepts: check, money order

NEW EARTH DESIGNS/JEANNE BENJAMIN

(formerly Jeanne Benjamin)
81 Lake Rd.
Brookfield MA 01506
Phone: (508)867-8114
E-mail: newearthdesign@juno.com
Offers: Silkscreened patterns for traditional rug hooking—over 400 designs of all types. Hand-dyed wool swatches, spots, skies and yardage. Some kits available.
Catalog: Pattern catalog, $6 ppd. Swatch and wool listing, $2, prepaid. Kit listing, #10 SASE.
Phone Orders: 9-5 EST or leave message.
Mail Orders: US and Canada.
Discounts: To legitimate teachers and stores.

POLKA'S YARN FARM

RR 2, Box 317
Vandergrift PA 15690
Contact: Alvina Polka
Phone: (724)845-6883
Store Location: RR 2, Spruce Hollow Rd., Vandergrift PA.
Offers: Locker hooks and supplies, rug backing, carded wool, kits, books and video.
Catalog: Yes.
Phone Orders: Yes.
Mail Orders: Yes.

PRIMITIVE PASTIMES

(formerly Kim Dubay)
37 Bow St.
Freeport ME 04032
Contact: Kim Dubay
Phone: (207)865-6897
E-mail: rogdubay@aol.com
Store Location: At above address.
Offers: "Primitive Pastimes" line of original primitive pre-cut hooked rug kits and patterns. Also carry some supplies for rug making: wool (as is and hand-dyed), hooks, pattern books by Kindred Spirits, burlap by the yard and more.
Catalog: $5 ppd, color. Send check or money order.
Phone Orders: To prequalified wholesale orders only.
Mail Orders: Will ship to street address in US; Canada for an additional charge.
Discounts: Wholesale available to qualified teachers and shops.
Accepts: personal check, money order

RED CLOVER RUGS

84554 Parkway Rd.
Pleasant Hill OR 97455
Contact: Barbara Benner
Phone: (800)858-YARN or (541) 744-5934
E-mail: barbararcr@msn.com
Offers: Over 145 Shelburne Museum and original Red Clover patterns for both punch needle and traditional rug hooking. Over 325 colors of wool rug yarn. Punch needle rug kits, books and the Oxford Punch needle also available. Also offers custom designing of punch-hooked rugs.

Catalog: New 32 pages, color. $4.
Phone Orders: M-F, 8-3 PST.
Accepts: MasterCard, Visa

RIGBY CLOTH STRIPPING MACHINES

P.O. Box 158
Bridgton ME 04009
Contact: J. David Paulson
Phone: (207)647-5679
Store Location: At above address.
Offers: The original cloth-stripping machine, which cuts wool into narrow strips for hooking or wider strips for braiding or weaving. Available in 4 models and 10 sizes of cutter heads. Offers cutter regrinding service. Manufacturer.
Catalog: Yes.
Phone Orders: Yes.
Mail Orders: Best way.
Discounts: Yes.
Accepts: check

RUG HOOKING, INC.

3603 Johnston St., Suite Q
Lafayette LA 70503
Contact: Tanya Bourque
Phone: (318)993-3460
Fax: (318)993-3460
E-mail: rughooking@sminet.com
Store Location: At above address. T-F, 10-4; Sat, 10-3.
Offers: 100% virgin wool rug yarn, 100% cotton monk's cloth, patterns, frames, oxford punch needle, ball winders and more. Kits and custom rugs.
Catalog: $4 (refundable).
Phone Orders: T-F, 10-4.
Mail Orders: Will ship to US and Canada. Prepayment required.
Discounts: Discount for teachers/professional groups.
Accepts: American Express, MasterCard, Visa

SAX ARTS & CRAFTS

P.O. Box 510710
2405 S. Calhoun Rd.
New Berlin WI 53151
Phone: (414)784-6880
Offers: A variety of supplies (known brands), including a full line of weaving looms and aids, yarns, weaving kits, rug/craft yarns, embroidery/crewel threads, rug hook frames and aids, canvas hoops, burlap and felt. Native American beading, beads, feathers, macrame, basketry and batik supplies, fabric paints, airbrush kits and inks, stencil films, trims, foam, stained glass kits, etching and beveled glass supplies and supplies for decoupage, jewelry making, leather, casting, plastics, wood and metalworking are also available.
Catalog: $5 (refundable).
Discounts: Quantity; sells wholesale to legitimate businesses.

SEA HOLLY HOOKED RUGS
1906 M. Bay Dr.
Kill Devil Hills NC 27948
Contact: Jean Edmonds
Phone: (252)441-8961
Store Location: By appointment.
Offers: Traditional rug-hooking kits/patterns. Wools by the yard or pound and hand-dyed wool. Also offers hooks, rug shears and frames, including Heritage lap frame with gripper strips. Also offers burlap, rug binding and other aids and supplies. Books are also available.
Catalog: Coming soon.
Phone Orders: Yes.
Mail Orders: Yes.
Accepts: major credit cards

SHILLCRAFT
8899 Kelso Dr.
Baltimore MD 21221
Phone: (410)682-3060
Fax: (410)682-3130
Offers: Latchhook kits (for rugs, pillows and wall hangings)—designs stenciled on canvas with precut wool or acrylic yarn, interchangeable colors available), traditional and contemporary motifs: Kamariah and Persian, florals, animals, Southwestern, children's, patriotic, inspirational, Christmas and others. Tools and aids, cross-stitch and other needlecraft kits.
Catalog: $1.
Discounts: Sells wholesale to legitimate businesses.

SPRUCE TOP RUG HOOKING STUDIO, INC.
255 W. Main St.
Mahone Bay, Nova Scotia B0J 2E0
Canada
Contact: Carol Harvey-Clark
Phone: (902)624-1923 or (888)RUG-HOOK
Store Location: At above address.
Offers: Gallery of fine hooked rugs, supplies for rug hooking, classes and books. Open year-round.
Catalog: Free.
Phone Orders: (888)RUG-HOOK.
Mail Orders: Yes.
Discounts: Teachers' discount.
Accepts: American Express, MasterCard, Visa

SWEET BRIAR STUDIO
P.O. Box 731
Hope Valley RI 02832
Phone: (401)539-1009

Offers: Traditional and primitive supplies for rug making, custom designs and designer patterns.
Catalog: Send for catalog. $5.
Mail Orders: Yes.
Accepts: American Express, Discover, MasterCard, Visa

TRIPLE OVER DYE
187 Jane Dr.
Syracuse NY 13219
Phone: (315)468-2616
Offers: TOD dye formulas books (over 100 formulas per book)—*TOD Book I* and *TOD Book II* by Lydia Hicks and *TOD Book III* by Janet Matthews. Includes TOD snips (8 shade samples to put with each formula in TOD books). Also offers measuring spoons—¼-¹⁄₃₂ teaspoon.
Catalog: Free brochure.
Discounts: Quantity; teachers and institutions.

THE WOOL WINDER
RR 1
Manilla, Ontario K0M 2J0
Canada
Contact: Lois Glanville
Phone: (705)786-1358
Store Location: 1 hour northeast of Toronto.
Offers: Primitive rug-hooking as well as braiding supplies. New Locker hooking and Penny rug supplies. Wool fabric, backings, books and more. All supplies required for the mentioned crafts.
Catalog: Price list.
Phone Orders: Yes.
Mail Orders: Yes.
Discounts: To teachers and shops.
Accepts: check, C.O.D.

WOOL WORKS PLUS
1246 Oak Ridge Dr.
South Bend IN 46617
Phone: (219)234-2587
Offers: Line of rug-hooking and braiding supplies and accessories.
Catalog: $1 (refundable).
Discounts: Teachers and dealers.

YANKEE PEDDLER HOOKED RUGS
57 Saxonwood Rd.
Fairfield CT 06430
Phone: (203)255-5399
Offers: Rug-hooking wool by yard or pound, line of other supplies including hooks, frames, new designs for spot-dyed wools and others.
Catalog: $5; send large SASE for flyer.

Sewing

Also see other categories of Section II.

ALL BRANDS

9789 Florida Blvd.
Baton Rouge LA 70815
Phone: (504)923-1285 or (800)739-7374
Fax: (800)866-1261 or (504)923-1261
E-mail: sewserg@aol.com
Website: allbrands.com
Offers: Sewing machines, sergers and embroidery machines: Bernina, Baby Lock, Pfaff, New Home, Juki, Elna, Viking, White, Necchi, Riccar, Brother, Simplicity and Singer; commercial brands—Johnson, Thompson, Singer, Juki and others. Monogrammers—Toyota, Brother, Melco, Pfaff and others. Also offers smocking pleaters, machine accessories, cabinets, tables, pressing equipment and warehouse locations nationwide.
Catalog: Send SASE for list (specify product, brand and price levels).
Accepts: American Express, Discover, MasterCard, Visa, Home Source 90-day interest free

AMAZON DRYGOODS

2218 E. 11th St.
Davenport IA 52803
Phone: (319)322-6800
Fax: (319)322-4008
Offers: Nineteenth-century-inspired products: over 11,000 historic/ethnic clothes patterns, up to the 1950s, with emphasis on the 1800s; men's and women's clothing including corsets and military uniforms. Supplies/aids: hoop wire, boning, stays and feathers. Fabrics: Nainsook, batiste and other cottons, flannels, taffeta, satins, gold "bouillon" frieze and tradecloth. Also offers hat veilings, trims, military buttons and yard goods (blue, butternut, gray wool and others). Books available on costuming, fashions, accessories and lace making and Victorian and Indian clothing. Carries ready-made historic clothes, shoes, hats and accessories, plus washboards, buckets, washtubs and others.
Catalog: General, $3. Patterns, $7. Shoe, $5. Windows, $2.
Accepts: American Express, Discover, MasterCard, Visa

AMERICAN & EFIRD, INC.

P.O. Box 507
Mount Holly NC 28120
Contact: Jim Guin
Phone: (704)822-6014
Fax: (800)847-3236

Website: http://www.amefird.com
Offers: Maxi-Lock 100% polyester serger threads, signature gallery of threads, including 298 colors of all-purpose thread and an extended array of specialty threads. A&E is also the exclusive US importer of Mettler premium quality threads and the exclusive US distributor of the YKK home sewing products line and Blue Ridge yarns. Contact your dealer or send SASE.

ATLANTA THREAD & SUPPLY CO.

695 Red Oak Rd.
Stockbridge GA 30281
Phone: (800)847-1001
Offers: Sewing supplies/aids (some known brands): cone threads, closures, markers, linings/pockets, interfacings and shoulder pads. Also offers pliers, measurers, dress forms, hampers, caddies, gauges, notions, pleaters, cords, weights and pressing aids (irons, machines and steamers). High-speed sewing machines: Tacsew, Singer, Pfaff and Consew. Racks: counter, spiral, adjustable, garment and others. Also offers cutting machines.
Catalog: Free.
Discounts: Quantity.

BERNINA CANADA

(formerly Bernina Sewing Center)
660 Denison St.
Markham, Ontario L3R 1C1
Canada
Contact: Mario Stoller
Phone: (905)475-9365
Fax: (905)475-7022
Offers: Importers of Bernina sewing machines, embroidery machines and Bernette sergers.

THE BUTTON SHOP

7023 Roosevelt Rd.
Berwyn IL 60402
Phone: (708)795-1234
Offers: Sewing supplies: line of zippers, bindings and interfacings. Threads: mercerized, specialty, invisible, machine, carpet and metallics, including Talon American and others. Buttons: usuals, military and decoratives. Also offers trims, elastics, tapes, cords, bra parts, pockets, ribbons, knit cuffs, measurers, closures, buckles, markers and notions. Carries old treadle and other sewing machine parts, plus new parts. Also offers scissors.
Catalog: Free.
Discounts: Quantity; sells wholesale.

CAROL'S CREATIONS

(formerly C. Cummings)
67 DeRow Court
Sacramento CA 95833
Contact: Carol Cummings
Phone: (916)927-8801
Offers: Writing publications, including copyright/marketing pattern designs and other. *How to Copyright, Professionally Package and Nationally Market Your Original Pattern Designs for Big Money.* $12 ppd.
Catalog: Free.
Mail Orders: Yes.
Accepts: check

CHILDREN'S CORNER, INC.

3814 Cleghorn Ave.
Nashville TN 37215
Contact: Ginger Caldwell
Phone: (615)385-0303
Fax: (615)385-0837
E-mail: lthomcson@nashville.com
Website: http://www.childrenscornerfabric.com
Store Location: At above address.
Offers: Designer children's clothing patterns for classics, smocking and French hand sewing. Also patterns for 17½"-19½" dolls, books, fabric and fine trims.
Catalog: $2.50. 32 pages.
Phone Orders: 9-3 CST.
Mail Orders: Will ship US, Canada and Australia.
Discounts: Sells wholesale to legitimate businesses.
Accepts: MasterCard, Visa

CREANATIVITY

P.O. Box 335
Thiensville WI 53092
Phone: (414)242-5477 or (800)929-2386
Offers: Soft sculpture craft patterns: hands-on Nativity set and large Noah's ark set. Send SASE.
Accepts: American Express, Discover, MasterCard, Visa

CROWNING TOUCH, INC.

2410 Glory C Rd.
Medford OR 97501
Contact: Emma Graham
Phone: (541)772-8430
Fax: (541)772-5106
Store Location: 3859 S. Stage Rd., Medford OR 97501.
Offers: Fasturn products, universal presser foot lifter, sewing tools and notions, patterns and Pear Blossom doll patterns.
Catalog: Yes.
Phone Orders: Yes.
Mail Orders: Yes.
Discounts: 10% to American Sewing Guild members. 10% to teachers.
Accepts: Discover, MasterCard, Visa

CSZ ENTERPRISES, INC.

1288 W. 11th St., Suite 200
Tracy CA 95376
Phone: (209)832-4324
Offers: Dress forms and pants forms kits: exactly duplicates body (make own or custom made). Also offers instructional videos and form stands. Send SASE.

DELECTABLE MOUNTAIN CLOTH

125 Main St.
Brattleboro VT 05301
Phone: (802)257-4456
E-mail: jan@delectablemountain.com
Website: www.delectablemountain.com
Store Location: At above address.
Offers: Silks, velvets, jacquards, scrim and linens. Buttons: glass, metal shell and tagua nut.
Catalog: Sampling of fabrics, repro Victorian, many silks, $10. Button brochure, $2. SASE.
Phone Orders: With sampling, M-Sat, 10-5.
Mail Orders: With sampling. Will ship to US.
Discounts: No wholesale.
Accepts: American Express, MasterCard, Visa

DOGWOOD LANE

P.O. Box 145
Dugger IN 47848
Phone: (800)648-2213
Offers: Handmade porcelain buttons (folk shapes), classic clothing and patterns.
Catalog: $2.50.

DRESS RITE FORMS

3817 N. Pulaski
Chicago IL 60614
Phone: (773)588-5761
Offers: Dress forms for all sizes and shapes; male and female. Send for custom forms.

EASTMAN MACHINE CO.

779 Washington St.
Buffalo NY 14203
Contact: Deborah Flemming
Phone: (716)856-2200
Fax: (716)856-2068
E-mail: sales@eastmanww.com
Website: eastmanww.com
Offers: Cutting equipment, electric rotary shears, scissors, thread trimmers, markers, thread winders, chalk, pattern marking and CAD software.
Phone Orders: M-F, 7:30-5:30 EST.
Mail Orders: Will ship to any location. Prepayment required.
Discounts: Sells wholesale to legitimate businesses.
Accepts: MasterCard, Visa

ELNA USA

1760 Gilsinn Lane
Fenton MO 63026
Phone: (800)848-ELNA (US) or (800)263-2313 (Canada)
Fax: (800)270-ELNA
Website: www.elnausa.com
Offers: Complete line of computerized and mechanical sewing machines, sergers, accessories and attachments. Available through independent dealer network. Also offer ironing presses.

FASHION FABRICS CLUB/NATURAL FIBER FABRICS

10490-10512 Baur Blvd.
St. Louis MO 63132
Phone: (314)993-4919 or (800)468-0602
Offers: Fabrics from clothing lines of designers, such as Liz Claiborne, Jones New York and Leslie Fay. Natural synthetic fibers, including silks, wools, cottons, linens, rayons and blends.
Catalog: Send SASE for brochure.

GREENBERG & HAMMER, INC.

24 W. 57th St.
New York NY 10019
Contact: Frank T. Piazza, president
Phone: (212)246-2835 or (800)955-5135
Fax: (212)765-8475
E-mail: Soon.
Website: Soon.
Store Location: At above address.
Offers: Interfacings, sewing notions, accessories and supplies for dressmakers, costumers, milliners and others. Also offers professional steamers.
Catalog: Free.
Phone Orders: M-F, 9-6; Sat, 10-5 EST.
Mail Orders: Will ship worldwide. Will accept C.O.D.—cash only.
Discounts: Sells wholesale. Discounts apply depending on quantity.
Accepts: American Express, MasterCard, Visa

HANCOCK'S OF PADUCAH

(formerly Hancock Fabrics)
3841 Hinkleville Rd.
Paducah KY 42001
Contact: Justin Hancock
Phone: (502)443-4410
Fax: (502)442-2164
E-mail: hanpad@sunsix.infi.net or email@hancocks-paducah.com
Website: www.hancocks-paducah.com
Store Location: I-24, exit 4 at State Highway 62.
Offers: World's largest supply of cotton fabrics for quilters. Also a huge selection of Waverly drapery and upholstery fabrics. Quilting notions, supplies and tools are offered at a substantial discount to retail.
Catalog: Free. 4 color, 72 pages.
Phone Orders: (800)845-8723.

Mail Orders: Shipping to all points worldwide. Ship by USPS, UPS or FedEx.
Accepts: Discover, MasterCard, Visa, cashier's check, personal check (US funds)

HOME-SEW

Dept. CS1
P.O. Box 4099
Bethlehem PA 18018
Contact: Lucy W. Perusse
Phone: (800)344-4739 or (610)867-3833
Fax: (610)867-9717
Offers: Sewing and craft supplies. Home-Sew is known for its famous assortments of trims, laces, appliqués, ricrac and bows. Offers cotton polyester, allover laces, cluny, venice, lace sets and eyelets. Also elastics, quilting supplies, cone thread, sewing aids, felt, muslin, battenberg, doilies, ribbon and doll supplies.
Catalog: Free. Add 50¢ to join sample club.
Mail Orders: Will ship overseas.
Discounts: Wholesale. Free postage on mail orders over $50. Quantity discounts.
Accepts: MasterCard, Novus, Visa

ISLANDER SEWING SYSTEMS

(formerly Islander—Video Division)
P.O. Box 66
Grants Pass OR 97528
Contact: Karen Calvert
Phone: (541)479-3906
Fax: (541)479-3906
E-mail: sew-tech@chatlink.com
Website: http://www.islandersewing.com
Store Location: Office: 396 Calvert Dr., Grants Pass OR 97526.
Offers: Seminars, instruction in drafting, production-line sewing and couture/fine sewing. Travels to hosted seminars; will schedule throughout US and Canada and other locations.
Catalog: Call or write to above.
Phone Orders: 24-hour answering machine.
Mail Orders: At P.O. Box.
Discounts: Wholesale. Case lot and package discounts.
Accepts: Discover, MasterCard, Visa, check, money order (US funds)

JUDITH M MILLINERY

104 S. Detroit St.
LaGrange IN 46761-1806
Contact: Judith Mishler
Phone: (219)499-4407
E-mail: Coming.
Website: Coming.
Store Location: At above address. M-Th, 12-6; F-Sat, 10:30-6.
Offers: Millinery supplies: hat blocks, boxes, stands, felt and straw bodies, ribbons, nonrusting needles, pins and pushpins, sizing, veiling, glues, wires, horsehair, buckram by the yard, feathers, flower trims and 50 book titles.

Catalog: Free.
Phone Orders: During shop hours or leave a message.
Mail Orders: Will ship US, Canada and international.
Discounts: Quantity. Teachers and institutions.
Accepts: MasterCard, Visa

LIFETIME CAREER SCHOOLS
Dept. CSS9918
101 Harrison St.
Archbald PA 18403
Phone: (800)326-9221 or (717)876-6340
Fax: (717)876-8179
Offers: Home study diploma programs in landscaping, flower arranging and floristry, sewing/dressmaking, doll repair, secretarial, bookkeeping, cooking and small business management.
Catalog: Free color brochure.
Phone Orders: M-F, 8:30-5 EST.
Mail Orders: Will ship to US, Canada and foreign countries.
Accepts: MasterCard, Visa

LIVE GUIDES
10306 64th Place W.
Mukilteo WA 98275
Phone: (206)353-0240
Offers: Generic serger instructional video—all aspects of serger sewing on 9 models of sergers (purchase or rent). Send SASE.
Accepts: MasterCard, Visa

MARY'S PRODUCTIONS
Dept. CSS
P.O. Box 87
217 N. Main
Aurora MN 55705
Phone: (218)229-2804
Fax: (218)229-2533
E-mail: mbmulari@virginia.k12.mn.us
Offers: Sewing books: appliqué, accents, sweatshirts, travel gear/gifts, squeakers and others.
Catalog: Send SASE for free brochure.
Discounts: Sells wholesale.

NANCY'S NOTIONS
Dept. 32
P.O. Box 683
Beaver Dam WI 53916-0683
Phone: (800)833-0690
Fax: (800)255-8119
Website: http://www.nancysnotions.com
Offers: A source for unique sewing and quilting supplies and accessories, including thread for any type of plain or decorative stitching, specialty presser feet, hundreds of handy notions, important machine care tools, practical serger products and beautiful fabrics, plus educational videos and references from the *Sewing With Nancy* public television program. Nancy's Notions offers Value Priced products, staff-tested quality, guaranteed satisfaction, knowledgeable and

friendly customer service and speedy delivery.
Catalog: Free.
Discounts: Qualified sewing professionals and wholesale accounts.

NANCY'S VIDEO LIBRARY
P.O. Box 3000
Beaver Dam WI 53916-3000
Phone: (800)336-8373
Fax: (800)255-8119
Website: http://www.nancysvideolibrary.com
Offers: Over 200 sewing, quilting and craft videos for rent. Subjects include basic to advanced sewing skills, crafts and gifts, creating and embellishing, embroidery, home decorating and furnishings, fitting and wardrobing, machine care, needlework and hobbies, quilting and serging. Rental costs range from $4.95 to $8.95 per video for Video Library members ($2 per video higher for nonmembers). One time membership fee includes members-only specials and quarterly updates. Video rental period is 7 days. Prepaid postage return bag/box provided. Rent 11 videos and get 12th rental free with Video Library Bonus Program.
Catalog: Free.

NATIONAL THREAD & SUPPLY CO.
695 Red Oak Rd.
Stockbridge GA 30281
Phone: (800)331-7600
Offers: Sewing threads—over 40 types, including Coats & Clark serging thread (in 250 colors). Also offers Wiss and Gingher scissors, Sussman irons, Dritz notions and others.
Catalog: Free.
Accepts: American Express, MasterCard, Visa

NEW YORK FELT, INC.
107 Court St., Suite 17
Watertown NY 13601
Contact: Todd Badalato
Phone: (800)635-3267 (US); (800)782-5763 (Canada)
Fax: (315)788-4087
E-mail: nyfelt@gisco.net
Store Location: 6 Fisher Dr., Watertown NY 13601.
Offers: Pressed wool felts, burlap, and vinyl.
Catalog: Felt and burlap color cards, $3 (refundable).
Phone Orders: M-F, 8-4 EST.
Mail Orders: Will ship across US. Prompt delivery.
Discounts: Quantity, teachers and institutions.
Accepts: MasterCard, Visa

112 SEWING SUPPLIES
142 Medford Ave.
Patchogue NY 11772
Phone: (516)475-8282
Store Location: At above address.
Offers: Sewing machine parts, attachments, accessories for home/commercial models and hard-to-find items.
Catalog: $1.
Discounts: Teachers and institutions.

PATTERN STUDIO

P.O. Box 15874
Cincinnati OH 45215-0874
Contact: Dee Atkinson
Phone: (513)821-HATS
Offers: Millinery patterns and supplies, glove-making patterns and supplies, books related to millinery and gloves, general sewing supplies, glove-making starter kits, hat pins, glove-making fabrics and linings, beading kits, interfacings, plastic for hat visors, rulers, proportional scales, warm and natural batting, wire ribbon, millinery and glove-making seminars and workshops.
Catalog: $3 (not refundable).
Phone Orders: Leave message with details if no answer.
Mail Orders: At above address. Will ship to Canada (add $3 postage) and US. Allow 4 weeks for delivery.
Discounts: Sells patterns wholesale to legitimate businesses.
Accepts: MasterCard, Visa, check, money order

PURCHASE FOR LESS

P.O. Box 363
Philo CA 95466
Phone: (707)895-9500
Fax: (707)895-9500
E-mail: pfl@pacific.net
Website: http://www.purchaseforless.com
Offers: New quilting/sewing books. Appliqué, patchwork, foundation method, samplers, imagery, modular, traditional and contemporary, basic, advanced, shortcuts and others. Sewing subjects include clothing/quilting, serging, cutting, colors, couture, embroidery and other fiber arts.
Catalog: $2, mailed out first-class mail.
Phone Orders: Yes.
Mail Orders: At above address.
Discounts: Average discount 33% with reasonable shipping charges.
Accepts: call for payment instruction

RANITA CORP.—SURE-FIT DESIGNS/FABRIQUE

P.O. Box 5698
Eugene OR 97405-0698
Contact: Glenda Sparling
Phone: (541)344-0422
Fax: (541)344-3944
E-mail: crickett@jb.com
Website: getcreativeshow.com
Offers: Patterns, fitting tools and fabric embellishment books.
Phone Orders: Yes.
Mail Orders: At above address.
Accepts: MasterCard, Visa, check

SARAH'S SEWING SUPPLIES

7267-A Mobile Hwy.
Pensacola FL 32526
Contact: Sarah Doyle
Phone: (850)944-2960
E-mail: sarah@wordsetc.com

Website: http://www.wordsetc.com
Offers: Sewing supplies, patternmaking books and videos, craft and how-to books and sewing machine and serger repair books.
Catalog: $2 (refundable).
Phone Orders: M-Sat, 8-8 CST.
Mail Orders: Ship to US, Canada and overseas.
Accepts: MasterCard, Visa

SEW FANCY

4745 Eighth Line
RR 1
Beeton, Ontario L0G 1A0
Canada
Contact: Beverly Johnson
Phone: (905)775-1396
Fax: (905)775-0107
E-mail: email@sewfancy.com
Website: www.sewfancy.com
Store Location: M-Sat, 9-4.
Offers: Supplies for sewing heirlooms and intimates, including heirloom (French hand) sewing, smocking, embroidery and now bra making and fine lingerie. Complete line of hard-to-find notions and designer patterns.
Catalog: Full-size 8½×11. $5 (refundable), upon request.
Phone Orders: (800)SEW-FNCY.
Mail Orders: Orders sent by post or courier.
Discounts: 25% discount with business documents.
Accepts: MasterCard, Visa

SEWIN' IN VERMONT

84 Concord Ave.
St. Johnsbury VT 05819
Phone: (802)748-3803 or (800)451-5124 or (888)451-5124
Fax: (802)748-2165
Store Location: At above address.
Offers: Major brand sewing machines, sergers and presses with discounted prices. Also offers notions and machine embroidery supplies.
Catalog: Brochures.
Phone Orders: M-F, 9:30-5 EST.
Mail Orders: Will ship to US and Canada.
Discounts: All our products have a discounted price.
Accepts: Discover, MasterCard, Visa

SILKPAINT CORP.

P.O. Box 18
18220 Waldron Dr.
Waldron, MO 64092
Phone: (816)891-7774
Fax: (816)891-7775
Website: www.silkpaint.com
Offers: Fiber-Etch Fabric Remover (removes plant fibers within embroidered area for "instant cutwork"). Also offers silk-painting items.
Catalog: Free.
Discounts: Sells wholesale to legitimate businesses.
Accepts: MasterCard, Visa

THE SMOCKING BONNET

1341 W. Liberty Rd.
Sykesville MD 21784
Contact: Kathleen Hamblet
Phone: (410)552-3380
Fax: (410)552-3396
Store Location: At above address.
Offers: Fine fabrics, laces, patterns, books and plates for the smocker, and French/heirloom sewing services available. Friendly, prompt service; most orders shipped same day.
Catalog: Current (1997) edition, $5.
Phone Orders: (800)524-1678. M-F, 10-4; Sat, 10-2.
Mail Orders: P.O. Box 53, Lisbon MD 21765. Will ship anywhere US Mail or UPS will take it.
Discounts: 25% off retail to legitimate business. $50 minimum order.
Accepts: American Express, Discover, MasterCard, Visa

SOLO SLIDE FASTENERS, INC.

(formerly Solo Sewing Supplies)
P.O. Box 378
8 Spring Brook Rd.
Foxboro MA 02035
Contact: Michael C. Flatto
Phone: (508)698-0303
Fax: (508)698-2813
E-mail: solozip@tiac.net
Offers: Alteration and sewing supplies, including zippers, thread, scissors, irons and sewing machines.
Catalog: Yes.
Phone Orders: Yes.
Mail Orders: Yes.

SOUTHSTAR SUPPLY

(formerly Scissors & Snips)
P.O. Box 90147
Nashville TN 37209
Contact: Diane Kuykendall
Phone: (615)353-7000
Fax: (615)353-7155
E-mail: southstar@worldnet.att.net
Website: www.southstarsupply.com
Store Location: At above address.
Offers: Parts, supplies and equipment for patternmaking, cutting, sewing and finishing of sewn products.
Catalog: Available upon request.
Phone Orders: M-F, 7-5 CST.
Mail Orders: Contact SouthStar by phone, fax or E-mail first to get quote of current pricing, taxes and freight.
Discounts: Based on quantity ordered.
Accepts: American Express, MasterCard, Visa

SUCCESSFUL SEWING BOOK CLUB

1507 Dana Ave.
Cincinnati OH 45207
Contact: Mary Dacres, editor
Phone: (513)531-2690
Fax: (513)531-4744

Offers: The club catalog and newsletter, describing the main selection book, several alternates and dozens of other book offerings arrives about every 4 weeks. It includes hard-to-find tools and gadgets, videos and more—all at a discount price.

THINGS JAPANESE

9805 NE 116th St., Suite 7160
Kirkland WA 98034
Contact: Maggie Backman
Phone: (425)821-2287
Fax: (425)821-3554
E-mail: thingsjapanese@seanet.com
Offers: Silk notions, including thread, ribbon, bias ribbon and instant-set fabric dyes and paints to "color" and embellish silk fibers. Also offers instructional guides and kits for coloring, stenciling and stamping silks. New video: *Dyeing in a Teacup*.
Catalog: $1.
Phone Orders: Yes.
Mail Orders: Yes.
Discounts: Wholesale and retail.

THREADBARE PATTERN CO.

P.O. Box 1484
Havelock NC 28532
Phone: (800)4-PATTERN
Fax: (919)447-7957
E-mail: patterns@coastalnet.com
Offers: Wearable art patterns.
Catalog: Flyers with orders.
Phone Orders: Yes.
Mail Orders: Yes.
Accepts: American Express, Discover, MasterCard, Visa, check, cash

TIMBERLINE SEWING KITS

P.O. Box 126-CS
16 Clark St.
Pittsfield NH 03263-0126
Contact: "Fuzz" Freese
Phone: (603)435-8888
Store Location: At above address.
Offers: Ready-to-sew kits for outerwear and outdoor gear; jackets, vests, totes, garment and cargo bags, packs, bike bags, drawstring sacks, billfolds, wallets, accessory pouches, ski bags, gaiters and others. Also offers comforter kits (4 bed sizes). Manufacturer.
Catalog: Brochure, $1. Raw materials list included upon request.
Phone Orders: Yes.
Mail Orders: At above address.
Discounts: 10% discounts to school and educational groups; $50 minimum.
Accepts: check, money order

TREADLEART

25834 Narbonne Ave.
Lomita CA 90717
Contact: Janet Stocker
Phone: (310)534-5122
Fax: (310)534-8372
E-mail: treadleart@aol.com
Website: treadleart.com
Store Location: At above address. Also 1965 Mendocino Ave., Santa Rosa CA 95401. (707)523-2122.
Offers: Books, patterns, notions, thread, sewing supplies and machine accessories. Also sewing machines and fabric.
Catalog: $3 (refundable).
Phone Orders: 8-6 weekdays.
Mail Orders: Ship anywhere.
Discounts: Have a separate wholesale catalog.
Accepts: American Express, Discover, MasterCard, Visa

A VERY UNUSUAL PLACE

4683 Clearview St.
Salt Lake City UT 84117
Contact: Bea Proctor
Phone: (801)277-4914
E-mail: bproctor@aros.net
Website: needlearts.com
Store Location: At above address. By appointment.
Offers: Smocking, heirloom sewing, silk ribbon embroidery and tatting (needle and shuttle).
Catalog: 64 pages. $8 (credit coupon $3 on first $25 order).
Phone Orders: Yes.
Mail Orders: At above address.
Accepts: MasterCard, Visa

WELLSPRING GALLERY

P.O. Box 64429
Los Angeles CA 90064
Phone: (310)441-4204
Fax: (310)470-6424
Website: www.wellspringgallery.com
Offers: Art/specialty sewing products, including threads—tire silk, Sulky metallic, rayon and hand embroidery types. Also offers stabilizers, including interfacing, iron-ons and liquids. Specialty books, including technique, art sewing, beading, design, paper and basketry titles available. Also carries other supplies. Call or send SASE.

WINSOR TRADING, INC./SOBUCK

P.O. Box 16367
Seattle WA 98116
Contact: Jon Cook
Phone: (206)937-4082
Fax: (206)935-5310
E-mail: winsortr@sprynet.com
Website: http://home.sprynet.com/sprynet/winsortr
Store Location: Seattle WA location.
Offers: Buckwheat hulls and buckwheat seed, birdseed and spray millet.

YLI CORP.

161 W. Main St.
Rock Hill SC 29730
Phone: (800)296-8139
Offers: Silk embroidery products, including ribbons in 185 colors, thread, floss, kits, patterns, videos and books. Also offers serging threads, including Wooly Nylon, Candlelight Metallic, monofilament, lingerie/bobbin and 100% cotton quilting thread.

Spinning & Weaving

Also see General Needlecraft Supplies; Knitting & Crochet; Knotting; Rug Making; Yarns; other related categories.

BLUSTER BAY WOODWORKS
P.O. Box 1970
Sitka AK 99835
Contact: Terry Lavallee
Phone: (888)747-7533
Offers: 34 styles of shuttles in 8 different hardwoods—all designed especially for handweavers—including 4 styles of end-feed shuttles.
Catalog: With color photo. Free.
Phone Orders: M-F, 9-5 Alaska time; 24-hour voice mail.
Mail Orders: Will ship worldwide. Allow 4-6 weeks for delivery.
Discounts: Wholesale inquiries welcome.
Accepts: MasterCard, Visa

BARE HILL STUDIOS/FIBER LOFT
P.O. Box 327
Rt. 111 (Post Office Bldg.)
Harvard MA 01451
Contact: Reba Maisel
Phone: (800)874-YARN
Fax: (978)456-8480
Store Location: At above address.
Offers: Natural fiber yarns for machine/hand crochet/knitting and weaving: Rowan, Tahki, Elite, Sirdar, Noro, Jaeger, Reynolds and more. Also offers mill ends and exotic fibers (silks, angoras and ribbons).
Catalog: Yarn samples, $5.25. Additional exotic fibers, ribbon, $2.75.
Phone Orders: Yes.
Mail Orders: At above address.
Discounts: Quantity discount.
Accepts: Discover, MasterCard, Visa, check

BOUNTIFUL
P.O. Box 1727
125-B Moraine Ave.
Estes Park CO 80517
Contact: Lois or Bud Scarbrough
Phone: (970)586-9332
E-mail: bountiful@earthlink.net
Store Location: At above address. Hours vary; call.
Offers: Spinning wheels and looms from Schacht, Jensen, Louet, Ashford, Lendrum, Reeves, Timbertops, Majacraft, Dundas, Norwood, Cranbrook, Hagen, Harrisville, Glimakra, Leclerc and Beka, as well as Spin Now kits, children's kits, Navajo and tapestry looms, books, videos, fibers, yarns, knitting, parts and accessories. Has layaway service.
Catalog: Spinner's and Weaver's catalog, $3 each.
Phone Orders: 7 days a week, 9-8 MST.
Mail Orders: Ships to US, Canada and overseas.
Discounts: To schools and teachers.
Accepts: American Express, Discover, MasterCard, Visa

MAURICE BRASSARD ET FILS, INC.
1972 Simoneau
CP 4
Plessisville, Quebec G6L 2Y6
Canada
Offers: Weaving yarns: cottons, polyester, Orlon, linen, boucle and silk—all in several colors. Also offers Lamieux yarn (wool) and Nilus Leclerc looms.
Catalog: Free price list; list with samples, $9.95.

BY THE BAY CREATIONS/THE BAG LADY
1887 Union Ave.
North Bend OR 97459
Contact: Elaine Almquist
Phone: (541)756-7978
Fax: (541)756-9719
E-mail: baglady@harborside.com
Website: Pending.
Store Location: At above address.
Offers: Full line of spinning and weaving supplies, tools, yarns and knitting needles. Felting supplies. Books on related subjects. Dyes—extensive color/surface design book selection. Only manufacturer of quality spinning wheel tote bags and portable loom covers.
Catalog: $5 (refundable with first order).
Phone Orders: (888)756-7978.
Mail Orders: Ship worldwide.
Discounts: Wholesale to legitimate business.
Accepts: MasterCard, Visa

CAMERON FIBRE ARTS
RR 3
Ashton, Ontario K0H 1B0
Canada
Contact: Dini Cameron
Phone: (613)838-5000
Fax: (613)838-3763
E-mail: cfa@proweave.com
Website: http://www.proweave.com
Store Location: At above address.
Offers: Textile design software and training.
Phone Orders: Yes.

Mail Orders: Will ship anywhere.
Accepts: Visa

CAROLINA HOMESPUN
190 Eastridge Rd.
Ridgeway VA 24148
Contact: Merike Saarniit, owner
Phone: (540)957-1174
Fax: (540)957-2644
E-mail: carolina_homespun@msn.com
Store Location: At above address. By appointment only.
Offers: Spinning, weaving, knitting, fibercrafting equipment and supplies including spinning wheels, looms, dyes, fibers, yarns, books, videos. Merike teaches workshops at the sheep farm and on the road.
Catalog: $2.
Phone Orders: Anytime (leave message if calling after hours).
Mail Orders: UPS shipper. Will ship anywhere.
Discounts: Some wholesale to legitimate businesses.
Accepts: American Express, Discover, MasterCard, Visa

COBUN CREEK FARM
408 Cobun Creek Rd.
Morgantown WV 26508
Contact: Susan Elkin
Phone: (304)292-1907
Store Location: Outside Morgantown.
Offers: Raw and washed fleece for spinning and dolls/Santas. Coopworth 5-6″ high luster, white and natural grays.
Catalog: Sample price list, SASE with 25¢.
Phone Orders: 8 a.m.-9 p.m.
Mail Orders: Prefer.
Discounts: Volume; inquire.
Accepts: MasterCard, Visa

COTTON CLOUDS
5176 S. 14th Ave.
Safford AZ 85546
Contact: Irene Schmoller
Phone: (800)322-7888
Fax: (520)428-6630
E-mail: cottonclouds@az.org
Website: cottonclouds.com
Store Location: Safford AZ location.
Offers: Cotton and cotton blend yarns as well as rayon chenille yarns. Cotton spinning fibers and spinning wheels. Knitting machines, books and exclusively designed kits.
Catalog: $6.50 ($5 refundable).
Phone Orders: M-F, 8-3.
Mail Orders: Yes.
Discounts: Bulk discounts. Weekly specials.
Accepts: MasterCard, Visa

CUSTOM COLORS
P.O. Box 906
Dallas OR 97338
Contact: Kay Fielding

Phone: (503)623-3404
Fax: (503)623-3801
E-mail: custom@teleport.com
Offers: Sterling silver or 14 karat gold charms and jewelry. Fine quality alpacas, llamas, sheep, horses and other fiber animals, alone or on chains, charm bracelets and others. Also fiber animals in pins—great prizes for 4-H or breed shows or gifts to friends.
Catalog: Call for information.
Phone Orders: Yes.
Mail Orders: At above address. Prepayment required.
Discounts: Wholesale. Quantity to organizations.
Accepts: Discover, MasterCard, Visa

CYREFCO
P.O. Box 2559
Menlo Park CA 94026
Phone: (650)324-1796
Offers: 16 shaft Compumarche dobby systems to retrofit Cyrefco, Glimakra, Woolhouse and Cranbrook looms. End-delivery shuttles.
Catalog: $3.

DAFT DAMES HANDCRAFTS
P.O. Box 148-B
Akron NY 14001
Phone: (716)542-4235
Offers: Yarns, including pearl and mercerized cottons, cotton flake, silks, Shetland wool/polyesters and rayon chenille. Natural cotton warps.
Catalog: Send 75¢ for each sample.

THE DESIGNERY
(formerly Ayottes Designery)
P.O. Box 308-CSS
43 Maple St.
Center Sandwich NH 03227
Phone: (603)284-6915
Store Location: 43 Maple Street is shown on most maps as Rt. 113. T-Sat, 10-5.
Offers: Suppliers for weavers, knitters and spinners, including equipment, books, yarns, fibers, videos and other items from Brittany, Interweave Press, Leclerc, Louet, Schacht, Skacel and others. Also publishes weaving home study course. Package deals for new weavers and spinners. We're here to help!
Catalog: Supply catalog: Send 5 first-class stamps. Finished goods catalog: Send $5. For both, send check for $6.50 and specify both.
Phone Orders: T-Sat, 10-5.
Mail Orders: Yes.
Discounts: We offer package deals on a variety of items and supplies. These offers change, so check for our latest specials.
Accepts: Discover, MasterCard, Visa, money order

DUNDAS LOOM CO.
P.O. Box 7522
Missoula MT 59807
Phone: (406)728-3050

Fax: (406)728-4695
Offers: Floor and table looms in 3 sizes each; spinning wheels, tapestry looms, weaving and spinning accessories.
Catalog: Brochure, $2.50.
Discounts: Sells wholesale through dealers.

EATON YARNS

P.O. Box 665
Tarrytown NY 10591
Phone: (914)631-1550
Offers: Yarns from Finland: Tow and line linens, wools, cottons and seine twines. Also offers Poppana bias-cut cotton strips.
Catalog: Color cards, $2 each.

THE EWE TREE

61 Geoppert Rd.
Peninsula OH 44264
Phone: (216)650-6777
Offers: Fabric rolls, 6-12″ wide, for rug weaving, rug and basket crochet and other crafts; 40 lb. minimum.
Catalog: Send SASE for samples.
Accepts: American Express, Discover, MasterCard, Visa

FAIRMOUNT FARM FLEECES

Fairmount Farm, Thomas Rd.
Rindge NH 03461
Phone: (603)899-5445
Store Location: At above location.
Offers: Fleece for spinning and weaving: natural colors—white, cream, light/dark grays, browns and blacks. Also offers Finnsheep, Finnsheep Xs and Merino Xs. Send SASE.

THE FIBER STUDIO

P.O. Box 637-CSS
Foster Hill Rd.
Henniker NH 03242
Phone: (603)428-7830
Website: http://www.conknet.com/fiberstudio
Offers: Yarns: novelties, Shetlands, rug wools, chenilles, cottons, silks, brushed mohair, perle cottons (3/2-5/2), Berber wool, 10/6 rug linen and Tahki wools. Spinning fibers: New Zealand fleeces, yak, mohair, camel hair, alpaca, silk rovings and flax. Also offers weaving looms and spinning wheels, studio knitting machines, exotic wood buttons, mill ends and closeouts.
Catalog: $1. Yarn samples, $5. Fiber samples, $4.
Discounts: Quantity.
Accepts: MasterCard, Visa

FIBERWORKS

27 Suffolk St. W.
Guelph, Ontario N1H 2H9
Canada
Contact: Ingrid Boesel or Bob Keates
Phone: (519)822-5988
Fax: (519)822-3095
E-mail: fiberworks.pcw@sympatico.ca

Website: http://www3.sympatico.ca/fiberworks.pcw
Offers: Software for weavers.
Catalog: Brochure.
Phone Orders: 9-9 EST.
Mail Orders: Will ship anywhere, usually next day. Small shipping charge overseas.
Accepts: MasterCard, Visa

FINGERLAKES WOOLEN MILL

1193 Stewarts Corners Rd.
Genoa NY 13071
Phone: (800)441-WOOL
E-mail: yarn@fingerlakes-yarns.com
Website: http://www.fingerlakes-yarns.com
Offers: Fingerlake yarns: wools, angora/wool, silk/wool blends, brushed mohair and Unspun in 23 colors. Sock, stocking and sweater kits. Fulled kits for felting (hats, mittens, socks, tams and backpacks), spinning kits and roving and sheep pins also available.
Catalog: $4 for samples.
Discounts: Sells wholesale to yarn stores and professional designers.

FIRESIDE FIBERARTS

1060 Olele Point Rd.
Port Ludlow WA 98365
Phone: (360)437-0733
Fax: (360)437-5060
E-mail: firesidelooms@olympus.net
Offers: Custom-made weaving looms: floor, tapestry and other types. Also offers weaving accessories. Benches with moving seats and display fixtures. Previously owned looms information.
Catalog: $3.

FLAX FACTORY/SPINNING & WEAVING

RFD 1, Box 2410
Troy ME 04987
Contact: Paulette Schmidt
Phone: (207)948-2286
Fax: (207)948-2286
Store Location: Troy ME location.
Offers: Dyed flax and wool/flax blends for hand spinners. Custom-spun linen and lindsey woolsey yarns, spinning and weaving equipment and supplies, books and finished products—teddy bears and embroidered heirloom linens.
Catalog: Gift: 27 pages, $3. Equipment and supplies: 100 pages, $6.
Phone Orders: Yes.
Mail Orders: At above address.
Discounts: Wholesale and retail.
Accepts: MasterCard, Visa

FLEECE & FROMAGE FARMS

P.O. Box 15
Saratoga Springs NY 12866
Phone: (518)885-9290
Offers: Chemical-free yarns, exotic blends of kid mohair and silk, Rambouillet raw fleece, ready-to-spin roving and batting, and washable lambskins.
Catalog: Samples, $1 (specify interest).

FOOTHILLS FIBERWORKS

2235 Chesterfield Dr.
Maryville TN 37803
Contact: Melissa Tallent
Phone: (423)681-5000
E-mail: missy3448@aol.com
Store Location: At above address. T-Sat, 10-4.
Offers: Spinning wheels, looms and accessories. Full line of spinning fibers, yarns, natural and synthetic dyes and fiber preparation equipment. Doll hair and beard hair. Reproduction textiles. Pet hair spinning.
Catalog: Full listing and samples, $5 (refunded with first order).
Phone Orders: (800)808-7087. M-Sat, 10-10.
Mail Orders: Will ship anywhere.
Discounts: Wholesale to legitimate businesses.
Accepts: MasterCard, Visa

FRICKE ENTERPRISES

8702 State Rd. 92
Granite Falls WA 98252-9779
Contact: Jo Fricke
Phone: (360)691-5779
Fax: (360)691-7590
E-mail: frickent@gte.net
Offers: Manufacturer of Fricke chain-drive drum carders for wool and exotic fibers; tools included; manual and motorized. Spinning wheels, skein winders, "Big Ball" Winder and wool and cotton hand cards.
Catalog: Yes.
Phone Orders: Yes.
Mail Orders: Yes.
Accepts: check, money order

FROM THE FARM

52772 Sunquist Rd.
Milton-Freewater OR 97862
Contact: Vanessa Thew Thompson
Phone: (541)558-3767
Fax: (541)558-3767
E-mail: vanessa@bmi.net
Website: http://members.tripod.com/~fromthefarm/ftfindex.htm
Store Location: On a farm, in an old dairy barn. Hwy. 11 north through Milton-Freewater to Oregon-Washington border, turn west (left), go 2 miles, turn south (left) onto Trolley Rd. (gravel, ends at Sunquist). Turn west (right) onto Sunquist. Go about ½ mile to "From the Farm" sign. Drive down the lane until you reach the end. Very easy to find.
Offers: Classes in all types of fiber techniques, mill end yarns, kits, bath items (handmade soaps, woolly washers, foot soaks, bath salts and more), hand-spun yarns, small equipment, large equipment, books of all kinds, Louet equipment and Harrisville equipment.
Catalog: Flyers; working on catalog.
Phone Orders: Leave a message if no answer.
Mail Orders: Yes.
Discounts: Not usually, but every once in a while.
Accepts: MasterCard, Visa

GENERAL BAILEY HOMESTEAD FARM

340 Spier Falls Rd.
Greenfield Center NY 12833-2005
Contact: Kathy
Phone: (518)893-2015
Fax: (518)893-0778
E-mail: kathygbhfewe@compuserve
Website: www.generalbaileyfarm.com
Store Location: At above address. Open all year.
Offers: Spinning and knitting supplies and equipment. Spinning wheels—Ashford, Jensen, Schacht. Louet, Columbine and Majacraft. Natural and chemical dyes. Large selection of patterns, books, buttons, knitting needles and hooks. Rughooking supplies, spinning fibers. Classes and consultation. Natural fiber yarns and knitwear kits.
Catalog: 40 pages. $2 (refundable).
Phone Orders: Yes.
Mail Orders: Yes.
Discounts: Wholesale to qualified vendors.
Accepts: Discover, MasterCard, Visa, check, money order

GILMORE LOOMS

1032 N. Broadway
Stockton CA 95205
Phone: (209)463-1545
Fax: (209)465-9627
E-mail: gilmorelom@aol.com
Website: http://www.quikpage.com/g/gilmorelooms
Offers: Handweaving looms: 4 & 8 harness, 26", 32", 40" and 46". Most loom equipment and inkle looms.
Catalog: Free brochure.

THE GLEANERS YARN BARN

P.O. Box 1191
Canton GA 30114
Phone: (404)479-5083
Offers: Mill end yarns and threads in natural, synthetic and blends, in a variety of sizes and types. Wool rug yarn by the pound also available.
Catalog: Sample catalog and mailing list (1 year), $3. Wool yarn samples, $1.

GOOD WOOD

Rt. 2, Box 447A
Bethel VT 05032
Phone: (802)234-5534

E-mail: goodwood@sover.net

Offers: Good Wood frame and slant weaving looms in small sizes; mini inkle loom. Magic Heddle lets weaver warp looms without threading warp through holes or slots. Also offers wood "inchworms" for making knitted cord. Call or write.

Accepts: MasterCard, Visa

LOUISE HEITE, ICELANDIC WOOL

P.O. Box 53

Camden Wyoming DE 19934

Phone: (800)777-9665

E-mail: eheite@dmv.com

Website: dmv.com/~iceland

Offers: Icelandic wool for spinning and weaving (also knitting and felt work). Annual wool camp in Iceland. Write.

JANE'S FIBER & BEADS

(formerly Jane's Fiber Works)

604 Franklin St.

Greeneville TN 37745

Contact: Jane Overman

Phone: (423)639-7919

Fax: (423)638-5676

E-mail: fiber@greene.xtn.net

Website: http://fiber.xtn.net

Store Location: 602 Franklin St., Greeneville TN 37745.

Offers: Spinning wheels and weaving looms by Ashford, Beka, Charkha, Cranbook, Glimakra, Louet, Leclerc, Lendrum, Majacraft, Mirrix and Schacht. Dyes, yarn, books, tassel supplies, fibers, knitting needles and yarns and beads.

Catalog: On-line or request one.

Phone Orders: (888)497-2665, 9-6 EST.

Mail Orders: Ships within 48 hours on items in stock.

KESSENICH LOOMS CO.

P.O. Box 156

Allegan MI 49010-1056

Phone: (616)673-5204

Offers: Red oak table and floor looms that weave anything from rugs to fine cloth. Size range: table looms 10″, 14″, 20″ and 25″ and floor looms 30″, 36″, 42″ and 46″ all in either 4- or 8-harness models. Other custom or specialized weaving equipment available, such as accessories and handicapped floor looms.

Catalog: Brochure, $1.

KNOTS & TREADLES

P.O. Box 394

103 E. Pittsburgh St.

Delmont PA 15626

Contact: Peggy Cost

Phone: (724)468-4265

Offers: Yarns, spinning and weaving supplies and equipment, Eweseful Gifts (anything with a sheep on it—shoelaces, socks, rubbers stamps and much more!), video rental library via UPS—Learn how-to in your own home. Established Delmont 1980!

Catalog: Please send 3 stamps. Sheep print fabric swatches, $5.

Phone Orders: Yes.

Mail Orders: Yes.

Accepts: MasterCard, Visa, check, C.O.D.

LA LANA WOOLS

136 Paseo Norte

Taos NM 87571

Phone: (505)758-9631

Offers: Plant-dyed, hand-spun and mill-spun yarns, carded blends and fleeces. Also offers Schacht equipment.

Catalog: Sample card set, $25.

LAMBSPUN OF COLORADO

(formerly Lambspun Bulky Sample Club)

1101 E. Lincoln

Fort Collins CO 80524

Contact: Shirley Ellsworth

Phone: (970)484-1998

Fax: (970)484-1998

E-mail: lambspun@fortnet.org

Store Location: At above address.

Offers: Lambspun brand of yarns and fibers. 7 rooms of yarns, fibers, equipment, books for weavers, spinners and knitters. Classes and workshops. Knitting groups. Lambspun Bulky Club—mail-order club for fibers and yarns. $7 per year. New Lambspun swatch club for knitters, $15 per year includes newsletter and yarns to swatch. 6 bimonthly mailings.

Catalog: Yarn catalog, $5. Complete catalog of yarns and fibers, $15.

Phone Orders: (800)558-5262.

Mail Orders: Dept. D, P.O. Box 300, Ft. Collins CO 80524.

Discounts: Mail-order club features closeouts and test-market yarns. Wholesale also.

Accepts: MasterCard, Visa

LECLERC LOOMS

P.O. Box 4

1972 Simoneau

Plessisville, Quebec G6L 2Y6

Canada

Contact: Francois Brassard

Phone: (819)362-2408

Fax: (819)362-2045

E-mail: leclerc@login.net

Website: www.oricom.ca/leclerc

Store Location: Plessisville, Quebec location.

Offers: Handweaving loom.

Catalog: $2.

Mail Orders: Yes.

CAROL LEIGH'S SPECIALTIES

7001 Hill Creek Rd.

Columbia MO 65203

Phone: (573)874-2233

Offers: Spinning and weaving tools, equipment, supplies and

books. Line of natural dyes and kits, and permanent moth-proofing. Triangular frame looms that weave in 6 sizes. Holds classes in spinning, natural dyeing, weaving and felting.
Catalog: Product catalog, $2. Free workshop brochure.
Accepts: MasterCard, Visa

LOUET SALES, INC.
P.O. Box 267
Ogdensburg NY 13669
Contact: Trudy Nan Stralen
Phone: (613)925-4502
Fax: (613)925-1405
E-mail: trudy@louet.com
Website: www.louet.com
Store Location: Showroom in Prescott, Ontario.
Offers: Spinning wheels—12 sizes and accessories; carding equipment; floor looms with various weaving widths, featuring countermarche system; 24-harness table Magic Dobby Loom. Also offers a variety of natural fibers, dyed Merino and Corriedale for felting. British mohair and Merino yarns, Euroflak wetspun, dyed linen and silk embroidery yarns, including hand-dyed with natural dyes. Also lace-making and felting equipment, range of dyes, patterns and books.
Catalog: Catalog, price list and local dealer information, $5.
Phone Orders: M-F, 9-5 EST.
Mail Orders: Ship worldwide.
Discounts: Sells wholesale to stores and production persons.

THE LUNATIC FRINGE
161 Ave. C
Apalachicola FL 32320
Contact: David or Michele Belson
Phone: (850)653-8747
E-mail: belzonni@juno.com
Store Location: At above address. Call for current hours and show schedule.
Offers: A complete line of cotton yarns, mercerized and not, naturals and dyed, including the Tubular Spectrum color gamp kit—brilliant colors by the ounce, pound or ton in 10/2 and 5/2 mercerized cotton—and lots of other great yarns and kits for weavers and knitters (and crocheters, beaders, embroiderers and others). Source for fine yarns including 40/2 mercerized cotton, and 140/2 reeled silks. Interlacements hand-painted warps and skeins, Schacht weaving and spinning products and other weaving equipment, Design and Sew patterns plus Socka, Economy and Jagger spun wools, fun sock kits and the fabulous Sheep Kabobs, fiberglass composite knitting needles. Also the proud sponsor of LunaSea, an annual February Florida Fiber Retreat with seminars and workshops in weaving, sewing, knitting, beadwork and other fiber techniques, with a bonfire and beach fun.
Catalog: Free and fun.
Phone Orders: (800)483-8749. M-Sat, 10-6 EST.
Mail Orders: Will ship worldwide.
Accepts: MasterCard, Visa, cash

MACOMBER LOOMS
P.O. Box 186
York ME 03909
Contact: Rick Hart
Phone: (207)363-2808
Fax: (207)363-2808
Store Location: 130 Beech Ridge Rd., York ME 03909.
Offers: Traditional Ad-A-Harness Looms, weaving widths 16"-146". Designer's Delight air dobby systems, Power Cloth Advance Fly Shuttle Beaters and loom accessories.
Catalog: $3.
Phone Orders: Yes.
Mail Orders: At P.O. Box.
Accepts: Discover, MasterCard, Visa

THE MANNINGS
P.O. Box 687
East Berlin PA 17316
Contact: Carol J. Woolcock
Phone: (717)624-2223
E-mail: mannings@sun-link.com
Website: http://www.the-mannings.com
Store Location: 1132 Green Ridge Rd., East Berlin PA 17316.
Offers: Weaving looms by Schacht, Norwood, Gilmakra, Cranbrook, Louet, Harrisville, LeClerc, Gallinger and Toika. Spinning wheels by Ashford, Dundas, Louet, Lendrum, Schacht, Reeves and Timbertops. Wide variety of yarns from most major manufacturers and mill end yarns. Books for knitters, spinners and weavers. Dyeing and felt making also available. Classes for spinning, weaving and knitting.
Catalog: Catalog and yarn style card, $2.50.
Phone Orders: M-F, 9-4:30.
Mail Orders: Ship worldwide. Prepayment required.
Accepts: Discover, MasterCard, Visa

MODERN LOOPERS
526 W. Lebanon St.
Mt. Airy NC 27030
Contact: Ray Arnold
Phone: (888)955-0714
Fax: (336)786-7780
Store Location: At above address.
Offers: 26 colorfast loopers plus natural and white loopers for weavers.
Catalog: Write or call for free samples.
Phone Orders: Leave message.
Mail Orders: At above address.
Accepts: MasterCard, Visa

MOONS SHADOW FARMS
11252 Kekke Rd.
Chisholm MN 55719
Contact: Liz Voelker or Kitty Castro
Phone: (218)254-3190 or (218)262-3267
Store Location: At above address. Anytime.
Offers: Coated spinning fleeces, felting batts, felting fleeces, quilting batts, wool rovings, dyed mohair, wool/mohair blend

rovings, wool top, lambskins and "Santa Beard" washed white wool.
Catalog: Sample sheets, $3.
Phone Orders: Anytime. Prepayment required for shipping.
Mail Orders: Will ship US and Canada via UPS and prepayment required.
Accepts: personal check, money order

MOUNTAIN LOOM CO.

P.O. Box 509
Vader WA 98593
Phone: (800)238-0296 or (360)295-3856
Fax: (360)295-3287
E-mail: johnanderson@mtnloom.com
Website: www.mtnloom.com
Offers: Looms: 12-28″ table models; 4-, 8-, 12- and 16-harness models. Also offers transportable floor, tapestry and countermarch floor-style looms. Carries Maru Dai for Kumihimo, plus accessories and books.
Catalog: Color. $2.
Accepts: MasterCard, Visa

NORSK FJORD FIBER

P.O. Box 271
Lexington GA 30648
Contact: Noel Thurner
Phone: (706)743-5120
Store Location: 82 Stephens Rd., Lexington GA 30648. M-Sat, 9:30-5:30 EST.
Offers: Tapestry looms, yarns, books. Felting batts, from Swedish Gotland, spinning rovings from Norwegian, Spelsau and Swedish Gotland felt making supplies, pewter buttons and clasps and Novi knitting needles.
Catalog: $2.
Phone Orders: Yes.
Mail Orders: Worldwide.
Discounts: Wholesale to licensed businesses.
Accepts: MasterCard, Visa, check from US bank

NORTHWEST LOOMS

P.O. Box 1854
Ridgecrest CA 93556
Contact: Tony Klissus
Phone: (760)375-3179
E-mail: klissus@ridgecrest.ca.us
Website: http://www.ridgecrest.ca.us/~klissus/northwest.htm
Offers: Handweaving looms and equipment, including Pioneer open-heddle/reed and traditional weaving looms, double-beam hardwood bead looms, shuttles and related specialty weaving items.
Catalog: On request.
Phone Orders: Yes.
Mail Orders: Yes.

OREGON WORSTED CO.

P.O. Box 82098
Portland OR 97282
Phone: (503)786-1234

Fax: (503)786-2022
Offers: Line of wool handweaving yarns, including Wilamette 2-ply, and Nehalem 3-ply; 12 basic and 30 promotional colors. Sold in cones.
Catalog: Send $3 and SASE for color card.

PINTLER SHEEPCAMP

530 Faucher
Moxee WA 98936
Phone: (509)453-0183
E-mail: ztxp87a@prodigy.com
Offers: Rovings: Lincoln, Romney, mohair, Merino, silk and alpaca—natural colors and dyed.
Catalog: Send SASE for list.

RIO GRANDE WEAVER'S SUPPLY

216 Pueblo Norte Rd.
Taos NM 87571
Phone: (505)758-0433 or (800)765-1272
Offers: Rio Grande weaving loom and spinning wheel. Rio Grande yarns: hand-dyed wool rug/tapestry/apparel types. Also offers Glimakra and Schacht equipment, wool warp yarns, natural and synthetic dyes and books.
Catalog: Full color catalog, $3.
Discounts: Quantity.

THE RIVER FARM

P.O. Box 895
New Market VA 22844
Phone: (800)USA-WOOL
E-mail: riverfam@gte.net
Offers: Fleece—black, brown, gray and white Corriedale (skirted and sorted). Weaving looms and spinning wheels: Schacht, Ashford, Country Craftsman and Louet Workshops.
Catalog: $2.
Accepts: MasterCard, Visa

SUZANNE RODDY—HANDWEAVER

1519 Memorial
Conroe TX 77304
Contact: Suzanne T. Roddy
Phone: (409)441-1718
Fax: (409)788-1730
E-mail: suzier@lcc.net
Store Location: At above address. M-F, 9-1.
Offers: Quality service and discount prices since 1986. Natural yarns, fibers and dyes—our specialty! Wide selection of books and weaving/spinning equipment. Free shipping and SRH sample catalog with floor looms/wheels. Needlework skeins and knitting needles.
Catalog: Yarn sample catalog, $20; fiber sample catalog, $15; both together, $25 (refundable with $50 yarn/fiber order). Price list, $2 mailed, or E-mailed free.
Phone Orders: Yes.
Mail Orders: Yes. Prepayment or C.O.D. unless established customer; then net on receipt of invoice.

Discounts: Most items already discounted. Further discounts to businesses with sales tax number.
Accepts: no credit cards

ROSKOS FARMS
W-74, Sauer Mill Rd.
Arcadia WI 54612
Contact: Patrice Roskos
Phone: (608)323-7072
Offers: Wool from our Cheviot, Corriedale, Lincoln and Romney sheep. Raw or washed fleeces; natural or dyed rovings, felting, spinning and quilting batts; craft hair; yarn; and sheep pelts.
Catalog: Brochure and samples, $2 (specify color/breed).
Phone Orders: 7 days a week, 8-6 CST.
Mail Orders: Yes. Prepayment required.
Accepts: check, money order

ST. PETER WOOLEN MILL
101 W. Broadway
St. Peter MN 56082
Phone: (507)931-3734
Fax: (507)931-9040
E-mail: spwoolen@prairie.lakes.com
Website: www.woolenmill.com
Store Location: At above address.
Offers: Wool batting, wool roving, alpaca roving, curly mohair. Service: custom scouring and carding of new and used wool.
Catalog: Free brochure.
Discounts: Quantity; teachers and institutions; sells wholesale to legitimate businesses.
Accepts: American Express, Discover, MasterCard, Visa

SAJAMA ALPACA
P.O. Box 1209
Ashland OR 97520
Phone: (800)736-0949
Offers: Line of alpaca yarns on skeins and cones in 19 natural and dyed colors.
Catalog: Call for free samples.

SALT LAKE WEAVER'S STORE
1227 E. 3300 S.
Salt Lake City UT 84106
Contact: Annie Taylor
Phone: (802)486-1610
Store Location: At above address.
Offers: Looms, spinning wheels, all related support equipment, yarns, mill ends, raw wool, roving, spinning fibers, Procion and Cushing dyes and natural dyes. Also books on all the above. Offer year-round classes.
Catalog: $1.
Phone Orders: (800)363-5585. M-S, 10-6.
Mail Orders: Will ship anywhere.
Discounts: 10% to guilds and professionals.
Accepts: American Express, Discover, MasterCard, Visa

SALT SPRING ISLAND FIBRE STUDIOS
121 Mountain Rd.
Salt Spring Island, British Columbia V8K 1T8
Canada
Contact: Mary Paddon or Pat Daniel
Phone: (250)653-4033
Fax: (250)537-9930
E-mail: susanb@islandnet.com
Website: Under construction.
Store Location: 7 studios on Salt Spring. Call to arrange visit.
Offers: Alpaca, mohair, llama, wool yarns, raw fleece and rovings. Also knitting patterns, tools and knit kits. Custom spinning, dyeing and weaving.
Catalog: $4.
Phone Orders: M-F, 9-5 PST.
Mail Orders: Will ship anywhere the post goes. Allow 6 weeks for delivery.
Accepts: MasterCard, money order

SAX ARTS & CRAFTS
P.O. Box 510710
2405 S. Calhoun Rd.
New Berlin WI 53151
Phone: (414)784-6880
Offers: A variety of supplies (known brands), including a full line of weaving looms and aids, yarns, weaving kits, rug/craft yarns, embroidery/crewel threads, rug hook frames and aids, canvas, hoops, burlap and felt. Native American beading, beads, feathers, macrame, basketry and batik supplies, fabric paints, airbrush kits and inks, stencil films, trims, foam, stained glass kits, etching and beveled glass supplies and supplies for decoupage, jewelry making, leather, casting, plastics, wood and metalworking are also available.
Catalog: $5 (refundable).
Discounts: Quantity, sells wholesale to legitimate businesses.

SCHACHT SPINDLE CO., INC.
6101 Ben Place
Boulder CO 80301
Phone: (800)228-2553
Offers: Spinning wheels for fine-medium-heavyweight yarns. Weaving looms: floor models, table, tapestry and rigid-heddle type table models, plus inkle looms and rope machines. Accessories and tools: winders, shuttles, beaters, heddles, spindles, umbrella swift and others.
Catalog: See your weaving and spinning supply shop; or send $3 for catalog and address of nearest dealer.

SCHOOLHOUSE YARNS
P.O. Box 1152
Worland WY 82401
Phone: (307)347-4485
Offers: Finnish weaving yarns: wool blanket type and other wools, worsted, plus linens and linen warp, seine twines and

cotton Pilvi. Also offers cotton bias strips, and Toika looms and loom equipment.
Catalog: Sample cards, $2 each, plus 75¢ shipping.

SHADEYSIDE FARM
P.O. Box 48
Chenango Bridge NY 13745
Contact: Nancy Morey
Phone: (607)656-4737
E-mail: shadeyside@juno.com
Offers: Fibers for hand spinners: silk and silk blend tops, raw and degummed cocoons, dyed fibers, Rainbow Dyeing book, and tussah/wool yarns.
Catalog: Send #10 SASE with 52¢ postage.
Phone Orders: Yes.
Mail Orders: With prepayment.
Accepts: MasterCard, Visa, check, cash

SHANNOCK TAPESTRY LOOMS
10402 NW 11th Ave.
Vancouver WA 98685
Phone: (360)573-7264
Offers: Shannock tapestry looms—high-tension, heavy-duty, professional type, with roller beams and weaving accessories. Also imports a line of fine Australian yarns in 371 colors. Sells Swedish, Finnish and domestic warp twine. Also weighted brass beaters, wooden beaters and various types of tapestry bobbins. Write.

THE SILK TREE
20297 Stanton Ave.
Maple Ridge, British Columbia V2X 9A5
Canada
Phone: (604)465-9816
Fax: (604)465-0976
E-mail: aurum@axionet.com
Offers: Line of silk yarns and fibers, natural and dyed silk.
Catalog: Samples, $5.

SILVERBROOK FARMS/SHOPPE
P.O. Box 133
16040 US Hwy. 119 N.
Marchand PA 15758
Contact: Ginger Maine
Phone: (724)286-3317
Fax: (724)286-1241
E-mail: Soon.
Website: Soon.
Store Location: Intersection of US 119 and SR 1043 in Marchand (8 miles south of Punxsutawney).
Offers: Areas' largest and most complete fibre arts center for weaving, spinning, machine and hand knitters, crochet, dyeing, and fiber crafts. 10 rooms of equipment, supplies and finished goods. Natural fiber farm raising wide range of wools, mohair, angora, camel and linen. Also stocks silk, yak, cottons, alpaca, ramie, synthetics, looms, spinning wheels and knitting machines. Classes. Tours: area history and History of Fibre Processing Museum.

Catalog: Free.
Phone Orders: Year round. Must be prepaid.
Discounts: With tax number on file. Minimum $100.
Accepts: Discover, MasterCard, Visa, check

SONOMA COUNTY FIBERTRAILS
P.O. Box 91
Occidental CA 95465
Contact: JoAnn Slissman
Phone: (707)874-3374
Store Location: Various farms in Sonoma County CA.
Offers: Hand-spinning fibers produced on member farms. Many breeds of sheep, llamas, alpacas, mohair and angora. Dye plants, sheepskins and livestock. All collective members are knowledgeable hand spinners.
Catalog: List of producers and products available by mail.

SOUTHWEST CORNER
P.O. Box 418
Bisbee AZ 85603
Contact: Joan Ruane
Phone: (520)432-3603
E-mail: jsruane@aol.com
Store Location: 114 Tombstone Canyon, Bisbee AZ 85603. Open by appointment.
Offers: Class in spinning and weaving; cotton-spinning supplies, fiber and equipment.
Catalog: Free with SASE.
Phone Orders: (800)879-8412. 8-8 MST.
Mail Orders: Ship anywhere.
Discounts: 20% on some items to legitimate fiber shop.
Accepts: check, money order

SPIN CRAFT
P.O. Box 327
Salmon ID 83467
Contact: Connie Delaney
Phone: (208)756-3076
Fax: (208)756-3076
E-mail: spincraft@aol.com
Store Location: 300 Monroe St., Salmon ID 83467.
Offers: Knitting, crochet and weaving patterns for hand-spun or exotic yarns. Knit-to-Fit patterns include easy calculations for any size from any yarn.
Catalog: Free.
Phone Orders: Call for free catalog.
Mail Orders: At P.O. Box. Quick response.
Discounts Buy 5 patterns, get 1 free.
Accepts: check, money order

STEEL HEDDLE
P.O. Box 550
Greenville GA 30222
Phone: (706)672-4238
Offers: Reeds: Steel Heddle brand, in standard and pattern reeds. Also offers custom-made reeds.
Catalog: Send for order information/prices.
Discounts: Sells wholesale.

STEPHANIE'S STUDIO & YARN

1637 Appian Rd.
Bybee TN 37713
Contact: Bill or Stephanie Widmann
Phone: (423)623-1986 or (800)323-9411
Fax: (423)623-9565
E-mail: yarn@planetc.com
Website: http://members.aol.com/dsgneryarn
Store Location: At above address. M-F, 8:30-5.
Offers: Cone yarns for machine knitting, weaving, crocheting, hand knitting and crafts. Also acrylics, cottons, blends and metallic yarns. Stephanie's Yarn Club $14 a year. Receive yarn sample catalog, patterns, quarterly newsletter, 5% off regular prices, sales and toll-free number.
Catalog: Stephanie's Yarn Club includes catalog.
Phone Orders: Yes.
Mail Orders: Ship UPS.
Discounts: Below wholesale prices every day. Sales often.
Accepts: Discover, MasterCard, Visa, check, money order

STONY MOUNTAIN FIBERS

939 Hammocks Gap Rds.
Charlottesville VA 22911
Phone: (804)295-2008
E-mail: stonymtn@aol.com
Offers: Spinning wheels, looms, carders, combs, fibers, dyes and books.
Catalog: $2 (refundable).

SWEET GRASS WOOL

P.O. Box 266
Green Ranch Rd.
Melville MT 59055
Contact: Carolyn Green
Phone: (406)537-4472
E-mail: greenranch@mcn.net
Website: http://www.mcn.net/~greenranch/
Store Location: At above address.
Offers: 6 different kinds of mule-spun wool yarn (natural white and gray) and roving from our flock of Targhee sheep. Targhee combed top also. The yarns and combed top are available in 27 different hand-painted colors.
Catalog: Samples of all yarns and all colors, $7.50.
Phone Orders: M-Sat, 9-7 MST. OK to leave message.
Mail Orders: Prepayment required. Natural yarns shipped right away. Allow 6 weeks for hand-painted yarns.
Discounts: Wholesale inquiries invited for legitimate businesses.
Accepts: check, money order, cash

TREENWAY SILKS, LTD.

(formerly Treenway Crafts Ltd.)
725 Caledonia Ave.
Victoria, British Columbia V8T 1E4
Canada
Phone: (604)383-1661
Fax: (604)383-0543
Offers: Silk yarns in 26 weights/sizes; hand-dyed yarns in 72 colors; representative for Treetops dyed silk fibre, Ashford product line. Publishes newsletter.
Catalog: Complete samples and price list, $5; complete samples with Treetops fibres, $10.

BONNIE TRIOLA YARNS

343 E. Gore Rd.
Erie PA 16509
Contact: Bonnie Triola
Phone: (814)825-7821
Fax: (814)824-5418
E-mail: btriola@moose.erie.net
Website: http://moose.erie.net/~btriola
Offers: Cone yarn for machine knitters, weavers and crafters. Wholesale and retail. Specializes in high-quality designer closeouts at fantastic prices.
Catalog: $10.
Phone Orders: Yes.
Mail Orders: Yes.
Discounts: Yes.
Accepts: MasterCard, Visa, check

VICTORIAN VIDEO

930 Massachusetts
Lawrence KS 66044
Contact: Susan Bateman
Phone: (785)842-4333 or (800)848-0284
Fax: (785)842-0794
E-mail: yarnbarn@idir.net
Website: www.victorianvid.com
Store Location: At above address.
Offers: Over 180 instructional videos on weaving, spinning, dyeing, knitting, crochet, beadwork, rug making, quilting, sewing, lace making and more.
Catalog: Free.
Phone Orders: (800)848-0284. M-Sat, 9-5:30 CST.
Mail Orders: Prepayment required. Prompt shipping.
Discounts: Sells wholesale to legitimate businesses.
Accepts: Discover, MasterCard, Visa, check, money order

VILLAGE WOOLS, INC.

3801 San Mateo NE
Albuquerque NM 87110
Phone: (800)766-4553 or (505)883-2919
Store Location: At above address.
Offers: Brown sheep yarn, Rowan stockist, Jo Sharp, Alice Starmore, Classic Elite, creative yarns and others. Supplies and equipment for weaving, knitting, crocheting, spinning and silk painting. Dyes, books and patterns.
Catalog: Free.

THE WEAVER'S LOFT

P.O. Box 13
308 S. Pennsylvania Ave.
Centre Hall PA 16828
Contact: Molly Mahaffy
Phone: (800)693-7242 or (814)364-1433
E-mail: yarnshop@aol.com

Website: www.shopsite.com/yarnshop
Store Location: At above address. T-Sat, 10-6.
Offers: Full line of fine knitting and weaving yarns and equipment. Also spinning supplies.
Catalog: Free. $18 yarn sample set (partially refundable).
Phone Orders: T-Sat, 10-6 EST.
Mail Orders: Both domestic and foreign. Orders mailed within 3 days.
Discounts: Wholesales Ann Grout drop spindles and Jamieson & Smith Shetland wool to legitimate shops.
Accepts: Discover, MasterCard, Visa

WEAVER'S WAY

P.O. Box 70
Columbus NC 28722
Offers: Yarns, including mercerized perle cottons, natural and novelty cottons and other name brands. Alternatives, Weaver's Way Wool and equipment also available.
Catalog: Catalog and sample cards, $3.

THE WEAVING WORKS

4717 Brooklyn Ave. NE
Seattle WA 98105-4410
Contact: Mary Ashton
Phone: (206)524-1221
Fax: (206)524-0250
Store Location: At above address. Near University of Washington.
Offers: Supplies/classes/books on basketry, book arts, dyeing, knitting, papermaking, spinning, surface design, miscellaneous textile arts and weaving.
Catalog: Catalog and price list. Classes and workshops newsletter.
Phone Orders: (888)524-1221.
Mail Orders: At above address.
Discounts: 10% schools with appropriate documentation.
Accepts: Discover, MasterCard, Visa, check

WEBS

Service Center Rd.
P.O. Box 147
Northampton MA 01061
Phone: (413)584-2225
Fax: (413)584-1603
E-mail: webs@yarn.com
Website: yarn.com
Offers: Name-brand yarns, closeouts, mill ends and Webs lines in rayon, chenille, cottons, mohair, linen, silk and wools on cones and skeins for knitters, machine knitters and hand weavers. Also has looms, spinning wheels, knitting supplies and books.
Catalog: Samples, $2. Equipment brochure, $1.
Discounts: Quantity; institutions. Discounts on yarn to all.

THE WOOLERY

1193 Stewarts' Corners Rd.
Genoa NY 13071
Phone: (315)497-1542

Fax: (315)497-3620
E-mail: jive@woolery.com
Website: http://www.woolery.com
Offers: Weaving looms: Glimakra, Harrisville, Leclerc, Schacht and Norwood/Cranbrook. Also offers accessories, spinning wheels, hand-spinning equipment and supplies, dyes, Fingerlakes yarns (wools/blends) and kits.
Catalog: 32 pages. $3.
Phone Orders: M-F, 9-6:30 EST.
Mail Orders: Will ship to US, Canada and overseas.
Discounts: On spinning wheels, looms and many accessories.
Accepts: MasterCard, Visa

YARN BARN

930 Massachusetts
Lawrence KS 66044
Contact: Susan Bateman
Phone: (785)842-4333 or (800)468-0035
Fax: (785)842-0794
E-mail: yarnbarn@idir.net
Website: www.yarnbarn-ks.com
Store Location: At above address. 7 days a week.
Offers: Large selection of knitting and weaving yarns with supplies and equipment to cover those areas as well as spinning, dyeing, rug braiding and needlepoint. Hundreds of books covering most textile arts; over 180 videos on same.
Catalog: 3 free options: (1) knitting and crochet, (2) weaving, spinning and equipment and (3) videos.
Phone Orders: (800)468-0035. M-Sat. 9:30-5:30 CST.
Mail Orders: Any location. Prepayment please.
Discounts: Quantity discounts on yarns and fibers. Looms and spinning wheels competitively priced.
Accepts: Discover, MasterCard, Visa, check, money order

THE YARN SHOP AND FIBRES

549 Main St.
Laconia NH 03246
Contact: Ellen or Ely
Phone: (603)528-1221 or (800)375-1221
E-mail: yarnshop@cyberportal.net
Website: www.cyberportal.net/yarnshop
Store Location: At above address.
Offers: Full range of yarns, classes, books, spinning equipment and supplies, cross-stitch charts, floss and fabric.
Phone Orders: Yes.
Mail Orders: Yes.
Accepts: American Express, Discover, MasterCard, Visa

YOLO WOOL PRODUCTS

41501 County Rd. 27
Woodland CA 95776
Phone: (916)666-1473
Offers: Sliver for spinning, weaving yarns, plus wool batting and knitting yarns.
Catalog: Flyers, samples, $2.
Discounts: Quantity; sells wholesale to legitimate businesses.

Yarns—Multipurpose

Also see General Needlecraft Supplies; Knitting & Crochet; Spinning & Weaving; other related categories.

ARTFIBERS GALLERY
124 Sutter St., 2nd Floor
San Francisco CA 94104
Contact: Roxanne Seabright
Phone: (415)956-6319 or (888)326-1112
Fax: (415)421-1734
E-mail: yarn@artfibers.com
Website: www.artfibers.com
Store Location: At above address.
Offers: America's leading discount importer of spectacular fashion and exotic yarns for knitting, weaving and fiber art from Europe. Fashion patterns in pattern library plus custom patterns. Workshops and tutorials. Further discounts for bulk purchases.
Catalog: On website. CD-ROM for $4 ppd.
Phone Orders: Yes.
Mail Orders: Shipping within US is a flat fee of $5 regardless of size of order.
Discounts: See above. 1,000 gram purchase is $2 off per ball.
Accepts: MasterCard, Visa, check, cash

BROADWAY YARN CO.
P.O. Box 1350
Sanford NC 27331-1350
Phone: (919)774-1300
Offers: Yarns for weaving, crochet, knitting and macrame: poly/cottons, nylon, wools and blends and polyester. Also offers loom selvage and others.
Catalog: Swatch cards, $3 (refundable).
Discounts: Sells wholesale.

CREATURE COMFORTS
P.O. Box 606
Vashon Island WA 98070
Contact: Carolyn Smith
Phone: (206)463-2004
Fax: (206)463-6137
E-mail: viva@nwrain.com
Website: www.nwrain.net/creaturecomforts
Offers: Chinchilla yarns, patterns, kits, roving and raw fibers.
Catalog: Yes.
Phone Orders: Anytime—answering machine.
Mail Orders: Priority Mail worldwide.
Accepts: MasterCard, Visa

CUMBERLAND YARN SHOP
51 Buchwood Lane #11
Crossville TN 38555
Contact: Jean Marr
Phone: (931)707-1026 or (931)456-8065
Store Location: At above address. Near Food City.
Offers: Quality yarns and lessons. Assistance with problems: T-F, 10-5; Sat, 10-2.
Phone Orders: Yes.
Mail Orders: Yes.
Accepts: MasterCard, Visa

FIESTA YARNS
P.O. Box 2548
Corrales NM 87048
Phone: (505)897-4485
Offers: Hand-dyed yarns—mohair, rayon, cotton, silk and wools—in a variety of plies, colors and textures.
Catalog: Color cards, $10.

THE GLEANERS YARN BARN
P.O. Box 1191
Canton GA 30114
Phone: (404)479-5083
Offers: First-quality mill end yarns: cottons, rayons and blends, cotton/nylon, acrylics, wools, polyesters, Orlon, Lurex, angora blends, wool rug, bouclé and novelty types. Available by the pound.
Catalog: Current samples (year's mailing), $3.

GREAT YARNS, INC.
1208 Ridge Rd.
Raleigh NC 27607
Contact: Jane C. Weir
Phone: (919)832-3599
Fax: (919)836-9702
E-mail: greatyrn@gte.net
Website: www.great-yarns.com
Store Location: At above address in Ridgewood Shopping Center. M-F, 10-6; Sat, 10-5.
Offers: Large selection of hand-knitting yarns, patterns and buttons. Classes, workshops and Spring Mountain Knitting Retreat.
Catalog: Combined with quarterly mailing. $5 or put on E-mail address and distribution.
Phone Orders: (800)810-0045. M-F, 10-6; Sat, 10-5.
Mail Orders: Yes.
Accepts: MasterCard, Visa, check, cash

HALCYON YARN

12 School St.
Bath ME 04530
Contact: Halcyon Blake
Phone: (800)341-0282
Fax: (207)442-0633
E-mail: service@halcyonyarn.com
Website: www.halcyonyarn.com
Store Location: At above address. M,T,Th and F, 8-5; W, 8-8; Sat, 10-4.
Offers: Yarns, fibers, books, dyes, equipment for weavers, hand and machine knitters, spinners, felters, dyers, rug hookers, crocheters and lace makers. Available by mail order or visit on website.
Catalog: 64 pages, color.
Phone Orders: M-F, 8-5 EST.
Mail Orders: Will ship worldwide.
Discounts: Based on quantity purchased for yarn, fiber and books.
Accepts: American Express, Discover, MasterCard, Visa

HANEKE WOOL FASHIONS

(formerly Haneke Merino Wool)
630 N. Black Cat Rd.
Meridian ID 83642
Contact: Charlotte Marston
Phone: (208)888-3129 or (800)523-WOOL
Fax: (208)888-2776
E-mail: kathyhaneke@msn.com
Store Location: At above address.
Offers: Naturally processed 100% Merino wool yarn and Merino blends. 100% alpaca yarn and various exotic blends. Exclusive distributor of Heaven Sent. Knitting notions, books and spinning equipment and supplies.
Catalog: Sample card and kit catalog available.
Phone Orders: Yes.
Mail Orders: Will ship to US and Canada. Prepayment required.
Discounts: Dealer inquiries welcome.
Accepts: MasterCard, Visa, check

JAMIE HARMON

Rt. 3, Box 464
Jericho VT 05465
Offers: Hand-spun and naturally dyed wool yarn, worsted weights and others. Also offers Rainbow Ridge children's sweater kits.
Catalog: Samples and brochure, $4.

HARRISVILLE DESIGNS INC.

Box 806-Center Village
Harrisville NH 03450
Contact: Sharon Driscoll
Phone: (603)827-3333
Fax: (603)827-3335
E-mail: info@harrisville.com
Website: www.harrisville.com
Store Location: At above address. M-F, 9-5.

Offers: Handweaving floor looms and accessories. 100% virgin wool yarn for knitting and weaving. Children's looms and craft kits.
Catalog: Yarn catalog, $6. Friendly Loom catalog, $2. Loom catalog, $2.
Phone Orders: Yes.
Mail Orders: Prepayment. Orders shipped within one week.
Discount: Sell wholesale to legitimate businesses.
Accepts: Discover, MasterCard, Visa

HENRY'S ATTIC

5 Mercury Ave.
Monroe NY 10950-9736
Contact: Samira Galler
Phone: (914)783-3930
Fax: (914)782-2548
Offers: Undyed natural fiber yarns and fibers. Also dyed brushed mohair: yarns suitable for hand dyeing, hand knitting, hand weaving and doll hair. Fibers (wool, alpaca, flax and mohair) suitable for hand spinning and doll hair.
Catalog: Sample set, $20.
Phone Orders: M-F, 9-6 EST.
Discounts: Sells wholesale only to legitimate businesses.

THE HILL KNITTERY, INC.

10720 Yonge St.
Richmond Hill, Ontario L4C 3C9
Canada
Contact: Bev Nimon
Phone: (905)770-4341
Fax: (905)770-8701
E-mail: dnimon@idirect.com
Store Location: M-Sat, 10-6.
Offers: Wide range of imported, natural fibre yarns, patterns, books and accessories. Excellent lessons and workshops provided.
Phone Orders: Yes.
Mail Orders: We will ship Canada or US on prepaid orders.
Accepts: Interac, MasterCard, Visa

CHERYL KOLANDER'S AURORA SILK

5806 N. Vancouver Ave.
Portland OR 97217
Phone: (503)286-4149
E-mail: silkhemp@teleport.com
Offers: Line of silk yarns, naturally hand-dyed, in 4 sizes and 180 colors for weaving, knitting, crochet and needlework. Also offers hemp spinning fiber, including 5 yarns for knitting, weaving and needlework in 24 naturally hand-dyed colors and a book on hemp. Also offers natural dyes and custom dyeing service.
Catalog: Samples, $2.
Accepts: MasterCard, Visa

LUCHI YARNS INTERNATIONAL

1055 Paramount Pkwy., Unit E
Batavia IL 60510
Contact: David Lu

Phone: (630)761-9674
Fax: (630)761-9675
E-mail: lysilk@aol.com
Store Location: At above address.
Offers: Silk scarves, silk fabrics, silk yarn and fiber for fiber artists.
Catalog: Brochure.
Phone Orders: 24 hours.
Mail Orders: Will ship to US and Canada.
Accepts: MasterCard, Visa

MARR HAVEN

Dept CSS
772 39th St.
Allegan MI 49010
Contact: Barbara Marr
Phone: (616)673-8800
Fax: (616)686-0341
E-mail: mhyarn@accn.org
Website: http://www.accn.org/~mhyarn
Store Location: At the farm.
Offers: Wool yarn, from Merino-Rambouillet sheep, by skeins or cones in natural and dyed colors. Supplies for hand and machine knitters. Locker hooks and spinning supplies also available.
Catalog: Send long SASE.
Phone Orders: (800)653-8810. Orders only with credit card.
Mail Orders: Shipping normally by next business day, UPS or Priority Mail. Prepayment required.
Accepts: MasterCard, Visa

MIZ BEARS CREATIONS

2248 Obispo Ave. #206
Signal Hill CA 90806
Contact: Nancy Long
Phone: (562)498-7168 or (800)774-9988
Fax: (562)494-6795
E-mail: mizbearsakanancylong@worldnet.att.net
Store Location: At above address. M-F, 9-6 PST.
Offers: Complete line of Paternayan Persian yarn in twist braids, Red Heart precut rug yarn, knit patterns, crochet patterns, complete Clover needle assortments, DMC Floss, Erica Wilson Persian yarns, assorted hand-painted canvas and afghan kits (knit and crochet).
Catalog: $2 (refundable).
Phone Orders: M-F, 9-6 PST.
Mail Orders: Will ship to US, Canada and US territories. Payment required at time of order. Allow 4-7 days for shipping.
Discounts: Wholesale to legitimate businesses with proper identification.
Accepts: Discover, MasterCard, Visa

MOUNTAIN COLORS YARN

P.O. Box 156
Corvallis MT 59828
Contact: Leslie Taylor
Phone: (406)777-3377

Fax: (406)777-7313
E-mail: redfox@bitterroot.net
Store Location: 4072 Eastside Hwy., Stevensville MT 59870. In the creamery.
Offers: Hand-painted yarns, including multicolored wool, mohair and novelty in 26 different colors. Patterns and kits for assorted sweaters, vests, socks, hats, mittens and more.
Catalog: Free. Catalog and color cards, $7.
Phone Orders: M-F, 9-3.
Mail Orders: Ship to US and Canada.
Discounts: Sell wholesale to legitimate businesses.
Accepts: MasterCard, Visa

OLD MILL YARN

(formerly Davidsons Old Mill Yarns)
109 E. Elizabeth
Eaton Rapids MI 48827
Phone: (517)663-2711
Fax: (517)663-5911
Store Location: At above address.
Offers: Knitting, weaving and spinning supplies. Also has mill end yarns.
Catalog: On weaving supplies only, $5.
Phone Orders: (800)257-2711.
Accepts: Discover, MasterCard, Visa, check (with proper ID)

THE OHIO HEMPERY, INC.

P.O. Box 18
Guysville OH 45735
Contact: D. Daniels
Phone: (800)BUY-HEMP
Fax: (740)662-6446
E-mail: hempery@hempery.com
Website: www.hempery.com
Offers: Hemp products, including twine, webbing, rope, fabric, paper, raw fiber materials, oils, seeds, books, accessories, clothing and others.
Catalog: Free retail catalog.
Phone Orders: M-F, 8-8; Sat, 9-5 EST.
Mail Orders: Standard UPS ground unless otherwise requested. All orders prepaid. Most orders shipped within 24 hours of receipt.
Discounts: Wholesale prices are available to legitimate retailers who present a valid tax ID number, vendor license number or tax exemption form.
Accepts: all major credit cards

PERSONAL THREADS BOUTIQUE

8025 West Dodge Rd.
Omaha NE 68114-3413
Contact: Carolyn Lewis
Phone: (402)391-7733
Fax: (402)391-0039
E-mail: carolyn@personalthreads.com
Website: http://www.personalthreads.com
Store Location: At above address. M-F, 9-6; Sat, 9-3 CST.
Offers: The finest knitting, weaving and needlecraft supplies. Hand-dyed wools, hand-painted needlepoint canvases,

yarns, flosses, needles and crochet hooks, pattern books and looms. Colinette, Tahki, Dale, Plymouth, Annabell Fox, Amy Blatt, Caron, Classic Elite, Gloria Tracy, Prism, Noro, Muench and many more.
Catalog: Free quarterly newsletter/catalog (must be requested in writing). On-line searchable catalog.
Phone Orders: (800)306-7733. M-F, 9-6; Sat, 9-3 CST.
Mail Orders: Use form in catalog, or order on-line.
Discounts: Annual New Year's sale 12/26-1/15; 20% off all merchandise.
Accepts: American Express, MasterCard, Visa

PINE TREE KNITS
Rt. 2, Box 840
East Lebanon ME 04027
Contact: Faye Krause
Phone: (207)457-3949 or (888)953-5809
E-mail: fkrause840@ime.net
Store Location: East Lebanon ME location. M,F, Sat, 10-5; T,W,Th, 7 p.m.-9 p.m.
Offers: Studio knitting machines, cone yarn, patterns and accessories. Hand knitting yarn, patterns and accessories. Custom-designed knitwear, patterns, kits and buttons.
Catalog: Color brochure.
Phone Orders: During store hours.
Mail Orders: 4-6 weeks delivery.
Discounts: Sells wholesale.
Accepts: MasterCard, Visa, check, cash

RICHLAN FARM
313 Richlan Rd.
Sharpsburg KY 40374
Contact: Lanette Freitag
Phone: (606)383-4454
Fax: (606)269-0605
E-mail: lanette@richlan.com
Website: richlan.com
Store Location: At above address. By appointment.
Offers: Wool from sheep, and alpaca for spinning and crafting.
Phone Orders: (606)293-9145.
Accepts: check

ROVINGS CUSTOM CARDING & DYEING
Box 192
Oakbank, Manitoba R0E 1J0
Canada
Contact: Francine Ruiter or Michelle Ruiter
Phone: (204)444-3040 or (800)266-5536
Fax: (204)222-6129
Store Location: 7-449 Main St., Oakbank, Manitoba R0E 1J0 Canada.
Offers: Custom carding and dyeing. North American distributors of Wendy Dennis Australian Polwarth and Polwarth/ Leicester coated fleece. We carry exotic fibres. Polwarth and Polwarth blended yarns. Natural and hand-dyed colors. We will custom dye. Lace sock and shawl kits. Distributors for

Louet and Ashford. Small handcrafted (locally) spinning tools. Books and magazines.
Catalog: Price lists available. Sample card packages, $10.
Phone Orders: T-F, 10-4; Sat, 10-1.
Mail Orders: We'll ship anywhere. Allow 6-8 weeks delivery on stock items.
Discounts: We give quantity discounts on purchases and processing. Wholesale inquiries welcome.
Accepts: MasterCard, Visa, check

SALT LAKE WEAVER'S STORE
1227 E. 3300 S.
Salt Lake City UT 84106
Contact: Annie Taylor
Phone: (801)486-1610
Store Location: At above address.
Offers: Looms, spinning wheels, all related support equipment, yarns, mill ends, raw wool, roving, spinning fibers, Procion and Cushing dyes and natural dyes. Also books on all the above. Offer year-round classes.
Catalog: $1.
Phone Orders: (800)363-5585. M-Sat, 10-6.
Mail Orders: Will ship anywhere.
Discounts: 10% to guilds and professionals.
Accepts: American Express, Discover, MasterCard, Visa

SALT SPRING ISLAND FIBRE STUDIOS
121 Mountain Rd.
Salt Spring Island, British Columbia V8K 1T8
Canada
Contact: Mary Paddon or Pat Daniel
Phone: (250)653-4033
Fax: (250)537-9930
E-mail: susanb@islandnet.com
Website: Under construction.
Store Location: 7 studios on Salt Spring. Call to arrange visit.
Offers: Alpaca, mohair, llama, wool yarns, raw fleece and rovings. Also knitting patterns, tools and knit kits. Custom spinning, dyeing and weaving.
Catalog: $4.
Phone Orders: M-F, 9-5 PST.
Mail Orders: Will ship anywhere the post goes. Allow 6 weeks for delivery.
Accepts: MasterCard, money order

SPINNING WHEEL
2 Ridge St.
Dover NH 03820
Contact: Martha Hauschka
Phone: (603)749-4246
Fax: (603)332-7007
E-mail: kurttoy@nh.ultranet.com
Website: www.nh.ultranet.com/~kurttoy/
Store Location: At above address. Closed Sundays.
Offers: Alice Starmore stockist. Retail yarn and accessory store.
Catalog: Color card, $20 ppd.

Phone Orders: Yes.
Mail Orders: Yes.
Accepts: MasterCard, Novus, Visa

STONE FOX FIBRE WORKS

1544 E. River Rd.
Grafton WI 53024
Contact: Nancy Fox
Phone: (414)375-2779
E-mail: stonefox@execpc.com
Website: www.impossibledream.com/fiber/
Offers: Yarns of 100% llama and 100% llama plied with British mohair yarn. Kits-to-Knit for sweaters, scarves, throw pillows, more. You pick from a wide selection of colors. Finished items from the same styles and more in your size and choice of colors. Llamas for sale as pets and fiber producers.
Catalog: With samples, $5 (refundable with order).
Mail Orders: Free shipping within US. Extra shipping charges outside US.

2JP RANCH

4735 W. Quince Ave.
Silver Springs NV 89429
Contact: Polly Holmes
Phone: (702)577-2100
Website: http://www.ramblin.com
Store Location: At ranch. Call for appointment.
Offers: Sheep wool, fleeces, roving and yarns—white and natural. Mohair (Angora goats) fleeces and roving—white and natural colored. Angora rabbit fiber and yarns.
Catalog: Free price list.
Phone Orders: PST.
Mail Orders: Prepayment required.

WANDERINGS' COUNTRY STORE

1944 Washington Valley Rd.
Martinsville NJ 08836
Contact: Suzanne Johnson or Grace Petrany
Phone: (800)456-KNIT
Fax: (908)647-6234
E-mail: wanderknit@aol.com
Website: www.wanderings.com
Store Location: At above address.
Offers: Large selection of yarns, knit kits, patterns, accessories, Brittany and Inox needles. Encore, Galway, Snuggly, Gaelic aran, Naturspun Lopi, mohair, Red/Heart Yarns and much more! Also hand-knit sweaters and Dale of Norway sweaters. Knitters' gifts, country crafts, hand lotions and more.
Catalog: $2.
Phone Orders: M-Sat, 10-5 EST.
Mail Orders: Worldwide.
Discounts: 10% to Frequent Knitter's Club members.
Accepts: American Express, Discover, MasterCard, Visa

WEAVER'S WAY

P.O. Box 70
Columbus NC 28722
Offers: Mercerized/perle, natural and novelty cotton yarns

and wools. Also offers weaving equipment.
Catalog: Catalog, sample cards set, $3 (cash).
Discounts: On volume orders.

THE WEB-STERS: HANDSPINNERS, WEAVERS & KNITTERS

11 N. Main St.
Ashland OR 97520
Phone: (541)482-9801
Store Location: At above address. Open daily 10-6 PST.
Offers: Books, yarn and tools for knitters, weavers and hand spinners.
Catalog: 40 pages, color. Free. Knitting, weaving, and spinning supplies.
Phone Orders: Yes.
Mail Orders: Call for stock confirmation and shipping charges.
Discounts: Retail.
Accepts: American Express, Discover, MasterCard, Visa

WHIPPLETREE YARN AND GIFTS

3504 Chicago Dr.
Hudsonville MI 49426
Phone: (616)669-4487
Offers: Wide variety of yarns. Also books and supplies for knitters and crocheters.

WILDE YARNS

P.O. Box 4662
3737 Main St.
Philadelphia PA 19127
Phone: (215)482-8800
Store Location: At above address.
Offers: Wool yarns for weaving and knitting in variety of weights and colors. Carded wool in natural and dyed colors for hand spinning and felt making.
Catalog: Sample pack, $7.50.
Discounts: Available to retailers, institutions and production craftspeople.

THE WOOLERY

R.D. 1, Stewarts' Corners
Genoa NY 13071
Phone: (315)497-1542 or (800)441-9665
Fax: (315)497-3620
E-mail: jive@woolery.com
Website: www.woolery.com
Offers: Yarns: soft wools and angoras in 29 colors. Un-Spun yarns also available. Also mohair and cotton yarns.
Catalog: $4.
Phone Orders: M-F, 9-6:30 EST.
Mail Orders: Will ship to US, Canada and overseas.
Accepts: MasterCard, Visa

YARN BARN

918 Massachusetts St.
Lawrence KS 66044
Contact: Susan Bateman
Phone: (785)842-4333 or (800)468-0035
Fax: (785)842-6794

E-mail: yarnbarn@idir.net
Website: www.yarnbarn-ks.com
Store Location: At above address. 7 days a week.
Offers: Large selection of knitting and weaving yarns with supplies and equipment to cover those areas as well as spinning, dyeing, rug braiding and needlepoint. Hundreds of books covering most textile arts. Over 180 videos on same.
Catalog: 3 free options: (1) knitting and crochet, (2) weaving, spinning and equipment and (3) videos.
Phone Orders: (800)468-0035. M-Sat, 9:30-5:30 CST.
Mail Orders: Any location. Prepayment please.
Discounts: Quantity discounts on yarn and fibers. Looms and spinning wheels competitively priced.
Accepts: Discover, MasterCard, Visa, check, money order

THE YARN BASKET
150 Falling Spring Rd.
Chambersburg PA 17201
Contact: Sue Sollenberger
Phone: (717)263-3236
Store Location: I-81, exit 6 and Rt. 30, behind Shoney's.
Offers: Knitting and crochet yarns, patterns and accessories. Needlepoint yarns and accessories. Cross-stitch, ribbon embroidery and crewel classes.
Phone Orders: (888)YRN-BSKT.
Mail Orders: Will ship UPS, Priority Mail and regular mail.
Accepts: Discover, MasterCard, Visa

YARNS BY DESIGN
247 E. Wisconsin Ave.
Neenah WI 54956
Contact: Ron Busha

Phone: (920)727-0530
Fax: (920)727-0550
E-mail: yarns@juno.com
Store Location: At above address. M,Th, F, 10-8; T,W, Sat, 10-5.
Offers: Fibers for spinning, knitting and weaving. Sell spinning wheels, looms and accessories. Specialty designed sweaters.
Catalog: Product listing and prices, $1.
Phone Orders: During business hours.
Mail Orders: Will ship within US. Prepayment required. Allow 2-4 weeks for delivery.
Discounts: Refer to our newsletter.
Accepts: MasterCard, Visa

YARNS BY MAIL
2215 Louise Lane
Norman OK 73071
Phone: (405) 360-0140
Offers: Natural fibers for machine and hand knitting.
Catalog: Green Mountain Spinnery samples, $6. Fingerlake Woolen Mill samples, $4.
Mail Orders: At above address. Orders sent by Priority Mail at US Postal Service rates; no added handling charge.
Discounts: Yarn prices are less than retail. No charge to turn skeins into balls.
Accepts: check, money order, cashier's check (no credit cards)

Resources

Associations

Also see General Craft Supplies; Publications.
Include a business-size, stamped, self-addressed envelope with inquiries to associations.

AMERICAN ASSOCIATION OF WOODTURNERS

3200 Lexington Ave.
Shoreview MN 55126
Phone: (612)484-9094
Fax: (612)484-1724
E-mail: aaw@compuserve.com
Offers: This international nonprofit association is dedicated to providing education and information to those interested in this craft. Members get a quarterly journal, *American Woodturner*, and annual resources directory and other benefits.

AMERICAN CRAFT COUNCIL

72 Spring St.
New York NY 10019
Offers: This nonprofit educational organization promotes excellence in contemporary craft (clay, fiber, glass, metal, wood and other media) through a variety of programs. Publishes *American Craft*, a bimonthly magazine, and holds juried craft shows annually across the country. Also offers a research library. Send SASE.

AMERICAN NEEDLEPOINT GUILD, INC.

3410 Valley Creek Circle
Middleton WI 53562
Contact: Cathy Felten
Phone: (608)831-3328
Fax: (608)831-0651
E-mail: president@needlepoint.org
Website: www.needlepoint.org
Offers: Educational nonprofit organization whose main purpose is educational and cultural development through participation in and encouragement of interest in the art of needlepoint (stitchery worked by hand with a threaded needle on a readily countable ground). ANG offers education to at-large and chapter members through correspondence courses, audiovisual programs, national seminars, both teacher and judging certification programs, and *Needle Pointers* magazine published 6 times a year. Members are from throughout the world.

AMERICAN QUILTER'S SOCIETY

P.O. Box 3290
Paducah KY 42002
Phone: (502)898-7903
Fax: (502)898-8890

Offers: Members of this society of professional and amateur quilters join to carry on this American tradition. They receive *American Quilter* magazine 4 times yearly, the *Update* bimonthly newsletter, discount admission to the Annual National Quilt Show and Contest (that awards over $80,000 in cash prizes) and receive member discounts of up to 20% on books and other resources. They also share experiences, ideas and advice with other members nationwide.

AMERICAN SOCIETY OF ARTISTS, INC.

P.O. Box 1326
Palatine IL 60078
Phone: (312)751-2500
E-mail: socofartist@webtv.com
Offers: This is a professional service organization for artists and artisans; membership is juried. Membership benefits include publicity, art shows and art/craft shows. Those qualified may participate in lecture and demonstration services. Also offers *A.S.A. Artisan*, a quarterly publication.

ASSOCIATION OF TRADITIONAL HOOKING ARTISTS (ATHA)

1360 Newman Ave.
Seekonk MA 02771-2611
Contact: Nancy Martin
Phone: (508)399-8230
Offers: Nonprofit association of rug hookers. 45-page colored-cover newsletter, complimentary issue with membership information. Write to above address.
Accepts: check only for membership

THE EMBROIDERERS GUILD OF AMERICA, INC.

335 W. Broadway, Suite 100
Louisville KY 40202
Contact: Bonnie Key
Phone: (502)589-6956
Fax: (502)584-7900
E-mail: egahq@aol.com
Store Location: National headquarters only with 355 chapters.
Offers: *Needle Arts* magazine. Available only to members.

THE KNITTING GUILD OF AMERICA

P.O. Box 1606
Knoxville TN 37901-1606
Contact: Mindi Efurd
Phone: (423)524-2401
Fax: (423)524-8677
E-mail: tkga@tkga.com
Website: www.tkga.com
Store Location: At above address.

Offers: *Cast On* magazine 5 times per year. Education programs; Master Hand and Machine program, correspondence courses, Learn-A-Stitch kits, videos and slide show. Local guild affiliation, conventions and conferences.
Catalog: Educational program brochure. Convention and conference brochures.
Phone Orders: (800)274-6034.
Mail Orders: At above address.
Accepts: MasterCard, Visa, check

NATIONAL CLOTH DOLL MAKERS ASSOCIATION

1601 Provincetown Dr.
San Jose CA 95129
E-mail: brnmrk@sjm.infi.net
Offers: This association whose members love and make cloth dolls is open to any who shares that experience. For information, send long SASE.

NATIONAL INSTITUTE OF AMERICAN DOLL ARTISTS (NIADA)

P.O. Box 87
Bybee TN 37713
Phone: (914)687-7949
Offers: This is an organization of professional doll artists and its devoted patrons. For patron membership information, contact: Kathy Van Winkle, 101 Rainbow Dr., Apt. 8085, Livingston TX 77351. For artist membership information, contact Shelly Thornton, 1600 S. 22nd St., Lincoln NE 68502.

NATIONAL MODEL RAILROAD ASSOCIATION

4121 Cromwell Rd.
Chattanooga TN 37421
Phone: (423)892-2846
Fax: (423)899-4869
Offers: Membership to this national group is open to all age groups—youth to elders—who are interested in model railroading. Members receive the NMRA bulletin of news, events and related information.

ORIGAMI USA

(formerly The Friends of the Origami Center of America)
15 W. 77th St.
New York NY 10024-5192
Phone: (212)769-5635
Fax: (212)769-5668
Website: www.origami-usa.org
Offers: Origami books and instructional videos; a full range of origami papers from around the world.
Catalog: Write for a free catalog.
Accepts: MasterCard, Visa

STENCIL ARTISANS LEAGUE, INC.

10521 St. Charles Rock Rd., Suite 1
St. Ann MO 63074-1838
Contact: Rosemary Jost
Phone: (314)429-3459
Fax: (314)429-0334
E-mail: salistl@aol.com
Website: www.sali.org
Offers: An international nonprofit organization dedicated to the promotion and preservation of the art of stenciling and related decorative painting. Membership provides for opportunities in artistic and professional growth. Annual convention. Quarterly 48-page publication. Liability insurance.
Accepts: MasterCard, Visa

SURFACE DESIGN ASSOCIATION

P.O. Box 20799
Oakland CA 94620
Phone: (707)829-3110
Offers: This is a nonprofit, educational association. Members receive a quarterly *Textile Journal* and *Newsletter* with surface design data, news and technical and business information.

Books & Booksellers

Also see specific categories throughout the book.

BETTER HOMES & GARDENS/MEREDITH BOOKS
(formerly Meredith Books)
1716 Locust St.
Des Moines IA 50309-3023
Contact: Tom Wierzbicki
Phone: (515)284-3604
Fax: (515)284-3912
E-mail: twierzbi@mdp.com
Offers: Selection of quilting, kids' and cross-stitch books, including two Mary Engelbreit cross-stitch books.
Phone Orders: (800)678-8091. Also fax orders to (515)284-3371.

BETTERWAY BOOKS
F&W Publications
1507 Dana Ave.
Cincinnati OH 45207
Phone: (513)531-2222
Offers: Publisher of a variety of woodworking and craft titles. Craft titles include *The Teddy Bear Sourcebook*; *The Doll Sourcebook*; *How to Start Making Money With Your Crafts*, by Kathy Ruzek; *Picture-Perfect Worry-Free Wedding*, by Diane Warner; and *How to Start Making Money With Your Sewing*, by Karen Maslowski.
Catalog: Request a free catalog from the above address.
Phone Orders: (800)289-0963.

DECORATIVE ARTIST'S BOOK CLUB
P.O. Box 12577
Cincinnati OH 45212-0577
Phone: (513)531-8250
E-mail: dabcservice@fwpubs.com
Offers: Each month you'll receive a bulletin offering 50+ books in all areas of decorative painting—each book is discounted at least 15% off the retail price. Each book is hand picked by the editor of the club, a decorative artist herself, with your needs in mind. Decorative Artist's Book Club also provides expert tips and techniques, book excerpts, a calendar of events and a page dedicated to individual club members and their artwork. Drop us a note or call to find out about the latest new member offer.

DOVER PUBLICATIONS, INC.
31 E. Second St.
Mineola NY 11501
Phone: (516)294-7000
Offers: Craft/needlecraft books including a series of copy-right-free design books and cut-and-use stencil books. Craft books include glass crafts, silkscreen, paper, woodworking and needlecrafts (quilt, knit, crochet, lace, cross-stitch and others). Also offers textiles, photography, architecture, art instruction, children's activities, Native American crafts and designs, stencil books, plus non-art/craft titles.
Catalog: Free needlecraft catalog.

I LOVE QUILTING BOOK CLUB
1507 Dana Ave.
Cincinnati OH 45207
Contact: Mary Dacres, editor
Phone: (513)531-2690
Fax: (513)531-4744
Offers: About every 4 weeks a free issue of the club catalog and newsletter, describing the main selection book, several alternates and dozens of other book offerings including hard-to-find tools and gadgets, videos and more—all at a discount price.

MOUNTAIN LAUREL BOOKS
26 Florence Ave.
Ellington CT 06029-4117
Contact: Kathleen Vaiciulis
Phone: (860)871-6250
Fax: (860)870-8965
E-mail: mtlaurel@tiac.net
Website: www.tiac.net/users/mtlaurel
Offers: Free international book search for books of all genre.
Catalog: $4 for 50+ page catalog of needlework books.
Phone Orders: M-F, 9-5 EST.
Mail Orders: Worldwide delivery.
Accepts: All major credit cards

NORTH LIGHT BOOK CLUB
P.O. Box 12171
Cincinnati OH 45212-0411
Phone: (513)531-8250
Offers: Each month you'll get a free issue of *North Light Magazine*, offering 100 or more books on all areas of fine art—each book discounted at least 15% off the retail price. North Light also provides book excerpts, step-by-step lessons and tips from renowned art instructors, and devotes a full page to a club member's work in each issue. Drop North Light a note or call to find out what the latest new member offer is. Currently, it's a book of your choice free with another one for just half price.

NORTH LIGHT BOOKS
1507 Dana Ave.
Cincinnati OH 45207
Offers: Arts/crafts how-to books. Fine art titles include wa-

tercolor, pastel, oil, acrylic, airbrush, screen printing, design, graphics, drawing, perspective, pencil and others. Crafts titles include decorative painting, gift making, silk painting, dough craft, paper sculpture, nature projects, home building, log homes, playhouses, masonry, woodworking, furniture making, molding and others.

Catalog: Free.

Discounts: Quantity; teachers and institutions; sells wholesale to legitimate businesses.

POPULAR WOODWORKING BOOKS

F&W Publications
1507 Dana Ave.
Cincinnati OH 45207
Phone: (513)531-2222
Offers: Publisher of a variety of woodworking and craft titles. Woodworking titles include project books, how-to books and informational titles, such as *The Woodworker's Guide to Furniture Design*, by Garth Graves; *Good Wood Joints*, by Jackson and Day; *Creating Beautiful Boxes With Inlay Techniques*, by Doug Stowe; and *The Best of Wood Boxes*, edited by R. Adam Blake.
Catalog: Request a free catalog from the above address.
Phone Orders: (800)289-0963.

MARY ROEHR BOOKS & VIDEO

500 Saddlerock Circle
Sedona AZ 86336
Contact: Mary Roehr
Phone: (520)282-4971
Fax: (520)282-4971
E-mail: maryroehr@kachina.net
Website: www.sewnet.com/maryroehr
Offers: Books and videos on sewing and crafting businesses, altering ready-to-wear, speed tailoring and sewing's first cartoon book. Also hard-to-find tailoring, sewing and pressing supplies.
Catalog: Free.
Phone Orders: 24 hours.
Mail Orders: At above address.
Discounts: Inquire for wholesale and distributor pricing.
Accepts: American Express, MasterCard, Novus, Visa, check, money order

STOREY PUBLISHING

Schoolhouse Rd.
Pownal VT 05261
Phone: (800)441-5700
Offers: Over 130 country skills booklets, including rug mak-

ing, furniture, stencils, curtains and quilts, insulated window shutters, homemade wine, clay flowerpots, canoes, solar-heated pit greenhouse, chair caning, hearth and root cellar construction, pole woodshed, cold-frame construction and other country booklets.
Catalog: Free.
Discounts: Quantity; sells wholesale to legitimate businesses.
Accepts: MasterCard, Visa

SUCCESSFUL SEWING BOOK CLUB

1507 Dana Ave.
Cincinnati OH 45207
Contact: Mary Dacres, editor
Phone: (513)531-290
Fax: (513)531-4744
Offers: The club catalog and newsletter, describing the main selection book, several alternates and dozens of other book offerings arrives about every 4 weeks. It includes hard-to-find tools and gadgets, videos and more—all at a discount price.

THE TAUTON PRESS

P.O. Box 5506
63 S. Main St.
Newtown CT 06470-5506
Contact: Ellen Williams
Phone: (800)926-8776, ext. 453
Fax: (203)426-3434
E-mail: ewilliams@taunton.com
Website: www.taunton.com
Offers: Finely illustrated and how-to books in woodworking, home remodeling, sewing and needlecrafts. For professionals, experienced hobbyists and beginners.
Catalog: Free catalog available. Also available through website.
Phone Orders: (800)888-8286.
Mail Orders: At above address.
Discounts: Sells wholesale to businesses.
Accepts: MasterCard, Visa

WOODWORKER'S BOOK CLUB

P.O. Box 12171
Cincinnati OH 45212-0171
Phone: (513)531-8250
Offers: A free monthly issue of the club newsletter, describing the main selection and dozens of other selections. You always have at least 10 days to decide which books you want to buy. Drop a note to find out about the latest membership opening offer or call for further information.

General Craft Business

Also see Supportive Materials & Aids. This category aids those who have gone from hobby status to professional with crafts work—those who are suppliers, service providers or otherwise in business, and those who desire to be in business.

ART CALENDAR
P.O. Box 199
Upper Fairmount MD 21867
Phone: (410)651-9151 or (800)597-5988
Website: www.artcalendar.com
Offers: This monthly publication connects artists with exhibition and income opportunities and includes over 5,000 listings of shows and other possibilities for exhibiting. It also includes information on marketing one's artwork, examines legal issues affecting artists and discusses trends in the visual arts marketplace.

BARBARA BRABEC PRODUCTIONS
P.O. Box 2137
Naperville IL 60567
Phone: (630)717-4188
Fax: (630)717-5198
Offers: Crafts marketing reports and books by Barbara Brabec (a home-based business authority): *Homemade Money*, 5th ed. rev. (Betterway, 1997); *Homemade for Profit* (Evans, 1996); *The Craft Business Answer Book* (Evans, 1998); and *Creative Cash* (New Century Edition, Prima, 1998).
Catalog: Send for free brochure.

BLACK DIAMOND ENTERPRISE
(formerly Carris Pottery)
105 Monticello Rd.
Oak Ridge TN 37830
Contact: Tom Carris
Phone: (423)483-7167
Fax: (423)482-8059
E-mail: bdetom@aol.com
Offers: The Digital Image Showcase: computer software that creates digital, full-color catalogs averaging 20-50 color pictures on a floppy disk. Can be used as a floppy mailer, with websites or home pages, or to E-mail to your customers. Full and LE versions available for sale, or BDE can create your catalog for you.
Catalog: Ask for Digital Image Showcase free brochure.
Phone Orders: Yes.
Mail Orders: At above address.
Accepts: American Express, Discover, MasterCard, Visa

THE BUSINESS OF HERBS
439 Ponderosa Way
Jemez Springs NM 87025-8036
Offers: This bimonthly newsletter reports trade news, market tips, grower resources, sources and more. Herbal facts, interviews, ideas, forums, book reviews, events and business ideas round out issues. Advertising.

FRONT ROOM PUBLISHERS
P.O. Box 1541
Clifton NJ 07015-1541
Phone: (973)773-4215
Fax: (973)815-1235
E-mail: rjp@intac.com
Website: http://www.intac.com/~rjp
Offers: Publications on craft marketing/home business: *Directory of Craft Shops and Galleries*; *Directory of Craft Malls and Rent-A-Space Shops*; *Directory of Seasonal/Holiday Boutiques*; *Directory of Wholesale Reps for Craft Professionals*; *Creative Crafters Directory*; *How to Sell to Craft Shops* and *How to Start and Run a Successful Handcraft Co-Op*. Special reports on selling, debts, credit collections, hangtags, displays and current craft marketing concerns.
Catalog: Flyer for #10 SASE.
Phone Orders: M-F, 10-4 EST.
Mail Orders: Prepayment required.
Accepts: MasterCard, Visa, check, money order

THE NATIONAL DIRECTORY OF ARTISTS & CRAFTSMEN
P.O. Box 424
Devault PA 19432
Phone: (610)640-ARTS
Offers: Frequently updated resource publication of artists and craftsmen of the twentieth and twenty-first centuries. For further information, send SASE and/or send for forms. Cost to order is $45. Basic cost to be in it is $25.

NORTHWOODS TRADING CO.
13451 Essex Court
Eden Prairie MN 55347
Offers: *Directory of Wholesale Reps for Craft Professionals* lists sales reps selling to department stores, gift shops, museums and galleries, with descriptions of each company, and tips and data on presenting crafts work. An aid to making the right connections. Directory, $16.95.

THE REP REGISTRY
P.O. Box 2306
Capistrano Beach CA 92624
Phone: (714)240-3333
Fax: (714)493-2627

E-mail: repregistr@aol.com

Offers: Rep sourcing service. Over 5,000 registered gift industry reps, many of whom work with producers of handcrafted product. Also *Gift Trade Marketing: The Handbook for Manufacturers New to Wholesaling*. Send SASE for details.

REVENUE SERVICE CO., INC.

P.O. Box 200205
Denver CO 80220
Phone: (800)453-1127
Fax: (303)355-5338
Offers: Nationwide collection service for crafts accounts collecting. Send SASE.

SYLVIA'S STUDIO

1090 Cambridge St.
Novato CA 94947
Phone: (415)883-6206
Fax: (415)883-4546
E-mail: studio@crl.com
Website: http://www.crl.com/~studio
Offers: Publications by Sylvia Landman. Books include *Make Your Quilting Pay for Itself* and *Crafting for Dollars*. 28-page business reports on operating a teaching studio, writing for the crafts market, marketing crafts and mail-order selling. Audiotapes of small business college classes, including arts/crafts marketing, mail order, starting a home business, couples in business and time management. Send SASE.

Publications

Publications in your areas of interest can be treasures of source information, technical inspiration and networking cooperation. Check a newsstand or library for a single issue of a publication that interests you. If you inquire regarding subscriptions to publications, include a business-size, stamped, self-addressed envelope, or try requesting a current single issue of the publication and include a check or money order of at least $6.00 to cover cost and postage.

AIRBRUSH MAGAZINE
P.O. Box 70
Cosby TN 37722
Offers: Articles in this airbrushing publication feature color step-by-step instruction from known instructors.

THE AMERICAN NEEDLECRAFTER
23 Old Pecan Rd.
Big Sandy TX 75755
Offers: This is the official newspaper of American Needlecraft Association. It is published quarterly, with articles of interest to needlecrafters from members and manufacturers, special savings for members, calendar of nationwide stitching events, pattern book review and Needlepals—pen pals with needlecrafting interests.

AMERICAN QUILTER
P.O. Box 3290
Paducah KY 42002
Phone: (502)898-7903
Offers: This official magazine of the American Quilter's Society displays quilts and techniques that promote the art form and preserve the craft. Among the features: who's who, historical notes, show listings and events and more.

ANNA CREATIVE NEEDLEWORK & CRAFTS
GLP International
153 S. Dean St.
Englewood NJ 07631
Phone: (201)871-1010
Fax: (201)871-0870
E-mail: info@glpnews.com
Website: http://www.glpnews.com/crafts.html
Offers: Mail-order subscriptions to *Anna Creative Needlework & Crafts*.
Catalog: Call.
Phone Orders: M-F, 9-5 EST.
Discounts: Magazines available to retailers. Call (800)457-4443 for dealer terms.
Accepts: American Express, MasterCard, Visa

ART CALENDAR
P.O. Box 199
Upper Fairmount MD 21867
Phone: (410)651-9151 or (800)597-5988
Website: www.artcalendar.com
Offers: This monthly publication connects artists with exhibition and income opportunities and includes over 5,000 listings of shows and other possibilities for exhibiting. It also includes information on marketing one's artwork, examines legal issues affecting artists and discusses trends in the visual arts marketplace.

THE ARTISTS' MAGAZINE
F&W Publications
1507 Dana Ave.
Cincinnati OH 45207
Contact: Jennifer King
Phone: (513)531-2690, ext. 467
Fax: (513)531-2902
E-mail: tamedit@aol.com
Offers: This monthly magazine features step-by-step art instruction in a variety of media, from oil and watercolor to acrylic and colored pencil. Each issue presents tips and techniques from professional artists, plus complete listings of markets to show and sell your work.

ART/QUILT MAGAZINE
Dept. CS
P.O. Box 630927
Houston TX 77263-0927
Contact: Lynn Young
Fax: (713)975-6072
E-mail: Coming.
Website: http://www.gcx.com/artquilt/magi.htm
Offers: *Art/Quilt Magazine* by subscription; back issues also available; sample copy $7 ($10 overseas). Also book service offering art, quilt and other books by mail. *Art/Quilt Magazine* is a quarterly magazine devoted to art quilts. High-quality reproductions of quilts accompany articles about artists, shows and more in an art magazine format.
Catalog: Send SASE.
Mail Orders: Will ship overseas. Prepayment required on retail orders.
Discounts: No for retail; wholesale for magazine orders; send for information.
Accepts: MasterCard, Visa, check (US funds, US account)

BLACK SHEEP NEWSLETTER
25455 NW Dixie Mountain Rd.
Scappoose OR 97056
Contact: Peggy Lundquist

Phone: (503)621-3063
E-mail: bsnewsltr@aol.com
Offers: This quarterly newsletter is meant for growers, spinners and textile artists interested in black sheep wool and other animal fibers. Upcoming events and book reviews are included. Advertising.

BURDA A WORLD OF FASHION

GLP International
153 S. Dean St.
Englewood NJ 07631
Phone: (201)871-1010
Fax: (201)871-0870
E-mail: info@glpnews.com
Website: http://www.glpnews.com/crafts.html
Offers: Mail-order subscriptions to *Burda A World of Fashion*.
Catalog: Call.
Phone Orders: M-F, 9-5 EST.
Discounts: Magazines available to retailers. Call (800)457-4443 for dealer terms.
Accepts: American Express, MasterCard, Visa

THE BUSINESS OF HERBS

439 Ponderosa Way
Jemez Springs NM 87025-8036
Offers: This bimonthly newsletter reports trade news, market tips, grower resources, sources and more. Herbal facts, interviews, ideas, forums, book reviews, events and business ideas round out issues. Advertising.

CAR MODELER

Kalmbach Publishing Co.
P.O. Box 1612
21027 Crossroads Circle
Waukesha WI 53187-1612
Phone: (414)796-8776
Fax: (414)796-0126
E-mail: customerservice@kalmbach.com
Website: www.kalmbach.com
Offers: Over 200 hobby-related books, calendars and videos.
Catalog: Upon request.
Phone Orders: (800)533-6644.
Accepts: American Express, Discover, MasterCard, Visa

CERAMIC ARTS & CRAFTS

30595 Eight Mile Rd.
Livonia MI 48152-1798
Offers: This monthly magazine focuses on how-tos in hobby ceramics, with color projects, materials list and instructions. A variety of techniques are given in each issue, as are "See What's New" and "Worldwide Shows." Advertising.

CERAMICS MAGAZINE

30595 Eight Mile Rd.
Livonia MI 48152-1798
Offers: This monthly ceramics publication presents mold designs and products from known manufacturers, decorating techniques, contributions by world famous ceramic artists,

articles by professionals, tips and shortcuts. National show listings. Advertising.

CLASSIC TOY TRAINS

Kalmbach Publishing Co.
P.O. Box 1612
21027 Crossroads Circle
Waukesha WI 53187-1612
Phone: (414)796-8776
Fax: (414)796-0126
E-mail: customerservice@kalmbach.com
Website: www.kalmbach.com
Offers: Over 200 hobby-related books, calendars and videos.
Catalog: Upon request.
Phone Orders: (800)533-6644.
Accepts: American Express, Discover, MasterCard, Visa

THE CLOTH DOLL

P.O. Box 2167
Lake Oswego OR 97035-0051
Offers: This quarterly magazine serves the interest of cloth doll makers and collectors. Issues provide at least 3 doll and clothing patterns, articles on techniques, accessories, new products, feature artists, book reviews and doll show reviews. Advertising.

CONTEMPORARY DOLL COLLECTOR

Scott Publications
30595 Eight Mile Rd.
Livonia MI 48152-1798
Contact: Jeanette Foxe
Phone: (800)458-8237 or (248)477-6650
Fax: (248)477-6795
E-mail: 104137.1254@compuserve.com
Store Location: At above address. M-F, 8-5.
Offers: Magazines, books for ceramics, dolls and miniatures.
Catalog: Free. 31 pages.
Phone Orders: (800)458-8237.
Mail Orders: At above address.
Discounts: Dealers and distributors.
Accepts: Discover, MasterCard, Visa

THE CRAFT & ART SHOW CALENDAR

(formerly The Craft Show Calendar)
P.O. Box 424
Devault PA 19432
Contact: Rose Brein Finkel
Phone: (610)640-ARTS
Fax: (610)640-2332
Website: http://www.art-craftpa.com/finkel.html
Store Location: The Gallery at Cedar Hollow (CS).
Offers: All handcrafts, folk art, fine art, jewelry, clothing, furniture, pottery, woodworking, glass, metals and special exhibitions. Please send SASE for more information. The Craft & Art Show Calendar—shows, galleries and publications in the mid-Atlantic states—$18 subscription (1 issue $5).
Catalog: The Craft & Art Show Calendar for the Craft Show Goer.

Phone Orders: Yes.
Mail Orders: Yes.
Accepts: SASE to be in shows or The Craft & Art Show Calendar

CRAFT MARKETING NEWS
Front Room Publishers
P.O. Box 1541
Clifton NJ 07015-1541
Contact: Adele Patti, editor
Phone: (973)773-4215
Fax: (973)815-1235
E-mail: rjp@intac.com
Website: http://www.intac.com/~rjp
Offers: Published bimonthly for all wanting to sell their handcrafts, with listings of craft shops, galleries and craft malls in the US wanting finished items. Special reports, investigative craft reporters nationwide, comments and views. Published since 1984.
Catalog: Flyer with #10 SASE.
Phone Orders: M-F, 10-4 EST.
Mail Orders: Prepayment required.
Accepts: MasterCard, Visa, check, money order

CRAFTING TRADITIONS
P.O. Box 996
Greendale WI 53125
Offers: Published 6 times a year, this publication features more than 40 craft projects per issue. Full-size patterns and instructions for variety of crafts, including holiday and family-oriented crafts, are included.

THE CRAFTS FAIR GUIDE
P.O. Box 688
Corte Madera CA 94976
Phone: (415)924-3259 or (800)871-2341
E-mail: leecfg@pacbell.net
Offers: This quarterly publication covers in detail, and through reviews, over 1,000 fairs throughout the West. Fairs are rated for sales/enjoyment. Invaluable for show marketing. Shows listed by dates/town/state. Advertising. $45 per year.

CRAFTS MAGAZINE
P.O. Box 1790
Peoria IL 61656
Offers: How-to techniques and full-sized, foldout patterns are included in colorful monthly issues of this magazine that presents an array of crafts/needlecrafts techniques. Advertising.

CRAFTS 'N THINGS
2400 Devon, Suite 375
Des Plaines IL 60016
Contact: Nona Piorkowski, associate editor
Phone: (847)635-5800
Fax: (847)635-6311
Offers: This magazine carries a variety of general craft projects, craft ideas, how-tos and tips for beginner and advanced

craftspeople. Single-sided full-size patterns and step-by-step instructions are offered. Published 10 times yearly.

CROCHET HOME
23 Old Pecan Rd.
Big Sandy TX 75755
Offers: An assortment of crochet patterns with instructions and diagrams make up this bimonthly magazine, including projects for personal and home decor; women's and children's clothing and others. Also features letters, articles, pictures and directions and regular features.

CROCHET WITH HEART
P.O. Box 55595
Little Rock AR 72215
Offers: This magazine features crochet projects, including afghans, baby items and keepsakes, clothing and accessories. It includes gift suggestions, designer profiles, buyer's guide, advice, letters and reviews of Leisure Arts and Coats & Clark leaflets.

CROCHET WORLD
306 E. Parr Rd.
Berne IN 46711
Offers: This bimonthly crochet magazine presents illustrated project patterns for adult and children's apparel, dolls and doll clothes, toys and home decor items. Projects are marked for level of ability, easy to advanced. "Potpourri," reader trades/wants, and "Show-It-Off" are among regular features. Advertising.

CROSS COUNTRY STITCHING
Jeremiah Junction, Inc.
P.O. Box 710
Manchester CT 06045
Contact: Allen Coleman
Phone: (860)646-0665 or (800)231-8108
Fax: (860)643-1880
E-mail: akcoleman@worldnet.att.net
Website: www.crosscountryshopping.com
Offers: The counted cross-stitch store at your front door. Free copy of *Cross Country Stitching* magazine and catalog. French country decor, bright illustrated designs with verses and sayings. Lots of easy-to-stitch projects are delightful and enjoyable. Cross-stitch designs are fun and will be greatly appreciated as gifts.
Catalog: Cross Country Shopping, 24 pages, full color.
Phone Orders: (800)231-8108. M-F, 7:30-4:30 EST.
Mail Orders: Will ship worldwide. Prepayment required. 2 weeks delivery in US, 4 weeks outside US.
Discounts: Wholesale to legitimate retailers.
Accepts: MasterCard, Visa

CROSS STITCH! MAGAZINE
23 Old Pecan Rd.
Big Sandy TX 75755
Phone: (903)636-4011
Offers: Bimonthly magazine gives stitch basics and projects for many cross-stitch items, each with stitch and color charts,

materials lists and instructions. Readers' letters with hints and getting started columns are in each issue, along with patterns for everyone, from wall hangings to wearables.

THE CROSS STITCHER MAGAZINE

Dept. CSS2
701 Lee St.
Des Plaines IL 60016
Offers: This bimonthly magazine is devoted to cross-stitching, providing a variety of pattern illustrations, features and other information.

DECORATIVE ARTIST'S BOOK CLUB

P.O. Box 12577
Cincinnati OH 45212-0577
Phone: (513)531-8250
E-mail: dabcservice@fwpubs.com
Offers: Each month you'll receive a bulletin offering 50 + books in all areas of decorative painting—each book is discounted at least 15% off the retail price. Each book is hand picked by the editor of the club, a decorative artist herself, with your needs in mind. Decorative Artist's Book Club also provides expert tips and techniques, book excerpts, a calendar of events and a page dedicated to individual club members and their artwork. Drop us a note or call to find out about the latest new member offer.

DECORATIVE ARTIST'S WORKBOOK

F&W Publications
1507 Dana Ave.
Cincinnati OH 45207
Contact: Anne Hevener
Phone: (513)531-2690
Fax: (513)531-2902
E-mail: dawedit@aol.com
Offers: This bimonthly magazine is for decorative painters and crafters. Each issue features new designs to paint on wood, tin, fabric, glass and more. All projects are complete with materials lists, full-size patterns, step-by-step instructions and color photos to show the way.

DOLL ARTISAN

Jones Publishing, Inc.
P.O. Box 471
Iola WI 54945
Phone: (715)445-5000
Fax: (715)445-4053
E-mail: dollmaking@dollmakingartisan.com
Website: http://www.dollmakingartisan.com
Offers: Bimonthly magazine dedicated to people who make porcelain reproductions of antique dolls from the classic period (1840-1940) of dolls. An official publication of the Doll Artisan Guild. Subscription $29.95 US for 1 year.
Phone Orders: M-F, 9-5 CST.
Accepts: American Express, MasterCard, Visa

DOLL CRAFTER

30595 Eight Mile Rd.
Livonia MI 48152-1798
Offers: This is a monthly magazine for creators and collectors of dolls. Each issue contains a free clothing pattern and features collectible dolls.

DOLLHOUSE MINIATURES

Kalmbach Publishing
P.O. Box 1612
21027 Crossroads Circle
Waukesha WI 53187-1612
Contact: Kay M. Olson
Phone: (414)798-6618
Fax: (414)796-1383
E-mail: kayolson@dhminiatures.com
Website: http://www.dhminiatures.com
Offers: This is a monthly magazine of miniatures that offers profiles of craftspeople and displays of their work, plus how-to tips and techniques, visits to museums/collections and more. Miniature projects are diagrammed and directed. Regulars: show calendar, letters, reviews and others. Advertising. Sample copy, $3.95.
Phone Orders: (800)533-6444.

DOLLS IN MINIATURE

Dept. CSS
1040 Bentoak Lane
San Jose CA 95129
Phone: (408)252-6607
E-mail: dollsmini@aol.com
Offers: This quarterly magazine is concerned with making and collecting miniature dolls, dollhouse accessories and teddy bears. Sample issue, $5 ($9 outside US).

THE EMBROIDERERS GUILD OF AMERICA, INC.

335 W. Broadway, Suite 100
Louisville KY 40202
Contact: Bonnie Key
Phone: (502)589-6956
Fax: (502)584-7400
E-mail: egahq@aol.com
Store Location: National headquarters only, with 355 chapters.
Offers: Available only to members.

FIBERARTS: THE MAGAZINE OF TEXTILES

67 Broadway
Asheville NC 28801
Phone: (704)253-0467
Fax: (704)253-7952
E-mail: fiberarts@larkbooks.com
Offers: This magazine showcases contemporary and historical fiber, with articles on quilting, weaving, stitchery, soft sculpture surface designing and more. Also includes educational and travel listings and show opportunities and data. Advertising.

FINE TOOL JOURNAL

27 Fickett Rd.

Pownal ME 04069

Offers: This quarterly magazine on tools for craftspeople and collectors features absentee auctions, tools for sale, technical and historical information, coming events calendar and other topics.

FINESCALE MODELER

Kalmbach Publishing Co.

P.O. Box 1612

21027 Crossroads Circle

Waukesha WI 53187-1612

Phone: (414)796-8776

Fax: (414)796-0126

E-mail: customerservice@kalmbach.com

Website: www.kalmbach.com

Offers: This magazine, issued 10 times yearly, aids readers with crafting skills on all levels by presenting tips, projects and instructions in the realms of ships, cars, dioramas, military vehicles and others. Advertising. Over 200 hobby-related books, calendars and videos.

Catalog: Upon request.

Phone Orders: (800)533-6644.

Accepts: American Express, Discover, MasterCard, Visa

FOR THE LOVE OF CROSS STITCH

P.O. Box 55595

Little Rock AR 72215

Offers: This is a magazine for cross-stitch lovers. Each issue is devoted to cross-stitch, with new projects and techniques, designs for every skill level.

GARDEN RAILWAY

Kalmbach Publishing Co.

P.O. Box 1612

21027 Crossroads Circle

Waukesha WI 53187-1612

Phone: (414)796-8776

Fax: (414)796-0126

E-mail: customerservice@kalmbach.com

Website: www.kalmbach.com

Offers: Over 200 hobby-related books, calendars and videos.

Catalog: Upon request.

Phone Orders: (800)533-6644.

Accepts: American Express, Discover, MasterCard, Visa

HAND PAPERMAKING

P.O. Box 77027

Washington DC 20013

Phone: (800)821-6604

Fax: (301)220-2394

E-mail: handpapermaking@bookarts.com

Website: www.bookarts.com/handpapermaking

Offers: Semiannual journal and quarterly newsletter with information on the art and craft for western and eastern papermaking.

HANDCRAFT ILLUSTRATED

P.O. Box 7450

Red Oak IA 51591-0450

Offers: Quarterly published crafts. Project and resources magazine, with decorating ideas, quick projects, field guide and reader's notes.

HANDWOVEN

Interweave Press

201 E. Fourth St.

Loveland CO 80537

Offers: This weaving magazine is issued 5 times yearly, with photographed weaving projects to provide ideas, inspiration and instruction to handweavers of all skill levels, plus articles of lore, history, techniques, profiles and functional pieces for the home. Includes woven fashions, accessories, fabrics. Advertising.

HARRIET'S THEN & NOW

P.O. Box 1363

Winchester VA 22604-1363

Contact: Harriet Engler

Phone: (540)667-2541

Fax: (540)722-4618

Website: www.harriets.com

Offers: Nineteenth-century how-to magazine. $6 per issue or $30 yearly. Original articles, diaries and fashion plates.

THE HERB QUARTERLY

P.O. Box 689

San Anselmo CA 94960

Offers: Published quarterly. Includes articles on herb crafting; also medicinal, gardening, culinary and folklore.

HERBALGRAM

P.O. Box 201660

Austin TX 78720

Contact: Gayle Engels

Phone: (512)331-8868

Fax: (512)331-1924

E-mail: abc@herbalgram.org

Website: www.herbalgram.org

Offers: This quarterly journal is published by the American Botanical Council and the Herb Research Foundation. Includes reviews, media coverage, herb data, updates, legalities, conference data, book reviews and an events calendar—all edited by an advisory board.

Catalog: $2.50 or free with order (included in HerbalGram).

Phone Orders: (800)373-7105 (automated).

Accepts: MasterCard, Visa

THE HOME SHOP MACHINIST

P.O. Box 1810

Traverse City MI 49685

Offers: This bimonthly magazine provides expert guidance, information and resources to all who enjoy working with metal for pleasure or profit in their home shops.

HOOKED ON CROCHET

23 Old Pecan Rd.
Big Sandy TX 75755

Offers: An assortment of crochet projects with instructions and diagrams make up this bimonthly magazine, including projects for home decor and gifts, women's and children's clothing, and home decorator items. Letters and stitch illustrations are regular features.

HOW MAGAZINE

1507 Dana Ave.
Cincinnati OH 45207

Offers: The focal point of this bimonthly magazine is graphics—design, creativity and technology. Design experts share their wisdom on topics including design techniques, tools, problem solving, color separations, papers, computer systems, business, legalities, self-promotion and more.

I LOVE QUILTING BOOK CLUB

1507 Dana Ave.
Cincinnati OH 45207
Contact: Mary Dacres, editor
Phone: (513)531-2690
Fax: (513)531-4744

Offers: About every 4 weeks a free issue of the club catalog and newsletter, describing the main selection book, several alternates and dozens of other book offerings including hard-to-find tools and gadgets, videos and more—all at a discount price.

INTERWEAVE KNITS

Interweave Press
201 E. Fourth St.
Loveland CO 80537
Contact: Nancy Arndt
Phone: (970)669-7672
Fax: (970)669-6117
Website: http://www.interweave.com

Offers: *Piecework* is meant for those who love handwork and those who value its past and present role—exploring historic and ethnic, fabric-related needlework in articles and selected projects. The bimonthly magazine presents handwork to inspire both novice and advanced creators in quilting, knitting, crochet, basketry, applique and lace making.

A KID'S GUIDE TO CRAFTS

500 Vaughn St.
Harrisburg PA 17110

Offers: Stackpole Magazines, a division of Stackpole, Inc., of Mechanicsburg PA has successfully produced highly regarded, highly specialized craft magazines that attract and retain loyal readers. For more than a decade, this division has maintained a strong presence in the craft industry, which has experienced tremendous growth during that time.

Stackpole Magazines offers adult crafters a variety of useful, educational and entertaining publications, and now it offers young crafters the same. The need for craft guides dedicated solely to children is there, and Stackpole is filling it with a new crafting series called *A Kid's Guide to Crafts*. Each guide in the series will feature anywhere from 7 to 10 projects on a particular topic. The second set of 3 guides in this ongoing series is dedicated to a hodgepodge of projects, fall and winter holiday crafts, and fun with threads, fabric and yarn. Subsequent guides will feature spring and summer holiday crafts, dollhouse construction and cardboard concoctions.

For futher information about all our fine publications, please write to Stackpole Magazines at above address. Distributed by Stackpole Books. Trade accounts, call (800)732-3669.

KITE LINES

P.O. Box 466
Randallstown MD 21133-0466

Offers: This is the comprehensive international journal of kiting and a major source of news, plans, techniques, reviews of new kites and books, profiles of kiting personalities, in-depth features. With event and supplier lists. Advertising.

KNITTER'S MAGAZINE/WEAVER'S MAGAZINE

P.O. Box 1525
Sioux Falls SD 57101-1525

Offers: This magazine includes several knitting projects.

KNITTERS NEWS

Box 65004
358 Danforth
Toronto, Ontario M4Y 3Z2
Canada
E-mail: stp@interlog.com

Offers: This knitting newsletter, published 5 times yearly, includes patterns, techniques, projects and more.

LAPIDARY JOURNAL

60 Chestnut Ave., Suite 201
Devon PA 19333-1312
Phone: (610)293-1112
Fax: (610)293-1717
E-mail: ljmagazine@aol.com
Website: www.lapidaryjournal.com

Offers: For over 50 years, *Lapidary Journal* has been the premier source of information about the gem, bead, jewelry-making, mineral and fossil fields. Spectacular full-color photography of beads and jewelry and the sensational "Jewelry Journal" section inspire thousands of readers to try new easy-to-follow gemstone and jewelry-making projects. Special editions include the *Bead Annual*, the *Annual Buyers' Directory*, the *Gemstone Arts Annual* and the *Design and Tools & Supplies Editions*. Glossy, 180 pages monthly, $4.95 cover price.

Catalog: Request the free *Lapidary Journal Book & Video Catalog* by calling (610)676-GEMS.

Phone Orders: For subscriptions call (800)676-4336.

THE LEATHER CRAFTERS & SADDLERS JOURNAL

331 Annette Court
Rhinelander WI 54501-2902
Offers: This bimonthly leatherworking publication with how-tos, step-by-step instructional articles, including full-sized patterns of leather craft, leather art, custom saddle and boot making; all skill levels. It covers leather, tools, machinery and allied materials, plus leather-craft industry news.

LEISURE ARTS-THE MAGAZINE

P.O. Box 55595
Little Rock AR 72215

MEMORY MAKERS MAGAZINE

475 W. 115th Ave. #6
Denver CO 80234
Contact: Customer service
Phone: (800)366-6465
Fax: (303)452-3582
E-mail: letters@memorymakers.com
Website: www.memorymakers.com
Offers: A bimonthly scrapbooking magazine, plus various craft books, including *Punch Your Art Out*, Volume 1. Subscriptions: 1 year (6 issues), $24.95. In Canada please add $10 for postage (US funds).
Phone Orders: Subscriptions taken by phone.
Discounts: Wholesale to businesses.
Accepts: American Express, Discover, MasterCard, Visa

MINIATURE COLLECTOR MAGAZINE

30595 Eight Mile
Livonia MI 48152-1798
Contact: Ruth Keessen
Phone: (800)458-8237 or (248)477-6650
Fax: (248)477-6795
E-mail: 104137.1254@compuserve.com
Offers: Eight times per year, magazine for creators, collectors and crafters of miniatures and dollhouses. Sample issue, $3.95.
Phone Orders: M-F, 8-5 EST.
Accepts: Discover, MasterCard, Visa

MODEL RAILROADER

Kalmbach Publishing
P.O. Box 1612
21027 Crossroads Circle
Waukesha WI 53187-1612
Phone: (414)796-8776
Fax: (414)796-0126
E-mail: customerservice@kalmbach.com
Website: www.kalmbach.com
Offers: This monthly magazine presents inspirational tours of the world's layouts, including prototype data and how-to information. Also included are tips, projects and photographs. Advertising.
Catalog: Upon request.
Phone Orders: (800)533-6644.
Accepts: American Express, Discover, MasterCard, Visa

THE NATIONAL DIRECTORY OF ARTISTS & CRAFTSMEN

P.O. Box 424
Devault PA 19432
Phone: (610)640-ARTS
Offers: Frequently updated resource publication of artists and craftsmen of the twentieth and twenty-first centuries. For further information, send SASE and/or send for forms. Cost to order is $45. Basic cost to be in it is $25.

NATIONAL STAMPAGRAPHIC

P.O. Box 370985
Las Vegas NV 89137-0985
Contact: Melody H. Stein
Phone: (702)396-2188
Fax: (702)396-2189
E-mail: natstamp@aol.com
Store Location: 3109 N. Rainbow Blvd., Las Vegas NV 89108.
Offers: Quarterly art stamp magazine. How-to articles, stamping information, contests and exchanges. Single issue, $5.
Phone Orders: M-Sat, 10-6 PST.
Mail Orders: Prepayment required.
Discounts: Sells wholesale to retail stores.
Accepts: Discover, MasterCard, Visa

THE NEEDLECRAFT SHOP, INC.

23 Old Pecan Rd.
Big Sandy TX 75755
Offers: Plastic canvas kits, pattern books, plastic canvas in a variety of shapes and sizes, 67 colors of plastic canvas yarn, crochet pattern books, kits, dolls and doll clothing.
Catalog: Free.

OLD-TIME CROCHET

P.O. Box 9009
Big Sandy TX 75755
Offers: This quarterly crochet magazine features patterns from cover to cover—classic and traditional apparel, accessories and home decor. Advertising.

ORNAMENT

P.O. Box 2349
San Marcos CA 92079
Phone: (760)599-0222
Fax: (760)599-0228
E-mail: ornament@cts.com
Store Location: 1230 Keystone Way, Vista CA 92083.
Offers: *Ornament* covers ancient, contemporary and ethnic jewelry, beads and clothing through insightful, scholarly articles and beautifully imaginative full-color photography. This international journal provides an in-depth guide to the finest artists, artworks, museums and gallery exhibitions, special events and news and publication reviews pertinent to the exciting world of personal adornment.
Phone Orders: Yes.
Mail Orders: At P.O. Box.
Accepts: MasterCard, Visa

PAINTING MAGAZINE

Dept. 49126

2400 Devon Ave., Suite 375

Des Plaines IL 60018-4618

Offers: This bimonthly magazine is devoted to decorative painting. It includes how-to instructions for projects and techniques for wood, fabric, metal, rocks and other surfaces with all kinds of paints. Ideas, hints and education articles complement the issues.

PINE MEADOW KNITTING NEWS

490 Woodland View Dr.

York PA 17402-1248

Contact: Joan L. Hamer

Phone: (717)846-0762

E-mail: jlhamer@blazenet.net

Website: www.benefitslink.com/knit/pmkn

Offers: Knitting newsletter with emphasis on knitting for charity, published quarterly. Pattern book from past issues, $7 ppd.

Accepts: check, money order

PLASTIC CANVAS CORNER

P.O. Box 55595

Little Rock AR 72215

Offers: Created for plastic canvas lovers, this magazine offers 6 issues yearly with quick and easy projects, including original designs, tips and color charts with instruction for home accessories of every kind for a variety of skill levels and styles, traditional to contemporary. Letters and hints, book reviews and a buyer's guide, contests and designers' interviews are also featured.

PLASTIC CANVAS! MAGAZINE

23 Old Pecan Rd.

Big Sandy TX 75755

Offers: Bimonthly magazine gives stitch basics and projects for many plastic canvas needlepoint items, each with stitch and color charts, materials lists and instructions. Typical patterns include wall hangings, baskets, boxes, tissue holders, organizers, banks, vases and others.

PROJECTS IN METAL

P.O. Box 1810

Traverse City MI 49685

Offers: This bimonthly magazine is meant for those serious about shopwork and includes complete plans for valuable tools and accessories which are presented to prepare the home metalworker for hobby projects offered in every issue.

QUICK & EASY PLASTIC CANVAS

23 Old Pecan Rd.

Big Sandy TX 75755

Offers: This bimonthly magazine presents easy projects with stitch and color charts, materials lists and instructions for a wide range of home decor items, from baskets to hangings, organizers, cubes and others.

QUICK & EASY QUILTING

306 E. Parr Rd.

Berne IN 46711

Offers: This is a bimonthly magazine with a comprehensive selection of quilting projects.

QUILT WORLD

306 E. Parr Rd.

Berne IN 46711

Offers: This bimonthly magazine presents full-size patterns throughout—motifs, diagrams and photographs for a variety of quilts—from heritage to contemporary style. Includes international news, "Notes & Quotes," "Pieces and Patches" rundown, book reviews, "Quilters Queries & Quotes," "Show Directory" and "Classifieds."

RADIO CONTROL CAR ACTION

P.O. Box 427

Mt. Morris IL 61054

Phone: (800)877-5169 or (815)734-1116 (foreign)

Fax: (815)734-1188

Offers: This R/C car magazine features the newest models and trends, plus photo features on cars, bodies, accessories, driver models. Includes information on engines, parts, pit tips, plus articles, product news and advertising.

RAILFAN & RAILROAD

Carstens Publications

108 Phil Hardin Rd.

Newton NJ 07860

Contact: Henry Carstens

Phone: (973)383-3355

Fax: (973)383-4064

E-mail: carstens@nac.net.

Website: www.carstens-publications.com

Offers: This monthly railroad magazine puts emphasis on the contemporary scene with coverage of trains, railroads and facilities, runs and developments. Features on traction and light rail, narrow gauge, railroadiana, video and book reviews and coming events, trips and all for the dedicated rail enthusiast.

Phone Orders: (800)474-6995.

RUBBERSTAMPMADNESS

408 SW Monroe #210

Corvallis OR 97333

Offers: A world of rubber stamping is represented in this bimonthly publication that is color-covered; includes reviews of catalogs, news, mail art, how-tos, letters and trends. Advertising.

RUG HOOKING

500 Vaughn St.

Harrisburg PA 17110

Phone: (717)234-7519

Fax: (717)234-1359

Website: www.rughookingonline.com

Offers: This magazine is published 5 times per year and is devoted to all aspects of rug hooking, including pictured projects (4 to 5 per issue) from hooking experts to instruct and inspire. Features techniques, beginnner and pro designs, preparing and dyeing wools, ideas, profiles of professionals, and photographs. Advertising.

SAC NEWSMONTHLY
P.O. Box 159
Bogalusa LA 70429
Contact: Wayne Smith
Phone: (800)825-3722
Fax: (504)732-3744
E-mail: sacrafts@aol.com
Store Location: 414 Ave. B., Bogalusa LA 70427
Offers: This monthly publication gives nationwide listings and articles for art and craft show opportunities. Includes details on place, time, deadline and fees involved. Has display and classified advertising. Single issue, $3; 1-year subscription, $24 ($24.96 in Louisana).
Mail Orders: Subscription in US. Prepayment required. Allow 6-8 weeks for first issue.
Accepts: Discover, MasterCard, Visa, check, money order

SCALE AUTO ENTHUSIAST
Kalmbach Publishing Co.
P.O. Box 1612
21027 Crossroads Circle
Waukesha WI 53187-1612
Phone: (414)796-8776
Fax: (414)796-0126
E-mail: customerservice@kalmbach.com
Website: www.kalmbach.com
Offers: Over 200 hobby-related books, calendars and videos.
Catalog: Upon request.
Phone Orders: (800)533-6644.
Accepts: American Express, Discover, MasterCard, Visa

SCULPTURE
International Sculpture Center
1050 17th St. NW, Suite 250
Washington DC 20036
Offers: Subscribe to the premiere magazine of contemporary sculpture. Published 10 times a year, *Sculpture* features criticism, reviews from around the world, studio visits and interviews with established and emerging artists, as well as technical articles on materials and methods. Advertising.

SEW BEAUTIFUL
720 Madison St.
Huntsville AL 35800
Offers: Magazine of sewing projects and features, suppliers' guide and answer column.

SEW NEWS
P.O. Box 1790
Peoria IL 61656
Offers: This sewing publication appears monthly, reporting on fashions, fabrics, sewing savvy and projects. Features projects and suggestions (illustrated) on color, dyeing, coordinating and others. Sewing patterns reviewed and hints

given; includes resources, product data, book reviews, tips, latest products, videos and shoppers. Advertising.

SILK PAINTERS INTERNATIONAL, INC.
P.O. Box 887
Riverdale MD 20738
Contact: Diane Tuckman
Phone: (301)474-7347
Fax: (301)441-2395
E-mail: paintsilk@aol.com
Offers: *The Silkworm Newsletter*: 1 year (6 issues) for $18 ($25 international).
Phone Orders: Yes.
Mail Orders: Yes.
Accepts: American Express, Discover, MasterCard, Visa

SIMPLY CROSS STITCH
23 Old Pecan Rd.
Big Sandy TX 75755
Offers: Cross-stitch projects in this bimonthly magazine are shown with stitch and color charts and instructions and materials lists. Patterns for home decor and wearables, letters, hints and a getting started column are in each issue.

SOFT DOLLS & ANIMALS
30595 Eight Mile
Livonia MI 48152-1798
Contact: Barbara Campbell
Phone: (800)458-8237 or (248)477-6650
Fax: (248)477-6795
E-mail: 104137.1254@compuserve.com
Offers: Quarterly magazine to creators and crafters of cloth dolls, animals with fabric figures. Sample issue, $4.95.
Phone Orders: M-F, 8-5 EST.
Accepts: Discover, MasterCard, Visa

SPIN-OFF
201 E. Fourth St.
Loveland CO 80537
Offers: This quarterly magazine is meant for hand spinner enthusiasts. It is a resource for information on fibers, spinning and dyeing techniques, project ideas and equipment. Feature topics have included hand-spun yarns and fiber, equipment and other data. Advertising.

SUCCESSFUL SEWING BOOK CLUB
1507 Dana Ave.
Cincinnati OH 45207
Contact: Mary Dacres, editor
Phone: (513)531-290
Fax: (513)531-4744
Offers: The club catalog and newsletter, describing the main selection book, several alternates and dozens of other book offerings, arrives about every 4 weeks. It includes hard-to-find tools and gadgets, videos and more—all at a discount price.

TEDDY BEAR REVIEW

170 Fifth Ave.
New York NY 10010
Offers: This quarterly publication on teddy bears presents teddy history. Projects are shown, as are profiles, holiday topics, collections and more.

TRAINS

Kalmbach Publishing Co.
P.O. Box 1612
21027 Crossroads Circle
Waukesha WI 53187-1612
Phone: (414)796-8776
Fax: (414)796-0126
E-mail: customerservice@kalmbach.com
Website: www.kalmbach.com
Offers: Over 200 hobby-related books, calendars and videos.
Catalog: Upon request.
Phone Orders: (800)533-6644.
Accepts: American Express, Discover, MasterCard, Visa

TREADLEART SEWING & QUILTING SUPPLY CATALOG & SUPPLEMENTS & COMPLETE THREAD CATALOG

25834 Narbonne Ave.
Lomita CA 90717
Offers: This bimonthly magazine is geared to sewing embellishment—projects, hints, topics—illustrated, diagrammed and described.

WACKY WOOLIES KNIT'N CLUB

250 E. Madison Ave.
Crescent City CA 95531
Contact: Sharon Philbrick
Phone: (707)464-4330
E-mail: wwkc@gte.net
Website: http://www.angelfire.com/biz/knitknuts/index.html
Store Location: At above address.
Offers: 6 newsletters per year plus several patterns for knitting and crochet. 36-inch yarn samples of all yarns featured. Interact with fellow club members and participate in contests, campaigns, yarn trades—too much to mention. $14/year club membership.
Catalog: Will send complimentary newsletter and free pattern upon request.
Phone Orders: M-F, 10-4 only.
Accepts: check

THE WATERCOLOUR GAZETTE

Kor Publications
P.O. Box 66047, RPO Unicity
Winnipeg, Manitoba R3K 2E7
Canada
Contact: Eileen Korponay

Phone: (204)889-6467
Fax: (204)889-6467
E-mail: kor@solutions.mb.ca
Website: http://personal.solutions.net/kor
Offers: 12-page watercolor self-help newsletter and self-help watercolor reports. Send $2 postage for free sample copy and our information brochure.
Catalog: 5-page information brochure.
Mail Orders: Will ship to Canada, US and other countries. Prepayment required.
Accepts: MasterCard

WESTART

P.O. Box 6868
Auburn CA 95604-6868
Offers: This semimonthly tabloid has a readership of artists, craftpeople and students. It features current reviews and listings of fine art competitions and arts and crafts fairs and festivals.

WILDFOWL CARVING & COLLECTING

500 Vaughn St.
Harrisburg PA 17110

WOODWORK MAGAZINE

P.O. Box 1529
Ross CA 94957
Contact: John Lavine, editor
Phone: (415)382-0580
Fax: (415)382-0587
E-mail: woodwrkmag@aol.com
Offers: This bimonthly magazine covers woodworking today, with topics for all skill levels. Presents cabinetmaking design and how-tos, profiles of professionals and their work, and technical theory. Includes quality photography and diagramming throughout for projects and other features—on contemporary and other furnishings. Regular features include techniques, questions and answers. Advertising.

THE WORKBASKET

Flower & Garden Crafts Edition
700 W. 47th St., Suite 810
Kansas City MO 64111
Contact: Roberta Schneider, editor
Offers: This home magazine presents features on knitting, crochet, sewing, embroidery, quilting, other needlecrafts and crafts. Projects are diagrammed. Included are projects for home, decor, wearables and accessories for all. Advertising.

Supportive Materials & Aids

Also see General Craft Supplies.

ACTION BAG & DISPLAY CO.

501 N. Edgewood Ave.
Wood Dale IL 60191
Phone: (708)766-2881 or (800)824-2247
Fax: (800)400-4451
E-mail: actionbg@ix.netcom.com
Offers: Bags: Ziploc and other plastic bags in a variety of sizes, including Floss-a-Way cotton drawstring bags, retail shopping bags and shipping supplies. Manufacturer.
Catalog: Free.
Discounts: Sells wholesale.

AIM FIXTURES, INC.

(formerly A.I.M. Displays)
4007 Riverside Dr. #202
Tampa FL 33603
Contact: Doug Curtis
Phone: (813)237-0303
Fax: (813)239-9526
E-mail: aimer@mci2000.com
Website: www.aimfixtures.com
Offers: Aluminum display/exhibit panels and modular components in a variety of sizes. Open frames, mesh- and fabric-covered inserts and shelving units configured to any requirement. Lightweight, durable and attractive. Exceeds all mall fire codes.
Catalog: Full color. Free.
Phone Orders: M-F, 9-6 EST.
Mail Orders: Will ship to US and Canada. All orders f.o.b. Hendersonville NC. Allow 10 working days for shipment.
Discounts: Sells wholesale to legitimate businesses.
Accepts: check, money order, cash

ALLYSON'S TITLE PLATES

(formerly Allyson's)
21-C Cote Dr.
Epping NH 03042
Contact: Dick Allyson
Phone: (603)679-5266
Fax: (603)679-5266
Store Location: At above address.
Offers: Engraved brass plates for artists, crafters, modelers and others.
Catalog: Free brochure.
Mail Orders: Yes.
Discounts: 1 free with 6.

ALPHA IMPRESSIONS

4161 S. Main St.
Los Angeles CA 90037
Phone: (213)234-8221
Fax: (213)234-8215
E-mail: alphaimp@aol.com
Store Location: At above address.
Offers: Labels—woven and custom printed.
Catalog: Free brochures.
Discounts: Quantity.

ALTHOR PRODUCTS

2 Turnage Lane
Bethel CT 06801
Contact: Judy Vivone
Phone: (800)688-2693
Fax: (203)830-6064
Store Location: At above address. 9-5 EST.
Offers: Plastic packaging, over 800 sizes in stock.
Catalog: 24 pages.
Phone Orders: M-F, 9-5 EST.
Mail Orders: Will ship US and internationally.
Accepts: MasterCard, Visa

ALUMA-PANEL, INC.

2410 Oak St. W.
Cumming GA 30041
Contact: Carter Barnes
Phone: (800)258-3003
Fax: (800)258-6201
Store Location: M-F, 8:15-5. Cumming GA, Greer SC and Columbus GA locations.
Offers: Sign blanks and stands: aluminum, styrene and D-board types, variety of sizes. Also offers flexible magnetic sheeting, Sparcal vinyl, corrugated plastic, blank banners, sandblast stencil and Chromatic paints.
Catalog: Upon request.
Mail Orders: No Canada shipments.
Discounts: Sells wholesale to sign shops.
Accepts: American Express, Discover, MasterCard, Visa

JERRY ANTHONY PHOTOGRAPHY

3952 Shattuck Ave.
Columbus OH 43220
Contact: Sharon Richwine
Phone: (614)451-5207
Fax: (614)457-3123
E-mail: janthonyphoto@iwaynet.net
Offers: Product photography and color postcards and catalog sheets for 16 years. We work exclusively with artists. Ship

your work or visit our studio. Call for an appoinment or free color flyer. We help you sell your work.
Phone Orders: M-F, 9-5 EST.
Accepts: American Express, Discover, MasterCard, Visa

ARIZONA CASE
5755 N. 51st Ave. #3
Glendale AZ 85301
Phone: (800)528-0195 or (602)931-3691
Fax: (602)931-3692
Store Location: Showroom at above address. M-Th, 9-4:30; F, 9-3.
Offers: Collapsible display cases, store fixtures, portable halogen lighting systems, jewelers trays, Riker mounts, gemstone displays, countertop Lucite displays and jewelry displays.
Catalog: 48 pages, color. Free.
Phone Orders: M-Th, 8:30-4:30; F, 8:30-3.
Mail Orders: In-stock items ship within 48 hours. Out-of-stock or special orders, 2-4 weeks lead time.
Discounts: Based on quantity, as outlined on price list.
Accepts: Discover, MasterCard, Visa

ARMSTRONG PRODUCTS
P.O. Box 979
Guthrie OK 73044
Phone: (800)278-4279
Offers: Ultra-System display panels including portable style, perforated to allow hanging shelves and items; interchangeable with other System panels.
Catalog: Call or write for free catalog.

BADGE-A-MINIT
P.O. Box 800
La Salle IL 61301
Phone: (800)223-4103
Offers: Our starter kit, for only $29.95 + $4.50 p&h, includes a button assembly press and enough pinback parts for 10 buttons. Additional button parts are available in our free catalog.
Catalog: Free. Color.

BAGS PLUS
640 Country Club Ln., Suite 201
Itasca IL 60143
E-mail: bagsplus@aol.com
Website: www.bagsplus.com
Offers: Bags, including poly-zip close, heavyweight and with hand holes. Also offers cellophane in 11 sizes, with a cloth drawstring. Shopping bags and gift totes and T-shirt bags also available. Handles small orders. Send SASE.

COLLECTOR'S HOUSE
1739 Hwy 9 N.
Howell NJ 07731
Phone: (800)448-9298
Fax: (732)845-3236
E-mail: collectorshouse@iop.com
Website: www.cardmail.com/collectors-house
Offers: Jewelry displays—jewelry trays, bracelet T-bars,

necklace stands/easels, Allstate portable tabletop showcases and Riker mount display boxes (cardboard with glass top, variety of sizes, with cotton-velvet). Fitted table covers, price tags, bags, boxes, bubble wrap and dealers supplies.
Catalog: Send for catalog.
Phone Orders: Yes.
Mail Orders: Worldwide.
Discounts: Quantity.
Accepts: all credit cards, check, C.O.D.

CREATIVE ENERGIES, INC.
1607 N. Magnolia Ave.
Ocala FL 34475
Phone: (800)351-8889
Offers: Stackable display panels. Also offers the Light-Dome—a waterproof canopy with ease of setup—hand trucks, director chair and indoor booths.
Catalog: Free brochure. Video, $5.

DEALERS SUPPLY, INC.
P.O. Box 717
Matawan NJ 07747
Phone: (800)524-0576
Fax: (732)591-8571
Offers: Booth supplies: fire-retardant fitted table covers and drapes, showcases, display grids and risers, folding tables, lighting, black lights, security aids and alarms, booth sign, moving supplies, KD Kanopies and more.
Catalog: Free.
Discounts: Quantity.
Accepts: Discover, MasterCard, Visa

DOVER PUBLICATIONS, INC.
31 E. Second St.
Mineola NY 11501
Phone: (516)294-7000
Offers: Copyright-free design books—black on glossy white, clip/use: borders, holiday motifs, seasons, art nouveau/deco, contemporary motifs, patriotic, sports, office, children's, silhouettes, old-fashioned, travel, transportation, health, symbols, florals, ethnic, early ads and calligraphy.
Catalog: Free pictorial archive catalogs and clip art.

DREW ENGINEERING
P.O. Box 150
19202 Birchtree Lane
Melta VA 23410-0150
Contact: Don Drew
Phone: (757)787-3797
Fax: (757)787-3797
E-mail: carver@shore.intercom.net
Store Location: At above address. M-F, 8-5.
Offers: Handcrafted metal display stands for shore bird and fish decoys.
Catalog: Price list available.
Phone Orders: M-Sat, 8-8.

Mail Orders: Will ship to US and Canada. 6-8 weeks delivery.
Discounts: Discounts for quantity orders.

EVERGREEN BAG CO.
22 Ash St.
East Hartford CT 06108
Phone: (800)775-3595
E-mail: sales@everbag.com
Website: www.everbag.com
Offers: Paper and plastic packaging, including retail containers and poly bags. Also offers shipping supplies, including cord-handled shopper bag, white T-shirt bags, textured and other gift boxes and others.
Catalog: Free.

FETPAK, INC.
70 Austin Blvd.
Commack NY 11725
Phone: (800)88-FETPAK
Fax: (888)FAX-4600
E-mail: info@fetpak.com
Website: www.fetpak.com
Store Location: Warehouse/offices at above address. M-F, 9-4.
Offers: Packaging supplies for resale and for end users. All types of plastic bags, gift bags, gift boxes, tissue paper, jewelry boxes, jewelry displays and supplies, labels, pricing guns, tags and tagging supplies, store supplies, sign cards, drawstring pouches, adhesive tapes, bubble mailers, corrugated cartons, stretch wrap cutters, shrink film and poly tubing.
Catalog: Free. 32 pages, full color.
Phone Orders: M-F, 9-5 EST.
Mail Orders: Orders shipped same day received if received before 1 p.m. EST. We ship worldwide.
Discounts: We are distributors and sell for resale or to business end users.
Accepts: American Express, Discover, MasterCard, Visa, check

FLOURISH CO.
5763 Wheeler Rd.
Fayetteville AR 72704
Contact: Bob Morison
Phone: (800) 296-0049
Fax: (501)444-8480
E-mail: info@flourish.com
Website: www.flourish.com
Store Location: Fayetteville AR location.
Offers: The Archtop and TrimLine canopies, the Protector canopy and the ProMaster and Vendor indoor booth frames. Custom drapery in flame-resistant fabrics. Free fabric samples.
Catalog: Free.
Phone Orders: Yes.
Mail Orders: Yes.

Discounts: Call for quantity quote.
Accepts: Discover, MasterCard, Visa

GENERAL LABEL MFG.
P.O. Box 640371
Miami FL 33164
Contact: Eric Gerard
Phone: (305)944-4696
Fax: (305)949-2662
Store Location: North Miami Beach FL location.
Offers: Printed fabric labels, custom name labels with logos or special lettering. Care content and size labels ready to ship. Iron-on labels for camps, nursing homes, and schools. Small orders or large. Affordable prices.
Catalog: Write or call (800)944-4696.
Phone Orders: Yes.
Mail Orders: At above address.
Accepts: MasterCard, Visa, check, money order

HEIRLOOM WOVEN LABELS
P.O. Box 488, CSS
Moorestown NJ 08057
Contact: Lois Rudy
Phone: (609)722-1618
Fax: (609)722-8905
E-mail: heirlooml@aol.com
Website: http://members.aol.com/heirlooml
Offers: 100% woven (not printed) personalized labels in wide range of colors/styles/motifs. Name tapes and care/content/size tabs. New 1" satin labels. New woven luggage straps.
Catalog: Free brochure upon request.
Phone Orders: M-F, 9-5 EST.
Mail Orders: Allow 3-4 weeks for delivery.
Discounts: 20% discount on orders of 500 or 1,000 labels.
Accepts: American Express, MasterCard, Visa, check, money order

IDENT-IFY LABEL CORP.
P.O. Box 140204
Brooklyn NY 11214-0204
Contact: Anthony Diserio
Phone: (718)436-3126
Fax: (718)436-9302
E-mail: identify0l@aol.com
Store Location: 3913 14th Ave., Brooklyn NY 11218.
Offers: Personalized printed cotton labels, woven labels, custom-printed labels with your logo and name tapes for schools, camps and institutions. Also care and content labels, size labels and sewing notions.
Catalog: $1.
Phone Orders: M-F, 6:30 a.m.-2 p.m. EST.
Mail Orders: Ship anywhere. 3-4 weeks delivery.
Discounts: Quantity.
Accepts: MasterCard, Visa, check, money order

IMPACT IMAGES

4919 Windplay Dr.
El Dorado Hills CA 95762
Contact: Dave Pavao
Phone: (800)233-2630
Fax: (916)933-4717
E-mail: impactimages@prodigy.net.
Offers: Crystal-clear plastic bags for packaging art and photography (and other flat objects) for retail sale. Great for greeting cards. Bags have resealable flap. Protect mats and artwork from fingerprints, smudges and dirt. Keeps product looking fresh and clean. Also have backing board and hanging tabs.
Catalog: Free samples and price list.
Phone Orders: M-F, 8-5 PST.
Mail Orders: Can ship worldwide. Ships within 48 hours by method specified.
Discounts: Volume discounts.
Accepts: MasterCard, Visa, check, money order, cash

JEFF'S DECAL COMPANY

1747 Selby Ave.
St. Paul MN 55014
Phone: (612)646-5069
Fax: (612)644-2695
Offers: Custom water-slide decals and labels for all crafts. Minimum orders are 25 sheets or more for single-color decals and 1,000 sheets or more for multicolor. Labels start at a press run for 250 minimum.
Catalog: Sample and listing, $1, or fax ideas on amounts, colors and sizes.

JENKINS CRAFTED CANOPIES

(formerly Jenkins)
3950-A Valley Blvd.
Walnut CA 91789
Phone: (909)594-1349/1471
Offers: Canopies for indoor/outdoor use, canopy connectors, hardware, sawhorses, signs and sign frames, racks and other accessories.
Catalog: Call or write for free brochure.

JULE-ART

P.O. Box 91748
Albuquerque NM 87199
Contact: Art Pippert
Phone: (800)833-8980
Fax: (505)344-6306
E-mail: info@jule-art.com
Website: http://www.jule-art.com/displays/
Store Location: Showroom at 7215 Washington NE, Albuquerque NM 87109.
Offers: Wholesale only. Acrylic displays and store fixtures, risers, easels, brochure holders and sign holders.
Catalog: 120 pages.
Phone Orders: Yes.
Mail Orders: Yes.

Discounts: Yes.
Accepts: Credit cards

K.I.A. PHOTOGRAPHY

453-5 Main St.
Nashua NH 03060
Phone: (603)888-0357
Offers: Promotional items—color postcards, business cards, catalog sheets, brochures and others in a variety of sizes, from photo to slide. 1-5 week production, 1,000 minimum.
Catalog: Call or send $3 for 28-page catalog.

KIMMERIC STUDIO

Dept. CSS
P.O. Box 10749
South Lake Tahoe CA 96158
Contact: Carol Carlson
Phone: (530)573-1616
Fax: (888)824-7178
E-mail: kimmeric@sierra.net
Website: Coming.
Offers: Craft handtags to personalize or price your crafts and gifts. Also custom orders. I specialize in pen and ink product illustration, offering "crafty" business cards, brochures and catalogs—all to help you sell your goods on paper. Established 1983.
Catalog: 38 pages. $2.
Phone Orders: Always accepted. If I am not in, please leave a message and I will return your call.
Mail Orders: Will ship anywhere. All orders satisfaction guaranteed.
Discounts: Bulk tags and wholesale available.
Accepts: MasterCard, Visa, check, money order

LR PUBLICATIONS/ACCESS PR

16 Fairwood View Court
Phoenix MD 21131
Contact: Laura W. Rosen, president
Phone: (410)527-0104
Fax: (410)527-0104
E-mail: lrpubl@aol.com
Website: Coming.
Offers: Quality editorial services, including news releases, marketing brochures, artists' biographies and curriculum vitae and buyer newsletters. L. Rosen is the former editor of *Niche Crafts* magazine.
Catalog: Send SASE for current brochure.
Accepts: MasterCard, Visa

M.D. ENTERPRISES DISPLAY SYSTEMS

9738 Abernathy
Dallas TX 75220
Fax: (214)350-7372
Offers: Display systems for the professional artist. KD Kanopies shelters.
Catalog: Call or write for brochure.

ELAINE MARTIN, INC.
25685 Hillview Court #E
Mundelein IL 60060
Phone: (800)642-1043
Fax: (847)726-1240
Website: www.emartin.com
Offers: Show/display equipment—snap-joint canopies in 3 standard colors, with slant, flat or peak roof models. Also E-Z Up and KD canopies, display booth, side panels, display grids and panels, display pedestals and folding tables. Director chair and accessories.
Catalog: Free.
Accepts: American Express, Discover, MasterCard, Visa

JOHN MEE CANOPIES
P.O. Box 11220
Birmingham AL 35202
Phone: (205)967-1885
Offers: KD Majestic canopies, 3 sizes. E-Z Up 500 canopies, 4 sizes with double-truss frame and polyester top. Also offers package specials and items from Showoff, Graphic Display Systems and Armstrong, including replacement tops, chairs and others.
Catalog: Write or call for free catalog.
Accepts: MasterCard, Visa

MITCHELL GRAPHICS
2363 Mitchell Park Dr.
Petoskey MI 49770
Phone: (800)583-9401
Offers: Printing of full-color postcards on recycled paper with soy ink.
Catalog: Free product and sample package.

NEATNIKS
104 Oakhill Court
St. Charles IL 60174
Contact: Maxine Peretz Prange
Phone: (630)443-0706
Fax: (630)443-0706
E-mail: neatniksl@aol.com
Website: http://members.aol.com/neatniksl/
Offers: Small storage containers in nine sizes—ideal for beads, buttons, components, etc. Built-in hinged lids with rectangular shape.
Catalog: Free.
Phone Orders: Yes.
Mail Orders: Yes.
Discounts: To stores for resale.
Accepts: Discover, MasterCard, Visa

NEW VENTURE PRODUCTS
1411-B 63rd Way N.
Clearwater FL 33760
Phone: (800)771-SHOW
Website: www.vp.com
Offers: The Showoff Line of canopy and display systems—

portable, easy-setup displays in a variety of sizes and types. Call or write.

ON DISPLAY
P.O. Box 42007
Richmond VA 23225
Phone: (804)231-1942
Fax: (804)232-5906
Offers: Bases for display of items, including plug-in and battery-powered models lighted for effects with glass or crystal in 24 stock shapes/sizes, revolving and custom-made solid bases for awards or special projects. Call or write.

OTT-LITE TECHNOLOGY
1214 W. Cass St.
Tampa FL 33606
Phone: (800)842-8848
Fax: (813)626-8790
Website: www.ott-lite.com
Offers: Match colors easily! See details clearly! OTT-LITE True Color Lighing lets you see colors and details accurately. Designed for arts, crafts and hobbies, it makes projects easier, faster and more enjoyable!
Catalog: Free.
Phone Orders: Yes.
Discounts: Wholesale, distributor, retailer.
Accepts: All major credit cards

PLASTIC BAGMART
554 Haddon Ave.
Collingswood NJ 08108
Phone: (800)360-BAGS
Offers: Plastic bags—clear, zip-lock and carryout types—plus shipping tapes, bubble pack bags, tissue, boxes and more.
Catalog: Free price lists. Full catalog, $3 (refunded with purchase).
Discounts: Quantity; sells wholesale to legitimate businesses and professionals.
Accepts: MasterCard, Visa

PNTA (PACIFIC NORTHWEST THEATRE ASSOCIATES)
333 Westlake Ave., N.
Seattle WA 98109
Phone: (206)622-7850 or (800)622-7850
Fax: (206)628-3162
E-mail: sales@pnta.com
Website: www.pnta.com
Store Location: At above address.
Offers: Full line of theater, stage and studio supplies, including scenic paints, fabrics, hardware, books and materials. Thermoplastics, including nontoxic workable fabric-form, sheets and pellets for molding and free-form sculpture are also available. Colors include gold leaf, bronzing powders, fiber dyes, fluorescents and others. Also carries makeup material and tools, books on making theater props and masks, scenic design, lighting and more.
Catalog: Free. 104 pages.

Phone Orders: M-F, 9-6; Sat, 11-5.
Mail Orders: Prepayment required. Same-day shipping on most orders placed by 1 p.m.
Accepts: MasterCard, Visa, purchase order on approved credit

SAKET CO.

7249 Atoll Ave.
North Hollywood CA 91605
Phone: (818)764-0110
Store Location: At above address.
Offers: Plastic bags in all sizes, small and large quantities, for crafts/hobbies, commercial and office use and industry. Cellophane bags.
Catalog: Free.
Discounts: Quantity; teachers and institutions; sells wholesale to legitimate businesses and professionals.

STERLING NAME TAPE CO.

9 Willow St.
Winsted CT 06098
Contact: Polly
Phone: (888)312-0113
Fax: (860)379-0394
E-mail: colwash@esslink.com
Offers: Custom labels printed with name, logo, artwork and more in one or more ink colors with care or content information on back.
Catalog: Includes samples, $1.
Phone Orders: Yes.
Mail Orders: Yes.
Accepts: American Express, MasterCard, Visa

SUNBURST BOTTLE COMPANY

5710 Auburn Blvd. #7
Sacramento CA 95841
Contact: Linda or Edie
Phone: (916)348-5576
Fax: (916)348-3803
E-mail: sunburst@cwo.com
Website: www.sunburstbottle.com
Store Location: At above address. M-F, 8-4.

Offers: Bottles, jars, vials, droppers, tea bags, cellophane bags, muslin bags, sprayers, pumps, corks, lip balm containers and related containers.
Catalog: $2.
Phone Orders: 24 hours.
Mail Orders: Will ship anywhere within 48 hours.
Discounts: With volume.
Accepts: MasterCard, Visa, C.O.D.

T.S.I. MANUFACTURING JEWELERS

(formerly T.S.I. Wholesale Mfg. Jewelers and Refiners)
2275 Morris Rd.
Lapeer MI 48446
Contact: John Desaye
Phone: (810)664-8291
Fax: (810)664-2466
E-mail: tsi@cardina.net
Website: http://www.cardina.net/~tsi/redalert.html
Store Location: At above address. 9-5.
Offers: Specializing in carving pictures of pets, dogs, cats and others, and making rings, pendants, earrings, pins and tie tacks, out of 14 karat gold and sterling silver, from the photo. Will even make up this item for the nose. One-of-a-kind, your finished product will be the same as the photo, or you may choose from our catalog.
Catalog: Yes.
Phone Orders: Yes.
Mail Orders: At above address. Allow 3-4 weeks for delivery.
Discounts: Depends on amount ordered.
Accepts: American Express, Discover, MasterCard, Visa

THE WOOD FACTORY

1225 Red Cedar Circle
Fort Collins CO 80524
Phone: (800)842-9663
Fax: (970)224-1949
Offers: Portable wood displays and accessories, including arches, revolving panel displays, bin and basket units, crates and custom designs.
Catalog: Free.
Phone Orders: M-F, 8:30-4:30 MST.
Accepts: American Express, Discover, MasterCard, Visa

Index